CAMBRIDGE
Brighter Thinking

A Level Further Mathematics for AQA
Student Book 2 (Year 2)
Stephen Ward, Paul Fannon, Vesna Kadelburg and Ben Woolley

CAMBRIDGE
UNIVERSITY PRESS

University Printing House, Cambridge CB2 8BS, United Kingdom

One Liberty Plaza, 20th Floor, New York, NY 10006, USA

477 Williamstown Road, Port Melbourne, VIC 3207, Australia

314–321, 3rd Floor, Plot 3, Splendor Forum, Jasola District Centre, New Delhi – 110025, India

79 Anson Road, #06-04/06, Singapore 079906

Cambridge University Press is part of the University of Cambridge.

It furthers the University's mission by disseminating knowledge in the pursuit of education, learning and research at the highest international levels of excellence.

www.cambridge.org
Information on this title:
www.cambridge.org/ 9781316644478 (Paperback)
www.cambridge.org/ 9781316644317 (Paperback with Cambridge Elevate edition)

© Cambridge University Press 2018

This publication is in copyright. Subject to statutory exception and to the provisions of relevant collective licensing agreements, no reproduction of any part may take place without the written permission of Cambridge University Press.

First published 2018

20 19 18 17 16 15 14 13 12 11 10 9 8 7 6 5 4 3 2

Printed in Italy by Rotolito S.p.A.

A catalogue record for this publication is available from the British Library

ISBN 978-1-316-64447-8 Paperback
ISBN 978-1-316-64431-7 Paperback with Cambridge Elevate edition

Additional resources for this publication at www.cambridge.org/education

Cambridge University Press has no responsibility for the persistence or accuracy of URLs for external or third-party internet websites referred to in this publication, and does not guarantee that any content on such websites is, or will remain, accurate or appropriate.

....

NOTICE TO TEACHERS IN THE UK

It is illegal to reproduce any part of this work in material form (including photocopying and electronic storage) except under the following circumstances:
(i) where you are abiding by a licence granted to your school or institution by the Copyright Licensing Agency;
(ii) where no such licence exists, or where you wish to exceed the terms of a licence, and you have gained the written permission of Cambridge University Press;
(iii) where you are allowed to reproduce without permission under the provisions of Chapter 3 of the Copyright, Designs and Patents Act 1988, which covers, for example, the reproduction of short passages within certain types of educational anthology and reproduction for the purposes of setting examination questions.

Message from AQA

This textbook has been approved by AQA for use with our qualification. This means that we have checked that it broadly covers the specification and we are satisfied with the overall quality. Full details of our approval process can be found on our website.

We approve textbooks because we know how important it is for teachers and students to have the right resources to support their teaching and learning. However, the publisher is ultimately responsible for the editorial control and quality of this book.

Please note that when teaching the A/AS Level Further Mathematics (7366, 7367) course, you must refer to AQA's specification as your definitive source of information. While this book has been written to match the specification, it cannot provide complete coverage of every aspect of the course.

A wide range of other useful resources can be found on the relevant subject pages of our website: www.aqa.org.uk

IMPORTANT NOTE
AQA has not checked or approved the practice question marks. AQA has not approved any Cambridge Elevate content.

Contents

Introduction iv
How to use this book v

1 Further complex numbers: powers and roots — 1
1: De Moivre's theorem 2
2: Complex exponents 7
3: Roots of complex numbers 11
4: Roots of unity 15
5: Further factorising 20
6: Geometry of complex numbers 22

2 Further complex numbers: trigonometry — 31
1: Deriving multiple-angle formulae 32
2: Application to polynomial equations 34
3: Powers of trigonometric functions 37
4: Trigonometric series 40

3 Further transformations of the ellipse, hyperbola and parabola — 47
1: Parametric and polar form 48
2: Rotations and enlargements 51
3: Combined transformations 53

4 Further graphs and inequalities — 61
1: The graph of $\frac{1}{f(x)}$ 62
2: The graph of $|f(x)|$ 66
3: Modulus equations and inequalities 70

5 Further vectors — 77
1: The vector product 78
2: Equation of a plane 85
3: Intersections between lines and planes 93
4: Angles between lines and planes 101
5: Distance between a point and a plane 104

6 Further matrices — 113
1: Transposes and inverses 114
2: Row and column operations 120
3: Solving linear systems with three unknowns 127
4: Geometrical interpretation of 3-variable simultaneous equations 129
5: Eigenvalues and eigenvectors 137
6: Diagonalisation and applications 143

Focus on ... Proof 1 154
Focus on ... Problem solving 1 156
Focus on ... Modelling 1 160
Cross-topic review exercise 1 161

7 Further polar coordinates — 167
1: Area enclosed by a curve 167
2: Area between two curves 171

8 Further hyperbolic functions — 178
1: Domain and range of hyperbolic and inverse hyperbolic functions 180
2: Reciprocal hyperbolic functions 183
3: Using hyperbolic identities to solve equations 186
4: Differentiation 188
5: Integration 191

9 Further calculus — 201
1: Differentiation of inverse trigonometric functions 202
2: Differentiation of inverse hyperbolic functions 204
3: Using inverse trigonometric and hyperbolic functions in integration 206
4: Using partial fractions in integration 211
5: Reduction formulae 214
6: Length of an arc 220
7: Area of a surface of revolution 223

10 Maclaurin series and limits — 229
1: Maclaurin series 230
2: Limits 234
3: Improper integrals 240

11 Differential equations — 248
1: Terminology of differential equations 248
2: The integrating factor 253
3: Homogeneous second order linear differential equations with constant coefficients 257
4: Inhomogeneous second order linear differential equations with constant coefficients 261

12 Applications of differential equations — 270
1: Forming differential equations 270
2: Simple harmonic motion and Hooke's law 273
3: Damping and damped oscillations 281
4: Coupled first order differential equations 285

13 Numerical methods — 294
1: Mid-ordinate rule 295
2: Simpson's rule 298
3: Euler's method 302
4: Improved Euler's method 305

Focus on ... Proof 2 312
Focus on ... Problem solving 2 314
Focus on ... Modelling 2 317
Cross-topic review exercise 2 319
Practice paper 327
Formulae 329
Answers to exercises 335
Glossary 389
Index 391
Acknowledgements 394

Introduction

You have probably been told that mathematics is very useful, yet it can often seem like a lot of techniques that just have to be learnt to answer examination questions. You are now getting to the point where you will start to see where some of these techniques can be applied in solving real problems. We hope, however, that anyone working through this book, as well as seeing how maths can be useful, will realise that it can also be incredibly frustrating, surprising and ultimately beautiful.

The book is woven around three key themes from the new curriculum.

Proof

Maths is valued because it trains you to think logically and communicate precisely. At a high level maths is far less concerned about answers and more about the clear communication of ideas. It is not about being neat – although that might help! It is about creating a coherent argument that other people can easily follow but find difficult to refute. Have you ever tried looking at your own work? If you cannot follow it yourself it is unlikely anybody else will be able to understand it. In maths we communicate by using a variety of means – feel free to use combinations of diagrams, words and algebra to aid your argument. And once you have attempted a proof, try presenting it to your peers. Look critically (but positively) at some other people's attempts. It is only through having your own attempts evaluated and trying to find flaws in other proofs that you will develop sophisticated mathematical thinking. This is why we have included lots of common errors in our Work it out boxes – just in case your friends don't make any mistakes!

Problem solving

Maths is valued because it trains you to look at situations in unusual, creative ways, to persevere and to evaluate solutions along the way. We have been heavily influenced by a great mathematician and maths educator George Polya, who believed that students were not just born with problem-solving skills – these were developed by seeing problems being solved and reflecting on their solutions before trying similar problems. You may not realise it but good mathematicians spend most of their time being stuck. You need to spend some time on problems you can't do, trying out different possibilities. If after a while you have not cracked it then look at the solution and try a similar problem. Don't be disheartened if you cannot get it immediately – in fact, the longer you spend puzzling over a problem the more you will learn from the solution. You may never need to integrate a rational function in the future, but we firmly believe that the problem-solving skills you will develop by trying it can be applied in many other situations.

Modelling

Maths is valued because it helps us solve real-world problems. However, maths describes ideal situations and the real world is messy! Modelling is about deciding on the important features needed to describe the essence of a situation and turning that into a mathematical form, then using it to make predictions, compare to reality and possibly improve the model. In many situations the technical maths is actually the easy part – especially with modern technology. Deciding which features of reality to include or ignore and anticipating the consequences of these decisions is the hard part. Yet it is amazing how some fairly drastic assumptions – such as pretending a car is a single point or that people's votes are independent – can result in models that are surprisingly accurate.

More than anything else this book is about making links – links between the different chapters, the topics covered and the themes above, links to other subjects and links to the real world. We hope that you will grow to see maths as one great complex but beautiful web of interlinking ideas.

Maths is about so much more than examinations, but we hope that if you absorb these ideas (and do plenty of practice!) you will find maths examinations a much more approachable and possibly even enjoyable experience. However, always remember that the results of what you write down in a few hours by yourself, in silence, under exam conditions are not the only measure you should consider when judging your mathematical ability – it is only one variable in a much more complicated mathematical model!

How to use this book

Throughout this book you will notice particular features that are designed to aid your learning. This section provides a brief overview of these features.

In this chapter you will learn how to:
- use De Moivre's theorem to derive trigonometric identities
- find sums of some trigonometric series.

Chapter 1, Section 1	You should be able to use De Moivre's theorem to raise a complex number to a power.	1 Find $\left(2\left(\cos\frac{\pi}{7} + i\sin\frac{\pi}{7}\right)\right)^4$ in modulus-argument form.
Chapter 1, Section 2	You should be able to use the exponential form of a complex number.	2 a Write $4e^{-i\frac{\pi}{3}}$ in exact Cartesian form. b Write down the complex conjugate of $2 + e^{ix}$.

Learning objectives
A short summary of the content that you will learn in each chapter.

Before you start
Points you should know from your previous learning and questions to check that you're ready to start the chapter.

WORKED EXAMPLE

The left-hand side shows you how to set out your working. The right-hand side explains the more difficult steps and helps you understand why a particular method was chosen.

Key point

A summary of the most important methods, facts and formulae.

PROOF

Step-by-step walkthroughs of standard proofs and methods of proof.

Common error

Specific mistakes that are often made. These typically appear next to the point in the Worked example where the error could occur.

WORK IT OUT

Can you identify the correct solution and find the mistakes in the two incorrect solutions?

Tip

Useful guidance, including ways of calculating or checking answers and using technology.

Each chapter ends with a **Checklist of learning and understanding** and a **Mixed practice exercise**, which includes **past paper questions** marked with the icon.

After every few chapters, you will find extra sections that bring together topics in a more synoptic way.

FOCUS ON...

Unique sections relating to the preceding chapters that develop your skills in proof, problem-solving and modelling.

CROSS-TOPIC REVIEW EXERCISE

Questions covering topics from across the preceding chapters, testing your ability to apply what you have learned.

You will find **practice papers** towards the end of the book, as well as a **glossary** of key terms (picked out in colour within the chapters), and **answers** to all questions. Full **worked solutions** can be found on the Cambridge Elevate digital platform, along with a **digital version** of this Student Book.

A Level Further Mathematics for AQA Student Book 2

Maths is all about making links, which is why throughout this book you will find signposts emphasising connections between different topics, applications and suggestions for further research.

⏮ Rewind
Reminders of where to find useful information from earlier in your study.

📷 Focus on...
Links to problem-solving, modelling or proof exercises that relate to the topic currently being studied.

⏭ Fast forward
Links to topics that you may cover in greater detail later in your study.

ⓘ Did you know?
Interesting or historical information and links with other subjects to improve your awareness about how mathematics contributes to society.

Colour coding of exercises

The questions in the exercises are designed to provide careful progression, ranging from basic fluency to practice questions. They are uniquely colour-coded, as shown here.

1. A sequence is defined by $u_n = 2 \times 3^{n-1}$. Use the principle of mathematical induction to prove that $u_1 + u_2 + \ldots + u_n = 3^n - 1$.
2. Show that $1^2 + 2^2 + \ldots + n^2 = \dfrac{n(n+1)(2n+1)}{6}$.
3. Show that $1^3 + 2^3 + \ldots + n^3 = \dfrac{n^2(n+1)^2}{4}$.
4. Prove by induction that $\dfrac{1}{1 \times 2} + \dfrac{1}{2 \times 3} + \dfrac{1}{3 \times 4} + \ldots + \dfrac{1}{n(n+1)} = \dfrac{n}{n+1}$.
5. Prove by induction that $\dfrac{1}{1 \times 3} + \dfrac{1}{3 \times 5} + \dfrac{1}{5 \times 7} + \ldots + \dfrac{1}{(2n-1) \times (2n+1)} = \dfrac{n}{2n+1}$.
6. Prove that $1 \times 1! + 2 \times 2! + 3 \times 3! + \ldots + n \times n! = (n+1)! - 1$.
7. Use the principle of mathematical induction to show that $1^2 - 2^2 + 3^2 - 4^2 + \ldots + (-1)^{n-1} n^2 = (-1)^{n-1} \dfrac{n(n+1)}{2}$.
8. Prove that $(n+1) + (n+2) + (n+3) + \ldots + (2n) = \dfrac{1}{2}n(3n+1)$.
9. Prove using induction that $\sin\theta + \sin 3\theta + \ldots + \sin(2n-1)\theta = \dfrac{\sin^2 n\theta}{\sin\theta}$, $n \in \mathbb{Z}^+$.
10. Prove that $\sum_{k=1}^{n} k\, 2^k = (n-1) 2^{n+1} + 2$.

Black – practice questions which come in several parts, each with subparts i and ii. You only need attempt subpart i at first; subpart ii is essentially the same question, which you can use for further practice if you got part i wrong, for homework, or when you revisit the exercise during revision.

Green – practice questions at a basic level.

Blue – practice questions at an intermediate level.

Red – practice questions at an advanced level.

Purple – challenging questions that apply the concept of the current chapter across other areas of maths.

Yellow – designed to encourage reflection and discussion.

🖩 indicates a question that requires a calculator

1 Further complex numbers: powers and roots

In this chapter you will learn how to:

- raise complex numbers to integer powers (De Moivre's theorem)
- work with complex exponents
- find roots of complex numbers
- use roots of unity
- find quadratic factors of polynomials
- use a relationship between complex number multiplication and geometric transformations.

Before you start…

Further Mathematics Student Book 1, Chapter 1	You should know how to find the modulus and argument of a complex number.	1	Find the modulus and argument of $-3 + 4i$.
Further Mathematics Student Book 1, Chapter 1	You should be able to represent complex numbers on an Argand diagram.	2	Write down the complex numbers corresponding to the points A and B.
Further Mathematics Student Book 1, Chapter 1	You should know how to work with complex numbers in Cartesian form.	3	Given that $z = 3 - 2i$ and $w = 2 + i$, evaluate: a $z - w$ b $\dfrac{z}{w}$.
Further Mathematics Student Book 1, Chapter 1	You should be able to multiply and divide complex numbers in modulus–argument form.	4	Given that $z = 10\left(\cos\dfrac{3\pi}{4} + i\sin\dfrac{3\pi}{4}\right)$ and $w = 2\left(\cos\dfrac{2\pi}{3} + i\sin\dfrac{2\pi}{3}\right)$, find: a zw b $\dfrac{z}{w}$. Give the arguments in the range $(-\pi, \pi]$.

Further Mathematics Student Book 1, Chapter 1	You should be able to work with complex conjugates.	5 Write down the complex conjugate of: a $5i - 3$ b $3\left(\cos \frac{\pi}{4} + i \sin \frac{\pi}{4}\right)$.
Further Mathematics Student Book 1, Chapter 1	You should know how to relate operations with complex numbers to transformations on an Argand diagram.	6 Let $a = 2 + i$ and z be any complex number. Describe a geometrical transformation that maps: a z to z^* b z to $z + a$.

Extending arithmetic with complex numbers

You already know how to perform basic operations with complex numbers, both in Cartesian and in modulus–argument forms. Modulus–argument form is particularly well suited to multiplication and division. In this chapter you will see how you can use this to find powers and roots of complex numbers. This chapter also includes a definition of complex powers that can make calculations even simpler.

You will also meet roots of unity, which are the solutions of the equation $z^n = 1$. They have some useful algebraic and geometric properties. Some of the applications include finding exact values of trigonometric functions.

Because you can represent complex numbers as points on an Argand diagram, operations with complex numbers have a geometric interpretation. You can use this fact to solve some problems that at first sight have nothing to do with complex numbers. This is just one example of the use of complex numbers to solve real-life problems.

Rewind

You met complex numbers in Further Mathematics Student Book 1, Chapter 1.

Fast forward

You will learn more about links between complex numbers and trigonometry in Chapter 2.

Section 1: De Moivre's theorem

In Further Mathematics Student Book 1, Chapter 1, you learnt that you can write complex numbers in Cartesian form, $x + iy$, or in modulus-argument form, $r(\cos\theta + i\sin\theta)$. You also learnt the rules for multiplying complex numbers in modulus-argument form:

$$|zw| = |z||w| \text{ and } \arg(zw) = \arg z + \arg w$$

You can apply this result to find powers of complex numbers. If a complex number has modulus r and argument θ, then multiplying $z \times z$ gives that z^2 has modulus r^2 and argument 2θ. Repeating this process, you can see that

$$|z^n| = |z|^n \text{ and } \arg(z^n) = n \arg z$$

In other words, when you raise a complex number to a power, you raise the modulus to the same power and multiply the argument by the power.

1 Further complex numbers: powers and roots

Key point 1.1

De Moivre's theorem

For a complex number, z, with modulus r and argument θ:

$$z^n = (r(\cos\theta + i\sin\theta))^n = r^n(\cos n\theta + i\sin n\theta)$$

for every integer power n.

For positive integer powers, you can prove this result by induction.

Rewind

Proof by induction was covered in Further Mathematics Student Book 1, Chapter 12. For Proof 1 you will also need the compound angle formulae from A Level Mathematics Student Book 2, Chapter 8.

Focus on...

See Focus on ... Proof 1 for a proof that extends De Moivre's theorem to all rational n.

PROOF 1

When $n = 1$:
$(r(\cos\theta + i\sin\theta))^1 = r(\cos\theta + i\sin\theta)$
so the result is true for $n = 1$.

Check that the result is true for $n = 1$.

Assuming that the result is true for some k:
$(r(\cos\theta + i\sin\theta))^k = r^k(\cos k\theta + i\sin k\theta)$

Assume that the result is true for some k and write down what that means.

Then for $n = k + 1$:
$(r(\cos\theta + i\sin\theta))^{k+1} = r^k(\cos k\theta + i\sin k\theta) \times r(\cos\theta + i\sin\theta)$

Make a link between $n = k$ and $n = k + 1$. In this case use $z^{k+1} = z^k z$.

$= r^{k+1}(\cos k\theta \cos\theta + i\cos k\theta \sin\theta + i\sin k\theta \cos\theta - \sin k\theta \sin\theta)$
$= r^{k+1}((\cos k\theta \cos\theta - \sin k\theta \sin\theta) + i(\cos k\theta \sin\theta + \sin k\theta \cos\theta))$
$= r^{k+1}(\cos(k+1)\theta + i\sin(k+1)\theta)$

Group real and imaginary parts.

Use:
$\cos(A + B) = \cos A \cos B - \sin A \sin B$
and
$\sin(A + B) = \sin A \cos B + \cos A \sin B$

Hence the result is true for $n = k + 1$.

This is the result you are trying to prove, but with n replaced by $k + 1$.

The result is true for $n = 1$, and if it is true for some k then it is also true for $k + 1$. Therefore it is true for all n integers ≥ 1 by induction.

Remember to write the full conclusion.

A Level Further Mathematics for AQA Student Book 2

You can use De Moivre's theorem to evaluate powers of complex numbers.

WORKED EXAMPLE 1.1

Evaluate, without a calculator, $\dfrac{(1+i)^{10}}{4i}$.

$|1+i| = \sqrt{1^2 + 1^2} = \sqrt{2}$

$\arg(1+i) = \arctan\left(\dfrac{1}{1}\right) = \dfrac{\pi}{4}$

$\therefore 1 + i = \sqrt{2}\left(\cos\dfrac{\pi}{4} + i\sin\dfrac{\pi}{4}\right)$

First find the modulus and argument of each number.

$|4i| = 4,\ \arg(4i) = \dfrac{\pi}{2}$

$\therefore 4i = 4\left(\cos\dfrac{\pi}{2} + i\sin\dfrac{\pi}{2}\right)$

By De Moivre's theorem:

$\left(\sqrt{2}\left(\cos\dfrac{\pi}{4} + i\sin\dfrac{\pi}{4}\right)\right)^{10} = (\sqrt{2})^{10}\left(\cos\dfrac{10\pi}{4} + i\sin\dfrac{10\pi}{4}\right)$

The argument needs to be between $-\pi$ and π:

$\dfrac{5\pi}{2} - 2\pi = \dfrac{\pi}{2}$

$= 2^5\left(\cos\dfrac{5\pi}{2} + i\sin\dfrac{5\pi}{2}\right)$

$= 32\left(\cos\dfrac{\pi}{2} + i\sin\dfrac{\pi}{2}\right)$

Dividing the moduli and subtracting the arguments:

$\dfrac{(1+i)^{10}}{4i} = \dfrac{32\left(\cos\dfrac{\pi}{2} + i\sin\dfrac{\pi}{2}\right)}{4\left(\cos\dfrac{\pi}{2} + i\sin\dfrac{\pi}{2}\right)}$

$= \dfrac{32}{4}(\cos 0 + i\sin 0)$

$= 8$

WORK IT OUT 1.1

Evaluate $(1 + i\sqrt{3})^6$.

Which is the correct solution? Identify the errors made in the incorrect solutions.

Solution 1

$(1 + i\sqrt{3})^6 = 1 + 6(i\sqrt{3})^1 + 15(i\sqrt{3})^2 + 20(i\sqrt{3})^3 + 15(i\sqrt{3})^4 + 6(i\sqrt{3})^5 + (i\sqrt{3})^6$

$= 1 + 6i\sqrt{3} - 45 - 60i\sqrt{3} + 135 + 54i\sqrt{3} - 27$

$= 64$

Continues on next page

Solution 2 $1 + i\sqrt{3} = 2\cos\dfrac{\pi}{6} + i\sin\dfrac{\pi}{6}$

So, using De Moivre's theorem:

$$\left(1 + i\sqrt{3}\right)^6 = 2^6 \cos\left(\dfrac{\pi}{6} \times 6\right) + i\sin\left(\dfrac{\pi}{6} \times 6\right)$$
$$= 64\cos\pi + i\sin\pi$$
$$= -64$$

Solution 3 $\left(1 + i\sqrt{3}\right)^6 = 1^6 + \left(i\sqrt{3}\right)^6$
$$= 1 + 27$$
$$= 28$$

You can also prove that De Moivre's theorem works for negative integer powers.

WORKED EXAMPLE 1.2

Let $z = r(\cos\theta + i\sin\theta)$.

a Find the modulus and argument of $\dfrac{1}{z}$.

b Hence prove De Moivre's theorem for negative integer powers.

a Multiplying top and bottom by the complex conjugate:

$$\dfrac{1}{z} = \dfrac{1}{r(\cos\theta + i\sin\theta)} \times \dfrac{(\cos\theta - i\sin\theta)}{(\cos\theta - i\sin\theta)}$$

$$= \dfrac{\cos\theta - i\sin\theta}{r(\cos^2\theta + \sin^2\theta)}$$

$$= \dfrac{1}{r}(\cos\theta - i\sin\theta) \qquad \text{Use } \cos^2\theta + \sin^2\theta = 1$$

$$= \dfrac{1}{r}(\cos(-\theta) + i\sin(-\theta)) \qquad \text{To find the modulus and argument, you need to write the number in this form. Remember that } \cos(-\theta) = \cos\theta \text{ and } \sin(-\theta) = -\sin\theta.$$

Hence $\left|\dfrac{1}{z}\right| = \dfrac{1}{r}$ and $\arg\left(\dfrac{1}{z}\right) = -\theta$.

This means that you can write $\dfrac{1}{z} = \dfrac{1}{r}(\cos(-\theta) + i\sin(-\theta))$.

b

You need to prove that $z^{-n} = r^{-n}(\cos(-n\theta) + i\sin(-n\theta))$.

Using De Moivre's theorem for positive powers:

$$\left(\dfrac{1}{z}\right)^n = \left(\dfrac{1}{r}(\cos(-\theta) + i\sin(-\theta))\right)^n$$

$$= \left(\dfrac{1}{r}\right)^n (\cos(-n\theta) + i\sin(-n\theta))$$

Since you have already proved De Moivre's theorem for positive powers, you can use $z^{-n} = (z^{-1})^n = \left(\dfrac{1}{z}\right)^n$ with the modulus and argument of $\dfrac{1}{z}$ found in part **a**.

Hence $z^{-n} = r^{-n}(\cos(-n\theta) + i\sin(-n\theta))$, as required.

A Level Further Mathematics for AQA Student Book 2

WORKED EXAMPLE 1.3

Find the modulus and argument of $\dfrac{1}{(1-i\sqrt{3})^7}$.

Modulus and argument of $1 - i\sqrt{3}$:

> The best way to find the modulus and argument is to sketch a diagram.

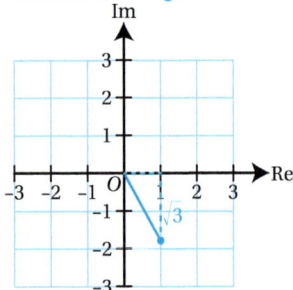

$\sqrt{1^2 + \sqrt{3}^2} = 2$

$\tan^{-1} \dfrac{\sqrt{3}}{1} = \dfrac{\pi}{3}$

$z = 2\left(\cos\left(-\dfrac{\pi}{3}\right) + i\sin\left(-\dfrac{\pi}{3}\right)\right)$

Applying De Moivre's theorem for negative powers:

$z^{-7} = 2^{-7}\left(\cos\left(-7 \times -\dfrac{\pi}{3}\right) + i\sin\left(-7 \times -\dfrac{\pi}{3}\right)\right)$

$= \dfrac{1}{128}\left(\cos\dfrac{7\pi}{3} + i\sin\dfrac{7\pi}{3}\right)$

> This is in the form $r(\cos\theta + i\sin\theta)$ so you can just read off the modulus and the argument.

The modulus is $\dfrac{1}{128}$ and the argument is $\dfrac{7\pi}{3} - 2\pi = \dfrac{\pi}{3}$.

> The argument needs to be between 0 and 2π, so you need to take away 2π.

EXERCISE 1A

1 Evaluate each expression, giving your answer in the form $r(\cos\theta + i\sin\theta)$.

   a   **i** $\left(2\left(\cos\dfrac{\pi}{5} + i\sin\dfrac{\pi}{5}\right)\right)^6$ **ii** $\left(3\left(\cos\left(-\dfrac{\pi}{3}\right) + i\sin\left(-\dfrac{\pi}{3}\right)\right)\right)^4$

   b   **i** $\left(\cos\dfrac{\pi}{6} + i\sin\dfrac{\pi}{6}\right)^2\left(\cos\dfrac{\pi}{4} + i\sin\dfrac{\pi}{4}\right)^3$ **ii** $\left(\cos\dfrac{\pi}{8} + i\sin\dfrac{\pi}{8}\right)^4\left(\cos\dfrac{\pi}{3} + i\sin\dfrac{\pi}{3}\right)^2$

   c   **i** $\dfrac{\left(\cos\dfrac{2\pi}{3} + i\sin\dfrac{2\pi}{3}\right)^6}{\left(\cos\dfrac{\pi}{6} + i\sin\dfrac{\pi}{6}\right)^3}$ **ii** $\dfrac{\left(\cos\dfrac{\pi}{4} + i\sin\dfrac{\pi}{4}\right)^2}{\left(\cos\dfrac{\pi}{3} + i\sin\dfrac{\pi}{3}\right)^6}$

2. Given that $z = \cos\frac{\pi}{6} + i\sin\frac{\pi}{6}$:

   a write z^2, z^3 and z^4 in the form $r(\cos\theta + i\sin\theta)$

   b represent z, z^2, z^3 and z^4 on the same Argand diagram.

3. a Given that $z = \cos\frac{2\pi}{3} + i\sin\frac{2\pi}{3}$:

   i write z^2, z^3 and z^4 in modulus-argument form

   ii represent z, z^2, z^3 and z^4 on the same Argand diagram.

   b For which natural numbers n is $z^n = z$?

4. a Find the modulus and argument of $1 + i\sqrt{3}$.

   Hence, clearly showing your working, find:

   b $(1 + i\sqrt{3})^5$ in modulus-argument form.

   c $(1 + i\sqrt{3})^5$ in Cartesian form.

5. a Write $-\sqrt{2} + i\sqrt{2}$ in the form $r(\cos\theta + i\sin\theta)$.

   b Hence, clearly showing your working, find $(-\sqrt{2} + i\sqrt{2})^6$ in simplified Cartesian form.

6. Find the smallest positive integer value of n for which $\left(\cos\frac{5\pi}{12} + i\sin\frac{5\pi}{12}\right)^n$ is real.

7. Find the smallest positive integer value of k such that $\left(\cos\frac{3\pi}{28} + i\sin\frac{3\pi}{28}\right)^k$ is pure imaginary.

Section 2: Complex exponents

The rules for multiplying complex numbers in modulus–argument form look just like the rules of indices.

Compare

$$r_1(\cos\theta_1 + i\sin\theta_1) \times r_2(\cos\theta_2 + i\sin\theta_2) = r_1 r_2(\cos(\theta_1 + \theta_2) + i\sin(\theta_1 + \theta_2))$$

with

$$k_1 e^{x_1} \times k_2 e^{x_2} = k_1 k_2 e^{x_1 + x_2}.$$

You can extend the definition of powers to imaginary numbers so that all the rules of indices still apply.

Key point 1.2

Euler's formula:

$$e^{i\theta} \equiv \cos\theta + i\sin\theta$$

Did you know?

Substituting $\theta = \pi$ into Euler's formula and rearranging gives $e^{i\pi} + 1 = 0$. This equation, called Euler's identity, connects five important numbers from different areas of mathematics. It is often cited as 'the most beautiful' equation in mathematics.

The Maclaurin series you know for e^x, $\sin x$ and $\cos x$ provide a justification for Euler's formula if you accept that the series for e^x converges for imaginary as well as for real numbers.

You can write a complex number with modulus r and argument θ in **exponential form** as $re^{i\theta}$. You now have two different ways of writing complex numbers with a given modulus and argument.

 **Rewind**

See Further Mathematics Student Book 1, Chapter 11, for a reminder of the Maclaurin series. You will meet these again in Chapter 10.

 Key point 1.3

$$re^{i\theta} = r(\cos\theta + i\sin\theta)$$

When working with complex numbers in exponential form you can use all the normal rules of indices.

WORKED EXAMPLE 1.4

Given that $z = 2e^{\frac{i\pi}{12}}$ and $w = \frac{1}{2}e^{\frac{i\pi}{4}}$, find $z^5 w^3$ in the form $x + iy$.

$z^5 w^3 = \left(2e^{\frac{i\pi}{12}}\right)^5 \left(\frac{1}{2}e^{\frac{i\pi}{4}}\right)^3$

You can do all the calculations in exponential form and then convert to Cartesian form at the end.

$= 2^5 e^{\frac{5i\pi}{12}} \times \frac{1}{2^3} e^{\frac{3i\pi}{4}}$

Use rules of indices for the powers: $\frac{5}{12} + \frac{3}{4} = \frac{7}{6}$

$= 4e^{\frac{7i\pi}{6}}$

$= 4\left(\cos\left(\frac{7\pi}{6}\right) + i\sin\left(\frac{7\pi}{6}\right)\right)$

Now write in terms of trigonometric functions and evaluate.

$= 4\left(-\frac{\sqrt{3}}{2} - \frac{1}{2}i\right)$

$= -2\sqrt{3} - 2i$

You can combine Euler's formula with rules of indices to raise any real number to any complex power.

WORKED EXAMPLE 1.5

Find, correct to three significant figures, the value of:

a e^{2+3i} **b** 3^{2+3i}.

a $e^{2+3i} = e^2 e^{3i}$

Use rules of indices to separate the real and imaginary parts of the power.

$= e^2(\cos 3 + i\sin 3)$

Use Euler's formula for the imaginary power.

$= -7.32 + 1.04i$

Expand the brackets and give the answer to 3 s.f. Remember that the arguments of the trigonometric functions are in radians.

— Continues on next page

b $3^{2+3i} = (e^{\ln 3})^{2+3i}$
$= e^{2\ln 3} e^{(3\ln 3)i}$
$= 9(\cos(\ln 27) + i\sin(\ln 27))$
$= -8.89 - 1.38i$

> You only know how to raise e to a complex power, so express 3 as a power of e.

> Use rules of indices and then Euler's formula. Note that $e^{2\ln 3} = e^{\ln 9} = 9$ and $3\ln 3 = \ln 27$.

The complex conjugate of a number is easy to find when written in exponential form. This is best seen on an Argand diagram, where taking the complex conjugate is represented by a reflection in the real axis. In this case it is best to take the argument between $-\pi$ and π.

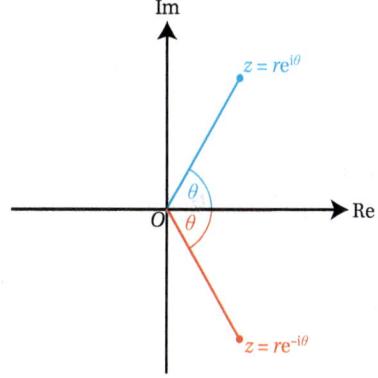

⏩ Fast forward

You will use the exponential form of complex numbers when solving second-order differential equations in Chapter 11.

🔑 Key point 1.4

The complex conjugate of $z = re^{i\theta}$ is $z^* = re^{-i\theta}$.

💡 Tip

Note that if $r = 1$, you also have $z^* = \frac{1}{z} = e^{-i\theta}$.

In Further Mathematics Student Book 1, Chapter 2, you used complex conjugates when solving polynomial equations.

WORKED EXAMPLE 1.6

A cubic equation has real coefficients and two of its roots are 1 and $2e^{\frac{i\pi}{3}}$. Find the equation in the form $x^3 + ax^2 + bx + c = 0$.

The roots are: 1, $2e^{\frac{i\pi}{3}}$ and $2e^{-\frac{i\pi}{3}}$.

> Complex roots occur in conjugate pairs, so you can write down the third root.

$-a = 1 + 2e^{\frac{i\pi}{3}} + 2e^{-\frac{i\pi}{3}}$
$= 1 + 4\cos\frac{\pi}{3}$
$= 3$
$\therefore a = -3$

> Use the formulae for sums and products of roots to find the coefficients of the equation: $-a = x_1 + x_2 + x_3$

> Remember that $z + z^* = 2\text{Re}(z)$, and that $\text{Re}(e^{\frac{i\pi}{3}}) = \cos\frac{\pi}{3} = \frac{1}{2}$

$b = \left(1 \times 2e^{\frac{i\pi}{3}}\right) + \left(1 \times 2e^{-\frac{i\pi}{3}}\right) + \left(2e^{\frac{i\pi}{3}} \times 2e^{-\frac{i\pi}{3}}\right)$
$= 4\cos\left(\frac{\pi}{3}\right) + 4$
$= 6$

> $b = x_1x_2 + x_2x_3 + x_3x_1$

Continues on next page

A Level Further Mathematics for AQA Student Book 2

$-c = 1 \times 2e^{\frac{i\pi}{3}} \times 2e^{-\frac{i\pi}{3}} = 4$ .... $-c = x_1 x_2 x_3$
$\therefore c = -4$

Hence the equation is $x^3 - 3x^2 + 6x - 4 = 0$.

EXERCISE 1B

You can use your calculator to perform operations with complex numbers in Cartesian, modulus-argument and exponential forms, as well as to convert from one form to another. Do the questions in this exercise without a calculator first, then use a calculator to check your answers.

1 Write each complex number in Cartesian form without using trigonometric functions.

    a **i** $3e^{i\frac{\pi}{6}}$ **ii** $4e^{\frac{i\pi}{4}}$

    b **i** $4e^{i\pi}$ **ii** $5e^{2\pi i}$

    c **i** $e^{\frac{2\pi i}{3}}$ **ii** $2e^{\frac{3\pi}{2}i}$

2 Write each complex number in the form $re^{i\theta}$.

    a **i** $5 + 5i$ **ii** $2\sqrt{3} - 2i$

    b **i** $-\frac{1}{2} + \frac{1}{2}i$ **ii** $1 - i\sqrt{3}$

    c **i** $-4i$ **ii** -5

3 Write the answer to each calculation in the form $re^{i\theta}$.

    a **i** $4e^{i\frac{\pi}{6}} \times 5e^{i\frac{\pi}{4}}$ **ii** $\dfrac{5e^{i\frac{3\pi}{4}}}{10e^{i\frac{\pi}{4}}}$

    b **i** $\dfrac{\left(2e^{i\frac{\pi}{4}}\right)^3}{\left(5e^{i\frac{\pi}{3}}\right)^2}$ **ii** $\dfrac{2e^{i\frac{\pi}{3}}}{\left(e^{i\frac{\pi}{6}}\right)^5}$

4 Represent each complex number on an Argand diagram.

    a **i** $e^{i\frac{\pi}{3}}$ **ii** $e^{i\frac{3\pi}{4}}$

    b **i** $5e^{i\frac{\pi}{2}}$ **ii** $2e^{-i\frac{\pi}{2}}$

5 Let $z = 2e^{\frac{i\pi}{12}}$ and $w = 4e^{\frac{i\pi}{3}}$. Show that $z^2 + w = 2(1+i)(1+\sqrt{3})$.

6 Let $z = 2e^{\frac{i\pi}{3}}$ and $w = 3e^{\frac{-i\pi}{6}}$. Write each complex number in the form $x + iy$.

    a $\dfrac{z}{w}$ **b** $z^5 w^3$.

7 Write e^{4+3i} in the form $x + iy$, where x and y are real, giving your answer correct to three significant figures.

8 Write $e^{2-i\frac{\pi}{3}}$ in exact Cartesian form.

9. The equation $x^3 + ax^2 + bx + c = 0$ has real coefficients, and two of its roots are 2 and $e^{\frac{i\pi}{3}}$. Find the values of a, b and c.

10. A quartic equation has real coefficients and two of its roots are $e^{\frac{i\pi}{6}}$ and $2e^{-\frac{i\pi}{3}}$. Find the equation in the form $x^4 + ax^3 + bx^2 + cx + d = 0$.

11. Find 5^i in the form $x + iy$.

12. Find 3^{2-i} in the form $x + iy$.

Section 3: Roots of complex numbers

Now that you can use De Moivre's theorem to find powers of complex numbers, it makes sense to ask whether you can also find roots.

In Further Mathematics Student Book 1, you learnt how to find the two square roots of a complex number by writing $z = x + iy$ and comparing real and imaginary parts. You also know that a polynomial equation of degree n has n complex roots. Just as a complex number has two square roots, it will have three cube roots, four fourth roots, and so on.

You can't always use the algebraic method to find all those roots. De Moivre's theorem gives an alternative method.

> ⏪ **Rewind**
>
> See Further Mathematics Student Book 1, Chapter 1, for an example of finding square roots of a complex number.

WORKED EXAMPLE 1.7

Solve the equation $z^3 = 4\sqrt{3} + 4i$.

Let $z = r(\cos\theta + i\sin\theta)$.　　　　Use the modulus-argument form since raising to a power is easier in this form than in Cartesian form.

Then the equation is equivalent to
$r^3(\cos 3\theta + i\sin 3\theta) = 4\sqrt{3} + 4i$　　　Use De Moivre's theorem and then compare the modulus and the argument of both sides.

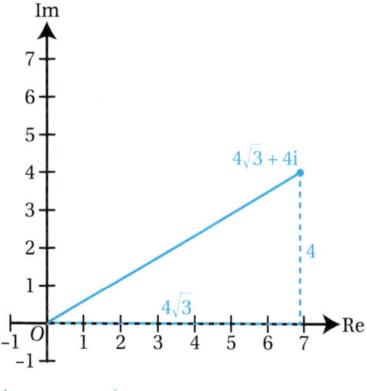

Find the modulus and argument of $4\sqrt{3} + 4i$

$\left|4\sqrt{3} + 4i\right| = \sqrt{\left(4\sqrt{3}\right)^2 + 4^2} = 8$

$\arg\left(4\sqrt{3} + 4i\right) = \arctan\left(\dfrac{4}{4\sqrt{3}}\right) = \dfrac{\pi}{6}$

Continues on next page

Therefore,

$r^3(\cos 3\theta + i \sin 3\theta) = 8\left(\cos \dfrac{\pi}{6} + i \sin \dfrac{\pi}{6}\right)$

Comparing the moduli:
$r^3 = 8 \Rightarrow r = 2$ .... Remember that, by definition, r is a positive real number.

Comparing the arguments:

$3\theta = \dfrac{\pi}{6}, \dfrac{13\pi}{6}$ or $\dfrac{25\pi}{6}$

$\theta = \dfrac{\pi}{18}, \dfrac{13\pi}{18}, \dfrac{25\pi}{18}$

If $0 < \theta < 2\pi$ then $0 < 3\theta < 6\pi$.
Since adding on 2π to the argument returns to the same complex number, there are three possible values for 3θ between 0 and 6π.

The solutions are:

$z_1 = 2\left(\cos \dfrac{\pi}{18} + i \sin \dfrac{\pi}{18}\right)$

$z_2 = 2\left(\cos \dfrac{13\pi}{18} + i \sin \dfrac{13\pi}{18}\right)$

$z_3 = 2\left(\cos \dfrac{25\pi}{18} + i \sin \dfrac{25\pi}{18}\right)$

Write down all three solutions in modulus-argument form.

If you plot the three solutions from Worked example 1.7 on an Argand diagram, you will notice an interesting pattern. They all have the same modulus so they lie on a circle of radius 2. The arguments differ by $\dfrac{2\pi}{3}$ so they are equally spaced around the circle. Therefore, the three points form an equilateral triangle.

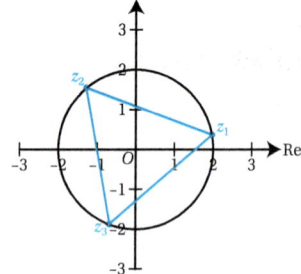

🔑 Key point 1.5

To solve $z^n = w$:

- write w in modulus-argument form
- use De Moivre's theorem to write $z^n = r^n(\cos n\theta + i \sin n\theta)$
- compare moduli, remembering that they are always real
- compare arguments, remembering that adding 2π onto the argument does not change the number
- write n different solutions in modulus-argument form.

All n solutions will have the same modulus, and their arguments will differ by $\dfrac{2\pi}{n}$. This means that the Argand diagram will always show the pattern you noticed in Worked example 1.7.

🔑 Key point 1.6

The solutions of $z^n = w$ form a regular polygon with vertices on a circle centred at the origin.

1 Further complex numbers: powers and roots

WORKED EXAMPLE 1.8

Draw an Argand diagram showing the solutions of the equation $z^6 = 729$.

One solution is $z_1 = \sqrt[6]{729} = 3$

There are six solutions, forming a regular hexagon.

You only need to find one solution and then complete the diagram.

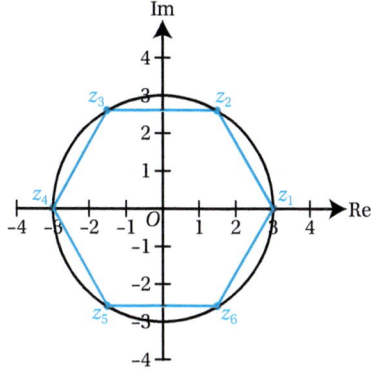

You can also find the equation with solutions that form a given regular polygon.

WORKED EXAMPLE 1.9

The diagram shows a regular pentagon inscribed in a circle on an Argand diagram. One of the vertices lies on the positive imaginary axis.

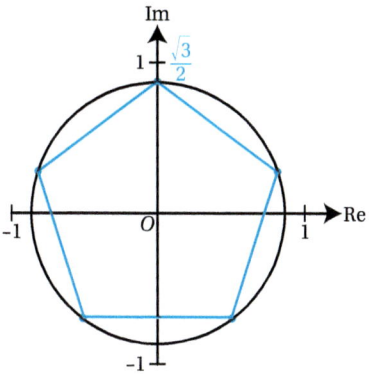

The five vertices of the pentagon correspond to the solutions of an equation of the form $z^n = w$, where w is a complex number. Find the values of n and w.

There are five solutions, so $n = 5$.

Any equation of the form $z^n = w$ has n complex solutions.

From the diagram:
$z = \frac{\sqrt{3}}{2}$ i is a solution.

Use the fact that one solution is given in the question.

Hence $w = \left(\frac{\sqrt{3}}{2}\text{i}\right)^5 = \frac{9\sqrt{3}}{32}\text{i}$

Remember that $\text{i}^5 = \text{i}$.

A Level Further Mathematics for AQA Student Book 2

EXERCISE 1C

In this exercise you must clearly show your working.

1. Find all three cube roots of each number, giving your answers in the form $re^{i\theta}$.

   a i 27   ii 100

   b i 8i   ii i

   c i 1 + i   ii $2 - \sqrt{3}i$

2. Find the fourth roots of each number. Give your answers in the form $r(\cos\theta + i\sin\theta)$ and show them on an Argand diagram.

   a i −16   ii 81i

   b i $128\sqrt{2} + 128i\sqrt{2}$ ii $-\dfrac{1}{2} + \dfrac{\sqrt{3}}{2}i$

3. Solve the equation $z^3 = -8$ for $z \in \mathbb{C}$. Give your answers in the form $x + iy$.

4. a Find the modulus and the argument of $8\sqrt{3} - 8i$.

   b Solve the equation $z^4 = 8\sqrt{3} - 8i$, giving your answers in the form $r\left(\cos\left(\dfrac{p}{q}\pi\right) + i\sin\left(\dfrac{p}{q}\pi\right)\right)$, where p and q are integers.

5. Solve the equation $z^3 - \sqrt{2}(4 - 4i) = 0$, giving your answers in Cartesian form.

6. Find all complex solutions of the equation $z^4 + 81i = 0$, giving your answers in the form $r\left(\cos\left(\dfrac{p}{q}\pi\right) + i\sin\left(\dfrac{p}{q}\pi\right)\right)$, where p and q are integers.

7. a Write $4 + 4\sqrt{3}i$ in the form $re^{i\theta}$.

   b Hence solve the equation $z^4 = 4 + 4\sqrt{3}i$, giving your answers in the form $re^{i\theta}$.

   c Show your solutions on an Argand diagram.

8. The diagram shows a square with one vertex at (2, 2). The complex numbers corresponding to the vertices of the square are solutions of an equation of the form $z^n = w$, where $n \in \mathbb{N}$ and $w \in \mathbb{R}$.

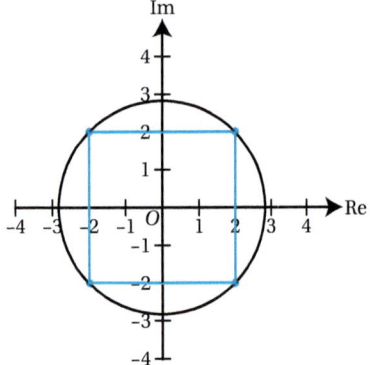

Find the values of n and w.

9　a　Solve the equation $z^4 = -16$, giving your answers in Cartesian form.

　　b　Hence express $z^4 + 16$ as a product of two real quadratic factors.

10　a　Find all the solutions of the equation $z^3 = -8i$.

　　b　Hence solve the equation $w^3 + 8i(w-1)^3 = 0$. Give your answers in exact Cartesian form.

11　Consider the equation $z^3 + (4\sqrt{2} - 4\sqrt{2}i) = 0$.

　　a　Solve the equation, giving your answers in the form $r(\cos\theta + i\sin\theta)$.

　　The solutions are represented on an Argand diagram by points A, B and C, labelled clockwise with A in the first quadrant. D is the midpoint of AB and the corresponding complex number is d.

　　b　Find the modulus and argument of d.

　　c　Write d^3 in exact Cartesian form.

12　a　Find, in exponential form, the three solutions of the equation $z^3 = -1$.

　　b　Expand $(x+2)^3$.

　　c　Hence or otherwise solve the equation $z^3 + 6z^2 + 12z + 9 = 0$, giving any complex solution in exact Cartesian form.

Section 4: Roots of unity

In Section 3 you learnt a method for finding all complex roots of a number. A special case of this is solving the equation $z^n = 1$. Its solutions are called **roots of unity**.

WORKED EXAMPLE 1.10

Find the fifth roots of unity, giving your answers in exponential form.

Let the roots be $z = re^{i\theta}$. Then: 　$(re^{i\theta})^5 = 1$	Write z in exponential form and use De Moivre's theorem.
$\Rightarrow r^5 e^{5i\theta} = 1e^{0i}$	1 has modulus 1 and argument 0.
Comparing the moduli: 　$r = 1$	
Comparing the arguments: $5\theta = 0, 2\pi, 4\pi, 6\pi, 8\pi$ $\theta = 0, \dfrac{2\pi}{5}, \dfrac{4\pi}{5}, \dfrac{6\pi}{5}, \dfrac{8\pi}{5}$	Remember that there should be five solutions.

The fifth roots of unity are: $1, e^{\frac{2i\pi}{5}}, e^{\frac{4i\pi}{5}}, e^{\frac{6i\pi}{5}}, e^{\frac{8i\pi}{5}}$

As in Section 3, the five roots form a regular pentagon on the Argand diagram:

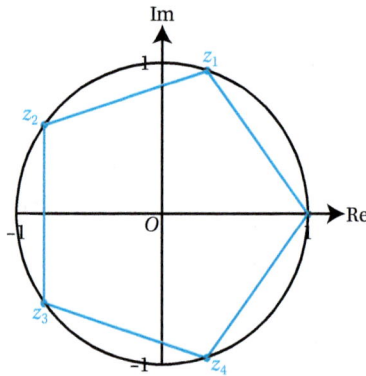

The same procedure works for any power n: there will be n distinct roots, each with modulus 1, and with arguments differing by $\frac{2\pi}{n}$. Remembering that one of the roots always equals 1, you can write down the full set of roots.

> ### Key point 1.7
>
> The nth roots of unity are:
> $$1, e^{\frac{2\pi i}{n}}, e^{\frac{4\pi i}{n}}, \ldots, e^{\frac{2(n-1)\pi i}{n}}$$
> They form a regular n-gon on an Argand diagram.

Notice that all the arguments are multiples of $\frac{2\pi}{n}$. But multiplying an argument by a number k corresponds to raising the complex number to the power of k. Hence all the nth roots of unity are powers of $e^{\frac{2\pi i}{n}}$. It is usual to denote the n roots $\omega_0, \omega_1, \ldots, \omega_{n-1}$.

> ### Key point 1.8
>
> You can write the nth root of unity as:
> $$\omega_k = \left(e^{\frac{2\pi i}{n}}\right)^k = \omega_1^k, \text{ where } k = 0, 1, \ldots, n-1$$

You can use the fact that the roots form a regular polygon to deduce various relationships between them. For example, for $n = 5$, you can use the symmetry of the pentagon to see that $\omega_4 = \omega_1^*$ and $\omega_3 = \omega_2^*$.

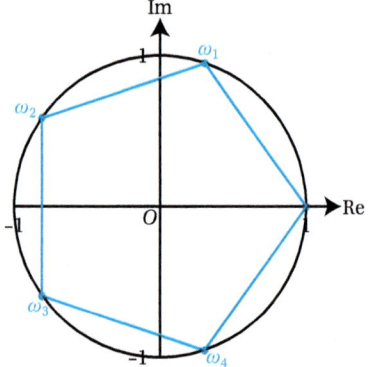

1 Further complex numbers: powers and roots

One of the most useful results concerns the sum of all n roots. You know from Further Mathematics Student Book 1, Chapter 1, that adding complex numbers corresponds to adding vectors on an Argand diagram. Since the points corresponding to the n roots of unity are equally spaced around the circle, the sum of the corresponding vectors should be zero.

You can also prove this result algebraically.

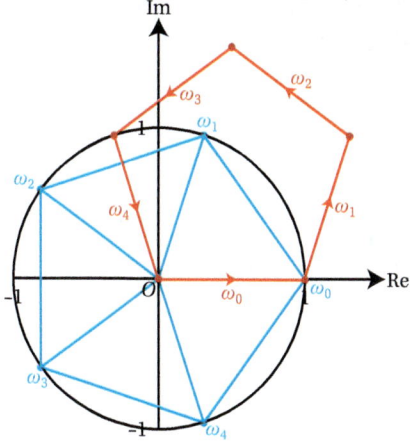

WORKED EXAMPLE 1.11

Let n be a natural number, and let $\omega = e^{\frac{2\pi i}{n}}$. Let $1, \omega_1, \omega_2, \ldots, \omega_{n-1}$ be the nth roots of unity.

a Express ω_k in terms of ω.
b Hence show that $1 + \omega_1 + \ldots + \omega_{n-1} = 0$.

a $\omega_k = \omega^k$ — This is the result from Key point 1.8.

b $1 + \omega_1 + \ldots + \omega_{n-1} = 1 + \omega + \omega^2 + \ldots + \omega^{n-1}$
$$= \frac{1 - \omega^n}{1 - \omega}$$
$$= 0 \text{ (since } \omega^n = 1\text{)}$$

This is a geometric series with first term 1 and common ratio ω.
Note that $\omega \neq 1$ so you can use the formula for the sum of the geometric series.

ω is an nth root of unity, which means that $\omega^n = 1$.

🔑 Key point 1.9

If $1, \omega_1, \omega_2, \ldots, \omega_{n-1}$ are the nth roots of unity, then
$$1 + \omega_1 + \ldots + \omega_{n-1} = 0.$$

⏮ Rewind

You learnt about sums and products of roots of polynomials in Further Mathematics Student Book 1, Chapter 2.

💡 Tip

You could also prove the result in Key point 1.9 by using the result about the sum of the roots of a polynomial: these are the roots of the equation $z^n - 1 = 0$, so their sum equals minus the coefficient of z^{n-1} which is 0.

⏭ Fast forward

You will learn more about the links between complex numbers and trigonometry in Chapter 2.

You can use the result in Key point 1.9 with a specific value of n to find some special values of trigonometric functions.

17

WORKED EXAMPLE 1.12

Let $\omega = e^{\frac{2\pi i}{5}}$.

a Show that $\text{Re}(\omega) + \text{Re}(\omega^2) = -\frac{1}{2}$.

b Hence find the exact value of $\cos \frac{2\pi}{5}$.

a From the diagram:

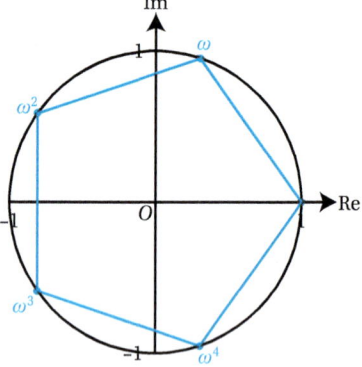

The five points form a regular pentagon.

$\omega^4 = \omega^*$ and $\omega^3 = (\omega^2)^*$

Hence $\text{Re}(\omega^4) = \text{Re}(\omega)$ and $\text{Re}(\omega^3) = \text{Re}(\omega^2)$ .... You are interested in the real parts.

Using the result $1 + \omega + \omega^2 + \omega^3 + \omega^4 = 0$ .... This is the result from Key point 1.9.
and taking the real part:
$1 + \text{Re}(\omega) + \text{Re}(\omega^2) + \text{Re}(\omega^3) + \text{Re}(\omega^4) = 0$

$1 + 2\text{Re}(\omega) + 2\text{Re}(\omega^2) = 0$ .... Pair up the terms with equal real parts.

$\text{Re}(\omega) + \text{Re}(\omega^2) = -\frac{1}{2}$

b $\text{Re}(\omega) = \cos \frac{2\pi}{5}$, $\text{Re}(\omega^2) = \cos \frac{4\pi}{5}$ .... Use the fact that $\omega = e^{\frac{2\pi i}{5}} = \cos \frac{2\pi}{5} + i \sin \frac{2\pi}{5}$
and $\omega^2 = \cos \frac{4\pi}{5} + i \sin \frac{4\pi}{5}$.

$\therefore \cos \frac{2\pi}{5} + \cos \frac{4\pi}{5} = -\frac{1}{2}$

$\cos \frac{2\pi}{5} + 2\cos^2 \frac{2\pi}{5} - 1 = -\frac{1}{2}$ .... Use $\cos \frac{4\pi}{5} = 2\cos^2 \frac{2\pi}{5} - 1$.

$4\cos^2 \frac{2\pi}{5} + 2\cos \frac{2\pi}{5} - 1 = 0$ .... This is a quadratic equation in $\cos \frac{2\pi}{5}$.

$\cos \frac{2\pi}{5} = \frac{-2 + \sqrt{4+16}}{8}$ .... Take the positive root since $\cos \frac{2\pi}{5} > 0$.

$= \frac{-1 + \sqrt{5}}{4}$

1 Further complex numbers: powers and roots

EXERCISE 1D

1 Write down, in the form $r(\cos\theta + i\sin\theta)$, all the solutions of each equation.

   a   **i** $z^3 = 1$ **ii** $z^2 = 1$

   b   **i** $z^6 = 1$ **ii** $z^4 = 1$

2 For each equation from Question 1, write the solutions in exact Cartesian form.

3 **a** Write down, in the form $e^{i\theta}$, the solutions of the equation $z^5 = 1$.

    b Represent the solutions on an Argand diagram.

4 The diagram shows all the solutions of an equation $z^n = 1$.

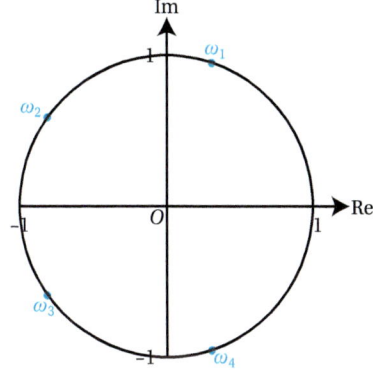

    a Write down the value of n.

    b Write down the value of $\omega_1 + \omega_2 + \omega_3 + \omega_4$.

    c Which statements are correct? Choose from these options.

       A $\omega_3 = \omega_1^3$ **B** $\omega_4 = \omega_2^2$ **C** $\omega_3^5 = 1$ **D** $\omega_1^3 = -\omega_1^2$

5 Let $\omega = e^{\frac{2\pi i}{7}}$.

    a Express the seventh roots of unity in terms of ω.

    b Is there an integer k such that $\omega^k = -\omega$? Justify your answer.

    c Write down the smallest positive integer p such that $\omega^{17} = \omega^p$.

    d Write down an integer m such that $\omega^m = (\omega^2)^*$.

6 Let $1, \omega_1, \omega_2, \omega_3, \omega_4, \omega_5$ be the distinct sixth roots of unity.

    a Show that $\omega_n = \omega_1^n$ for $n = 2, 3, 4, 5$.

    b Hence show that $1 + \omega_1 + \omega_2 + \omega_3 + \omega_4 + \omega_5 = 0$.

7 **In this question you must clearly show your working.**

    a Find, in exact Cartesian form, all the complex solutions of the equation $z^3 = 1$.

    b Hence find the exact solutions of the equation $(z-1)^3 = (z+2)^3$.

8 Multiply out and simplify $(a+b\omega)(a-b\omega^2)$, where $\omega = e^{\frac{i\pi}{3}}$.

9 Let $\omega = e^{\frac{2\pi i}{5}}$.

   a Write, in terms of ω, the complex roots of the equation $z^5 = 1$.

   Consider the equation $(z-1)^5 = (z+1)^5$.

   b Find, in terms of ω, all solutions of the equation.

   c Show that the solutions can be written as $i\cot\left(\frac{k\pi}{5}\right)$ for $k = 1, 2, 3, 4$.

   d Show that $(z-1)^5 = (z+1)^5$ is equivalent to $5z^4 + 10z^2 + 1 = 0$.

   e Hence show that $\cot^2 \frac{\pi}{5} + \cot^2 \frac{2\pi}{5} = 2$.

10 Let $1, \omega, \omega^2, \omega^3, \omega^4, \omega^5$ be the solutions of the equation $z^6 = 1$, where ω is the one with the smallest positive argument.

   a Show these solutions on an Argand diagram.

   b Write in the form $re^{i\theta}$:

      i $\dfrac{1+\omega}{2}$ ii $\dfrac{\omega^3 + \omega^4}{2}$.

11 a Show that $\cos 3\theta = 4\cos^3\theta - 3\cos\theta$.

   Let $\omega = \cos \frac{2\pi}{7} + i\sin \frac{2\pi}{7}$.

   b i Show that $1 + \omega + \omega^2 + \omega^3 + \omega^4 + \omega^5 + \omega^6 = 0$.

      ii Hence deduce the value of $\cos \frac{2\pi}{7} + \cos \frac{4\pi}{7} + \cos \frac{6\pi}{7}$.

   c Show that $\cos \frac{2\pi}{7}$ is a root of the equation $8t^3 + 4t^2 - 4t - 1 = 0$.

Section 5: Further factorising

In Further Mathematics Student Book 1, Chapter 2, you learnt that complex roots of a real polynomial come in conjugate pairs, and how you can use this fact to factorise a polynomial. You used the important result that, for any complex number w,

$$(z-w)(z-w^*) = z^2 - 2\mathrm{Re}(w) + |w|^2$$

You can now combine this with your knowledge of roots of complex numbers to factorise expressions of the form $z^n + c$.

WORKED EXAMPLE 1.13

a Find all the complex solutions of $z^4 = -81$, giving your answers in Cartesian form.
b Hence write $z^4 + 81$ as a product of two real quadratic factors.

a Let $z = re^{i\theta}$.
> Write z in exponential form to find the roots, then turn answers into Cartesian form.

Then $r^4 e^{i4\theta} = -81 = 81 e^{i\pi}$
> The argument of -81 is π.

Comparing the moduli:
$r^4 = 81$, so $r = 3$

Comparing the arguments:
$4\theta = \pi, 3\pi, 5\pi, 7\pi$
$\theta = \dfrac{\pi}{4}, \dfrac{3\pi}{4}, \dfrac{5\pi}{4}, \dfrac{7\pi}{4}$
> You are looking for 4 solutions, so add 2π three times.

The solutions are:
$z_1 = \dfrac{3\sqrt{2}}{2} + \dfrac{3\sqrt{2}}{2}i$
$z_2 = -\dfrac{3\sqrt{2}}{2} + \dfrac{3\sqrt{2}}{2}i$
$z_3 = -\dfrac{3\sqrt{2}}{2} - \dfrac{3\sqrt{2}}{2}i$
$z_4 = \dfrac{3\sqrt{2}}{2} - \dfrac{3\sqrt{2}}{2}i$
> Find the Cartesian form
> $x + iy = (r\cos\theta) + i(r\sin\theta)$

b $z^4 + 81 = (z - z_1)(z - z_2)(z - z_3)(z - z_4)$
> The factors of $z^4 + 81$ correspond to the roots of the equation $z^4 + 81 = 0$, which you found in part **a**.

$(z - z_1)(z - z_4) = z^2 - 2\text{Re}(z_1) + |z_1|^2$
$\qquad\qquad\qquad = z^2 - 3\sqrt{2}z + 9$

$(z - z_2)(z - z_3) = z^2 - 2\text{Re}(z_2) + |z_2|^2$
$\qquad\qquad\qquad = z^2 + 3\sqrt{2}z + 9$

> To get real quadratic factors you need to pair up the factors corresponding to the conjugate roots. You can use the shortcut
> $(z - w)(z - w^*) = z^2 - 2\text{Re}(w) + |w|^2$ and $|z_k| = 3$.

$\therefore z^4 + 81 = (z^2 - 3\sqrt{2}z + 9)(z^2 + 3\sqrt{2}z + 9)$

EXERCISE 1E

In this exercise you must clearly show your working.

1 **a** Find, in exponential form, all the complex solutions of the equation $z^4 = -16$.
  b Write your answers from part **a** in exact Cartesian form.
  c Hence express $z^4 + 16$ as a product of two real quadratic factors.

2 By solving the equation $z^8 = 16$, express $z^8 - 16$ as a product of four real quadratic factors.

3 Show that $z^5 - 1 = (z - 1)(z^2 - (2\cos\theta)z + 1)(z^2 - (2\cos\phi)z + 1)$, where $\theta, \phi \in (0, \pi)$.

4 Let $\omega = e^{\frac{2i\pi}{5}}$.

   a Write the solutions of the equation $z^5 - 1 = 0$ in terms of ω.

   b Hence evaluate $(2-\omega)(2-\omega^2)(2-\omega^3)(2-\omega^4)$.

5 a Show that $t^2 + t + 1 = \left(t - e^{\frac{2i\pi}{3}}\right)\left(t - e^{-\frac{2i\pi}{3}}\right)$.

   b Solve the equation $z^4 = e^{\frac{2i\pi}{3}}$.

   c Hence write $z^8 + z^4 + 1$ as a product of four real quadratic factors.

6 Let $\omega = e^{\frac{2i\pi}{7}}$.

   a Write down the non-real roots of the equation $z^7 = 1$ in terms of ω.

   b Show that $\cos\frac{2\pi}{7} + \cos\frac{4\pi}{7} + \cos\frac{6\pi}{7} = -\frac{1}{2}$.

   c Hence show that $\cos\frac{2\pi}{7}$ is a solution of the equation $8t^3 + 4t^2 - 4t - 1 = 0$.

Section 6: Geometry of complex numbers

Multiplication of complex numbers has an interesting geometrical interpretation. On an Argand diagram, let A be the point corresponding to the complex number $z_1 = r_1(\cos\theta_1 + i\sin\theta_1)$, and let B be the point corresponding to the complex number $z_1 \times (r_2(\cos\theta_2 + i\sin\theta_2)) = r_1 r_2(\cos(\theta_1 + \theta_2) + i\sin(\theta_1 + \theta_2))$.

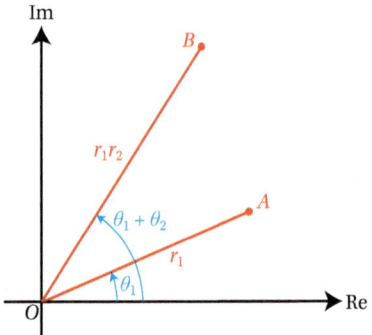

Then $OA = r_1$, $OB = r_1 r_2$, and $\angle AOB = (\theta_1 + \theta_2) - \theta_1 = \theta_2$. Hence the transformation that takes point A to point B is a rotation through angle θ_2 followed by an enlargement with scale factor r_2.

Key point 1.10

Multiplication by $r(\cos\theta + i\sin\theta)$ corresponds to a rotation about the origin though angle θ and an enlargement with scale factor r.

⏮ Rewind

You already know, from Further Mathematics Student Book 1, Chapter 1, that adding a complex number $a + ib$ corresponds to a translation with vector $\binom{a}{b}$, and that taking the complex conjugate corresponds to a reflection in the real axis.

1 Further complex numbers: powers and roots

WORKED EXAMPLE 1.14

Points A and B on an Argand diagram represent complex numbers $a = \sqrt{3} + i$ and $b = 2\sqrt{2} + 2i\sqrt{2}$, respectively.

a Find the modulus and argument of a and b.
b Hence describe a combination of two transformations that maps A to B.

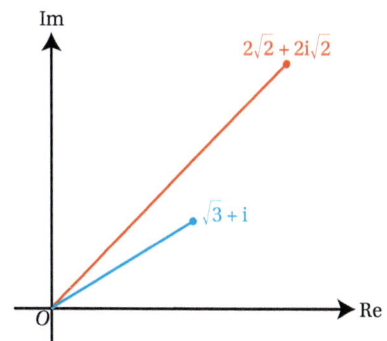

A diagram helps to find the modulus and the argument.

a $|a| = \sqrt{3+1} = 2$, $\arg(a) = \arctan\left(\dfrac{1}{\sqrt{3}}\right) = \dfrac{\pi}{6}$

$|b| = \sqrt{8+8} = 4$, $\arg(b) = \arctan\left(\dfrac{2\sqrt{2}}{2\sqrt{2}}\right) = \dfrac{\pi}{4}$

b Enlargement with scale factor 2

$|b| = 2|a|$

and rotation through $\dfrac{\pi}{4} - \dfrac{\pi}{6} = \dfrac{\pi}{12}$ about the origin.

The angle of rotation is the difference between the arguments.

The result from Key point 1.10 is remarkably powerful in some situations that have nothing to do with complex numbers.

WORKED EXAMPLE 1.15

An equilateral triangle has one vertex at the origin and another at (1, 2). Find one possible set of coordinates of the third vertex.

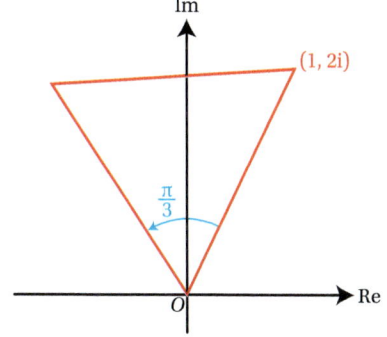

On an Argand diagram the point (1, 2) corresponds to the complex number $1 + 2i$. You can obtain the third vertex by rotation through 60° anticlockwise about the origin and no enlargement. This corresponds to multiplication by the complex number with modulus 1 and argument $\dfrac{\pi}{3}$.

Continues on next page

23

A Level Further Mathematics for AQA Student Book 2

The complex number corresponding to the third vertex is

$$(1 + 2i)\left(\cos \frac{\pi}{3} + i \sin \frac{\pi}{3}\right) = (1 + 2i)\left(\frac{1}{2} + \frac{\sqrt{3}}{2}i\right)$$
$$= \left(\frac{1}{2} - \sqrt{3}\right) + \left(\frac{\sqrt{3}}{2} + 1\right)i$$

So the coordinates are $\left(\frac{1}{2} - \sqrt{3}, \frac{\sqrt{3}}{2} + 1\right)$.

Tip

There is another equilateral triangle with vertices (0, 0) and (1, 2). You can obtain it by rotating clockwise through 60°, corresponding to multiplication by $\cos\left(-\frac{\pi}{3}\right) + i \sin\left(-\frac{\pi}{3}\right)$.

Focus on...

You can use several different approaches to solve the problem from Worked example 1.15. You could use coordinate geometry and trigonometry, or you could use a matrix to carry out the rotation. In Focus on ... Problem solving 1 you will explore different approaches to similar problems.

Rewind

You studied rotation matrices in Further Mathematics Student Book 1, Chapter 8.

EXERCISE 1F

1 Points A and B represent complex numbers $a = 4 + i$ and $b = 5 + 3i$ on an Argand diagram.

   a Find the modulus and argument of a and b.

   b Point A is mapped to point B by a combination of an enlargement and a rotation. Find the scale factor of the enlargement and the angle of rotation.

2 Points P and Q represent complex numbers $p = 3 + 5i$ and $q = -\sqrt{30} + 2i$, respectively.

   a Show that $|p| = |q|$. b Describe a single transformation that maps P to Q.

3 The complex number corresponding to the point A in the diagram is $z_1 = 3 + 2i$. The distance $OB = OA$. Find, in surd form, the complex number corresponding to the point B.

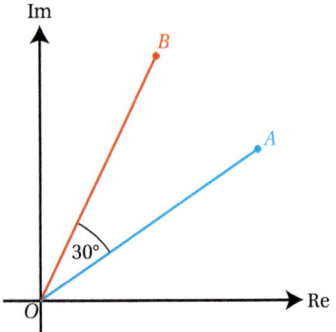

24

4 The diagram shows a square *OABC*, where *A* has coordinates (5, 2).

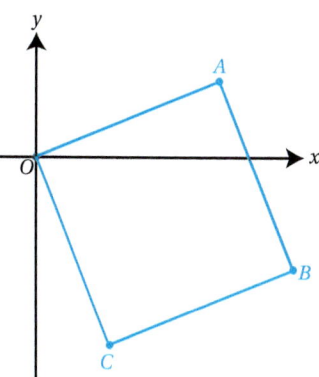

Find the exact coordinates of *B* and *C*.

5 The diagram shows a right-angled triangle *OAB* with angle *AOB* = 30°. The coordinates of *A* are (6, 3).

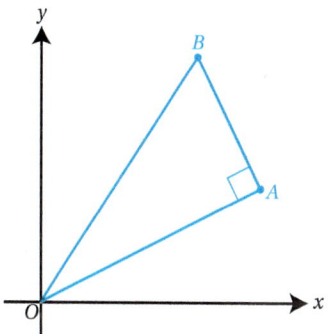

a Find the exact length *OB*.

b Using complex numbers, or otherwise, find the coordinates of *B*.

6 Let $z = 0.6 + 0.8i$.

a Represent z, z^2 and z^3 on an Argand diagram.

b Describe fully the transformation mapping z to z^3.

7 The diagram shows an equilateral triangle with its centre at the origin and one vertex *A*(4, −1).

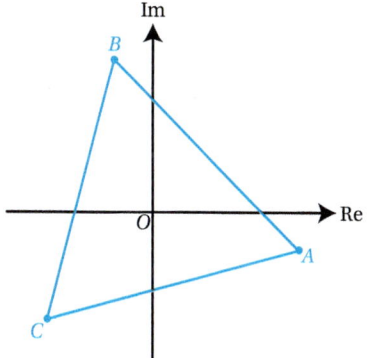

a Write down the complex number corresponding to the vertex *A*.

b Hence find the coordinates of the other two vertices.

8 The diagram shows line l through the origin, with gradient $\sqrt{3}$, and the point A representing the complex number $\sqrt{2} + i\sqrt{2}$.

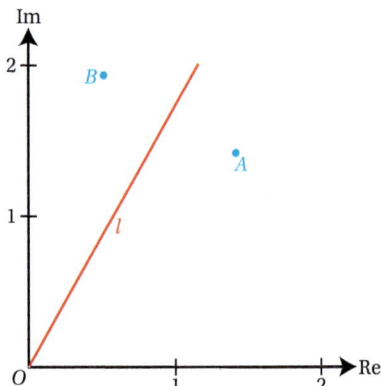

a The line l is the locus of $z \in \mathbb{C}$ which satisfy $\arg z = \theta$. Find the exact value of θ.

Point B is the reflection of point A in the line l.

b Find the size of the angle AOB.

c Use complex numbers to find the exact coordinates of B.

9 a The point representing a complex number z on an Argand diagram is reflected in the real axis and then rotated 90° anticlockwise about the origin. Write down, in terms of z, the complex number representing the resulting image.

b If the rotation is applied before the reflection, show that the resulting image represents the complex number $-iz^*$.

10 a The point representing the complex number p on an Argand diagram is rotated through angle θ about the point representing the complex number a. The resulting point represents complex number q. Explain why $q - a = (p - a)e^{i\theta}$.

b Find the exact coordinates of the image when the point $P(1, 3)$ is rotated 60° anticlockwise about the point $A(2, -1)$.

11 a On an Argand diagram, points A, B and C represent complex numbers a, b and c, respectively. C is the image of B after a rotation through angle θ, anticlockwise, about A.

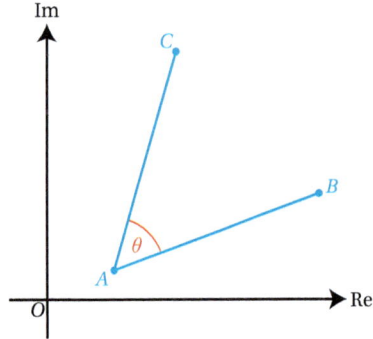

Express the complex number $c - a$ in terms of $b - a$.

b The point $(4, 1)$ is rotated 45° anticlockwise about the origin. The image is then rotated 30° anticlockwise about the point $(-1, 2)$. Find the coordinates of the final image.

12 The diagram shows two equilateral triangles on an Argand diagram.

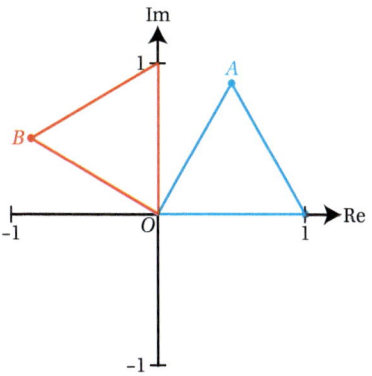

Find the complex number corresponding to the midpoint of AB. Give your answer in exact Cartesian form.

Checklist of learning and understanding

- De Moivre's theorem: $(r(\cos\theta + i\sin\theta))^n = r^n(\cos n\theta + i\sin n\theta)$ for $n \in \mathbb{Z}$.
- Exponential form of a complex number: $re^{i\theta} = [r, \theta] = r(\cos\theta + i\sin\theta)$.
- To solve $z^n = w$:
  - write w in modulus–argument form and write $z^n = r^n(\cos n\theta + i\sin n\theta)$
  - compare moduli, remembering that they are always real
  - compare arguments, remembering that adding 2π onto the argument does not change the number
  - the n solutions form a regular polygon on an Argand diagram.
- The nth roots of unity (solutions of $z^n = 1$) are $1, e^{\frac{2\pi i}{n}}, e^{\frac{4\pi i}{n}}, \ldots, e^{\frac{2(n-1)\pi i}{n}}$.
  - You can write them as ω^k, where $\omega = e^{\frac{2\pi i}{n}}$ and $k = 0, 1, 2, \ldots, n-1$.
  - $1 + \omega_1 + \ldots + \omega_{n-1} = 0$.
- You can use roots of the equation $z^n = a$ to factorise the expression $z^n - a$. Real quadratic factors are found by combining each root with its complex conjugate:
$$(z - re^{i\theta})(z - re^{-i\theta}) = z^2 - 2r\cos\theta + r^2$$
- Multiplication by $re^{i\theta}$ corresponds to an enlargement with scale factor r and a rotation through angle θ anticlockwise about the origin.

Mixed practice 1

1 If $z^* = re^{i\theta}$, find $\frac{1}{z}$ in exponential form.

Choose from these options.

A $\frac{1}{r}e^{i\theta}$ **B** $re^{i\theta}$ **C** $\frac{1}{r}e^{-i\theta}$ **D** $re^{-i\theta}$

2   **a** Find the modulus and argument of $-1 + i\sqrt{3}$.

       b Hence find $(-1 + i\sqrt{3})^5$ in exact Cartesian form.

3   **a** Write down, in the form $re^{i\theta}$, all the solutions of the equation $z^5 = 1$.

       b Show the solutions on an Argand diagram.

4 Find $\left(\cos\frac{\pi}{3} + i\sin\frac{\pi}{3}\right)^4 \left(\cos\frac{\pi}{4} + i\sin\frac{\pi}{4}\right)^5$ in the form $re^{i\theta}$, where $-\pi < \theta \leq \pi$.

5   **a** Find the modulus and argument of $8 - 8i$.

       b Hence solve the equation $z^4 = 8 - 8i$, giving your answers in the form $r(\cos\theta + i\sin\theta)$.

6   **a** Find the modulus and argument of $1 + i$.

       b A regular hexagon is inscribed in a circle, centred at the origin, on an Argand diagram and one of its vertices is $1 + i$. Find an equation with solutions represented by the six vertices of the hexagon.

7   **a** Express $-9i$ in the form $re^{i\theta}$, where $r > 0$ and $-\pi < \theta \leq \pi$.

       b Solve the equation $z^4 + 9i = 0$, giving your answers in the form $re^{i\theta}$, where $r > 0$ and $-\pi < \theta \leq \pi$.

[© AQA 2014]

8 If $\arg((a+i)^3) = \pi$, where a is real and positive, find the exact value of a.

Choose from these options.

A $\frac{1}{3}$ **B** 3 **C** $\frac{\sqrt{3}}{3}$ **D** $\sqrt{3}$

9 Find the exact value of $\dfrac{1}{(\sqrt{3} + i)^6}$, clearly showing your working.

10   **a** Express $\dfrac{\sqrt{3}}{2} - \dfrac{1}{2}i$ in the form $r(\cos\theta + i\sin\theta)$.

       b Hence show that $\left(\dfrac{\sqrt{3}}{2} - \dfrac{1}{2}i\right)^9 = ci$ where c is a real number to be found.

       c Find one pair of possible values of positive integers m and n such that $\left(\dfrac{\sqrt{3}}{2} - \dfrac{1}{2}i\right)^m = \left(\dfrac{\sqrt{2}}{2} + \dfrac{\sqrt{2}}{2}i\right)^n$.

11 If ω is a complex third root of unity and a and b are real numbers, prove that:

   a $1 + \omega + \omega^2 = 0$

   b $(\omega a + \omega^2 b)(\omega^2 a + \omega b) = a^2 - ab + b^2$.

1 Further complex numbers: powers and roots

12 If $0 < \theta < \frac{\pi}{2}$ and $z = (\sin \theta + i(1 - \cos \theta))^2$, find in its simplest form arg z.

13 If $z = \cos \theta + i \sin \theta$, prove that $\dfrac{z^2 - 1}{z^2 + 1} = i \tan \theta$.

14 a Express i in the form $re^{i\theta}$.

b Hence state the exact value of i^i.

15 Let $\omega = e^{\frac{2i\pi}{5}}$.

a Write ω^2, ω^3 and ω^4 in the form $e^{i\theta}$.

b Explain why $\omega^1 + \omega^2 + \omega^3 + \omega^4 = -1$.

c Show that $\omega + \omega^4 = 2 \cos \dfrac{2\pi}{5}$ and $\omega^2 + \omega^3 = 2 \cos \dfrac{4\pi}{5}$.

d Form a quadratic equation in $\cos \dfrac{2\pi}{5}$ and hence show that $\cos \dfrac{2\pi}{5} = \dfrac{\sqrt{5} - 1}{4}$.

16 Let $1, \omega, \omega^2$ be the solutions of the equation $z^3 = 1$.

a Show that $1 + \omega + \omega^2 = 0$.

b Find the value of

   i $(1 + \omega)(1 + \omega^2)$ 　　ii $\dfrac{1}{1 + \omega} + \dfrac{1}{1 + \omega^2}$.

c Hence find a cubic equation with integer coefficients and roots 3, $\dfrac{1}{1 + \omega}$ and $\dfrac{1}{1 + \omega^2}$.

17 Let Z and A be points on an Argand diagram representing complex numbers z and a, respectively. The complex number z_1 represents the point obtained by translating Z using the vector $\overrightarrow{OA}$ and then rotating the image through angle θ anticlockwise about the origin. The complex number z_2 corresponds to the point obtained by first rotating Z anticlockwise through angle θ about the origin and then translating Z by vector $\overrightarrow{OA}$.

Show that the distance between the points represented by z_1 and z_2 is independent of z.

18 a Express $-4 + 4\sqrt{3}i$ in the form $re^{i\theta}$, where $r > 0$ and $-\pi < \theta \leq \pi$.

b i Solve the equation $z^3 = -4 + 4\sqrt{3}i$, giving your answers in the form $re^{i\theta}$, where $r > 0$ and $-\pi < \theta \leq \pi$.

ii The roots of the equation $z^3 = -4 + 4\sqrt{3}i$ are represented by the points P, Q and R on an Argand diagram.

Find the area of the triangle PQR, giving your answer in the form $k\sqrt{3}$ where k is an integer.

c By considering the roots of the equation $z^3 = -4 + 4\sqrt{3}i$, show that $\cos \dfrac{2\pi}{9} + \cos \dfrac{4\pi}{9} + \cos \dfrac{8\pi}{9} = 0$.

[© AQA 2013]

A Level Further Mathematics for AQA Student Book 2

19 Point A represents the complex number $3 + i$ on an Argand diagram. Point A is rotated $\frac{\pi}{3}$ radians anticlockwise about the origin to point B. Point B is then translated by $\begin{pmatrix} -2 \\ 1 \end{pmatrix}$ to obtain point C.

   a Find, in Cartesian form, the complex number corresponding to B.

   b Find the distance AC.

20 a Points P and Q on an Argand diagram correspond to complex numbers $z_1 = x_1 + iy_1$ and $z_2 = x_2 + iy_2$. Show that $PQ = |z_1 - z_2|$.

   b The diagram shows a triangle with one vertex at the origin, one vertex at the point $A(a, 0)$ and one vertex at the point B such that $OB = b$ and $\angle AOB = \theta$.

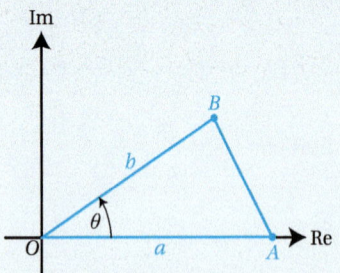

   i Write down the complex number corresponding to point A.

   ii Write down the number corresponding to point B in modulus-argument form.

   iii Write down an expression for the length of AB in terms of a, b and θ.

   iv Hence prove the cosine rule for the triangle AOB: $AB^2 = OA^2 + OB^2 - 2(OA)(OB) \cos \theta$.

2 Further complex numbers: trigonometry

In this chapter you will learn how to:

- use De Moivre's theorem to derive trigonometric identities
- find sums of some trigonometric series.

Before you start…

Chapter 1, Section 1	You should be able to use De Moivre's theorem to raise a complex number to a power.	1 Find $\left(2\left(\cos\frac{\pi}{7} + i\sin\frac{\pi}{7}\right)\right)^5$ in modulus–argument form.
Chapter 1, Section 2	You should be able to use the exponential form of a complex number.	2 a Write $4e^{-\frac{i\pi}{3}}$ in exact Cartesian form. b Write down the complex conjugate of $2 + e^{3i}$.
A Level Mathematics Student Book 1, Chapter 9	You should be able to use the binomial expansion for positive integer powers.	3 Expand and simplify $(x - 2y)^5$.
Further Mathematics Student Book 1, Chapter 1	You should know how to divide complex numbers.	4 Find the real and imaginary parts of $\frac{1 - e^{ix}}{1 + e^{ix}}$, where x is real.
A Level Mathematics Student Book 2, Chapter 4	You should be able to use the formulae for the sum of a geometric series.	5 a Find an expression for the sum of the first n terms of the geometric series $e^x + e^{2x} + e^{3x} + \ldots$ b For which values of x does the series in part **a** have a sum to infinity?

Using complex numbers to derive trigonometric identities

The modulus–argument form of a complex number provides a link between complex numbers and trigonometry. This is a powerful tool for deriving new trigonometric identities.

These trigonometric identities are one example of the use of complex numbers to establish facts about real numbers and functions. Other such applications include a formula for cubic equations, calculations involving alternating current, and analysing the motion of waves. The fact that complex numbers proved correct results in a concise way was a major factor in convincing mathematicians that they should be accepted.

Section 1: Deriving multiple-angle formulae

You can raise a complex number to a power in two different ways. You can either use the Cartesian form and multiply out the brackets, or you can write the complex number in modulus–argument form and use De Moivre's theorem. Equating these two answers allows you to derive formulae for trigonometric ratios of multiple angles.

> ⏮ **Rewind**
>
> You have already met double-angle formulae, such as $\cos 2\theta = 2\cos^2 \theta - 1$, in A Level Mathematics Student Book 2, Chapter 8.

WORKED EXAMPLE 2.1

Derive a formula for $\cos 4\theta$ in terms of $\cos \theta$.

Let $z = \cos \theta + i \sin \theta$.
Then $z^4 = (\cos \theta + i \sin \theta)^4$.
    Start with an expression for a complex number involving $\cos \theta$, and find z^4 in two different ways.

First, using the binomial theorem:
$$z^4 = \cos^4 \theta + 4\cos^3 \theta (i \sin \theta) + 6\cos^2 \theta (i \sin \theta)^2$$
$$\quad + 4\cos \theta (i \sin \theta)^3 + (i \sin \theta)^4$$
$$= \cos^4 \theta + 4i \cos^3 \theta \sin \theta - 6\cos^2 \theta \sin^2 \theta$$
$$\quad - 4i \cos \theta \sin^3 \theta + \sin^4 \theta$$
    $i^2 = -1$, $i^3 = -i$, $i^4 = 1$.

Now, using De Moivre's theorem:
$$z^4 = \cos 4\theta + i \sin 4\theta$$

Equating real parts:
$$\cos 4\theta = \cos^4 \theta - 6\cos^2 \theta \sin^2 \theta + \sin^4 \theta$$
    The two expressions for z^4 must have equal real parts and equal imaginary parts.
$$= \cos^4 \theta - 6\cos^2 \theta (1 - \cos^2 \theta) + (1 - \cos^2 \theta)^2$$
    You want the answer in terms of $\cos \theta$ only, so use $\sin^2 \theta = 1 - \cos^2 \theta$.
$$= 8\cos^4 \theta - 8\cos^2 \theta + 1$$
    Simplify the final expression.

> ⏭ **Fast forward**
>
> By equating imaginary parts of the two expressions in Worked example 2.1, you can obtain a similar expression for $\sin 4\theta$ – see Question 1 in Exercise 2A.

> ℹ **Did you know?**
>
> These expressions for sines and cosines of multiple angles can also be derived through repeated application of compound angle identities. However, the calculations become increasingly long.

2 Further complex numbers: trigonometry

WORK IT OUT 2.1

Express $\sin 5\theta$ in terms of $\sin \theta$.

Which is the correct solution? Identify the errors made in the incorrect solutions.

Solution 1

$\sin \theta = \dfrac{1}{2i}(e^{i\theta} - e^{-i\theta})$

So

$$\sin^5 \theta = \dfrac{1}{2i} \times \left(\dfrac{1}{2i}\right)^4 (e^{i\theta} - e^{-i\theta})^5$$

$$= \dfrac{1}{2i} \times \dfrac{1}{16}(e^{5i\theta} - 5e^{3i\theta} + 10e^{i\theta} - 10e^{-i\theta} + 5e^{3i\theta} - e^{-5i\theta})$$

$$= \dfrac{1}{16}\left(\dfrac{e^{5i\theta} - e^{-5i\theta}}{2i} - 5\dfrac{e^{3i\theta} - e^{-3i\theta}}{2i} + 10\dfrac{e^{i\theta} - e^{-i\theta}}{2i}\right)$$

$$= \dfrac{\sin 5\theta - 5\sin 3\theta + 10\sin\theta}{16}$$

$\therefore 16 \sin^5 \theta = \sin 5\theta - 5\sin 3\theta + 10\sin\theta$

$\sin 5\theta = 16\sin^5 \theta + 5\sin 3\theta - 10\sin\theta$

Solution 2

$(\cos\theta + i\sin\theta)^5 = \cos^5\theta + 5i\cos^4\theta\sin\theta - 10\cos^3\theta\sin^2\theta - 10i\cos^2\theta\sin^3\theta + 5\cos\theta\sin^4\theta + i\sin^5\theta$

Taking the imaginary part:

$\sin 5\theta = 5\cos^4\theta\sin\theta - 10\cos^2\theta\sin^3\theta + \sin^5\theta$
$= 5(1 - \sin^2\theta)^2\sin\theta - 10(1 - \sin^2\theta)\sin^3\theta + \sin^5\theta$

Solution 3

$\sin 5\theta = \operatorname{Im}[(\cos\theta + i\sin\theta)^5]$
$= \operatorname{Im}[\cos^5\theta + 5i\cos^4\theta\sin\theta - 10\cos^3\theta\sin^2\theta - 10i\cos^2\theta\sin^3\theta + 5\cos\theta\sin^4\theta + i\sin^5\theta]$
$= 5i\cos^4\theta\sin\theta - 10i\cos^2\theta\sin^3\theta + i\sin^5\theta$
$= 5i(1 - \sin^4\theta)\sin\theta - 10i(1 - \sin^2\theta)\sin^3\theta + i\sin^5\theta$

EXERCISE 2A

1 **a** Find the imaginary part of $(\cos\theta + i\sin\theta)^4$.

   b Hence show that $\sin 4\theta = 4\cos\theta(\sin\theta - 2\sin^3\theta)$.

2 Use the binomial expansion to find the real and imaginary parts of $(\cos\theta + i\sin\theta)^3$. Hence find an expression for $\sin 3\theta$ in terms of $\sin\theta$.

3 **a** Expand $(\cos\theta + i\sin\theta)^5$.

   b Hence or otherwise express $\sin 5\theta$ in terms of $\sin\theta$.

4 **a** Show that $\cos 5\theta = 16\cos^5\theta - 20\cos^3\theta + 5\cos\theta$.

   b Hence solve the equation $\cos 5\theta = 5\cos\theta$ for $\theta \in [0, 2\pi]$.

5 **a** Find the values of A, B and C such that $\sin 5\theta = A\sin^5\theta - B\sin^3\theta + C\sin\theta$.

   b Given that $4\sin^5\theta + \sin 5\theta = 0$, find the possible values of $\sin\theta$.

6 **a** Find the real and imaginary parts of $(\cos\theta + i\sin\theta)^4$.

  b Hence express $\tan 4\theta$ in terms of $\tan\theta$.

7 **a** Show that $\tan 6\theta = \dfrac{6\tan\theta - 20\tan^3\theta + 6\tan^5\theta}{1 - 15\tan^2\theta + 15\tan^4\theta - \tan^6\theta}$.

  b Hence solve the equation:
  $$\tan^6\theta + 6\tan^5\theta - 15\tan^4\theta - 20\tan^3\theta + 15\tan^2\theta + 6\tan\theta - 1 = 0$$
  for $\theta \in \left[0, \dfrac{\pi}{2}\right)$.

8 **a** Use the binomial expansion to find the real and imaginary parts of $(\cos\theta + i\sin\theta)^5$.

  b Hence show that $\dfrac{\sin 5\theta}{\sin\theta} = 16\cos^4\theta - 12\cos^2\theta + 1$.

  c Assuming that θ is small enough that the terms in θ^4 and higher can be ignored, find an approximate expression, in increasing powers of θ, for $\dfrac{\sin 5\theta}{\sin\theta}$.

Section 2: Application to polynomial equations

In Section 1 you learnt how to express $\sin n\theta$ and $\cos n\theta$ as a polynomial in $\sin\theta$ or $\cos\theta$. For example, $\cos 4\theta = 8\cos^4\theta - 8\cos^2\theta + 1$. You can now use the roots of the polynomial and the solutions of $\cos 4\theta = 0$ to find the values of $\cos\theta$.

WORKED EXAMPLE 2.2

  a Find all the values of $\theta \in [0, 2\pi)$ for which $\cos 4\theta = 0$.

You are given that $\cos 4\theta = 8\cos^4\theta - 8\cos^2\theta + 1$.

  b Write down the roots of the equation $8c^2 - 8c^4 = 1$ in the form $\cos\theta$, where $\theta \in [0, \pi)$.

  c Hence find the exact value of $\cos\dfrac{3\pi}{8}$.

a $\theta \in [0, 2\pi) \Rightarrow 4\theta \in [0, 8\pi)$
$\cos 4\theta = 0$
$$4\theta = \dfrac{\pi}{2}, \dfrac{3\pi}{2}, \dfrac{5\pi}{2}, \dfrac{7\pi}{2}, \dfrac{9\pi}{2}, \dfrac{11\pi}{2}, \dfrac{13\pi}{2}, \dfrac{15\pi}{2}$$
$$\theta = \dfrac{\pi}{8}, \dfrac{3\pi}{8}, \dfrac{5\pi}{8}, \dfrac{7\pi}{8}, \dfrac{9\pi}{8}, \dfrac{11\pi}{8}, \dfrac{13\pi}{8}, \dfrac{15\pi}{8}$$

b Write $c = \cos\theta$.
Then
$8c^2 - 8c^4 = 1$
$\Leftrightarrow 8c^4 - 8c^2 + 1 = 0$
$\Leftrightarrow \cos 4\theta = 0$

*Making the substitution relates the equations from parts **a** and **b**.*

Continues on next page

Hence
$c = \cos\theta$
$= \cos\dfrac{\pi}{8}, \cos\dfrac{3\pi}{8}, \cos\dfrac{5\pi}{8}, \cos\dfrac{7\pi}{8}.$

The equation from part **a** has eight solutions but the equation from part **b** should only have four (since it is a degree 4 polynomial). This is because, for example, $\cos\dfrac{\pi}{8} = \cos\dfrac{15\pi}{8}$.

c $8c^4 - 8c^2 + 1 = 0$

$c^2 = \dfrac{2 \pm \sqrt{2}}{4}$

$c = \pm\sqrt{\dfrac{2 \pm \sqrt{2}}{4}}$

You can actually solve the equation from part **b** exactly, as it is a quadratic in c^2.

$\cos\dfrac{3\pi}{8}$ is the smallest positive solution from part **b**:

$\cos\dfrac{3\pi}{8}$ is one of these four solutions. You can see from the cos graph that it is the smallest positive one of the four numbers.

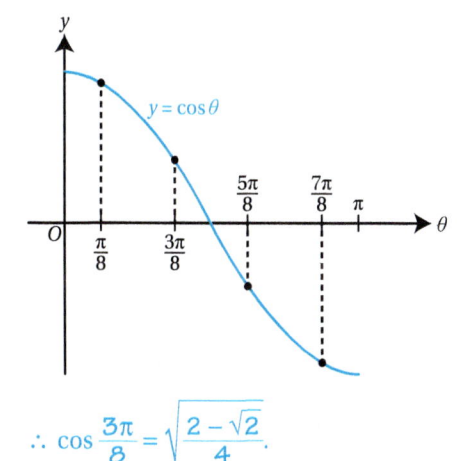

$\therefore \cos\dfrac{3\pi}{8} = \sqrt{\dfrac{2-\sqrt{2}}{4}}.$

Sometimes you can't solve the polynomial equation, but you can still use the results about sums and products of roots to derive expressions involving combinations of trigonometric ratios.

> **⏮ Rewind**
>
> See Further Mathematics Student Book 1, Chapter 2, for a reminder about roots of polynomials.

WORKED EXAMPLE 2.3

a Show that $\tan 3\theta = \dfrac{3\tan\theta - \tan^3\theta}{1 - 3\tan^2\theta}.$

b Show that the equation $t^3 - 3t^2 - 3t + 1 = 0$ can be written as $\tan 3\theta = k$, where $t = \tan\theta$, and state the value of k.

c Hence find the exact value of $\tan\dfrac{\pi}{12} + \tan\dfrac{5\pi}{12}.$

a Write $c = \cos\theta$ and $s = \sin\theta$.
Then
$\cos 3\theta + i\sin 3\theta = (\cos\theta + i\sin\theta)^3$
$\qquad\qquad\qquad\quad = c^3 + 3ic^2s - 3cs^2 - is^3$

Use De Moivre's theorem.

Continues on next page

Hence
$$\tan 3\theta = \frac{\sin 3\theta}{\cos 3\theta} = \frac{3c^2s - s^3}{c^3 - 3cs^2}$$
$$= \frac{3t - t^3}{1 - 3t^2}$$
where $t = \tan\theta$.

Separate real and imaginary parts to find sin and cos.

Divide top and bottom by c^3 and use $\frac{s}{c} = \tan\theta$.

b $t^3 - 3t^2 - 3t + 1 = 0$
$\Leftrightarrow 1 - 3t^2 = 3t - t^3$
$\Leftrightarrow \frac{3t - t^3}{1 - 3t^2} = 1$
$\Leftrightarrow \tan 3\theta = 1$
so $k = 1$

Rearrange the equation into the form from part a.

c $\tan 3\theta = 1$
$3\theta = \frac{\pi}{4}, \frac{5\pi}{4}, \frac{9\pi}{4} \ldots$
$\theta = \frac{\pi}{12}, \frac{5\pi}{12}, \frac{9\pi}{12} \ldots$
$t = \tan\theta = \tan\frac{\pi}{12}, \tan\frac{5\pi}{12}$ or $\tan\frac{9\pi}{12}$
Hence
$\tan\frac{\pi}{12} + \tan\frac{5\pi}{12} + \tan\frac{9\pi}{12} = -\frac{-3}{1} = 3$
$\tan\frac{\pi}{12} + \tan\frac{5\pi}{12} + (-1) = 3$
$\tan\frac{\pi}{12} + \tan\frac{5\pi}{12} = 4$

Solve the cubic equation by solving $\tan 3\theta = 1$.

Although there are infinitely many values of θ, they only give three different values of $\tan\theta$ (since tan is a periodic function).

Use the result about the sum of the roots of a cubic polynomial: $p + q + r = -\frac{b}{a}$

$\tan\frac{9\pi}{12} = \tan\frac{3\pi}{4} = -1$

EXERCISE 2B

1 a Write down an expression for $\cos 2\theta$ in terms of $\cos\theta$.

b Given that $\cos 2\theta = \frac{\sqrt{3}}{2}$, find a quadratic equation in c, where $c = \cos\theta$.

c Hence find the exact value of $\cos\frac{\pi}{12}$.

2 a Given that $\tan 2\theta = 1$, show that $t^2 + 2t - 1 = 0$, where $t = \tan\theta$.

b Solve the equation $\tan 2\theta = 1$ for $\theta \in (0, \pi)$.

c Hence find the exact value of $\tan\frac{5\pi}{8}$.

3 You are given that $\cos 5\theta = 16\cos^5\theta - 20\cos^3\theta + 5\cos\theta$.

a Find the possible values of $\theta \in [0, \pi]$ for which $16\cos^4\theta - 20\cos^2\theta + 5 = 0$.

b Hence show that $\cos\left(\frac{\pi}{10}\right)\cos\left(\frac{3\pi}{10}\right) = \frac{\sqrt{5}}{4}$.

4 **a** Show that $\sin 3\theta = 3\sin\theta - 4\sin^3\theta$.

   b Given that $\theta \in [0, 2\pi]$ and that $\sin 3\theta = \frac{1}{2}$, find the possible values of θ.

   c Hence show that $\sin\frac{\pi}{18}$ is a root of the equation $8x^3 - 6x + 1 = 0$ and find, in a similar form, the other two roots.

5 You are given that $\tan 4\theta + \tan 3\theta = 0$.

   a Show that $\tan 7\theta = 0$.

   b Let $t = \tan\theta$. Express $\tan 4\theta$ and $\tan 3\theta$ in terms of t. Hence show that $t^7 - 21t^5 + 35t^3 - 7t = 0$.

6 You are given that $\sin 7\theta = 7\sin\theta - 56\sin^3\theta + 112\sin^5\theta - 64\sin^7\theta$.

   a Show that the equation $64s^6 - 112s^4 + 56s^2 - 7 = 0$ has roots $\pm\sin\frac{\pi}{7}$, $\pm\sin\frac{3\pi}{7}$ and $\pm\sin\frac{5\pi}{7}$.

   b Hence find the exact value of $\sin\left(\frac{\pi}{7}\right)\sin\left(\frac{3\pi}{7}\right)\sin\left(\frac{5\pi}{7}\right)$.

Section 3: Powers of trigonometric functions

Another important link with trigonometry comes from considering the exponential form of complex numbers:
$$e^{i\theta} = \cos\theta + i\sin\theta$$
and
$$\begin{aligned}e^{-i\theta} &= \cos(-\theta) + i\sin(-\theta)\\ &= \cos\theta - i\sin\theta\end{aligned}$$

By adding and subtracting these two equations you can establish two very useful identities.

🔑 Key point 2.1

$$\cos\theta = \frac{e^{i\theta} + e^{-i\theta}}{2}$$
$$\sin\theta = \frac{e^{i\theta} - e^{-i\theta}}{2i}$$

You can further generalise this result.

🔑 Key point 2.2

If $z = e^{i\theta}$, then
$$z^n + \frac{1}{z^n} = 2\cos n\theta$$
$$z^n - \frac{1}{z^n} = 2i\sin n\theta$$

PROOF 2

Using De Moivre's theorem for positive and negative integers:

$z^n = \cos n\theta + i \sin n\theta$

$\dfrac{1}{z^n} = z^{-n} = \cos n\theta - i \sin n\theta$

> Remember that $\cos(-x) = \cos(x)$ and $\sin(-x) = -\sin x$.

Adding the two equations:

$z^n + \dfrac{1}{z^n} = 2\cos n\theta$

Subtracting the two equations:

$z^n - \dfrac{1}{z^n} = 2i \sin n\theta$

You can use the results in Key point 2.2 to derive another class of trigonometric identities, expressing powers of trigonometric functions in terms of functions of multiple angles. For example: $\cos^2\theta = \dfrac{1}{2}(\cos 2\theta + 1)$.

WORKED EXAMPLE 2.4

Show that $\sin^5\theta = \dfrac{1}{16}\sin 5\theta - \dfrac{5}{16}\sin 3\theta + \dfrac{5}{8}\sin\theta$.

Let $z = \cos\theta + i\sin\theta$.

Using the binomial expansion:

$\left(z - \dfrac{1}{z}\right)^5 = z^5 + 5z^4\left(-\dfrac{1}{z}\right) + 10z^3\left(-\dfrac{1}{z}\right)^2 + 10z^2\left(-\dfrac{1}{z}\right)^3$

$\qquad\qquad + 5z\left(-\dfrac{1}{z}\right)^4 + \left(-\dfrac{1}{z}\right)^5$

$= z^5 - 5z^3 + 10z - \dfrac{10}{z} + \dfrac{5}{z^3} - \dfrac{1}{z^5}$

> Simplify the fractions, taking care with negative signs.

$= \left(z^5 - \dfrac{1}{z^5}\right) - 5\left(z^3 - \dfrac{1}{z^3}\right) + 10\left(z - \dfrac{1}{z}\right)$

> Group the terms to get expressions of the form $z^n - \dfrac{1}{z^n}$.

So

$(2i\sin\theta)^5 = 2i\sin 5\theta - 10i\sin 3\theta + 20i\sin\theta$

$32i\sin^5\theta = 2i\sin 5\theta - 10i\sin 3\theta + 20i\sin\theta$

$\therefore \sin^5\theta = \dfrac{1}{16}\sin 5\theta - \dfrac{5}{16}\sin 3\theta + \dfrac{5}{8}\sin\theta$

> On both sides of the equation, use the result from Key point 2.2:
> $z^n - \dfrac{1}{z^n} = 2i\sin n\theta$

2 Further complex numbers: trigonometry

Trigonometric identities such as these are very useful when integrating powers of trigonometric functions.

> **⏮ Rewind**
>
> In A Level Mathematics Student Book 2, Chapter 11, you used the identity $\cos^2\theta = \frac{1}{2}(\cos 2\theta + 1)$ to find $\int \cos^2 x \, dx$.

WORKED EXAMPLE 2.5

a Expand and simplify $\left(z + \frac{1}{z}\right)^6$.

b Show that $\cos^6 x = \frac{1}{32}\cos 6x + \frac{3}{16}\cos 4x + \frac{15}{32}\cos 2x + \frac{5}{16}$.

c Hence find $\int \cos^6 x \, dx$.

a Using the binomial expansion:
$$\left(z + \frac{1}{z}\right)^6 = z^6 + 6z^5\left(\frac{1}{z}\right) + 15z^4\left(\frac{1}{z}\right)^2 + 20z^3\left(\frac{1}{z}\right)^3$$
$$+ 15z^2\left(\frac{1}{z}\right)^4 + 6z\left(\frac{1}{z}\right)^5 + \left(\frac{1}{z}\right)^6$$
$$= z^6 + 6z^4 + 15z^2 + 20 + \frac{15}{z^2} + \frac{6}{z^4} + \frac{1}{z^6}$$

b Let $z = \cos x + i\sin x$.

$$\left(z + \frac{1}{z}\right) = \left(z^6 + \frac{1}{z^6}\right) + 6\left(z^4 + \frac{1}{z^4}\right) + 15\left(z^2 + \frac{1}{z^2}\right) + 20$$

Group the terms on the right so that you can use the result from Key point 2.2.

$$\Rightarrow (2\cos x)^6 = (2\cos 6x) + 6(2\cos 4x) + 15(2\cos 2x) + 20$$

$$\Rightarrow \cos^6 x = \frac{1}{32}\cos 6x + \frac{3}{16}\cos 4x + \frac{15}{32}\cos 2x + \frac{5}{16}$$

Divide by $2^6 = 64$.

c Using the result from part a:

$$\int \cos^6 x \, dx = \int\left(\frac{1}{32}\cos 6x + \frac{3}{16}\cos 4x + \frac{15}{32}\cos 2x + \frac{5}{16}\right)dx$$

Don't forget to divide by the coefficient of x.

$$= \frac{1}{192}\sin 6x + \frac{3}{64}\sin 4x + \frac{15}{64}\sin 2x + \frac{5}{16}x + c$$

EXERCISE 2C

1 Let $z = \cos\theta + i\sin\theta$. Express each of these expressions as a sum of terms of the form $\cos k\theta$ or $\sin k\theta$.

   a **i** $\left(z + \frac{1}{z}\right)^3$ **ii** $\left(z + \frac{1}{z}\right)^4$

   b **i** $\left(z - \frac{1}{z}\right)^4$ **ii** $\left(z - \frac{1}{z}\right)^5$

2 Let $z = \cos\theta + i\sin\theta$.

   a Show that $z^n + z^{-n} = 2\cos n\theta$.

   b Hence show that $32\cos^5\theta = A\cos 5\theta + B\cos 3\theta + C\cos\theta$, where A, B and C are constants to be found.

3 **a** Use the expansion of $\left(z - \dfrac{1}{z}\right)^6$, where $z = e^{i\theta}$, to show that $32\sin^6\theta = 10 - 15\cos 2\theta + 6\cos 4\theta - \cos 6\theta$.

   b Hence find the exact value of $\displaystyle\int_0^{\frac{\pi}{3}} \sin^6\theta\, d\theta$.

4 A complex number is defined by $z = \cos\theta + i\sin\theta$.

   a **i** Show that $\dfrac{1}{z} = \cos\theta - i\sin\theta$.

   ii Use De Moivre's theorem to deduce that $z^n - \dfrac{1}{z^n} = 2i\sin n\theta$.

   b **i** Expand $\left(z - \dfrac{1}{z}\right)^5$.

   ii Hence find integers a, b and c such that
   $16\sin^5\theta = a\sin 5\theta + b\sin 3\theta + c\sin\theta$.

   c Find $\displaystyle\int \sin^5 2x\, dx$.

5 Let $z = \cos\theta + i\sin\theta$.

   a Show that $z^n - z^{-n} = 2i\sin n\theta$.

   b Expand $(z + z^{-1})^6$ and $(z - z^{-1})^6$.

   c Hence show that $\cos^6\theta + \sin^6\theta = \dfrac{1}{8}(3\cos 4\theta + 5)$.

6 **a** Write down expressions for $\sin x$ and $\cos x$ in terms of e^{ix}.

   b Hence evaluate $\displaystyle\int_0^{\pi} \sin^3 x \cos^4 x\, dx$, clearly showing your working.

Section 4: Trigonometric series

In Section 1 you learnt about expressions for sine and cosine of multiple angles. What happens if you add several such expressions together? For example, is it possible to simplify a sum such as
$\sin x + \sin 2x + \sin 3x + \sin 4x$?

Did you know?

Sums like these come up when combining waves (interference). They are also used in Fourier series, which is a way of writing other functions in terms of sines and cosines.

2 Further complex numbers: trigonometry

You can simplify certain sums of this type, using the exponential form of complex numbers and the formula for the sum of geometric series. This is because $\sin kx$ is the imaginary part of e^{ikx}, and the numbers $e^{ix}, e^{2ix}, e^{3ix}, e^{4ix}$ form a geometric series.

> **Rewind**
>
> You met geometric series in A Level Mathematics Student Book 2, Chapter 4.

WORKED EXAMPLE 2.6

a Find an expression for $e^{ix} + e^{2ix} + e^{3ix} + \ldots + e^{nix}$.

b Hence show that $\sin x + \sin 2x + \sin 3x + \ldots \sin 10x = \dfrac{\sin x + \sin 10x - \sin 11x}{4\sin^2\left(\dfrac{x}{2}\right)}$.

a Geometric series with $a = e^{ix}, r = e^{ix}$.

$\therefore e^{ix} + e^{2ix} + e^{3ix} + \ldots + e^{nix} = \dfrac{e^{ix}(1 - e^{nix})}{1 - e^{ix}}$

This is a geometric series with common ratio e^{ix}.

Use $S_n = \dfrac{a(1-r^n)}{1-r}$ for the sum of the first n terms.

b $\sin x + \sin 2x + \ldots + \sin 10x = \operatorname{Im}(e^{ix} + e^{2ix} + \ldots + e^{10ix})$

*This is the imaginary part of the series from part **a**, with $n = 10$.*

$= \operatorname{Im}\left(\dfrac{e^{ix}(1 - e^{10ix})}{1 - e^{ix}}\right)$

$= \operatorname{Im}\left(\dfrac{e^{ix}(1 - e^{10ix})}{1 - e^{ix}} \times \dfrac{1 - e^{-ix}}{1 - e^{-ix}}\right)$

Multiply top and bottom by the complex conjugate of the denominator in order to separate real and imaginary parts.

$= \operatorname{Im}\left(\dfrac{e^{ix} - 1 - e^{11ix} + e^{10ix}}{1 - e^{ix} - e^{-ix} + 1}\right)$

$= \operatorname{Im}\left(\dfrac{e^{ix} - 1 - e^{11ix} + e^{10ix}}{2 - 2\cos x}\right)$

Use $e^{ix} + e^{-ix} = 2\cos x$ in the denominator.

The imaginary part is:

$\dfrac{\sin x - \sin 11x + \sin 10x}{2 - 2\cos x}$

Now the denominator is real, so you just need to take the imaginary part of the numerator.

$= \dfrac{\sin x + \sin 10x - \sin 11x}{4\sin^2\left(\dfrac{x}{2}\right)}$

Use the double angle formula in the denominator:
$2\cos x = 2\left(1 - 2\sin^2\left(\dfrac{x}{2}\right)\right)$.

If the modulus of the common ratio is smaller than 1, a geometric series also has a sum to infinity.

A Level Further Mathematics for AQA Student Book 2

WORKED EXAMPLE 2.7

a Show that the geometric series $1 + \frac{1}{2}e^{i\theta} + \frac{1}{4}e^{2i\theta} + \ldots$ converges, and find an expression for its sum to infinity.

b Hence evaluate $\sum_{k=0}^{\infty} \frac{1}{2^k} \cos k\theta$.

a The geometric series has $|r| = \left|\frac{1}{2}e^{i\theta}\right| = \frac{1}{2} < 1$, hence it converges.

The common ratio is $\frac{1}{2}e^{i\theta}$.

Using $S_\infty = \frac{a}{1-r}$:

$$S_\infty = \frac{1}{1 - \frac{1}{2}e^{i\theta}} = \frac{2}{2 - e^{i\theta}}$$

b $\sum_{k=0}^{\infty} \frac{1}{2^k} \cos k\theta = \text{Re}\left(1 + \frac{1}{2}e^{i\theta} + \frac{1}{4}e^{2i\theta} + \ldots\right)$

*The required sum is the real part of the sum from part **a**.*

$$= \text{Re}\left(\frac{2}{2 - e^{i\theta}}\right)$$

$$= \text{Re}\left(\frac{2}{2 - e^{i\theta}} \times \frac{2 - e^{-i\theta}}{2 - e^{-i\theta}}\right)$$

Multiply top and bottom by the complex conjugate of the denominator to separate real and imaginary parts.

$$= \text{Re}\left(\frac{4 - 2e^{-i\theta}}{4 - 2e^{i\theta} - 2e^{-i\theta} + 1}\right)$$

$$= \text{Re}\left(\frac{4 - 2e^{-i\theta}}{5 - 4\cos\theta}\right)$$

Use $e^{i\theta} + e^{-i\theta} = 2\cos\theta$.

$$= \frac{4 - 2\cos\theta}{5 - 4\cos\theta}$$

Now take the real part of the numerator, using $e^{-i\theta} = \cos\theta - i\sin\theta$.

Another series you know how to sum is the binomial expansion.

WORKED EXAMPLE 2.8

By considering the expansion of $(e^{i\theta} + 1)^5$, or otherwise, show that
$\sin 5\theta + 5\sin 4\theta + 10\sin 3\theta + 10\sin 2\theta + 5\sin\theta = 32\cos^5\left(\frac{\theta}{2}\right)\sin\left(\frac{5\theta}{2}\right)$.

Using the binomial expansion:

$(e^{i\theta} + 1)^5 = e^{5i\theta} + 5e^{4i\theta} + 10e^{3i\theta} + 10e^{2i\theta} + 5e^{i\theta} + 1$

$\sin 5\theta + 5\sin 4\theta + 10\sin 3\theta + 10\sin 2\theta + 5\sin\theta = \text{Im}\left((e^{i\theta} + 1)^5\right)$

The required series is the imaginary part of this.

Continues on next page

$e^{i\theta} + 1 = (\cos\theta + 1) + i\sin\theta$ *Use the double angle formulae.*

$\qquad = 2\cos^2\dfrac{\theta}{2} + 2i\sin\dfrac{\theta}{2}\cos\dfrac{\theta}{2}$

$\qquad = 2\cos\dfrac{\theta}{2}\left(\cos\dfrac{\theta}{2} + i\sin\dfrac{\theta}{2}\right)$

$\qquad = \left(2\cos\dfrac{\theta}{2}\right)e^{i\frac{\theta}{2}}$

Hence

$(e^{i\theta} + 1)^5 = \left(2\cos\dfrac{\theta}{2}\right)^5 e^{i\frac{5\theta}{2}}$

so

$\operatorname{Im}\left((e^{i\theta} + 1)^5\right) = \left(2\cos\dfrac{\theta}{2}\right)^5 \sin\dfrac{5\theta}{2}$

$\therefore \sin 5\theta + 5\sin 4\theta + 10\sin 3\theta + 10\sin 2\theta + 5\sin\theta = 32\cos^5\left(\dfrac{\theta}{2}\right)\sin\left(\dfrac{5\theta}{2}\right)$

EXERCISE 2D

1 a Find an expression for the sum to infinity of the geometric series $1 + \dfrac{1}{3}e^{i\theta} + \dfrac{1}{9}e^{2i\theta} + \ldots$

   b Hence evaluate $\displaystyle\sum_{k=0}^{\infty} \dfrac{1}{3^k}\cos k$.

2 a Show that the geometric series $1 + \dfrac{1}{2}e^{i\theta} + \dfrac{1}{4}e^{2i\theta} + \ldots$ converges and find an expression for its sum to infinity.

   b Hence show that $\dfrac{1}{2}\sin\theta + \dfrac{1}{4}\sin 2\theta + \dfrac{1}{8}\sin 3\theta + \ldots = \dfrac{2\sin\theta}{5 - 4\cos\theta}$.

3 Use the geometric series $e^{ix} - \dfrac{1}{2}e^{3ix} + \dfrac{1}{4}e^{5ix} - \ldots$ to evaluate $\sin 1 - \dfrac{1}{2}\sin 3 + \dfrac{1}{4}\sin 5 - \ldots$

4 Use the expansion of $(e^{i\theta} + 1)^4$ to show that $\cos 4\theta + 4\cos 3\theta + 6\cos 2\theta + 4\cos\theta + 1 = 16\cos^4\left(\dfrac{\theta}{2}\right)\cos 2\theta$.

5 By considering $(e^{i\theta} - 1)^5$ or otherwise, show that

$\sin 5\theta - 5\sin 4\theta + 10\sin 3\theta - 10\sin 2\theta + 5\sin\theta = 32\sin^5\left(\dfrac{\theta}{2}\right)\cos\left(\dfrac{5\theta}{2}\right)$

6 a Find an expression for the sum of the series $e^{i\theta} + e^{3i\theta} + e^{5i\theta} \ldots + e^{(2n-1)i\theta}$.

   b Hence prove that $\cos\theta + \cos 3\theta + \cos 5\theta \ldots + \cos((2n-1)\theta) = \dfrac{\sin 2n\theta}{2\sin\theta}$.

   c Find all the solutions to the equation $\cos\theta + \cos 3\theta + \cos 5\theta = 0$ for $0 < \theta < \pi$.

Checklist of learning and understanding

- By expanding $(\cos\theta + i\sin\theta)^n$ and comparing the real and imaginary parts to $\cos n\theta + i\sin\theta$, you can derive expressions for $\sin n\theta$ and $\cos n\theta$ in terms of powers of $\sin\theta$ and $\cos\theta$.
  - Considering these expressions as polynomials in $\sin\theta$ or $\cos\theta$, you can find some exact values of trigonometric functions.
- If $z = e^{i\theta}$, then $z^n + \dfrac{1}{z^n} = 2\cos n\theta$ and $z^n - \dfrac{1}{z^n} = 2i\sin n\theta$.
  - In particular, $\cos\theta = \dfrac{e^{i\theta} + e^{-i\theta}}{2}$ and $\sin\theta = \dfrac{e^{i\theta} - e^{-i\theta}}{2i}$.
  - You can use these expressions, together with the binomial expansion, to express powers of $\sin\theta$ and $\cos\theta$ in terms of sin and cos of multiples of θ.
- By considering real and imaginary parts of geometric or binomial series involving $e^{i\theta}$, you can derive expressions for sums of trigonometric series.

Mixed practice 2

1 **a** Expand and simplify $(\cos\theta + i\sin\theta)^4$.

    b Hence find constants A and B such that $\dfrac{\sin 4\theta}{\cos\theta} = A\sin\theta - B\sin^3\theta$.

2 Use De Moivre's theorem to show that $\cos 5\theta = 16\cos^5\theta - 20\cos^3\theta + 5\cos\theta$. Hence find the largest and smallest values of $\cos\theta - 4\cos^3\theta + \dfrac{16}{5}\cos^5\theta$.

3 **a** By considering $\left(z + \dfrac{1}{z}\right)^5$, where $z = \cos\theta + i\sin\theta$, find the values of constants A, B and C such that $\cos^5\theta = A\cos 5\theta + B\cos 3\theta + C\cos\theta$.

    b Hence find the exact value of $\displaystyle\int_0^{\frac{\pi}{2}} \cos^5\theta\, d\theta$.

4 Show that $\sin 5\theta = 16\sin^5\theta - 20\sin^3\theta + 5\sin\theta$. Hence show that $\sin\dfrac{13\pi}{30}$ is a root of the equation $32x^5 - 40x^3 + 10x - 1 = 0$.

5 By considering the expansion of $(1+i)^{10}$, show that $\binom{10}{1} - \binom{10}{3} + \binom{10}{5} - \binom{10}{7} + \binom{10}{9} = 32$.

6 Show that $1 + 4\cos 2\theta + 6\cos 4\theta + 4\cos 6\theta + \cos 8\theta = 16\cos 4\theta\cos^4\theta$.

7 Let $z = \cos\theta + i\sin\theta$.

    a Show that $2\cos\theta = z + \dfrac{1}{z}$.

    b Show that $2\cos n\theta = z^n + \dfrac{1}{z^n}$.

    c Consider the equation $3z^4 - z^3 + 2z^2 - z + 3 = 0$.

       i Show that the equation can be written as $6\cos 2\theta - 2\cos\theta + 2 = 0$.

       ii Find all four complex roots of the original equation.

8 **a** By considering $(\cos\theta + i\sin\theta)^3$, find expressions for $\cos 3\theta$ and $\sin 3\theta$.

    b Show that $\tan 3\theta = \dfrac{3\tan\theta - \tan^3\theta}{1 - 3\tan^2\theta}$.

    c Hence show that $\tan\dfrac{\pi}{12}$ is a root of the equation $x^3 - 3x^2 - 3x + 1 = 0$.

    d Show that $(x+1)$ is a factor of $x^3 - 3x^2 - 3x + 1$ and hence find the exact solutions of the equation $x^3 - 3x^2 - 3x + 1 = 0$.

    e By considering $\tan\dfrac{\pi}{4}$, explain why $\tan\dfrac{\pi}{12} < 1$.

    f Hence state the exact value of $\tan\dfrac{\pi}{12}$.

45

9 a i Use De Moivre's theorem to show that

$$\cos 5\theta = \cos^5 \theta - 10 \cos^3 \theta \sin^2 \theta + 5 \cos \theta \sin^4 \theta$$

and find a similar expression for $\sin 5\theta$.

ii Deduce that

$$\tan 5\theta = \frac{\tan \theta (5 - 10 \tan^2 \theta + \tan^4 \theta)}{1 - 10 \tan^2 \theta + 5 \tan^4 \theta}.$$

b Explain why $t = \tan \frac{\pi}{5}$ is a root of the equation

$$t^4 - 10t^2 + 5 = 0$$

and write down the three other roots of this equation in trigonometrical form.

c Deduce that

$$\tan \frac{\pi}{5} \tan \frac{2\pi}{5} = \sqrt{5}.$$

[© AQA 2011]

10 a Use De Moivre's theorem to show that, if $z = \cos \theta + i \sin \theta$, then

$$z^n + \frac{1}{z^n} = 2 \cos n\theta$$

b i Expand $\left(z^2 + \frac{1}{z^2}\right)^4$.

ii Show that

$$\cos^4 2\theta = A \cos 8\theta + B \cos 4\theta + C$$

where A, B and C are rational numbers.

c Hence solve the equation

$$8 \cos^4 2\theta = \cos 8\theta + 5$$

for $0 \leq \theta \leq \pi$, giving each solution in the form $k\pi$.

d Show that

$$\int_0^{\frac{\pi}{2}} \cos^4 2\theta \, d\theta = \frac{3\pi}{16}.$$

[© AQA 2012]

3 Further transformations of the ellipse, hyperbola and parabola

In this chapter you will learn how to:

- recognise an ellipse, a hyperbola or a parabola from its parametric or polar equation
- find the equation of a curve after a combination of rotations, reflections and stretches
- identify a transformation, or a sequence of transformations, by considering the transformed equation.

Before you start…

Further Mathematics Student Book 1, Chapter 3	You should be able to recognise the equation and main features of an ellipse, hyperbola and parabola.	1	Name the curve described by the equation $\dfrac{x^2}{16} - \dfrac{y^2}{9} = 1$ and find the equations of any asymptotes and the coordinates of any axis intercepts.
Further Mathematics Student Book 1, Chapter 3	You should know how to find the equation of a curve after a translation, reflection of stretch.	2	Find the equation of the curve $y^2 = 6x$ after: a a translation with vector $\begin{pmatrix} -2 \\ 5 \end{pmatrix}$ b a reflection in the line $y = -x$.
A Level Mathematics Student Book 2, Chapter 3	You should be able to recognise a transformation, or combination of transformations, that map one function onto another.	3	Describe two transformations which map the graph of $y = f(x)$ onto the graph of $y = -f(3x)$.

Conic sections

Conic sections is a collective name for a group of curves that can be obtained as cross-sections of a cone. There are three distinct types: the ellipse (with a circle as a special case), hyperbola and parabola. In Further Mathematics Student Book 1, Chapter 3, you met Cartesian equations of these curves and also learnt how the equations are changed by translations, reflections and stretches. In this chapter you will add enlargements and rotations to this list of transformations. You will also see how you can apply techniques of parametric equations and polar coordinates to describe the curves in several different ways.

A Level Further Mathematics for AQA Student Book 2

Section 1: Parametric and polar form

Ellipse

$\dfrac{x^2}{a^2} + \dfrac{y^2}{a^2} = 1$

Hyperbola

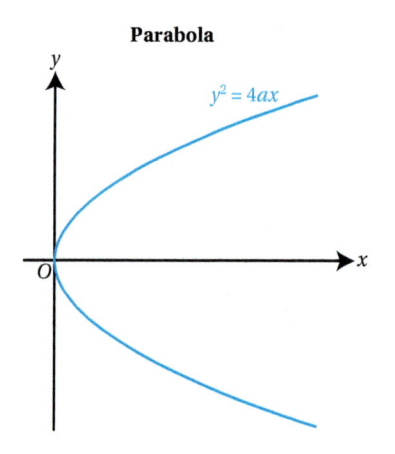

$y = -\dfrac{b}{a}x$, $y = \dfrac{b}{a}x$

$\dfrac{x^2}{a^2} - \dfrac{y^2}{a^2} = 1$

Parabola

$y^2 = 4ax$

You can also describe these curves using parametric and polar equations.

> **Rewind**
>
> You met parametric equations in A Level Mathematics Student Book 2, Chapter 12, and polar coordinates in Further Mathematics Student Book 1, Chapter 6.

WORKED EXAMPLE 3.1

Show that the curve described by the parametric equations

$x = 1 + \tan^2 t$, $y = 3 \sec t$, $t \in \left(-\dfrac{\pi}{2}, \dfrac{\pi}{2}\right)$ is a parabola.

$y^2 = 9 \sec^2 t$
$ = 9(1 + \tan^2 t)$
$ = 9x$

You need to find a Cartesian equation. It looks like y^2 is related to x.

Hence the Cartesian equation is $y^2 = 9x$, which is the equation of a parabola.

Recognise the standard equation of a parabola.

WORKED EXAMPLE 3.2

Find a Cartesian equation of the curve with polar equation $r^2 = \dfrac{36}{13\cos^2\theta - 4}$. Hence sketch the curve.

Using $\cos\theta = \dfrac{x}{r}$:

$r^2 = \dfrac{36}{\dfrac{13x^2}{r^2} - 4}$

The connection between polar and Cartesian coordinates is: $r^2 = x^2 + y^2$, $x = r\cos\theta$ and $y = r\sin\theta$. It is often useful to start by expressing $\cos\theta$ in terms of x and r and see if any r terms cancel.

$\Leftrightarrow r^2 = \dfrac{36r^2}{13x^2 - 4r^2}$

$\Leftrightarrow 13x^2 - 4r^2 = 36$

$\Leftrightarrow 13x^2 - 4(x^2 + y^2) = 36$

Now use $r^2 = x^2 + y^2$.

$\Leftrightarrow 9x^2 - 4y^2 = 36$

$\Leftrightarrow \dfrac{x^2}{4} - \dfrac{y^2}{9} = 1$

Divide by 36 to get 1 on the right.

Continues on next page

3 Further transformations of the ellipse, hyperbola and parabola

This is a hyperbola with x-intercepts $(\pm 2, 0)$ and asymptotes $y = \pm \dfrac{3}{2} x$.

This is the equation of a hyperbola $\left(\dfrac{x^2}{a^2} - \dfrac{y^2}{b^2} = 1 \right)$ with $a = 2$ and $b = 3$.

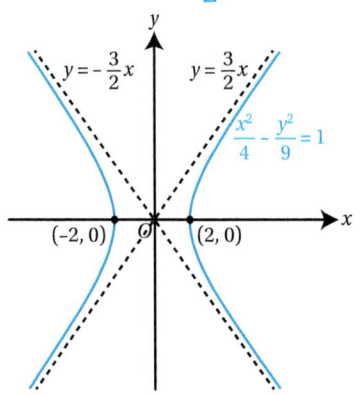

Transformations of curves

You already know how to apply certain transformations to curves by changing the equation.

Transformation	Change to equation
translation with vector $\begin{pmatrix} p \\ q \end{pmatrix}$	replace x by $(x - p)$ and y by $(y - q)$
reflection in the x-axis	replace y by $-y$
reflection in the y-axis	replace x by $-x$
reflection in the line $y = x$	swap x and y
reflection in the line $y = -x$	replace x by $-y$ and y by $-x$
stretch horizontally with scale factor a and vertically with scale factor b	replace x by $\left(\dfrac{x}{a}\right)$ and y by $\left(\dfrac{y}{b}\right)$

WORKED EXAMPLE 3.3

Show that the curve with polar equation $r = \dfrac{3}{2 + \cos \theta}$ is an ellipse and state the equations of its axes of symmetry.

Using $x = r \cos \theta$:
$$r = \dfrac{3}{2 + \dfrac{x}{r}} = \dfrac{3r}{2r + x}$$

$\Leftrightarrow 2r + x = 3$
$\Leftrightarrow 4r^2 = (3 - x)^2$
$\Leftrightarrow 4x^2 + 4y^2 = 9 - 6x + x^2$
$\Leftrightarrow 3x^2 + 6x + 4y^2 = 9$
$\Leftrightarrow 3(x + 1)^2 - 3 + 4y^2 = 9$
$\Leftrightarrow 3(x + 1)^2 + 4y^2 = 12$
$\Leftrightarrow \dfrac{(x + 1)^2}{4} + \dfrac{y^2}{3} = 1$

Start by expressing $\cos \theta$ in terms of x and r.

Note that r can't be zero, so you can divide by it.

$r = \sqrt{x^2 + y^2}$, so isolate r on the left before squaring both sides. (r is, by definition, positive, so squaring both sides is fine.)

You are looking for an equation of the ellipse, so complete the square for x and make the RHS equal to 1.

Continues on next page

49

This is an ellipse translated −1 units horizontally.   Recognise the translation with vector $\begin{pmatrix} -1 \\ 0 \end{pmatrix}$.

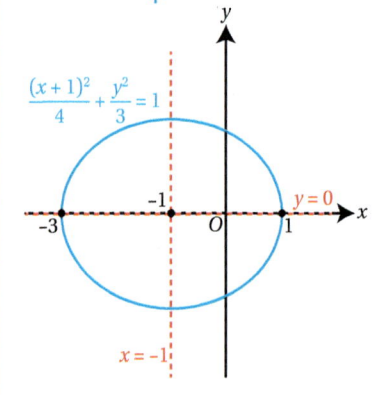

$\dfrac{(x+1)^2}{4} + \dfrac{y^2}{3} = 1$

Hence its axes of symmetry are $y = 0$ and $x = −1$.

Did you know?

The equation of an ellipse in the form shown in Worked example 3.3 is normally used to describe planetary orbits.

EXERCISE 3A

1. Show that the curve described by the parametric equations $x = 3t^2$, $y = 6t$, $t \in \mathbb{R}$ is a parabola.

2. Show that the curve with equations $x = 2t^2 + 1$, $y = 5t − 2$ is a parabola and state the coordinates of its vertex.

3. Find the Cartesian equation of the curve with parametric equations $x = 4\cos t$, $y = 5\sin t$, $t \in [0, 2\pi)$. Hence sketch the curve.

4. Show that the curve with parametric equations $x = 7\cosh t$, $y = 3\sinh t$ is a hyperbola and find the equations of its asymptotes.

5. Sketch the curve with parametric equations $x = 5\sec t$, $y = 5\tan t$.

6. Show that the curve with parametric equations $x = 3 − 5\cos\theta$, $y = 1 + 2\sin\theta$ is an ellipse and state the equations of its axes of symmetry.

7. Show that the curve with parametric equations $x = \cos 2\theta$, $y = \cos\theta$, $\theta \in [0, 2\pi)$ is a parabola. State the coordinates of its vertex.

8. Find the Cartesian equation of the curve with polar equation $r^2 = \dfrac{5}{2\cos^2\theta - 1}$. What is the name given to this curve?

9. Find the Cartesian equation of the polar curve $r^2 = \dfrac{2}{3\sin^2\theta + 1}$. What is the name given to this curve?

3 Further transformations of the ellipse, hyperbola and parabola

10 A curve is described by the polar equation $r = \dfrac{9}{1 + 2\cos\theta}$.

    a Find the Cartesian equation of the curve.

    b Hence sketch the curve, indicating the position of the intercepts with the coordinate axes.

11 Find the Cartesian equation of the curve given by polar equation $r = \dfrac{40}{3 - \sin\theta}$. State the name given to this curve and write down the equations of its axes of symmetry.

12 Curve C_1 has equation $5x^2 + 12y^2 = 32$.

    a Find the equation of the tangent to C_1 at the point $(2, 1)$. Give your answer in the form $ax + by = c$, where a, b and c are integers.

    Curve C_2 has equation $5x^2 - 30x + 12y^2 + 48y + 61 = 0$.

    b Describe the transformation that transforms C_1 to C_2.

    c Hence find the equation of the tangent to C_2 at the point $(5, -1)$.

13 An ellipse is obtained from the circle $x^2 + y^2 = 18$ by a horizontal stretch with scale factor 5.

    a Find the equation of the ellipse.

    b Write down the equation of the tangent to the circle at the point $(3, 3)$.

    c Hence find the equation of the tangent to the ellipse at the point $(15, 3)$.

14 The parabola C_1 has equation $y^2 = 16(x - 2)$.

    a Find the equations of the tangents to C_1 that pass through the origin.

    The parabola C_2 has parametric equations $x = t^2 + 8$, $y = 2t$, $t \in \mathbb{R}$.

    b Describe the single transformation that maps C_1 to C_2.

    c Hence find the equations of the tangents to C_2 that pass through the origin.

Section 2: Rotations and enlargements

> **Key point 3.1**
>
> You can rotate a curve by changing its equation:
>
> | Rotation anticlockwise | Change to equation |
> | --- | --- |
> | 90° | replace x by y and y by $-x$ |
> | 180° | replace x by $-x$ and y by $-y$ |
> | 270° | replace x by $-y$ and y by x |

On this course, you only need to be able to use rotations through 90°, 180° and 270°.

WORKED EXAMPLE 3.4

The parabola with equation $y^2 = 6x$ is rotated 90° clockwise about the origin. Find the equation of the resulting curve.

$x^2 = 6(-y)$ …………… A 90° clockwise rotation is the same as a 270°
$\Leftrightarrow y = -\dfrac{1}{6}x^2$ rotation anticlockwise. Replace x by $-y$ and y by x.

An enlargement (with the centre at the origin) is a combination of a horizontal and a vertical stretch, both with the same scale factor.

Key point 3.2

Replacing x by $\dfrac{x}{c}$ and y by $\dfrac{y}{c}$ results in an enlargement with scale factor c and centre at the origin.

WORKED EXAMPLE 3.5

Describe fully the transformation that transforms the curve $\dfrac{x^2}{2} + \dfrac{y^2}{5} = 1$ into the curve $50x^2 + 20y^2 = 1$.

$50x^2 + 20y^2 = 1$ …………… Relate the transformed equation to the original equation.
$\Leftrightarrow \dfrac{100x^2}{2} + \dfrac{100y^2}{5} = 1$
$\Leftrightarrow \dfrac{(10x)^2}{2} + \dfrac{(10y)^2}{5} = 1$ …………… Decide what x and y have been replaced by.

This is an enlargement with centre at the origin and scale factor $\dfrac{1}{10}$.   …………… x and y have been replaced by $10x$ and $10y$, respectively.

EXERCISE 3B

1 Find the equation of each given curve after a 90°, 180° and 270° rotation anticlockwise. Which of the rotations leave the curve unchanged?

  a Ellipse $\dfrac{x^2}{4} + \dfrac{y^2}{7} = 1$
  b Hyperbola $\dfrac{x^2}{4} - \dfrac{y^2}{7} = 1$
  c Parabola $y^2 = 8x$

2 Find the equation of each curve after it has been rotated 90° anticlockwise about the origin. Which reflections result in the same curve?

  a Ellipse $\dfrac{x^2}{5} + \dfrac{y^2}{2} = 1$
  b Hyperbola $\dfrac{x^2}{12} - \dfrac{y^2}{5} = 1$
  c Parabola $y^2 = 5x$

3 Find the equation of the hyperbola $\dfrac{x^2}{5} - \dfrac{y^2}{12} = 1$ after it is rotated 90° anticlockwise about the origin.

4 Find the equation of the parabola $y^2 = 6x$ after it is rotated 90° anticlockwise about the origin.

5 Find the equation of the hyperbola $x^2 - 2y^2 = 1$ after enlargement by scale factor 3.

3 Further transformations of the ellipse, hyperbola and parabola

6   **a**   Sketch the curve C_1 with equation $y^2 = 5x$.

The curve C_2 is an enlargement of C_1 with scale factor 3 (and centre at the origin).

   b   Find the equation of C_2.

   c   Describe a horizontal stretch that transforms C_2 back to C_1.

7   Describe fully the transformation that maps the hyperbola $\frac{x^2}{3} - \frac{y^2}{5} = 1$ onto the hyperbola $5x^2 - 3y^2 = 105$.

8   Describe fully a possible transformation that maps the curve $x^2 - 3y^2 = 3$ onto the curve $y^2 - 3x^2 = 3$. Hence state the equations of the asymptotes of the curve $y^2 - 3x^2 = 3$.

9   **a**   Sketch the hyperbola with equation $\frac{x^2}{3} - \frac{y^2}{12} = 1$.

   b   Show that an enlargement with centre at the origin does not change the equations of the asymptotes.

10   Show that the curve with equation $\frac{y^2}{9} - \frac{x^2}{16} = 1$ is a hyperbola and find the equations of its asymptotes.

Section 3: Combined transformations

You can combine any of the transformations from Sections 1 and 2. You know that sometimes the order of transformations matters – performing transformations in a different order may produce a different curve.

> **Rewind**
>
> You met combined transformations in A Level Mathematics Student Book 2, Chapter 3.

WORKED EXAMPLE 3.6

Find the equation of the ellipse $\frac{x^2}{16} + \frac{y^2}{9} = 1$ after each sequence of transformations.

a   Enlargement with scale factor 3 followed by a translation with vector $\begin{pmatrix} -1 \\ 4 \end{pmatrix}$.

b   Translation with vector $\begin{pmatrix} -1 \\ 4 \end{pmatrix}$ followed by an enlargement with scale factor 3.

a   After the enlargement: *The enlargement replaces x by $\frac{x}{3}$ and y by $\frac{y}{3}$.*

$\dfrac{\left(\frac{x}{3}\right)^2}{16} + \dfrac{\left(\frac{y}{3}\right)^2}{9} = 1$ *Remember that both variables are squared.*

$\Leftrightarrow \dfrac{x^2}{144} + \dfrac{y^2}{81} = 1$

After the translation: *Replace x by $x + 1$ and y by $y - 4$.*

$\dfrac{(x+1)^2}{144} + \dfrac{(y-4)^2}{81} = 1$

b   After the translation: *Now do the translation first.*

$\dfrac{(x+1)^2}{16} + \dfrac{(y-4)^2}{9} = 1$

Continues on next page

53

After the enlargement:

$$\frac{\left(\frac{x}{3}+1\right)^2}{16}+\frac{\left(\frac{y}{3}-4\right)^2}{9}=1$$

$$\Leftrightarrow \frac{(x+3)^2}{144}+\frac{(y-12)^2}{81}=1$$

> For the enlargement, the x and y **inside** the brackets need to be replaced.
> You can see that this curve has the same shape as the one in part **a** but is in a different position.

You also need to be able to identify the sequence of transformations that maps one curve to another. You have already seen that sometimes there are several transformations giving the same result for a given curve (for example, because of the symmetry of the ellipse, a 90° rotation gives the same result as a reflection in the line $y = x$). It is also possible that transformations can be carried out in a different order. Therefore there might be more than one correct answer to a question.

WORKED EXAMPLE 3.7

The parabola $y^2 = 2x$ is transformed to the parabola $x^2 = -6y$ by a rotation followed by a horizontal stretch.

a Describe fully both transformations.
b The rotation from part **a** can be replaced by a reflection and still result in the same curve. What is the reflection?
c The same curve can also be obtained by a horizontal stretch followed by a rotation. Find the scale factor of the stretch.

a The rotation is 90° clockwise about the origin. .... The rotation replaces x by $-y$ (and y by x or $-x$).

The equation after the rotation is $x^2 = -2y$.
After the enlargement:

$$\left(\frac{x}{k}\right)^2 = -2y$$

$$\Leftrightarrow x^2 = -2k^2 y$$

Hence $k^2 = 3$. .... Compare the last equation to $x^2 = -6y$.

The enlargement has centre at the origin and scale factor $\sqrt{3}$.

b The reflection is in the line $y = -x$. .... The reflection needs to replace x by $-y$ and y by x or $-x$. (See the table in Key point 3.1)

The horizontal stretch with scale factor k replaces x by $\frac{x}{k}$.

c After the stretch:

$$y^2 = 2\left(\frac{x}{k}\right)$$

After the rotation:

$$x^2 = \frac{2}{k}(-y) = -\frac{2}{k}y$$

Hence $\frac{2}{k} = 6$, so the scale factor is $\frac{1}{3}$. .... Compare this to $x^2 = -6y$.

The rotation still needs to be 90° clockwise.

3 Further transformations of the ellipse, hyperbola and parabola

WORK IT OUT 3.1

Describe a sequence of three transformations that transforms the circle $x^2 + y^2 = 1$ into the ellipse with equation $\dfrac{(x-3)^2}{25} + \dfrac{(y+2)^2}{9} = 1$.

Which is the correct solution? Identify the errors made in the incorrect solutions.

Solution 1	Solution 2	Solution 3
1 Translation with vector $\begin{pmatrix} 3 \\ -2 \end{pmatrix}$; 2 Horizontal stretch with scale factor 25; 3 Vertical stretch with scale factor 9.	1 Horizontal stretch with scale factor 25; 2 Vertical stretch with scale factor $\dfrac{1}{9}$; 3 Translation with vector $\begin{pmatrix} 3 \\ 2 \end{pmatrix}$.	1 Translation with vector $\begin{pmatrix} \dfrac{3}{5} \\ -\dfrac{2}{3} \end{pmatrix}$; 2 Horizontal stretch with scale factor 5; 3 Vertical stretch with scale factor 3.

EXERCISE 3C

1 Find the equation of each curve after the given sequence of transformations.

a **i** $\dfrac{x^2}{3} + \dfrac{y^2}{5} = 1$;

rotation through 90° anticlockwise about the origin; translation with vector $\begin{pmatrix} 3 \\ -1 \end{pmatrix}$.

ii $\dfrac{x^2}{4} - \dfrac{y^2}{3} = 1$;

rotation through 90° anticlockwise about the origin; translation with vector $\begin{pmatrix} -2 \\ 5 \end{pmatrix}$.

b **i** $y^2 = 6x$;

horizontal translation 3 units to the right; rotation through 90° clockwise about the origin.

ii $y^2 = 10x$;

vertical translation 5 units up; rotation through 90° clockwise about the origin.

c **i** $x^2 - y^2 = 16$;

vertical stretch with scale factor 2; translation 3 units in the positive y-direction; horizontal stretch with scale factor 5.

ii $x^2 + y^2 = 12$;

horizontal stretch with scale factor 2; vertical stretch with scale factor 3; translation 2 units in the negative x-direction.

d **i** $y^2 = 4x$;

enlargement with scale factor 2; translation 6 units in the positive x-direction; enlargement with scale factor $\dfrac{1}{2}$.

ii $y^2 = 8x$;

translation 3 units in the negative x-direction; enlargement with scale factor 2; translation 3 units in the positive x-direction.

55

2. Describe a possible sequence of transformations that transforms:
   a i $x^2 + y^2 = 1$ to $(x-1)^2 + (y+5)^2 = 9$
      ii $x^2 - y^2 = 1$ to $(x-3)^2 + (x-2)^2 = 16$
   b i $x^2 + 2y^2 = 5$ to $9(x-2)^2 + 8y^2 = 5$
      ii $3x^2 + 5y^2 = 15$ to $3(x+5)^2 + 5(y-3)^2 = 45$
   c i $\frac{x^2}{5} + \frac{y^2}{3} = 1$ to $\frac{(x-2)^2}{3} + \frac{(y-4)^2}{5} = 1$
      ii $\frac{x^2}{4} - \frac{y^2}{3} = 1$ to $\frac{(y+3)^2}{4} - \frac{(x-4)^2}{3} = 1$
   d i $y^2 = 5x$ to $(x-3)^2 = 10y$
      ii $y^2 = 12x$ to $x^2 = 3(y-1)$.

3. Curve C is obtained from the parabola $y^2 = 4x$ by this sequence of transformations: translation 5 units in the positive x-direction; enlargement with scale factor 3.

   Find the equation of C and find the coordinates of its vertex.

4. The parabola $y^2 = 2x$ is transformed by this sequence of transformations: translation p units in the negative x-direction; enlargement with scale factor $\frac{1}{2}$.
   The resulting curve has equation $y^2 = x + 4$. Find the value of p.

5. The ellipse $\frac{x^2}{4} + \frac{y^2}{25} = 1$ is rotated $90°$ anticlockwise about the origin and then translated. The equation of the resulting curve is $\frac{(x-3)^2}{25} + \frac{(y+1)^2}{4} = 1$.
   Find the translation vector.

6. The hyperbola $\frac{x^2}{12} - \frac{y^2}{7} = 1$ is rotated $90°$ **clockwise** about the origin and then translated. The equation of the resulting curve is $\frac{(y+3)^2}{12} - \frac{(x-5)^2}{7} = 1$.
   Find the translation vector.

7. a Sketch the curve with equation $\frac{x^2}{5} + \frac{y^2}{3} = 1$, labelling the axes intercepts.
   b Find the equation of the curve after this sequence of transformations: translation 3 units in the positive x-direction; enlargement with scale factor $\frac{1}{2}$; rotation through $90°$ anticlockwise about the origin.

8. Curve C has equation $\frac{x^2}{12} - \frac{y^2}{7} = 1$.
   a State the name given to this curve and find the equations of its asymptotes.

   This sequence of transformations is applied to C: translation 5 units in the positive y-direction; enlargement with scale factor $\frac{1}{3}$; rotation through $90°$ anticlockwise about the origin.
   The resulting curve is C_1.
   b Find the equation of C_1.
   c Find the equations of the asymptotes of C_1.

3 Further transformations of the ellipse, hyperbola and parabola

9 **a** Find the equations of the asymptotes of the hyperbola $(x+4)(y-7) = 22$.

b Describe a single transformation that transforms this hyperbola to $(x+8)(y-14) = 88$.

10 **a** Describe a combination of transformations that maps the circle $x^2 + y^2 = 1$ onto the ellipse with equation $\dfrac{x^2}{a^2} + \dfrac{y^2}{b^2} = 1$.

b Hence find an expression for the area of the ellipse.

11 The curve C has parametric equations $x = \cos 2t$, $y = 8 \cos t$, for $t \in [0, 2\pi)$.

a Find the Cartesian equation of C.

C can be obtained from the parabola $y^2 = 4x$ by a combination of a horizontal translation and a vertical stretch.

b Describe fully each of the two transformations.

12 The hyperbola with equation $\dfrac{x^2}{4} - \dfrac{y^2}{9} = 1$ is translated 2 units to the right and stretched vertically with scale factor 2.

Find the equation of the resulting curve and the equations of its asymptotes.

13 **a** Show that the curve C with equation $9x^2 - 18x - y^2 = 27$ can be obtained from the hyperbola $\dfrac{x^2}{4} - \dfrac{y^2}{9} = 1$ by a combination of a translation and a stretch.

b Hence find the asymptotes of C.

14 The ellipse $\dfrac{x^2}{3} + \dfrac{y^2}{5} = 1$ is translated and then rotated 90° anticlockwise about the origin. The equation of the resulting curve is $\dfrac{(x-3)^2}{5} + \dfrac{(y+1)^2}{3} = 1$.

Find the translation vector.

15 The curve $\dfrac{x^2}{4} + \dfrac{y^2}{3} = 1$ is transformed into the curve $\dfrac{(3x-1)^2}{4} + \dfrac{(y-2)^2}{12} = 1$ by a translation followed by two stretches.

Describe fully each of the three transformations.

57

Checklist of learning and understanding

- You need to be able to transform curves using any combination of these transformations:

Transformation	Change to equation
translation with vector $\begin{pmatrix} p \\ q \end{pmatrix}$	replace x by $(x - p)$ and y by $(y - q)$
reflection in the x-axis	replace y by $-y$
reflection in the y-axis	replace x by $-x$
reflection in the line $y = x$	swap x and y
reflection in the line $y = -x$	replace x by $-y$ and y by $-x$
stretch horizontally with scale factor a and vertically with scale factor b	replace x by $\left(\dfrac{x}{a}\right)$ and y by $\left(\dfrac{y}{b}\right)$
enlargement with scale factor c and the centre at the origin	replace x by $\dfrac{x}{c}$ and y by $\dfrac{y}{c}$
rotation through 90° anticlockwise	replace x by y and y by $-x$
rotation through 180° anticlockwise	replace x by $-x$ and y by $-y$
rotation through 270° anticlockwise	replace x by $-y$ and y by x

- Because of the symmetries of the ellipse, hyperbola and parabola, some of the listed transformations appear to have the same effect.
- You can identify a transformation, or a sequence of transformations, by considering how to get from one equation to another.

3 Further transformations of the ellipse, hyperbola and parabola

Mixed practice 3

1. Find the scale factor of the enlargement that, when combined, transforms the curve $xy = 4$ into the curve $xy = 12$.

   Choose from these options.

   A 3 **B** $\dfrac{1}{3}$ **C** $\sqrt{3}$ **D** $\dfrac{1}{\sqrt{3}}$

2. **a** Sketch the curve with equation $\dfrac{x^2}{3} + \dfrac{y^2}{9} = 1$, showing the coordinates of any intercepts with the axes.

   b The curve is rotated 90° anticlockwise about the origin and then stretched horizontally with scale factor $\dfrac{1}{3}$. Find the equation of the resulting curve.

3. The parabola $y^2 = 3x$ is enlarged with scale factor 5 and then translated by vector $\begin{pmatrix} -1 \\ 4 \end{pmatrix}$.

   Find the equation of the resulting curve and the coordinates of its vertex.

4. The hyperbola $x^2 - y^2 = 5$ is enlarged with scale factor 3 and then translated by vector $\begin{pmatrix} -2 \\ 2 \end{pmatrix}$.

   Find the equation of the resulting curve, and the equations of its asymptotes.

5. The parabola C_1 has equation $y^2 = 6x$. The parabola C_2 is obtained from C_1 by a reflection in the line $y = x$ followed by a horizontal stretch with scale factor 3.

   Find the coordinates of the points of intersection of C_1 and C_2.

6. **a** Find the coordinates of the points where the line $y = x$ intersects the circle $x^2 + y^2 = 32$.

   b Describe fully two transformations that, when combined, map the circle $x^2 + y^2 = 32$ onto the ellipse $\dfrac{(x-3)^2}{32} + \dfrac{y^2}{8} = 1$.

   c Hence find the points of intersection of the line $2y = x - 3$ with the ellipse $\dfrac{(x-3)^2}{32} + \dfrac{y^2}{8} = 1$.

7. The parabola $y^2 = 5x$ is translated by $\begin{pmatrix} -4 \\ 1 \end{pmatrix}$ and then rotated 90° **clockwise** about the origin.

   What is the equation of the resulting curve?

   Choose from these options.

   A $(x-1)^2 = -5(y-4)$ **B** $(x-1)^2 = -5(y+4)$

   C $(x+1)^2 = 5(y+4)$ **D** $(x+1)^2 = 5(y-4)$

8. Find the equation of the parabola $y^2 = 7x$ after it has been translated by $\begin{pmatrix} 3 \\ 5 \end{pmatrix}$ and then rotated 180° about the origin.

   State the coordinates of the vertex of the transformed curve.

9. **a** Show that the line $y = x + 6$ is tangent to the circle $x^2 + y^2 = 18$.

   b Hence find the positive value of k for which the line $y = kx + 8$ is tangent to the ellipse $\dfrac{x^2}{54} + \dfrac{(y-2)^2}{18} = 1$.

10 a Find the exact values of k such that the line $x + y = k$ is tangent to the ellipse $\frac{x^2}{9} + \frac{y^2}{4} = 1$.

The ellipse $\frac{x^2}{9} + \frac{y^2}{4} = 1$ is translated by $\begin{pmatrix} -3 \\ 2 \end{pmatrix}$ and then enlarged with scale factor $\frac{1}{3}$.

   b Find the equation of the transformed ellipse.

   c Find the exact value of c such that the line $x + y = c$ is tangent to the transformed ellipse.

11 a The curve with Cartesian equation $\frac{x^2}{c} + \frac{y^2}{d} = 1$ is mapped onto the curve with polar equation $r = \frac{10}{3 - 2\cos\theta}$ by a single geometrical transformation.

By writing the polar equation as a Cartesian equation in a suitable form, find the values of the constants c and d.

   b Hence describe the geometrical transformation referred to in part **a**.

[©AQA 2016]

12 Find the equations of the asymptotes of the curve $4(3y - 5)^2 - 9(2x + 7)^2 = 36$.

Choose from these options.

   A $6x + 6y = 11$ and $6x - 6y = 31$

   B $6x + 6y + 11 = 0$ and $6x - 6y + 31 = 0$

   C $6x + 6y = 31$ and $6x - 6y = 11$

   D $6x + 6y + 31 = 0$ and $6x - 6y + 11 = 0$

13 Curve E_1 is an ellipse with equation $\frac{x^2}{a^2} + \frac{y^2}{b^2} = 1$. Curve E_2 is obtained by rotating E_1 90° anticlockwise about the origin. E_1 and E_2 intersect at four points, which form a square. Find, in terms of a and b, the area of the square.

14 Curve C has parametric equations $x = 1 + 4\sinh t$, $y = 2 + 5\cosh t$ ($t \in \mathbb{R}$). Curve H is a part of the hyperbola $\frac{x^2}{25} - \frac{y^2}{16} = 1$ with $x \geq 0$.

   a Find the Cartesian equation of C.

   b Describe a possible sequence of two transformations that transforms H into C.

   c Hence sketch C, stating the coordinates of its vertex and the equations of its asymptotes.

15 The curve C has polar equation $r = \frac{3}{\sqrt{5} + 2\cos\theta}$.

   a Find the Cartesian equation of C.

   b Describe a sequence of two transformations that transforms C into the circle $x^2 + y^2 = 45$.

   c Hence find the exact area enclosed by C.

4 Further graphs and inequalities

In this chapter you will learn how to:

- draw graphs of $y = \dfrac{1}{f(x)}$
- draw graphs of $y = |f(x)|$ for non-linear $f(x)$
- solve modulus equations and inequalities.

Before you start…

Further Mathematics Student Book 1, Chapter 4	You should be able to sketch graphs of rational functions.	1	Sketch the graphs of: a $y = \dfrac{x+3}{x-2}$ b $y = \dfrac{2x^2 - 3x - 2}{x^2 + 2x - 3}$.
Further Mathematics Student Book 1, Chapter 5	You should be able to sketch graphs of hyperbolic functions.	2	Sketch the graphs of: a $y = \sinh(x+2)$ b $y = \cosh x - 4$.
A Level Mathematics Student Book 2, Chapter 3	You should be able to sketch modulus graphs for linear functions.	3	On the same axes, sketch the graphs of $y = |2x - 3|$ and $y = |x + 1|$.
A Level Mathematics Student Book 2, Chapter 3	You should be able to solve modulus equations and inequalities for linear functions.	4	Solve the inequality $|2x - 3| < |x + 1|$.

Sketching reciprocal and modulus graphs

This chapter focuses on extending further the types of functions you can sketch. Building in particular on your knowledge of rational functions from Further Mathematics Student Book 1, Chapter 4, you will first look at techniques for drawing reciprocal graphs, i.e. graphs of $y = \dfrac{1}{f(x)}$ for some given function $f(x)$. You will then look at sketching general modulus functions rather than just the linear modulus functions you worked with in A Level Mathematics Student Book 2, Chapter 3. As in that chapter, you will be able to use these modulus graphs to help solve modulus equations and inequalities.

Section 1: The graph of $\frac{1}{f(x)}$

A **reciprocal transformation** turns the graph of $y = f(x)$ into the graph of $y = \frac{1}{f(x)}$.

The simplest reciprocal transformation turns $y = x$ into $y = \frac{1}{x}$.

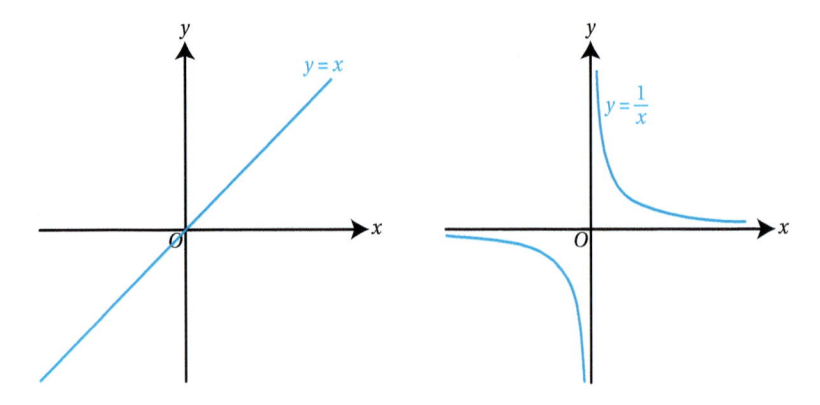

This example illustrates the behaviour of the graph of any function $g(x) = \frac{1}{f(x)}$.

Key point 4.1

f(x)	$g(x) = \frac{1}{f(x)}$
$f(a) = 0$	The line $x = a$ is a vertical asymptote.
The line $x = a$ is a vertical asymptote.	$g(a) = 0$
$f(x) \to +\infty$	$g(x) \to 0$ (tends to zero from above)
$f(x) \to -\infty$	$g(x) \to 0$ (tends to zero from below)
$f(x) \to 0$	$g(x) \to +\infty$ or $g(x) \to -\infty$
$f(x)$ has a horizontal asymptote $y = b$.	$g(x)$ has a horizontal asymptote $y = \frac{1}{b}$.
$0 < f(x) < 1$	$g(x) > 1$
$f(x) = 1$	$g(x) = 1$
$f(x) > 1$	$0 < g(x) < 1$
$-1 < f(x) < 0$	$g(x) < -1$
$f(x) = -1$	$g(x) = -1$
$f(x) < -1$	$-1 < g(x) < 0$
$(a, f(a))$ is a turning point.	$(a, g(a))$ is the opposite turning point, if $g(a)$ is finite.

Tip

If you are unsure about which side of an asymptote to sketch the graph, check a point on each side.

4 Further graphs and inequalities

Using Key point 4.1 as a guide, it is possible to make a rough sketch of the reciprocal for any given graph.

WORKED EXAMPLE 4.1

The diagram shows the graph of function f(x), with a root at a and asymptotes $x = b$ and $y = -c$. Sketch the corresponding graph of $g(x) = \dfrac{1}{f(x)}$.

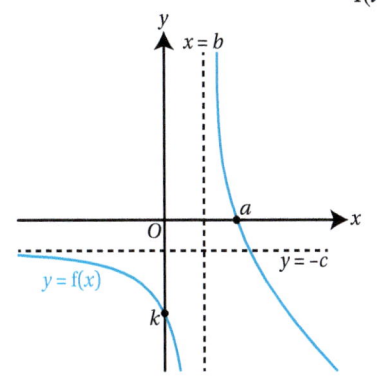

As $x \to -\infty$, $f(x) \to -c$ ∴ $g(x) \to -\dfrac{1}{c}$ — Consider what happens when x is large and negative.

So $y = -\dfrac{1}{c}$ is a horizontal asymptote of $g(x)$.

As $x \to +\infty$, $f(x) \to -\infty$ ∴ $g(x) \to 0$ — Consider what happens when x is large and positive.
So $y = 0$ is a horizontal asymptote of $g(x)$.

$f(a) = 0$ so $x = a$ is a vertical asymptote of $g(x)$. — Consider what happens when $f(x)$ has a root.

$x = b$ is a vertical asymptote of $f(x)$ so $g(b) = 0$. — Consider what happens when $f(x)$ has a vertical asymptote.

$f(x)$ has no turning points so $g(x)$ has no turning points. — Consider what happens when $f(x)$ has a turning point.

Put this information together.

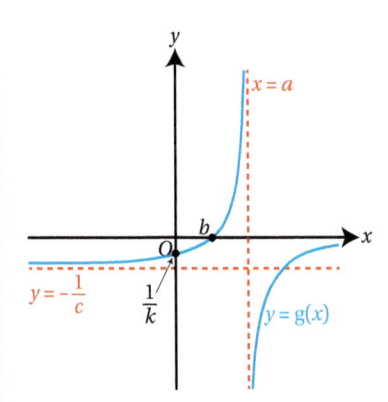

A Level Further Mathematics for AQA Student Book 2

EXERCISE 4A

1 By first sketching the graph of $y = f(x)$, sketch the graph of $y = \dfrac{1}{f(x)}$, indicating the positions of any axes intercepts and asymptotes.

- **a** **i** $f(x) = x - 3$ **ii** $f(x) = x - 5$
- **b** **i** $f(x) = x + 1$ **ii** $f(x) = x + 3$
- **c** **i** $f(x) = x^2$ **ii** $f(x) = (x - 1)^2$
- **d** **i** $f(x) = x^2 - 4$ **ii** $f(x) = x^2 + x - 6$
- **e** **i** $f(x) = e^x + 1$ **ii** $f(x) = e^{x+2}$
- **f** **i** $f(x) = \ln x + 2$ **ii** $f(x) = \ln(x + 3)$
- **g** **i** $f(x) = \sin x$ **ii** $f(x) = \tan x$

2 For each function $f(x)$:

A find any axis intercepts and vertical asymptotes for $y = f(x)$

B write down any axis intercepts and vertical asymptotes for $y = \dfrac{1}{f(x)}$.

- **a** **i** $f(x) = \dfrac{2 - x}{x^2 - 5}$ **ii** $f(x) = \dfrac{x^2 - 4}{2x^2 + 3x + 1}$
- **b** **i** $f(x) = \dfrac{\sin\left(\dfrac{\pi}{2}x\right)}{x^2 - 4x + 3}$ for $-2 < x < 4$ **ii** $f(x) = 1 + \dfrac{4x}{x^2 - 2x - 3}$

3 The graph of $y = f(x)$ is shown. Sketch the graph of $y = \dfrac{1}{f(x)}$.

a **i**

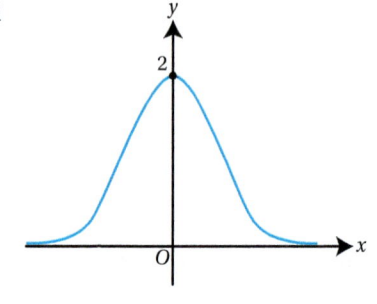

ii

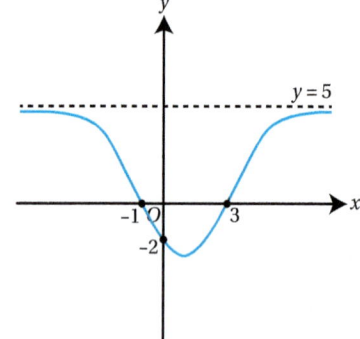

b **i**

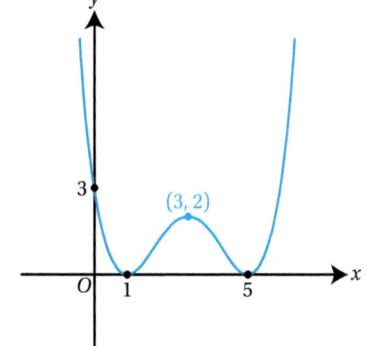

ii

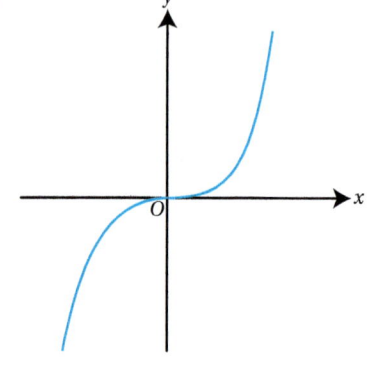

c i

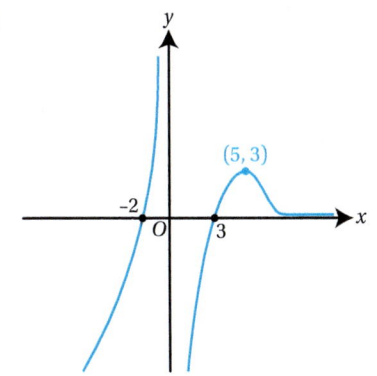

(5, 3), crosses at -2 and 3

ii

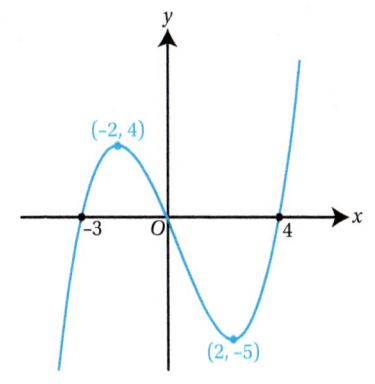

(−2, 4), (2, −5), crosses at -3 and 4

d i

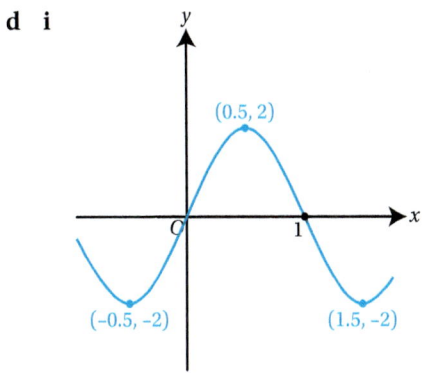

(0.5, 2), (−0.5, −2), (1.5, −2), crosses at 1

ii

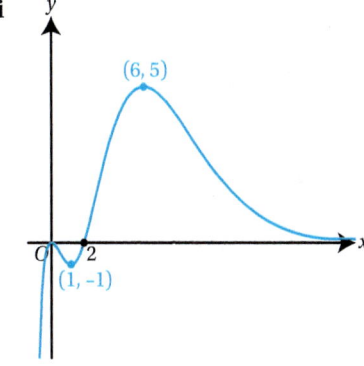

(6, 5), (1, −1), crosses at 2

e i

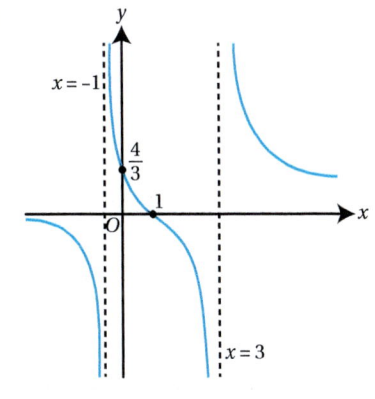

$x = -1$, $x = 3$ asymptotes; passes through $\frac{4}{3}$ and 1

ii

$x = -1$ asymptote, $y = x - 1$ asymptote; crosses at -2 and 2, $y = -4$

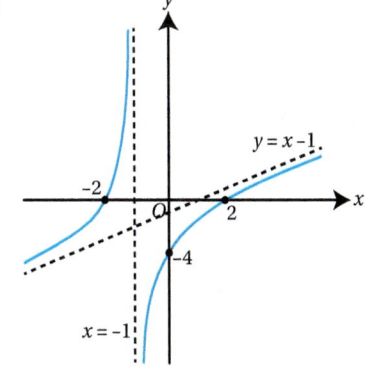

4. This is a graph of $y = \text{f}(x)$. Sketch the graph of $y = \dfrac{1}{\text{f}(x)}$, indicating clearly the positions of any asymptotes and coordinates of any maximum and minimum points.

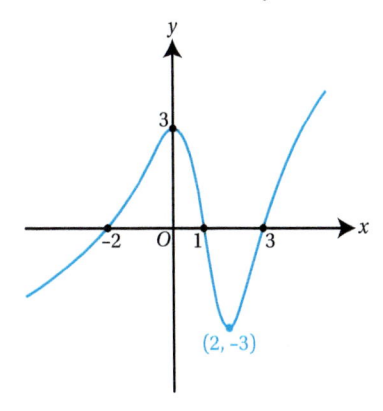

Graph passes through $(0, 3)$, crosses x-axis at -2, 1, and 3, with minimum at $(2, -3)$.

5. This is a graph of $y = f(x)$.

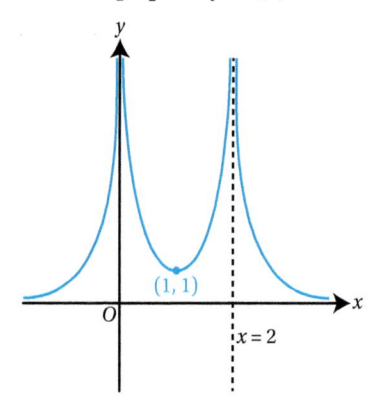

On a separate diagram, sketch the graph of $y = \dfrac{1}{f(x)} - 2$.

6. $f(x)$ is a function of the form $f(x) = \dfrac{ax^2 + bx + c}{x^2 + dx + e}$ where a is non-zero, and $f(x) = \dfrac{1}{g(x)}$.

Given that $f(x)$ has a single vertical asymptote at $x = 1$ and a horizontal asymptote at $y = 2$, while $g(x)$ has a single vertical asymptote at $x = 3$, find the values of a, b, c, d and e.

7. The graph of the functions $y = f(x)$ and $y = g(x)$ are shown. Copy $y = f(x)$ and $y = g(x)$ and, on the same axes, sketch the graph of $y = \dfrac{f(x)}{g(x)}$.

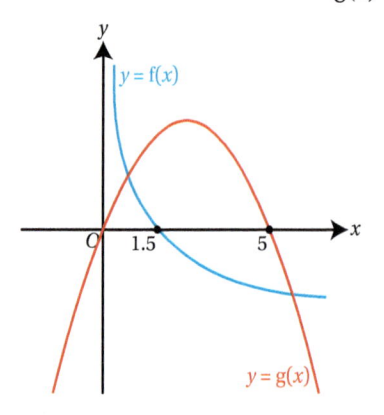

Section 2: The graph of $|f(x)|$

The modulus function has the property that any negative values are changed to positive values of the same magnitude. Hence the graph of $y = |f(x)|$ will be identical to that of $y = f(x)$ wherever $f(x)$ is positive, and will be the same as $y = -f(x)$ whenever $f(x)$ is negative.

Key point 4.2

To draw $y = |f(x)|$, reflect any parts of $f(x)$ that occur below the x-axis to appear above the x-axis.

4 Further graphs and inequalities

WORKED EXAMPLE 4.2

Given that f(x) = x(x − 2), draw the graph of y = |f(x)|.

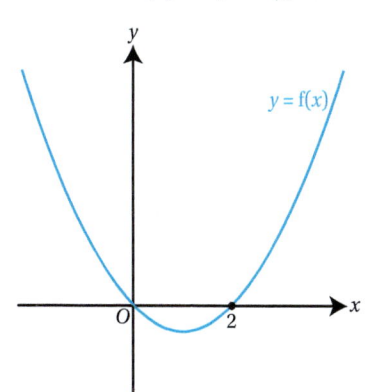

Draw the graph of f(x) to see which parts are above and which parts are below the x-axis.

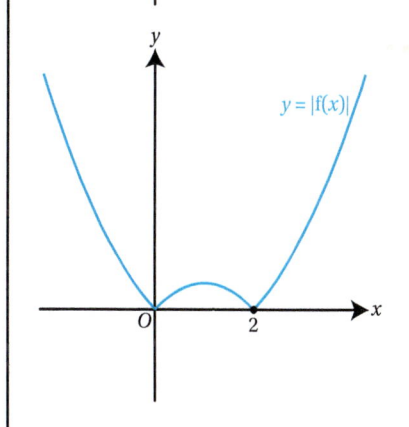

Reflect the parts of the graph that occur below the x-axis in the x-axis.

EXERCISE 4B

1 For each graph of f(x), sketch a graph for |f(x)|.

a i (0.5, 2), 1

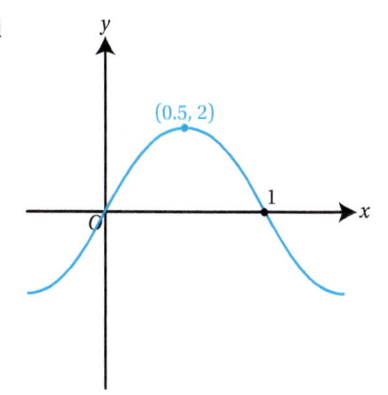

ii (6, 5), 2, (1, −1)

67

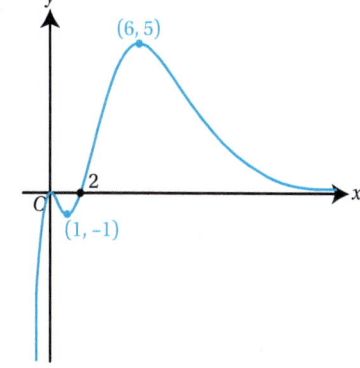

b i

(graph with asymptotes $x = -\frac{1}{2}$ and $x = 3$, point $\frac{4}{3}$)

ii

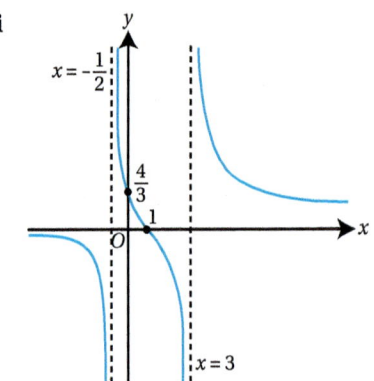

(graph with asymptote $x = -1$, intercepts -2 and -4)

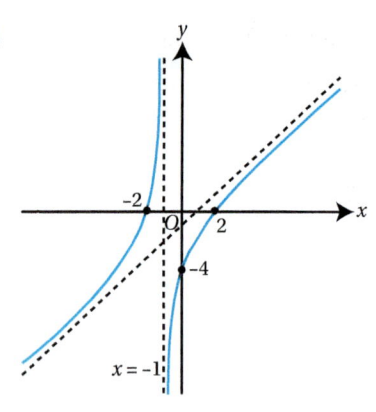

2 These are the graphs of f(x) and g(x).

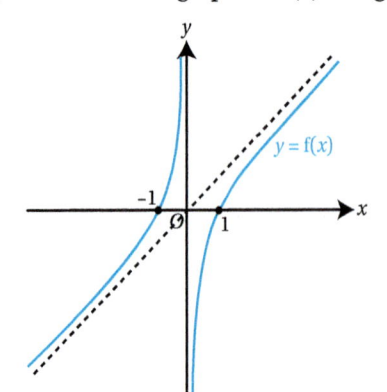

(graph of $y = f(x)$ with intercepts at -1 and 1)

(graph of $y = g(x)$ with intercepts at -2, 1, 2 and point 4)

Sketch:

a i $|f(x)|$ **ii** $|g(x)|$

b i $4 + 2|f(x)|$ **ii** $2|g(x)| - 2$

c i $2|2 + f(x)|$ **ii** $2|g(x) - 1|$

3 Sketch each graph, showing the axes intercepts and any asymptotes.

a i $y = |(x+2)(x-1)(x-3)|$ **ii** $y = |(x+3)(3-x)(x-5)|$

b i $y = |(x-5)(x+2)(x-1)^2|$ **ii** $y = |x^2(x-1)(x-2)|$

c i $y = |e^x - 2|$ **ii** $y = |e^{-x} - 3|$

d i $y = |\sinh x|$ **ii** $y = |\cosh x - 2|$

e i $y = \left|\dfrac{x-3}{x+2}\right|$ **ii** $y = \left|\dfrac{x+5}{x-3}\right|$

4 Sketch the graph of $y = |(x-a)(x-b)|$ given that $a < 0 < b$. Label all axis intercepts.

5 Use graphs to find the number of real solutions of the equation $|x^2 - 5x| = |\ln x|$.

6 Use graphs to find the number of real roots of the equation $|\sin x| = |x^2 - 1|$.

4 Further graphs and inequalities

7 a Find the minimum value of $y = x^2 - 4x$.

b For what values of k does the equation $|x^2 - 4x| = k$ have exactly two solutions?

> **Tip**
> You could approach part **a** of Question 7 by differentiating, completing the square or by using the fact that the minimum occurs halfway between the roots.

8 The diagram shows the graph of $y = f(x)$.

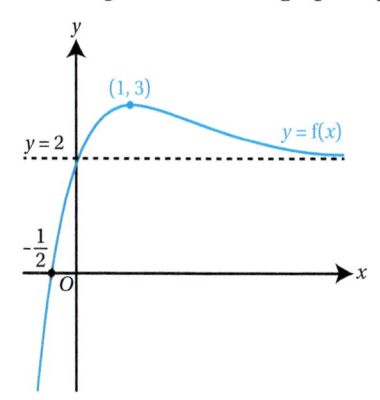

[Graph showing curve with maximum at $(1, 3)$, horizontal asymptote $y = 2$, passing through $-\frac{1}{2}$ on the x-axis]

a Sketch the graph of $y = |f(x)|$.

b State the set of values of k for the which the equation $|f(x)| = k$ has exactly three real roots.

9 Solve the equation $|x^2 - 7x + 10| = 7x - 10 - x^2$.

10 Find the range of the function $f(x) = |8e^{-x} - 5|$ for $x \geqslant 0$.

11 This is a graph of $y = f(x)$.

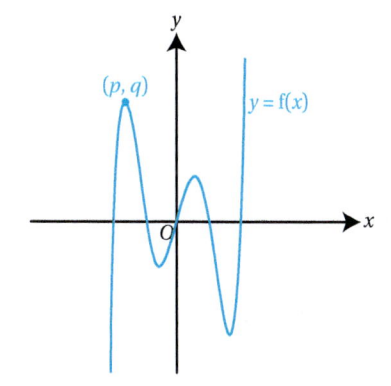

[Graph with point (p, q) marked]

Sketch the graph of $y = f(x) + |f(x)|$.

12 The diagram shows the graph of the function $y = f(x)$.

a Sketch the graph of $y = \frac{1}{2}(f(x) + |f(x)|)$.

b Solve the equation $\frac{1}{2}(f(x) + |f(x)|) = f(x)$.

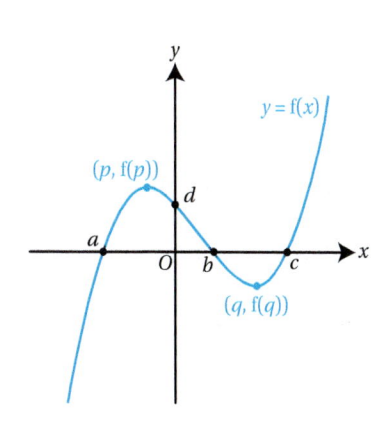

[Graph with points $(p, f(p))$, $(q, f(q))$, and x-axis crossings at a, b, c, with d marked on y-axis]

69

Section 3: Modulus equations and inequalities

In A Level Mathematics Student Book 2, Chapter 3, you learnt how to solve modulus equations and inequalities involving linear functions, for example: $|3x - 2| = |x + 5|$ or $|2x + 1| < x + 7$. You did this by sketching the graph and considering whether intersections occurred on the reflected part or the unreflected part of the graph. You can apply the same technique to equations and inequalities involving the modulus of other functions.

> **Tip**
>
> An alternative method is to square both sides, but this only works if both sides of the equation (or inequality) are positive.

WORKED EXAMPLE 4.3

Solve the equation $|x^2 - 7x + 10| = 5 - x$.

$x^2 - 7x + 10 = (x - 2)(x - 5)$ — Sketch the graph to locate the points of intersection.

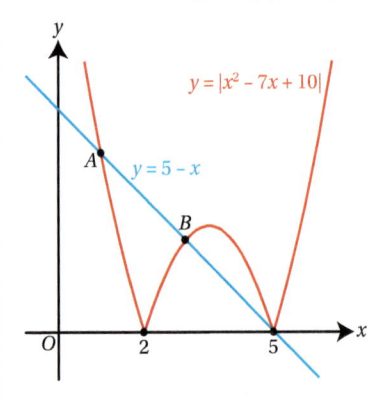

[Graph showing $y = |x^2 - 7x + 10|$ and $y = 5 - x$ with intersection points labelled A, B, and at x = 5]

From the graph, one intersection is at $x = 5$. There are two others: — The graph shows three points of intersection.

For A: $x^2 - 7x + 10 = 5 - x$ — A is on the unreflected part of the parabola.
$\Leftrightarrow x^2 - 6x + 5 = 0$
$\Leftrightarrow (x - 1)(x - 5) = 0$
Point A is at $x = 1$.

For B: $-x^2 + 7x - 10 = 5 - x$ — B is on the reflected part of the parabola, so make the expression negative.
$\Leftrightarrow x^2 - 8x + 15 = 0$
$\Leftrightarrow (x - 3)(x - 5) = 0$
Point B is at $x = 3$.

Hence the solutions are $x = 1, 3, 5$.

4 Further graphs and inequalities

WORKED EXAMPLE 4.4

Solve the inequality $|\tan 2x| \geq \sqrt{3}$ for $-\frac{\pi}{2} < x < \frac{\pi}{2}$.

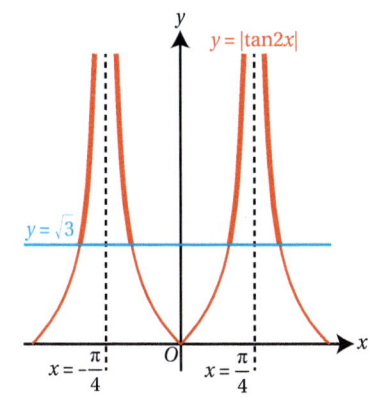

[graph of $y = |\tan 2x|$ with asymptotes at $x = -\frac{\pi}{4}$ and $x = \frac{\pi}{4}$, and horizontal line $y = \sqrt{3}$]	Sketch the graph, remembering the asymptotes.
Points of intersection: $\tan 2x = \sqrt{3} \text{ or } -\sqrt{3}$ $2x = \frac{\pi}{3}, -\frac{2\pi}{3}, -\frac{\pi}{3}, \frac{2\pi}{3}$ $x = -\frac{\pi}{3}, -\frac{\pi}{6}, \frac{\pi}{6}, \frac{\pi}{3}$	There are points of intersection on both the reflected part and the unreflected part of the graph.
The inequality holds when: $x \in \left[-\frac{\pi}{3}, -\frac{\pi}{4}\right) \cup \left(-\frac{\pi}{4}, -\frac{\pi}{6}\right] \cup \left[\frac{\pi}{6}, \frac{\pi}{4}\right) \cup \left(\frac{\pi}{4}, \frac{\pi}{3}\right]$	Describe the parts of the graph which are above the line $y = \sqrt{3}$, making sure you include the intersection points but exclude the asymptotes.

Sometimes it is possible to rearrange the equation or inequality before sketching graphs. Remember that you can multiply both sides of an inequality by an expression that is always positive.

WORKED EXAMPLE 4.5

Solve the inequality $\left|\dfrac{2x+1}{x-3}\right| \geq 3$.

$\left|\dfrac{2x+1}{x-3}\right| \geq 3$	Use $\left|\dfrac{a}{b}\right| = \dfrac{|a|}{|b|}$.
$\Leftrightarrow \dfrac{|2x+1|}{|x-3|} \geq 3$	
$\Leftrightarrow |2x+1| \geq 3|x-3|$	Since the denominator is positive, you can multiply without changing the direction of the inequality.
$\Leftrightarrow |2x+1| \geq |3x-9|$	Use $3|a| = |3a|$

Continues on next page

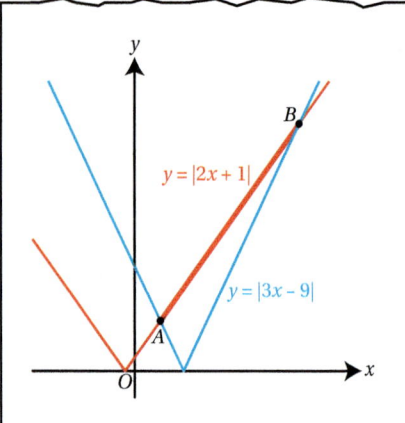

You can now use the method from A Level Mathematics Student Book 2, Chapter 3: sketch the graph and find intersection points.

Point A:
$2x + 1 = -3x + 9$
$5x = 8$
$x = \dfrac{8}{5}$

A is on the unreflected part of the red graph and the reflected part of the blue graph.

Point B:
$2x + 1 = 3x - 9$
$x = 10$

B is on the unreflected part of both graphs.

Hence
$\dfrac{8}{5} \leq x \leq 10$

The red graph is above the blue graph between A and B.

WORK IT OUT 4.1

Solve $|x + 1| > 2 - x$.
Which is the correct solution? Identify the errors made in the incorrect solutions.

Solution 1	Solution 2	Solution 3
Squaring both sides to remove the modulus: $(x + 1)^2 > (2 - x)^2$ $x^2 + 2x + 1 > 4 - 4x + x^2$ $6x > 3$ $x > 0.5$	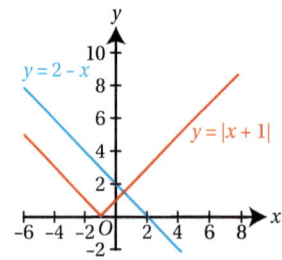 The intersection point is on the right-hand branch of the modulus function. $x + 1 = 2 - x$ $2x = 1$ $x = 0.5$ The inequality is satisfied to the right of this intersection, so the solution is $x > 0.5$.	If $x < 1$, then the inequality becomes $-(x + 1) > 2 - x$ $0 > 3$ which is a contradiction, so no solution here. If $x > 1$, then the inequality becomes $x + 1 > 2 - x$ $x > 0.5$ which is also a contradiction, so no solution here either. Hence there is no solution.

EXERCISE 4C

1. Solve the equation $|x^2 - 8| = |10 - x^2|$.

2. Solve the inequality $|x^2 - x - 6| < 3 - x$.

3. Solve the inequality $|x^2 - 2x - 8| > |x - 4|$.

4. Solve the equation $|x^2 - 4| = 8x$.

5. Solve the inequality $|2\sin x| \geq 1$.

6. Solve the inequality $|7e^{-x} - 5| \geq 1$.

7. Solve the inequality $\left|\dfrac{2x+1}{x-3}\right| < 1$.

8. Solve the inequality $\left|\dfrac{5x-7}{x+1}\right| \geq 2$.

9. Solve the equation $x|x| = 4x$.

10. By sketching appropriate graphs or otherwise, solve $|x+1| + |x-1| = x + 4$.

11. Solve the inequality $|\arcsin x| > \dfrac{\pi}{4}$.

12. Solve the inequality $|\cosh x - 3| \leq 1$, giving your answer to three significant figures.

13. Solve the equation $|x + q^2| = |x - 2q^2|$, giving your answer in terms of q.

14. If $|x + y| = |x| + |y|$ for $x, y \in \mathbb{R}$, what can you say about xy?

73

Checklist of learning and understanding

- For a reciprocal transformation:

f(x)	$g(x) = \dfrac{1}{f(x)}$
f(a) = 0	The line $x = a$ is a vertical asymptote.
The line $x = a$ is a vertical asymptote.	g(a) = 0
f(x) → +∞	g(x) → 0 (tends to zero from above)
f(x) → −∞	g(x) → 0 (tends to zero from below)
f(x) → 0	g(x) → +∞ or g(x) → −∞
f(x) has a horizontal asymptote $y = b$.	g(x) has a horizontal asymptote $y = \dfrac{1}{b}$.
0 < f(x) < 1	g(x) > 1
f(x) = 1	g(x) = 1
f(x) > 1	0 < g(x) < 1
−1 < f(x) < 0	g(x) < −1
f(x) = −1	g(x) = −1
f(x) < −1	−1 < g(x) < 0
(a, f(a)) is a turning point.	(a, g(a)) is the opposite turning point, if g(a) is finite.

- $|x| = \begin{cases} x & x \geq 0 \\ -x & x < 0 \end{cases}$
- To draw $y = |f(x)|$, reflect any parts of f(x) that occur below the x-axis so they appear above the x-axis.
- You can use a graph to solve modulus equations and inequalities.
- When rearranging modulus equations and inequalities you can use $|ab| = |a||b|$ and $\left|\dfrac{a}{b}\right| = \dfrac{|a|}{|b|}$.

Mixed practice 4

1 Given that $f(x) = x^2 + 2x - 15$, find the complete set of possible values of the constant k for which $|f(x)| = k$ has two solutions.

Choose from these options.

   A All real numbers   **B** $x < -1$ **C** $-5 < k < 3$ **D** $x = 0$ or $x > 16$

2 The graph of $y = f(x)$ is shown.

   a Sketch the graph of $y = \dfrac{1}{f(x)}$.

   b State the coordinates of the maximum points of $\dfrac{1}{f(x)}$.

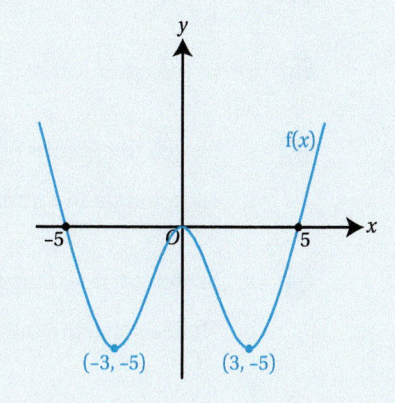

3 Solve the inequality $|2x - 1| < x$.

4 A function is defined by $f(x) = \dfrac{x^2 - 4x}{x - 2}$ and $g(x) = |f(x)|$.

   Find all asymptotes of $g(x)$ and sketch $g(x)$ for $-3 < x < 7$.

5 The graph of $y = f(x)$ is shown.

   Sketch $\dfrac{1}{f(x)}$. Indicate clearly the positions of any x-intercepts and asymptotes.

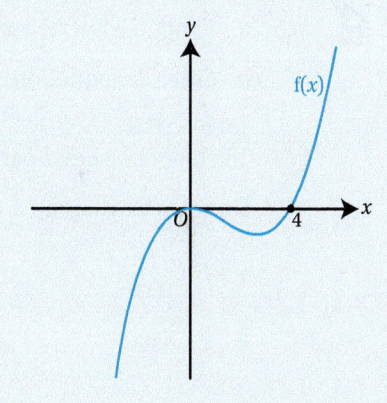

6 **a** Sketch the graph of $y = |4 \ln (x - e)|$, indicating the exact value of the x-coordinate where the curve meets the x-axis.

   b **i** Solve the equation $|4 \ln (x - e)| = 4$.

       ii Hence, or otherwise, solve the inequality $|4 \ln (x - e)| \geqslant 4$.

[©AQA 2012]

7 **a** On separate diagrams, sketch:

      i the curve with equation $y = |3x + 3|$

      ii the curve with equation $y = |x^2 - 1|$.

   b **i** Solve the equation $|3x + 3| = |x^2 - 1|$.

       ii Hence solve the inequality $|3x + 3| < |x^2 - 1|$.

[©AQA 2011]

75

8 a Solve the equation $|2x - 1| = 5 - 3|x|$.

   b Write down the solution of the inequality $|2x - 1| \leq 5 - 3|x|$.

9 Solve the inequality $\left|\dfrac{x+1}{x-2}\right| \geq 2$.

10 Solve the inequality $\left|\dfrac{x-1}{x+3}\right| < 3$.

11 Solve the equation $|x^2 - 3x| = 2|x|$.

12 a Sketch the graphs of $y = |e^x - 1|$ and $y = |\ln(x - 1)|$.

   b Hence state the number of solutions of the equation $|e^x - 1| = |\ln(x - 1)|$.

13 a Sketch on the same set of axes the graphs of $y = |x^2 - 3x|$ and $y = \dfrac{1}{x^2 - 3x}$.

   b Hence solve the inequality $|x^2 - 3x| > \dfrac{1}{x^2 - 3x}$.

14 For which values of the real number x is $|x + k| = |x| + k$, where k is a positive real number?

15 a Explain why $|x|^2 \equiv x^2$.

   b Solve the equation $|x - 1| + |x + 1| = \dfrac{8}{|x + 1| - |x - 1|}$.

16 The diagram shows part of the graph of $y = f(x)$.

   On separate diagrams, sketch the graphs of:

   a $y = \dfrac{1}{f(x)}$

   b $y = x f(x)$.

17 The hyperbolic secant is defined by $\operatorname{sech} x = \dfrac{1}{\cosh x}$ for $x \in \mathbb{R}$.

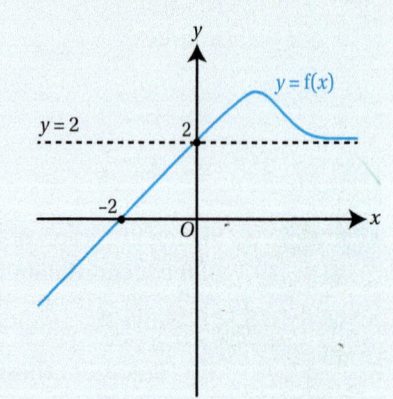

   a Sketch the graph of $y = \operatorname{sech} x$, indicating the coordinates of any stationary points and the equations of any asymptotes.

   b Find the exact solutions of the equation $\operatorname{sech} x = \dfrac{1}{3}$.

18 a Given that $\cosh x - \sinh x = 2$, find the exact value of x.

   b By sketching the graphs of $y = |\cosh x - 2|$ and $y = \sinh x$, or otherwise, solve the inequality $|\cosh x - 2| \leq \sinh x$.

5 Further vectors

In this chapter you will learn how to:

- find a vector perpendicular to two given vectors (using the vector product)
- find the equation of a plane in several different forms
- find intersections between lines and planes
- calculate angles between lines and planes
- calculate the distance from a point to a plane.

Before you start…

Further Mathematics Student Book 1, Chapter 9	You should be able to find the vector and Cartesian equation of a line in three dimensions.	1	A line passes through the points $(3, -1, 2)$ and $(5, 1, 8)$. a Find a vector equation of the line. b Write down a Cartesian equation of the line.
Further Mathematics Student Book 1, Chapter 9	You should be able to find the point of intersection of two lines.	2	Find the point of intersection of the line from Question **1** and the line $\mathbf{r} = \begin{pmatrix} 2 \\ 2 \\ 9 \end{pmatrix} + \mu \begin{pmatrix} -1 \\ 1 \\ 2 \end{pmatrix}$.
Further Mathematics Student Book 1, Chapter 9	You should know how to calculate the scalar product of two vectors and use it to calculate an angle between two lines.	3	Find the acute angle between the two lines from Question **2**.
Further Mathematics Student Book 1, Chapter 9	You should know how to use the scalar product to find the distance from a point to a line and the distance between two skew lines.	4	Find the shortest distance between the skew lines $\mathbf{r} = \begin{pmatrix} -3 \\ 3 \\ 18 \end{pmatrix} + \lambda \begin{pmatrix} 2 \\ -1 \\ -8 \end{pmatrix}$ and $\mathbf{r} = \begin{pmatrix} 5 \\ 0 \\ 2 \end{pmatrix} + \mu \begin{pmatrix} 1 \\ 1 \\ -1 \end{pmatrix}$.

Another way of multiplying vectors

You already know from Further Mathematics Student Book 1, Chapter 9, how to find the scalar or dot product of two vectors. In this chapter you will learn about a second way of multiplying together two vectors – the vector product or cross product. This provides a convenient way for finding a vector that is perpendicular to the two original vectors, and has many applications in Mechanics and Physics such as calculating the moment of a force and finding the effect of magnetic fields on charged particles.

> ⏩ **Fast forward**
>
> If you are studying the Mechanics option of Further Mathematics you will meet the cross product in Chapter 9 when looking at moments and couples of forces.

A Level Further Mathematics for AQA Student Book 2

As well as using the cross product to express the vector equation of a line in an alternative form, you will also use it to help you find the equation of a plane (a surface in three-dimensional space).

Section 1: The vector product

You know that you can use the scalar product to check whether two lines are perpendicular, but you also need to be able to find a line that is perpendicular to a given line.

In two dimensions, if a line has gradient m then a perpendicular line has gradient $-\frac{1}{m}$. Furthermore, there is only one perpendicular line passing through any given point.

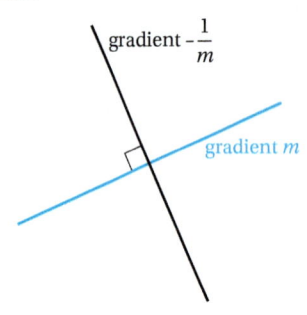

> **Rewind**
>
> You saw in Further Mathematics Student Book 1, Chapter 9, that lines $\mathbf{r} = \mathbf{a} + \lambda \mathbf{d}_1$ and $\mathbf{r} = \mathbf{b} + \mu \mathbf{d}_2$ are perpendicular if $\mathbf{d}_1 \cdot \mathbf{d}_2 = 0$.

In three dimensions, if you try to find a line through a given point and a perpendicular to a given line, you will find that there is more than one possible answer. In fact, there are infinitely many such lines.

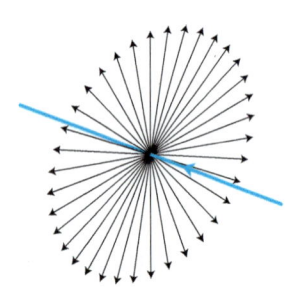

However, if you are given two lines, then there is only one direction that is perpendicular to both of them. This direction is given by the **vector product** (or **cross product**).

> **Key point 5.1**
>
> The vector product of two vectors, $\mathbf{a} \times \mathbf{b}$, is defined as
>
> $$\mathbf{a} \times \mathbf{b} = |\mathbf{a}||\mathbf{b}| \sin \theta \, \hat{\mathbf{n}}$$
>
> where θ is the angle between the vectors $\mathbf{a}$ and $\mathbf{b}$, and $\hat{\mathbf{n}}$ is a unit vector perpendicular to $\mathbf{a}$ and $\mathbf{b}$.

> **Fast forward**
>
> Later in this section you will use the magnitude of the vector product: $|\mathbf{a} \times \mathbf{b}| = |\mathbf{a}||\mathbf{b}| \sin \theta$.

> **Tip**
>
> It is important to use the × symbol to denote the vector product, so that it is distinct from the scalar product.

5 Further vectors

This means that the vector $\mathbf{c} = \mathbf{a} \times \mathbf{b}$ is perpendicular to both $\mathbf{a}$ and $\mathbf{b}$.

The definition in Key point 5.1 leads to a formula for finding the vector product from the components of the two vectors.

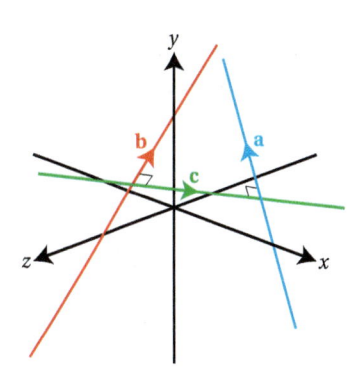

Key point 5.2

If $\mathbf{a} = \begin{pmatrix} a_1 \\ a_2 \\ a_3 \end{pmatrix}$ and $\mathbf{b} = \begin{pmatrix} b_1 \\ b_2 \\ b_3 \end{pmatrix}$, then:

$$\mathbf{a} \times \mathbf{b} = \begin{pmatrix} a_2 b_3 - a_3 b_2 \\ a_3 b_1 - a_1 b_3 \\ a_1 b_2 - a_2 b_1 \end{pmatrix}$$

Tip

The formula for the vector product can also be written using the notation of the determinant of a matrix:

$$\mathbf{a} \times \mathbf{b} = \begin{pmatrix} \mathbf{i} & a_1 & b_1 \\ \mathbf{j} & a_2 & b_2 \\ \mathbf{k} & a_3 & b_3 \end{pmatrix}$$

WORKED EXAMPLE 5.1

Find a vector perpendicular to both $\mathbf{a} = \begin{pmatrix} 1 \\ 1 \\ -2 \end{pmatrix}$ and $\mathbf{b} = \begin{pmatrix} -5 \\ 1 \\ 3 \end{pmatrix}$.

$\mathbf{a} \times \mathbf{b} = \begin{pmatrix} 1 \\ 1 \\ -2 \end{pmatrix} \times \begin{pmatrix} -5 \\ 1 \\ 3 \end{pmatrix}$ The vector $\mathbf{a} \times \mathbf{b}$ will be perpendicular to both $\mathbf{a}$ and $\mathbf{b}$.

$= \begin{pmatrix} 1 \times 3 - 1 \times (-2) \\ (-2) \times (-5) - 1 \times 3 \\ 1 \times 1 - 1 \times (-5) \end{pmatrix}$ Use the formula from Key point 5.2:

$$\begin{pmatrix} a_1 \\ a_2 \\ a_3 \end{pmatrix} \times \begin{pmatrix} b_1 \\ b_2 \\ b_3 \end{pmatrix} = \begin{pmatrix} a_2 b_3 - a_3 b_2 \\ a_3 b_1 - a_1 b_3 \\ a_1 b_2 - a_2 b_1 \end{pmatrix}$$

$= \begin{pmatrix} 5 \\ 7 \\ 6 \end{pmatrix}$

Did you know?

The vector product has many uses, both in pure mathematics and in its applications. For example, you can calculate the area of a triangle from the magnitude of the vector product.

In Mechanics, the moment of a force is actually a vector, given by $\mathbf{M} = \mathbf{F} \times \mathbf{r}$. You might also know the 'right-hand rule' for determining the direction of the magnetic force.

Tip

One important example of perpendicular vectors are the base vectors; for example, you can check that $\mathbf{i} \times \mathbf{j} = \mathbf{k}$ and $\mathbf{i} \times \mathbf{k} = -\mathbf{j}$.

WORK IT OUT 5.1

Find a vector perpendicular to $\begin{pmatrix} 1 \\ -1 \\ 1 \end{pmatrix}$ and $\begin{pmatrix} 1 \\ 2 \\ 3 \end{pmatrix}$.

Which is the correct solution? Identify the errors made in the incorrect solutions.

Solution 1	Solution 2	Solution 3
A vector perpendicular is given by: $$\begin{pmatrix} 1 \\ -1 \\ 1 \end{pmatrix} \times \begin{pmatrix} 1 \\ 2 \\ 3 \end{pmatrix} = \begin{pmatrix} +(-3-2) \\ -(3-1) \\ +(2-1) \end{pmatrix}$$ $$= \begin{pmatrix} -5 \\ -2 \\ 1 \end{pmatrix}$$	Let the perpendicular vector be $\begin{pmatrix} a \\ b \\ c \end{pmatrix}$. Then $\begin{pmatrix} a \\ b \\ c \end{pmatrix} \cdot \begin{pmatrix} 1 \\ -1 \\ 1 \end{pmatrix} = 0$ so $a - b + c = 0$ and $\begin{pmatrix} a \\ b \\ c \end{pmatrix} \cdot \begin{pmatrix} 1 \\ 2 \\ 3 \end{pmatrix} = 0$ so $a + 2b + 3c = 0$. Choose $c = 0$. Then $\begin{cases} a - b = 0 \\ a + 2b = 0 \end{cases}$ $\Leftrightarrow a = 0, b = 0$ So the vector is $\begin{pmatrix} 0 \\ 0 \\ 0 \end{pmatrix}$. Checking shows that the dot product is zero with both vectors.	$$\begin{pmatrix} 1 \\ -1 \\ 1 \end{pmatrix} \times \begin{pmatrix} 1 \\ 2 \\ 3 \end{pmatrix} = \begin{pmatrix} +(-3-2) \\ -(3-1) \\ +(2+1) \end{pmatrix}$$ $$= \begin{pmatrix} -5 \\ -2 \\ 3 \end{pmatrix}$$ So $\begin{pmatrix} 5 \\ 2 \\ -3 \end{pmatrix}$ is a perpendicular vector.

WORKED EXAMPLE 5.2

Lines l_1 and l_2 have equations $l_1: r = \begin{pmatrix} 1 \\ 5 \\ -2 \end{pmatrix} + \lambda \begin{pmatrix} 3 \\ -4 \\ 1 \end{pmatrix}$ and $l_2: r = \begin{pmatrix} 1 \\ 5 \\ -2 \end{pmatrix} + \mu \begin{pmatrix} 3 \\ 5 \\ 2 \end{pmatrix}$.

a Calculate $\begin{pmatrix} 3 \\ -4 \\ 1 \end{pmatrix} \times \begin{pmatrix} 3 \\ 5 \\ 2 \end{pmatrix}$.

b Hence find the equation of the line through the point $(1, 5, -2)$ that is perpendicular to both l_1 and l_2.

a $\begin{pmatrix} 3 \\ -4 \\ 1 \end{pmatrix} \times \begin{pmatrix} 3 \\ 5 \\ 2 \end{pmatrix} = \begin{pmatrix} (-4) \times 2 - 1 \times 5 \\ 1 \times 3 - 3 \times 2 \\ 3 \times 5 - (-4) \times 3 \end{pmatrix}$

$= \begin{pmatrix} -13 \\ -3 \\ 27 \end{pmatrix}$

Use the formula from Key point 5.2:
$$\begin{pmatrix} a_1 \\ a_2 \\ a_3 \end{pmatrix} \times \begin{pmatrix} b_1 \\ b_2 \\ b_3 \end{pmatrix} = \begin{pmatrix} a_2 b_3 - a_3 b_2 \\ a_3 b_1 - a_1 b_3 \\ a_1 b_2 - a_2 b_1 \end{pmatrix}$$

Continues on next page

b $\mathbf{r} = \begin{pmatrix} 1 \\ 5 \\ -2 \end{pmatrix} + \lambda \begin{pmatrix} -13 \\ -3 \\ 27 \end{pmatrix}$

> The vector equation of a line is $\mathbf{r} = \mathbf{a} + \lambda \mathbf{d}$.
>
> The direction is the perpendicular vector you have found in part **a**.
>
> The line passes through $(1, 5, -2)$.

The vector product has many properties similar to multiplication of real numbers but, like matrix multiplication, the vector product isn't commutative.

▶▶) **Fast forward**

In Section 2 you will use the vector product to find the equation of a plane.

🔑 **Key point 5.3**

Properties of the vector product:

- $\mathbf{a} \times \mathbf{b} = -\mathbf{b} \times \mathbf{a}$
- $(k\mathbf{a}) \times \mathbf{b} = k(\mathbf{a} \times \mathbf{b})$
- $(\mathbf{a} \times \mathbf{b}) \times \mathbf{c} = \mathbf{a} \times (\mathbf{b} \times \mathbf{c})$
- $\mathbf{a} \times (\mathbf{b} + \mathbf{c}) = (\mathbf{a} \times \mathbf{b}) + (\mathbf{a} \times \mathbf{c})$

Also, from the definition in Key point 5.2, you can see that

$$\mathbf{a} \times \mathbf{a} = \begin{pmatrix} a_2 a_3 - a_3 a_2 \\ a_3 a_1 - a_1 a_3 \\ a_1 a_2 - a_2 a_1 \end{pmatrix} = \mathbf{0}$$

In fact, this is a specific case of the fact that the cross product of any two parallel vectors is the zero vector.

🔑 **Key point 5.4**

- If vectors **a** and **b** are parallel then $\mathbf{a} \times \mathbf{b} = \mathbf{0}$.
- In particular, $\mathbf{a} \times \mathbf{a} = \mathbf{0}$.

WORKED EXAMPLE 5.3

Prove that $(2\mathbf{a} - \mathbf{b}) \times (\mathbf{a} + 3\mathbf{b}) = 7\mathbf{a} \times \mathbf{b}$.

$(2\underline{a} - \underline{b}) \times (\underline{a} + 3\underline{b}) = 2\underline{a} \times \underline{a} + 2\underline{a} \times 3\underline{b} - \underline{b} \times \underline{a} - \underline{b} \times 3\underline{b}$

$\qquad = 2\underline{a} \times 3\underline{b} - \underline{b} \times \underline{a}$

$\qquad = 6\underline{a} \times \underline{b} + \underline{a} \times \underline{b}$

$\qquad = 7\underline{a} \times \underline{b}$

> Expand exactly as you would with real numbers.
> $2\mathbf{a} \times (\mathbf{a} + 3\mathbf{b}) = 2\mathbf{a} \times \mathbf{a} + 2\mathbf{a} \times 3\mathbf{b}$ and $-\mathbf{b} \times (\mathbf{a} + 3\mathbf{b}) = -\mathbf{b} \times \mathbf{a} - \mathbf{b} \times 3\mathbf{b}$
>
> $\mathbf{a} \times \mathbf{a} = \mathbf{0}$ and $\mathbf{b} \times \mathbf{b} = \mathbf{0}$.
>
> $-\mathbf{b} \times \mathbf{a} = \mathbf{a} \times \mathbf{b}$

Equation of a line

In Further Mathematics Student Book 1, Chapter 9, you saw that the vector $\vec{AR} = \mathbf{r} - \mathbf{a}$ from a point on the line, A, to a general point, R, is parallel to the direction vector $\mathbf{d}$.

$$\mathbf{r} - \mathbf{a} = \lambda \mathbf{d} \Rightarrow \mathbf{r} = \mathbf{a} + \lambda \mathbf{d}$$

Using the vector product and the parallel vectors $\mathbf{r} - \mathbf{a}$ and $\mathbf{d}$, you now have an alternative vector equation of a line.

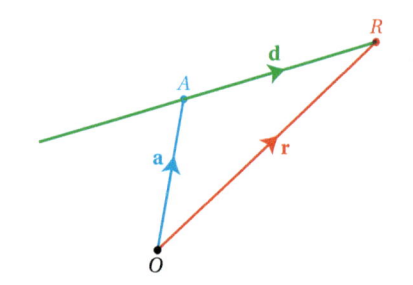

Key point 5.5

A line passing through the point with position vector $\mathbf{a}$ and parallel to the vector $\mathbf{d}$ has equation:
$$(\mathbf{r} - \mathbf{a}) \times \mathbf{d} = \mathbf{0}$$

Tip

Using the properties of the vector product, this can also be written as $\mathbf{r} \times \mathbf{d} = \mathbf{a} \times \mathbf{d}$.

WORKED EXAMPLE 5.4

Find a vector equation of the line that passes through the points $A(2, -3, 1)$ and $B(6, 1, -2)$, giving your answer in the form $\mathbf{r} \times \mathbf{d} = \mathbf{c}$.

The line is parallel to:

$$\mathbf{d} = \begin{pmatrix} 6 \\ 1 \\ -2 \end{pmatrix} - \begin{pmatrix} 2 \\ -3 \\ 1 \end{pmatrix} = \begin{pmatrix} 4 \\ 4 \\ -3 \end{pmatrix}$$

Find the direction of the line.
$\mathbf{d} = \mathbf{b} - \mathbf{a}$

So an equation is:

$$\left(\mathbf{r} - \begin{pmatrix} 2 \\ -3 \\ 1 \end{pmatrix} \right) \times \begin{pmatrix} 4 \\ 4 \\ -3 \end{pmatrix} = \mathbf{0}$$

Use $(\mathbf{r} - \mathbf{a}) \times \mathbf{d} = \mathbf{0}$ with either $\mathbf{a}$ or $\mathbf{b}$.

$$\mathbf{r} \times \begin{pmatrix} 4 \\ 4 \\ -3 \end{pmatrix} - \begin{pmatrix} 2 \\ -3 \\ 1 \end{pmatrix} \times \begin{pmatrix} 4 \\ 4 \\ -3 \end{pmatrix} = \mathbf{0}$$

Expand: $\mathbf{r} \times \mathbf{d} - \mathbf{a} \times \mathbf{d} = \mathbf{0}$

$$\mathbf{r} \times \begin{pmatrix} 4 \\ 4 \\ -3 \end{pmatrix} - \begin{pmatrix} 5 \\ 10 \\ 20 \end{pmatrix} = \mathbf{0}$$

Evaluate the cross product:
$$\begin{pmatrix} 2 \\ -3 \\ 1 \end{pmatrix} \times \begin{pmatrix} 4 \\ 4 \\ -3 \end{pmatrix} = \begin{pmatrix} 5 \\ 10 \\ 20 \end{pmatrix}$$

$$\therefore \mathbf{r} \times \begin{pmatrix} 4 \\ 4 \\ -3 \end{pmatrix} = \begin{pmatrix} 5 \\ 10 \\ 20 \end{pmatrix}$$

The magnitude of the vector product

The magnitude of the vector product is related to the area of the triangle determined by vectors **a** and **b**.

> **Key point 5.6**
>
> The area of a triangle with sides **a** and **b** is $\frac{1}{2}|\mathbf{a} \times \mathbf{b}|$.

> **Rewind**
>
> You met the formula $\frac{1}{2}ab\sin C$ for the area of a triangle in A Level Mathematics Student Book 1, Chapter 11.

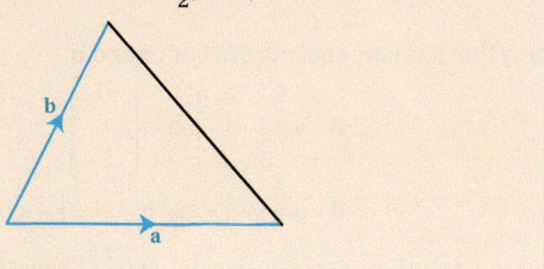

WORKED EXAMPLE 5.5

Find the area of the triangle with vertices $M\begin{pmatrix}1\\4\\2\end{pmatrix}$, $N\begin{pmatrix}3\\-3\\0\end{pmatrix}$, $P\begin{pmatrix}-1\\8\\9\end{pmatrix}$.

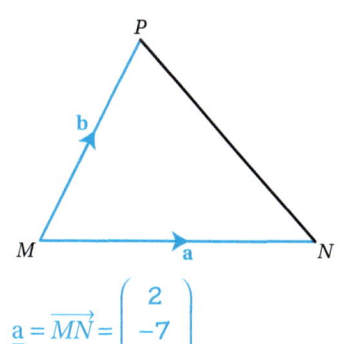

You need to find the two vectors that define the sides of the triangle. Drawing a diagram will help you to see which vectors to use.

$\mathbf{a} = \overrightarrow{MN} = \begin{pmatrix}2\\-7\\-2\end{pmatrix}$

$\mathbf{b} = \overrightarrow{MP} = \begin{pmatrix}-2\\4\\7\end{pmatrix}$

$\mathbf{a} \times \mathbf{b} = \begin{pmatrix}2\\-7\\-2\end{pmatrix} \times \begin{pmatrix}-2\\4\\7\end{pmatrix}$

You need to calculate $\mathbf{a} \times \mathbf{b}$ first, and then find its magnitude.

$= \begin{pmatrix}-49+8\\4-14\\8-14\end{pmatrix} = \begin{pmatrix}-41\\-10\\-6\end{pmatrix}$

Area $= \frac{1}{2}|\mathbf{a} \times \mathbf{b}|$

$= \frac{1}{2}\sqrt{41^2 + 10^2 + 6^2} = 21.3$

EXERCISE 5A

1 In each case, calculate $\mathbf{a} \times \mathbf{b}$ and state the vector $\mathbf{b} \times \mathbf{a}$.

   a   **i** $\mathbf{a} = \begin{pmatrix} 3 \\ 4 \\ 1 \end{pmatrix}, \mathbf{b} = \begin{pmatrix} 2 \\ 1 \\ 5 \end{pmatrix}$ **ii** $\mathbf{a} = \begin{pmatrix} 1 \\ -4 \\ 1 \end{pmatrix}, \mathbf{b} = \begin{pmatrix} -2 \\ 2 \\ 3 \end{pmatrix}$

   b   **i** $\mathbf{a} = 4\mathbf{i} + 3\mathbf{j}, \mathbf{b} = 5\mathbf{i} - \mathbf{j} + 2\mathbf{k}$ **ii** $\mathbf{a} = \mathbf{i} + 2\mathbf{j} - \mathbf{k}, \mathbf{b} = 3\mathbf{i} - \mathbf{k}$

2 In each case, calculate $\mathbf{a} \times \mathbf{b}$ and verify that it is perpendicular to both $\mathbf{a}$ and $\mathbf{b}$.

   a   **i** $\mathbf{a} = \begin{pmatrix} 1 \\ 1 \\ 2 \end{pmatrix}, \mathbf{b} = \begin{pmatrix} -1 \\ 2 \\ 5 \end{pmatrix}$ **ii** $\mathbf{a} = \begin{pmatrix} 2 \\ 3 \\ -7 \end{pmatrix}, \mathbf{b} = \begin{pmatrix} -1 \\ 1 \\ 3 \end{pmatrix}$

   b   **i** $\mathbf{a} = 4\mathbf{i} + \mathbf{j} - 3\mathbf{k}, \mathbf{b} = \mathbf{i} - \mathbf{j} + 3\mathbf{k}$ **ii** $\mathbf{a} = \mathbf{i} - \mathbf{j} + 5\mathbf{k}, \mathbf{b} = 2\mathbf{i} + \mathbf{j} - \mathbf{k}$

3 Find, in radians, the acute angle between the directions of vectors $\mathbf{a}$ and $\mathbf{b}$ given that:

   a $|\mathbf{a}| = 2, |\mathbf{b}| = 5$ and $|\mathbf{a} \times \mathbf{b}| = 7$ **b** $|\mathbf{a}| = 12, |\mathbf{b}| = 3$ and $\mathbf{a} \times \mathbf{b} = \begin{pmatrix} 2 \\ 1 \\ 4 \end{pmatrix}$

   c $|\mathbf{a}| = 7, |\mathbf{b}| = 1$ and $\mathbf{a} \times \mathbf{b} = 2\mathbf{i} - 3\mathbf{j} - 2\mathbf{k}$ **d** $|\mathbf{a}| = 4, |\mathbf{b}| = 4$ and $|\mathbf{a} \times \mathbf{b}| = 0$

4 Find, in the form $(\mathbf{r} - \mathbf{a}) \times \mathbf{d} = \mathbf{0}$, a vector equation of the line that passes through the points with coordinates:

   a (4, 3, 7) and (2, −5, 0)   **b** (−3, 0, 1) and (−4, −1, 10).

5 Find, in the form $(\mathbf{r} - \mathbf{a}) \times \mathbf{d} = \mathbf{0}$, a vector equation of the line given by the equation:

   a $\mathbf{r} = \mathbf{i} + \mathbf{j} - \mathbf{k} + \lambda(2\mathbf{i} - 3\mathbf{k})$ **b** $\mathbf{r} = 3\mathbf{i} - 4\mathbf{k} + \lambda(\mathbf{i} - 5\mathbf{j} + 2\mathbf{k})$.

6 Calculate the area of the triangle with vertices:

   a   **i** (1, 3, 3), (−1, 1, 2) and (1, −2, 4)   **ii** (3, −5, 1), (−1, 1, 3) and (−1, −5, 2)

   b   **i** (−3, −5, 1), (4, 7, 2) and (−1, 2, 2)   **ii** (4, 0, 2), (4, 1, 5) and (4, −3, 2).

7 Find a vector that is perpendicular to both $\mathbf{a} = 3\mathbf{i} - \mathbf{j} + 5\mathbf{k}$ and $\mathbf{b} = \mathbf{j} - 3\mathbf{k}$.

8 A line is perpendicular to vectors $\begin{pmatrix} -1 \\ 0 \\ 2 \end{pmatrix}$ and $\begin{pmatrix} 1 \\ 0 \\ 1 \end{pmatrix}$ and passes through the point (−1, 1, 7). Find the vector equation of the line.

9 The points $A(3, 1, 2)$, $B(-1, 1, 5)$ and $C(7, -2, 3)$ are vertices of a parallelogram $ABCD$.

   a Find the coordinates of D.   **b** Calculate the area of the parallelogram.

10 A line passes through the point (3, 1, 6) and is perpendicular to the lines with equations

$\mathbf{r} = \begin{pmatrix} 2 \\ 0 \\ 1 \end{pmatrix} + t\begin{pmatrix} -1 \\ 0 \\ 2 \end{pmatrix}$ and $\mathbf{r} = \begin{pmatrix} 2 \\ 0 \\ 0 \end{pmatrix} + s\begin{pmatrix} -3 \\ 3 \\ 2 \end{pmatrix}$. Find the equation of the line in vector form.

11 Find the Cartesian equation of the line that passes through the point (3, 1, 2) and is perpendicular to the lines with equations $\dfrac{x+1}{3} = \dfrac{y-2}{5} = \dfrac{(z-1)}{2}$ and $\dfrac{x-3}{4} = \dfrac{y-1}{5} = \dfrac{z+1}{1}$.

12 Given that |**a**| = 5, |**b**| = 7 and the angle between **a** and **b** is 30°, find the exact value of |**a** × **b**|.

13 a Prove that (**a** − **b**) × (**a** + **b**) = 2**a** × **b**. **b** Simplify (2**a** − 3**b**) × (3**a** + 2**b**).

14 a Explain why (**a** × **b**) • **a** = 0. **b** Evaluate (**a** × **b**) • (**a** − **b**).

15 Find the Cartesian equation of the line through the point (−3, 1, 1) that is perpendicular to lines $\frac{x}{3} = \frac{y}{3} = \frac{z-1}{1}$ and $\frac{x+1}{3} = \frac{y}{1} = \frac{z-1}{5}$.

16 Prove that for any two vectors **a** and **b**, |**a** × **b**|² + (**a** • **b**)² = |**a**|² |**b**|².

17 Given that **u** + **v** + **w** = **0**, show that **u** × **v** = **v** × **w** = **w** × **u**.

18 a Show that the lines $l_1 : \mathbf{r} = \begin{pmatrix} -3 \\ 3 \\ 18 \end{pmatrix} + \lambda \begin{pmatrix} 2 \\ -1 \\ -8 \end{pmatrix}$ and $l_2 : \mathbf{r} = \begin{pmatrix} 5 \\ 0 \\ 2 \end{pmatrix} + \mu \begin{pmatrix} 1 \\ 1 \\ -1 \end{pmatrix}$ do not intersect.

b Points P and Q lie on l_1 and l_2 respectively, such that PQ is perpendicular to both lines.

  i Write down $\overrightarrow{PQ}$ in terms of λ and μ. **ii** Show that $9\mu − 69\lambda + 147 = 0$.

  iii Find a second equation for λ and μ. **iv** Find the coordinates of P and Q.

  v Hence find the shortest distance between l_1 and l_2.

Section 2: Equation of a plane

You are already used to describing positions of points by using unit vectors parallel to the x- and y-axes: for example, the position vector of the point $P(3, 2)$ is $\mathbf{r}_p = 3\mathbf{i} + 2\mathbf{j}$.

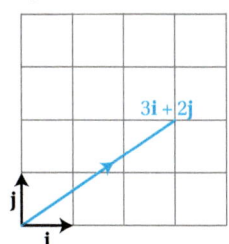

However, you can also use two directions other than those of **i** and **j**. The same point P can be reached from the origin by moving 2 units in the direction of vector $\mathbf{d}_1$ and 2 units in the direction of vector $\mathbf{d}_2$. Hence its position vector is $\mathbf{r}_p = 2\mathbf{d}_1 + 2\mathbf{d}_2$.

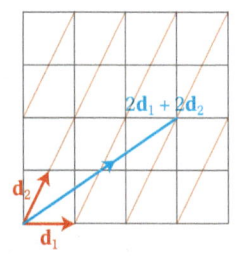

In the same way, every point in the plane has a position vector of the form $\lambda \mathbf{d}_1 + \mu \mathbf{d}_2$, where λ and μ are scalars.

A Level Further Mathematics for AQA Student Book 2

Consider now a plane that does not pass through the origin. To reach a point in the plane starting from the origin, you can go to some other point in the plane first, and then move along two directions that lie in the plane, as shown.

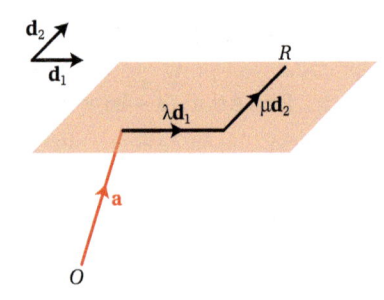

Key point 5.7

The vector equation of the plane containing point **a** and parallel to the directions of vectors $\mathbf{d}_1$ and $\mathbf{d}_2$ is $\mathbf{r} = \mathbf{a} + \lambda\mathbf{d}_1 + \mu\mathbf{d}_2$.

WORKED EXAMPLE 5.6

Find a vector equation of the plane containing points $M(3, 4, -2)$, $N(1, -1, 3)$ and $P(5, 0, 2)$.

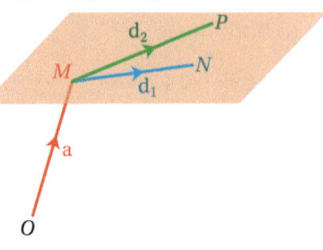

$\mathbf{r} = \mathbf{a} + \lambda\mathbf{d}_1 + \mu\mathbf{d}_2$ .... You need one point and two vectors parallel to the plane. Draw a diagram to see which vectors to use.

$\mathbf{a} = \begin{pmatrix} 3 \\ 4 \\ -2 \end{pmatrix}$ .... You can choose any of the three given points to be **a**, as they all lie in the plane.

$\mathbf{d}_1 = \overrightarrow{MN} = \begin{pmatrix} 1 \\ -1 \\ 3 \end{pmatrix} - \begin{pmatrix} 3 \\ 4 \\ -2 \end{pmatrix} = \begin{pmatrix} -2 \\ -5 \\ 5 \end{pmatrix}$ .... Vectors $\overrightarrow{MN}$ and $\overrightarrow{MP}$ are parallel to the plane.

$\mathbf{d}_2 = \overrightarrow{MP} = \begin{pmatrix} 5 \\ 0 \\ 2 \end{pmatrix} - \begin{pmatrix} 3 \\ 4 \\ -2 \end{pmatrix} = \begin{pmatrix} 2 \\ -4 \\ 4 \end{pmatrix}$

$\mathbf{r} = \begin{pmatrix} 3 \\ 4 \\ -2 \end{pmatrix} + \lambda \begin{pmatrix} -2 \\ -5 \\ 5 \end{pmatrix} + \mu \begin{pmatrix} 2 \\ -4 \\ 4 \end{pmatrix}$ .... Use $\mathbf{r} = \mathbf{a} + \lambda\mathbf{d}_1 + \mu\mathbf{d}_2$.

In Worked example 5.6, the plane was determined by three points. Two points do not determine a plane: there is more than one plane containing the line determined by points A and B, as shown in this diagram.

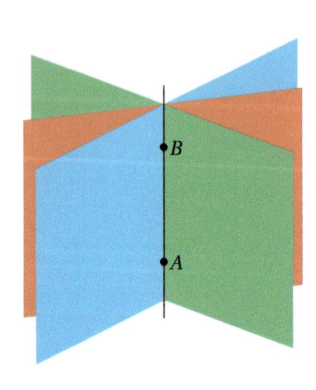

5 Further vectors

You can pick out one of these planes by requiring that it also passes through a third point, point C for example, which is not on the line AB, as illustrated here. This suggests that a plane can also be determined by a line and a point outside of that line.

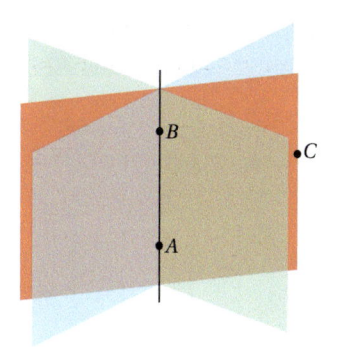

WORKED EXAMPLE 5.7

Find a vector equation of the plane containing the line $\mathbf{r} = \begin{pmatrix} -2 \\ 1 \\ 2 \end{pmatrix} + t \begin{pmatrix} -3 \\ 1 \\ 1 \end{pmatrix}$ and the point $A(4, -1, 2)$.

$\mathbf{a} = \begin{pmatrix} 4 \\ -1 \\ 2 \end{pmatrix}$ .... Point A lies in the plane.

$\mathbf{d}_1 = \begin{pmatrix} -3 \\ 1 \\ 1 \end{pmatrix}$ .... The direction vector of the line is parallel to the plane.

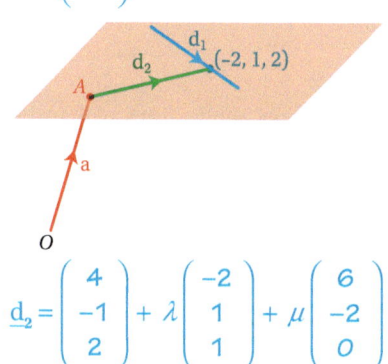

.... You need another vector parallel to the plane. You can use any vector between two points in the plane. One point in the plane is A. For the second point, you can pick any point on the line, for example $(-2, 1, 2)$.

$\mathbf{d}_2 = \begin{pmatrix} 4 \\ -1 \\ 2 \end{pmatrix} + \lambda \begin{pmatrix} -2 \\ 1 \\ 1 \end{pmatrix} + \mu \begin{pmatrix} 6 \\ -2 \\ 0 \end{pmatrix}$

$\mathbf{r} = \begin{pmatrix} 4 \\ -1 \\ 2 \end{pmatrix} + \lambda \begin{pmatrix} -3 \\ 1 \\ 1 \end{pmatrix} + \mu \begin{pmatrix} 6 \\ -2 \\ 0 \end{pmatrix}$ .... Now use $\mathbf{r} = \mathbf{a} + \lambda \mathbf{d}_1 + \mu \mathbf{d}_2$.

You can also determine a plane by two intersecting lines, and the two direction vectors are parallel to the plane.

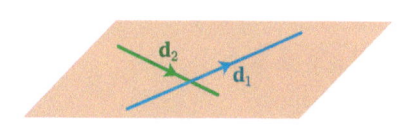

A Level Further Mathematics for AQA Student Book 2

WORKED EXAMPLE 5.8

Find a vector equation of the plane containing the lines $\mathbf{r} = \begin{pmatrix} 3 \\ -1 \\ 2 \end{pmatrix} + \lambda \begin{pmatrix} -1 \\ 1 \\ 2 \end{pmatrix}$ and $\mathbf{r} = \begin{pmatrix} 3 \\ -1 \\ 2 \end{pmatrix} + \mu \begin{pmatrix} 3 \\ 0 \\ 2 \end{pmatrix}$.

$\mathbf{r} = \begin{pmatrix} 3 \\ -1 \\ 2 \end{pmatrix} + \lambda \begin{pmatrix} -1 \\ 1 \\ 2 \end{pmatrix} + \mu \begin{pmatrix} 3 \\ 0 \\ 2 \end{pmatrix}$ .... You can tell that the two lines intersect at the point (3, −1, 2), so you can take that as one point in the plane. The two lines' direction vectors give two different directions in the plane.

If you have four points, they don't all necessarily lie in the same plane.

WORKED EXAMPLE 5.9

Determine whether points $A(2, -1, 3)$, $B(4, 1, 1)$, $C(3, 3, 2)$, and $D(-3, 1, 5)$ lie in the same plane.

Plane containing A, B, C: .... The plan is to find the equation of the plane containing points A, B and C (as in Worked example 5.6) and then check whether the point D lies in that plane.
$\mathbf{r} = \overrightarrow{OA} + \lambda \overrightarrow{AB} + \mu \overrightarrow{AC}$

$\mathbf{r} = \begin{pmatrix} 2 \\ -1 \\ -3 \end{pmatrix} + \lambda \begin{pmatrix} 2 \\ 2 \\ -2 \end{pmatrix} + \mu \begin{pmatrix} 1 \\ 4 \\ -1 \end{pmatrix}$

$\mathbf{r} = \overrightarrow{OD}$: .... For D to lie in the plane, you need values of λ and μ that make $\mathbf{r}$ equal to the position vector of D.
$\begin{cases} 2 + 2\lambda + \mu = -3 \\ -1 + 2\lambda + 4\mu = 1 \\ 3 - 2\lambda - \mu = 5 \end{cases}$

$\begin{cases} 2\lambda + \mu = -5 \\ 2\lambda + 4\mu = 2 \end{cases}$ .... You can solve the first two equations, and then check whether the solutions satisfy the third equation.

$\lambda = -\frac{11}{3}, \mu = \frac{7}{3}$

$3 - 2 \times \left(-\frac{11}{3}\right) - \frac{7}{3} = 8 \neq 5$

D does not lie in the same plane as A, B and C. .... There are no values of λ and μ that satisfy all three equations.

Key point 5.8 gives a list of possible ways to describe a plane.

🔑 Key point 5.8

A plane is uniquely determined by

- three points, not on the same line, or
- a line and a point outside that line, or
- two intersecting lines.

Cartesian equation of a plane

The vector equation of the plane can be a little difficult to work with, as it contains two parameters. It is also difficult to see whether two equations represent the same plane, because the two vectors parallel to the plane are not unique.

Now you will look at the question: Is there a way to describe the 'direction' of the plane, using just one direction vector?

The diagram shows a plane and a vector **n** perpendicular to it. This vector is perpendicular to every line in the plane, and it is called the **normal vector** of the plane.

Suppose A is a fixed point in the plane and let P be any other point. The normal vector is perpendicular to the line AP, so $\overrightarrow{AP} \bullet \mathbf{n} = 0$. This means that $(\mathbf{r} - \mathbf{a}) \bullet \mathbf{n} = 0$, which gives another form of an equation of the plane.

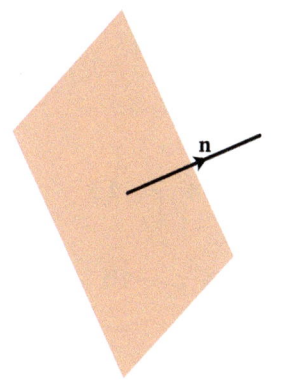

Key point 5.9

The scalar product equation of the plane is:

$$\mathbf{r} \bullet \mathbf{n} = \mathbf{a} \bullet \mathbf{n}$$

where **n** is the normal to the plane and **a** is the position vector of a point in the plane.

Remember that the position vector of a point is related to its coordinates. This means that you can use the scalar product equation to write the Cartesian equation of a plane.

Key point 5.10

Writing $\mathbf{r} = \begin{pmatrix} x \\ y \\ z \end{pmatrix}$ and expanding the scalar product gives the Cartesian equation of the plane in the form $n_1 x + n_2 y + n_3 z = d$.

WORKED EXAMPLE 5.10

Vector $\mathbf{n} = \begin{pmatrix} 2 \\ 4 \\ -1 \end{pmatrix}$ is perpendicular to the plane Π that contains point $A(3, -5, 1)$.

a Write an equation of Π in the form $\mathbf{r} \bullet \mathbf{n} = d$.
b Find the Cartesian equation of the plane.

Continues on next page

> **Tip**
>
> The letter Π (capital π) is often used as the name for a plane.

a $\underline{r} \cdot \underline{n} = \begin{pmatrix} 3 \\ -5 \\ 1 \end{pmatrix} \cdot \begin{pmatrix} 2 \\ 4 \\ -1 \end{pmatrix} = 6 - 20 - 1$ ┈┈┈ The equation of the plane is $\mathbf{r} \cdot \mathbf{n} = \mathbf{a} \cdot \mathbf{n}$.

$\underline{r} \cdot \underline{n} = -15$

b $\begin{pmatrix} x \\ y \\ z \end{pmatrix} \cdot \begin{pmatrix} 2 \\ 4 \\ -1 \end{pmatrix} = -15$ ┈┈┈ The Cartesian equation involves x, y, and z (the coordinates of P), which are the components of the position vector **r**.

$2x + 4y - z = -15$

You can convert from a vector to a Cartesian equation of the plane. This involves using the vector product to find the normal. The Cartesian equation is very convenient for checking whether a point lies in the plane: you just need to check that the coordinates of the point satisfy the equation.

> ⏮ **Rewind**
>
> You met the vector product in Section 1.

WORKED EXAMPLE 5.11

a Find the Cartesian equation of the plane with vector equation $\mathbf{r} = \begin{pmatrix} 1 \\ -2 \\ 5 \end{pmatrix} + \lambda \begin{pmatrix} 1 \\ 1 \\ 3 \end{pmatrix} + \mu \begin{pmatrix} 2 \\ -3 \\ 5 \end{pmatrix}$.

b Show that the point (2, 9, 10) lies in the plane.

a $\underline{r} \cdot \underline{n} = \underline{a} \cdot \underline{n}$ ┈┈┈ To find the Cartesian equation you need the normal vector and one point.

$\underline{a} = \begin{pmatrix} 1 \\ -2 \\ 5 \end{pmatrix}$ ┈┈┈ Point $(1, -2, 5)$ lies in the plane.

$\underline{n} = \begin{pmatrix} 1 \\ 1 \\ 3 \end{pmatrix} \times \begin{pmatrix} 2 \\ -3 \\ 5 \end{pmatrix} = \begin{pmatrix} 14 \\ 1 \\ -5 \end{pmatrix}$ ┈┈┈ **n** is perpendicular to all lines in the plane, so it is perpendicular to the direction vectors $\begin{pmatrix} 1 \\ 1 \\ 3 \end{pmatrix}$ and $\begin{pmatrix} 2 \\ -3 \\ 5 \end{pmatrix}$. The vector product of two vectors is perpendicular to both of them.

$\underline{r} \cdot \begin{pmatrix} 14 \\ 1 \\ -5 \end{pmatrix} = \begin{pmatrix} 1 \\ -2 \\ 5 \end{pmatrix} \cdot \begin{pmatrix} 14 \\ 1 \\ -5 \end{pmatrix}$

$14x + y - 5z = -13$ ┈┈┈ To get the Cartesian equation, write **r** as $\begin{pmatrix} x \\ y \\ z \end{pmatrix}$.

b $14(2) + 9 - 5(10) = -13$ ┈┈┈ A point lies in the plane if its coordinates satisfy the Cartesian equation.

Hence the point lies in the plane.

5 Further vectors

You can also convert from a Cartesian to a vector equation by finding two vectors that are perpendicular to the normal.

WORKED EXAMPLE 5.12

Find a vector equation of the plane with Cartesian equation $2x - 5y + z = 15$.

Finding two vectors perpendicular to $\begin{pmatrix} 2 \\ -5 \\ 1 \end{pmatrix}$:	You need two directions in the plane that are both perpendicular to the plane's normal.
$\begin{pmatrix} 2 \\ -5 \\ 1 \end{pmatrix} \cdot \begin{pmatrix} 1 \\ 0 \\ r \end{pmatrix} = 0 \Rightarrow r = -2$	These vectors satisfy $\begin{pmatrix} 2 \\ -5 \\ 1 \end{pmatrix} \cdot \begin{pmatrix} p \\ q \\ r \end{pmatrix} = 0$.
$\begin{pmatrix} 2 \\ -5 \\ 1 \end{pmatrix} \cdot \begin{pmatrix} 0 \\ 1 \\ r \end{pmatrix} = 0 \Rightarrow r = 5$	This gives one equation, which means that you can select values for two of the variables and then find the third one.
The two direction vectors are $\begin{pmatrix} 1 \\ 0 \\ -2 \end{pmatrix}$ and $\begin{pmatrix} 0 \\ 1 \\ 5 \end{pmatrix}$.	
For a point on the plane $(0, 0, z)$: $2(0) - 5(0) + z = 15 \Rightarrow z = 15$ So $(0, 0, 15)$ is a point in the plane.	To find a point in the plane, pick its x- and y- coordinates and then find z from the equation of the plane.
A vector equation of the plane is: $\mathbf{r} = \begin{pmatrix} 0 \\ 0 \\ 15 \end{pmatrix} + \lambda \begin{pmatrix} 1 \\ 0 \\ -2 \end{pmatrix} + \mu \begin{pmatrix} 0 \\ 1 \\ 5 \end{pmatrix}$	Now use $\mathbf{r} = \mathbf{a} + \lambda \mathbf{d}_1 + \mu \mathbf{d}_2$.

EXERCISE 5B

1 Write down the vector equation of the plane parallel to vectors **a** and **b** and containing point P.

   a   **i** $\mathbf{a} = \begin{pmatrix} -1 \\ 5 \\ 2 \end{pmatrix}, \mathbf{b} = \begin{pmatrix} 1 \\ -2 \\ 3 \end{pmatrix}, P(1, 0, 2)$ **ii** $\mathbf{a} = \begin{pmatrix} 0 \\ 4 \\ -1 \end{pmatrix}, \mathbf{b} = \begin{pmatrix} 5 \\ 3 \\ 0 \end{pmatrix}, P(0, 2, 0)$

   b   **i** $\mathbf{a} = 3\mathbf{i} + \mathbf{j} - 3\mathbf{k}, \mathbf{b} = \mathbf{i} - 3\mathbf{j}, \mathbf{p} = \mathbf{j} + \mathbf{k}$ **ii** $\mathbf{a} = 5\mathbf{i} - 6\mathbf{j}, \mathbf{b} = -\mathbf{i} + 3\mathbf{j} - \mathbf{k}, P(1, -6, 2)$

2 Find a vector equation of the plane containing points A, B and C.

   a   **i** $A(3, -1, 3), B(1, 1, 2), C(4, -1, 2)$ **ii** $A(-1, -1, 5), B(4, 1, 2), C(-7, 1, 1)$

   b   **i** $A(9, 0, 0), B(-2, 1, 0), C(1, -1, 2)$ **ii** $A(11, -7, 3), B(1, 14, 2), C(-5, 10, 0)$

3 Find a vector equation of the plane containing line l and point P.

   a   **i** $l : \mathbf{r} = \begin{pmatrix} -3 \\ 5 \\ 1 \end{pmatrix} + t \begin{pmatrix} 4 \\ 1 \\ 2 \end{pmatrix}, P(-1, 4, 3)$ **ii** $l : \mathbf{r} = \begin{pmatrix} 9 \\ -3 \\ 7 \end{pmatrix} + t \begin{pmatrix} 6 \\ -3 \\ 1 \end{pmatrix}, P(11, 12, 13)$

   b   **i** $l : \mathbf{r} = \begin{pmatrix} 4 \\ 4 \\ 1 \end{pmatrix} + t \begin{pmatrix} 0 \\ 0 \\ 1 \end{pmatrix}, P(-3, 1, 0)$ **ii** $l : \mathbf{r} = t \begin{pmatrix} 2 \\ 1 \\ 1 \end{pmatrix}, P(4, 0, 2)$

4 A plane has normal vector **n** and contains point A. Find the equation of the plane in the form $\mathbf{r} \cdot \mathbf{n} = d$, and the Cartesian equation of the plane.

 a i $\mathbf{n} = \begin{pmatrix} 3 \\ -5 \\ 2 \end{pmatrix}$, $A(3, 3, 1)$
 ii $\mathbf{n} = \begin{pmatrix} 6 \\ -1 \\ 2 \end{pmatrix}$, $A(4, 3, -1)$

 b i $\mathbf{n} = \begin{pmatrix} 3 \\ -1 \\ 0 \end{pmatrix}$, $A(-3, 0, 2)$
 ii $\mathbf{n} = \begin{pmatrix} 4 \\ 0 \\ -5 \end{pmatrix}$, $A(0, 0, 2)$

5 Find a normal vector to the plane given by the vector equation.

 a i $\mathbf{r} = \begin{pmatrix} 5 \\ 0 \\ 1 \end{pmatrix} + \lambda \begin{pmatrix} 1 \\ 2 \\ 3 \end{pmatrix} + \mu \begin{pmatrix} 5 \\ -2 \\ 2 \end{pmatrix}$
 ii $\mathbf{r} = \begin{pmatrix} 0 \\ 0 \\ 1 \end{pmatrix} + \lambda \begin{pmatrix} -3 \\ 6 \\ 2 \end{pmatrix} + \mu \begin{pmatrix} -1 \\ 1 \\ 2 \end{pmatrix}$

 b i $\mathbf{r} = \begin{pmatrix} 7 \\ 3 \\ 5 \end{pmatrix} + \lambda \begin{pmatrix} -5 \\ 1 \\ 2 \end{pmatrix} + \mu \begin{pmatrix} 0 \\ 0 \\ 1 \end{pmatrix}$
 ii $\mathbf{r} = \begin{pmatrix} 3 \\ 5 \\ 7 \end{pmatrix} + \lambda \begin{pmatrix} 6 \\ -1 \\ 2 \end{pmatrix} + \mu \begin{pmatrix} -1 \\ -1 \\ 3 \end{pmatrix}$

6 Find the equations of the planes from Question **5** in the form $\mathbf{r} \cdot \mathbf{n} = d$.

7 Find the Cartesian equations of the planes from Question **5**.

8 Find the Cartesian equation of the plane containing points A, B and C.

 a i $A(7, 1, 2)$, $B(-1, 4, 7)$, $C(5, 2, 3)$
 ii $A(1, 1, 2)$, $B(4, -6, 2)$, $C(12, 12, 2)$

 b i $A(12, 4, 10)$, $B(13, 4, 5)$, $C(15, -4, 0)$
 ii $A(1, 0, 0)$, $B(0, 1, 0)$, $C(0, 0, 1)$

9 Show that point P lies in the plane Π.

 a $P(-4, 8, 13)$, $\Pi : \mathbf{r} = \begin{pmatrix} 2 \\ 1 \\ 1 \end{pmatrix} + \lambda \begin{pmatrix} 4 \\ 1 \\ 2 \end{pmatrix} + \mu \begin{pmatrix} -1 \\ 4 \\ 7 \end{pmatrix}$
 b $P(4, 7, 5)$, $\Pi : \mathbf{r} \cdot \begin{pmatrix} 4 \\ -1 \\ 2 \end{pmatrix} = 19$

 c $P(1, 1, -2)$, $\Pi : 2x - 3y - 7z = 12$

10 A plane contains the point $(3, -2, 5)$. The vector $6\mathbf{i} + \mathbf{j} - 3\mathbf{k}$ is perpendicular to the plane. Find the Cartesian equation of the plane.

11 A plane contains points $A(5, 1, 5)$, $B(-3, 1, 2)$ and $C(0, 1, 5)$.

 Find the vector equation of the plane in the form $\mathbf{r} = \mathbf{a} + \lambda \mathbf{d}_1 + \mu \mathbf{d}_2$.

12 A plane contains points $P(3, 0, 2)$, $Q(-1, 1, 2)$ and $R(0, 5, 1)$.

 a Find $\overrightarrow{PQ} \times \overrightarrow{PR}$.

 b Hence find the Cartesian equation of the plane.

13 A plane is determined by the points $A(3, 1, 5)$, $B(-1, 4, 0)$ and $C(0, 0, 3)$.

 a Find the equation of the plane in the form $\mathbf{r} \cdot \mathbf{n} = k$.

 b Determine whether the point $D(1, 1, 4)$ lies in the same plane.

14 a Calculate $\begin{pmatrix} 4 \\ 4 \\ 1 \end{pmatrix} \times \begin{pmatrix} 1 \\ -1 \\ 3 \end{pmatrix}$.

b Hence find the Cartesian equation of the plane with vector equation $\mathbf{r} = \begin{pmatrix} 1 \\ 1 \\ 5 \end{pmatrix} + \lambda \begin{pmatrix} 4 \\ 4 \\ 1 \end{pmatrix} + \mu \begin{pmatrix} 1 \\ -1 \\ 3 \end{pmatrix}$.

15 a Calculate $\begin{pmatrix} -1 \\ 0 \\ 2 \end{pmatrix} \times \begin{pmatrix} 0 \\ 1 \\ 3 \end{pmatrix}$.

b Two lines have equations

$$l_1 : \mathbf{r} = \begin{pmatrix} 7 \\ -3 \\ 2 \end{pmatrix} + t \begin{pmatrix} -1 \\ 0 \\ 2 \end{pmatrix} \text{ and } l_2 : \mathbf{r} = \begin{pmatrix} 1 \\ 1 \\ 26 \end{pmatrix} + s \begin{pmatrix} 0 \\ 1 \\ 3 \end{pmatrix}$$

  i Show that l_1 and l_2 intersect.

  ii Find the coordinates of the point of intersection.

c Plane Π contains lines l_1 and l_2. Find the Cartesian equation of Π.

16 Determine whether the points (0, 3, 1), (1, 1, 5), (1, 0, 4) and (3, 8, 5) lie in the same plane.

17 A plane has Cartesian equation $x - 3y + 4z = 16$.

a Write down the normal vector, $\mathbf{n}$, of the plane.

b Find the values of p and q such that the vectors $\begin{pmatrix} 1 \\ 0 \\ p \end{pmatrix}$ and $\begin{pmatrix} 0 \\ 1 \\ q \end{pmatrix}$ are perpendicular to $\mathbf{n}$.

c Hence find a vector equation of the plane in the form $\mathbf{r} = \mathbf{a} + \lambda \mathbf{d}_1 + \pi \mathbf{d}_2$.

18 a Find the Cartesian equation of the plane with vector equation $\mathbf{r} = \begin{pmatrix} 0 \\ 1 \\ 5 \end{pmatrix} + \lambda \begin{pmatrix} -3 \\ 1 \\ 2 \end{pmatrix} + \mu \begin{pmatrix} 2 \\ 5 \\ 2 \end{pmatrix}$.

b Another plane has Cartesian equation $x - 3y + z = 7$. Find a vector equation of this plane in the form $\mathbf{r} = \mathbf{a} + \lambda \mathbf{d}_1 + \pi \mathbf{d}_2$.

19 Find, in the form $\mathbf{r} = \mathbf{a} + \lambda \mathbf{d}_1 + \pi \mathbf{d}_2$, a vector equation of the plane $3y - z = 5$.

Section 3: Intersections between lines and planes

The methods introduced in this section require equations of planes to be in Cartesian form and equations of lines to be in vector form. If in a question they are given in a different form, you might need to convert them first.

A Level Further Mathematics for AQA Student Book 2

Intersection between a line and a plane

The coordinates of the intersection point (if there is one) must satisfy both the equation of the line and the equation of the plane.

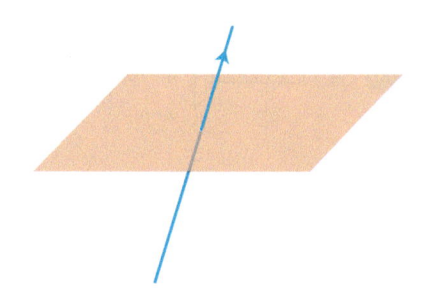

WORKED EXAMPLE 5.13

Find the intersection between the given line and plane, or show that they do not intersect.

a $\mathbf{r} = \begin{pmatrix} 4 \\ -3 \\ 1 \end{pmatrix} + \lambda \begin{pmatrix} 3 \\ 0 \\ -2 \end{pmatrix}$ and $2x - y + 2z = 5$

b $\dfrac{x-1}{-1} = \dfrac{y}{-3} = \dfrac{z+4}{2}$ and $x - 3y - 4z = 12$

a $2(4 + 3\lambda) - (-3) + 2(1 - 2\lambda) = 5$
$2\lambda = -6$
$\lambda = -3$

Substitute $x = 4 + 3\lambda$, $y = -3$, $z = 1 - 2\lambda$ into the equation of the plane.

$\mathbf{r} = \begin{pmatrix} 4 \\ -3 \\ 1 \end{pmatrix} - 3\begin{pmatrix} 3 \\ 0 \\ -2 \end{pmatrix} = \begin{pmatrix} -5 \\ -3 \\ 7 \end{pmatrix}$

Now use this value of λ to find the coordinates.

The intersection point is $(-5, -3, 7)$.

b $\begin{cases} x - 1 = -\mu \\ y = -3\mu \\ z + 4 = 2\mu \end{cases}$

*Change the equation of the line into the vector form and then follow the same procedure as in part **a**.*

$\begin{pmatrix} x \\ y \\ z \end{pmatrix} = \begin{pmatrix} 1 - \mu \\ -3\mu \\ -4 + 2\mu \end{pmatrix}$

$(1 - \mu) - 3(-3\mu) - 4(-4 + 2\mu) = 12$
$17 = 12$

Impossible to find μ. The line and plane do not intersect.

It is impossible to find a value of μ for a point which satisfies both equations. This means that the line is parallel to the plane.

It is possible for a line to lie entirely in a given plane.

WORKED EXAMPLE 5.14

Show that the line $\mathbf{r} = \begin{pmatrix} 3 \\ -1 \\ 1 \end{pmatrix} + t\begin{pmatrix} 3 \\ 1 \\ 0 \end{pmatrix}$ lies in the plane $x - 3y = 6$.

$(3 + 3t) - 3(-1 + t) = 6$
$6 = 6$

Continues on next page

| Every *t* is a solution. | The equation is satisfied for all values of *t*. |
| So, the line lies in the plane. | This means that every point on the line also lies in the plane. |

Intersection of two planes

If two planes intersect, they do so along a straight line. As the line lies in both planes, it must be perpendicular to both normal vectors. You can therefore find the direction of the line.

🔑 Key point 5.11

The line of intersection of planes with normals $\mathbf{n}_1$ and $\mathbf{n}_2$ has direction $\mathbf{n}_1 \times \mathbf{n}_2$.

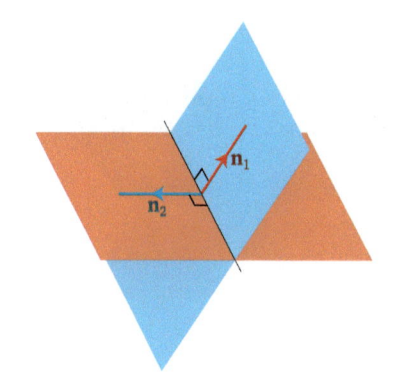

To find the equation of the intersection line you also need to find the position vector of one point on the line.

WORKED EXAMPLE 5.15

Find the line of intersection of the planes with equations $4x + 5y - z = 7$ and $x - 4z = -7$.

Direction vector:

$$\mathbf{n}_1 \times \mathbf{n}_2 = \begin{pmatrix} 4 \\ 5 \\ -1 \end{pmatrix} \times \begin{pmatrix} 1 \\ 0 \\ -4 \end{pmatrix}$$

$$= \begin{pmatrix} -20 \\ 15 \\ -5 \end{pmatrix}$$

The direction vector is perpendicular to both normal vectors.

The vector product of two vectors is perpendicular to both of them.

$$\mathbf{d} = \begin{pmatrix} -4 \\ 3 \\ -1 \end{pmatrix}$$

You can change the magnitude of the direction vector.

$$\begin{cases} 4x + 5y - z = 7 \\ x - 4z = -7 \end{cases}$$

You also need one point on the line; its (x, y, z) coordinates will satisfy both planes' equations.

Taking $x = 1$:

$$\begin{cases} 4 + 5y - z = 7 \\ 1 - 4z = -7 \end{cases}$$

$z = 2$

$5y = 5 \Rightarrow y = 1$

There are three unknowns but only two equations, so you can pick a value for one of the unknowns and then solve for the other two.

$$\mathbf{a} = \begin{pmatrix} 1 \\ 1 \\ 2 \end{pmatrix}$$

These values give the coordinates of one point on the line.

$\mathbf{r} = \mathbf{a} + \lambda \mathbf{d}$

You can now write down the equation of the line.

$$\mathbf{r} = \begin{pmatrix} 1 \\ 1 \\ 2 \end{pmatrix} + \lambda \begin{pmatrix} -4 \\ 3 \\ -1 \end{pmatrix}$$

Intersection of three planes

Two different planes are either parallel or intersect in a line. With three planes, there are more options.

If two of the planes are parallel, the third plane can either intersect both of them (in two different lines) or be parallel to them.

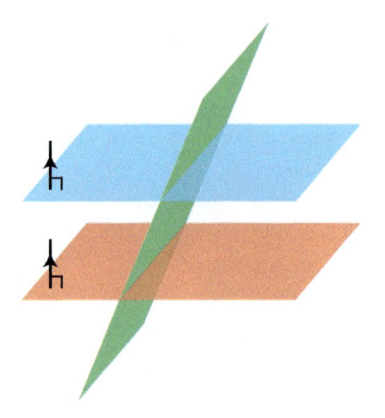

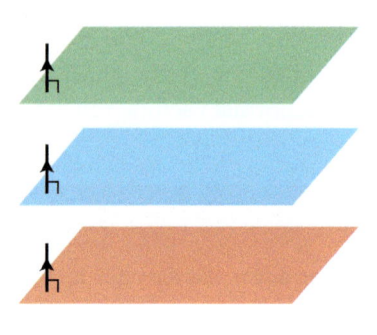

> **Tip**
>
> If two planes are parallel, their normals are multiples of each other. For example, the planes $x + 2y - 5z = 11$ and $2x + 4y - 10z = 4$ are parallel.

If two planes intersect in a line, there are three different options for the third plane.

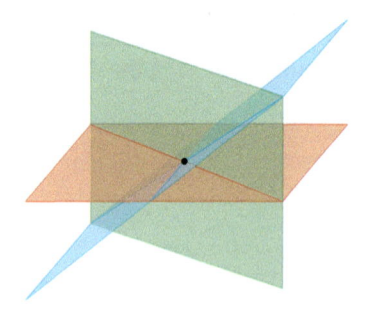

The third plane intersects the line of intersection of the first two planes.

The three planes intersect at a unique point.

The third plane contains the line of intersection of the other two.

The three planes intersect along a line and form a sheaf.

The third plane is parallel to the line of intersection of the other two planes.

The three planes form a triangular prism.

You already know how to find the line of intersection of two planes. You can then try to find the intersection of this line with the third plane.

WORKED EXAMPLE 5.16

The planes Π_1, Π_2 and Π_3 are given by the equations:

$\Pi_1: 3x - y + z = 17$ $\Pi_2: x + 2y - z = 8$ $\Pi_3: 3x + y + 2z = 19$

Π_1 and Π_2 intersect along a line l.

a   Find a vector equation of l.
b   Find the point of intersection of all three planes.

Continues on next page

a Direction vector of l:
$$\begin{pmatrix} 3 \\ -1 \\ 1 \end{pmatrix} \times \begin{pmatrix} 1 \\ 2 \\ -1 \end{pmatrix} = \begin{pmatrix} -1 \\ 4 \\ 7 \end{pmatrix}$$

The direction vector of the line is the cross product of the normals.

For a point on l, set $x = 0$:
$$\begin{cases} -y + z = 17 \\ 2y - z = 8 \end{cases}$$
$\Rightarrow y = 25,\ z = 42$

To find one point on the line, you can pick a value for its x-coordinate and then use the equations to find y and z.

The equation of l is
$$\mathbf{r} = \begin{pmatrix} 0 \\ 25 \\ 42 \end{pmatrix} + \lambda \begin{pmatrix} -1 \\ 4 \\ 7 \end{pmatrix}$$

Use $\mathbf{r} = \mathbf{a} + \lambda \mathbf{d}$.

b Intersection of l and Π_3:
$$3(-\lambda) + (25 + 4\lambda) + 2(42 + 7\lambda) = 19$$
$$15\lambda + 109 = 19$$
$$\lambda = -6$$

Substitute $x = -\lambda,\ y = 25 + 4\lambda,\ z = 42 + 7\lambda$ from the equation of the line into the equation of the plane.

Then
$$\begin{pmatrix} 0 \\ 25 \\ 42 \end{pmatrix} - 6 \begin{pmatrix} -1 \\ 4 \\ 7 \end{pmatrix} = \begin{pmatrix} 6 \\ 1 \\ 0 \end{pmatrix}$$

Substitute λ back into the equation of the line to find the intersection point.

So, the three planes intersect at the point $(6, 1, 0)$.

Worked example 5.17 shows two possibilities when three planes do not intersect at a single point. It uses planes Π_1 and Π_2 from Worked example 5.16.

WORKED EXAMPLE 5.17

The planes Π_1, Π_2 and Π_4 are given by the equations:

$\Pi_1: 3x - y + z = 17$ $\qquad$ $\Pi_2: x + 2y - z = 8$ $\qquad$ $\Pi_4: 2x - 3y + 2z = k$.

Π_1 and Π_2 intersect along a line l with equation $\mathbf{r} = \begin{pmatrix} 0 \\ 25 \\ 42 \end{pmatrix} + \lambda \begin{pmatrix} -1 \\ 4 \\ 7 \end{pmatrix}$.

a Show that, when $k = 3$, the three planes form a triangular prism.
b Find the value of k for which the three planes intersect along a line.

a When $k = 3$:
$$2(-\lambda) - 3(25 + 4\lambda) + 2(42 + 7\lambda) = 3$$
$$0\lambda + 9 = 3$$

Try to find the intersection between Π_4 and l.

No solution for λ, so l and Π_4 do not intersect.

It is impossible to find λ such that $0\lambda + 9 = 3$.

Continues on next page

Hence the three planes form a triangular prism.

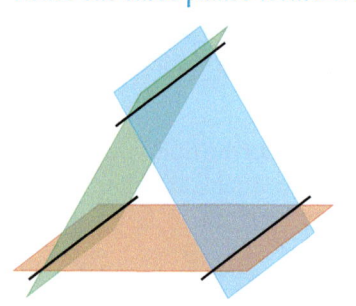

You can also check that l is parallel to Π_4. This is because the direction of l is perpendicular to the normal vector of Π_4:

$$\begin{pmatrix} -1 \\ 4 \\ 7 \end{pmatrix} \cdot \begin{pmatrix} 2 \\ -3 \\ 2 \end{pmatrix} = -2 - 12 + 14 = 0$$

b $2(-\lambda) - 3(25 + 4\lambda) + 2(42 + 7\lambda) = k$
$0\lambda + 9 = k$

The equation is satisfied for all λ when $k = 9$.

You now want l to lie in the plane Π_4. This will happen when the equation for intersection is satisfied for all λ.

Fast forward

In Chapter 6 you will learn that you can also use matrices to find the intersection of three planes and distinguish between different cases when the intersection is not a single point.

EXERCISE 5C

1 Find the coordinates of the point of intersection of line l and plane Π.

a **i** $l : \mathbf{r} = \begin{pmatrix} 2 \\ 1 \\ 2 \end{pmatrix} + \lambda \begin{pmatrix} 5 \\ 0 \\ -1 \end{pmatrix}, \Pi : 4x + 2y - z = 29$

  ii $l : \mathbf{r} = \begin{pmatrix} -5 \\ 1 \\ 1 \end{pmatrix} + \lambda \begin{pmatrix} 7 \\ 3 \\ -3 \end{pmatrix}, \Pi : x + y + 5z = 11$

b **i** $l : \dfrac{x-2}{5} = \dfrac{y+1}{2} = \dfrac{z}{6}, \Pi : \mathbf{r} \cdot \begin{pmatrix} 1 \\ -4 \\ 1 \end{pmatrix} = 4$

  ii $l : \dfrac{x-5}{-1} = \dfrac{y-3}{2} = \dfrac{z-5}{1}, \Pi : \mathbf{r} \cdot \begin{pmatrix} 2 \\ -1 \\ 1 \end{pmatrix} = 21$

5 Further vectors

2 Show that plane Π contains line l.

  a $\Pi: x + 6y + 2z = 7$, $l: \mathbf{r} = \begin{pmatrix} 5 \\ 0 \\ 1 \end{pmatrix} + t \begin{pmatrix} 2 \\ -1 \\ 2 \end{pmatrix}$

  b $\Pi: 5x + y - 2z = 15 \quad l: \dfrac{x-4}{1} = \dfrac{y+1}{1} = \dfrac{z-2}{3}$

  c $\Pi: \mathbf{r} \bullet \begin{pmatrix} 1 \\ 0 \\ -4 \end{pmatrix} = -5$, $l: \mathbf{r} = \begin{pmatrix} -1 \\ 0 \\ 1 \end{pmatrix} + t \begin{pmatrix} 8 \\ 3 \\ 2 \end{pmatrix}$

  d $\Pi: \mathbf{r} \bullet \begin{pmatrix} -2 \\ -2 \\ 5 \end{pmatrix} = \begin{pmatrix} 5 \\ 3 \\ 1 \end{pmatrix} \bullet \begin{pmatrix} -2 \\ -2 \\ 5 \end{pmatrix}$, $l: \dfrac{x-3}{2} = \dfrac{y}{3} = \dfrac{z+1}{2}$

3 Find a vector equation of the line of intersection of each pair of planes.

  a i $3x + y - z = 5$ and $x - 2y + 4z = -5$ **ii** $x + y = 3$ and $x - y = 5$

  b i $2x - y = 4$ and $2y + z = 5$ **ii** $x + 2y - 5z = 6$ and $z = 0$

4 Find the point of intersection of the line $\mathbf{r} = \begin{pmatrix} 3 \\ -1 \\ 2 \end{pmatrix} + \lambda \begin{pmatrix} 2 \\ 1 \\ 1 \end{pmatrix}$ and the plane $x - y + z = 18$.

5 A line has equation $\left(\mathbf{r} - \begin{pmatrix} 2 \\ -1 \\ 2 \end{pmatrix} \right) \times \begin{pmatrix} -1 \\ 2 \\ 1 \end{pmatrix} = \mathbf{0}$.

  a Write down the direction vector of the line.

  b Find the coordinates of the point where the line intersects the plane with equation $\mathbf{r} \bullet \begin{pmatrix} 3 \\ 3 \\ 2 \end{pmatrix} = 16$.

6 Find the coordinates of the point of intersection of the line $\dfrac{x-2}{3} = \dfrac{y-1}{2} = z + 1$ with the plane $2x - y - 2z = 7$.

7 a Calculate $\begin{pmatrix} 3 \\ -1 \\ 3 \end{pmatrix} \times \begin{pmatrix} 2 \\ 2 \\ 1 \end{pmatrix}$.

  b Hence find the equation of the line of intersection of the planes $3x - y + 3z = 20$ and $2x + 2y + z = 10$.

8 Let $\mathbf{p} = 3\mathbf{i} - 2\mathbf{j} + \mathbf{k}$ and $\mathbf{q} = \mathbf{i} - 4\mathbf{k}$.

  a Calculate $\mathbf{p} \times \mathbf{q}$.

  b Hence find the equation of the line of intersection of the planes with equations $\mathbf{r} \bullet \mathbf{p} = 3$ and $\mathbf{r} \bullet \mathbf{q} = -7$. Give your answer in the form $(\mathbf{r} - \mathbf{a}) \times \mathbf{d} = \mathbf{0}$.

9 The plane with equation $12x - 3y + 5z = 60$ intersects the x, y, and z axes at points P, Q, R, respectively.

  a Find the coordinates of P, Q and R.

  b Find the area of the triangle PQR.

10 The line *l* is the intersection of the planes with equations $3x + y + z = 8$ and $-7x + 3y + z = 2$.

   a Find a vector equation of *l*.

   A third plane has equation $x + y + 3z = 0$.

   b By considering the intersection between this plane and *l*, find the coordinates of the point of intersection of all three planes.

11 a Find the line of intersection of the planes:

   $\Pi_1 : 2x - y + z = 6$ and $\Pi_2 : 3x + y + 5z = -7$.

   b Another plane is $\Pi_3 : x - 3y - 3z = 8$.

   Show that the three planes form a triangular prism.

12 Three planes have equations:

   $\Pi_1 : 2x + y - 2z = 0$

   $\Pi_2 : x - 2y - z = 2$

   $\Pi_3 : 3x + 4y - 3z = d$.

   a Find an equation of the line of intersection of Π_1 and Π_2.

   b Find the value of *d* for which the three planes form a sheaf.

13 Show that the intersection of the planes:

   $\Pi_1 : x + y = 0$

   $\Pi_2 : x - 4y - 2z = 0$

   $\Pi_3 : \frac{1}{2}x + 3y + z = 0$

   is a line and find its direction vector in the form $a\mathbf{i} + b\mathbf{j} + c\mathbf{k}$.

14 Three planes have equations:

   $\Pi_1 : x - 2y - z = -2$

   $\Pi_2 : 2x + y - 3z = 9$

   $\Pi_3 : x + y - az = 3$.

   a Find the Cartesian equation of the line of intersection of Π_1 and Π_2.

   b Find the value of *a* for which the three planes do not intersect.

   c For this value of *a*, describe the geometrical configuration of the three planes.

Section 4: Angles between lines and planes

The angle between a line l and a plane Π is the smallest possible angle that l makes with any of the lines in Π. In the diagram, this is the angle, labelled θ, between l and the line AP. Drawing a two-dimensional diagram of triangle APR makes it clearer what the angles are.

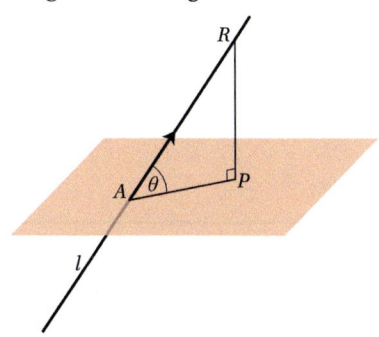

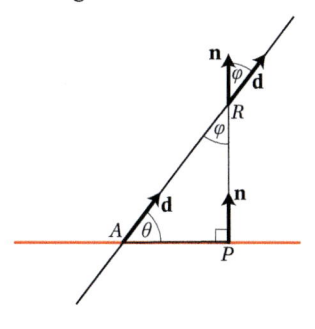

Key point 5.12

The angle between the line with direction vector **d** and the plane with normal **n** is $90° - \phi$, where ϕ is the acute angle between **d** and **n**.

Rewind

You can find the angle between two vectors by using the scalar product, which you met in Further Mathematics Student Book 1, Chapter 9.

WORKED EXAMPLE 5.18

Find the angle between line l with equation $\mathbf{r} = \begin{pmatrix} 4 \\ 0 \\ 7 \end{pmatrix} + \lambda \begin{pmatrix} 3 \\ 3 \\ 2 \end{pmatrix}$ and the plane with equation $5x - y + z = 7$.

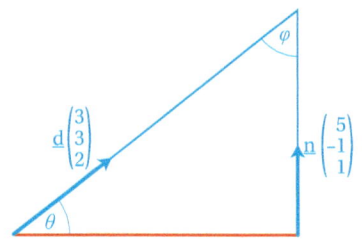

$\cos \phi = \dfrac{\mathbf{d} \cdot \mathbf{n}}{|\mathbf{d}||\mathbf{n}|}$

$= \dfrac{\begin{pmatrix} 3 \\ 3 \\ 2 \end{pmatrix} \cdot \begin{pmatrix} 5 \\ -1 \\ 1 \end{pmatrix}}{\sqrt{9+9+4}\sqrt{25+1+1}}$

$= \dfrac{14}{\sqrt{22}\sqrt{27}}$

$\therefore \phi = 54.9°$

The angle between the line and the plane is $\theta = 90° - \phi = 35.1°$

The angle between a line and a plane is 90° − (angle between the lines' direction vector and the plane's normal).

You can use a similar method to find the angle between two planes. Again a diagram is helpful so you can see where the relevant angle is. The sum of angles in a quadrilateral is 360°, so the two angles marked θ are equal.

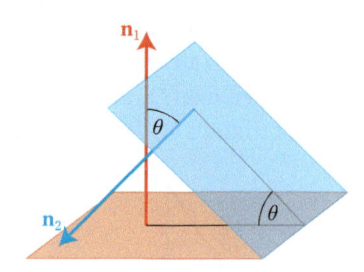

Key point 5.13

The angle between two planes is equal to the angle between their normals.

WORKED EXAMPLE 5.19

Find the acute angle between planes with equations $4x - y + 5z = 11$ and $x + y - 3z = 3$.

$\cos \theta = \dfrac{\mathbf{n}_1 \cdot \mathbf{n}_2}{|\mathbf{n}_1||\mathbf{n}_2|}$ .... You need to find the angle between the normals. The components of the normal vector are the coefficients in the Cartesian equation.

$= \dfrac{\begin{pmatrix} 4 \\ -1 \\ 5 \end{pmatrix} \cdot \begin{pmatrix} 1 \\ 1 \\ -3 \end{pmatrix}}{\sqrt{16+1+25}\sqrt{1+1+9}}$

$= \dfrac{-12}{\sqrt{42}\sqrt{11}}$

$\therefore \theta = 123.9°$

$180° - 123.9° = 56.1°$ .... You need the acute angle.

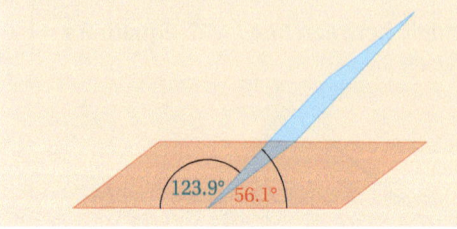

The angle between the planes is 56.1° (1 d.p.).

EXERCISE 5D

1 Find the acute angle between line l and plane Π, correct to the nearest 0.1°.

a **i** $l : \mathbf{r} = \begin{pmatrix} 4 \\ -1 \\ 2 \end{pmatrix} + \lambda \begin{pmatrix} 1 \\ -1 \\ 3 \end{pmatrix}$, $\Pi : \mathbf{r} \cdot \begin{pmatrix} 4 \\ -1 \\ 2 \end{pmatrix} = 7$

ii $l : \mathbf{r} = \begin{pmatrix} 2 \\ -3 \\ 1 \end{pmatrix} + \lambda \begin{pmatrix} -3 \\ 1 \\ 1 \end{pmatrix}$, $\Pi : \mathbf{r} \cdot \begin{pmatrix} -1 \\ -2 \\ 2 \end{pmatrix} = 1$

b **i** $l : \dfrac{x}{2} = \dfrac{y-1}{5} = \dfrac{z-2}{5}$, $\Pi : x - y - 3z = 1$

ii $l : \dfrac{x+1}{-1} = \dfrac{y-3}{3} = \dfrac{z+2}{-3}$, $\Pi : 2x + y + z = 14$

5 Further vectors

2 Find the acute angle between each pair of planes.

  a $3x - 7y + z = 4$ and $x + y - 4z = 5$

  b $x - z = 4$ and $y + z = 1$

3 Line l has Cartesian equation $\dfrac{x-3}{2} = \dfrac{y+1}{3} = \dfrac{z-5}{-1}$.

  a Write down the direction vector of l.

  b Find the acute angle between l and the plane with equation $x - 3y + 5z = 7$.

4 Plane Π_1 has Cartesian equation $3x - y + z = 7$.

  a Write down a normal vector of Π_1.

  Plane Π_2 has equation $x - 5y + 5z = 11$.

  b Find, correct to the nearest degree, the acute angle between Π_1 and Π_2.

5 Line l has equation $\left(\mathbf{r} - \begin{pmatrix} 5 \\ -1 \\ 2 \end{pmatrix} \right) \times \begin{pmatrix} 4 \\ 2 \\ 3 \end{pmatrix} = \mathbf{0}$.

  a Write down the direction vector of l.

  b Find the acute angle that l makes with the plane $\mathbf{r} \cdot \begin{pmatrix} -1 \\ 4 \\ 3 \end{pmatrix} = 7$.

6 A plane has vector equation $\mathbf{r} = \begin{pmatrix} 3 \\ 7 \\ 1 \end{pmatrix} + \lambda \begin{pmatrix} -1 \\ 3 \\ 1 \end{pmatrix} + \mu \begin{pmatrix} 2 \\ 2 \\ 5 \end{pmatrix}$.

  a Find the normal vector of the plane.

  b Find the acute angle that the plane makes with the line $\mathbf{r} = \begin{pmatrix} 1 \\ 2 \\ -1 \end{pmatrix} + \lambda \begin{pmatrix} 3 \\ 1 \\ 5 \end{pmatrix}$.

7 Show that the planes with equations $3x + y + 4z = 7$ and $x + 9y - 3z = 8$ are perpendicular to each other.

8 Line l has Cartesian equation $\dfrac{4-x}{5} = z + 1$, $y = -3$.

  a Find the direction vector of l.

  b Find the acute angle that l makes with the plane $4x - 3z = 0$.

9 Plane Π has equation $5x - 3y - z = 1$.

  a Show that point $P(2, 1, 6)$ lies in the plane Π.

  b Point Q has coordinates $(7, -1, 2)$. Find the exact value of the sine of the angle between PQ and Π.

  c Find the exact distance PQ.

  d Hence find the exact distance of Q from Π.

> **▶▶| Fast forward**
>
> In Section 5 you will see another method to find the distance from a point to a plane.

103

A Level Further Mathematics for AQA Student Book 2

Section 5: Distance between a point and a plane

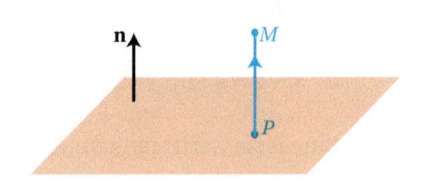

Given a plane with equation $\mathbf{r} \cdot \mathbf{n} = d$ and a point M outside of the plane, the distance from M to the plane is equal to the distance MP, where the line MP is perpendicular to the plane. This means that the direction of MP is $\mathbf{n}$.

To find the distance MP:

- write down the vector equation of the line with direction $\mathbf{n}$ through point M
- find the intersection, P, between the line and the plane
- calculate the distance MP.

Point P is called the foot of the perpendicular from the point to the plane.

WORKED EXAMPLE 5.20

Plane Π has Cartesian equation $3x - y + z = 8$.

a Find the equation of the line that is perpendicular to Π and passes through the point $M(13, -3, 10)$.
b Hence find the distance from M to Π.

a $\underline{\mathbf{r}} = \begin{pmatrix} 13 \\ -3 \\ 10 \end{pmatrix} + \lambda \begin{pmatrix} 3 \\ -1 \\ 1 \end{pmatrix}$

The perpendicular line is the direction of the normal to the plane.

b Intersection with Π:
$3(13 + 3\lambda) - (-3 - \lambda) + (10 + \lambda) = 8$
$11\lambda = -44$
$\lambda = -4$

You need the distance from M to the point where the perpendicular line intersects the plane.

The intersection point is $\begin{pmatrix} 13 \\ -3 \\ 10 \end{pmatrix} - 4\begin{pmatrix} 3 \\ -1 \\ 1 \end{pmatrix} = \begin{pmatrix} 1 \\ 1 \\ 6 \end{pmatrix}$

The distance is
$\sqrt{(13-1)^2 + (-3-1)^2 + (10-6)^2} = 4\sqrt{11}$

Find the distance between $M(13, -3, 10)$ and the point $(1, 1, 6)$.

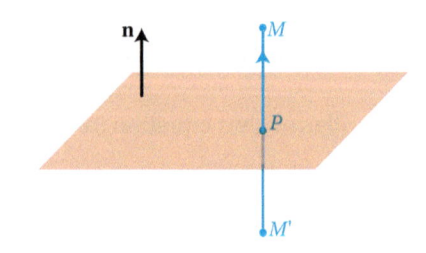

You can use the same idea to find the reflection of a point in a plane. The reflection of M in Π is the point M' such that MM' is perpendicular to the plane and the distance of M' from Π is the same as the distance of M from Π. This means that $\overrightarrow{PM'} = \overrightarrow{MP}$.

WORKED EXAMPLE 5.21

Find the coordinates of the reflection of the point $M(13, -3, 10)$ in the plane $\Pi : 3x - y + z = 8$.

Let P be the foot of the perpendicular from M to Π. Then P has coordinates $(1, 1, 6)$.

> These are the plane and the point from Worked example 5.20, so you have already found the coordinates of P.

Let M' be the reflection of M.

Then
$\overrightarrow{PM'} = \overrightarrow{MP}$
$\underline{m}' - \underline{p} = \underline{p} - \underline{m}$

> You need to find a point M' such that $\overrightarrow{PM'} = \overrightarrow{MP}$.

$\underline{m}' = 2\underline{p} - \underline{m}$

$= 2\begin{pmatrix} 1 \\ 1 \\ 6 \end{pmatrix} - \begin{pmatrix} 13 \\ -3 \\ 10 \end{pmatrix} = \begin{pmatrix} -11 \\ 5 \\ 2 \end{pmatrix}$

> The vector between two points equals the difference between their position vectors.

The coordinates of the reflection are $(-11, 5, 2)$.

EXERCISE 5E

1. Plane Π has equation $x - 3y + z = 6$. Line l is perpendicular to Π and passes through the point $A(3, -7, 4)$.
   a. Write down the direction vector of l.
   b. Find the coordinates of the point of intersection of l and Π.
   c. Hence find the exact distance of A from Π.

2. Plane Π has equation $2x + 2y - z = 11$. Line l is perpendicular to Π and passes through the point $P(-3, -3, 4)$.
   a. Find the equation of l.
   b. Find the coordinates of the point Q where l intersects Π.
   c. Find the shortest distance from P to Π.

3. Plane Π has equation $6x - 2y + z = 16$. Line l is perpendicular to Π and passes through the origin.
   a. Find the coordinates of the point of intersection of l and Π.
   b. Find the shortest distance of Π from the origin, giving your answer in exact form.

4. Plane Π has equation $\mathbf{r} \cdot \begin{pmatrix} 4 \\ 6 \\ -3 \end{pmatrix} = 1$. Point $B(-3, -4, 8)$ is reflected in Π and the image is point C. The line BC intersects Π at Q.
   a. Write down a vector equation of the line BC.
   b. Find the coordinates of Q.
   c. Hence find the coordinates of C.

5 Four points have coordinates $A(7, 0, 1)$, $B(8, -1, 4)$, $C(9, 0, 2)$, $D(6, 5, 3)$.
   a Show that $\overrightarrow{AD}$ is perpendicular to both $\overrightarrow{AB}$ and $\overrightarrow{AC}$.
   b Write down the equation of the plane Π containing the points A, B and C in the form $\mathbf{r} \cdot \mathbf{n} = k$.
   c Find the exact distance of point D from plane Π.
   d Point D_1 is the reflection of D in Π. Find the coordinates of D_1.

6 Points $A(8, 0, 4)$, $B(12, -1, 5)$ and $C(10, 0, 7)$ lie in the plane Π.
   a Find $\overrightarrow{AB} \times \overrightarrow{AC}$.
   b Hence find the area of the triangle ABC, correct to three significant figures.
   c Find the Cartesian equation of Π.
   Point D has coordinates $(-7, -28, 11)$.
   d Find a vector equation of the line through D perpendicular to the plane.
   e Find the intersection of this line with Π, and hence find the perpendicular distance of D from Π.
   f Find the volume of the pyramid $ABCD$.

7 Two planes have equations:
   $\Pi_1: x - 3y + z = 6$, and $\Pi_2: 3x - 9y + 3z = 0$.
   a Show that Π_1 and Π_2 are parallel.
   b Show that Π_2 passes through the origin.
   c Write down the equation of the line through the origin which is perpendicular to Π_2.
   d Hence find the distance between the planes Π_1 and Π_2.

8 a Show that the planes $\Pi_1: x - z = 4$ and $\Pi_2: z - x = 8$ are parallel.
   b Write down a vector equation of the line through the origin which is perpendicular to the two planes.
   c i   Find the coordinates of the foot of the perpendicular from the origin to Π_1.
      ii Find the coordinates of the foot of the perpendicular from the origin to Π_2.
   d Use your answers from part c to find the exact distance between the two planes.

5 Further vectors

Checklist of learning and understanding

- The vector product of two vectors, $\mathbf{a} \times \mathbf{b}$, is defined as

$$\mathbf{a} \times \mathbf{b} = |\mathbf{a}||\mathbf{b}| \sin \theta \, \hat{\mathbf{n}}$$

  where θ is the angle between the vectors $\mathbf{a}$ and $\mathbf{b}$, and $\hat{\mathbf{n}}$ is a unit vector perpendicular to $\mathbf{a}$ and $\mathbf{b}$.

- The vector product can be calculated as

$$\mathbf{a} \times \mathbf{b} = \begin{pmatrix} a_2 b_3 - a_3 b_2 \\ a_3 b_1 - a_1 b_3 \\ a_1 b_2 - a_2 b_1 \end{pmatrix}$$

- The vector $\mathbf{a} \times \mathbf{b}$ is perpendicular to both $\mathbf{a}$ and $\mathbf{b}$.
- Properties of the vector product:
    - $\mathbf{a} \times \mathbf{b} = -\mathbf{b} \times \mathbf{a}$
    - $(k\mathbf{a}) \times \mathbf{b} = k(\mathbf{a} \times \mathbf{b})$
    - $(\mathbf{a} \times \mathbf{b}) \times \mathbf{c} = \mathbf{a} \times (\mathbf{b} \times \mathbf{c})$
    - $\mathbf{a} \times (\mathbf{b} + \mathbf{c}) = (\mathbf{a} \times \mathbf{b}) + (\mathbf{a} \times \mathbf{c})$
- If vectors $\mathbf{a}$ and $\mathbf{b}$ are parallel then $\mathbf{a} \times \mathbf{b} = \mathbf{0}$.
  In particular, $\mathbf{a} \times \mathbf{a} = \mathbf{0}$.
- The vector equation of a line passing through the point with position vector $\mathbf{a}$ and parallel to the vector $\mathbf{d}$ can also be written as $(\mathbf{r} - \mathbf{a}) \times \mathbf{d} = \mathbf{0}$
    - The area of a triangle with sides $\mathbf{a}$ and $\mathbf{b}$ is $\frac{1}{2}|\mathbf{a} \times \mathbf{b}|$.
- The vector equation of a plane is $\mathbf{r} = \mathbf{a} + \lambda \mathbf{d}_1 + \mu \mathbf{d}_2$, where $\mathbf{d}_1$ and $\mathbf{d}_2$ are two vectors parallel to the plane and $\mathbf{a}$ is the position vector of one point in the plane.
- The Cartesian equation of a plane has the form $n_1 x + n_2 y + n_3 z = k$. This can also be written in the scalar product form $\mathbf{r} \cdot \mathbf{n} = \mathbf{a} \cdot \mathbf{n}$, where $\mathbf{n} = \begin{pmatrix} n_1 \\ n_2 \\ n_3 \end{pmatrix}$ is the normal vector of the plane, which is perpendicular to every line in the plane. To derive the Cartesian equation from a vector equation, use $\mathbf{n} = \mathbf{d}_1 \times \mathbf{d}_2$.
- The angle between two planes is the angle between their normals.
- The angle between a line and a plane is
  $90°$ – (angle between the line direction vector and the plane's normal).
- To find the intersection between a line and a plane, express x, y, z for the line in terms of λ and substitute into the Cartesian equation of the plane.
- To find the distance between a point and a plane:
    - find the equation of the line in the direction of the normal, passing through the point
    - find where this line intersects the plane
    - find the distance between this and the original point.
- If two planes intersect, the line of intersection has direction parallel to $\mathbf{n}_1 \times \mathbf{n}_2$.
- Three different planes could:
    - intersect at a single point
    - intersect along a line (form a sheaf)
    - not intersect because the line of intersection of two of the planes is parallel to the third plane (form a triangular prism)
    - not intersect because two of the planes are parallel.
- To find the intersection of three planes, first find the line of intersection of two of the planes, and then intersect this line with the third plane.

Mixed practice 5

1 Find a vector perpendicular to $\mathbf{a} = 3\mathbf{i} - 5\mathbf{j} - \mathbf{k}$ and $\mathbf{b} = 3\mathbf{i} - \mathbf{k}$.

2 Given that $\mathbf{a} = 2\mathbf{i} + \mathbf{j} - 3\mathbf{k}$, $\mathbf{b} = -3\mathbf{i} + 2\mathbf{k}$ and $\mathbf{c} = \mathbf{i} - 3\mathbf{j} + 4\mathbf{k}$, find $(\mathbf{a} \times \mathbf{b}) \cdot \mathbf{c}$.

3 The vector $\mathbf{n} = 3\mathbf{i} + \mathbf{j} - \mathbf{k}$ is normal to a plane that passes through the point $(3, -1, 2)$.

   a Find an equation for the plane.

   b Find a if the point $(a, 2a, a-1)$ lies on the plane.

4 The plane Π has equation $x - 2y + z = 20$ and the point A has coordinates $(4, -1, 2)$.

   a Write down the vector equation of the line l through A that is perpendicular to Π.

   b Find the coordinates of the point of intersection of line l and plane Π.

   c Hence find the shortest distance from point A to plane Π.

5 **a** Calculate $\begin{pmatrix} 2 \\ -1 \\ 1 \end{pmatrix} \times \begin{pmatrix} 3 \\ 1 \\ -1 \end{pmatrix}$.

   b Plane Π_1 has normal vector $\begin{pmatrix} 2 \\ -1 \\ 1 \end{pmatrix}$ and contains point $A(3, 4, -2)$.

   Find the Cartesian equation of the plane.

   c Plane Π_2 has equation $3x + y - z = 15$. Show that Π_2 contains point A.

   d Write down the vector equation of the line of intersection of the two planes.

   e A third plane, Π_3, has equation $\mathbf{r} \cdot \begin{pmatrix} 2 \\ 1 \\ 2 \end{pmatrix} = 12$.

   Find the coordinates of the point of intersection of all three planes.

   f Find the angle between Π_1 and Π_3 in degrees.

6 Plane Π has equation $x - 4y + 2z = 7$ and point P has coordinates $(9, -7, 6)$.

   a Show that point $R(5, 1, 3)$ lies in the plane Π.

   b Find the vector equation of the line PR.

   c Write down the vector equation of the line through P perpendicular to Π.

   d N is the foot of the perpendicular from P to Π.
   Find the coordinates of N.

   e Find the exact distance of point P from the plane Π.

5 Further vectors

7 The fixed points A and B and the variable point C have position vectors

$$\mathbf{a} = \begin{pmatrix} 3 \\ -4 \\ 1 \end{pmatrix}, \mathbf{b} = \begin{pmatrix} 2 \\ 1 \\ -3 \end{pmatrix} \text{ and } \mathbf{c} = \begin{pmatrix} 2-t \\ t \\ 5 \end{pmatrix}$$

respectively, relative to the origin O, where t is a scalar parameter.

a Find an equation of the line AB in the form $(\mathbf{r} - \mathbf{u}) \times \mathbf{v} = \mathbf{0}$.

b Determine $\mathbf{b} \times \mathbf{c}$ in terms of t.

c i Show that $\mathbf{a} \cdot (\mathbf{b} \times \mathbf{c})$ is constant for all values of t, and state the value of this constant.

  ii Write down a geometrical conclusion that can be deduced from the answer to part **c i**.

[©AQA 2010]

8 Two planes have equations

$x + 2y + 2z = 5$ and $px + 3y = 10$

where p is a non-zero constant.

Given that the acute angle, θ, between the planes is such that $\cos \theta = \frac{2}{3}$, find the value of p.

[©AQA 2013]

9 Line L_1 has equation $r = \begin{pmatrix} 5 \\ 1 \\ 2 \end{pmatrix} + t \begin{pmatrix} -1 \\ 1 \\ 3 \end{pmatrix}$ and line L_2 has equation $r = \begin{pmatrix} 5 \\ 4 \\ 9 \end{pmatrix} + s \begin{pmatrix} 2 \\ 1 \\ 1 \end{pmatrix}$.

a Find $\begin{pmatrix} -1 \\ 1 \\ 3 \end{pmatrix} \times \begin{pmatrix} 2 \\ 1 \\ 1 \end{pmatrix}$.

b Find the coordinates of the point of intersection of the two lines.

c Write down a vector perpendicular to the plane containing the two lines.

d Hence find the Cartesian equation of the plane containing the two lines.

10 The position vectors of points N and L are:

$\mathbf{n} = 2\mathbf{i} - 5\mathbf{j} + \mathbf{k}$

$\mathbf{l} = \mathbf{i} + \mathbf{j} - 2\mathbf{k}$

a Find the vector product $\mathbf{n} \times \mathbf{l}$.

b Using your answer to part **a**, or otherwise, find the area of the parallelogram with two sides $\overrightarrow{ON}$ and $\overrightarrow{OL}$.

11 The vectors **p**, **q** and **r** are such that:

p × **q** = **p** × **r**

where **p** ≠ **0** and **q** ≠ **r**.

What can you say about **p**, **q** and **r**?

Choose from these options.

   A   **q** is parallel to **r**.   **B**   **q** is perpendicular to **r**.

   C   **p** is parallel to **q** − **r**.   **D**   **p** is perpendicular to **q** − **r**.

12   **a**   Find the coordinates of the point of intersection of lines

$$l_1: \frac{x-1}{3} = \frac{y+1}{4} = \frac{3-z}{3} \text{ and } l_2: \frac{x+12}{2} = \frac{y}{1} = \frac{z+17}{1}.$$

   b   Find a vector perpendicular to both lines.

   c   Hence find the Cartesian equation of the plane containing l_1 and l_2.

13 Point A (3, 1, −4) lies on line L which is perpendicular to plane $\Pi: 3x - y - z = 1$.

   a   Find the Cartesian equation of L.

   b   Find the point of intersection of the line L and the plane Π.

   c   Point A is reflected in Π. Find the coordinates of the image of A.

   d   Point B has coordinates (1, 1, 1). Show that B lies in Π.

   e   Find the distance between B and L.

14 The planes Π_1, Π_2 and Π_3 have Cartesian equations

$$2x + y - z = 3$$
$$3x - 2y + z = 5$$
$$12x - y - z = 40$$

respectively.

   a   Find, in the form **r** = **a** + λ**d**, a vector equation for the line L which is the intersection of Π_1 and Π_2.

   b   **i**   Determine whether L meets Π_3, and use your answer to decide whether the system given by the equations of these three planes is consistent or inconsistent.

       ii   Describe geometrically the arrangement of the three planes.

   c   **i**   Find the coordinates of a common point of Π_2 and Π_3.

       ii   Deduce a vector equation for the line of intersection of Π_2 and Π_3.

[©AQA 2012]

5 Further vectors

15 Consider the tetrahedron shown in the diagram and define vectors $\mathbf{a} = \overrightarrow{CB}$, $\mathbf{b} = \overrightarrow{CD}$ and $\mathbf{c} = \overrightarrow{CA}$.

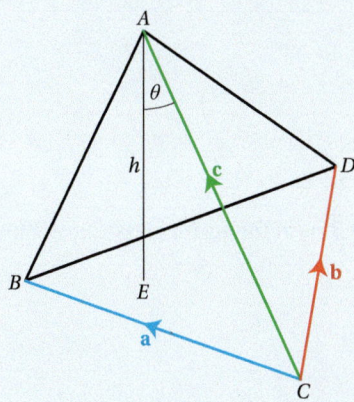

  a Write down an expression for the area of the base BCD in terms of vectors $\mathbf{a}$ and $\mathbf{b}$ only.

  b AE is the height of the tetrahedron, $|AE| = h$ and $\angle CAE = \theta$. Express h in terms of c and θ.

  c Use the results from parts **a** and **b** to prove that the volume of the tetrahedron is given by $\frac{1}{6}|(\mathbf{a} \times \mathbf{b}) \cdot \mathbf{c}|$.

  d Find the volume of the tetrahedron with vertices $(0, 4, 0)$, $(0, 6, 0)$, $(1, 6, 1)$ and $(3, -1, 2)$.

16 Line l passes through point $A(-1, 1, 4)$ and has direction vector $\mathbf{d} = \begin{pmatrix} 6 \\ 1 \\ 5 \end{pmatrix}$. Point B has coordinates $(3, 3, 1)$. Plane Π has normal vector $\mathbf{n}$, and contains the line l and the point B.

  a Write down a vector equation for l.

  b Explain why $\overrightarrow{AB}$ and $\mathbf{d}$ are both perpendicular to $\mathbf{n}$.

  c Hence find one possible vector $\mathbf{n}$.

  d Find the Cartesian equation of plane Π.

17 The plane $3x + 2y - z = 2$ contains the line $x - 3 = \frac{2y + 2}{5} = \frac{z - 5}{k}$. Find k.

18 Find the Cartesian equation of the plane containing the lines
$x = \frac{3 - y}{2} = z - 1$ and $\frac{x - 2}{3} = \frac{y + 1}{-3} = \frac{z - 3}{5}$.

19 Two planes have equations $\Pi_1: 3x - y + z = 17$ and $\Pi_2: x + 2y - z = 4$.

  a Calculate $\begin{pmatrix} 3 \\ -1 \\ 1 \end{pmatrix} \times \begin{pmatrix} 1 \\ 2 \\ -1 \end{pmatrix}$.

  b Show that Π_1 and Π_2 are perpendicular.

  c Show that the point $M(1, 1, 2)$ does not lie in either of the two planes.

  d Find a vector equation of the line through M which is parallel to both planes.

111

20 The lines L_1 and L_2 have equations

$$\mathbf{r} = \begin{pmatrix} 7 \\ -25 \\ 9 \end{pmatrix} + \alpha \begin{pmatrix} 3 \\ -4 \\ 7 \end{pmatrix} \text{ and } \mathbf{r} = \begin{pmatrix} 7 \\ 19 \\ -2 \end{pmatrix} + \beta \begin{pmatrix} 2 \\ -2 \\ 3 \end{pmatrix}$$

respectively.

a Determine a vector, **n**, which is perpendicular to both lines.

b i The point A on L_1 and the point B on L_2 are such that $\overrightarrow{AB} = \lambda\mathbf{n}$ for some constant λ. Show that:

$3\alpha - 2\beta + 2\lambda = 0$
$4\alpha - 2\beta - 5\lambda = -44$
$7\alpha - 3\beta + 2\lambda = -11$

ii Find the position vectors of A and B.

iii Deduce the shortest distance between L_1 and L_2.

[©AQA 2012]

21 a The plane Π_1 is perpendicular to the line $\left(\mathbf{r} - \begin{pmatrix} 2 \\ 4 \\ -3 \end{pmatrix} \right) \times \begin{pmatrix} 5 \\ 2 \\ -1 \end{pmatrix} = \begin{pmatrix} 0 \\ 0 \\ 0 \end{pmatrix}$.

The point $(3, -1, 2)$ lies on Π_1. Find an equation for Π_1 in the form $\mathbf{r} \cdot \mathbf{n} = c$.

b The plane Π_2 contains the points $(2, 3, 2)$, $(4, 1, -1)$ and $(0, -1, 2)$.

Show that an equation for Π_2 is $2x - y + 2z = d$, where d is an integer to be found.

c Show that the acute angle, θ, between the planes Π_1 and Π_2 is such that $\cos\theta = \dfrac{\sqrt{30}}{15}$.

d The plane Π_3 has the equation $4(k-2)x + (k+1)y - 4k^2z = 8$, where k is an integer. The three planes Π_1, Π_2 and Π_3 have no point in common.

i Show that one possible value of k is 1 and find the other possible value.

ii State the geometrical configuration of the three planes for each of the two cases in part **d i**, giving reasons for your answers.

[©AQA 2016]

6 Further matrices

In this chapter you will learn how to:

- calculate determinants and inverses for 3×3 matrices
- use matrices to solve simultaneous equations in three variables
- interpret geometrically instances where there is no unique solution to three simultaneous equations in three unknowns
- carry out row and column operations and understand how these affect the determinant of a matrix
- find eigenvalues and eigenvectors for 2×2 and 3×3 matrices
- use eigenvalues and eigenvectors to diagonalise a matrix.

Before you start…

Further Mathematics Student Book 1, Chapter 7	You should know how to add, subtract and perform scalar multiplication with matrices and carry out multiplication of matrices.	1	$\mathbf{A} = \begin{pmatrix} 1 & 3 \\ 2 & -4 \end{pmatrix}$ and $\mathbf{B} = \begin{pmatrix} 1 & -2 \\ -5 & -1 \end{pmatrix}$. Calculate: a $\mathbf{A} - 3\mathbf{B}$ b $\mathbf{BA}$.
Further Mathematics Student Book 1, Chapter 7	You should know how to calculate the determinant of a 2×2 matrix.	2	Calculate $\det \begin{pmatrix} 3 & -1 \\ 2 & 2 \end{pmatrix}$.
Further Mathematics Student Book 1, Chapter 7	You should know how to calculate the inverse of a non-singular 2×2 matrix.	3	Find $\begin{pmatrix} 3 & 1 \\ -4 & 2 \end{pmatrix}^{-1}$.
Further Mathematics Student Book 1, Chapter 7	You should know how to calculate the transpose of a matrix.	4	Given that $\mathbf{A} = \begin{pmatrix} 1 & 3 & 2 \\ 6 & 3 & -4 \end{pmatrix}$, find $\mathbf{A}^\mathrm{T}$.
Further Mathematics Student Book 1, Chapter 7	You should be able to use matrices to solve a simultaneous equation in two unknowns.	5	Express the system of simultaneous equations $\begin{cases} 2x - 3y = 2 \\ 5x - 8y = 3 \end{cases}$ in the form $\mathbf{M} \begin{pmatrix} x \\ y \end{pmatrix} = \begin{pmatrix} a \\ b \end{pmatrix}$. Find $\mathbf{M}^{-1}$ and hence find x and y.
Chapter 5	You should be able to express a plane in vector sum, vector normal or Cartesian equation form.	6	Points A, B and C have coordinates $(1, 2, 1)$, $(2, 3, -3)$ and $(0, 1, 2)$ respectively. Find the plane containing A, B and C, giving your answer in the form: a $\mathbf{r} = \mathbf{a} + \lambda \mathbf{d}_1 + \mu \mathbf{d}_2$ b $\mathbf{r} \cdot \mathbf{n} = k$ c $ax + by + cz = d$.

113

A Level Further Mathematics for AQA Student Book 2

Chapter 5	You should know how to find the equation of the line of intersections of two planes.	7	Find the vector equation of the line of intersections of the planes $2x + 2y + z = 7$ and $5x - y + z = 4$.
A Level Mathematics Student Book 2, Chapter 5	You should be able to use the factor theorem to find factors of polynomials.	8	$f(x) = 2x^3 - x^2 - 18x + 9$ a Show that $(x - 3)$ is a factor of $f(x)$. b Express $f(x)$ as a product of linear factors.
Further Mathematics Student Book 1, Chapter 8	You should know how to find invariant lines for a linear transformation.	9	Transformation T is given by matrix $\begin{pmatrix} 6 & 2 \\ 5 & -3 \end{pmatrix}$. Find any invariant lines under transformation T and determine whether any are a line of invariant points.

Further uses of matrices

In Further Mathematics Student Book 1, Chapters 7 and 8, you learnt about matrices and how to use them to solve equations and represent linear transformations. You can extend the ideas of determinants and inverses to 3×3 matrices and then use them to solve systems of three linear equations. Such systems have many applications, including solving problems about planes, which you met in Chapter 5.

The idea of invariant lines (lines that are mapped to themselves by a transformation) leads to the concept of eigenvectors and eigenvalues. You will learn how to use these to find a diagonalised form of a matrix, but they have many other uses beyond the scope of this course.

> **Focus on...**
>
> Matrices have applications in many other situations. See Focus on... Modelling 1 for an application in biology.

Section 1: Transposes and inverses

Transposes

You met the idea of transposes in your previous study of matrices. The **transpose** of a matrix is formed by swapping its rows and columns. There are some rules associated with transposes that you might find useful.

> **Key point 6.1**
>
> The transpose of a matrix obeys these rules:
> - $(\mathbf{AB})^T = \mathbf{B}^T \mathbf{A}^T$
> - $(\mathbf{A} + \mathbf{B})^T = \mathbf{A}^T + \mathbf{B}^T$

Determinant of a 3×3 matrix

There are several ways to calculate the determinant of a 3×3 matrix. Here you will learn the standard method, which can be extended for calculating the determinant of a square matrix of any size.

> **Rewind**
>
> You saw how to find the determinant of a 2×2 matrix in Further Mathematics Student Book 1, Chapter 7.

First you need a few concepts and terms that will make the calculation easier.

- For each element of the matrix, the **submatrix** is what remains when you delete that element's row and column.

  So for matrix $\mathbf{A} = \begin{pmatrix} a_{11} & a_{12} & a_{13} \\ a_{21} & a_{22} & a_{23} \\ a_{31} & a_{32} & a_{33} \end{pmatrix}$, the submatrix of element a_{12} is the 2×2 matrix $\begin{pmatrix} a_{21} & a_{23} \\ a_{31} & a_{33} \end{pmatrix}$, which you find by deleting row 1 and column 2 from the original matrix.

- You call the determinant of the submatrix of element a_{12} the **minor** of element a_{12}.

- The **cofactor** c_{ij} for element a_{ij} is equal to its minor multiplied by $(-1)^{i+j}$. It can help to envisage this power change as a checkerboard pattern of signs.

  The 3×3 sign change matrix $(-1)^{i+j}$ looks like this: $\begin{pmatrix} + & - & + \\ - & + & - \\ + & - & + \end{pmatrix}$

- Finally, to find the determinant of a matrix, select any row or column and total the product of each element and its cofactor. It does not matter which row or column you choose, the value will be the same.

Key point 6.2

To find the determinant of a 3×3 matrix $\mathbf{A}$:

- select a row or column
- for each element a_{ij} in that row or column, calculate the cofactor c_{ij}
- the determinant is the sum of the products $a_{ij}c_{ij}$ for the row or column selected.

You will most often expand along the first row, giving this rule:

$$\det \begin{pmatrix} a_{11} & a_{12} & a_{13} \\ a_{21} & a_{22} & a_{23} \\ a_{31} & a_{32} & a_{33} \end{pmatrix} = a_{11}\begin{vmatrix} a_{22} & a_{23} \\ a_{32} & a_{33} \end{vmatrix} - a_{12}\begin{vmatrix} a_{21} & a_{23} \\ a_{31} & a_{33} \end{vmatrix} + a_{13}\begin{vmatrix} a_{21} & a_{22} \\ a_{31} & a_{32} \end{vmatrix}$$

> **Tip**
>
> If the matrix has an unknown, expand along the row or column containing the unknown.

However, if the first row doesn't contain a zero but another row or column does, then choose the one that does to expand along. This will make the calculation easier.

WORKED EXAMPLE 6.1

Find the determinant of matrix $\mathbf{A} = \begin{pmatrix} 1 & 2 & 0 \\ 2 & -1 & 3 \\ -2 & 0 & 1 \end{pmatrix}$.

$\mathbf{A} = \begin{pmatrix} 1 & 2 & 0 \\ 2 & -1 & 3 \\ -2 & 0 & 1 \end{pmatrix}$ — Select a row or column, ideally containing at least one zero, to simplify the calculation.

Continues on next page

A Level Further Mathematics for AQA Student Book 2

Expanding about the first row:

$$\det A = +1 \times \begin{vmatrix} -1 & 3 \\ 0 & 1 \end{vmatrix}$$
$$-2 \times \begin{vmatrix} 2 & 3 \\ -2 & 1 \end{vmatrix}$$
$$+0 \times \begin{vmatrix} 2 & -1 \\ -2 & 0 \end{vmatrix}$$
$$= +1 \times (-1) - 2 \times 8 + 0 \times (-2)$$
$$= -17$$

For each element in the top row, multiply by the sign change $(-1)^{i+j}$ and then by the determinant of its submatrix.

Tip

You are permitted to use a calculator to find determinants (and inverses) of numerical 3×3 matrices. You are expected to know how to calculate by hand as well, in the event of non-numerical entries.

You can always check your answer on a calculator by substituting one or more trial values for any unknowns and checking that your formula matches the numerical output from your calculator!

Rewind

Remember from Further Mathematics Student Book 1, Chapter 7, that a matrix that has a zero determinant is said to be singular.

WORKED EXAMPLE 6.2

Find the value of a for which matrix $\mathbf{A} = \begin{pmatrix} 1 & 2 & 0 \\ 2 & a & 3 \\ -2 & 0 & 1 \end{pmatrix}$ is singular.

Using the middle column:

$$\mathbf{A} = \begin{pmatrix} 1 & 2 & 0 \\ 2 & a & 3 \\ -2 & 0 & 1 \end{pmatrix}$$

Select a row or column containing that unknown to minimise working.

The centre column also contains a zero so is the easiest option.

$$\det A = -2 \times \begin{vmatrix} 2 & 3 \\ -2 & 1 \end{vmatrix}$$
$$+a \times \begin{vmatrix} 1 & 0 \\ -2 & 1 \end{vmatrix}$$
$$-0 \times \begin{vmatrix} 1 & 0 \\ 2 & 3 \end{vmatrix}$$
$$= -2 \times 8 + a \times 1 - 0 \times 3$$
$$= a - 16$$

For each element in the centre column, multiply by the sign change $(-1)^{i+j}$ and then by the determinant of its submatrix.

For $\mathbf{A}$ to be singular, $\det A = 0$, so $a = 16$.

As you learned in Further Mathematics Student Book 1, Chapter 8, the determinant of a 2×2 matrix gives the area scale factor of the linear transformation it describes. The determinant of a 3×3 matrix gives the volume scale factor of the transformation, where a negative determinant indicates that the orientation of the object is reversed by the transformation.

6 Further matrices

🔑 Key point 6.3

For a linear transformation in three dimensions defined by a 3×3 matrix **T**:

- for an object A with volume V, the image of A under **T** will have volume $V |\det \mathbf{T}|$
- if $\det \mathbf{T}$ is negative, the transformation involves a reflection so that an object and its image have opposite orientations.

The inverse of a 3×3 matrix

For the inverse, you now have to calculate cofactors for each of the nine elements, and assemble these into a **cofactor matrix** $\mathbf{C} = \begin{pmatrix} c_{11} & c_{12} & c_{13} \\ c_{21} & c_{22} & c_{23} \\ c_{31} & c_{32} & c_{33} \end{pmatrix}$.

For a non-singular matrix **A**, the inverse $\mathbf{A}^{-1}$ equals the transpose of the cofactor matrix, multiplied by the reciprocal of the determinant of **A**.

> ⏪ **Rewind**
>
> You saw how to find the inverse of a 2×2 matrix in Further Mathematics Student Book 1, Chapter 7.

🔑 Key point 6.4

For non-singular matrix **A**, where **C** is the matrix of cofactors of **A**,

$$\mathbf{A}^{-1} = \frac{1}{\det \mathbf{A}} \mathbf{C}^{\mathrm{T}}$$

WORKED EXAMPLE 6.3

Find the inverse of non-singular matrix $\mathbf{A} = \begin{pmatrix} 1 & 4 & -1 \\ 2 & 4 & -3 \\ -2 & 1 & 1 \end{pmatrix}$.

The matrix of cofactors:

$\mathbf{C} = \begin{pmatrix} +\begin{vmatrix} 4 & -3 \\ 1 & 1 \end{vmatrix} & -\begin{vmatrix} 2 & -3 \\ -2 & 1 \end{vmatrix} & +\begin{vmatrix} 2 & 4 \\ -2 & 1 \end{vmatrix} \\ -\begin{vmatrix} 4 & -1 \\ 1 & 1 \end{vmatrix} & +\begin{vmatrix} 1 & -1 \\ -2 & 1 \end{vmatrix} & -\begin{vmatrix} 1 & 4 \\ -2 & 1 \end{vmatrix} \\ +\begin{vmatrix} 4 & -1 \\ 4 & -3 \end{vmatrix} & -\begin{vmatrix} 1 & -1 \\ 2 & -3 \end{vmatrix} & +\begin{vmatrix} 1 & 4 \\ 2 & 4 \end{vmatrix} \end{pmatrix}$

$= \begin{pmatrix} 7 & 4 & 10 \\ -5 & -1 & -9 \\ -8 & 1 & -4 \end{pmatrix}$

For each cofactor, find the determinant of the relevant submatrix and apply the sign-change $(-1)^{i+j}$.

$\mathbf{C}^{\mathrm{T}} = \begin{pmatrix} 7 & -5 & -8 \\ 4 & -1 & 1 \\ 10 & -9 & -4 \end{pmatrix}$

Write down $\mathbf{C}^{\mathrm{T}}$.

The determinant of **A** equals any lead diagonal element of $\mathbf{AC}^{\mathrm{T}}$:

$\det \mathbf{A} = 1 \times 7 + 4 \times 4 - 1 \times 10$
$\qquad = 13$

$\mathbf{AC}^{\mathrm{T}} = (\det \mathbf{A})\mathbf{I}$, so calculate the upper left element of $\mathbf{AC}^{\mathrm{T}}$ to find $\det \mathbf{A}$.

$\mathbf{A}^{-1} = \frac{1}{13}\mathbf{C}^{\mathrm{T}} = \frac{1}{13}\begin{pmatrix} 7 & -5 & -8 \\ 4 & -1 & 1 \\ 10 & -9 & -4 \end{pmatrix}$

WORKED EXAMPLE 6.4

$\mathbf{M} = \begin{pmatrix} 2 & 1 & 4 \\ -1 & 0 & a \\ 2 & 2 & -2 \end{pmatrix}$ is a non-singular matrix. Find the possible values for a and give $\mathbf{M}^{-1}$ in terms of a.

The matrix of cofactors:

$\mathbf{C} = \begin{pmatrix} +\begin{vmatrix} 0 & a \\ 2 & -2 \end{vmatrix} & -\begin{vmatrix} -1 & a \\ 2 & -2 \end{vmatrix} & +\begin{vmatrix} -1 & 0 \\ 2 & 2 \end{vmatrix} \\ -\begin{vmatrix} 1 & 4 \\ 2 & -2 \end{vmatrix} & +\begin{vmatrix} 2 & 4 \\ 2 & -2 \end{vmatrix} & -\begin{vmatrix} 2 & 1 \\ 2 & 2 \end{vmatrix} \\ +\begin{vmatrix} 1 & 4 \\ 0 & a \end{vmatrix} & -\begin{vmatrix} 2 & 4 \\ -1 & a \end{vmatrix} & +\begin{vmatrix} 2 & 1 \\ -1 & 0 \end{vmatrix} \end{pmatrix}$

> Rather than working out the determinant first to find the possible values of a, you can move straight to finding the inverse in terms of a and calculate the determinant in the course of the calculations. For each cofactor, find the determinant of the relevant submatrix and apply the sign-change $(-1)^{i+j}$.

$= \begin{pmatrix} -2a & 2a-2 & -2 \\ 10 & -12 & -2 \\ a & -2a-4 & 1 \end{pmatrix}$

$\mathbf{C}^T = \begin{pmatrix} -2a & 10 & a \\ 2a-2 & -12 & -2a-4 \\ -2 & -2 & 1 \end{pmatrix}$

> Write down $\mathbf{C}^T$.

The determinant of $\mathbf{M}$ equals any lead diagonal element of $\mathbf{MC}^T$:

> $\mathbf{MC}^T = (\det \mathbf{M})\mathbf{I}$, so calculate the upper left element of $\mathbf{MC}^T$ to find $\det \mathbf{M}$.

$\det \mathbf{M} = 2 \times (-2a) + 1 \times (2a-2) + 4 \times (-2)$
$= -10 - 2a$

> For $\mathbf{M}$ to be non-singular, $\det \mathbf{M} \neq 0$.

So $\mathbf{M}$ is non-singular for $a \neq -5$.

$\mathbf{M}^{-1} = \dfrac{1}{-10-2a} \mathbf{C}^T = \dfrac{1}{2a+10} \begin{pmatrix} 2a & -10 & -a \\ 2-2a & 12 & 2a+4 \\ 2 & 2 & -1 \end{pmatrix}$

Tip

Even with a matrix containing an unknown, you can still use your calculator. Assign to a the value 0.01 and then calculate $\det \mathbf{A}$ and $(\det \mathbf{A})\mathbf{A}^{-1}$. Since all the other elements are integers, multiples and powers of a should be easy to read off from the display, as long as the coefficients are less than 100.

However, you will be expected to answer any question of this form showing full working, so you can only use your calculator to check your working.

EXERCISE 6A

1 Write down the transpose of each matrix.

a i $\begin{pmatrix} 1 & 2 \\ 1 & 3 \end{pmatrix}$ **ii** $\begin{pmatrix} 1 & 5 \\ 2 & 3 \\ 1 & -3 \end{pmatrix}$ **b i** $\begin{pmatrix} 2 & 6 & 0 \\ 4 & 1 & 0 \end{pmatrix}$ **ii** $\begin{pmatrix} 1 & 2 & -4 \\ 8 & -3 & 3 \\ -1 & 7 & 22 \\ -5 & -2 & 0 \end{pmatrix}$

6 Further matrices

2 Find the determinant of each matrix.

a i $\begin{pmatrix} 1 & 3 & 2 \\ 2 & 4 & 0 \\ 5 & -3 & 0 \end{pmatrix}$ ii $\begin{pmatrix} 1 & 0 & -2 \\ 2 & 2 & -3 \\ 1 & -4 & 0 \end{pmatrix}$ b i $\begin{pmatrix} 3 & 1 & -4 \\ -5 & 1 & 0 \\ 1 & -2 & 6 \end{pmatrix}$ ii $\begin{pmatrix} 2 & 4 & 1 \\ 1 & 2 & 6 \\ -3 & -6 & 8 \end{pmatrix}$

c i $\begin{pmatrix} 2 & a & 1 \\ -2 & 1 & 1 \\ 3 & 0 & 2 \end{pmatrix}$ ii $\begin{pmatrix} 3 & b & 2 \\ -4 & 2 & -3 \\ 0 & 1 & -1 \end{pmatrix}$ d i $\begin{pmatrix} c & 1 & -1 \\ 2 & 7 & c \\ 1 & -3 & 2 \end{pmatrix}$ ii $\begin{pmatrix} 2 & 0 & d \\ -3 & 2 & 5 \\ 1 & d & -1 \end{pmatrix}$

3 Find the inverse of each non-singular matrix in Question 2.

4 By considering $A = \begin{pmatrix} 2 & -8 \\ 4 & 3 \end{pmatrix}$, $B = \begin{pmatrix} -6 & 2 \\ 1 & 5 \end{pmatrix}$, demonstrate that:

a $(\mathbf{AB})^T = \mathbf{B}^T\mathbf{A}^T$

b $(\mathbf{A}+\mathbf{B})^T = \mathbf{A}^T + \mathbf{B}^T$.

5 Find all possible values of k for which $\begin{pmatrix} 1 & k & 0 \\ 2 & -3 & k \\ 1 & k & 2 \end{pmatrix}$ is singular.

6 Find all possible solutions for $\det \begin{pmatrix} x & 6 & -9 \\ 2 & 4 & x \\ -1 & -2 & 3 \end{pmatrix} = 0$.

7 Prove that $(\mathbf{AB})^T = \mathbf{B}^T\mathbf{A}^T$ if $\mathbf{A}$ and $\mathbf{B}$ are 2×2 square matrices.

8 Matrices $\mathbf{A}$ and $\mathbf{B}$ are given by $\mathbf{A} = \begin{pmatrix} a & 2 & 3 \\ 0 & 4 & 1 \\ 1 & 1 & 2 \end{pmatrix}$ and $\mathbf{B} = \begin{pmatrix} 1 & -2 & b \\ 3 & 0 & 1 \\ 0 & 2 & 1 \end{pmatrix}$.

Given that both $\mathbf{A}+\mathbf{B}$ and $\mathbf{A}-\mathbf{B}$ are singular, find the values of a and b.

9 Matrices $\mathbf{A}$ and $\mathbf{B}$ are given by $\mathbf{A} = \begin{pmatrix} 1 & k & 0 \\ 3 & 1 & 4 \\ -1 & 3 & -2 \end{pmatrix}$ and $\mathbf{B} = \begin{pmatrix} -2 & k & -5 \\ -2 & 0 & -3 \\ k & 1 & 2 \end{pmatrix}$.

a Find each of $\det \mathbf{A}$ and $\det \mathbf{B}$ in terms of k.

b Without finding $\mathbf{AB}$, determine all values of k for which $\mathbf{AB}$ is singular.

10 Matrix $\mathbf{M}$ is given by $\mathbf{M} = \begin{pmatrix} 2 & -1 & -1 \\ 1 & 3 & 1 \\ 1 & 2 & 2 \end{pmatrix}$.

a Find $\det \mathbf{M}$.

b A three-dimensional object A with volume 2.5 cm^3 is transformed by a linear transformation with matrix $\mathbf{T}$. Write down the volume of the image of A when:

i $\mathbf{T} = \mathbf{M}$

ii $\mathbf{T} = \mathbf{A}^{-1}\mathbf{M}\mathbf{A}$ for some non-singular matrix $\mathbf{A}$

iii $\mathbf{T} = \mathbf{MB}^2$ where $\mathbf{B}$ is a 3×3 matrix with determinant 0.2.

A Level Further Mathematics for AQA Student Book 2

11 Transformation T is defined by matrix $\mathbf{M} = \begin{pmatrix} 1 & 1 & -4 \\ 2 & 3 & 0 \\ 1 & 0 & -2 \end{pmatrix}$.

The image of point A under transformation T has coordinates $(1, 1, 7)$. Find the coordinates of A.

12 Transformation T is given by matrix $\mathbf{M}$ where $\mathbf{M} = \begin{pmatrix} 2 & 1 & p \\ 3 & -2 & 1 \\ q & 4 & -1 \end{pmatrix}$.

a Given $\mathbf{M}^{-1} = \dfrac{1}{8}\begin{pmatrix} -2 & 5 & 3 \\ 2 & -1 & 1 \\ r & 1-r & 3-r \end{pmatrix}$, find p, q and r.

b Given that T maps point A to $(1, 1, -1)$, find the coordinates of A.

13 Two invertible transformations $\mathbf{A}$ and $\mathbf{B}$ are defined by matrices $\mathbf{A} = \begin{pmatrix} 1 & a & 2 \\ 0 & 3 & 1 \\ 2 & 2 & 1 \end{pmatrix}$ and $\mathbf{B} = \begin{pmatrix} 0 & 4 & b \\ 1 & 1 & 2 \\ 1 & 2 & -1 \end{pmatrix}$.

Point C has image $(-2, 1, 8)$ under both matrices.

Find a, b and the coordinates of point C.

14 An orthogonal matrix is defined as a matrix $\mathbf{M}$ satisfying $\mathbf{M}\mathbf{M}^T = \mathbf{I}$. Prove that if $\mathbf{A}$ and $\mathbf{B}$ are orthogonal matrices, then so is $\mathbf{AB}$.

Section 2: Row and column operations

You have seen how you can use matrices to solve simultaneous equations. You know that swapping the two equations doesn't change the solution – this is an example of a **row operation**.

There are three elementary row operations that you can perform on a matrix:

- swapping two rows
- multiplying a row by a non-zero constant
- adding a non-zero multiple of one row to another row.

There are three equivalent types of column operations, and all the results shown here for row operations apply equally when considering columns instead of rows.

> **Rewind**
>
> See Further Mathematics Student Book 1, Chapter 7, for a reminder of solving simultaneous equations using 2×2 matrices.

Key point 6.5

If matrix $\mathbf{N}$ is obtained from matrix $\mathbf{M}$ by:

- swapping two rows (or two columns), then $\det \mathbf{N} = -\det \mathbf{M}$
- multiplying one row (or one column) by constant k, then $\det \mathbf{N} = k \det \mathbf{M}$
- adding a multiple of one row to another row (or a multiple of one column to another column), then $\det \mathbf{N} = \det \mathbf{M}$.

6 Further matrices

For example, if you start from the matrix **M**:

$$\mathbf{M} = \begin{pmatrix} 1 & 2 & 3 \\ 4 & 5 & 6 \\ 2 & 4 & 8 \end{pmatrix}$$

you can form a new matrix **N** by adding -2 lots of the top row to the bottom row, getting:

$$\mathbf{N} = \begin{pmatrix} 1 & 2 & 3 \\ 4 & 5 & 6 \\ 2-2\times 1 & 4-2\times 2 & 8-2\times 3 \end{pmatrix} = \begin{pmatrix} 1 & 2 & 3 \\ 4 & 5 & 6 \\ 0 & 0 & 2 \end{pmatrix}$$

Matrix **N** will be much easier to work with because it has a row with two zeros.

You can use the property of determinants that $\det(\mathbf{AB}) = \det \mathbf{A} \times \det \mathbf{B}$ to prove the results in Key point 6.5.

PROOF 3

Each of these three row operations is equivalent to multiplying the original matrix by a matrix **T**, where **T** is formed from the identity matrix by performing the desired operation. Left-multiplication by **T** mimics a row operation and right-multiplication by **T** mimics a column operation.

Swapping two rows

Swapping the first and second row of a matrix is the same as left-multiplying it by $\begin{pmatrix} 0 & 1 & 0 \\ 1 & 0 & 0 \\ 0 & 0 & 1 \end{pmatrix}$.

$$\begin{pmatrix} 0 & 1 & 0 \\ 1 & 0 & 0 \\ 0 & 0 & 1 \end{pmatrix} \begin{pmatrix} a_{11} & a_{12} & a_{13} \\ a_{21} & a_{22} & a_{23} \\ a_{31} & a_{32} & a_{33} \end{pmatrix} = \begin{pmatrix} a_{21} & a_{22} & a_{23} \\ a_{11} & a_{12} & a_{13} \\ a_{31} & a_{32} & a_{33} \end{pmatrix}$$

So if **N** is formed by swapping two rows of **M**, $\mathbf{N} = \mathbf{RM}$ for some reflection **R**.
Therefore, $\det \mathbf{N} = \det \mathbf{R} \times \det \mathbf{M} = -\det \mathbf{M}$

> As you know from Further Mathematics Student Book 1, Chapter 8, the matrix $\begin{pmatrix} 0 & 1 & 0 \\ 1 & 0 & 0 \\ 0 & 0 & 1 \end{pmatrix}$ represents a reflection through the plane $y = x$, and so has determinant -1; each of the other row swaps can be similarly represented by a reflection.

Multiplying a row by a non-zero constant

Multiplying the third row of a matrix by a non-zero constant k is the same as left-multiplying it by $\begin{pmatrix} 1 & 0 & 0 \\ 0 & 1 & 0 \\ 0 & 0 & k \end{pmatrix}$:

$$\begin{pmatrix} 1 & 0 & 0 \\ 0 & 1 & 0 \\ 0 & 0 & k \end{pmatrix} \begin{pmatrix} a_{11} & a_{12} & a_{13} \\ a_{21} & a_{22} & a_{23} \\ a_{31} & a_{32} & a_{33} \end{pmatrix} = \begin{pmatrix} a_{11} & a_{12} & a_{13} \\ a_{21} & a_{22} & a_{23} \\ ka_{31} & ka_{32} & ka_{33} \end{pmatrix}$$

So if **N** is formed by multiplying a row of **M** by a non-zero constant k, $\mathbf{N} = \mathbf{SM}$ for some stretch **S**.
Therefore, $\det \mathbf{N} = \det \mathbf{S} \times \det \mathbf{M} = k \det \mathbf{M}$

> As you know from Further Mathematics Student Book 1, Chapter 8, the matrix $\begin{pmatrix} 1 & 0 & 0 \\ 0 & 1 & 0 \\ 0 & 0 & k \end{pmatrix}$ represents a stretch in the z-direction, and has determinant k.

Continues on next page

Adding a non-zero multiple of one row to another row

Adding k lots of the third row to the second row of a matrix is the same as left-multiplying it by $\begin{pmatrix} 1 & 0 & 0 \\ 0 & 1 & k \\ 0 & 0 & 1 \end{pmatrix}$:

The matrix $\begin{pmatrix} 1 & 0 & 0 \\ 0 & 1 & k \\ 0 & 0 & 1 \end{pmatrix}$ represents a transformation that you have not encountered in three dimensions, a shear in the planes perpendicular to the x-axis, and has determinant 1.

$$\begin{pmatrix} 1 & 0 & 0 \\ 0 & 1 & k \\ 0 & 0 & 1 \end{pmatrix} \begin{pmatrix} a_{11} & a_{12} & a_{13} \\ a_{21} & a_{22} & a_{23} \\ a_{31} & a_{32} & a_{33} \end{pmatrix} = \begin{pmatrix} a_{11} & a_{12} & a_{13} \\ a_{21}+ka_{31} & a_{22}+ka_{32} & a_{23}+ka_{33} \\ a_{31} & a_{32} & a_{33} \end{pmatrix}$$

So if **N** is formed by adding a multiple of one row of **M** to another row, **N = VM** for some shear **V**.
Therefore, $\det \mathbf{N} = \det \mathbf{V} \times \det \mathbf{M} = \det \mathbf{M}$

Using row and column operations to factorise determinants

You can use these properties of row and column operations to deduce the results shown here; you can use the shorthand R_i for the ith row and C_i for the ith column to keep the notation simple.

- If every element of a row (or column) has a common factor, the determinant of the matrix can be factorised by dividing through by that factor.

  For example:
  $$\det \begin{pmatrix} 2 & 5 & 4 \\ 2 & 9 & 2 \\ 3 & 9 & 6 \end{pmatrix} = 3 \det \begin{pmatrix} 2 & 5 & 4 \\ 2 & 9 & 2 \\ 1 & 3 & 2 \end{pmatrix} \text{ taking a factor of 3 from } R_3$$

  $$= 6 \det \begin{pmatrix} 2 & 5 & 2 \\ 2 & 9 & 1 \\ 1 & 3 & 1 \end{pmatrix} \text{ taking a factor of 2 from } C_3$$

- A matrix with a row (or column) equal to a multiple of another row (or column) must be singular.

  For example: $\det \begin{pmatrix} 1 & 4 & 2 \\ 3 & -1 & 2 \\ 2 & 8 & 4 \end{pmatrix} = 0$ because $R_3 = 2R_1$ so you could use

  the row operation $R_3 - 2R_1$ to form a matrix with a row of zeros.

WORKED EXAMPLE 6.5

Factorise completely $\det \begin{pmatrix} x & y & z \\ x^2 & y^2 & z^2 \\ x^3 & y^3 & z^3 \end{pmatrix}$.

$\det \begin{pmatrix} x & y & z \\ x^2 & y^2 & z^2 \\ x^3 & y^3 & z^3 \end{pmatrix}$

Rather than calculating the determinant immediately, use row and column operations to simplify the calculation.

Continues on next page

$$= xyz \det \begin{pmatrix} 1 & 1 & 1 \\ x & y & z \\ x^2 & y^2 & z^2 \end{pmatrix}$$ .... Factorise x from C_1, y from C_2 and z from C_3.

$$= xyz \det \begin{pmatrix} 1 & 0 & 0 \\ x & y-x & z-x \\ x^2 & y^2-x^2 & z^2-x^2 \end{pmatrix}$$ .... Column operations:
$C_2 \to C_2 - C_1$
$C_3 \to C_3 - C_1$

$$= xyz \begin{vmatrix} y-x & z-x \\ y^2-x^2 & z^2-x^2 \end{vmatrix}$$ .... Calculate the determinant, expanding through R_1.

$$= xyz\,(y-x)(z-x) \begin{vmatrix} 1 & 1 \\ y+x & z+x \end{vmatrix}$$ .... Factorise $(y-x)$ from C_1 and $(z-x)$ from C_2.

$$= xyz\,(y-x)(z-x)(z-y)$$ .... Calculate the determinant.

$$= xyz\,(x-y)(y-z)(z-x)$$ .... Rearrange for symmetry.

It is important to notice that in Worked example 6.5, the repeated pattern through x, y and z must inevitably lead to a similarly consistent pattern cycle in the determinant.

Sometimes symmetry in the matrix can help in finding the factorised form of a determinant. For example, if two rows are identical when $a = b$, then subtracting these two rows would produce a row of zeros when $a = b$. You could then use the factor theorem to deduce that $(a - b)$ is a factor of the determinant.

WORKED EXAMPLE 6.6

a Show that $(a-b)$ is a factor of $\mathbf{D} = \begin{vmatrix} 1 & a & bc \\ 1 & b & ac \\ 1 & c & ab \end{vmatrix}$.

b Factorise $\mathbf{D}$ completely into linear factors.

a Replacing the top row with the difference of the two rows:

$$\mathbf{D} = \begin{vmatrix} 0 & a-b & -c(a-b) \\ 1 & b & ac \\ 1 & c & ab \end{vmatrix}$$

.... Since the top two rows are equal when $a = b$, their difference is useful to consider. Factorising it highlights the factor of $(a-b)$. From Key point 6.5 this operation does not change the value of $\mathbf{D}$.

$$= (a-b) \begin{vmatrix} 0 & 1 & -c \\ 1 & b & ac \\ 1 & c & ab \end{vmatrix}$$

.... Use Key point 6.5 to take out to factor of $(a-b)$.

b $$\mathbf{D} = (a-b) \begin{vmatrix} 0 & 1 & -c \\ 0 & b-c & -a(b-c) \\ 1 & c & ab \end{vmatrix}$$

.... Use $R_2 \to R_2 - R_3$.

Continues on next page

$$= (a-b)(b-c)\begin{vmatrix} 0 & 1 & -c \\ 0 & 1 & -a \\ 1 & c & ab \end{vmatrix}$$ .... Take out a factor from the middle row.

$$= (a-b)(b-c)\begin{vmatrix} 0 & 1 & -c \\ 0 & 0 & c-a \\ 1 & c & ab \end{vmatrix}$$ .... You can use $R_2 \to R_2 - R_1$.

$$= (a-b)(b-c)(c-a)\begin{vmatrix} 0 & 1 & -c \\ 0 & 0 & 1 \\ 1 & c & ab \end{vmatrix}$$ .... Take out a factor from the middle row.

$$= (a-b)(b-c)(c-a)\left(0 - 0 + 1\begin{vmatrix} 1 & -c \\ 0 & 1 \end{vmatrix}\right)$$ .... Expand the determinant along the first column.

$$= (a-b)(b-c)(c-a)$$ .... Since the 2×2 determinant equals 1.

WORK IT OUT 6.1

Find the determinant of $\begin{pmatrix} x & x & 0 \\ 0 & x & x \\ x & 0 & x \end{pmatrix}$.

Which is the correct solution? Identify the errors made in the incorrect solutions.

Solution 1	Using your calculator to find the determinant with numerical matrix: $\begin{vmatrix} x & x & 0 \\ 0 & x & x \\ x & 0 & x \end{vmatrix} = x \begin{vmatrix} 1 & 1 & 0 \\ 0 & 1 & 1 \\ 1 & 0 & 1 \end{vmatrix} = x(2) = 2x$
Solution 2	Subtracting row 3 from row 1 and expanding along the first column: $\begin{vmatrix} x & x & 0 \\ 0 & x & x \\ x & 0 & x \end{vmatrix} = \begin{vmatrix} 0 & x & -x \\ 0 & x & x \\ x & 0 & x \end{vmatrix} = 0 - 0 + x(x^2 - -x^2) = 2x^3$
Solution 3	$\det\begin{pmatrix} x & x & 0 \\ 0 & x & x \\ x & 0 & x \end{pmatrix} = x(x^2 - 0) + x(0 - x^2) + 0(0 - x^2) = x^3 - x^3 = 0$

Using the determinant to calculate a vector product

You learned in Chapter 5, Section 1, how to calculate the vector product using the formula

$$\mathbf{a} \times \mathbf{b} = \begin{pmatrix} a_1 \\ a_2 \\ a_3 \end{pmatrix} \times \begin{pmatrix} b_1 \\ b_2 \\ b_3 \end{pmatrix} = \begin{pmatrix} a_2 b_3 - a_3 b_2 \\ a_3 b_1 - a_1 b_3 \\ a_1 b_2 - a_2 b_1 \end{pmatrix}.$$

If the vectors **a** and **b** are written as sums of the unit vectors **i**, **j** and **k**, then you can also express the vector product using determinant notation.

6 Further matrices

Key point 6.6

If $\mathbf{a} = a_1\mathbf{i} + a_2\mathbf{j} + a_3\mathbf{k}$ and $\mathbf{b} = b_1\mathbf{i} + b_2\mathbf{j} + b_3\mathbf{k}$, then

$$\mathbf{a} \times \mathbf{b} = \det\begin{pmatrix} \mathbf{i} & a_1 & b_1 \\ \mathbf{j} & a_2 & b_2 \\ \mathbf{k} & a_3 & b_3 \end{pmatrix}.$$

This result will be given in your formula book.

Since the result in Key point 6.6 is a determinant, you can use column operations to simplify the determinant before calculating.

WORKED EXAMPLE 6.7

Vectors **a** and **b** are given by $\mathbf{a} = \mathbf{i} + 2\mathbf{j} - 4\mathbf{k}$ and $\mathbf{b} = -6\mathbf{i} + 3\mathbf{j} + \mathbf{k}$.

Find $\mathbf{a} \times \mathbf{b}$.

$\mathbf{a} \times \mathbf{b} = \det\begin{pmatrix} \mathbf{i} & 1 & -6 \\ \mathbf{j} & 2 & 3 \\ \mathbf{k} & -4 & 1 \end{pmatrix}$ 　Use $\mathbf{a} \times \mathbf{b} = \det\begin{pmatrix} \mathbf{i} & a_1 & b_1 \\ \mathbf{j} & a_2 & b_2 \\ \mathbf{k} & a_3 & b_3 \end{pmatrix}$.

$= \mathbf{i}\begin{vmatrix} 2 & 3 \\ -4 & 1 \end{vmatrix} - \mathbf{j}\begin{vmatrix} 1 & -6 \\ -4 & 1 \end{vmatrix} + \mathbf{k}\begin{vmatrix} 1 & -6 \\ 2 & 3 \end{vmatrix}$ 　Expand along the first column.

$= 14\mathbf{i} + 23\mathbf{j} + 15\mathbf{k}$

EXERCISE 6B

1 Factorise each determinant completely.

a i $\begin{vmatrix} x & 2 & 3 \\ x^2 & 4 & 9 \\ x^4 & 16 & 81 \end{vmatrix}$　　**ii** $\begin{vmatrix} a+b & a^2+b^2 & a^3+b^3 \\ 2 & 2 & 2 \\ 4 & 8 & 16 \end{vmatrix}$

b i $\begin{vmatrix} x & xy & xyz \\ xy & xy^2 & xy^2z \\ xyz & xy^2z & xy^2z^2 \end{vmatrix}$　　**ii** $\begin{vmatrix} x & y & z \\ x+1 & y+1 & z+1 \\ x+3 & y+3 & z+3 \end{vmatrix}$

c i $\begin{vmatrix} 1 & 1 & 1 \\ 1 & \sin t & \cos t \\ 1 & \sin^2 t & \cos^2 t \end{vmatrix}$　　**ii** $\begin{vmatrix} 1 & a & bc \\ 1 & b & ac \\ 1 & c & ab \end{vmatrix}$

2 Use $\mathbf{a} \times \mathbf{b} = \det\begin{pmatrix} \mathbf{i} & a_1 & b_1 \\ \mathbf{j} & a_2 & b_2 \\ \mathbf{k} & a_3 & b_3 \end{pmatrix}$ to find the vector product $\mathbf{a} \times \mathbf{b}$ for the given vectors.

a i $\mathbf{a} = \begin{pmatrix} 3 \\ 1 \\ -2 \end{pmatrix}, \mathbf{b} = \begin{pmatrix} 1 \\ 5 \\ 3 \end{pmatrix}$　　**ii** $\mathbf{a} = \begin{pmatrix} -3 \\ 2 \\ -4 \end{pmatrix}, \mathbf{b} = \begin{pmatrix} -1 \\ 2 \\ 7 \end{pmatrix}$

b i $\mathbf{a} = -3\mathbf{i} + \mathbf{j} + 2\mathbf{k}, \mathbf{b} = 2\mathbf{i} - \mathbf{k}$　　**ii** $\mathbf{a} = 5\mathbf{i} + 2\mathbf{j} + 3\mathbf{k}, \mathbf{b} = -\mathbf{i} - \mathbf{j} - 4\mathbf{k}$

3 By using suitable row and column operations, show that each of these matrices is singular.

a **i** $\begin{pmatrix} 2 & 5 & 7 \\ 3 & 4 & -2 \\ 8 & 13 & 3 \end{pmatrix}$ **ii** $\begin{pmatrix} -1 & 3 & -5 \\ 2 & -2 & 4 \\ 5 & 1 & 1 \end{pmatrix}$ **b** **i** $\begin{pmatrix} a & b & c \\ b & a & c \\ a+c & b-c & c \end{pmatrix}$ **ii** $\begin{pmatrix} x & y & z \\ yz & xz & xy \\ (yz)^{-1} & (xz)^{-1} & (xy)^{-1} \end{pmatrix}$

4 Matrix **A** is given by $\begin{pmatrix} a & 3 & 6 \\ 2 & -4 & 8 \\ 1 & 7 & 1-a \end{pmatrix}$.

  a Show that **A** is singular if $a = 3$.

  b Calculate det **A** in terms of a.

5 Matrix **M** is given by $\begin{pmatrix} 2 & 4 & 8 \\ x & x^2 & x^3 \\ y & y^2 & y^3 \end{pmatrix}$.

  a Explain why the structure of the matrix shows that these must be factors of the determinant of **M**:

  i x **ii** $(x-y)$ **iii** $(x-2)$.

  b Find the determinant of **M**, factorising your answer as far as possible.

6 Matrix **M** and **N** are given by $\mathbf{M} = \begin{pmatrix} a & b & c \\ d & e & f \\ g & h & i \end{pmatrix}$ and $\mathbf{N} = \begin{pmatrix} a+bk & b & c \\ d+ek & e & f \\ g+hk & h & i \end{pmatrix}$.

  a Define the column operation which converts **M** to **N**.

  b By considering **M** = **NR** for some matrix **R**, show that det **M** = det **N**.

7 Factorise completely the determinant $\begin{vmatrix} 1 & 1 & 1 \\ b & a & 1 \\ a^2 & b^2 & 1 \end{vmatrix}$.

8 Three column vectors, **a**, **b** and **c** are written as an array, to form matrix **M**:

$\mathbf{M} = \begin{pmatrix} a_1 & b_1 & c_1 \\ a_2 & b_2 & c_2 \\ a_3 & b_3 & c_3 \end{pmatrix} = [\mathbf{a} \ \mathbf{b} \ \mathbf{c}]$

  a Show that det $\mathbf{M} = (\mathbf{a} \times \mathbf{b}) \cdot \mathbf{c}$.

  b Use the result in part **a** to show that:

  i exchanging the first two columns of a matrix changes the sign of its determinant but not the absolute value of the determinant

  ii rotating the columns ($[C_1 \ C_2 \ C_3] \to [C_3 \ C_1 \ C_2]$) does not change the determinant of a matrix

  iii if two columns of a matrix are multiples of each other, then the matrix determinant is zero

  iv if the three columns are such that $\lambda C_1 + \mu C_2 + \nu C_3 = 0$ for some non-zero values λ, μ and ν, then the matrix determinant is zero.

9 Express the determinant $\begin{vmatrix} 1 & 1 & 1 \\ p & q & r \\ p^3 & q^3 & r^3 \end{vmatrix}$ as the product of four linear factors.

6 Further matrices

10 Points A, B, and C have position vectors $\mathbf{a}$, $\mathbf{b}$ and $\mathbf{c}$ respectively, where $\mathbf{a} = \begin{pmatrix} 1 \\ 0 \\ 3 \end{pmatrix}$, $\mathbf{b} = \begin{pmatrix} -1 \\ 2 \\ 5 \end{pmatrix}$, $\mathbf{c} = \begin{pmatrix} 2 \\ -5 \\ 2 \end{pmatrix}$.

   a i Find the Cartesian equation of the plane Π containing O, A and B and show that the point C does not lie in Π.

   ii By considering the cross product $\mathbf{a} \times \mathbf{b}$, find the exact area of triangle OAB.

   iii Calculate the exact perpendicular distance between C and plane Π.

   iv Use your answers to parts **ii** and **iii** to calculate the volume of tetrahedron $OABC$.

   b Explain how your answer to part **a iv** relates to the value $\dfrac{1}{6} \begin{vmatrix} 1 & -1 & 2 \\ 0 & 2 & -5 \\ 3 & 5 & 2 \end{vmatrix}$.

> **Tip**
>
> The volume of any straight-edged tapering solid equals $\dfrac{Bh}{3}$ where B is the base area and h is the perpendicular distance from base plane to vertex.

> **Did you know?**
>
> Listing three vectors $\mathbf{a}$, $\mathbf{b}$ and $\mathbf{c}$ as the columns of a matrix and finding its determinant is a way of calculating the vector triple product $(\mathbf{a} \times \mathbf{b}) \cdot \mathbf{c} = (\mathbf{b} \times \mathbf{c}) \cdot \mathbf{a} = (\mathbf{c} \times \mathbf{a}) \cdot \mathbf{b}$ with many applications in geometry and beyond. The vector triple product can be used to calculate the volumes of parallelepipeds and other solids in three-dimensional space.

Section 3: Solving linear systems with three unknowns

In Further Mathematics Student Book 1, Chapter 7, you learnt how to recast a pair of simultaneous equations in two unknowns into a matrix problem, and use matrix inverses and multiplication to solve for the unknowns.

Geometrically, the solution represents the intersection of two straight lines. If the matrix $\mathbf{M}$ is singular then the two lines must be parallel, and so have no unique intersection point.

You can use exactly the same approach to solve a set of three simultaneous equations in three unknowns.

> **Key point 6.7**
>
> For simultaneous equations in three unknowns x, y and z, in the form
> $$ax + by + cz = p$$
> $$dx + ey + fz = q,$$
> $$gx + hy + iz = r$$
>
> rewrite as $\mathbf{Mr} = \mathbf{a}$ where $\mathbf{M} = \begin{pmatrix} a & b & c \\ d & e & f \\ g & h & i \end{pmatrix}$, $\mathbf{r} = \begin{pmatrix} x \\ y \\ z \end{pmatrix}$ and $\mathbf{a} = \begin{pmatrix} p \\ q \\ r \end{pmatrix}$.
>
> If $\mathbf{M}$ is non-singular, the solution is $\mathbf{r} = \mathbf{M}^{-1}\mathbf{a}$.

WORKED EXAMPLE 6.8

Using matrices, solve these linear simultaneous equations.

$4x + 3y - 2z = 3$
$2x - 6y = -5$
$6x - 7y + 5z = 1$

$\begin{pmatrix} 4 & 3 & -2 \\ 2 & -6 & 0 \\ 6 & -7 & 5 \end{pmatrix} \begin{pmatrix} x \\ y \\ z \end{pmatrix} = \begin{pmatrix} 3 \\ -5 \\ 1 \end{pmatrix}$

Recast the problem in matrix form as $\mathbf{M} \begin{pmatrix} x \\ y \\ z \end{pmatrix} = \begin{pmatrix} p \\ q \\ r \end{pmatrix}$.

$\begin{pmatrix} x \\ y \\ z \end{pmatrix} = \begin{pmatrix} 4 & 3 & -2 \\ 2 & -6 & 0 \\ 6 & -7 & 5 \end{pmatrix}^{-1} \begin{pmatrix} 3 \\ -5 \\ 1 \end{pmatrix}$

$= \dfrac{1}{194} \begin{pmatrix} 30 & 1 & 12 \\ 10 & -32 & 4 \\ -22 & -46 & 30 \end{pmatrix} \begin{pmatrix} 3 \\ -5 \\ 1 \end{pmatrix}$ (from calculator)

Rearrange to $\begin{pmatrix} x \\ y \\ z \end{pmatrix} = \mathbf{M}^{-1} \begin{pmatrix} p \\ q \\ r \end{pmatrix}$, find the inverse $\mathbf{M}^{-1}$ and solve to find the unknowns.

$= \begin{pmatrix} 0.5 \\ 1 \\ 1 \end{pmatrix}$

Solution: $x = \dfrac{1}{2}$, $y = 1$, $z = 1$

Remember to state the solution.

When **M** is non-singular, a unique solution to x, y and z can be found. When **M** is singular, there is no unique solution. You will look at the geometrical interpretations for these situations, and how to distinguish them, in Section 4.

EXERCISE 6C

1 By expressing the set of simultaneous equations as a matrix problem $\mathbf{Mr} = \mathbf{a}$, find the unique solution in each case, or determine that there is no unique solution.

a i $\begin{cases} 2x + 4y - z = 3 \\ 3x - 6y + z = 10 \\ 4x + 3y - 2z = 1 \end{cases}$ **ii** $\begin{cases} 2x + y - 5z = 15 \\ 5x + 6y + z = 7 \\ x - 8y + 5z = 1 \end{cases}$

b i $\begin{cases} 4x + y - 3z = -2 \\ 2x - 6y + z = 1 \\ -x + 3y + 4z = 7 \end{cases}$ **ii** $\begin{cases} x + 4y - 2z = -1 \\ 2x + 3y + 6z = 3 \\ 5x - 2y - z = -3 \end{cases}$

c i $\begin{cases} 2x + y = k \\ 3x - 2z = 1 - 3k \\ x + y + z = 2k \end{cases}$ **ii** $\begin{cases} 5x + y - 3z = k \\ 4x + 6y - z = k \\ 8x + 4y + z = k - 2 \end{cases}$

2 Show that the system of equations
$\begin{cases} 2x + 3y - 2z = 2 \\ 3x + 2y + z = 5 \\ 3x + 7y - 7z = 3 \end{cases}$
has no unique solution.

3 By calculating a matrix inverse, find the intersection between the planes $x + 2y - z = -5$, $x - y + 3z = 8$ and $3x - 5z = 1$.

4 For what values of k does the system of equations
$$\begin{cases} -x + (2k-5)y - 2z = 2 \\ (1+k)x - y + (k-1)z = 5 \\ x + y + 2z = 1 \end{cases}$$
have no unique solution?

5 Matrix **M** is given by $\mathbf{M} = \begin{pmatrix} a & 1 & 2 \\ 3 & a & -2 \\ -1 & 1 & 1 \end{pmatrix}$.

   a Show that **M** is non-singular for every real value a.

   b Find $\mathbf{M}^{-1}$ in terms of a.

   c Use $\mathbf{M}^{-1}$ to solve the equations $\begin{cases} x + y + 2z = 4 \\ 3x + y - 2z = 1 \\ -x + y + z = -2 \end{cases}$

6 **a** Show that the system of equations $\begin{cases} kx + 3y - z = -2 \\ -3x + (k+4)y + z = -8 \\ x + 3y + (k-2)z = 4 \end{cases}$

     has no unique solution for $k = 1$.

   b Find all values of k for which there is no unique solution.

   c For $k = 3$, find x, y and z.

Section 4: Geometrical interpretation of 3-variable simultaneous equations

Simultaneous equations in two variables describe lines. If there is a unique solution, it represents the intersection of the lines, and if there is no unique solution this arises because the lines are parallel (no solution) or identical (infinitely many solutions).

Equations in three variables describe **planes**. As with lines, two planes can either intersect (planes intersect in a line) or be parallel or identical.

> **Rewind**
>
> In Chapter 5, Section 3, you learnt how to use vectors to find the line of intersection of two planes. Matrix and vector calculations offer complementary approaches to problems involving planes.

planes intersecting in a line   parallel planes   coincident planes

With three planes there are several possibilities; altogether, there are eight different arrangements, but these fit into three cases:

1 **Consistent** system: unique solution
The matrix of coefficients is non-singular; therefore the three planes meet at a single point.
Using the working described in Section 3, you can find the point.

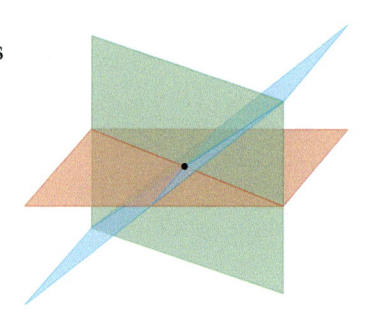

three distinct planes intersecting in a point

2 **Consistent** system: infinitely many solutions
The matrix of coefficients is singular. The three planes intersect either in a line or in a plane.

   a If all three equations describe the same plane, the solution is that plane.

coincident planes

   b If two of the equations describe the same plane, and the third plane is distinct and not parallel, the solution is a line.

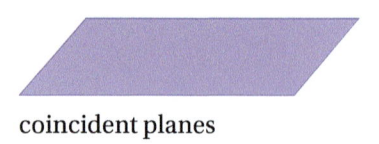

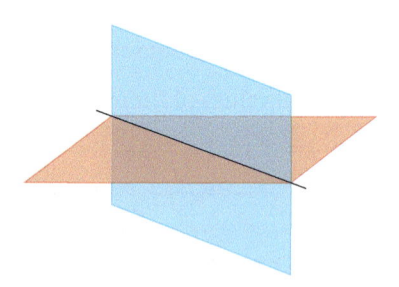

two distinct planes intersecting in a line

   c If the three equations describe different planes, all of which meet at the same line (the planes form a sheaf), the solution is that line.

three distinct planes intersecting in a line

3 **Inconsistent** system: no solutions
The matrix of coefficients is singular. The three planes coincide at no points.
   a All three planes are parallel and distinct.

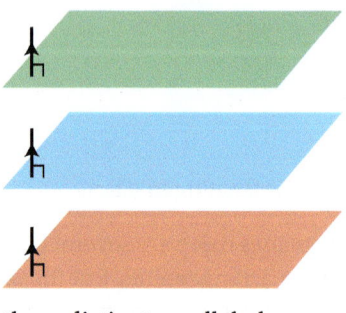

three distinct parallel planes

b Two of the equations describe the same plane and the third describes a distinct but parallel plane.

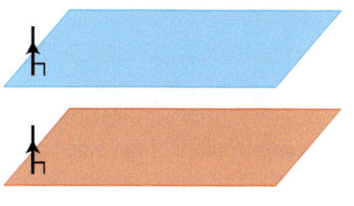

two distinct parallel planes

c Two of the equations describe distinct, parallel planes and the third describes a plane which is not parallel to the other two.

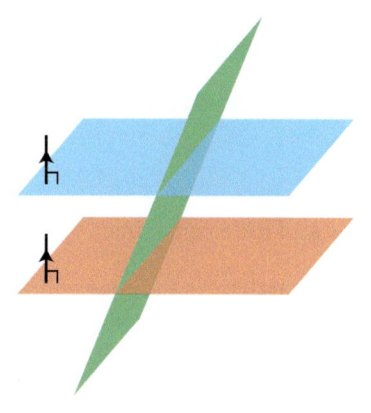

two parallel planes and one non-parallel plane

d The planes enclose a triangular prism, so that each pair of planes intersects in a line, with the three distinct lines running parallel to each other.

three planes forming a triangular prism

Cases 1 and 2 are said to arise from a **consistent** system of equations, because solving the equations (using algebraic elimination, for example) will reduce the three equations to:

- in case 1, a unique solution (such as $x = 1$, $y = 7$, $z = -3$)
- in case 2, algebraic elimination will lead to an equation that is obviously always true, such as $0 = 0$.

Case 3 arises from an **inconsistent** system; attempting to solve the equations simultaneously will produce a contradiction, such as $0 = 1$.

After finding whether or not the solution is unique and whether the system is consistent, you can then consider how many of the planes are parallel to determine the geometric configuration of the system.

A Level Further Mathematics for AQA Student Book 2

> **Key point 6.8**
>
> To determine the geometric configuration of a 3 by 3 system of equations:
> - find the determinant of the matrix of coefficients
> - if the matrix is singular, determine whether the system is consistent
> - consider how many of the planes are parallel to each other.

WORKED EXAMPLE 6.9

For the system of simultaneous equations
$$\begin{cases} x + y - 2z = 2 \\ ax + y + z = b \\ -2y + 3z = 1 \end{cases}$$
where a and b are constants:

a show that there is a unique solution if $a = 1$ and find that solution when $b = 5$
b find the value of a for which there is not a unique solution
c for the value of a found in part **b**, find the value of b such that the system is consistent. Interpret your solution geometrically.

a $\begin{pmatrix} 1 & 1 & -2 \\ a & 1 & 1 \\ 0 & -2 & 3 \end{pmatrix} \begin{pmatrix} x \\ y \\ z \end{pmatrix} = \begin{pmatrix} 2 \\ b \\ 1 \end{pmatrix}$ …… Recast the problem in matrix form as $\mathbf{M} \begin{pmatrix} x \\ y \\ z \end{pmatrix} = \begin{pmatrix} p \\ q \\ r \end{pmatrix}$.

Expanding about the first column:

$\det \begin{pmatrix} 1 & 1 & -2 \\ a & 1 & 1 \\ 0 & -2 & 3 \end{pmatrix} = 1 \begin{vmatrix} 1 & 1 \\ -2 & 3 \end{vmatrix} - a \begin{vmatrix} 1 & -2 \\ -2 & 3 \end{vmatrix}$ …… Show that $\det \mathbf{M} \neq 0$ to establish the existence of a unique solution.

$= 5 + a$

The matrix is non-singular for $a = 1$ and therefore there will be a unique solution.

For $a = 1$, $b = 5$:

$\begin{pmatrix} x \\ y \\ z \end{pmatrix} = \begin{pmatrix} 1 & 1 & -2 \\ 1 & 1 & 1 \\ 0 & -2 & 3 \end{pmatrix}^{-1} \begin{pmatrix} 2 \\ 5 \\ 1 \end{pmatrix}$ …… Rearrange to $\begin{pmatrix} x \\ y \\ z \end{pmatrix} = \mathbf{M}^{-1} \begin{pmatrix} p \\ q \\ r \end{pmatrix}$, find the inverse $\mathbf{M}^{-1}$ and solve to find the unknowns.

$= \begin{pmatrix} 3 \\ 1 \\ 1 \end{pmatrix}$ (from calculator)

Solution: $x = 3$, $y = 1$, $z = 1$ …… Remember to state the solution.

b There is no unique solution when the matrix determinant is 0. …… Use the result for the determinant that you found in part **a**.
$\therefore a = -5$

Continues on next page

6 Further matrices

c When $a = -5$:

$x + y - 2z = 2$ (1)
$-5x + y + z = b$ (2)
$-2y + 3z = 1$ (3)

$5 \times (1) + (2)$:   Eliminate x by using (1) and (2).
$6y - 9z = 10 + b$ (4)

$(4) + 3 \times (3)$:   Eliminate y from (3) and (4).
$0 = 13 + b$

For a consistent solution, $13 + b = 0$, so $b = -13$ The equation must reduce to $0 = 0$ for the system to be consistent.

There are infinitely many solutions since the system is consistent. Since all three normals are different, the planes are all different so they must intersect in a line. They form a sheaf of planes.   Being consistent but with no unique solution means that there are infinitely many solutions. You then only need to distinguish a plane of solutions from a line of solutions.

WORKED EXAMPLE 6.10

For the system of simultaneous equations

$$\begin{cases} kx - y + 3z = -2 \\ x + 6y - z = 3 \\ 3x - 8y + 7z = 6 \end{cases}$$

find the value of k for which there is no unique solution, and interpret this situation geometrically.

$\det \begin{pmatrix} k & -1 & 3 \\ 1 & 6 & -1 \\ 3 & -8 & 7 \end{pmatrix} = k \begin{vmatrix} 6 & -1 \\ -8 & 7 \end{vmatrix} + 1 \begin{vmatrix} 1 & -1 \\ 3 & 7 \end{vmatrix} + 3 \begin{vmatrix} 1 & 6 \\ 3 & -8 \end{vmatrix}$ No unique solution when det $\mathbf{M} = 0$.

$= 34k + 10 - 78$
$= 34(k - 2)$

There is no unique solution when $k = 2$.

When $k = 2$:   Now use elimination to decide if the system is consistent.

$2x - y + 3z = -2$ (1)
$x + 6y - z = 3$ (2)
$3x - 8y + 7z = 6$ (3)

$(2) + 6 \times (1)$:   Eliminate y from (1) and (2). You could choose any variable to eliminate, but the numbers for y look convenient.

$13x + 17z = -9$ (4)

$(3) - 8 \times (1)$:   Eliminate y from (1) and (3).

$-13x - 17z = 22$ (5)

Continues on next page

133

(4) + (5):

$$0 = 13$$

The system is therefore inconsistent.

All three normals are in different directions, so no two planes are parallel. Therefore, they form a triangular prism.

Eliminate x from (4) and (5). Because the determinant was zero, this step should also eliminate z.

This is since the last equation is clearly not true.

You need to distinguish between the four possible geometric configurations of the inconsistent system. You can do this by considering how many planes are parallel.

Finding the solution set to a consistent system

You already know that if the solution set to $\mathbf{Mr} = \mathbf{a}$ is a single point, you can find its position as

$$\mathbf{r} = \mathbf{M}^{-1}\mathbf{a}.$$

If the solution of the system is a line l, at least two of the planes must be distinct (and not parallel). You can find the direction vector of l by taking the cross product of the two distinct plane normals. To find a single point on line l, set one of x, y or z equal to zero (pick one whose element in the direction vector is not zero) and solve for the other two in any two of the plane equations simultaneously.

Rewind

You learnt how to find the line of intersection of two planes in Chapter 5, Section 3.

WORKED EXAMPLE 6.11

Three planes are described by the equations:
$$\begin{cases} x + 3y - 2z = 4 \\ 2x - 4y + z = 8 \\ -4x + 18y - 7z = -16 \end{cases}$$

Given that the system is consistent, find the solution of this system of equations and interpret it geometrically.

$$\mathbf{M}\begin{pmatrix} x \\ y \\ z \end{pmatrix} = \begin{pmatrix} 4 \\ 8 \\ -16 \end{pmatrix} \text{ where } \mathbf{M} = \begin{pmatrix} 1 & 3 & -2 \\ 2 & -4 & 1 \\ -4 & 18 & -7 \end{pmatrix}.$$

Recast the problem in matrix form as
$$\mathbf{M}\begin{pmatrix} x \\ y \\ z \end{pmatrix} = \begin{pmatrix} p \\ q \\ r \end{pmatrix}.$$

$\det \mathbf{M} = 0$, so there is not a single point of intersection.

You can find $\det \mathbf{M}$ by using technology.

Continues on next page

No row of the 3×3 matrix is a multiple of another, so there are no parallel planes. The three planes form a sheaf with a common intersecting line l.

You now need to distinguish between a plane of solutions and a line of solutions. You can do this by considering the number of parallel planes from looking at the normal of each plane.

From the original matrix **M**:

$$R_1^T \times R_2^T = \begin{pmatrix} 1 \\ 3 \\ -2 \end{pmatrix} \times \begin{pmatrix} 2 \\ -4 \\ 1 \end{pmatrix} = \begin{pmatrix} -5 \\ -5 \\ -10 \end{pmatrix}$$

The direction vector of l is $\begin{pmatrix} 5 \\ 5 \\ 10 \end{pmatrix}$.

To find the direction of the line, take the vector product of two rows of the matrix (equivalent to the vector product of the plane normals).

Setting $x = 0$ in the first two equations of the system:

$$\begin{cases} 3y - 2z = 4 & (1) \\ -4y + z = 8 & (2) \end{cases}$$

$(1) + 2(2)$: $-5y = 20$, so $y = -4$, $z = -8$
So the point $(0, -4, -8)$ lies on l.

Fix $x = 0$ (y or z would also work since the direction vector has no zero elements).

The planes intersect at line $r = \begin{pmatrix} 0 \\ -4 \\ -8 \end{pmatrix} + t \begin{pmatrix} 5 \\ 5 \\ 10 \end{pmatrix}$.

Remember to state the solution.

EXERCISE 6D

Questions 5 to 8 in this exercise also appear in Exercise 5C. Use this to compare the two methods of solving the equations.

1 For each set of simultaneous equations, determine whether they are consistent or inconsistent and interpret the geometrical relationship of the planes described by the equations. If there is a unique solution, find it.

a i $\begin{cases} 2x + y - z = 6 \\ -x + 2y + z = 3 \\ 3x - 5y + 2z = 3 \end{cases}$ **ii** $\begin{cases} 4x + 2y - z = 2 \\ 2x - y + z = 5 \\ 3x - 3y + 2z = 8 \end{cases}$

b i $\begin{cases} x + y - 2z = 6 \\ -x + 2y + z = 5 \\ 3x + 3y - 6z = 2 \end{cases}$ **ii** $\begin{cases} 5x - 3y + 2z = 4 \\ 2x - 2y + z = 2 \\ x + 5y - z = -2 \end{cases}$

c i $\begin{cases} 9x - 3y + 3z = 5 \\ 4x - 2y + z = 1 \\ x + 3y + 2z = 6 \end{cases}$ **ii** $\begin{cases} 4x + 2y - 6z = 6 \\ -x - 2y + 3z = -3 \\ 6x + 3y - 9z = -9 \end{cases}$

d i $\begin{cases} 2x + 3y + z = 2 \\ 5x - 6y + z = 1 \\ x + 3y + 2z = 3 \end{cases}$ **ii** $\begin{cases} 4x + 2y - z = -1 \\ -x + 3y + z = 5 \\ 3x - 5y + 2z = 7 \end{cases}$

2 A system of equations is given by $\begin{cases} 3x + y + z = 8 \\ -7x + 3y + z = 2 \\ x + y + 3z = 0 \end{cases}$

   a Show that the system has a unique solution and find this solution.

   b The three equations represent planes. Describe the configuration of the three planes.

3 A system of equations is given by $\begin{cases} x = 2 \\ x + y - z = 7 \\ 2x + y + z = 3 \end{cases}$.

   a Show that the system has a unique solution.

   b The three equations represent planes. Describe the configuration of the three planes.

4 Find the intersection of the planes

$$x - 2y + z = 5$$
$$2x + y + z = 1$$
$$x + 2y - z = -2$$

5 **a** Show that there is no unique solution to the equation system given by $\begin{cases} 2x - y + z = 6 \\ 3x + y + 5z = -7 \\ x - 3y - 3z = 8 \end{cases}$

   b Show that the system is inconsistent.

   c Interpret the system geometrically.

6 Consider this system of equations:

$\begin{cases} 2x + y - 2z = 0 \\ x - 2y - z = 2 \\ 3x + 4y - 3z = d \end{cases}$

   a Show that the system does not have a unique solution.

   b Find the value of d for which the system is consistent.

   c The three equations represent planes. For the value of d found in part **b**, describe the configuration of the three planes.

   d For the value of d found in part **b**, solve the system of equations.

7 **a** Show that the system of equations

$\begin{cases} x + y = 0 \\ x - 4y - 2z = 0 \\ \frac{1}{2}x + 3y + z = 0 \end{cases}$

   is consistent.

   The three equations in part **a** represent three planes.

   b Describe the geometrical configuration of the planes.

   c Find the solution of the system.

6 Further matrices

8 a Find the inverse of the matrix $\begin{pmatrix} 1 & -1 & 0 \\ 0 & 1 & 1 \\ 1 & 0 & -1 \end{pmatrix}$.

b Hence find, in terms of d, the coordinates of the point of intersection of the planes $x - y = 4$, $y + z = 1$ and $x - z = d$.

9 Consider the system of equations
$$\begin{cases} x - 2y - z = -2 \\ 2x + y - 3z = 9 \\ x + 3y - az = 3 \end{cases}$$

a Find the value of a for which the system does not have a unique solution.

b For the value of a found in part **a**, determine whether the system is consistent, and describe the geometric configuration of the three planes represented by the system.

10 a Find the value of p for which the system of equations $\begin{cases} x - y - z = -2 \\ 2x + 3y - 7z = a + 4 \\ x + 2y + pz = a^2 \end{cases}$ does not have a unique solution.

b For the value of p found in part **a**, find the two values of a for which the system is consistent.

c Describe the geometric configuration of the three planes represented by the three equations.

d Find the solution of the system for the value of p from part **a** and the larger of the two values of a from part **b**.

Section 5: Eigenvalues and eigenvectors

In Further Mathematics Student Book 1, Chapter 8, you learned how to find invariant lines for two-dimensional linear transformations.

For example, when finding an invariant line of the form $y = mx$ for the matrix $\mathbf{M} = \begin{pmatrix} 2 & 2 \\ 1 & 3 \end{pmatrix}$, you would set up an equation $\begin{pmatrix} 2 & 2 \\ 1 & 3 \end{pmatrix} \begin{pmatrix} 1 \\ m \end{pmatrix} = \lambda \begin{pmatrix} 1 \\ m \end{pmatrix}$.

You can turn this into simultaneous equations and solve to find m and λ. In this case $m = -0.5$, $\lambda = 1$ or $m = 1$, $\lambda = 4$.

λ is said to be an **eigenvalue** of $\mathbf{M}$, with associated **eigenvector** $\begin{pmatrix} 1 \\ m \end{pmatrix}$.

The eigenvector does not have a unique form; any non-zero multiple is valid since it only serves to define the direction of the invariant line.

Key point 6.9

If $\mathbf{Mv} = \lambda \mathbf{v}$ then λ is called an eigenvalue of $\mathbf{M}$ and $\mathbf{v}$ is its associated eigenvector.

The only constraint on the eigenvector is that it cannot be a zero vector as this does not describe any direction.

For any vector **v**, the identity matrix **I**, by its definition, has the property **v** = **Iv**.

Therefore,

$\quad$ **M** = λ**v**

$\Rightarrow$ **M** = λ**Iv**

$\Rightarrow$ (**M** − λ**I**)**v** = **0**

$\therefore$ det (**M** − λ**I**) = **0** (since if **M** − λ**I** were not singular, the equation could be solved to get **v** = **0**).

det (**M** − λ**I**) = 0 forms a polynomial in λ called the **characteristic equation** of matrix **M** and its roots are the eigenvalues of **M**.

To find the eigenvector or eigenvectors associated with each eigenvalue, substitute each value λ into the equation (**M** − λ**I**)**v** = **0** and solve the resulting equations. You will find that these equations do not have a unique solution, but you can set one (or sometimes more) of the components of **v** equal to a convenient value to find a solution.

> **Tip**
>
> This ability to set a component to a convenient value is equivalent to saying that the length of the eigenvector is not important.

WORKED EXAMPLE 6.12

Find the eigenvalues of $\begin{pmatrix} 2 & 2 \\ 1 & 3 \end{pmatrix}$ and their associated eigenvectors.

Characteristic equation:　　　　　　　　　　　　Solve the characteristic equation det (**M** − λ**I**) = 0 to find the eigenvalues.

$\det \begin{pmatrix} 2-\lambda & 2 \\ 1 & 3-\lambda \end{pmatrix} = 0$

$(2-\lambda)(3-\lambda) - 2 = 0$

$\lambda^2 - 5\lambda + 4 = 0$

$(\lambda - 1)(\lambda - 4) = 0$

$\lambda = 1$ or 4

For $\lambda = 4$:　　　　　　　　　　　　　　　　Substitute into the equation (**M** − λ**I**)**v** = **0** with $\mathbf{v} = \begin{pmatrix} x \\ y \end{pmatrix}$.

$\begin{pmatrix} -2 & 2 \\ 1 & -1 \end{pmatrix} \begin{pmatrix} x \\ y \end{pmatrix} = \begin{pmatrix} 0 \\ 0 \end{pmatrix}$

$\begin{cases} -2x + 2y = 0 \\ x - y = 0 \end{cases}$

Write the matrix equation in a standard algebraic form. You will usually find that the two equations are equivalent. This means that there are infinitely many solutions....

When $x = 1$ then $y = 1$, so an eigenvector associated with $\lambda = 4$ is $\begin{pmatrix} 1 \\ 1 \end{pmatrix}$.

... but you only want one, so you are free to choose the one with $x = 1$.

Continues on next page

6 Further matrices

For $\lambda = 1$:

$$\begin{pmatrix} 1 & 2 \\ 1 & 2 \end{pmatrix} \begin{pmatrix} x \\ y \end{pmatrix} = \begin{pmatrix} 0 \\ 0 \end{pmatrix}$$

Substitute into the equation $(\mathbf{M} - \lambda\mathbf{I})\mathbf{v} = \mathbf{0}$ with $\mathbf{v} = \begin{pmatrix} x \\ y \end{pmatrix}$.

Both rows give $x + 2y = 0$

Write the matrix equation in a standard algebraic form. Here you just get the same equation twice.

When $y = 1$ then $x = -2$, so an eigenvector associated with $\lambda = 1$ is $\begin{pmatrix} -2 \\ 1 \end{pmatrix}$

You are free to choose the one with $y = 1$ to keep all numbers as integers.

> **Tip**
>
> The **lead diagonal** of a square matrix runs from the top left element to the bottom right element. The sum of this lead diagonal is the sum of the eigenvalues, which provides a useful way of checking your answer.

Characteristic equations for 3 × 3 matrices

You can use exactly the same principle to find eigenvalues and eigenvectors for a 3 × 3 matrix.

WORKED EXAMPLE 6.13

Find the eigenvalues and eigenvectors of $\begin{pmatrix} -2 & -3 & -3 \\ -6 & -5 & -6 \\ 6 & 6 & 7 \end{pmatrix}$.

Characteristic equation:

$$\det \begin{pmatrix} -2-\lambda & -3 & -3 \\ -6 & -5-\lambda & -6 \\ 6 & 6 & 7-\lambda \end{pmatrix} = 0$$

Find the characteristic equation $\det(\mathbf{M} - \lambda\mathbf{I}) = 0$, whose roots are the eigenvalues.

Expanding about the first row:

$$(-2-\lambda)\begin{vmatrix} -5-\lambda & -6 \\ 6 & 7-\lambda \end{vmatrix} + 3\begin{vmatrix} -6 & -6 \\ 6 & 7-\lambda \end{vmatrix} - 3\begin{vmatrix} -6 & -5-\lambda \\ 6 & 6 \end{vmatrix} = 0$$

$(-2-\lambda)(\lambda^2 - 2\lambda + 1) + 3(6\lambda - 6) - 3(6\lambda - 6) = 0$

$-(\lambda + 2)(\lambda - 1)^2 = 0$

If you expand the cubic fully you will need to use the Factor theorem to show that 1 is a root. If possible, keep the cubic factorised to reduce working.

The eigenvalues are 1 (repeated) and -2.

$(\mathbf{M} - \lambda\mathbf{I})\underline{v} = \underline{0}$

Use $(\mathbf{M} - \lambda\mathbf{I})\mathbf{v} = \mathbf{0}$ to find the eigenvectors.

Continues on next page

139

For $\lambda = 1$:
$$\begin{pmatrix} -3 & -3 & -3 \\ -6 & -6 & -6 \\ 6 & 6 & 6 \end{pmatrix} \begin{pmatrix} x \\ y \\ z \end{pmatrix} = \begin{pmatrix} 0 \\ 0 \\ 0 \end{pmatrix}$$

All three rows give $x + y + z = 0$.

Choose $x = 1$, $y = 1$, then $z = -2$.

Choose $x = 0$, $y = 1$, then $z = -1$.

So the eigenvectors associated with $\lambda = -1$ are $\begin{pmatrix} 1 \\ 1 \\ -2 \end{pmatrix}$ and $\begin{pmatrix} 0 \\ 1 \\ -1 \end{pmatrix}$.

> Where all three rows are multiples of each other, a single plane is described. Pick any two non-parallel vectors in that plane as eigenvectors.

> To find these two vectors you are free to choose two values of the variables, then use the equation to find the third one. There are many possible choices, so there is no unique correct set.

For $\lambda = -2$:
$$\begin{pmatrix} 0 & -3 & -3 \\ -6 & -3 & -6 \\ 6 & 6 & 9 \end{pmatrix} \begin{pmatrix} x \\ y \\ z \end{pmatrix} = \begin{pmatrix} 0 \\ 0 \\ 0 \end{pmatrix}$$

$$\begin{cases} -3y - 3z = 0 & (1) \\ -6x - 3y - 6z = 0 & (2) \\ 6x + 6y + 9z = 0 & (3) \end{cases}$$

When $x = 1$, then:
$$\begin{cases} -3y - 3z = 0 & (1) \\ -6 - 3y - 6z = 0 & (2) \\ 6 + 6y + 9z = 0 & (3) \end{cases}$$

> You are free to choose a value of x.

$(1) - (2)$: $6 + 3z = 0$

So $z = -2$.

Substituting into (1) gives $y = 2$.

> Notice that you did not have to use equation (3) – this is normal when solving for eigenvectors as it is just a combination of the other two equations so does not give additional information. In this example, $(3) = -(2) - (1)$.

Therefore an eigenvector associated with $\lambda = -2$ is $\underline{v} = \begin{pmatrix} 1 \\ 2 \\ -2 \end{pmatrix}$.

ⓘ Did you know?

If an eigenvalue is a repeated solution of the characteristic equation with multiplicity m then there can be up to m eigenvectors associated with that eigenvalue. It is therefore possible for an n by n matrix to have fewer than n eigenvectors. If this is the case, then it is usually associated with a geometric transformation called a shear.

In finding the final eigenvector you might have wondered whether your choice of x might fail. The answer is, sadly, yes – if in Worked example 6.13 you had chosen $x = 0$, you would have found $y = 0$ and $z = 0$ which is not an allowed eigenvector. Sometimes you can get equations with no solutions. In either case you need to look for another possible value.

Sometimes, as in Worked example 6.14, you find that some values are constrained and only some are free to be chosen.

WORKED EXAMPLE 6.14

The matrix $\mathbf{M}$ is given by $\begin{pmatrix} 2 & 0 & 2 \\ 0 & 1 & 0 \\ 2 & 0 & -1 \end{pmatrix}$.

Find an eigenvector associated with an eigenvalue of 1.

$\begin{pmatrix} 1 & 0 & 2 \\ 0 & 0 & 0 \\ 2 & 0 & -2 \end{pmatrix} \begin{pmatrix} x \\ y \\ z \end{pmatrix} = \begin{pmatrix} 0 \\ 0 \\ 0 \end{pmatrix}$.

Put $\lambda = 1$ into the usual eigenvector equation.

This is equivalent to:
$\begin{cases} x + 2z = 0 & (1) \\ 0 = 0 & (2) \\ 2x - 2z = 0 & (3) \end{cases}$

Equation (2) seems very strange! Also, there is no mention of y in any equation.

(1) + (3):
$3x = 0$

Equations (1) and (2) can be solved directly, so you are not free to choose x or z.

So $x = 0$ and $z = 0$

There is no constraint on y, so choose $y = 1$.

However, you are free to choose any convenient value for y.

So an eigenvector is $\begin{pmatrix} 0 \\ 1 \\ 0 \end{pmatrix}$.

EXERCISE 6E

1 Find the eigenvalues and corresponding eigenvectors for each matrix.

a i $\begin{pmatrix} 1 & 4 \\ 2 & 3 \end{pmatrix}$ **ii** $\begin{pmatrix} 4 & -1 \\ 6 & -1 \end{pmatrix}$ **b i** $\begin{pmatrix} 3 & 1 \\ 1 & 3 \end{pmatrix}$ **ii** $\begin{pmatrix} 7 & 3 \\ -5 & -1 \end{pmatrix}$

c i $\begin{pmatrix} 4 & 1 \\ -1 & 2 \end{pmatrix}$ **ii** $\begin{pmatrix} 2 & -9 \\ 1 & 8 \end{pmatrix}$ **d i** $\begin{pmatrix} 2 & 5 \\ -1 & -2 \end{pmatrix}$ **ii** $\begin{pmatrix} 1 & 5 \\ -2 & -1 \end{pmatrix}$

2 Each matrix has only one eigenvalue.
Determine the unknown constant and find the eigenvalue and associated eigenvector.

a **i** $\begin{pmatrix} 3 & -1 \\ 1 & a \end{pmatrix}$ **ii** $\begin{pmatrix} p & 2 \\ -8 & -6 \end{pmatrix}$ **b** **i** $\begin{pmatrix} 5 & b \\ 2 & 3 \end{pmatrix}$ **ii** $\begin{pmatrix} 2 & 4 \\ q & -2 \end{pmatrix}$

3 Find the eigenvalues and eigenvectors of the matrix $\mathbf{M} = \begin{pmatrix} 4 & 1 \\ 3 & 6 \end{pmatrix}$.

4 Find the eigenvalues and eigenvectors of the matrix $\mathbf{M} = \begin{pmatrix} 4 & 2 \\ -6 & -4 \end{pmatrix}$.

5 Matrix **A** is given by $\mathbf{A} = \begin{pmatrix} 2.5 & 1 & 3 \\ -2 & -3 & -1 \\ -1.5 & -4 & 4 \end{pmatrix}$.

Show that 2 is an eigenvalue of **A** and find the remaining eigenvalues and all associated eigenvectors of the matrix.

6 A transformation T is given by $\mathbf{M} = \begin{pmatrix} -1 & 1 & 2 \\ 0 & 1 & 0 \\ 2 & 1 & -1 \end{pmatrix}$.

Given that T has a line of invariant points, find all eigenvalues and associated eigenvectors of the matrix.

7 A matrix is given by $\mathbf{A} = \begin{pmatrix} 3 & 2 & -1 \\ 0 & 5 & -1 \\ -3 & 1 & 4 \end{pmatrix}$.

a Show that 6 is an eigenvalue of **A**.

b Find all eigenvalues and associated eigenvectors of **A**.

8 Matrix $\mathbf{M} = \begin{pmatrix} 1 & p & -p \\ 0 & 6 & 0 \\ -10 & 10 & -4 \end{pmatrix}$.

$x - y + z = 0$ is the eigenplane associated with the eigenvalue q of **M**.

a Find p and q.

b Find the other eigenvalue and its associated eigenvector.

9 Transformation T is described by matrix $\mathbf{M} = \begin{pmatrix} 1 & -1 & 3 \\ -1 & 1 & 3 \\ 3 & 3 & 3 \end{pmatrix}$.

The sum of two of the eigenvalues of **M** is 8.

Find all the eigenvalues and associated eigenvectors of **M**.

10 Transformation T is described by matrix $\mathbf{M} = \begin{pmatrix} 1 & -8 & -4 \\ -8 & 1 & -4 \\ -4 & -4 & 7 \end{pmatrix}$.

a Determine the characteristic equation of **M** and show that **M** has eigenvalues k and $-k$, for some real value $k > 0$, where k is to be determined.

b i Find the eigenvectors associated with the eigenvalues.

  ii Show that all eigenvectors associated with $\lambda = k$ are perpendicular to all eigenvectors associated with $\lambda = -k$.

T is the composition of an enlargement with scale factor k and a second transformation R.

c Use your answer to part **b** to describe the effect of transformation R.

11 Matrix **A** is given by $\mathbf{A} = \begin{pmatrix} 80 & -30 & 6 \\ 195 & -73 & 15 \\ -78 & 30 & -4 \end{pmatrix}$ and has two eigenvalues. Find the eigenvalues and associated eigenvectors.

Section 6: Diagonalisation and applications

Suppose $n \times n$ matrix **M** has n linearly independent eigenvectors $\mathbf{v}_1, \mathbf{v}_2, \ldots, \mathbf{v}_n$ with associated eigenvalues $\lambda_1, \lambda_2, \ldots, \lambda_n$. You can now use your understanding of eigenvectors and eigenvalues from Section 5 to **diagonalise** matrix **M**; that is, you can express **M** in the form $\mathbf{UDU}^{-1}$ for some matrix **U** where **D** is a **diagonal matrix**. A diagonal matrix has zero for every element outside the lead diagonal.

> **Tip**
>
> Remember, the lead diagonal of a square matrix runs from the top left element to the bottom right element: $a_{11}, a_{22}, \ldots, a_{nn}$.

To illustrate this, you can use the matrix $\mathbf{M} = \begin{pmatrix} -2 & -3 & -3 \\ -6 & -5 & -6 \\ 6 & 6 & 7 \end{pmatrix}$ from Worked example 6.13, for which the eigenvalues and eigenvectors were:

$\lambda_1 = \lambda_2 = 1$ associated with $\mathbf{v}_1 = \begin{pmatrix} 1 \\ -1 \\ 0 \end{pmatrix}$ and $\mathbf{v}_2 = \begin{pmatrix} 1 \\ 0 \\ -1 \end{pmatrix}$

$\lambda_3 = -2$, associated with $\mathbf{v}_3 = \begin{pmatrix} 1 \\ 2 \\ -2 \end{pmatrix}$.

Construct **U**, with columns equal to the eigenvectors: $\mathbf{U} = [\mathbf{v}_1 \mathbf{v}_2 \mathbf{v}_3]$.

$$\mathbf{U} = \begin{pmatrix} 1 & 1 & 1 \\ -1 & 0 & 2 \\ 0 & -1 & -2 \end{pmatrix}$$

Remember that because the eigenvectors are linearly independent, you know from Section 2 that **U** must be non-singular.

Now since by definition $\mathbf{M}\mathbf{v}_i = \lambda_i \mathbf{v}_i$, it follows that

$$\mathbf{MU} = \mathbf{M}[\mathbf{v}_1 \, \mathbf{v}_2 \, \mathbf{v}_3]$$
$$= [(\lambda_1 \mathbf{v}_1) \, (\lambda_2 \mathbf{v}_2) \, (\lambda_3 \mathbf{v}_3)]$$
$$= [\mathbf{v}_1 \, \mathbf{v}_2 \, \mathbf{v}_3] \begin{pmatrix} \lambda_1 & 0 & 0 \\ 0 & \lambda_2 & 0 \\ 0 & 0 & \lambda_3 \end{pmatrix}$$
$$= \mathbf{UD}$$

where **D** is the diagonal matrix whose lead diagonal consists of the eigenvalues, listed in the same order as their associated eigenvectors in **U**.

But now, since **MU = UD** and **U** is non-singular, right-multiplication by $\mathbf{U}^{-1}$ gives

$$\mathbf{M} = \mathbf{UDU}^{-1}$$

$$\begin{pmatrix} -2 & -3 & -3 \\ -6 & -5 & -6 \\ 6 & 6 & 7 \end{pmatrix} = \begin{pmatrix} 1 & 1 & 1 \\ -1 & 0 & 2 \\ 0 & -1 & -2 \end{pmatrix} \begin{pmatrix} 1 & 0 & 0 \\ 0 & 1 & 0 \\ 0 & 0 & -2 \end{pmatrix} \begin{pmatrix} 1 & 1 & 1 \\ -1 & 0 & 2 \\ 0 & -1 & -2 \end{pmatrix}^{-1}$$

which is the diagonalised form required.

> **Key point 6.10**
>
> If $n \times n$ matrix **M** has n eigenvectors $\mathbf{v}_1, \ldots, \mathbf{v}_n$ with associated eigenvalues $\lambda_1, \ldots, \lambda_n$, then you can write **M** in diagonalised form
> $$\mathbf{M} = \mathbf{UDU}^{-1}$$
> where $\mathbf{U} = [\mathbf{v}_1 \ldots \mathbf{v}_n]$ and **D** is a diagonal matrix with $\lambda_1, \ldots, \lambda_n$ as the lead diagonal elements.

WORKED EXAMPLE 6.15

The matrix $\mathbf{M} = \begin{pmatrix} 2 & -3 \\ 1 & 6 \end{pmatrix}$ has eigenvalues $\lambda_1 = 3$ and $\lambda_2 = 5$ with associated eigenvectors $\mathbf{v}_1 = \begin{pmatrix} 3 \\ -1 \end{pmatrix}$ and $\mathbf{v}_2 = \begin{pmatrix} 1 \\ -1 \end{pmatrix}$.

Write **M** in the form $\mathbf{UDU}^{-1}$, where **D** is a diagonal matrix.

Let $\mathbf{U} = \begin{pmatrix} 3 & 1 \\ -1 & -1 \end{pmatrix}$, the matrix with the eigenvectors as columns and let $\mathbf{D} = \begin{pmatrix} 3 & 0 \\ 0 & 5 \end{pmatrix}$, the diagonal matrix with eigenvalues as elements of the lead diagonal.

*Set $\mathbf{U} = [\mathbf{v}_1 \mathbf{v}_2]$ and **D** the diagonal matrix of eigenvalues.*

Then

$$\mathbf{M} = \begin{pmatrix} 3 & 1 \\ -1 & -1 \end{pmatrix} \begin{pmatrix} 3 & 0 \\ 0 & 5 \end{pmatrix} \begin{pmatrix} 3 & 1 \\ -1 & -1 \end{pmatrix}^{-1}$$

Use $\mathbf{M} = \mathbf{UDU}^{-1}$

The method of diagonalisation relies on **U** being non-singular: that is, there must be three non-parallel eigenvectors. As you saw in Section 5, this will be the case when the characteristic equation has no repeated roots, but might not be true otherwise. An $n \times n$ matrix with fewer than n eigenvectors cannot be diagonalised.

The diagonalised form has several uses, but the most immediate application lies in calculating powers of a matrix.

If $\mathbf{M} = \mathbf{UDU}^{-1}$, then:

$$\begin{aligned}\mathbf{M}^k &= (\mathbf{UDU}^{-1})^k \\ &= (\mathbf{UDU}^{-1})(\mathbf{UDU}^{-1})\ldots(\mathbf{UDU}^{-1}) \\ &= \mathbf{U}(\mathbf{DU}^{-1}\mathbf{U})^{k-1}\mathbf{DU}^{-1} \quad \text{(matrix multiplication is associative)} \\ &= \mathbf{UD}^{k-1}\mathbf{DU}^{-1} \\ &= \mathbf{UD}^k\mathbf{U}^{-1}\end{aligned}$$

and because $\mathbf{D}$ is a diagonal matrix, you can write down $\mathbf{D}^k$ without needing any matrix multiplication.

> **Tip**
>
> You can easily show that Key point 6.11 is also true for negative integer values k as long as $\mathbf{M}$ is non-singular (equivalently, as long as all eigenvalues are non-zero). It is not valid for non-integer values of k.

> **Key point 6.11**
>
> If matrix $\mathbf{M}$ can be written as $\mathbf{M} = \mathbf{UDU}^{-1}$ for some matrices $\mathbf{U}$ and $\mathbf{D}$, then:
> $$\mathbf{M}^k = \mathbf{UD}^k\mathbf{U}^{-1}$$
> for any positive integer k.

WORKED EXAMPLE 6.16

It is known that the transformation given by $\mathbf{M} = \begin{pmatrix} 0 & -2 & -3 \\ 1 & 3 & 3 \\ -1 & -1 & -1 \end{pmatrix}$ has eigenvalues

$\lambda_1 = 1, \lambda_2 = -1$ and $\lambda_3 = 2$ with associated eigenvectors $\mathbf{v}_1 = \begin{pmatrix} 1 \\ 1 \\ -1 \end{pmatrix}, \mathbf{v}_2 = \begin{pmatrix} 1 \\ -1 \\ 1 \end{pmatrix}, \mathbf{v}_3 = \begin{pmatrix} 1 \\ -1 \\ 0 \end{pmatrix}$.

a Express $\mathbf{M}$ in the form $\mathbf{UDU}^{-1}$, where $\mathbf{D}$ is a diagonal matrix.
b Hence find $\mathbf{M}^n$ for odd integer n.

a Let $\mathbf{U} = \begin{pmatrix} 1 & 1 & 1 \\ 1 & -1 & -1 \\ -1 & 1 & 0 \end{pmatrix}$, the matrix with the eigenvectors .... Set $\mathbf{U} = [\mathbf{v}_1 \mathbf{v}_2 \mathbf{v}_3]$ and $\mathbf{D}$ the diagonal matrix of eigenvalues.

as columns and let $\mathbf{D} = \begin{pmatrix} 1 & 0 & 0 \\ 0 & -1 & 0 \\ 0 & 0 & 2 \end{pmatrix}$, the diagonal matrix with eigenvalues as elements of the lead diagonal.

Then

$\mathbf{M} = \begin{pmatrix} 1 & 1 & 1 \\ 1 & -1 & -1 \\ -1 & 1 & 0 \end{pmatrix}\begin{pmatrix} 1 & 0 & 0 \\ 0 & -1 & 0 \\ 0 & 0 & 2 \end{pmatrix}\begin{pmatrix} 1 & 1 & 1 \\ 1 & -1 & -1 \\ -1 & 1 & 0 \end{pmatrix}^{-1}$ .... Use $\mathbf{M} = \mathbf{UDU}^{-1}$

Continues on next page

b $U^{-1} = \dfrac{1}{2}\begin{pmatrix} 1 & 1 & 0 \\ 1 & 1 & 2 \\ 0 & -2 & -2 \end{pmatrix}$ .... Calculate U^{-1}, using your calculator.

$M^n = \dfrac{1}{2}\begin{pmatrix} 1 & 1 & 1 \\ 1 & -1 & -1 \\ -1 & 1 & 0 \end{pmatrix}\begin{pmatrix} 1 & 0 & 0 \\ 0 & -1 & 0 \\ 0 & 0 & 2 \end{pmatrix}^n\begin{pmatrix} 1 & 1 & 0 \\ 1 & 1 & 2 \\ 0 & -2 & -2 \end{pmatrix}$ .... $(UDU^{-1})^n = UD^nU^{-1}$

$= \dfrac{1}{2}\begin{pmatrix} 1 & 1 & 1 \\ 1 & -1 & -1 \\ -1 & 1 & 0 \end{pmatrix}\begin{pmatrix} 1^n & 0 & 0 \\ 0 & (-1)^n & 0 \\ 0 & 0 & 2^n \end{pmatrix}\begin{pmatrix} 1 & 1 & 0 \\ 1 & 1 & 2 \\ 0 & -2 & -2 \end{pmatrix}$ .... Find D^n by raising each eigenvalue to the power n.
n is odd so $(-1)^n = -1$.

$= \dfrac{1}{2}\begin{pmatrix} 1 & 1 & 1 \\ 1 & -1 & -1 \\ -1 & 1 & 0 \end{pmatrix}\begin{pmatrix} 1 & 1 & 0 \\ -1 & -1 & -2 \\ 0 & -2^{n+1} & -2^{n+1} \end{pmatrix}$

$= \dfrac{1}{2}\begin{pmatrix} 0 & -2^{n+1} & -2-2^{n+1} \\ 2 & 2+2^{n+1} & 2+2^{n+1} \\ -2 & -2 & -2 \end{pmatrix}$

$= \begin{pmatrix} 0 & -2^n & -1-2^n \\ 1 & 1+2^n & 1+2^n \\ -1 & -1 & -1 \end{pmatrix}$ .... Check that your answer is consistent with the original matrix M.

EXERCISE 6F

1 For each matrix, if the matrix can be given in the form UDU^{-1} where D is a diagonal matrix, give U and D.

a i $\begin{pmatrix} 3 & 4 \\ 8 & -1 \end{pmatrix}$ **ii** $\begin{pmatrix} 3 & 2 \\ 3 & 4 \end{pmatrix}$

b i $\begin{pmatrix} 3 & -4 \\ 1 & 7 \end{pmatrix}$ **ii** $\begin{pmatrix} -2 & 5 \\ -5 & 8 \end{pmatrix}$

> **Tip**
> There is not a unique diagonalised form. For example, reordering the eigenvalues and eigenvectors will produce different matrices U and D.

2 Each of these matrices has an eigenvalue 1. For each matrix, if it can be written in diagonalised form UDU^{-1} where D is a diagonal matrix, find U and D.

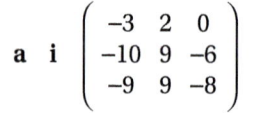

a i $\begin{pmatrix} -3 & 2 & 0 \\ -10 & 9 & -6 \\ -9 & 9 & -8 \end{pmatrix}$ **ii** $\begin{pmatrix} 2 & -2 & 4 \\ -10 & 9 & -4 \\ -15 & 14 & -11 \end{pmatrix}$

b i $\begin{pmatrix} 7 & 15 & -5 \\ -1 & -1 & 1 \\ 3 & 9 & -1 \end{pmatrix}$ **ii** $\begin{pmatrix} -3 & 12 & 8 \\ -1 & 4 & 2 \\ -1 & 3 & 3 \end{pmatrix}$

3 Express $\begin{pmatrix} 2 & -1 \\ 2 & 5 \end{pmatrix}$ in the form UDU^{-1}, where D is a diagonal matrix.

6 Further matrices

4 Explain why $\begin{pmatrix} 7 & 2 \\ -8 & -1 \end{pmatrix}$ cannot be written in the form $\mathbf{UDU}^{-1}$, where $\mathbf{D}$ is a diagonal matrix.

5 Matrix $\mathbf{M}$ has eigenvectors $\begin{pmatrix} 1 \\ 3 \end{pmatrix}$ and $\begin{pmatrix} 1 \\ 1 \end{pmatrix}$ and eigenvalues 1 and -2.

  a Find two possible matrices $\mathbf{M}_1$ and $\mathbf{M}_2$.

  b Find the product $\mathbf{M}_1\mathbf{M}_2$ and comment on your answer.

6 Matrix $\mathbf{A}$ is given by $\mathbf{A} = \begin{pmatrix} 4 & -4 \\ 3 & -4 \end{pmatrix}$.

  a Find a matrix $\mathbf{U}$ and a diagonal matrix $\mathbf{D}$ such that $\mathbf{A} = \mathbf{UDU}^{-1}$.

  b Find $\mathbf{A}^n$ for integer n when:

  i n is odd
  ii n is even.

7 Transformation T is described by matrix $\mathbf{M}$ where $\mathbf{M} = \begin{pmatrix} 1 & -\sqrt{3} \\ -\sqrt{3} & -1 \end{pmatrix}$.

  a If $\det \mathbf{M} = -k^2$ for some positive k, calculate k.

  b Find the two eigenvectors of $\mathbf{M}$ and their associated eigenvalues and show that the two eigenvectors are perpendicular.

  c T is the composition of an enlargement with scale factor k and another transformation R. Describe R.

  d By diagonalising $\mathbf{M}$, or otherwise, find $\mathbf{M}^{11}$.

8 a Express $\mathbf{M} = \begin{pmatrix} -9 & 14 & -5 \\ -2 & 4 & -2 \\ 16 & -22 & 6 \end{pmatrix}$ in the form $\mathbf{UDU}^{-1}$, where $\mathbf{D}$ is a diagonal matrix.

  b Hence find $\mathbf{M}^n$ for odd integer n, in terms of n.

9 a Describe the transformation given by matrix $\mathbf{A} = \dfrac{1}{2}\begin{pmatrix} \sqrt{3} & -1 \\ 1 & \sqrt{3} \end{pmatrix}$.

  b Show that $e^{i\frac{\pi}{6}}$ is an eigenvalue of $\mathbf{A}$ and find the other eigenvalue and the complex eigenvector associated with each.

  c Use your answer to part **b** to write $\mathbf{A}$ in the form $\mathbf{A} = \mathbf{UDU}^{-1}$ for some diagonal matrix $\mathbf{D}$.

  d Hence show that $\mathbf{A}^{12} = \mathbf{I}$.

Checklist of learning and understanding

- The transpose of a matrix obeys these rules:
  - $(\mathbf{AB})^T = \mathbf{B}^T\mathbf{A}^T$
  - $(\mathbf{A} + \mathbf{B})^T = \mathbf{A}^T + \mathbf{B}^T$.
- The determinant of a 3×3 matrix $\mathbf{A}$:
  - (expanding along the first row) is calculated as

  $$\det\begin{pmatrix} a_{11} & a_{12} & a_{13} \\ a_{21} & a_{22} & a_{23} \\ a_{31} & a_{32} & a_{33} \end{pmatrix} = a_{11}\begin{vmatrix} a_{22} & a_{23} \\ a_{32} & a_{33} \end{vmatrix} - a_{12}\begin{vmatrix} a_{21} & a_{23} \\ a_{31} & a_{33} \end{vmatrix} + a_{13}\begin{vmatrix} a_{21} & a_{22} \\ a_{31} & a_{32} \end{vmatrix}$$

  - the same value is obtained by expanding along any row or column
  - represents the volume scale factor of linear transformation $\mathbf{A}$.
- The inverse of a non-singular 3×3 matrix $\mathbf{A}$ is given by

  $$\mathbf{A}^{-1} = \frac{1}{\det \mathbf{A}}\mathbf{C}^T$$

  where $\mathbf{C}$ is the matrix of cofactors of $\mathbf{A}$.
- The vector product $\mathbf{a} \times \mathbf{b}$ can be calculated using matrix determinants:

  $$\begin{pmatrix} a_1 \\ a_2 \\ a_3 \end{pmatrix} \times \begin{pmatrix} b_1 \\ b_2 \\ b_3 \end{pmatrix} = \det\begin{pmatrix} \mathbf{i} & a_1 & b_1 \\ \mathbf{j} & a_2 & b_2 \\ \mathbf{k} & a_3 & b_3 \end{pmatrix}$$

- Three simple row operations affect the determinant in predictable ways.
  - Matrix $\mathbf{N}$ is obtained from matrix $\mathbf{M}$ by swapping two rows:

    $$\det \mathbf{N} = -\det \mathbf{M}.$$

  - Matrix $\mathbf{N}$ is obtained from matrix $\mathbf{M}$ by multiplying one row by constant k:

    $$\det \mathbf{N} = k \det \mathbf{M}.$$

  - Matrix $\mathbf{N}$ is obtained from matrix $\mathbf{M}$ by adding a multiple of one row to another row:

    $$\det \mathbf{N} = \det \mathbf{M}.$$

  - Equivalent column operations follow the same pattern.
- You can represent a system of three linear simultaneous equations in three unknowns in matrix form as

  $$\mathbf{Mr} = \mathbf{a} \text{ where } \mathbf{r} = \begin{pmatrix} x \\ y \\ z \end{pmatrix}.$$

  Each row of matrix $\mathbf{M}$ contains the coefficients of x, y and z in the planes described.
  - If $\det \mathbf{M} \neq 0$ there is a unique solution representing the point intersection of the three planes.

    $$\mathbf{r} = \mathbf{M}^{-1}\mathbf{a}$$

  - If $\det \mathbf{M} = 0$ then the three planes do not intersect at a single point and could be
    - inconsistent (no common intersection)
    - consistent (line or plane as the common intersection).
  - When $\det \mathbf{M} = 0$, you can determine the geometrical interpretation by considering the consistency of the system and the number of parallel planes.
- An eigenvalue λ and associated eigenvector $\mathbf{v}$ of a matrix $\mathbf{M}$ have the property that

  $$\mathbf{Mv} = \lambda \mathbf{v}.$$

- The eigenvalues of an $n \times n$ matrix $\mathbf{M}$ are the n roots of the polynomial

  $$\det(\mathbf{M} - \lambda \mathbf{I}) = 0$$

  - Each eigenvalue has an associated eigenvector.
  - Repeated eigenvalues can have multiple eigenvectors.

Continues on next page

- If an $n \times n$ matrix **M** has n non-parallel eigenvectors $\mathbf{v}_1, \ldots, \mathbf{v}_n$, then you can express **M** in diagonalised form as
$$\mathbf{M} = \mathbf{UDU}^{-1}$$
where $\mathbf{U} = [\,\mathbf{v}_1 \ldots \mathbf{v}_n\,]$ and **D** is a diagonal matrix with lead diagonal elements $\lambda_1 \ldots \lambda_n$.
- If $\mathbf{M} = \mathbf{UDU}^{-1}$, then $\mathbf{M}^k = \mathbf{UD}^k\mathbf{U}^{-1}$ for integer k.

Mixed practice 6

1 Find the sum of the eigenvalues of the matrix $\begin{pmatrix} 6 & 8 \\ 1 & 4 \end{pmatrix}$.

Choose from these options.

A 4 **B** 6 **C** 10 **D** 16

2 Find the value of k that results in the system of equations shown having a non-unique solution.

$$\begin{cases} x + y + z = k \\ x - y + z = k^2 \\ kx + 2ky + 3kz = k^3 \end{cases}$$

Choose from these options.

A 0 **B** 1 **C** 2 **D** 3

3 Find the eigenvalues and associated eigenvectors of $\mathbf{A} = \begin{pmatrix} 4 & -2 \\ -2 & 7 \end{pmatrix}$.

4 $\begin{pmatrix} 1 \\ 2 \end{pmatrix}$ is an eigenvector of matrix $\mathbf{M} = \begin{pmatrix} 3 & 1 \\ 4 & x \end{pmatrix}$.

  a Find the value of x.

  b Find the eigenvalue associated with $\begin{pmatrix} 1 \\ 2 \end{pmatrix}$ and find the remaining eigenvalue and associated eigenvector.

5 Let $\Delta = \begin{vmatrix} 1 & 2 & 3 \\ x & y & z \\ y+z & z+x & x+y \end{vmatrix}$.

  a Use a row operation to show that $(x + y + z)$ is a factor of Δ.

  b Hence, or otherwise, express Δ as a product of linear factors.

[©AQA 2011]

6 Matrix $\mathbf{A} = \begin{pmatrix} x & x & x+3 \\ 2 & 5 & x-1 \\ x & 4 & -4 \end{pmatrix}$ is singular.

Using row operations, or otherwise, show that $(x - 1)$ is a factor of det $\mathbf{A}$ and hence show there is only one real value x.

7 Let $\mathbf{X} = \begin{pmatrix} 3 & x \\ -1 & 7 \end{pmatrix}$.

  a Determine $\mathbf{X}\mathbf{X}^\mathrm{T}$.

  b Show that $\det(\mathbf{X}\mathbf{X}^\mathrm{T} - \mathbf{X}^\mathrm{T}\mathbf{X}) \leq 0$ for all real values of x.

  c Find the value of x for which the matrix $(\mathbf{X}\mathbf{X}^\mathrm{T} - \mathbf{X}^\mathrm{T}\mathbf{X})$ is singular.

[©AQA 2012]

8 **a** Find the values of t for which the system of equations

$$\begin{cases} tx + 2y + 3z = a \\ 2x + 3y - tz = b \\ 3x + 5y + (t+1)z = c \end{cases}$$

does not have a unique solution.

b For the integer value of t found in part **a**, find the relationship between a, b and c such that this system of equations is consistent.

[©AQA 2011]

9 Let $\Delta = \begin{vmatrix} yz & xz & xy \\ x & y & z \\ x^2 & -y^2 & z^2 \end{vmatrix}$.

a Show that $(y+z)$ is a factor of Δ.

b Factorise Δ as completely as possible.

[©AQA 2012]

10 **a** Determine the two values of k for which the system of equations

$$\begin{cases} x - 2y + kz = 5 \\ (k+1)x + 3y = k \\ x + 3y - z = -2 \end{cases}$$

does not have a unique solution.

b Show that this system of equations is consistent for one of these values of k, but is inconsistent for the other.

(You are not required to find any solutions to this system of equations.)

[©AQA 2010]

11 The matrices **A** and **B** are defined in terms of a real parameter t by

$$\mathbf{A} = \begin{pmatrix} 1 & 2 & 1 \\ 2 & t & 4 \\ 3 & 2 & -1 \end{pmatrix} \text{ and } \mathbf{B} = \begin{pmatrix} 15 & -4 & -1 \\ -2t & 4 & 2 \\ 17 & -4 & -3 \end{pmatrix}.$$

a Find, in terms of t, the matrix **AB** and deduce that there exists a value of t such that **AB** is a scalar multiple of the 3×3 identity matrix **I**.

b For this value of t, deduce $\mathbf{A}^{-1}$.

[©AQA 2010]

12 Factorise fully the determinant

$$\begin{vmatrix} x & y & z \\ x^2 & y^2 & z^2 \\ yz & zx & xy \end{vmatrix}.$$

[©AQA 2010]

13 Consider this system of equations, where a and b are real.
$$\begin{cases} ax + 9y + 6z = 6 \\ ay - z = b \\ x + 6y + z = 4 \end{cases}$$

   a Given that the system has no unique solution, find all possible values of a.

   b When the system has a unique solution, find that solution in terms of a when $b = -1$.

   c Find k such that the system is always consistent when $a = kb$.

14 The 3×3 matrices **A** and **B** satisfy
$$\mathbf{AB} = \begin{pmatrix} k & 8 & 1 \\ 1 & 1 & 0 \\ 1 & 4 & 0 \end{pmatrix}, \text{ where } \mathbf{A} = \begin{pmatrix} k & 6 & 8 \\ 0 & 1 & 2 \\ -3 & 4 & 8 \end{pmatrix}$$

   and k is constant.

   a Show that **AB** is non-singular.   b Find $(\mathbf{AB})^{-1}$ in terms of k.   c Find $\mathbf{B}^{-1}$.

[©AQA 2013]

15 Let $\Delta = \begin{vmatrix} a & -12 & 1 \\ 4 & -3a & a-3 \\ -3 & 4a & a+4 \end{vmatrix}$.

   a Use a row operation to show that $a - 4$ is a factor of Δ.

   b Factorise Δ as fully as possible.

[©AQA 2016]

16 The matrix **A** is given by $\mathbf{A} = \begin{pmatrix} 1 & 0 & -1 \\ 1 & 2 & 1 \\ 2 & 2 & 3 \end{pmatrix}$.

   a Given that $\mathbf{A}^2 = \begin{pmatrix} p & -2 & -4 \\ 5 & 6 & 4 \\ 10 & q & 9 \end{pmatrix}$, find the value of p and the value of q.

   b Given that $\mathbf{A}^3 - 6\mathbf{A}^2 + 11\mathbf{A} - 6\mathbf{I} = \mathbf{0}$, prove that
   $\mathbf{A}^{-1} = \frac{1}{6}(\mathbf{A}^2 - 6\mathbf{A} + 11\mathbf{I})$.

   c Given that $\mathbf{A}^{-1} = \frac{1}{6}\begin{pmatrix} r & -2 & 2 \\ -1 & 5 & -2 \\ -2 & s & 2 \end{pmatrix}$, find the value of r and the value of s.

   d Hence, or otherwise, find the solution of the system of equations
$$\begin{cases} x - z = k \\ x + 2y + z = 5 \\ 2x + 2y + 3z = 7 \end{cases}$$

   giving your answer in terms of k.

[©AQA 2013]

6 Further matrices

17 a By direct expansion, or otherwise, show that the value of $\begin{vmatrix} -3 & 5 & 3k+1 \\ -1 & 2 & k+1 \\ 2 & k-3 & 1 \end{vmatrix}$ is independent of k.

b i State, with a reason, whether the equations $\begin{cases} -3x + 5y + 7z = 3 \\ -x + 2y + 3z = 2 \\ 2x - y + z = 6 \end{cases}$ are consistent or inconsistent.

ii The three equations given in part **b i** are the Cartesian equations of three planes. State the geometrical configuration of these three planes.

18 The matrix $\mathbf{M} = \begin{pmatrix} 1 & 4 & 2 \\ 3 & k & 3 \\ 2 & k & 1 \end{pmatrix}$, where k is a constant.

a Show that $\mathbf{M}$ is non-singular for all values of k.

b Obtain $\mathbf{M}^{-1}$ in terms of k.

c Use $\mathbf{M}^{-1}$ to solve the equations

$$\begin{cases} x + 4y + 2z = 25 \\ 3x + ky + 3z = 3 \\ 2x + ky + z = 2 \end{cases}$$

giving your solution in terms of k.

[©AQA 2014]

19 The matrix $\mathbf{M} = \begin{pmatrix} 1 & 1 & 2 \\ 0 & 5 & -1 \\ 2 & p & 1 \end{pmatrix}$, where p is a constant, has three distinct eigenvalues λ_1, λ_2 and λ_3.

a Given that $\lambda_1 = 2$, find the value of p.

b Given that $\lambda_2 < 0$, find the values of λ_2 and λ_3.

c The transformation T has matrix $\mathbf{M}$. Find a vector equation for any one of the invariant lines of T.

[©AQA 2016]

20 The transformation T is represented by the matrix $\mathbf{M}$ with diagonalised form

$$\mathbf{M} = \mathbf{UDU}^{-1}$$

where $\mathbf{U} = \begin{pmatrix} 4 & -1 \\ 1 & 3 \end{pmatrix}$ and $\mathbf{D} = \begin{pmatrix} 27 & 0 \\ 0 & 1 \end{pmatrix}$.

a i State the eigenvalues, and corresponding eigenvectors, of $\mathbf{M}$.

ii Find a Cartesian equation for the line of invariant points of T.

b Write down $\mathbf{U}^{-1}$, and hence find the matrix $\mathbf{M}$ in the form $\begin{pmatrix} a & b \\ c & d \end{pmatrix}$ where a, b, c and d are integers.

c By finding the element in the first row, first column position of $\mathbf{M}^n$, prove that

$$4 \times 3^{3n+1} + 1$$

is a multiple of 13 for all positive integers n.

[©AQA 2010]

FOCUS ON ... PROOF 1

Extending the proof of De Moivre's theorem

De Moivre's theorem states that

$$(r(\cos\theta + i\sin\theta))^n = r^n(\cos n\theta + i\sin n\theta).$$

In Chapter 1, Section 1, you saw how to prove this result for integer values of n. However, the result extends, with a little bit of careful consideration of conventions, to rational values.

Proving the result for rational values

You have to be a little careful when raising a number to a rational power. For example, if you write z as $r(\cos\theta + i\sin\theta)$, then you can also write it as $r(\cos(\theta + 2k\pi) + i\sin(\theta + 2k\pi))$. If you could apply De Moivre's theorem with a rational power $\frac{a}{b}$ with a and b integers with no common factors, then $z^{\frac{a}{b}}$ would equal $r^{\frac{a}{b}}\left(\cos\left(\frac{a}{b}\theta + \frac{2ak\pi}{b}\right) + i\sin\left(\frac{a}{b}\theta + \frac{2ak\pi}{b}\right)\right)$.

This has b different values, corresponding to $k = 0, 1, \ldots, b-1$.

Multi-valued expressions are usually considered inconvenient, so you need to apply a convention that when raising to a rational power you choose θ to be the smallest positive value and $k = 0$. This is called the principal root.

> **Tip**
>
> Notice that when the power is an integer (for example: $b = 1$) then there is no problem – there is only one possible answer.

QUESTION

1 By considering $(r(\cos\theta + i\sin\theta))^{\frac{a}{b}} = r^n(\cos m\theta + i\sin m\theta)$, prove that one possible value for m and n is $\frac{a}{b}$.

[You can assume De Moivre's theorem for integer powers and that the normal rules for indices hold.]

Not proving the result for irrational numbers

It is tempting to think that if De Moivre's theorem can be proved for all rational numbers, then it must hold for irrational numbers. However, this turns out to be difficult to define. For example: consider 1^π.

As at the start of this section, you could write $1 = \cos 2k\pi + i\sin 2k\pi$. Then, if De Moivre's theorem did extend to irrational numbers, you would have

$$1^\pi = \cos 2k\pi^2 + i\sin 2k\pi^2.$$

Unlike in the rational case, there is no period to this expression.

Each different value of k therefore produces a different value for the expression. There are therefore infinitely many values (all lying on the circle with modulus 1), which makes this expression very hard to work with.

Focus on ... Proof 1

QUESTION

2 Use proof by contradiction to prove that if

$$\cos 2m\pi^2 + i \sin 2m\pi^2 = \cos 2p\pi^2 + i \sin 2p\pi^2,$$

then $m = p$.

[You can assume that the period of the $\cos \theta + i \sin \theta$ function is 2π and that π is an irrational number.]

FOCUS ON ... PROBLEM SOLVING 1

Using complex numbers to describe rotations

You know two different ways to describe rotations in a plane. The first method involves using matrices.

You can find the image of a point with position vector $\begin{pmatrix} x \\ y \end{pmatrix}$ after a rotation through an angle θ about the origin by multiplying it by the rotation matrix:

$$\begin{pmatrix} \cos\theta & -\sin\theta \\ \sin\theta & \cos\theta \end{pmatrix} \begin{pmatrix} x \\ y \end{pmatrix} = \begin{pmatrix} x\cos\theta - y\sin\theta \\ x\sin\theta + y\cos\theta \end{pmatrix}$$

> **Rewind**
>
> You met the rotation matrix in Further Mathematics Student Book 1, Chapter 8.

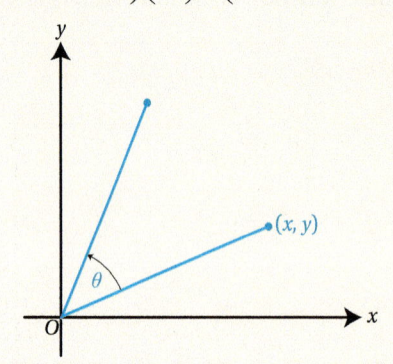

The second method involves using complex numbers. When a point corresponding to a complex number $z = x + iy$ is rotated through an angle θ about the origin, you can find the complex number corresponding to the image point by multiplying z by $e^{i\theta} = \cos\theta + i\sin\theta$:

$$(x + iy)(\cos\theta + i\sin\theta) = (x\cos\theta - y\sin\theta) + i(x\sin\theta + y\cos\theta)$$

> **Rewind**
>
> You met the idea of multiplication by $e^{i\theta}$ representing a rotation in Chapter 1, Section 6.

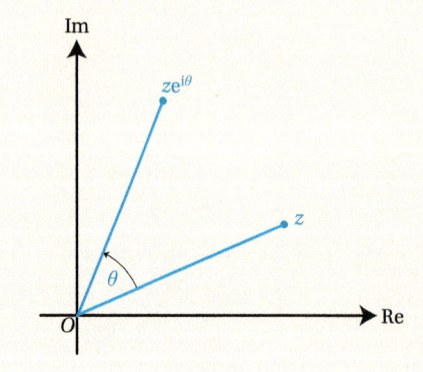

You can see that the two methods give the same coordinates of the image point. The advantage of the complex numbers method is that it results in a single equation, whereas the matrix method results in two equations (one for each component).

In this section you will compare the two methods when solving this problem:

> Three snails start at the vertices of an equilateral triangle. Each snail moves with a constant speed towards an adjacent snail: S_1 towards S_2, S_2 towards S_3 and S_3 towards S_1. Describe the path followed by each snail. After how long (if at all) do the snails meet?

Focus on ... Problem solving 1

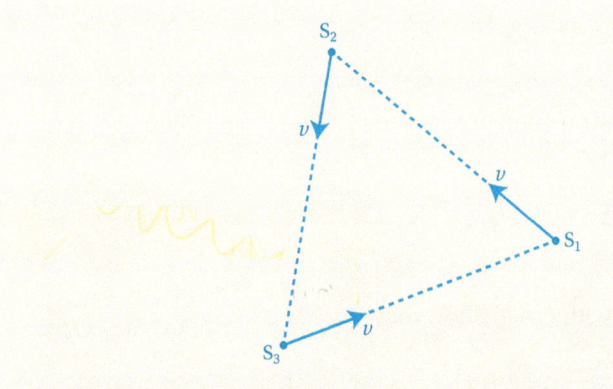

First you need to specify the problem a little more precisely. Set up the coordinate axes so that the origin is at the centre of the equilateral triangle and let the initial position of S_1 be at $(1, 0)$. Let v be the speed of each snail.

Because of the symmetry of the situation, the three snails will always form an equilateral triangle. You only need to find the path followed by S_1. You can find the position of S_2 by rotating S_1 through $120°$ anticlockwise about the origin, and you can find the position of S_3 by rotating S_2 through the same angle.

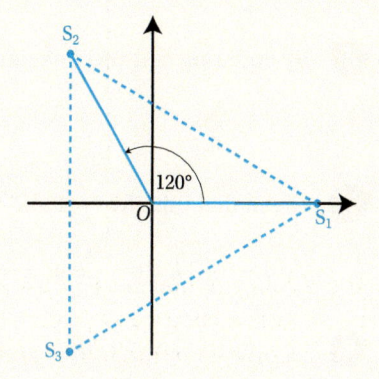

You will first approach the problem by using position vectors and matrices.

QUESTIONS

Let $\mathbf{r} = \begin{pmatrix} x \\ y \end{pmatrix}$ be the position vector of S_1 at time t.

1 Use a rotation matrix to write down the position vector of S_2 in terms of x and y.

2 Explain why $\dfrac{d\mathbf{r}}{dt} = k \begin{pmatrix} -\dfrac{3}{2}x - \dfrac{\sqrt{3}}{2}y \\ \dfrac{\sqrt{3}}{2}x - \dfrac{3}{2}y \end{pmatrix}$ for some constant k. Show that $k = \dfrac{v}{\sqrt{3}\sqrt{x^2 + y^2}}$.

3 Hence show that x and y satisfy this system of differential equations.

$$\begin{cases} 2\sqrt{x^2 + y^2}\,\dfrac{dx}{dt} = -v\sqrt{3}\,x - vy \\ 2\sqrt{x^2 + y^2}\,\dfrac{dy}{dt} = vx - v\sqrt{3}\,y \end{cases}$$

Although you will learn in Chapter 12 how to solve some systems of differential equations, these equations are non-linear so the methods from that chapter won't work here. You will return to the system of equations in Question 3 later, but for now you will consider a different approach.

QUESTIONS

Now, let z be the complex number corresponding to the position of S_1 at time t. Then the position of S_2 is given by $ze^{i\frac{2\pi}{3}}$.

4 Show that $\dfrac{dz}{dt} = \dfrac{v}{\sqrt{3}}\left(e^{i\frac{2\pi}{3}} - 1\right)\dfrac{z}{|z|}$.

5 Write $z = re^{i\theta}$. (Remember that both r and θ vary with time.) Show that:
$$\frac{dr}{dt} + ir\frac{d\theta}{dt} = \frac{v}{\sqrt{3}}\left(e^{i\frac{2\pi}{3}} - 1\right).$$

6 By equating real and imaginary parts, obtain this system of differential equations for r and θ.
$$\frac{dr}{dt} = -\frac{\sqrt{3}v}{2}, \quad \frac{d\theta}{dt} = \frac{v}{2r}$$

7 Given that initially $r = 1$ and $\theta = 0$, show that
$$r = 1 - \frac{\sqrt{3}v}{2}t, \quad \theta = -\frac{1}{\sqrt{3}}\ln\left(1 - \frac{\sqrt{3}v}{2}t\right).$$

8 The position of S_1 is then given by $z = re^{i\theta}$, S_2 by $re^{i\left(\theta + \frac{2\pi}{3}\right)}$ and S_3 by $re^{i\left(\theta + \frac{4\pi}{3}\right)}$.

At what time do the snails meet at the origin? What happens to the value of θ as t approaches this value?

The curve described by the equations in Question **7** is called a logarithmic spiral. Although each snail travels a finite distance $\left(v\dfrac{2}{\sqrt{3}v} = \dfrac{2}{\sqrt{3}}\right)$, it performs an infinite number of rotations. This diagram shows the paths of all three snails, and their positions when $t = 0$ and $t \approx \dfrac{0.7}{v}$.

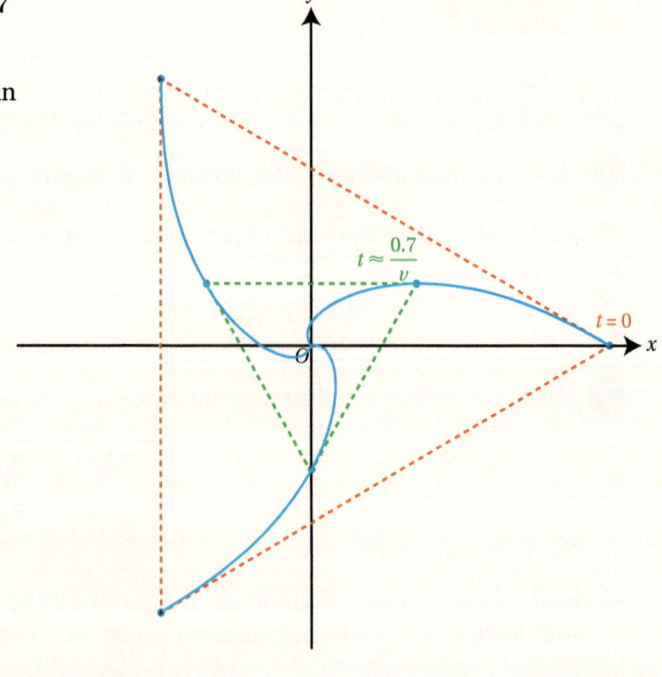

158

Focus on ... Problem solving 1

In this problem, using complex numbers resulted in equations you could solve, while this was not the case when using position vectors and matrices.

In Question **6**, you derived two separate differential equations for r and θ, which are the modulus and the argument of the complex number representing the position of S_1. This suggests that you might also be able to solve this problem by using polar coordinates, which are basically the same as the modulus and argument of a complex number.

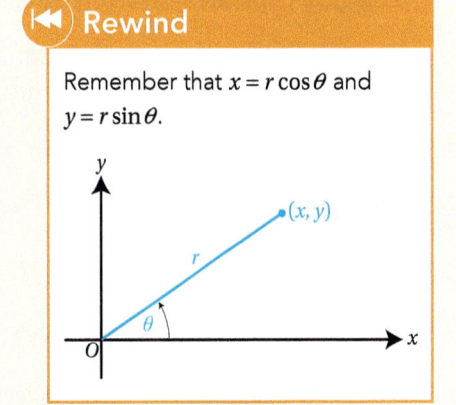

> ⏮ **Rewind**
>
> Remember that $x = r\cos\theta$ and $y = r\sin\theta$.

Look again at the system of equations from Question **3**:

$$\begin{cases} 2\sqrt{x^2+y^2}\,\dfrac{dx}{dt} = -v\sqrt{3}\,x - vy \\ 2\sqrt{x^2+y^2}\,\dfrac{dy}{dt} = vx - v\sqrt{3}\,y \end{cases}$$

Let r and θ be the polar coordinates of the point (x, y). Then the 'problem' term in the equations, $\sqrt{x^2+y^2}$, is simply r. You can rewrite the equations in terms of r and θ.

QUESTIONS

9 Show that $\dfrac{dx}{dt} = \dfrac{dr}{dt}\cos\theta - r\dfrac{d\theta}{dt}\sin\theta$ and obtain a similar expression for $\dfrac{dy}{dt}$.

10 Rewrite the system of equations in terms of r and θ. Combine the two equations to show that

$$\dfrac{dr}{dt} = -\dfrac{v\sqrt{3}}{2},\ \dfrac{d\theta}{dt} = \dfrac{v}{2r}.$$

> 💡 **Tip**
>
> Notice that these are the same equations you derived in Question **6**.

11 Obtain an expression for $\dfrac{dr}{d\theta}$ and hence show that $r = e^{-\sqrt{3}\,\theta}$.

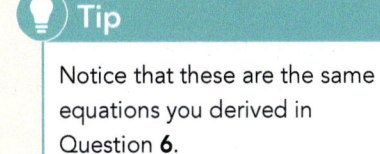

The final equation in Question **11** is the polar equation of a logarithmic spiral, the path followed by each snail.

FOCUS ON ... MODELLING 1

Leslie matrices

Matrices are applied in many different real-life situations. Leslie matrices have a particular application to a biological population structured into different groups such as adults and juveniles.

Imagine a group of rabbits. Each adult on average produces 3 juvenile rabbits each year. Each year 10% of adult rabbits die and 20% of juvenile rabbits die. Those juveniles who do not die become adults.

The number of adult rabbits in year n is denoted by a_n and the number of juvenile rabbits is denoted by j_n.

QUESTIONS

1 Explain why $a_{n+1} = 0.9a_n + 0.8j_n$.

2 Find an expression for j_{n+1} in terms of a_n.

3 The equations found in questions **1** and **2** can be written in a matrix form as $\begin{pmatrix} a_{n+1} \\ j_{n+1} \end{pmatrix} = \mathbf{M} \begin{pmatrix} a_n \\ j_n \end{pmatrix}$

Write down the matrix **M**.

4 An uninhabited island is populated with 200 adult rabbits in year 0. Use technology to find the number of adult rabbits in:

    a year 1   **b** year 10.

5 By investigating the sequence formed, find the long-term growth rate of the population.

6 Find the long-term ratio of juveniles to adults.

7 Find the eigenvalues and eigenvectors of **M**. What do you notice?

8 The population of rabbits is infected with a disease which decreases the average number of juvenile rabbits produced per adult rabbit each year to α. Find the smallest value of α so that the population will not become extinct.

9 Describe the assumptions made in creating this model.

10 In an alternative model each adult rabbit produces exactly one juvenile each year and there is no death. If the population starts with one (presumably pregnant) adult, investigate the number of adult rabbits after n years.

CROSS-TOPIC REVIEW EXERCISE 1

1 a Show that $\cos z = \dfrac{e^{iz} + e^{-iz}}{2}$.

b Hence find the value of $\cos 2i$ correct to three significant figures.

2 a Express $-8i$ in the form $re^{i\theta}$, where $r > 0$ and $-\pi < \theta \leqslant \pi$.

b Solve the equation $z^6 + 8i = 0$, giving your answers in the form $re^{i\theta}$, where $r > 0$ and $-\pi < \theta \leqslant \pi$.

3 The hyperbola H has equation $\dfrac{x^2}{8} - \dfrac{y^2}{3} = 1$.

Describe a sequence of two transformations that map H onto the curve with equation $x^2 = 4(2y^2 - x + 1)$.

4 The diagram shows the graph of $y = f(x)$.

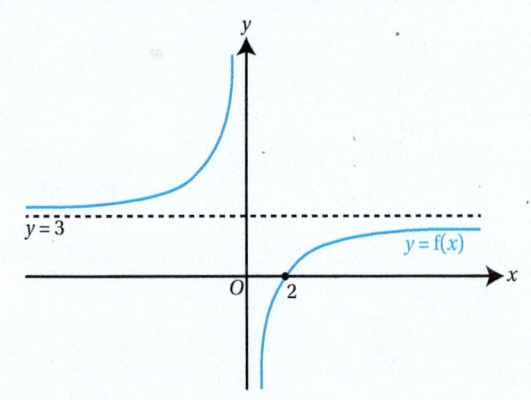

On separate axes, sketch the graphs of:

a $y = \dfrac{1}{f(x)}$ **b** $y = |f(x)|$.

5 a Sketch the graph of $y = |\operatorname{arsinh} x|$.

b Solve the inequality $|\operatorname{arsinh} x| > \ln 3$.

6 a On the same axes, sketch the graphs of:

i $y = |3x - 7|$ **ii** $y = |x^2 - x - 12|$.

b Solve the inequality $|x^2 - x - 12| < |3x - 7|$.

7 Points A, B and C have coordinates $(-3, 1, 1)$, $(0, 5, 2)$ and $(1, -3, 6)$ respectively.

a Find $\overrightarrow{AB} \times \overrightarrow{AC}$.

b Hence find the vector equation of the line through A that is perpendicular to AB and AC.

8 a Find the Cartesian equation of the plane Π_1 containing the points $(1, 1, 0)$, $(0, -2, 0)$ and $(0, 1, 2)$.

The plane Π_2 has Cartesian equation $2x + 3y - 4z = 5$.

   b Find, to three significant figures, the acute angle between the planes Π_1 and Π_2.

9 a Given that a and $(a + i)^5$ are both real, show that with $a > 0$, $a^2 = \dfrac{5 \pm 2\sqrt{5}}{5}$.

   b Find, in terms of a, the argument of $(a + i)^5$.

   c Hence show that $\cot \dfrac{\pi}{5} = \sqrt{\dfrac{5 + 2\sqrt{5}}{5}}$.

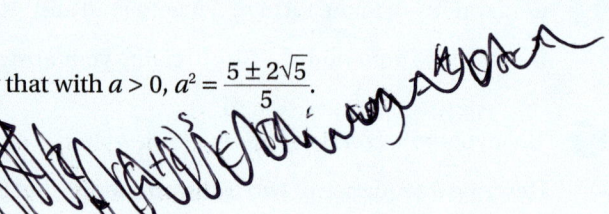

10 Find the smallest positive integer values of p and q for which
$$\frac{\left(\cos \dfrac{\pi}{8} + i \sin \dfrac{\pi}{8}\right)^p}{\left(\cos \dfrac{\pi}{12} - i \sin \dfrac{\pi}{12}\right)^q} = i.$$

[©AQA 2012]

11 Let $\mathbf{a} = 3\mathbf{i} + \mathbf{k}$, $\mathbf{b} = -\mathbf{i} + 5\mathbf{j} + p\mathbf{k}$ and $\mathbf{c} = \mathbf{i} + 4\mathbf{j} - 3\mathbf{k}$.

   a Find $\mathbf{a} \times \mathbf{b}$.

   b Find the value of p, given that $\mathbf{a} \times \mathbf{b}$ is parallel to $\mathbf{c}$.

12 a Expand and simplify, as far as possible, $(\mathbf{a} - 4\mathbf{b}) \times (\mathbf{a} + 3\mathbf{b})$ where $\mathbf{a}$ and $\mathbf{b}$ are vectors.

   b Given that $\mathbf{a}$ and $\mathbf{b}$ are perpendicular, deduce that $|(\mathbf{a} - 4\mathbf{b}) \times (\mathbf{a} + 3\mathbf{b})| = \lambda |\mathbf{a}||\mathbf{b}|$ where λ is an integer.

[©AQA 2013]

13 a Determine the two values of the integer n for which the system of equations
$$\begin{cases} 2x + ny + z = 5 \\ 3x - y + nz = 1 \\ -x + 7y + z = n \end{cases}$$
does not have a unique solution.

   b For the positive value of n found in part a, determine whether the system is consistent or inconsistent, and interpret this result geometrically.

[©AQA 2012]

14 The linear transformation T is represented by the matrix $\mathbf{M} = \begin{pmatrix} -k\sqrt{3} & 0 & -k \\ 0 & 2k & 0 \\ k & 0 & -k\sqrt{3} \end{pmatrix}$.

   a Find the determinant of $\mathbf{M}$ in terms of k.

   b The transformation T is the composition of two transformations. The first transformation, T_1, is an enlargement centre O and scale factor $2k\,(k>0)$, and the second is a transformation T_2. When T is applied to a solid shape of volume $48\,\text{cm}^3$, the volume of the image is $0.75\,\text{cm}^3$.

   i Find the value of k and hence state the scale factor of the enlargement.

   ii Give a full geometrical description of T_2.

   [©AQA 2016]

15 The matrix $\mathbf{A} = \begin{pmatrix} k & 1 & 2 \\ 2 & k & 1 \\ 1 & 2 & k \end{pmatrix}$, where k is a real constant.

   a **i** Show that there is a value of k for which

   $$\mathbf{AA}^\mathsf{T} = m\mathbf{I}$$

   where m is a rational number to be determined and $\mathbf{I}$ is the 3×3 identity matrix.

   ii Deduce the inverse matrix, $\mathbf{A}^{-1}$, of $\mathbf{A}$ for this value of k.

   b **i** Find $\det \mathbf{A}$ in terms of k.

   ii In the case when $\mathbf{A}$ is singular, find the integer value of k and show that there are no other possible real values of k.

   iii Find the value of k for which $\lambda = 7$ is a real eigenvalue of $\mathbf{A}$.

   [©AQA 2012]

16 Let $\mathbf{Y} = \begin{pmatrix} 3 & -1 & 1 \\ -1 & 3 & 1 \\ 1 & 1 & 3 \end{pmatrix}$.

   a Show that 4 is a repeated eigenvalue of $\mathbf{Y}$, and find the other eigenvalue of $\mathbf{Y}$.

   b For each eigenvalue of $\mathbf{Y}$, find a full set of eigenvectors.

   c The matrix $\mathbf{Y}$ represents the transformation T.

   Describe the geometrical significance of the eigenvectors of $\mathbf{Y}$ in relation to T.

   [©AQA 2011]

17 a Integrate e^{kx} with respect to x.

 b Show that for $x \in \mathbb{R}$, the imaginary part of $e^{(1+3i)x}$ is $e^x \sin 3x$.

 c Hence find the exact value of $\displaystyle\int_0^{\frac{\pi}{2}} e^x \sin 3x \, dx$.

18 a Show that $\cos z = \dfrac{e^{iz} + e^{-iz}}{2}$.

 b Hence find possible complex numbers z for which $\cos z = 2$.

19 a If $\mathbf{u} = \mathbf{i} + 2\mathbf{j} + 3\mathbf{k}$ and $\mathbf{v} = 2\mathbf{i} - \mathbf{j} + 2\mathbf{k}$, show that $\mathbf{u} \times \mathbf{v} = 7\mathbf{i} + 4\mathbf{j} - 5\mathbf{k}$.

 b Let $\mathbf{w} = \lambda\mathbf{u} + \mu\mathbf{v}$, where λ and μ are scalars. Show that $\mathbf{w}$ is perpendicular to the line of intersection of the planes $x + 2y + 3z = 5$ and $2x - y + 2z = 7$ for all values of λ and μ.

20 The matrix $\mathbf{M}$ is given by $\mathbf{M} = \begin{pmatrix} p & q \\ q & p \end{pmatrix}$ where p and q are constants and $q \neq 0$.

 a Find the eigenvalues of $\mathbf{M}$ in terms of p and q.

 b Find corresponding eigenvectors of $\mathbf{M}$.

 c Write down a matrix $\mathbf{U}$ and a diagonal matrix $\mathbf{D}$ such that $\mathbf{M} = \mathbf{UDU}^{-1}$.

 d Show that $\mathbf{M}^n = \mathbf{UD}^n\mathbf{U}^{-1}$.

 e Given that $p = 0.6$ and $q = 0.4$ and $\mathbf{M}^n \to \mathbf{L}$ as $n \to \infty$, find matrix $\mathbf{L}$.

[©AQA 2014]

21 The linear transformation T is represented by the matrix $\mathbf{M} = \begin{pmatrix} 1 & 2 & k \\ 0 & 3 & 4 \\ -1 & 1 & -1 \end{pmatrix}$.

 a In the case when $\mathbf{M}$ is a non-singular matrix:

  i find the possible values of k

  ii find $\mathbf{M}^{-1}$ in terms of k.

 b In the case when $k = 1$, the matrix $\mathbf{M}^{-1}$ is applied to a solid shape of volume 6 cm^3. Find the volume of the image.

 c In the case when $k = 5$, verify that the image of every point under T lies in the plane $x - y + z = 0$.

 d Find the value of k for which T has a line of invariant points and obtain the Cartesian equations of this line.

[©AQA 2015]

22 a i Use De Moivre's theorem to show that if $z = \cos\theta + i\sin\theta$, then
$$z^n - \frac{1}{z^n} = 2i\sin n\theta.$$

  ii Write down a similar expression for $z^n + \frac{1}{z^n}$.

b i Expand $\left(z - \frac{1}{z}\right)^2 \left(z + \frac{1}{z}\right)^2$ in terms of z.

  ii Hence show that
  $$8\sin^2\theta \cos^2\theta = A + B\cos 4\theta$$
  where A and B are integers.

c Hence, by means of the substitution $x = 2\sin\theta$, find the exact value of
$$\int_1^2 x^2\sqrt{4 - x^2}\, dx.$$

[©AQA 2014]

23 The plane transformation T is a rotation through θ radians anticlockwise about O, and maps points (x, y) onto image points (X, Y) such that
$$\begin{pmatrix} X \\ Y \end{pmatrix} = \begin{pmatrix} c & -s \\ s & c \end{pmatrix}\begin{pmatrix} x \\ y \end{pmatrix}$$
where $c = \cos\theta$ and $s = \sin\theta$.

a Write down the inverse of the matrix $\begin{pmatrix} c & -s \\ s & c \end{pmatrix}$ and hence show that
$$x = cX + sY \text{ and } y = -sX + cY.$$

b The curve C has equation $x^2 - 6xy - 7y^2 = 8$.

The image of C under T is the curve C' with equation $pX^2 + qXY + rY^2 = 8$.

  i Use the results of part **a** to show that
  $$q = 6s^2 + 16sc - 6c^2$$
  and express p and r in terms of c and s.

  ii Given that θ is an acute angle, find the values of c and s for which $q = 0$ and hence in this case express the equation of C' in the form
  $$\frac{X^2}{a^2} - \frac{Y^2}{b^2} = 1.$$

  iii Hence explain why C is a hyperbola.

[©AQA 2012]

24 The plane transformation T has matrix $\mathbf{A} = \begin{pmatrix} 1 & -2 \\ 2 & 1 \end{pmatrix}$, and maps points (x, y) onto image points (X, Y) such that

$$\begin{pmatrix} X \\ Y \end{pmatrix} = \mathbf{A} \begin{pmatrix} x \\ y \end{pmatrix}.$$

a   **i**   Find $\mathbf{A}^{-1}$.

    ii   Hence express each of x and y in terms of X and Y.

b   Give a full geometrical description of T.

c   **i**   Show that the curve E with equation $6x^2 + y^2 = 3$ is an ellipse.

    ii   Deduce that the image of the curve E under T has equation $2X^2 + 4XY + 5Y^2 = 15$.

    iii   Explain why the curve with equation $2x^2 + 4xy + 5y^2 = 15$ is an ellipse.

[©AQA 2009]

7 Further polar coordinates

In this chapter you will learn how to:
- find the area enclosed by a polar curve
- find the area enclosed between polar curves.

Before you start…

Further Mathematics Student Book 1, Chapter 6	You should be able to sketch polar curves.	1 Sketch the curve with polar equation $r = 2 - 2\cos\theta$.
Further Mathematics Student Book 1, Chapter 6	You should be able to convert between Cartesian and polar equations of a curve.	2 Find the polar equation of the curve with Cartesian equation $x^2 + (y-1)^2 = 1$.
A Level Mathematics Student Book 2, Chapter 11	You should be able to integrate trigonometric functions.	3 Evaluate: a $\int_0^{\frac{\pi}{6}} \cos 3\theta \, d\theta$ b $\int_0^{\frac{\pi}{2}} \sin^2\theta \, d\theta$.

Integration in polar coordinates

In Further Mathematics Student Book 1, Chapter 6, you were introduced to polar coordinates. You saw how to sketch polar curves and establish certain characteristics such as tangents at the pole. In this chapter you will combine your knowledge of polar curves with your knowledge of integration to find areas inside and between polar curves.

Section 1: Area enclosed by a curve

Finding the area bounded by a polar curve is similar to finding the area bounded by a Cartesian curve, except that rather than being the area between the curve, the x-axis and vertical lines $x = a$ and $x = b$, now it is the area between the curve, the pole and lines from the pole $\theta = \alpha$ and $\theta = \beta$.

Key point 7.1

The area enclosed between a polar curve and the half-lines $\theta = \alpha$ and $\theta = \beta$ is

$$A = \int_\alpha^\beta \frac{1}{2} r^2 \, d\theta.$$

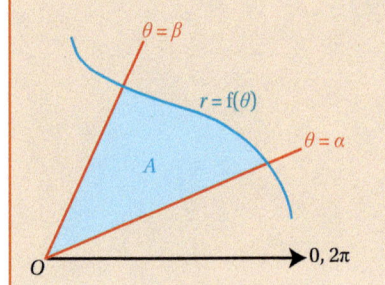

Focus on...

Focus on... Proof 2 extends the idea of integration in polar coordinates to deal with otherwise impossible integrals.

PROOF 4

Consider a curve $r = f(\theta)$, where $r \geq 0$ and $\alpha < \beta$.

You can split the region into small sectors of angle $\Delta\theta$ and area ΔA.

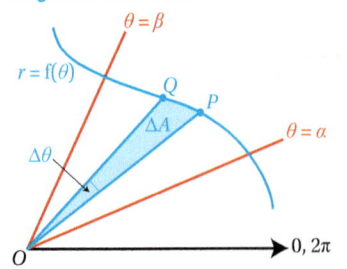

The polar coordinates of the point P are (r, θ) and the polar coordinates of the nearby point Q are $(r + \Delta r, \theta + \Delta\theta)$.

The area of each sector is approximately the same as the area of a sector of a circle with angle $\Delta\theta$ and radius r:

The area of a sector of a circle is $A = \frac{1}{2} r^2 \theta$.

$$\Delta A = \frac{1}{2} r^2 \Delta\theta$$

The total area is approximately:

$$A \approx \sum_{\theta=\alpha}^{\theta=\beta} \frac{1}{2} r^2 \Delta\theta$$

Summing all these sectors between $\theta = \alpha$ and $\theta = \beta$ gives the approximate total area.

$$A = \lim_{\Delta\theta \to 0} \sum_{\theta=\alpha}^{\theta=\beta} \frac{1}{2} r^2 \Delta\theta$$

$$= \int_\alpha^\beta \frac{1}{2} r^2 \, d\theta$$

The approximation becomes more and more accurate as the angle gets smaller. In the limit as $\Delta\theta \to 0$ the sum becomes an integral.

7 Further polar coordinates

WORKED EXAMPLE 7.1

The diagram shows the curve with polar equation $r = 3 - 2\sin\theta$.

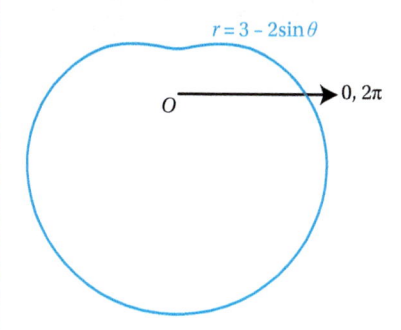

Find the area enclosed by the curve.

$A = \int_0^{2\pi} \frac{1}{2}(3 - 2\sin\theta)^2 \, d\theta$ — Use the formula $A = \int_\alpha^\beta \frac{1}{2}r^2 \, d\theta$.

$= \frac{1}{2}\int_0^{2\pi} (9 - 12\sin\theta + 4\sin^2\theta) \, d\theta$ — Expand the brackets.

$= \frac{1}{2}\int_0^{2\pi} (9 - 12\sin\theta + 2 - 2\cos 2\theta) \, d\theta$ — To integrate $\sin^2\theta$, use the $\cos 2\theta$ identity: $4\sin^2\theta = 2 - 2\cos 2\theta$.

$= \frac{1}{2}\int_0^{2\pi} (11 - 12\sin\theta - 2\cos 2\theta) \, d\theta$

$= \frac{1}{2}\Big[11\theta + 12\cos\theta - \sin 2\theta\Big]_0^{2\pi}$

$= \frac{1}{2}\Big[(22\pi + 12 - 0) - (0 + 12 - 0)\Big]$

$= 11\pi$

EXERCISE 7A

1 Find the area enclosed between these polar curves and half-lines.

   a **i** $r^2 = \cos 2\theta$; $a = -\frac{\pi}{4}$, $b = \frac{\pi}{4}$ **ii** $r^2 = \sin 3\theta$; $a = 0$, $b = \frac{\pi}{3}$

   b **i** $r = 2\theta$; $a = 0$, $b = \pi$ **ii** $r = \theta^2$; $a = 0$, $b = \pi$

   c **i** $r = 2e^\theta$; $a = 0$, $b = 2\pi$ **ii** $r = e^{\frac{\theta}{2}}$; $a = 0$, $b = 2\pi$

   d **i** $r = \cos\theta$; $a = 0$, $b = \frac{\pi}{2}$ **ii** $r = \sin\theta$; $a = \frac{\pi}{4}$, $b = \frac{\pi}{2}$

   e **i** $r = 1 + \sin\theta$; $a = -\frac{\pi}{2}$, $b = \frac{\pi}{2}$ **ii** $r = 1 - \cos\theta$; $a = 0$, $b = 2\pi$

> **Focus on...**
>
> Some areas can only be calculated exactly using polar coordinates. Focus on ... Proof 2 looks at one important example.

2 **a** Write down the polar equation of a circle of radius a with centre at the pole.

   b Using your answer to part **a**, show that the area of the circle is πa^2.

3. Find the exact value of the area enclosed between the curve $r = \tan\theta$, the initial line and the half-line $\theta = \frac{\pi}{4}$, clearly showing all your working.

4. The diagram shows the curve with polar equation $r = 2 + \cos\theta$, $0 \leq \theta < 2\pi$.

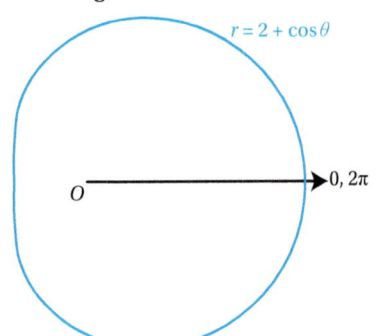

Show that the exact area enclosed by the curve is $\frac{9\pi}{2}$.

5. The diagram shows the curve with polar equation $r = 5 + 2\sin\theta$, $0 \leq \theta < 2\pi$.

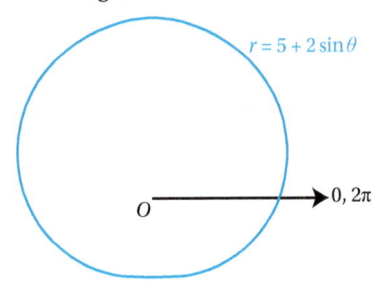

Find the exact area enclosed by the curve, clearly showing all your working.

6. a Sketch the curve with polar equation $r = \theta^{-\frac{1}{2}}$, $0 < \theta \leq 2\pi$.
   b Show that the area enclosed between the lines $\theta = a$ and $\theta = 2a$, where $0 < a \leq \pi$, is independent of a.

7. a Sketch the curve C with polar equation $r = 3\sin 2\theta$, $0 \leq \theta < 2\pi$.
   b Find the total area of the region enclosed by C, clearly showing all your working.

8. The curve C has polar equation $r = a\cos 2\theta$, for $r \geq 0$ and $0 \leq \theta < 2\pi$.
   a Sketch C, giving the equations of any tangents at the pole.
   b Find, in terms of a, the total area of the region enclosed by C, clearly showing all your working.

9. The area of the region enclosed between the curve with polar equation $r = a(1 + \tan\theta)$, the initial line and the half line $\theta = k$ is $a^2\left(\ln 2 + \frac{\sqrt{3}}{2}\right)$.
   Find the value of the positive constant k.

10 The diagram shows the curve with polar equation $r = a\sin\theta \sin 2\theta$, $0 \leq \theta < \frac{\pi}{2}$.

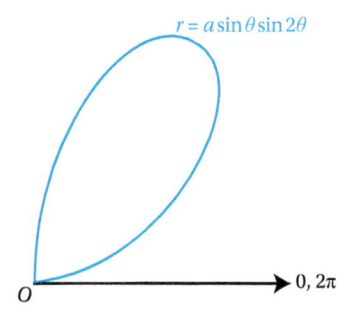

$r = a\sin\theta\sin 2\theta$

$0, 2\pi$

Show that the area of the region enclosed by the curve is $\frac{\pi a^2}{16}$.

Section 2: Area between two curves

To find the area enclosed between two polar curves, find the intersection points of the curves and calculate the part of the area bounded by each curve separately.

WORKED EXAMPLE 7.2

Two curves have polar equations:

$C_1: r = 3 + \cos\theta$

$C_2: r = 7\cos\theta$

for $0 \leq \theta < 2\pi$.

a Find the polar coordinates of the points of intersection of C_1 and C_2.
b Find the exact value of the area of the finite region enclosed between C_1 and C_2.

a The curves intersect where $3 + \cos\theta = 7\cos\theta$ $\cos\theta = \frac{1}{2}$	Equate the equations of the two curves.
$\theta = \frac{\pi}{3}, \frac{5\pi}{3}$	Solve for θ. There are two values between 0 and 2π.
From C_2: when $\cos\theta = \frac{1}{2}$, $r = \frac{7}{2}$.	Find the corresponding values of r.
The points of intersection are $\left(\frac{7}{2}, \frac{\pi}{3}\right)$ and $\left(\frac{7}{2}, \frac{5\pi}{3}\right)$.	

Continues on next page

b Sketching the curves:

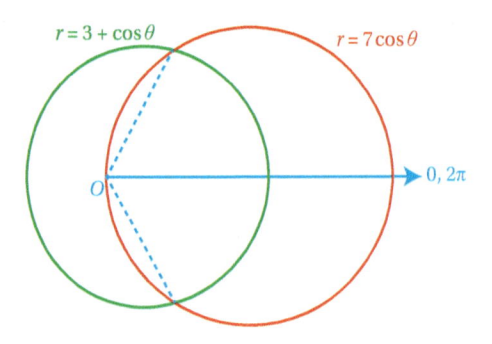

It is a good idea to sketch the curves to see where the required region is.

$$\text{Area} = 2\left[\int_0^{\frac{\pi}{3}} \frac{1}{2}(3+\cos\theta)^2 \, d\theta + \int_{\frac{\pi}{3}}^{\frac{\pi}{2}} \frac{1}{2}(7\cos\theta)^2 \, d\theta\right]$$

The required region above the initial line is made up of two parts: one bounded by C_1 between $\theta = 0$ and $\theta = \frac{\pi}{3}$ and one bounded by C_2 between $\theta = \frac{\pi}{3}$ and $\theta = \frac{\pi}{2}$.
By symmetry about the initial line, the full area is double this.

$$= \int_0^{\frac{\pi}{3}} (9 + 6\cos\theta + \cos^2\theta) \, d\theta + \int_{\frac{\pi}{3}}^{\frac{\pi}{2}} 49\cos^2\theta \, d\theta$$

$$= \int_0^{\frac{\pi}{3}} \left(9 + 6\cos\theta + \frac{\cos 2\theta + 1}{2}\right) d\theta + \int_{\frac{\pi}{3}}^{\frac{\pi}{2}} 49\left(\frac{\cos 2\theta + 1}{2}\right) d\theta$$

Expand and use $\cos^2\theta = \frac{\cos 2\theta + 1}{2}$.

$$= \left[9\theta + 6\sin\theta + \frac{1}{4}\sin 2\theta + \frac{1}{2}\theta\right]_0^{\frac{\pi}{3}} + \frac{49}{2}\left[\frac{1}{2}\sin 2\theta + \theta\right]_{\frac{\pi}{3}}^{\frac{\pi}{2}}$$

$$= \left[\left(\frac{19\pi}{6} + 3\sqrt{3} + \frac{\sqrt{3}}{8}\right) - (0)\right] + \frac{49}{2}\left[\left(\frac{\pi}{2}\right) - \left(\frac{\sqrt{3}}{4} + \frac{\pi}{3}\right)\right]$$

$$= \frac{29\pi}{4} - 3\sqrt{3}$$

ⓘ Common error

In more complicated questions where the region is between two curves, remember that in polar coordinates you are finding the area of a sector bounded by the curve and two half lines from the pole; not a region bounded by two vertical lines as in Cartesian coordinates.

7 Further polar coordinates

EXERCISE 7B

1 The diagram shows the curve with polar equation $r = 2$ and the line with polar equation $r = \sqrt{3}\sec\theta$, both defined for $0 \leqslant \theta < \dfrac{\pi}{2}$.

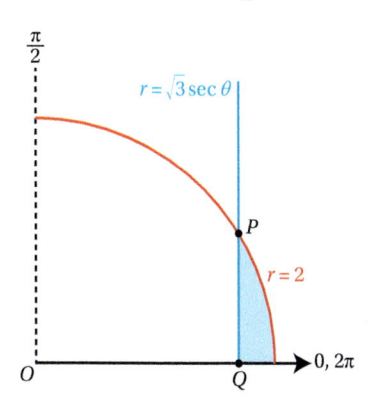

The line intersects the curve at the point P and intersects the initial line at the point Q.

a Find the polar coordinates of P.

b i Find the exact area of the triangle OPQ.

ii Hence show that the area of the shaded region is $\dfrac{2\pi - 3\sqrt{3}}{6}$.

2 The diagram shows the curve with polar equation $r = a(1 + \cos\theta)$, $0 \leqslant \theta < \pi$.

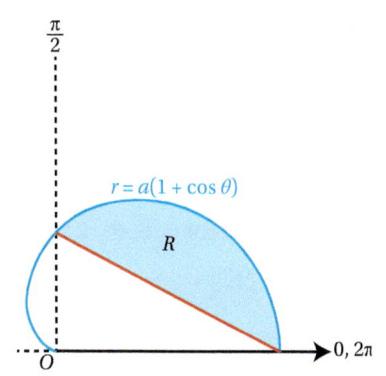

Find, in terms of a, the exact area of the shaded region R.

3 The diagram shows the curves with polar equations $r = a$ and $r = 2a\sin 2\theta$ for $0 \leqslant \theta < \dfrac{\pi}{2}$.

a Find the polar coordinates of the points of intersection of the two curves.

b Find the exact area of the shaded region enclosed within both curves.

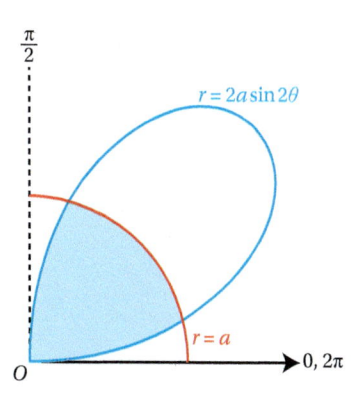

173

4 The diagram shows the curves with polar equations $r = \frac{1}{2}$ and $r = 1 - \sin\theta$, $0 \leq \theta < 2\pi$.

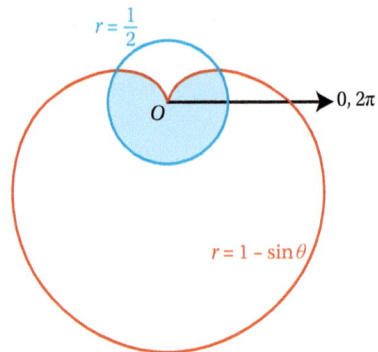

a Find the polar coordinates of the points of intersection of the two curves.

b Find the exact area of the shaded region enclosed inside both curves.

5 The diagram shows the curves C_1 and C_2 with polar equations $r = 6 - 6\cos\theta$ and $r = 2 + 2\cos\theta$, $0 \leq \theta < 2\pi$.

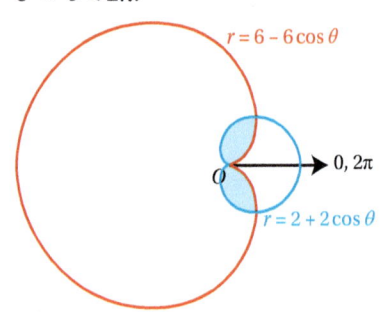

a Find the polar coordinates of the points of intersection of the two curves.

b Show that the area of the shaded region is $2(11\pi - 18\sqrt{3})$.

6 **a** On the same axes, sketch the curves with polar equations $r = 2$ and $r = 3 - 2\cos\theta$ for $0 \leq \theta < 2\pi$.

b Show that the exact value of the area inside $r = 3 - 2\cos\theta$ but outside $r = 2$ is $\dfrac{33\sqrt{3} + 28\pi}{6}$.

Checklist of learning and understanding

- The area enclosed between a polar curve and the half-lines $\theta = \alpha$ and $\theta = \beta$ is $A = \int_\alpha^\beta \frac{1}{2} r^2 \, d\theta$.
- To find the area enclosed between two polar curves, find the intersection points of the curves and calculate the part of the area bounded by each curve separately.

Mixed practice 7

1 Find the area of the region enclosed between the initial line and the curve with polar equation $r = \sqrt{2a}e^{\frac{\theta}{2}}, 0 \leq \theta < 2\pi$.

Choose from these options.

A $2a(e^{2\pi} - 1)$ **B** $a(e^{2\pi} - 1)$ **C** $\dfrac{\sqrt{2a}}{2}(e^{\pi} - 1)$ **D** $\sqrt{2a}(e^{\pi} - 1)$

2 a Sketch the curve with polar equation $r = \theta, 0 \leq \theta < 2\pi$.

   b Show that the area bounded by the curve and the initial line is $\dfrac{4\pi^3}{3}$.

3 a Sketch the curve with polar equation $r = 5 - 4\cos\theta, 0 \leq \theta < 2\pi$.

   b Find the exact area enclosed by the curve, clearly showing your working.

4 The Cartesian equation of a curve is $x^2 + y^2 - 2x = \sqrt{x^2 + y^2}, r \geq 0$.

   a Show that the polar equation of the curve is $r = 1 + 2\cos\theta$.

   b Find the equation of any tangents at the pole.

   c Hence sketch the curve for $0 \leq \theta < 2\pi$.

   d Show that the area enclosed by the curve is $2\pi + \dfrac{3\sqrt{3}}{2}$.

5 The diagram shows a sketch of a curve C, the pole O and the initial line.

The polar equation of C is $r = 2\sqrt{1 + \tan\theta}, -\dfrac{\pi}{4} \leq \theta \leq \dfrac{\pi}{4}$.

Show that the area of the shaded region, bounded by the curve C and the initial line, is $\dfrac{\pi}{2} - \ln 2$.

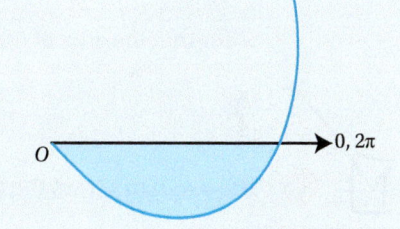

[© AQA 2012]

6 The diagram shows the curve with polar equation $r = 2 + 4\cos\theta, 0 \leq \theta < 2\pi$.

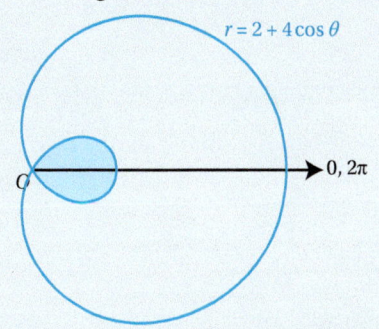

Find the exact value of the shaded area, clearly showing your working.

7 The diagram shows the curve C with polar equation $r = 10 - 10\cos\theta, 0 \leq \theta < 2\pi$.

   a Show that the area of the region bounded by C is 150π.

   The circle $x^2 + y^2 = 25$ intersects C at the points A and B.

   b Find the polar coordinates of A and B.

   c Find the area enclosed between the circle and C.

8 The diagram shows a sketch of a curve C.

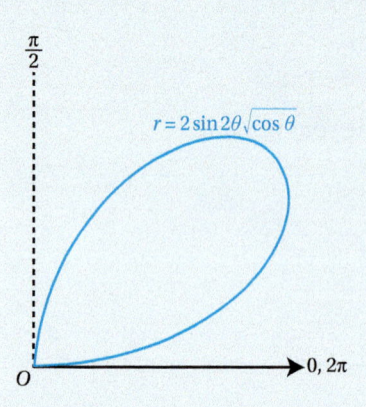

   The polar equation of the curve is $r = 2\sin 2\theta \sqrt{\cos\theta}, 0 \leq \theta \leq \frac{\pi}{2}$.

   Show that the area of the region bounded by C is $\frac{16}{15}$.

   [© AQA 2011]

9 The diagram shows the curve with polar equation $r = \cos\theta + \cos 3\theta, 0 \leq \theta < \pi$.

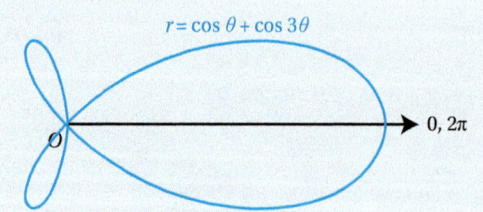

   a i Show that $\cos 3\theta \equiv 4\cos^3\theta - 3\cos\theta$.

      ii Hence find the equations of the tangents at the pole.

   b Show that the area enclosed in the large loop is $\frac{3\pi + 8}{12}$.

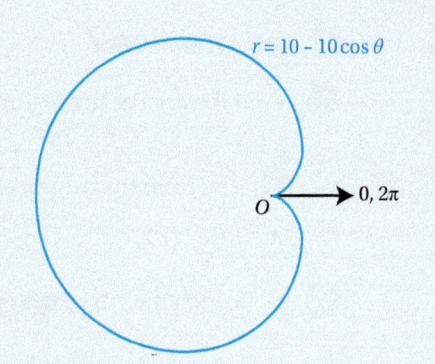

10 The diagram shows a sketch of a curve.

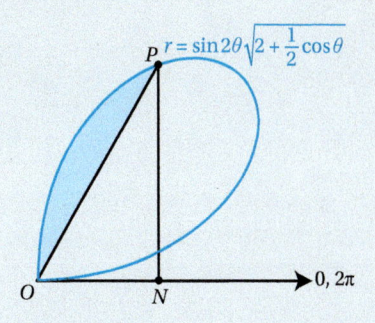

The polar equation of the curve is $r = \sin 2\theta \sqrt{2 + \frac{1}{2}\cos\theta}$, $0 \leq \theta \leq \frac{\pi}{2}$.

The point P is the point of the curve at which $\theta = \frac{\pi}{3}$.

The perpendicular from P to the initial line meets the initial line at the point N.

a i Find the exact value of r when $\theta = \frac{\pi}{3}$.

ii Show that the polar equation of the line PN is $r = \frac{3\sqrt{3}}{8}\sec\theta$.

iii Find the area of triangle ONP in the form $\frac{k\sqrt{3}}{128}$, where k is an integer.

b i Using the substitution $u = \sin\theta$, or otherwise, find $\int \sin^n\theta \cos\theta \, d\theta$, where $n \geq 2$.

ii Find the area of the shaded region bounded by the line OP and the arc OP of the curve. Give your answer in the form $a\pi + b\sqrt{3} + c$, where a, b and c are constants.

[© AQA 2013]

8 Further hyperbolic functions

In this chapter you will learn how to:

- define the reciprocal hyperbolic functions sech x, cosech x and coth x
- draw the graphs of reciprocal hyperbolic functions
- know the domain and range of hyperbolic, inverse hyperbolic and reciprocal hyperbolic functions and work with transformations of their graphs
- write the inverse reciprocal hyperbolic functions in terms of logarithms
- use further hyperbolic identities to solve equations
- differentiate and integrate hyperbolic and reciprocal hyperbolic functions.

Before you start…

Further Mathematics Student Book 1, Chapter 5	You should be able to use the definitions of sinh x, cosh x and tanh x.	1	Use the definitions of sinh x and cosh x to show that $\tanh x = \dfrac{e^{2x} - 1}{e^{2x} + 1}$.
Further Mathematics Student Book 1, Chapter 5	You should be able to draw the graphs of $y = \sinh x$, $y = \cosh x$ and $y = \tanh x$.	2	a On the same axes, sketch the graphs of $y = \cosh x$ and $y = 1 + \tanh x$. b Hence state the number of solutions to the equation $\cosh x = 1 + \tanh x$.
Further Mathematics Student Book 1, Chapter 5	You should be able to draw the graphs of $y = \operatorname{arsinh} x$, $y = \operatorname{arcosh} x$ and $y = \operatorname{artanh} x$.	3	On the same axes, sketch the graphs of $y = \sinh x$ and $y = \operatorname{arsinh} x$.
Further Mathematics Student Book 1, Chapter 5	You should know how to use the logarithmic form of arsinh x, arcosh x and artanh x.	4	Give exact values for: a $\operatorname{arsinh} \sqrt{3}$ b $\operatorname{artanh}\left(\dfrac{2}{3}\right)$.
Further Mathematics Student Book 1, Chapter 5	You should know how to use the identity $\cosh^2 x - \sinh^2 x \equiv 1$.	5	Solve the equation $6\sinh^2 x - 7\cosh x + 1 = 0$, giving your answers in terms of natural logarithms.
A Level Mathematics Student Book 2, Chapter 2	You should know how to understand the terms domain and range of a function.	6	For the function $f(x) = \sqrt{x - 3}$, state: a the largest possible domain b the corresponding range.

A Level Mathematics Student Book 2, Chapter 3	You should be able to draw a graph after two (or more) transformations.	7 The graph of $y = f(x)$ is shown. Points labelled: $(0, 0)$, $(-2, -8)$, $(2, -8)$. Sketch the graph of $y = 3 - f(2x)$, giving the new coordinates of the three labelled points on the original graph.
A Level Mathematics Student Book 2, Chapter 9	You should know how to differentiate and integrate the exponential function.	8 Find: a $\dfrac{d}{dx}(e^{2x})$ b $\int e^{-x} dx$.
A Level Mathematics Student Book 2, Chapter 9	You should know how to differentiate and integrate trigonometric functions.	9 Find: a $\dfrac{d}{dx}(\tan x)$ b $\int \cos x \, dx$.
A Level Mathematics Student Book 2, Chapter 10	You should know how to use the chain rule, product rule and quotient rule for differentiation.	10 Find $f'(x)$ for these functions. a $f(x) = \sin^2 3x$ b $f(x) = x \cos x$ c $f(x) = \dfrac{\tan 2x}{x}$
A Level Mathematics Student Book 2, Chapter 11	You should know how to integrate using trigonometric identities, the reverse chain rule and integration by parts.	11 Find: a $\int \tan^2 x \, dx$ b $\int \cos x \sin^3 x \, dx$ c $\int x \sin x \, dx$.

More techniques with hyperbolic functions

This chapter extends many of the ideas you met in Further Mathematics Student Book 1, Chapter 5, and introduces differentiation and integration of hyperbolic functions.

You will already be familiar with many of the ideas and methods in this chapter from those you have used with the corresponding trigonometric functions.

Section 1: Domain and range of hyperbolic and inverse hyperbolic functions

In Further Mathematics Student Book 1, Chapter 5, you met the graphs of the hyperbolic functions $\sinh x$, $\cosh x$ and $\tanh x$ and the graphs of the inverse hyperbolic functions $\sinh^{-1} x$, $\cosh^{-1} x$ and $\tanh^{-1} x$.

You now need to know the domain and range of these functions and be able to work with transformations of their graphs.

> **Rewind**
>
> You met domain and range in A Level Mathematics Student Book 2, Chapter 2.

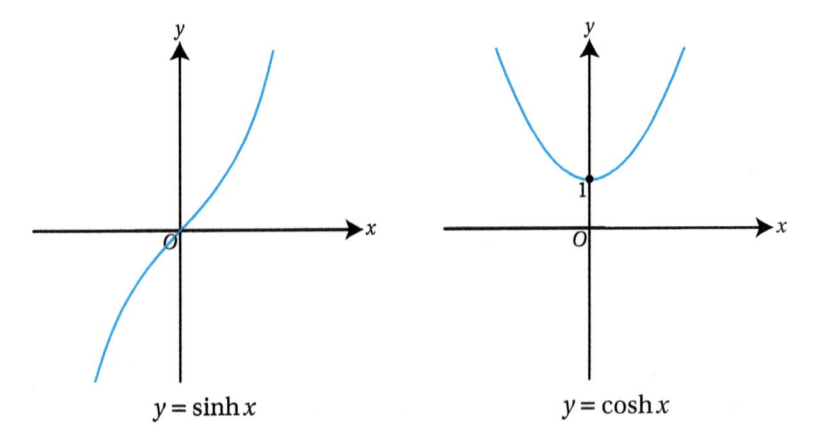

$y = \sinh x$

$y = \cosh x$

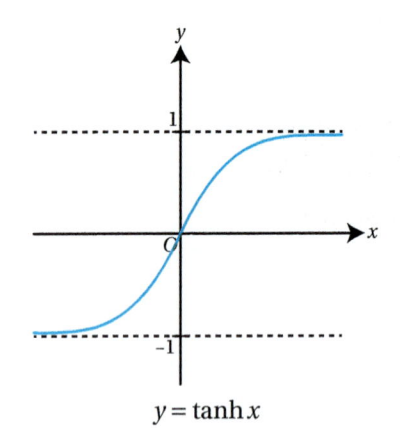

$y = \tanh x$

Key point 8.1

The domains and ranges of the hyperbolic functions $\sinh x$, $\cosh x$ and $\tanh x$ are given in the table.

Function	Domain	Range
$\sinh x$	$x \in \mathbb{R}$	$x \in \mathbb{R}$
$\cosh x$	$x \in \mathbb{R}$	$f(x) \geq 1$
$\tanh x$	$x \in \mathbb{R}$	$1 < f(x) < 1$

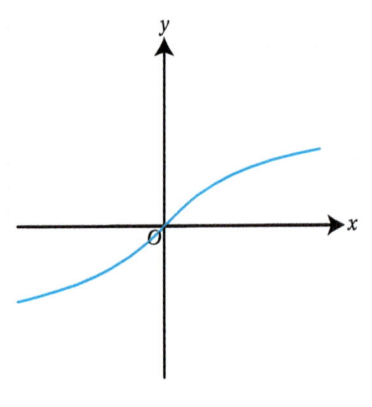

$y = \text{arsinh } x$

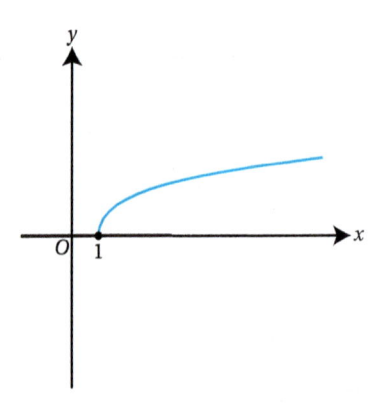

$y = \text{arcosh } x$

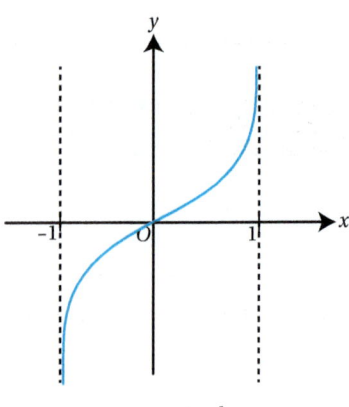

$y = \text{artanh } x$

180

8 Further hyperbolic functions

🔑 Key point 8.2

The domains and ranges of the inverse hyperbolic functions $\sinh^{-1} x$, $\cosh^{-1} x$ and $\tanh^{-1} x$ are given in the table.

Function	Domain	Range
$\cosh^{-1} x$	$x \geq 1$	$f(x) \in \mathbb{R}$
$\sinh^{-1} x$	$x \in \mathbb{R}$	$f(x) \in \mathbb{R}$
$\tanh^{-1} x$	$1 < x < 1$	$f(x) \in \mathbb{R}$

💡 Tip

$\sinh^{-1} x$, $\cosh^{-1} x$ and $\tanh^{-1} x$ are alternative notations for arsinh x, arcosh x and artanh x.

WORKED EXAMPLE 8.1

Given that $f(x) = 3\tanh x + 2$ for $x \in \mathbb{R}$,

a sketch the graph of $y = f(x)$
b state the range of $f(x)$.

a

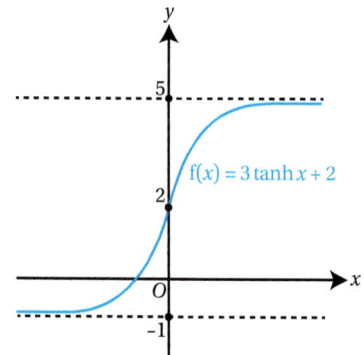

You need to apply two transformations to the graph of $y = \tanh x$:
- stretch by scale factor 3 parallel to the y-axis
- translation by $\begin{pmatrix} 0 \\ 2 \end{pmatrix}$.

The horizontal asymptote at $y = -1$ stays there, but the asymptote at $y = 1$ moves to $y = 5$.

b $-1 < f(x) < 5$

From the graph, the function is bounded by the asymptotes at $y = -1$ and $y = 5$.

WORKED EXAMPLE 8.2

Let $f(x) = 1 - \cosh^{-1}\left(\dfrac{x}{3}\right)$.

a State the largest possible domain of $f(x)$.
b For the domain in part **a**, find the range of $f(x)$.

a Domain: $x \geq 3$

The domain of $\cosh^{-1} x$ is $x \geq 1$, so $\dfrac{x}{3} \geq 1 \Rightarrow x \geq 3$.

Continues on next page

181

b

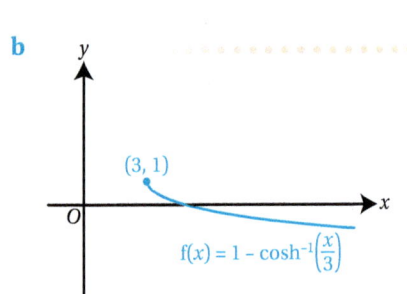

(3, 1)

$f(x) = 1 - \cosh^{-1}\left(\frac{x}{3}\right)$

Range: $f(x) \leq 1$

> It is always a good idea to sketch the graph when finding the range.
>
> You need to apply three transformations to the graph of $y = \cosh^{-1} x$:
> - stretch by scale factor 3 parallel to the x-axis
> - reflection in the x-axis
> - translation by $\begin{pmatrix} 0 \\ 1 \end{pmatrix}$.

EXERCISE 8A

1 For each hyperbolic function, sketch the graph of $y = f(x)$ and state the largest possible domain and the corresponding range.

   a **i** $f(x) = 3 - \sinh\left(\frac{x}{2}\right)$ **ii** $f(x) = 2\sinh(x - 1)$

   b **i** $f(x) = \cosh(2x + 3)$ **ii** $f(x) = 4 - \cosh x$

   c **i** $f(x) = 5 + 2\tanh x$ **ii** $f(x) = 4\tanh(-x)$

2 For each inverse hyperbolic function, sketch the graph of $y = f(x)$ and state the largest possible domain and the corresponding range.

   a **i** $f(x) = 3\sinh^{-1} x + 2$ **ii** $f(x) = 2 + \sinh^{-1}(-x)$

   b **i** $f(x) = 1 + \cosh^{-1} 2x$ **ii** $f(x) = 2\cosh^{-1}\left(\frac{x}{3}\right)$

   c **i** $f(x) = 2\tanh^{-1}(x + 1) + 3$ **ii** $f(x) = 3\tanh^{-1}(x - 2) + 1$

3 The diagram shows the graph of $y = a\cosh(x + b) - 5$, where a, and b are integers.

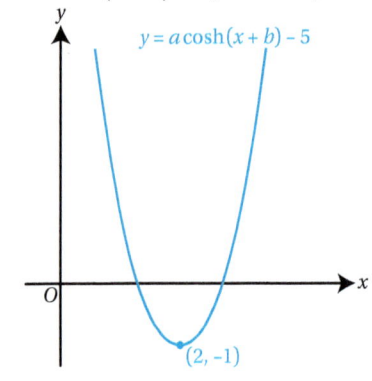

$y = a\cosh(x + b) - 5$

(2, −1)

Find the values of a and b.

8 Further hyperbolic functions

4 The diagram shows the graph of $y = a \tanh(2x + b)$, where a, and b are integers.

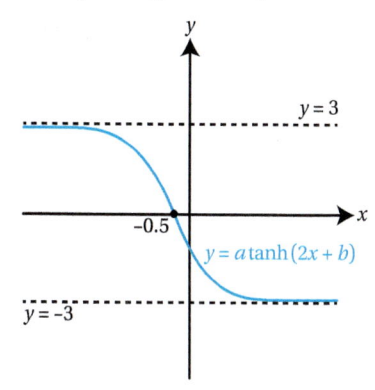

Find the values of a and b.

5 A function is given by $f(x) = \cosh^{-1}(x + a) + \tanh^{-1}(x + b)$, where a and b are constants.

Find, in terms of a, the set of values of the constant b so that $f(x)$ has the largest domain possible.

Section 2: Reciprocal hyperbolic functions

The **reciprocal hyperbolic functions** are defined in the same way as the reciprocal trigonometric functions you met in A Level Mathematics Student Book 2, Chapter 8.

Key point 8.3

The reciprocal hyperbolic functions are:

- $\operatorname{sech} x = \dfrac{1}{\cosh x}$
- $\operatorname{cosech} x = \dfrac{1}{\sinh x}$
- $\coth x = \dfrac{1}{\tanh x}$

Key point 8.4

The graph of $y = \operatorname{sech} x$

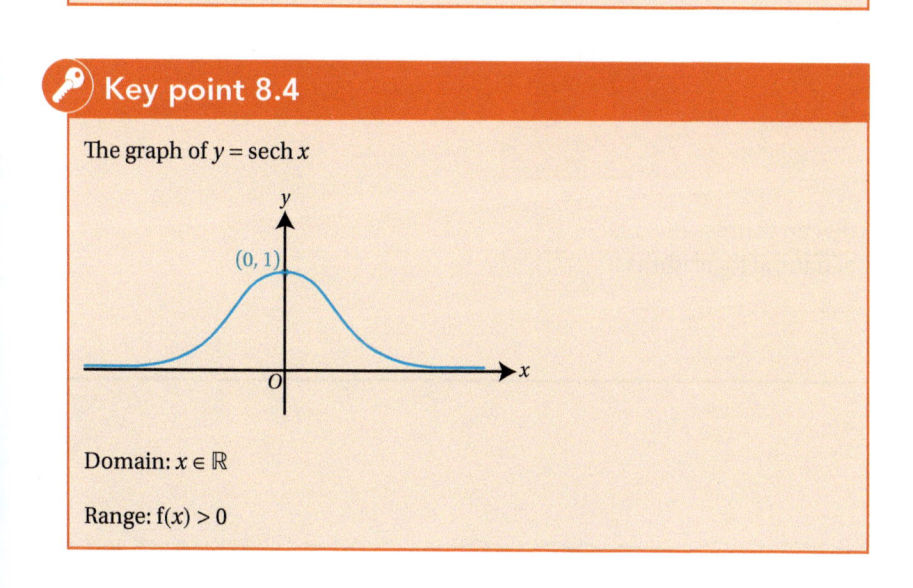

Domain: $x \in \mathbb{R}$

Range: $f(x) > 0$

Key point 8.5

The graph of $y = \text{cosech } x$

Domain: $x \neq 0$

Range: $f(x) \neq 0$

Key point 8.6

The graph of $y = \coth x$

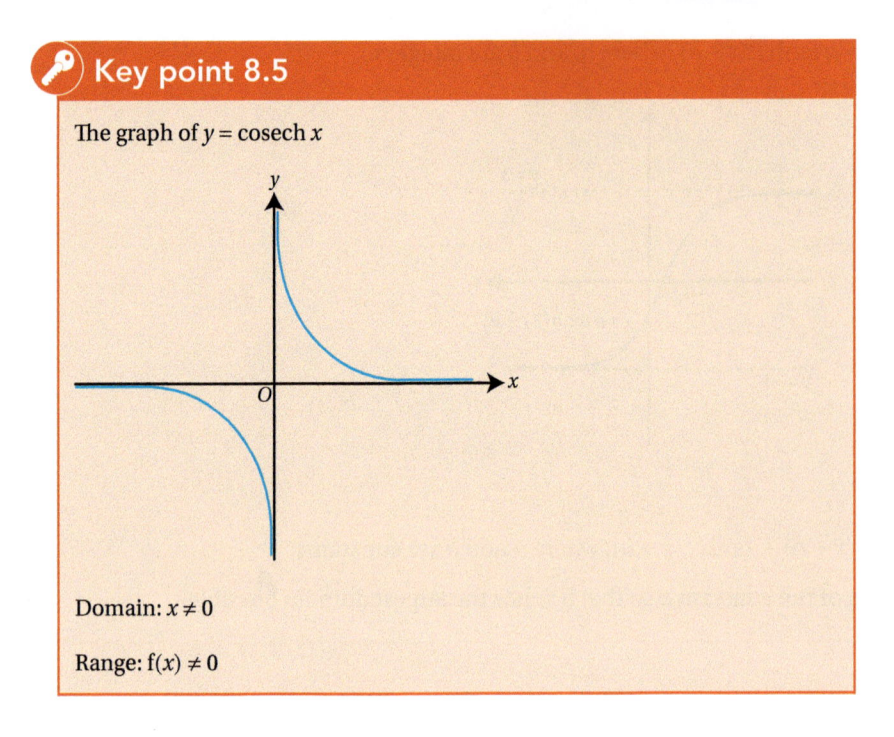

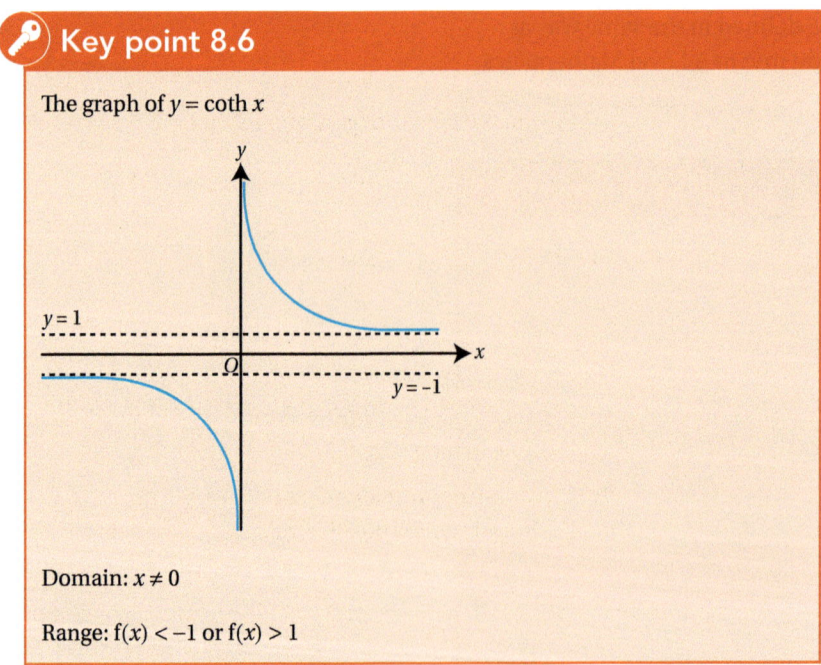

Domain: $x \neq 0$

Range: $f(x) < -1$ or $f(x) > 1$

Just as for inverse hyperbolic functions, you can express inverse reciprocal hyperbolic functions in terms of natural logarithms.

WORKED EXAMPLE 8.3

a Show that $\text{arsech } x = \ln\left(\dfrac{1 + \sqrt{1 - x^2}}{x}\right)$.

b State the domain of $\text{arsech } x$.

Continues on next page

a $y = \text{arsech } x$
$\Rightarrow \text{sech } y = x$

$$\frac{2}{e^y + e^{-y}} = x$$

> Use $\text{sech } x = \frac{1}{\cosh x}$ together with the definition of $\cosh x$.

$$e^y + e^{-y} = \frac{2}{x}$$

$$(e^y)^2 + 1 = \frac{2}{x} e^y$$

$$(e^y)^2 - \frac{2}{x} e^y + 1 = 0$$

$$\left(e^y - \frac{1}{x}\right)^2 - \frac{1}{x^2} + 1 = 0$$

> Complete the square (or use the quadratic formula).

$$\left(e^y - \frac{1}{x}\right)^2 = \frac{1}{x^2} - 1$$

> Solve for e^y.

$$e^y - \frac{1}{x} = \pm\sqrt{\frac{1}{x^2} - 1}$$

$$e^y = \frac{1}{x} \pm \sqrt{\frac{1 - x^2}{x^2}}$$

$$e^y = \frac{1}{x} \pm \frac{\sqrt{1 - x^2}}{x}$$

$$e^y = \frac{1 \pm \sqrt{1 - x^2}}{x}$$

If $x > 0$, then since $e^y > 0$:

$$e^y = \frac{1 + \sqrt{1 - x^2}}{x}$$

> Taking the positive root guarantees that $\frac{1 + \sqrt{1-x^2}}{x} > 0$ for positive x.

$$y = \ln\left(\frac{1 + \sqrt{1 - x^2}}{x}\right)$$

> Take natural log of both sides.

$$\therefore \text{arsech } x = \ln\left(\frac{1 + \sqrt{1 - x^2}}{x}\right)$$

b $1 - x^2 \geq 0 \Leftrightarrow -1 \leq x \leq 1$

> The expression $1 - x^2$ inside the square root must be non-negative.

Need $\frac{1 + \sqrt{1 - x^2}}{x} > 0$

> But the entire expression must be positive as ln is only defined for positive values.

$\therefore$ Domain: $0 < x \leq 1$

EXERCISE 8B

1 For each reciprocal hyperbolic function, sketch the graph of $y = f(x)$ and state the largest possible domain and the corresponding range.

   a **i** $f(x) = 3 - 2 \text{sech } x$ **ii** $f(x) = \text{sech }(x + 2) - 1$

   b **i** $f(x) = \text{cosech }(-x) + 2$ **ii** $f(x) = \text{cosech }(2x - 3)$

   c **i** $f(x) = 3 \coth x - 4$ **ii** $f(x) = 1 - 2 \coth x$

2 **a** On the same axes, sketch the graphs of $y = 2 \text{sech } x$ and $y = \coth (x + 1)$.

   b Hence state the number of solutions to the equation $2 \text{sech } x - \coth (x + 1) = 0$.

3 **a** On the same axes, sketch the graphs of $y = 2 - \operatorname{sech} x$ and $y = \operatorname{cosech} x + 1$.

b Hence state the number of solutions to the equation $\operatorname{sech} x + \operatorname{cosech} x = 1$.

4 Prove that $\operatorname{sech} x + \operatorname{cosech} x \equiv 2e^x \operatorname{cosech} 2x$.

5 **a** On the same axes, sketch the graphs of $y = \coth x$ and $y = \operatorname{arcoth} x$.

b For the function $\operatorname{arcoth} x$, state:

  i the largest possible domain

  ii the corresponding range.

c Prove that $\operatorname{arcoth} x = \frac{1}{2} \ln\left(\frac{x+1}{x-1}\right)$.

6 **a** Prove that for $x > 0$

$\operatorname{arcosech} x = \ln\left(\frac{1 + \sqrt{1 + x^2}}{x}\right)$.

b Hence prove that $\operatorname{arcosech} x = \operatorname{arsinh} \frac{1}{x}$ for all $x > 0$.

Section 3: Using hyperbolic identities to solve equations

In Further Mathematics Student Book 1, Chapter 5, you met the identities $\cosh^2 x - \sinh^2 x \equiv 1$ and $\tanh x \equiv \frac{\sinh x}{\cosh x}$. You now need to be familiar with some other identities and use these to solve hyperbolic equations.

Key point 8.7

- $\sinh 2x \equiv 2 \sinh x \cosh x$

- $\cosh 2x \equiv \begin{cases} \cosh^2 x + \sinh^2 x \\ 2\cosh^2 x - 1 \\ 2\sinh^2 x + 1 \end{cases}$

These will be given in your formula book.

WORKED EXAMPLE 8.4

Prove that $\cosh 2x \equiv \cosh^2 x + \sinh^2 x$.

$\cosh^2 x + \sinh^2 x \equiv \left(\frac{e^x + e^{-x}}{2}\right)^2 + \left(\frac{e^x - e^{-x}}{2}\right)^2$ .... Use the definitions of $\sinh x$ and $\cosh x$.

$\equiv \left(\frac{e^{2x} + 2 + e^{-2x}}{4}\right) + \left(\frac{e^{2x} - 2 + e^{-2x}}{4}\right)$ .... Expand and simplify.

$\equiv \frac{2e^{2x} + 2e^{-2x}}{4}$

$\equiv \frac{e^{2x} + e^{-2x}}{2}$

$\equiv \cosh 2x$

8 Further hyperbolic functions

Key point 8.8

- $\operatorname{sech}^2 x \equiv 1 - \tanh^2 x$
- $\operatorname{cosech}^2 x \equiv \coth^2 x - 1$

WORKED EXAMPLE 8.5

a Prove that $\operatorname{sech}^2 x \equiv 1 - \tanh^2 x$.

b Solve the equation $3 \operatorname{sech}^2 x + 4 \tanh x + 1 = 0$, giving your answer in the form $a \ln b$ where a and b are rational numbers.

a
$$1 - \tanh^2 x \equiv 1 - \left(\frac{e^x - e^{-x}}{e^x + e^{-x}}\right)^2$$

It is easiest to start with $1 - \tanh^2 x$. Use the definition of $\tanh x$.

$$\equiv \frac{(e^x + e^{-x})^2}{(e^x + e^{-x})^2} - \frac{(e^x - e^{-x})^2}{(e^x + e^{-x})^2}$$

Create a common denominator.

$$\equiv \frac{(e^{2x} + 2 + e^{-2x}) - (e^{2x} - 2 + e^{-2x})}{(e^x + e^{-x})^2}$$

$$\equiv \frac{4}{(e^x + e^{-x})^2}$$

$$\equiv \left(\frac{2}{e^x + e^{-x}}\right)^2$$

$$\equiv \operatorname{sech}^2 x$$

b
$$3 \operatorname{sech}^2 x + 4 \tanh x + 1 = 0$$
$$3(1 - \tanh^2 x) + 4 \tanh x + 1 = 0$$
$$3 - 3 \tanh^2 x + 4 \tanh x + 1 = 0$$
$$3 \tanh^2 x - 4 \tanh x - 4 = 0$$
$$(3 \tanh x + 2)(\tanh x - 2) = 0$$

Use $\operatorname{sech}^2 x \equiv 1 - \tanh^2 x$ to get a quadratic in $\tanh^2 x$.

Factorise and solve.

$$\tanh x = -\frac{2}{3}, 2$$

$$\therefore x = \frac{1}{2} \ln \left(\frac{1 + \left(-\frac{2}{3}\right)}{1 - \left(-\frac{2}{3}\right)}\right)$$

Then use $\operatorname{artanh} x = \frac{1}{2} \ln \left(\frac{1 + x}{1 - x}\right)$.

$$= \frac{1}{2} \ln \left(\frac{\frac{1}{3}}{\frac{5}{3}}\right)$$

$$= \frac{1}{2} \ln \left(\frac{1}{5}\right)$$

$$= -\frac{1}{2} \ln 5$$

187

A Level Further Mathematics for AQA Student Book 2

EXERCISE 8C

1 Prove each identity using the definitions of sinh x, cosh x and tanh x.

    a $\sinh 2x \equiv 2 \sinh x \cosh x$ **b** $\cosh 2x \equiv 2 \cosh^2 - 1$ **c** $\text{cosech}^2 x \equiv \coth^2 x - 1$

2 Solve the equation $\sinh 2x = 5 \sinh x$, giving your answers to three significant figures.

3 Solve the equation $\cosh 2x = \sinh x + 4$, giving your answers to three significant figures.

4 Solve the equation $\cosh 2x - 5 \cosh x - 2 = 0$, giving your answers in the form $\ln k$.

5 Solve the equation $2 \sinh 2x = 9 \tanh x$, giving exact answers.

6 Solve the equation $2 \,\text{sech}\, x = e^x$, giving your answer in the form $\ln k$.

7 Solve the equation $6 \tanh x - 7 \,\text{sech}\, x = 2$, giving your answer in the form $\ln k$, where k is a rational number.

8 Solve the equation $\text{cosech}^2 x - 2 \coth x = 2$, giving your answer in the form $a \ln b$, where a and b are rational numbers.

9 Solve the equation $2 \tanh^2 x = 4 - 5 \,\text{sech}\, x$, giving your answers in the form $\ln k$.

10 Prove that $\coth A + \text{cosech}\, A \equiv \coth \frac{A}{2}$.

11   **a** Prove that $\sinh 3x \equiv 4 \sinh^3 x + 3 \sinh x$.

    b Hence solve the equation $\sinh 6x = 6 + \sinh 2x$, giving your answer in the form $a \ln b$.

12   **a** Show that, for any real number k,

$$(\cosh x + \sinh x)^k + (\cosh x - \sinh x)^k \equiv 2 \cosh kx.$$

    b Hence solve the equation

$$(\cosh x + \sinh x)^6 + (\cosh x - \sinh x)^6 = 6,$$

    giving your answers in the form $a \ln b$.

Section 4: Differentiation

Key point 8.9

- $\frac{d}{dx}(\sinh x) = \cosh x$

- $\frac{d}{dx}(\cosh x) = \sinh x$

- $\frac{d}{dx}(\tanh x) = \text{sech}^2 x$

Only the final one of these will be given in your formula book.

8 Further hyperbolic functions

You can derive the results for the derivatives of sinh x and cosh x by returning to the definitions of these functions.

WORKED EXAMPLE 8.6

Show that $\frac{d}{dx}(\sinh x) = \cosh x$.

$y = \sinh x$ — Use the definition of sinh x.
$= \frac{e^x - e^{-x}}{2}$

Differentiating: $\frac{dy}{dx} = \frac{e^x - (-e^{-x})}{2}$

$= \frac{e^x + e^{-x}}{2}$

$= \cosh x$

You can show the result for tanh x either from the definition again or by using $\tanh x \equiv \frac{\sinh x}{\cosh x}$ and the quotient rule.

WORKED EXAMPLE 8.7

Use the derivatives of sinh x and cosh x to show that $\frac{d}{dx}(\tanh x) = \operatorname{sech}^2 x$.

$y = \tanh x$ — Use $\tanh x \equiv \frac{\sinh x}{\cosh x}$.
$= \frac{\sinh x}{\cosh x}$

Differentiating using the quotient rule:

$\frac{dy}{dx} = \frac{\cosh x \cosh x - \sinh x \sinh x}{\cosh^2 x}$

$= \frac{\cosh^2 x - \sinh^2 x}{\cosh^2 x}$

$= \frac{1}{\cosh^2 x}$ — Use $\cosh^2 x - \sinh^2 x \equiv 1$.

$= \operatorname{sech}^2 x$

WORKED EXAMPLE 8.8

Given that $y = x \tanh(x^2)$, find $\frac{dy}{dx}$.

Let $u = x$ and $v = \tanh(x^2)$ — Use the product rule.

Then $u' = 1$

Continues on next page

And

$v' = \text{sech}^2(x^2) \times 2x$

$\quad = 2x\,\text{sech}^2(x^2)$

$\dfrac{dy}{dx} = 1 \times \tanh(x^2) + x \times 2x\,\text{sech}^2(x^2)$

$\quad = \tanh(x^2) + 2x^2\,\text{sech}^2(x^2)$

> v is a composite function so use the chain rule to differentiate.

> Now apply the product rule formula.

Key point 8.10

- $\dfrac{d}{dx}(\text{sech}\,x) = -\text{sech}\,x\,\tanh x$
- $\dfrac{d}{dx}(\text{cosech}\,x) = -\text{cosech}\,x\,\coth x$
- $\dfrac{d}{dx}(\coth x) = -\text{cosech}^2 x$

You can show each of the results in Key point 8.10 in a similar way.

WORKED EXAMPLE 8.9

Prove that $\dfrac{d}{dx}(\text{sech}\,x) = -\text{sech}\,x\,\tanh x$.

$y = \text{sech}\,x$

$\quad = \dfrac{1}{\cosh x}$

$\quad = (\cosh x)^{-1}$

> Express $\text{sech}\,x$ in terms of $\cosh x$.

Differentiating, using the chain rule:

$\dfrac{dy}{dx} = -(\cosh x)^{-2} \times \sinh x$

$\quad = -\dfrac{\sinh x}{\cosh^2 x}$

$\quad = -\dfrac{1}{\cosh x} \times \dfrac{\sinh x}{\cosh x}$

$\quad = -\text{sech}\,x\,\tanh x$

> Rearrange into the form required.

WORKED EXAMPLE 8.10

Given that $f(x) = \text{cosech}^2(3x)$, find $f'(x)$.

$f(x) = \left[\text{cosech}(3x)\right]^2$

> Make sure you are thinking of $\text{cosech}^2 A$ as $(\text{cosech}\,A)^2$.

Using the chain rule:

$f'(x) = 2\,\text{cosech}(3x) \times \left(-\text{cosech}(3x)\coth(3x)\right) \times 3$

$\quad = -6\,\text{cosech}^2(3x)\coth(3x)$

> Remember to multiply by the derivative of $3x$ as well.

8 Further hyperbolic functions

EXERCISE 8D

1 Differentiate each function with respect to x.

a i $f(x) = \sinh 3x$
    ii $f(x) = \sinh \frac{1}{2}x$

b i $f(x) = \cosh(4x + 1)$
    ii $f(x) = \cosh \frac{1}{3}x$

c i $f(x) = \tanh \frac{2}{3}x$
    ii $f(x) = \tanh(1 - 2x)$

d i $f(x) = \operatorname{sech}(-\frac{1}{4}x)$
    ii $f(x) = \operatorname{sech} 3x$

e i $f(x) = \operatorname{cosech} 5x$
    ii $f(x) = \operatorname{cosech} \frac{1}{2}x$

f i $f(x) = \coth(3x - 1)$
    ii $f(x) = \coth(-4x)$

2 Differentiate each function with respect to x.

a $f(x) = x^2 \tanh 3x$
b $f(x) = \coth^2 5x$

3 Find the exact coordinates of the turning point on the curve $y = e^{\cosh x} - \cosh x$.

4 Find the exact coordinates of the minimum point on the curve $y = 3 \sinh x + 5 \cosh x$.

5 Show that the equation of the tangent to the curve $y = \tanh x$ at $x = \ln 2$ is $16x - 25y + 15 - 16 \ln 2 = 0$.

6 Find the equation of the normal to the curve $y = 2 \sinh x - \cosh x$ at $x = \ln 3$, giving your answer in the form $ax + by + c = 0$.

7 a Find the exact values of the x-coordinates of the turning points on the curve $y = \tanh 2x - x$.

   b Show that the maximum point has y-coordinate $\dfrac{\sqrt{2} - \ln(\sqrt{2} + 1)}{2}$.

8 Find the coordinates of the stationary point on the curve $y = e^{-x} \sinh \frac{1}{2}x$.

9 Show that the two points of inflection on the curve $y = \operatorname{sech} x$ have x-coordinates $\pm \ln k$, stating the value of k.

10 a Find the exact value of the x-coordinates of the stationary points on the curve with equation $y = 8 \sinh x - 27 \tanh x$.

    b Prove that one of the stationary points from part **a** is a local maximum and that one is a local minimum point.

Section 5: Integration

> **Key point 8.11**
>
> - $\int \sinh x \, dx = \cosh x + c$
> - $\int \cosh x \, dx = \sinh x + c$
> - $\int \tanh x \, dx = \ln \cosh x + c$
>
> **Only the final one of these will be given in your formula book.**

191

As with differentiation, you can derive the results for the integrals of sinh x and cosh x by returning to the definitions of these functions.

WORKED EXAMPLE 8.11

Show that $\int \sinh x \, dx = \cosh x + c$.

$\int \sinh x \, dx = \int \dfrac{e^x - e^{-x}}{2} \, dx$ — Use the definition of sinh x.

$\qquad = \dfrac{e^x - (-e^{-x})}{2} + c$

$\qquad = \dfrac{e^x + e^{-x}}{2} + c$

$\qquad = \cosh x + c$

You can show the result for the integral of tanh x either from the definition again or by using $\tanh x \equiv \dfrac{\sinh x}{\cosh x}$ and applying the reverse chain rule.

WORKED EXAMPLE 8.12

Show that $\int \tanh x \, dx = \ln \cosh x + c$.

$\int \tanh x \, dx = \int \dfrac{\sinh x}{\cosh x} \, dx$ — Use $\tanh x \equiv \dfrac{\sinh x}{\cosh x}$.

$\qquad = \ln \cosh x + c$ — This is of the form $\int \dfrac{f'(x)}{f(x)} \, dx$ so you can integrate it directly.

> **Tip**
>
> Look out for integrals of the form $\int f'(x)[f(x)]^n \, dx$ or $\int \dfrac{f'(x)}{f(x)} \, dx$ as you can integrate these without need for a substitution, by reversing the chain rule.

> **Rewind**
>
> See A Level Mathematics Student Book 2, Chapter 11, for a reminder about integrating trigonometric functions, using the reverse chain rule, trigonometric identities and integration by parts.

In Section 4, you differentiated sech x, cosech x and coth x. You can now reverse these standard derivatives and add them to the list of functions you can integrate:

- $\int -\text{sech } x \tanh x \, dx = \text{sech } x + c$
- $\int -\text{cosech } x \coth x \, dx = \text{cosech } x + c$
- $\int -\text{cosech}^2 x \, dx = \coth x + c$

> **Tip**
>
> When integrating hyperbolic functions, you can often use the same approach as with the corresponding trigonometric function.

Often you will need to use a hyperbolic identity before integrating.

8 Further hyperbolic functions

WORKED EXAMPLE 8.13

Find $\int \operatorname{sech} x (\tanh x + \sinh x) \, dx$.

$\int \operatorname{sech} x (\tanh x + \sinh x) \, dx = \int \operatorname{sech} x \tanh x + \operatorname{sech} x \sinh x \, dx$ — Expand the integrand.

$= \int \operatorname{sech} x \tanh x + \tanh x \, dx$ — Use $\operatorname{sech} x \sinh x \equiv \dfrac{1}{\cosh x} \sinh x \equiv \tanh x$.

$= -\operatorname{sech} x + \ln \cosh x + c$ — Both terms are now standard integrals.

WORKED EXAMPLE 8.14

Find $\int \cosh^2 x \, dx$.

$\cosh 2x \equiv 2\cosh^2 x - 1$ — Use the identity for $\cosh 2x$ in terms of $\cosh^2 x$.

$\Rightarrow \cosh^2 x \equiv \dfrac{\cosh 2x + 1}{2}$

$\therefore \int \cosh^2 x \, dx = \int \dfrac{\cosh 2x + 1}{2} \, dx$

$= \dfrac{1}{2}\left(\dfrac{1}{2} \sinh 2x + x\right) + c$ — Remember to divide by the coefficient of x when integrating $\cosh 2x$.

Sometimes it's better to use the definition of the hyperbolic function, rather than the method you would have used with the corresponding trigonometric function.

WORKED EXAMPLE 8.15

Find $\int e^x \cosh x \, dx$.

$\int e^x \cosh x \, dx = \int e^x \left(\dfrac{e^x + e^{-x}}{2}\right) dx$ — Use the definition of $\cosh x$.

$= \int \dfrac{e^{2x} + 1}{2} \, dx$

$= \dfrac{1}{2}\left(\dfrac{1}{2} e^{2x} + x\right) + c$

Rewind

If the integral in Worked example 8.15 had been $\int e^x \cos x \, dx$, you would have done integration by parts twice and rearranged.

EXERCISE 8E

1 Find:

a i $\int \sinh 3x \, dx$ ii $\int \sinh \dfrac{x}{2} \, dx$

b i $\int \cosh(2x + 1) \, dx$ ii $\int \cosh 4x \, dx$

c i $\int \tanh(-2x) \, dx$ ii $\int \tanh(3x - 2) \, dx$.

193

2 Find:

a i $\int \text{sech}^2(3-4x)\,dx$ 	ii $\int \text{sech}^2 2x\,dx$

b i $\int \text{sech}\frac{x}{3}\tanh\frac{x}{3}\,dx$ 	ii $\int \text{sech}(-3x)\tanh(-3x)\,dx$

c i $\int \text{cosech}\,4x\coth 4x\,dx$ 	ii $\int \text{cosech}\frac{x}{2}\coth\frac{x}{2}\,dx$

d i $\int \text{cosech}^2\left(-\frac{x}{4}\right)dx$ 	ii $\int \text{cosech}^2(2x-3)\,dx$.

3 Use an appropriate hyperbolic identity to find each integral.

a i $\int \sinh^2 2x\,dx$ 	ii $\int \cosh^2 3x\,dx$

b i $\int \tanh^2\frac{x}{2}\,dx$ 	ii $\int \coth^2 x\,dx$

c i $\int \sinh x\cosh x\,dx$ 	ii $\int \sinh 3x\cosh 3x\,dx$

4 Use a substitution or the reverse chain rule to find each integral.

a i $\int \sinh x\cosh^4 x\,dx$ 	ii $\int \text{sech}^2 x\tanh^3 x\,dx$

b i $\int \dfrac{\text{sech}^2 x}{2+\tanh x}\,dx$ 	ii $\int \dfrac{\cosh x}{\sinh x-3}\,dx$

c i $\int e^{\coth 2x}\text{cosech}^2 2x\,dx$ 	ii $\int \text{sech}\,x\tanh x\,e^{-\text{sech}\,x}\,dx$

5 Use integration by parts to find each integral.

a i $\int x\sinh x\,dx$ 	ii $\int x\sinh 2x\,dx$

b i $\int 3x\cosh x\,dx$ 	ii $\int x\cosh\frac{x}{2}\,dx$

c i $\int x^2\sinh x\,dx$ 	ii $\int x^2\sinh 3x\,dx$

d i $\int x^2\cosh 2x\,dx$ 	ii $\int 3x^2\cosh x\,dx$

6 Use the definitions of $\sinh x$ and/or $\cosh x$ to find each integral.

a i $\int e^x\sinh 2x\,dx$ 	ii $\int e^{2x}\cosh x\,dx$

b i $\int \sinh x\sinh 4x\,dx$ 	ii $\int \cosh 2x\cosh 3x\,dx$

7 Find $\int \dfrac{\sinh x+\cosh x}{4\cosh x}\,dx$.

8 By expressing $\sinh x$ and $\cosh x$ in terms of e^x, evaluate $\displaystyle\int_0^1 \dfrac{1}{\sinh x+\cosh x}\,dx$.

8 Further hyperbolic functions

9 **a** Find $\int \tanh x(1 - \text{sech}^2 x)\, dx$.

b Hence, or otherwise, find $\int \tanh^3 x\, dx$.

10 The diagram shows the region R, which is bounded by the curve $y = \sinh x$, the x-axis and the line $x = \ln 3$.

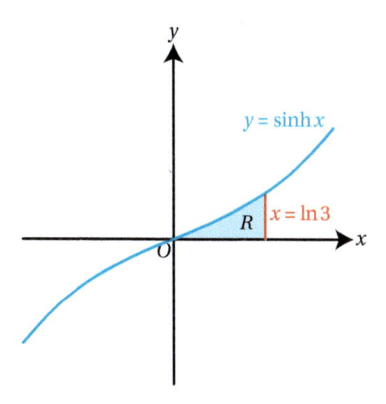

Show that the volume of the solid formed when the region R is rotated through 2π radians about the x-axis is given by $\frac{\pi}{18}(20 - 9\ln 3)$.

11 Find:

a $\int \cosh^3 x \sinh^2 x\, dx$

b $\int \frac{\cosh^3 x}{\sinh^2 x}\, dx$.

12 Find $\int \frac{x}{\cosh^2 x}\, dx$.

13 The diagram shows the region R bounded by curve $y = 4\cosh\frac{x}{2}$, for $x \geqslant 0$, the y-axis and the line $y = 3\sqrt{2}$.

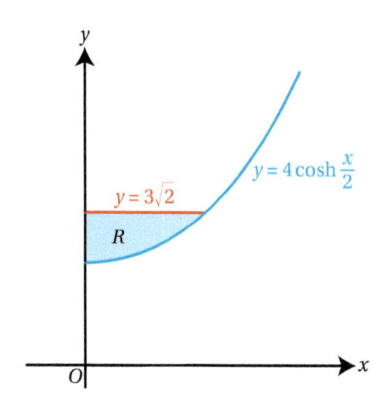

Find the exact volume of the solid formed when the region R is rotated through 2π radians about the x-axis.

14 **a** Using the substitution $u = e^x$, show that $\int \text{cosech}\, x\, dx = \ln\left|\frac{e^x - 1}{e^x + 1}\right| + c$.

b Hence find $\int \frac{3 - \tanh^2 4x}{\sinh 4x}\, dx$.

15 Using the substitution $u = \cosh x$, show that $\int_0^{\ln 2} \dfrac{\sinh^3 x}{\cosh x + 1} \, dx = \dfrac{1}{32}$.

16 Show that $\int_0^{\frac{\pi}{4}} \sin x \, \text{artanh}(\sin x) \, dx = \dfrac{\pi - \sqrt{2} \ln(3 + 2\sqrt{2})}{4}$.

Checklist of learning and understanding

- Domain and range of hyperbolic and inverse hyperbolic functions:

Function	Domain	Range
$\sinh x$	$f(x)$	$f(x) \in \mathbb{R}$
$\cosh x$	$f(x)$	$f(x) \geq 1$
$\tanh x$	$f(x)$	$1 < f(x) < 1$
$\sinh^{-1} x$	$f(x)$	$f(x) \in \mathbb{R}$
$\cosh^{-1} x$	$x \geq 1$	$f(x) \in \mathbb{R}$
$\tanh^{-1} x$	$1 < x < 1$	$f(x) \in \mathbb{R}$

- Definitions of reciprocal hyperbolic functions:
  - $\text{sech } x = \dfrac{1}{\cosh x}$
  - $\text{cosech } x = \dfrac{1}{\sinh x}$
  - $\coth x = \dfrac{1}{\tanh x}$

- Graphs of reciprocal hyperbolic functions:

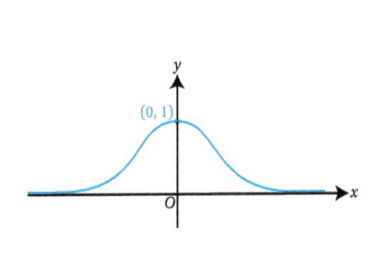

$y = \text{sech } x$ 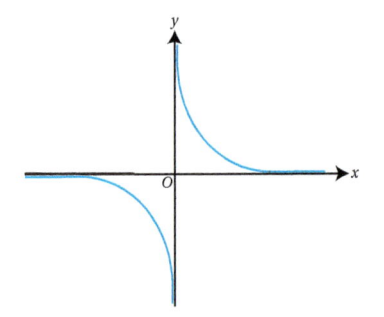 $y = \text{cosech } x$ 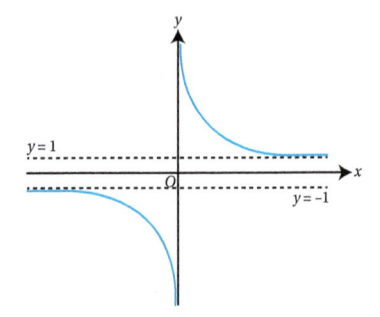 $y = \coth x$

- Domain and range of reciprocal hyperbolic functions:

Function	Domain	Range
$\text{sech } x$	$x \in \mathbb{R}$	$f(x) \in \mathbb{R}$
$\text{cosech } x$	$x \in \mathbb{R}$	$f(x) \geq 1$
$\coth x$	$x \in \mathbb{R}$	$1 < f(x) < 1$

Continues on next page

8 Further hyperbolic functions

- Identities:
  - $\sinh 2x \equiv 2 \sinh x \cosh x$
  - $\cosh 2x \equiv \begin{cases} \cosh^2 x + \sinh^2 x \\ 2\cosh^2 x - 1 \\ 2\sinh^2 x + 1 \end{cases}$
  - $\operatorname{sech}^2 x \equiv 1 - \tanh^2 x$
  - $\operatorname{cosech}^2 x \equiv \coth^2 x - 1$
- Derivatives of hyperbolic, reciprocal hyperbolic and inverse hyperbolic functions:
  - $\dfrac{d}{dx}(\sinh x) = \cosh x$
  - $\dfrac{d}{dx}(\cosh x) = \sinh x$
  - $\dfrac{d}{dx}(\tanh x) = \operatorname{sech}^2 x$
  - $\dfrac{d}{dx}(\operatorname{sech} x) = -\operatorname{sech} x \tanh x$
  - $\dfrac{d}{dx}(\operatorname{cosech} x) = -\operatorname{cosech} x \coth x$
  - $\dfrac{d}{dx}(\coth x) = -\operatorname{cosech}^2 x$
- Integrals of hyperbolic functions:
  - $\int \sinh dx = \cosh x + c$
  - $\int \cosh dx = \sinh x + c$
  - $\int \tanh dx = \ln \cosh x + c$
- Many hyperbolic integrals can be done by using the same method that you would have used for the corresponding trigonometric integral.

197

A Level Further Mathematics for AQA Student Book 2

Mixed practice 8

1 Given $f(x) = \sinh^2 3x$, find $f''(x)$.

Choose from these options.

A $6\cosh 3x$
B $18\cosh 6x$
C $3\cosh^2 3x$
D $9\sinh 6x$

2 Given that $f(x) = 3\tanh^2 x + 1$ for $x \in \mathbb{R}$,

   a sketch the graph of $y = f(x)$

   b state the range of $f(x)$.

3 Solve the equation $\sinh x = \text{sech } x$, giving your answer in the form $a \ln b$.

4 Show that the curve $y = e^x \cosh 2x$ has no points of inflection.

5 Given $f(x) = \text{cosech } x$, show that $f''(x) = 2\,\text{cosech}^3 x + \text{cosech } x$.

6 Given that $y = a\sinh nx + b\cosh nx$, show that $\dfrac{d^2y}{dx^2} = n^2 y$.

7 Find $\displaystyle\int \dfrac{\tanh 3x}{\cosh 3x}\,dx$.

8 Show that $\displaystyle\int_0^{\ln\sqrt{2}} e^{\cosh 4x} \sinh 4x\,dx = \dfrac{e}{4}\left(e^{\frac{9}{8}} - 1\right)$.

9 Solve the equation $4\tanh x - \text{sech } x = 1$, giving your answer in the form $\ln k$ where k is a rational number.

10 Solve the equation $6\,\text{sech}^2 x = 4 + \tanh x$, giving your answers in terms of natural logarithms.

11 Given that $y = \ln\left(\tanh \dfrac{x}{2}\right)$, where $x > 0$, show that $\dfrac{dy}{dx} = \text{cosech } x$.

12 Using the substitution $u = e^x$, find $\displaystyle\int \dfrac{1}{4\sinh x + 5\cosh x}\,dx$.

13 The diagram shows the graphs of $y = 5\cosh x$ and $y = \sinh x + 7$.

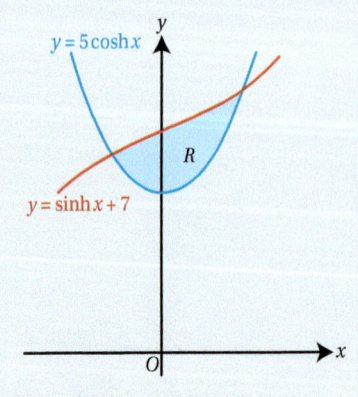

Find the exact value of the area of the shaded region.

8 Further hyperbolic functions

14 a Sketch the graph of $y = \tanh x$.

  b Given that $u = \tanh x$, use the definitions of $\sinh x$ and $\cosh x$ in terms of e^x and e^{-x} to show that
  $$x = \tfrac{1}{2}\ln\left(\frac{1+u}{1-u}\right).$$

  c i Show that the equation
  $$3\operatorname{sech}^2 x + 7\tanh x = 5$$
  can be written as
  $$3\tanh^2 x - 7\tanh x + 2 = 0.$$

  ii Show that the equation
  $$3\tanh^2 x - 7\tanh x + 2 = 0$$
  has only one solution for x.

  Find this solution in the form $\tfrac{1}{2}\ln a$, where a is an integer.

  [©AQA 2009]

15 a i Sketch the graphs of $y = \sinh x$ and $y = \cosh x$.

  ii Use your graphs to explain why the equation
  $$(k + \sinh x)\cosh x = 0$$
  where k is a constant, has exactly one solution.

  b A curve C has equation $y = 6\sinh x + \cosh^2 x$. Show that C has only one stationary point and show that its y-coordinate is an integer.

  [©AQA 2013]

16 a Prove that the curve
  $$y = 12\cosh x - 8\sinh x - x$$
  has exactly one stationary point.

  b Given that the coordinates of this stationary point are (a, b), show that $a + b = 9$.

  [©AQA 2011]

17 Prove that $\dfrac{\sinh x + \cosh x + 1}{\sinh x + \cosh x - 1} \equiv \coth \tfrac{1}{2}x$.

18 a Using the definition of $\cosh x$, show that $\cosh 3x \equiv 4\cosh^3 x - 3\cosh x$.

  b Hence solve the equation $\cosh 3x = 10\operatorname{sech} x$, giving your answer in the form $\ln k$.

19 a Given that $y = \sinh x$, use the definition of $\sinh x$ in terms of e^x and e^{-x} to show that
  $$x = \ln\left(y + \sqrt{y^2 + 1}\right).$$

  b A curve has equation $y = 6\cosh^2 x + 5\sinh x$.

  i Show that the curve has a single stationary point and find its x-coordinate, giving your answer in the form $\ln p$, where p is a rational number.

ii The curve lies entirely above the x-axis. The region bounded by the curve, the coordinate axes and the line $x = \cosh^{-1} 2$ has area A.

Show that
$$A = a\cosh^{-1} 2 + b\sqrt{3} + c$$
where a, b and c are integers.

[©AQA 2016]

9 Further calculus

In this chapter you will learn how to:

- differentiate inverse trigonometric and inverse hyperbolic functions
- reverse those results to find integrals of the form $(a^2 + x^2)^{-1}$, $(a^2 - x^2)^{-\frac{1}{2}}$, $(a^2 + x^2)^{-\frac{1}{2}}$ and $(x^2 - a^2)^{-\frac{1}{2}}$
- use trigonometric substitutions to find similar integrals
- integrate, using partial fractions with a quadratic expression in the denominator
- derive and use reduction formulae for integrals
- find the length of an arc and the area of a surface of revolution.

Before you start...

A Level Mathematics Student Book 2, Chapter 10	You should know how to differentiate functions defined implicitly.	1	Given that $x^2 - y^3 = 5x$, find an expression for $\dfrac{dy}{dx}$.
A Level Mathematics Student Book 2, Chapter 11	You should be able to integrate by using a substitution.	2	Use a suitable substitution to evaluate $\displaystyle\int_0^1 x^2\sqrt{1 + 2x^3}\,dx$.
A Level Mathematics Student Book 2, Chapter 11	You should be able to use integration by parts.	3	Find $\displaystyle\int x^3 \ln x\,dx$.
A Level Mathematics Student Book 2, Chapter 11	You should know how to integrate rational functions by splitting them into partial fractions.	4	Find $\displaystyle\int \dfrac{2x^2 - 9x + 8}{(x-1)(x-2)^2}\,dx$.

Some new integration techniques and applications

In this chapter you will extend the range of integration methods you can use and the range of functions you can integrate. Differentiation of inverse trigonometric functions leads to the rules for integrating functions of the form $\dfrac{1}{a^2 + x^2}$ and $\dfrac{1}{\sqrt{a^2 - x^2}}$ and suggests that you can use trigonometric substitution to find other similar integrals. Likewise, differentiation of inverse hyperbolic functions leads to rules for integrating $\dfrac{1}{\sqrt{a^2 + x^2}}$ and $\dfrac{1}{\sqrt{x^2 - a^2}}$. You can use these results in combination with partial fractions to integrate many rational functions.

You will also see how to extend the idea of repeated integration by parts to derive reduction formulae. These are recursive formulae that allow you to calculate more complex integrals from simpler ones.

So far you have used integration to find areas bounded by plane curves and volumes of revolution. You will now learn about formulae to calculate the length of an arc of a curve and the area of a surface of revolution.

Section 1: Differentiation of inverse trigonometric functions

You already know how to differentiate $\sin x$, $\cos x$ and $\tan x$. To differentiate their inverse functions you can use implicit differentiation.

> **Rewind**
>
> You met implicit differentiation in A Level Mathematics Student Book 2, Chapter 10.

WORKED EXAMPLE 9.1

Given that $y = \sin^{-1} x$, and that $|x| < 1$, find $\dfrac{dy}{dx}$ in terms of x.

$y = \sin^{-1} x$ $\Rightarrow \sin y = x$	You know how to differentiate sin, so express x in terms of y.
Differentiating each term with respect to x: $\cos y \dfrac{dy}{dx} = 1$	Remember the chain rule.
$\dfrac{dy}{dx} = \dfrac{1}{\cos y}$	
$= \dfrac{1}{\sqrt{1 - \sin^2 y}}$	You want the answer in terms of x, so you need to change cos to sin.
$= \dfrac{1}{\sqrt{1 - x^2}}$	

You should notice two important details in the derivation of the derivative of $\sin^{-1} x$ shown in Worked example 9.1. First, the $\sin^{-1} x$ function is defined for $|x| \leq 1$. However, you can see from the graph that the gradient at $x = \pm 1$ is not finite, so the condition $|x| < 1$ is required for the derivative to exist. (You can also see that the expression for $\dfrac{dy}{dx}$ is not defined when $x = \pm 1$.)

Second, you used $\cos^2 y = 1 - \sin^2 y$ to write $\cos y = \sqrt{1 - \sin^2 y}$. When taking a square root you need to ask whether it should be positive or negative (or both). In this case, the range of the $\sin^{-1} x$ function is $-\dfrac{\pi}{2} \leq y \leq \dfrac{\pi}{2}$ and in this range, $\cos y > 0$; this justifies taking the positive square root.

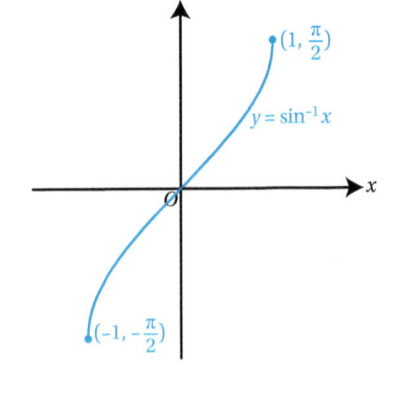

You can establish the results for the inverse cos and tan functions similarly.

🔑 Key point 9.1

- $\dfrac{d}{dx}(\sin^{-1} x) = \dfrac{1}{\sqrt{1 - x^2}}$, $|x| < 1$

- $\dfrac{d}{dx}(\cos^{-1} x) = \dfrac{-1}{\sqrt{1 - x^2}}$, $|x| < 1$

- $\dfrac{d}{dx}(\tan^{-1} x) = \dfrac{1}{1 + x^2}$

These will be given in your formula book.

9 Further calculus

Notice that the $\tan^{-1} x$ function is defined for all $x \in \mathbb{R}$, so there is no restriction on the domain of its derivative.

You can combine these results with other rules of differentiation.

> **Tip**
>
> Remember that $\arccos x$ is alternative notation for $\cos^{-1} x$.

WORKED EXAMPLE 9.2

Differentiate:

a $y = x^2 \tan^{-1} 4x$
b $y = \arccos \sqrt{x-3}$ and state the values for which the derivative is valid.

a Using the product rule:
$u = x^2$, $v = \tan^{-1} 4x$
$\dfrac{du}{dx} = 2x$
$\dfrac{dv}{dx} = \dfrac{1}{1+(4x)^2} \times 4$ .... Multiply by 4 (the derivative of $4x$) due to the chain rule.
$= \dfrac{4}{1+16x^2}$

$\therefore \dfrac{dy}{dx} = 2x \tan^{-1} 4x + \dfrac{4x^2}{1+16x^2}$ .... Use $\dfrac{dy}{dx} = \dfrac{du}{dx}v + u\dfrac{dv}{dx}$.

b Using the chain rule: .... Multiply by $\dfrac{1}{2}(x-3)^{-\frac{1}{2}}$ (the derivative of $\sqrt{x-3}$).
$\dfrac{dy}{dx} = \dfrac{-1}{\sqrt{1-\left(\sqrt{x-3}\right)^2}} \times \dfrac{1}{2}(x-3)^{-\frac{1}{2}}$
$= \dfrac{-1}{\sqrt{1-(x-3)}} \times \dfrac{1}{2\sqrt{x-3}}$
$= \dfrac{-1}{2\sqrt{(4-x)(x-3)}}$

The derivative is valid when .... The derivative of $\arccos x$ is only defined for $|x|<1$.
$|x-3|<1$
$\Leftrightarrow 2<x<4$

EXERCISE 9A

1 Find $\dfrac{dy}{dx}$ for each function.

  a i $y = \cos^{-1} 3x$ **ii** $y = \cos^{-1} 2x$

  b i $y = \tan^{-1}\left(\dfrac{x}{2}\right)$ **ii** $y = \tan^{-1}\left(\dfrac{2x}{5}\right)$

  c i $y = x \arcsin x$ **ii** $y = x^2 \arcsin x$

  d i $y = \arctan(x^2+1)$ **ii** $y = \arcsin(1-x^2)$, $0 < x < 1$

2 Find the exact value of the gradient of the graph of $y = \cos^{-1}\left(\dfrac{x}{2}\right)$ at the point where $x = \dfrac{1}{3}$.

3 Find the exact value of the gradient of the graph of $y = x \arctan 3x$ at the point where $x = -\dfrac{1}{3}$.

4 Differentiate $\arctan(3x+2)$, simplifying your answer as far as possible.

5 Find the derivative of $\arcsin(x^2-3)$, stating the range of values of x for which your answer is valid.

6 a Given that $y = \tan^{-1} x$, show that $\dfrac{dy}{dx} = \dfrac{1}{1+x^2}$.

   b Hence differentiate $\tan^{-1}\left(\dfrac{1}{x}\right)$ with respect to x.

7 Given that $y = \sin^{-1}\left(\dfrac{3x}{2}\right)$, show that $\dfrac{dy}{dx} = \dfrac{3}{\sqrt{4-9x^2}}$ and state the values of x for which the derivative is valid.

8 Given that $x \arctan y = 1$, show that $\dfrac{dy}{dx} = ax^b \sec^2(x^{-1})$, where a and b are integers to be found.

9 a Find $\dfrac{d}{dx}(x \sin^{-1} x)$.

   b Hence find $\displaystyle\int \sin^{-1} x \, dx$.

10 Show that the graph of $y = \arcsin(x^2)$ has no points of inflection.

Section 2: Differentiation of inverse hyperbolic functions

You also know how to differentiate hyperbolic functions, and so again you can use implicit differentiation to differentiate their inverse functions.

Rewind

See Chapter 8, Section 4, for differentiation of hyperbolic functions.

WORKED EXAMPLE 9.3

Given that $y = \sinh^{-1} x$, find $\dfrac{dy}{dx}$ in terms of x.

$y = \sinh^{-1} x$
$\Rightarrow \sinh y = x$ .... Rewrite in terms of $\sinh y$.

Differentiating with respect to y:

$\dfrac{dx}{dy} = \cosh y$

$\dfrac{dy}{dx} = \dfrac{1}{\cosh y}$ .... $\dfrac{dy}{dx} = \dfrac{1}{\left(\dfrac{dx}{dy}\right)}$, so take the reciprocal of both sides.

$= \dfrac{1}{\sqrt{\sinh^2 y + 1}}$ .... Use $\cosh^2 x - \sinh^2 x \equiv 1$.

$= \dfrac{1}{\sqrt{x^2 + 1}}$

You can establish the results for the inverse cosh and tanh functions in a similar way.

9 Further calculus

> **Key point 9.2**
>
> - $\frac{d}{dx}(\sinh^{-1} x) = \frac{1}{\sqrt{x^2 + 1}}$
> - $\frac{d}{dx}(\cosh^{-1} x) = \frac{1}{\sqrt{x^2 - 1}}, x > 1$
> - $\frac{d}{dx}(\tanh^{-1} x) = \frac{1}{1 - x^2}, |x| < 1$
>
> These will be given in your formula book.

WORKED EXAMPLE 9.4

Find the value of the x-coordinate of the point on the curve $y = \text{arcosh}\left(\frac{x}{2}\right)$ at which the tangent is parallel to the line $y = x$.

Differentiating, using the chain rule:	Remember to multiply by the derivative of $\frac{x}{2}$.
$y' = \dfrac{1}{\sqrt{\left(\frac{x}{2}\right)^2 - 1}} \times \dfrac{1}{2}$	
$= \dfrac{1}{2\sqrt{\frac{x^2}{4} - 1}}$	Simplify the denominator.
$= \dfrac{1}{2\sqrt{\frac{x^2 - 4}{4}}}$	
$= \dfrac{1}{\sqrt{x^2 - 4}}$	
So	$y = x$ has gradient 1, so set $y' = 1$ and solve for x.
$\dfrac{1}{\sqrt{x^2 - 4}} = 1$	
$\sqrt{x^2 - 4} = 1$	
$x^2 - 4 = 1$	
$x^2 = 5$	
$\therefore x = \sqrt{5}$	The domain of $y = \cosh^{-1}\left(\frac{x}{2}\right)$ is $x \geqslant 2$, so take the positive square root.

EXERCISE 9B

1 Differentiate each function with respect to x.

    a   **i** $f(x) = \text{arsinh } 2x$ **ii** $f(x) = \text{arsinh } (x + 2)$

    b   **i** $f(x) = \text{arcosh } (-x)$ **ii** $f(x) = \text{arcosh } 3x$

    c   **i** $f(x) = \text{artanh } 4x$ **ii** $f(x) = \text{artanh } (1 - 2x)$

2 Given that $f(x) = \text{arsinh}(\cosh x)$, find $f'(x)$.

3 Given that $f(x) = x\text{arcosh}(x^2)$, find $f'(x)$.

4 Given that $y = \text{artanh}\left(\dfrac{2}{x}\right)$ for $x > 2$, show that $\dfrac{dy}{dx} = \dfrac{a}{b - x^2}$ where a and b are integers to be found.

5 Find the equation of the tangent to the curve $y = \text{artanh}\, x$ at the point where $x = \dfrac{3}{5}$, giving your answer in the form $ax + by + c = 0$.

6 The tangents at $x = 0$ and $x = 1$ to the curve $y = \text{arsinh}\, x$ intersect at the point P. Show that the x-coordinate of P is $(2 + \sqrt{2})\ln(1 + \sqrt{2}) - (1 + \sqrt{2})$.

7 Find the coordinates of the point of inflection on the curve $y = \text{arsinh}(x + 1)$.

8 Show that $y = (\text{arcosh}\, x)^2$ satisfies $(x^2 - 1)\dfrac{d^2y}{dx^2} + x\dfrac{dy}{dx} = 2$.

9 Prove that the x-coordinate of the point on the curve $y = \text{artanh}(e^x)$ at which the gradient is $\sqrt{2}$ is $x = a\ln 2$, where a is a constant to be found.

10 a Prove that $\dfrac{d}{dx}(\text{arsech}\, x) = \dfrac{-1}{x\sqrt{1 - x^2}}$.

 b The tangent to the curve $y = \text{arsech}\, x$ at $x = \dfrac{4}{5}$ crosses the x-axis at the point P. The normal to the curve at $x = \dfrac{4}{5}$ crosses the x-axis at the point Q.

 Find the distance PQ, giving your answer in the form $k\ln 2$, where k is a rational number.

Section 3: Using inverse trigonometric and hyperbolic functions in integration

You can reverse the derivatives from Sections 1 and 2 to derive four more integration results:

$$\int \dfrac{1}{\sqrt{1 - x^2}}\, dx = \sin^{-1} x + c \qquad \int \dfrac{1}{\sqrt{1 + x^2}}\, dx = \sinh^{-1} x + c$$

$$\int \dfrac{1}{1 + x^2}\, dx = \tan^{-1} x + c \qquad \int \dfrac{1}{\sqrt{x^2 - 1}}\, dx = \cosh^{-1} x + c.$$

These results can be generalised slightly by making a linear substitution.

> **Tip**
>
> Notice that the results
> $\int \dfrac{-1}{\sqrt{x^2 - 1}}\, dx = \cos^{-1} x + c$ and
> $\int \dfrac{1}{x^2 - 1}\, dx = \tanh^{-1} x + c$ are not useful as the first is just the negative of $\sin^{-1} x$ and the second can be done by partial fractions.

9 Further calculus

🔑 Key point 9.3

- $\int \dfrac{1}{\sqrt{a^2 - x^2}}\, dx = \sin^{-1}\left(\dfrac{x}{a}\right) + c,\ |x| < a$

- $\int \dfrac{1}{a^2 + x^2}\, dx = \dfrac{1}{a}\tan^{-1}\left(\dfrac{x}{a}\right) + c$

- $\int \dfrac{1}{\sqrt{a^2 + x^2}}\, dx = \sinh^{-1}\left(\dfrac{x}{a}\right) + c$

- $\int \dfrac{1}{\sqrt{x^2 - a^2}}\, dx = \cosh^{-1}\left(\dfrac{x}{a}\right) + c,\ x > a$

These will be given in your formula book.

📷 Focus on…

See Focus on … Problem solving 2 for an example of using one of these integrals.

You also need to know how to derive these results, using trigonometric or hyperbolic substitutions.

WORKED EXAMPLE 9.5

Use the substitution $x = a \sin u$ to prove the result $\int \dfrac{1}{\sqrt{a^2 - x^2}}\, dx = \sin^{-1}\left(\dfrac{x}{a}\right) + c$ when $|x| < a$.

$\dfrac{dx}{du} = a \cos u$
$\Rightarrow dx = a \cos u\, du$
— Differentiate the substitution and express dx in terms of du.

$\dfrac{1}{\sqrt{a^2 - x^2}} = \dfrac{1}{\sqrt{a^2 - a^2 \sin^2 u}}$
$= \dfrac{1}{\sqrt{a^2(1 - \sin^2 u)}}$
— Express the integrand in terms of u.

$= \dfrac{1}{\sqrt{a^2 \cos^2 u}}$
— Use $\sin^2 u + \cos^2 u = 1$.

$= \dfrac{1}{a \cos u}$
— Since you are choosing the substitution, you can choose $a > 0$. For a given value of $\sin u$ there are two possible values of $\cos u$. You can choose the u that gives the positive value.

$\therefore \int \dfrac{1}{\sqrt{a^2 - x^2}}\, dx = \int \dfrac{1}{a \cos u}\, a \cos u\, du$
— Make the substitution and integrate.

$= \int 1\, du = u + c$

$= \sin^{-1}\left(\dfrac{x}{a}\right) + c$
— Write the answer in terms of x:
$x = a \sin u \Rightarrow u = \sin^{-1}\left(\dfrac{x}{a}\right)$.

You can derive the result $\int \dfrac{1}{a^2 + x^2}\, dx = \dfrac{1}{a}\tan^{-1}\left(\dfrac{x}{a}\right) + c$ similarly, using the substitution $x = a \tan u$ and the identity $1 + \tan^2 u = \sec^2 u$.

⏭ Fast forward

You will be asked to derive this result in Question 8 in Exercise 9C.

A Level Further Mathematics for AQA Student Book 2

WORKED EXAMPLE 9.6

Use the substitution $x = a \sinh u$ to prove the result $\int \dfrac{1}{\sqrt{a^2 + x^2}} \, dx = \sinh^{-1}\left(\dfrac{x}{a}\right) + c$.

$\dfrac{dx}{du} = a \cosh u$

$\Rightarrow dx = a \cosh u \, du$

Differentiate the substitution and express dx in terms of du.

$\dfrac{1}{\sqrt{a^2 + x^2}} = \dfrac{1}{\sqrt{a^2 + a^2 \sinh^2 u}}$

$= \dfrac{1}{\sqrt{a^2(1 + \sinh^2 u)}}$

Express the integrand in terms of u.

$= \dfrac{1}{\sqrt{a^2 \cosh^2 u}}$

Use $\cosh^2 u - \sinh^2 u = 1$.

$= \dfrac{1}{a \cosh u}$

Since you are choosing the substitution, you can choose $a > 0$.

$\therefore \int \dfrac{1}{\sqrt{a^2 + x^2}} \, dx = \int \dfrac{1}{a \cosh u} \, a \cosh u \, du$

Make the substitution and integrate.

$= \int 1 \, du = u + c$

$= \sinh^{-1}\left(\dfrac{x}{a}\right) + c$

Write the answer in terms of x: $x = a \sinh u \Rightarrow u = \sinh^{-1}\left(\dfrac{x}{a}\right)$.

You can derive the result $\int \dfrac{1}{\sqrt{x^2 - a^2}} \, dx = \cosh^{-1}\left(\dfrac{x}{a}\right) + c$ similarly, using the substitution $x = a \cosh u$ and the identity $\cosh^2 u - \sinh^2 u \equiv 1$.

> **▶▶ Fast forward**
>
> You will be asked to derive this result in Exercise 9C, Question 9.

You can combine these results with algebraic manipulation to integrate an even wider variety of functions.

WORKED EXAMPLE 9.7

Find $\int \dfrac{3}{9x^2 + 5} \, dx$.

$\int \dfrac{3}{9x^2 + 5} \, dx = \int \dfrac{3}{(3x)^2 + (\sqrt{5})^2} \, dx$

You can turn the integrand into the form $\dfrac{1}{u^2 + a^2}$ (with $a = \sqrt{5}$) by making a substitution $u = 3x$.

$= \dfrac{1}{3} \cdot \dfrac{3}{\sqrt{5}} \tan^{-1}\left(\dfrac{x}{\sqrt{5}}\right) + c$

Since the substitution is linear, you can simply divide by the coefficient of x.

$= \dfrac{1}{\sqrt{5}} \tan^{-1}\left(\dfrac{x}{\sqrt{5}}\right) + c$

If the denominator is not in the form $x^2 + a^2$ or $\sqrt{a^2 - x^2}$, you might need to complete the square to write it in this form.

WORKED EXAMPLE 9.8

Find $\int \dfrac{1}{\sqrt{4x^2 - 12x - 7}}\,dx$.

$$\begin{aligned}4x^2 - 12x - 7 &= (4x^2 - 12x) - 7 \\ &= (2x-3)^2 - 9 - 7 \\ &= (2x-3)^2 - 16\end{aligned}$$

The expression in the denominator is quadratic, so you should complete the square to write it in the form $u^2 - a^2$.

Hence

$$\int \dfrac{1}{\sqrt{4x^2 - 12x - 7}}\,dx = \int \dfrac{1}{\sqrt{(2x-3)^2 - 16}}\,dx$$
$$= \dfrac{1}{2}\cosh^{-1}\left(\dfrac{2x-3}{4}\right) + c$$

The integrand is of the form $\dfrac{1}{\sqrt{u^2 - a^2}}$ with $u = 2x - 3$ and $a = 4$. Remember to divide by the coefficient of x when integrating.

EXERCISE 9C

1 Find each indefinite integral.

 a **i** $\displaystyle\int \dfrac{3}{x^2 + 4}\,dx$ **ii** $\displaystyle\int \dfrac{5}{x^2 + 36}\,dx$

 b **i** $\displaystyle\int \dfrac{1}{9x^2 + 4}\,dx$ **ii** $\displaystyle\int \dfrac{4}{4x^2 + 25}\,dx$

 c **i** $\displaystyle\int \dfrac{6}{2x^2 + 3}\,dx$ **ii** $\displaystyle\int \dfrac{10}{5x^2 + 2}\,dx$

 d **i** $\displaystyle\int \dfrac{2}{\sqrt{9 - x^2}}\,dx$ **ii** $\displaystyle\int \dfrac{5}{\sqrt{4 - x^2}}\,dx$

 e **i** $\displaystyle\int \dfrac{1}{\sqrt{9 - 4x^2}}\,dx$ **ii** $\displaystyle\int \dfrac{3}{\sqrt{25 - 9x^2}}\,dx$

 f **i** $\displaystyle\int \dfrac{15}{\sqrt{5 - 3x^2}}\,dx$ **ii** $\displaystyle\int \dfrac{6}{\sqrt{7 - 12x^2}}\,dx$

2 Find each indefinite integral.

 a **i** $\displaystyle\int \dfrac{3}{\sqrt{16 + x^2}}\,dx$ **ii** $\displaystyle\int \dfrac{5}{\sqrt{25 + x^2}}\,dx$

 b **i** $\displaystyle\int \dfrac{10}{\sqrt{25 + 9x^2}}\,dx$ **ii** $\displaystyle\int \dfrac{3}{\sqrt{9 + 4x^2}}\,dx$

 c **i** $\displaystyle\int \dfrac{4}{\sqrt{3 + 2x^2}}\,dx$ **ii** $\displaystyle\int \dfrac{6}{\sqrt{5 + 7x^2}}\,dx$

 d **i** $\displaystyle\int \dfrac{2}{\sqrt{x^2 - 49}}\,dx$ **ii** $\displaystyle\int \dfrac{7}{\sqrt{x^2 - 36}}\,dx$

 e **i** $\displaystyle\int \dfrac{1}{\sqrt{9x^2 - 16}}\,dx$ **ii** $\displaystyle\int \dfrac{15}{\sqrt{25x^2 - 36}}\,dx$

 f **i** $\displaystyle\int \dfrac{4}{\sqrt{3x^2 - 7}}\,dx$ **ii** $\displaystyle\int \dfrac{2}{\sqrt{7x^2 - 11}}\,dx$

3 By first completing the square, find:

a i $\int \dfrac{1}{x^2 + 4x + 5}\, dx$ ii $\int \dfrac{1}{x^2 - 6x + 10}\, dx$

b i $\int \dfrac{1}{\sqrt{8x - x^2 - 15}}\, dx$ ii $\int \dfrac{1}{\sqrt{2x - x^2}}\, dx$

c i $\int \dfrac{6}{x^2 + 10x + 27}\, dx$ ii $\int \dfrac{5}{\sqrt{-4x^2 - 12x}}\, dx$

d i $\int \dfrac{1}{\sqrt{x^2 + 6x + 10}}\, dx$ ii $\int \dfrac{1}{\sqrt{x^2 + 4x + 5}}\, dx$

e i $\int \dfrac{1}{\sqrt{x^2 - 4x - 12}}\, dx$ ii $\int \dfrac{1}{\sqrt{x^2 - 2x}}\, dx$

f i $\int \dfrac{6}{\sqrt{4x^2 - 12x + 4}}\, dx$ ii $\int \dfrac{3}{\sqrt{x^2 + 2x + 5}}\, dx$.

4 Showing all your working clearly, find the exact value of $\displaystyle\int_0^4 \dfrac{1}{\sqrt{x^2 + 16}}\, dx$.

5 Show that $\displaystyle\int_0^{\frac{\sqrt{3}}{2}} \dfrac{3}{1 + 4x^2}\, dx = \dfrac{\pi}{2}$.

6 Show that $\displaystyle\int_{\frac{1}{\sqrt{3}}}^1 \dfrac{1}{\sqrt{4 - 3x^2}}\, dx = \dfrac{\pi\sqrt{3}}{18}$.

7 Find:

a $\int \dfrac{1}{1 + 9x^2}\, dx$ b $\int \dfrac{16}{16 + x^2}\, dx$.

8 a Use a trigonometric substitution to prove that $\int \dfrac{1}{a^2 + x^2}\, dx = \dfrac{1}{a}\tan^{-1}\left(\dfrac{x}{a}\right) + c$.

b Hence evaluate $\displaystyle\int_0^2 \dfrac{5}{4 + x^2}\, dx$.

9 a Use a hyperbolic substitution to prove that $\int \dfrac{1}{\sqrt{x^2 - a^2}}\, dx = \cosh^{-1}\left(\dfrac{x}{a}\right) + c,\ x > a$.

b Hence evaluate $\displaystyle\int_3^6 \dfrac{2}{\sqrt{x^2 - 9}}\, dx$, giving your answer in terms of a natural logarithm.

10 a Write $2x^2 + 4x + 11$ in the form $2(x + p)^2 + q$.

b Hence find $\int \dfrac{3}{2x^2 + 4x + 11}\, dx$.

11 a Write $1 + 6x - 3x^2$ in the form $a^2 - 3(x - b)^2$.

b Hence find the exact value of $\displaystyle\int_1^2 \dfrac{1}{\sqrt{1 + 6x - 3x^2}}\, dx$.

12 a Using a suitable substitution prove that, when $|x| < a$,

$\int \dfrac{1}{\sqrt{a^2 - x^2}}\, dx = \sin^{-1}\left(\dfrac{x}{a}\right) + c$.

b Find $\int \dfrac{3}{\sqrt{-4x^2 - 4x + 8}}\, dx$.

9 Further calculus

13 Use a suitable trigonometric substitution to show that

$$\int_{\frac{2}{5}}^{\frac{2\sqrt{3}}{5}} \frac{20}{25x^2 + 4} \, dx = \frac{\pi}{6}.$$

14 Find $\int \frac{1}{x^2 + 2x + 2} \, dx$.

15 Show that $\int_3^{5.5} \frac{10}{4x^2 - 24x + 61} \, dx = \frac{\pi}{4}$.

16 Find $\int \frac{4x + 5}{\sqrt{1 - x^2}} \, dx$.

17 Find $\int \frac{x + 1}{\sqrt{x^2 - 1}} \, dx$.

18 Find $\int \frac{6x - 5}{x^2 + 9} \, dx$.

19 **a** Write $2x^2 - 8x + 17$ in the form $a(x - p)^2 + q$.

   b Hence find $\int \frac{2x + 8}{2x^2 - 8x + 17} \, dx$.

20 Use a suitable hyperbolic substitution to show that

$$\int \sqrt{x^2 - 9} \, dx = \frac{x}{2}\sqrt{x^2 - 9} - \frac{9}{2}\cosh^{-1}\left(\frac{x}{3}\right) + c.$$

21 Use a suitable hyperbolic substitution to show that $\int \sqrt{4 - 9x^2} \, dx = \frac{x}{2}\sqrt{4 - 9x^2} + \frac{2}{3}\sin^{-1}\left(\frac{3x}{2}\right) + c$.

22 **a** Given that $\tan u = x$, express $\cos u$ and $\sin u$ in terms of x.

   b Use a suitable trigonometric substitution to show that

$$\int \frac{1}{1 + 2x^2 + x^4} \, dx = \frac{x}{2(1 + x^2)} + \frac{1}{2}\arctan x + c.$$

Section 4: Using partial fractions in integration

You have already used partial fractions to integrate rational expressions with linear and repeated linear factors in the denominator, such as $\int \frac{2x + 1}{(x - 1)(x + 2)^2} \, dx$. You can now use the results from Section 3 to extend the range of rational functions you can integrate to include those with denominators of the form $(x^2 + q^2)$.

In general, when there is a quadratic factor in the denominator, there are three possibilities.

- The quadratic factorises into two different linear factors, $(x - p)(x - q)$.

  The corresponding partial fractions are $\frac{A}{x - p} + \frac{B}{x - q}$.

> **Rewind**
>
> You met partial fractions in A Level Mathematics Student Book 2, Chapter 5, and then used them in integration in Chapter 11.

- The quadratic is a perfect square, $(x-p)^2$. The corresponding partial fractions are $\dfrac{A}{x-p} + \dfrac{B}{(x-p)^2}$.
- The quadratic does not factorise (the quadratic factor is **irreducible**). For example, (x^2+1) or (x^2+2x+5). Then there is only one corresponding partial fraction, with a numerator of the form $Bx+C$.

> **Key point 9.4**
>
> If $f(x)$ is a polynomial of order less than or equal to 2, then
> $$\frac{f(x)}{(x-p)(x^2+q^2)} = \frac{A}{x-p} + \frac{Bx+C}{x^2+q^2}.$$

WORKED EXAMPLE 9.9

a Express $\dfrac{3x}{(x-1)(x^2+2)}$ in partial fractions.

b Hence find $\displaystyle\int \dfrac{3x}{(x-1)(x^2+2)}\,dx$.

a $\dfrac{3x}{(x-1)(x^2+2)} = \dfrac{A}{x-1} + \dfrac{Bx+C}{x^2+2}$ — Use the result from Key point 9.4.

$3x = A(x^2+2) + (Bx+C)(x-1)$ — Multiply through by the common denominator.

$x=1: 3 = A(1+2) + 0 \Rightarrow A = 1$
$x=0: 0 = 1(0+2) + C(0-1) \Rightarrow C = 2$ — Substitute in the values of x which make some of the terms zero.

Comparing coefficients of x^2: — Look at the coefficient of x^2 to find B.
$0 = 1 + B$
$B = -1$

Hence
$\dfrac{3x}{(x-1)(x^2+2)} = \dfrac{1}{x-1} + \dfrac{-x+2}{x^2+2}$

b $\displaystyle\int \dfrac{3x}{(x-1)(x^2+2)}\,dx = \int\left(\dfrac{1}{x-1} + \dfrac{-x}{x^2+2} + \dfrac{2}{x^2+2}\right)dx$ — Integrate each term separately before applying limits. You need to split the second integral into two in order to apply standard results.

$\displaystyle\int \dfrac{1}{x-1}\,dx = \ln|x-1|$

$\displaystyle\int -\dfrac{x}{x^2+2}\,dx = -\dfrac{1}{2}\ln|x^2+2|$ — Here you can use a substitution $u = x^2+2$, or the reverse chain rule, as x is half the derivative of x^2+2.

$\displaystyle\int \dfrac{2}{x^2+2}\,dx = \dfrac{2}{\sqrt{2}}\arctan\left(\dfrac{x}{\sqrt{2}}\right)$ — Use $\displaystyle\int \dfrac{1}{x^2+a^2}\,dx = \dfrac{1}{a}\arctan\left(\dfrac{x}{a}\right)$ with $a = \sqrt{2}$.

Hence
$\displaystyle\int \dfrac{3x}{(x-1)(x^2+2)}\,dx = \ln|x-1| - \dfrac{1}{2}\ln|x^2+2| + \sqrt{2}\arctan\left(\dfrac{x}{\sqrt{2}}\right) + c$

If there is a quadratic factor in the denominator, you first need to check whether it is irreducible or whether it can be factorised. If a factor is irreducible, you need to write it in completed square form before you can apply standard integration results.

WORKED EXAMPLE 9.10

Given that $\dfrac{dy}{dx} = \dfrac{16x+36}{(x^2-4)(x^2+4x+5)}$, find an expression for y in terms of x.

The denominator is $(x-2)(x+2)(x^2+4x+5)$
Hence

$$\dfrac{16x+36}{(x^2-4)(x^2+4x+5)} = \dfrac{A}{x-2} + \dfrac{B}{x+2} + \dfrac{(Cx+D)}{x^2+4x+5}$$

$$16x+36 = A(x+2)(x^2+4x+5) + B(x-2)(x^2+4x+5)$$
$$+ (Cx+D)(x-2)(x+2)$$

$x = 2$: $68 = A(4)(17) \Rightarrow A = 1$
$x = -2$: $4 = B(-4)(1) \Rightarrow B = -1$
$x = 0$: $36 = 1(2)(5) - 1(-2)(5) + D(-2)(2) \Rightarrow D = -4$
$x = 1$: $52 = 1(3)(10) - 1(-1)(10) + (C-4)(-1)(3) \Rightarrow C = 0$

$$y = \int \left(\dfrac{1}{x-2} - \dfrac{1}{x+2} - \dfrac{4}{x^2+4x+5} \right) dx$$

$$\int \dfrac{4}{(x+2)^2+1} dx = 4 \arctan(x+2)$$

$$\therefore y = \ln\left|\dfrac{x-2}{x+2}\right| - 4\arctan(x+2) + c$$

You need to split the function into partial fractions before integrating.

Check whether the quadratic factors factorise. The second one has the discriminant $4^2 - 10 < 0$, so it is irreducible.

Multiply through by the denominator.

Substitute in suitable values of x.

For the third integral, you need to complete the square and then use $\int \dfrac{1}{x^2+a^2} dx = \arctan\left(\dfrac{x}{a}\right)$.

EXERCISE 9D

1 Use partial fractions to find each integral.

a i $\displaystyle\int \dfrac{2x^2+x+7}{(x^2+2)(x+3)} dx$ **ii** $\displaystyle\int \dfrac{-x^2+2x-5}{(x^2+1)(x-2)} dx$

b i $\displaystyle\int \dfrac{2x^2+13x+21}{(x+1)(x^2+6x+10)} dx$ **ii** $\displaystyle\int \dfrac{x^2-2x+12}{(x-2)(x^2+2x+5)} dx$

c i $\displaystyle\int \dfrac{-x^2+3x-2}{(x^2+1)(x+1)} dx$ **ii** $\displaystyle\int \dfrac{-3x-2}{(x^2+4)(x-1)} dx$

d i $\displaystyle\int \dfrac{x^3+2x^2+x+8}{(x+1)^2(x^2+3)} dx$ **ii** $\displaystyle\int \dfrac{x^3+x^2-7x+7}{(x-2)^2(x^2+1)} dx$

2 Showing all your working clearly, use partial fractions to find the exact value of $\int_0^1 \frac{-2x^2+x-1}{(x+1)(x^2+1)}dx$.

3 a Write $\frac{x^2-x+11}{(x-2)(x^2+9)}$ in partial fractions.

b Given that $\frac{dy}{dx} = \frac{x^2-x+11}{(x-2)(x^2+9)}$, and that $y=0$ when $x=0$, find y in terms of x.

4 Use partial fractions to integrate:

a $\frac{3x^2+x-5}{(x-2)(x^2+2x+1)}$

b $\frac{x^2+4x-2}{(x-2)(x^2+2x+2)}$.

5 Let $f(x) = \frac{2x^3+x^2+8x-16}{(x^2-16)(x^2+4)}$.

a Write $f(x)$ in partial fractions.

b Hence find the exact value of $\int_0^{2\sqrt{3}} f(x)\,dx$.

6 Let $f(x) = \frac{x^3+4x^2+3x+4}{(x+1)^2(x^2+1)}$.

Showing all your working clearly, use partial fractions to evaluate $\int_0^1 f(x)\,dx$.

7 Use partial fractions to find $\int \frac{2x^2+4x+18}{(x^2+2x-3)(x^2+2x+3)}dx$.

8 Show that

$$\int \frac{2x^2+3x-3}{(x^2+2x+5)(x+1)}dx = P\ln(x^2+2x+5) + Q\arctan\left(\frac{x+1}{2}\right) + R\ln|x-1| + c$$

where P, Q and R are constants to be found.

Section 5: Reduction formulae

In A Level Mathematics Student Book 2, Chapter 11, you saw examples where you had to use integration by parts more than once. For example:

$$\int x^2 e^x dx = x^2 e^x - \int 2xe^x\,dx \quad \text{(using } u=x^2,\ v=e^x\text{)}$$

$$= x^2 e^x - \left(2xe^x - \int 2e^x dx\right) \quad \text{(using } u=2x,\ v=e^x\text{)}$$

$$= x^2 e^x - 2xe^x + 2e^x + c$$

If you now wanted to find $\int x^3 e^x dx$, you would need to start by using integration by parts again:

$$\int x^3 e^x\,dx = x^3 e^x - \int 3x^2 e^x\,dx$$

However, rather than continuing with integration by parts, you can now use the answer you have already found:

$$\int x^3 e^x\,dx = x^3 e^x - 3\int x^2 e^x\,dx$$

$$= x^3 e^x - 3(x^2 e^x - 2xe^x + 2e^x) + c$$

You could now use this answer to find $\int x^4 e^x \, dx$, and so on.

For any positive integer n, if you write $I_n = \int x^n e^x \, dx$, then:

$$I_n = \int x^n e^x \, dx = x^n e^x - \int n x^{n-1} e^x \, dx$$

$$\therefore I_n = x^n e^x - n I_{n-1}$$

The last equation, which relates I_n to I_{n-1}, is an example of a **reduction formula**. Since you know that $I_0 = \int e^x \, dx = e^x + c$, you can use this formula to find I_n for any $n \geq 1$.

> **Rewind**
>
> This process of building up from I_0 to any I_n should remind you of proof by induction, which you met in Further Mathematics Student Book 1, Chapter 12.

WORKED EXAMPLE 9.11

Let $I_n = \int x^n e^{-3x} \, dx$.

a Derive the reduction formula $I_n = -\frac{1}{3} x^n e^{-3x} + \frac{1}{3} n I_{n-1}$.

b Hence find an expression for $I_3 = \int x^3 e^{-3x} \, dx$.

a Using integration by parts once:

$$u = x^n, \quad \frac{dv}{dx} = e^{-3x}$$

$$\Rightarrow \frac{du}{dx} = n x^{n-1}, \quad v = -\frac{1}{3} e^{-3x}$$

$$I_n = -\frac{1}{3} x^n e^{-3x} - \int -\frac{1}{3} e^{-3x} n x^{n-1} \, dx$$

$$= -\frac{1}{3} x^n e^{-3x} + \frac{1}{3} n \int e^{-3x} x^{n-1} \, dx \quad \text{........ Take the constants out of the integral and relate to } I_{n-1}.$$

$$\therefore I_n = -\frac{1}{3} x^n e^{-3x} + \frac{1}{3} n I_{n-1}$$

b $I_0 = \int e^{-3x} \, dx = -\frac{1}{3} e^{-3x} + c$ .... Start with I_0 and use the reduction formula until you get to I_3.

$$I_1 = -\frac{1}{3} x^1 e^{-3x} + \frac{1}{3}(1) I_0$$

$$= -\frac{1}{3} x e^{-3x} - \frac{1}{9} e^{-3x} + c$$

$$I_2 = -\frac{1}{3} x^2 e^{-3x} + \frac{1}{3}(2) I_1$$

$$= -\frac{1}{3} x^2 e^{-3x} - \frac{2}{9} x e^{-3x} - \frac{2}{27} e^{-3x} + c$$

$$I_3 = -\frac{1}{3} x^3 e^{-3x} + \frac{1}{3}(3) I_2$$

$$= -\frac{1}{3} x^3 e^{-3x} - \frac{1}{3} x^2 e^{-3x} - \frac{2}{9} x e^{-3x} - \frac{2}{27} e^{-3x} + c$$

Sometimes you need to use integration by parts more than once to get a reduction formula. Also, the formula does not need to relate I_n to I_{n-1}. In Worked example 9.12, the formula relates I_n to I_{n-2}. This example also illustrates how you can apply reduction formulae to evaluate definite integrals.

WORKED EXAMPLE 9.12

Let $I_n = \int_0^{\frac{\pi}{2}} x^n \cos x \, dx$.

a Express I_n in terms of I_{n-2}.

b Hence find the exact values of I_4 and I_5.

a $\int_0^{\frac{\pi}{2}} x^n \cos x \, dx = [x^n \sin x]_0^{\frac{\pi}{2}} - \int_0^{\frac{\pi}{2}} nx^{n-1} \sin x \, dx$

> Use integration by parts with $u = x^n$ and $\frac{dv}{dx} = \cos x$, so that $v = \sin x$.

$= \left(\frac{\pi}{2}\right)^n - \left([-nx^{n-1}\cos x]_0^{\frac{\pi}{2}} + \int_0^{\frac{\pi}{2}} n(n-1)x^{n-2}\cos x \, dx\right)$

> The integral is not directly related to I_{n-1}, so use integration by parts again with $u = nx^{n-1}$ and $\frac{dv}{dx} = \sin x$ so $v = -\cos x$.

$\therefore I_n = \left(\frac{\pi}{2}\right)^n - n(n-1)I_{n-2}$

> The remaining integral is now a multiple of I_{n-2}.

b
$I_0 = \int_0^{\frac{\pi}{2}} \cos x \, dx = [\sin x]_0^{\frac{\pi}{2}} = 1$

> To get I_4 you need to start from I_0.

$I_2 = \left(\frac{\pi}{2}\right)^2 - (2)(1)I_0 = \frac{\pi^2}{4} - 2$

$I_4 = \left(\frac{\pi}{2}\right)^4 - (4)(3)I_2 = \frac{\pi^4}{16} - 3\pi^2 + 24$

$I_1 = \int_0^{\frac{\pi}{2}} x \cos x \, dx$

> To get to I_5 you need to start from I_1, which you need to find using integration by parts.

$= [x \sin x]_0^{\frac{\pi}{2}} - \int_0^{\frac{\pi}{2}} \sin x \, dx$

$= \frac{\pi}{2} + [\cos x]_0^{\frac{\pi}{2}}$

$= \frac{\pi}{2} - 1$

$I_3 = \left(\frac{\pi}{2}\right)^3 - (3)(2)I_1 = \frac{\pi^3}{8} - 3\pi + 6$

$I_5 = \left(\frac{\pi}{2}\right)^5 - (5)(4)I_3 = \frac{\pi^5}{32} - \frac{5\pi^3}{2} + 60\pi - 120$

Reduction formulae do not always come from integration by parts. Another common way of deriving them is by using trigonometric identities.

WORKED EXAMPLE 9.13

a Show that $\tan^n x \equiv \sec^2 x \tan^{n-2} x - \tan^{n-2} x$.

b Hence evaluate $\int_0^{\frac{\pi}{3}} \tan^5 x \, dx$.

Continues on next page

a $\tan^n x \equiv \tan^2 x \tan^{n-2} x$
$ \equiv (\sec^2 x - 1)\tan^{n-2} x$
$ \equiv \sec^2 x \tan^{n-2} x - \tan^{n-2} x$

> The identity relating tan and sec is $1 + \tan^2 x \equiv \sec^2 x$.

b Let $I_n = \int_0^{\frac{\pi}{3}} \tan^n x \, dx$.

Then

$$I_n = \int_0^{\frac{\pi}{3}} (\sec^2 x \tan^{n-2} x - \tan^{n-2} x) \, dx$$

$$= \left[\frac{\tan^{n-1} x}{n-1}\right]_0^{\frac{\pi}{3}} - \int_0^{\frac{\pi}{3}} \tan^{n-2} x \, dx$$

$$\therefore I_n = \frac{(\sqrt{3})^{n-1}}{n-1} - I_{n-2}$$

> You can find $\int \sec^2 x \tan^{n-2} x \, dx$ using the reverse chain rule, as $\sec^2 x$ is the derivative of $\tan x$.

$$I_1 = \int_0^{\frac{\pi}{3}} \tan x \, dx = \left[\ln(\sec x)\right]_0^{\frac{\pi}{3}} = \ln 2$$

$$I_3 = \frac{(\sqrt{3})^2}{2} - I_1 = \frac{3}{2} - \ln 2$$

$$I_5 = \frac{(\sqrt{3})^4}{4} - I_3 = \frac{3}{4} + \ln 2$$

> Since I_n has been expressed in terms of I_{n-2}, you need to start from I_1 to build up to I_5.

In more complicated examples, after applying integration by parts, both I_{n-1} and I_n could appear on the right-hand side of the equations.

WORKED EXAMPLE 9.14

Find a reduction formula for $I_n = \int \frac{x^n}{\sqrt{x-1}} \, dx$.

$u = x^n$, $\frac{du}{dx} = nx^{n-1}$

$\frac{dv}{dx} = \frac{1}{\sqrt{x-1}}$, $v = 2\sqrt{x-1}$

> You can use integration by parts with $\frac{dv}{dx} = \frac{1}{\sqrt{x-1}}$ because this can be integrated to give $v = 2\sqrt{x-1}$.

$I_n = 2x^n\sqrt{x-1} - \int 2nx^{n-1}\sqrt{x-1} \, dx$

$ = 2x^n\sqrt{x-1} - 2n\int \frac{x^{n-1}(x-1)}{\sqrt{x-1}} \, dx$

$ = 2x^n\sqrt{x-1} - 2n\int \frac{x^n}{\sqrt{x-1}} \, dx + 2n\int \frac{x^{n-1}}{\sqrt{x-1}} \, dx$

> The integral on the right is not I_{n-1}, but you can make an expression with $\sqrt{x-1}$ in the denominator by writing $\sqrt{x-1} = \frac{x-1}{\sqrt{x-1}}$.

$\therefore I_n = 2x^n\sqrt{x-1} - 2nI_n + 2nI_{n-1}$
$\Leftrightarrow (2n+1)I_n = 2x^n\sqrt{x-1} + 2nI_{n-1}$

> The expression on the right contains both I_n and I_{n-1}. Add $2nI_n$ to both sides.

EXERCISE 9E

1 Use integration by parts to derive each reduction formula.

a i $I_n = \frac{1}{2}(x^n e^{2x} - nI_{n-1})$, where $I_n = \int x^n e^{2x} dx$

   ii $I_n = nI_{n-1} - x^n e^{-x}$, where $I_n = \int x^n e^{-x} dx$

b i $I_n = \frac{1}{2}x^n \sin 2x + \frac{n}{4}x^{n-1}\cos 2x + \frac{n}{4}(n-1)I_{n-2}$, where $I_n = \int x^n \cos 2x\, dx$

   ii $I_n = -3x^n \cos\left(\frac{x}{3}\right) + 9nx^{n-1}\sin\left(\frac{x}{3}\right) - 9n(n-1)I_{n-2}$, where $I_n = \int x^n \sin\left(\frac{x}{3}\right) dx$

c i $I_n = x^{2n} e^x - 2nx^{2n-1}e^x + 2n(2n-1)I_{n-1}$, where $I_n = \int x^{2n} e^x\, dx$

   ii $I_n = -x^{2n} e^{-x} - 2nx^{2n-1}e^{-x} + 2n(2n-1)I_{n-1}$, where $I_n = \int x^{2n} e^{-x}\, dx$

d i $2I_n = x^2(\ln x)^n - nI_{n-1}$, where $I_n = \int x(\ln x)^n dx$

   ii $4I_n = x^4(\ln x)^n - nI_{n-1}$, where $I_n = \int x^3 (\ln x)^n dx$

e i $(2n+1)I_n = 2x^n\sqrt{x+2} - 4nI_{n-1}$, where $I_n = \int \frac{x^n}{\sqrt{x+2}} dx$

   ii $(2n+1)I_n = 2nI_{n-1} - 2x^n\sqrt{1-x}$, where $I_n = \int \frac{x^n}{\sqrt{1-x}} dx$

2 Use the reduction formulae from Question **1** to find the exact value of each integral.

a i $\int_0^1 x^3 e^{2x} dx$ **ii** $\int_0^1 x^4 e^{-x} dx$

b i $\int_0^{\frac{\pi}{4}} x^5 \cos 2x\, dx$ **ii** $\int_0^{\pi} x^4 \sin\left(\frac{x}{3}\right) dx$

c i $\int_0^1 x^4 e^x dx$ **ii** $\int_0^1 x^4 e^{-x} dx$

d i $\int_1^e x(\ln x)^3 dx$ **ii** $\int_1^e x^3 (\ln x)^2 dx$

e i $\int_0^1 \frac{x^4}{\sqrt{x+2}} dx$ **ii** $\int_{-2}^0 \frac{x^3}{\sqrt{1-x}} dx$

3 Given that $I_n = \int_0^1 x^n e^x dx$:

  a show that $I_n = e - nI_{n-1}$

  b find the exact value of I_5.

4 a Find a reduction formula for $I_n = \int x(\ln x)^n dx$.

  b Hence evaluate $\int_{\frac{1}{e}}^e x(\ln x)^3 dx$.

5 **a** Use integration by parts to find $\int \ln x \, dx$.

  b Given that $I_n = \int_1^e (\ln x)^n \, dx$, show that $I_n = e - nI_{n-1}$.

  c Hence find the exact value of $\int_1^e (\ln x)^5 \, dx$.

6 Let $I_n = \int x^n e^{-2x} \, dx$.

  a Derive the reduction formula $I_n = -\frac{1}{2}x^n e^{-2x} + \frac{n}{2}I_{n-1}$.

  b Hence find $\int x^4 e^{-2x} \, dx$ in the form $e^{-2x}p(x) + c$, where p(x) is a polynomial.

7 Let $I_n = \int \tan^n x \, dx$.

  a Show that $I_n = \frac{\tan^{n-1} x}{n-1} - I_{n-2}$.

  b Hence find the exact value of $\int_0^{\frac{\pi}{4}} \tan^4 x \, dx$.

8 Given that $I_n = \int_0^\infty x^n e^{-ax} \, dx$, where $a > 0$:

  a show that $I_n = \frac{n}{a} I_{n-1}$

  b find $\int_0^\infty x^5 e^{-ax} \, dx$

  c use induction to show that $I_n = \frac{n!}{a^{n+1}}$.

9 Let $I_n = \int \sin^n x \, dx$.

  a By writing $\sin^n x$ as $\sin^{n-1} x \sin x$ and integrating by parts, show that $nI_n = (n-1)I_{n-2} - \sin^{n-1} x \cos x$.

  b Hence find the exact value of $\int_0^\pi \sin^5 x \, dx$.

10 **a** Given that $I_n = \int_0^{\ln 2} \tanh^n x \, dx$, show that $I_n = I_{n-2} - \frac{1}{n-1}\left(\frac{3}{5}\right)^{n-1}$.

  b Hence find the exact value of I_4.

11 Let $I_n = \int_0^1 \frac{x^n}{\sqrt{x+3}} \, dx$.

  a Show that $(2n+1)I_n = 4 - 6nI_{n-1}$.

  b Hence show that $I_2 = \frac{12}{5}(7 - 4\sqrt{3})$.

12 Let $I_n = \int_0^{\frac{\pi}{2}} \cos^n x \, dx$.

   a Show that $nI_n = (n-1)I_{n-2}$.

   b Hence find the exact value of $\int_0^{\frac{\pi}{2}} \cos^4 x \, dx$.

   c Prove by induction that $I_{2n} = \dfrac{(2n)!\pi}{2^{n+1}(n!)^2}$.

13 Use a reduction formula to find the exact value of $\int_0^{\pi} \sin^{10} x \, dx$.

Section 6: Length of an arc

You have already met the idea of a definite integral as a limit of a sum and using this to find the area under a curve. You can adapt this idea to calculate the length of an arc of a curve.

> **Rewind**
>
> See A Level Mathematics Student Book 1, Chapter 15, for a reminder of definite integration as the limit of the sum of areas of rectangles.

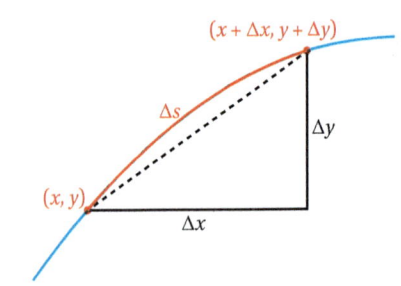

Consider a small section of a curve between points with coordinates (x, y) and $(x + \Delta x, y + \Delta y)$, and denote the length of this small section Δs. The small section of the curve is close to a straight line, so

$$\Delta s \approx \sqrt{(\Delta x)^2 + (\Delta y)^2} = (\Delta x)\sqrt{1 + \left(\dfrac{\Delta y}{\Delta x}\right)^2}$$

$$\Rightarrow \dfrac{\Delta s}{\Delta x} \approx \sqrt{1 + \left(\dfrac{\Delta y}{\Delta x}\right)^2}$$

As $\Delta x \to 0$, $\dfrac{\Delta s}{\Delta x} \to \dfrac{ds}{dx}$ and $\dfrac{\Delta y}{\Delta x} \to \dfrac{dy}{dx}$ and so

$$\dfrac{ds}{dx} = \sqrt{1 + \left(\dfrac{dy}{dx}\right)^2}$$

Integrating this expression between two x-values gives the length of the arc of the curve between two points.

> **Key point 9.5**
>
> The length of an arc of a curve between the point $x = a$ and $x = b$ is
>
> $$s = \int_b^a \sqrt{1 + \left(\dfrac{dy}{dx}\right)^2} \, dx.$$
>
> This will be given in your formula book.

> **Focus on...**
>
> The formula for the length of a curve is used in Focus on ... Problem solving 2 to find the equation of a hanging chain.

WORKED EXAMPLE 9.15

Find the length of the arc of the curve with equation $y = \ln(1-x^2)$ between the points $x = 0$ and $x = \frac{1}{2}$.

$$\frac{dy}{dx} = -\frac{2x}{1-x^2}$$

$$1 + \left(\frac{dy}{dx}\right)^2 = 1 + \frac{4x^2}{1-2x^2+x^4}$$

$$= \frac{1+2x^2+x^4}{1-2x^2+x^4}$$

$$= \frac{(1+x^2)^2}{(1-x^2)^2}$$

$$\therefore s = \int_0^{\frac{1}{2}} \frac{1+x^2}{1-x^2}\, dx \quad\quad\quad\quad \text{Use } s = \int_a^b \sqrt{1+\left(\frac{dy}{dx}\right)^2}\, dx.$$

$$\frac{1+x^2}{1-x^2} = \frac{A}{1-x} + \frac{B}{1+x} - 1 \quad\quad \text{Use partial fractions. This is an improper fraction because the highest power in both the numerator and the denominator is 2.}$$

$$1+x^2 = A(1+x) + B(1-x) - (1-x^2)$$

$$x = 1: 2 = 2A \Rightarrow A = 1$$

$$x = -1: 2 = 2B \Rightarrow B = 1$$

$$\therefore \frac{1+x^2}{1-x^2} = \frac{1}{1-x} + \frac{1}{1+x} - 1$$

$$s = \int_0^{\frac{1}{2}} \left(\frac{1}{1-x} + \frac{1}{1+x} - 1\right) dx$$

$$= \left[-\ln|1-x| + \ln|1+x| - x\right]_0^{\frac{1}{2}}$$

$$= \ln\left(\frac{\frac{3}{2}}{\frac{1}{2}}\right) - \frac{1}{2}$$

$$= \ln 3 - \frac{1}{2}$$

You can also use the formula for the length of an arc when the equation of the curve is given parametrically, using $\dfrac{dy}{dx} = \dfrac{\left(\frac{dy}{dt}\right)}{\left(\frac{dx}{dt}\right)}$.

🔑 Key point 9.6

The length of an arc of a curve between points with parameter values t_1 and t_2 is given by

$$s = \int_{t_1}^{t_2} \sqrt{\left(\frac{dx}{dt}\right)^2 + \left(\frac{dy}{dt}\right)^2}\, dt$$

This will be given in your formula book.

WORKED EXAMPLE 9.16

A circle with radius r has parametric equations $x = r \cos t$, $y = r \sin t$. Find the length of the arc of the circle between the points with $t = \dfrac{\pi}{6}$ and $t = \dfrac{\pi}{2}$.

$\dfrac{dx}{dt} = -r \sin t$, $\dfrac{dy}{dt} = r \cos t$

$s = \displaystyle\int_{\frac{\pi}{6}}^{\frac{\pi}{2}} \sqrt{(-r \sin t)^2 + (r \cos t)^2}\, dt$

$\quad\quad\quad\quad\quad\quad\quad\quad\quad\quad\quad\quad$ *Use $\sin^2 t + \cos^2 t = 1$.*

$= \displaystyle\int_{\frac{\pi}{6}}^{\frac{\pi}{2}} r\, dt$

$= r\left(\dfrac{\pi}{2} - \dfrac{\pi}{6}\right)$

$= \dfrac{\pi r}{3}$

EXERCISE 9F

1 Find and simplify an integral expression for the length of each arc and use technology to evaluate the integral.

  a i $y = x^2$ from $x = 0$ to $x = 3$.
  ii $y = \dfrac{1}{x}$ from $x = 1$ to $x = 2$.

  b i $y = \ln(4 - x^2)$ between $x = 0$ and $x = 1$.
  ii $y = \ln(1 - 4x^2)$ between $x = 0$ and $x = \dfrac{1}{4}$.

  c i $x = 3t^2 - 1$, $y = t^3$ from $t = 0$ to $t = 2$.
  ii $x = t^3 + 1$, $y = t(t - 1)$ from $t = 2$ to $t = 4$.

  d i $x = \sinh 2t$, $y = 4 \cosh t$ from $t = 0$ to $t = 1$.
  ii $x = \tanh t$, $y = \operatorname{sech} t$ from $t = 0$ to $t = \ln 2$.

2 Without using a calculator, find the exact value of the length of each arc.

  a i $y = 4x^{\frac{3}{2}}$ between $x = 1$ and $x = 4$.
  ii $y = \dfrac{1}{3}x^{\frac{3}{2}}$ between $x = 0$ and $x = 3$.

  b i $y = \cosh x$ between $x = 0$ and $x = \ln 2$.
  ii $y = \cosh x$ between $x = -\ln 3$ and $x = \ln 5$.

  c i $x = \dfrac{1}{3}t^3 - 4$, $y = 2t^2$ between $t = 0$ and $t = 3$.
  ii $x = \dfrac{1}{3}t^3 - 9$, $y = \dfrac{3}{2}t^2$ between $t = 1$ and $t = 5$.

  d i $x = 2 + 5 \cos \theta$, $y = 3 + 5 \sin \theta$ between $\theta = 0$ and $\theta = \dfrac{\pi}{2}$.

  ii $x = 4 - 2 \cos \theta$, $y = 2 \sin \theta - 1$ between $\theta = \dfrac{\pi}{4}$ and $\theta = \pi$.

3 Find the length of the graph of the curve with equation $y = \dfrac{2}{3}(x - 4)^{\frac{3}{2}}$ between the points $x = 4$ and $x = 7$.

4 Find the length of the arc of $y = \ln(\sec x)$ between $x = 0$ and $x = \dfrac{\pi}{4}$.

5 A curve has parametric equations $x = 2 \sin t + \cos t$, $y = 2 \cos t - \sin t$. Find the length of the arc of the curve between the points with parameter values $t = 0$ and $t = \dfrac{\pi}{2}$.

9 Further calculus

6 A curve has parametric equations $x = \cos^3 \theta$, $y = \sin^3 \theta$. The arc of the curve between $\theta = 0$ and $\theta = \frac{\pi}{2}$ has length s.

  a Show that $s = \int_0^{\frac{\pi}{2}} \frac{3}{2} \sin 2\theta \, d\theta$.

  b Hence find the length of the arc.

7 A curve has parametric equations $x = \theta - \sin \theta$, $y = 1 - \cos \theta$ for $\theta \in [0, 2\pi]$. Find the length of the curve.

8 A curve has parametric equations $x = 2\sinh t$, $y = \sinh^2 t$. s is the length of the arc of the curve between $t = 0$ and $t = P$.

  a Show that $s = P + \frac{1}{2}\sinh 2P$.

  b The Cartesian equation of the curve is $y = \frac{1}{4}x^2$. By considering the values of t corresponding to $x = 0$ and $x = 1$, find the exact length of the arc of the curve $y = \frac{1}{4}x^2$ between $x = 0$ and $x = 1$.

9 Consider the curve with parametric equations $x = \frac{1}{1+p^2}$, $y = \frac{p}{1+p^2}$.

  a Find the length of the arc of the curve between the points with $p = 0$ and $p = 1$.

  b Find the Cartesian equation of the curve. Sketch the portion of the curve for $0 \leq p \leq 1$.

10 A curve is defined parametrically by $x = t^3 + 5$, $y = 3t^2 - 5$. The length of the arc of the curve between the points with $t = 0$ and $t = 2$ is s.

  a Show that $s = \int_0^2 3t\sqrt{t^2 + k} \, dt$, stating the value of the constant k.

  b Find the exact value of s.

11 A curve is defined by $x = t - \tanh t$, $y = \operatorname{sech} t$. The length of the arc of the curve between the points with parameter 0 and t is $s(t)$.

  a Show that $\frac{ds}{dt} = \tanh t$.

  b Show that $y = e^{-s}$.

12 Let s denote the length of the arc of the curve $y = 6\sqrt{x}$ between $x = 0$ and $x = 1$.

  a Show that $s = \int_0^1 \sqrt{\frac{x+9}{x}} \, dx$.

  b Use the substitution $x = 9\sinh^2 \theta$ to show that $s = 9\sinh^{-1}\left(\frac{1}{3}\right) + \sqrt{A}$ and state the value of the integer A.

13 A curve has equation $y = \frac{1}{2}x^2$. Use the substitution $x = \sinh t$ to show that the length of the arc of the curve between $x = 0$ and $x = 1$ is $\frac{1}{2}(a + \ln b)$, where a and b are constants to be found.

Section 7: Area of a surface of revolution

In Further Mathematics Student Book 1, Chapter 10, you learned how to find volumes of solids of revolution, which are formed by rotating a region about the x- or the y-axis. It is also possible to calculate their surface area. You only need to be able to use the formulae for surfaces generated by rotation about the x-axis, and there is both a Cartesian and a parametric version.

A Level Further Mathematics for AQA Student Book 2

🔑 Key point 9.7

The area of a **surface of revolution** rotated about the x-axis:

$$S_x = \int_a^b 2\pi y \sqrt{1 + \left(\frac{dy}{dx}\right)^2}\, dx = \int_{t_1}^{t_2} 2\pi y \sqrt{\left(\frac{dx}{dt}\right)^2 + \left(\frac{dy}{dt}\right)^2}\, dt$$

This will be given in your formula book.

Note that the formula in Key point 9.7 gives the curved surface area, not including the base(s) of the resulting solid.

WORKED EXAMPLE 9.17

Find the curved surface area of the cone with base radius 5 and height 12.

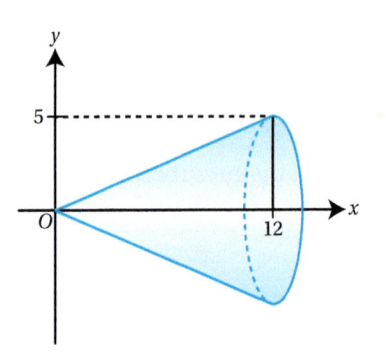

The curved surface area of the cone is generated by rotating the line segment about the x-axis. You can see from the diagram that the gradient of this line segment is $\frac{5}{12}$ so its equation is $y = \frac{5}{12}x$.

$\dfrac{dy}{dx} = \dfrac{5}{12}$

Use $\int_a^b 2\pi y \sqrt{1 + \left(\frac{dy}{dx}\right)^2}\, dx$. The x-values go from 0 to 12.

$S = \int_0^{12} 2\pi \left(\frac{5}{12}x\right)\sqrt{1 + \left(\frac{5}{12}\right)^2}\, dx$

$= 2\pi \int_0^{12} \frac{65}{144} x \, dx$

$= 2\pi \left[\frac{65}{288} x^2\right]_0^{12}$

$= \frac{65\pi}{144}(144 - 0)$

$= 65\pi$

You might recognise the formula $\pi r l$ for the curved surface area of the cone. In this case, $r = 5$ and $l = \sqrt{12^2 + 5^2} = 13$.

WORKED EXAMPLE 9.18

A semi-circle with radius r is given by parametric equations $x = r\cos\theta$, $y = r\sin\theta$ for $0 \leq \theta \leq \pi$. The semi-circle is rotated 2π radians about the x-axis. Show that the surface area of the resulting sphere is $4\pi r^2$.

Continues on next page

9 Further calculus

$$\left(\frac{dx}{d\theta}\right)^2 + \left(\frac{dy}{d\theta}\right)^2 = (-r\sin\theta)^2 + (r\cos\theta)^2 = r^2$$

Use $\int_0^\pi 2\pi y \sqrt{\left(\frac{dx}{d\theta}\right)^2 + \left(\frac{dy}{d\theta}\right)^2}\, d\theta$.

$$S = \int_0^\pi 2\pi r \sin\theta \sqrt{r^2}\, d\theta$$

$$= 2\pi r^2 \Big[-\cos\theta\Big]_0^\pi$$

$$= 2\pi r^2(1-(-1))$$

$$= 4\pi r^2$$

EXERCISE 9G

1 The given curve is rotated 2π radians about the x-axis. Write down and simplify the integral to evaluate the surface of revolution. Use technology to evaluate the integral.

a **i** $y = x^2$ from $x = 0$ to $x = 3$.
   ii $y = \dfrac{1}{x^2}$ from $x = 1$ to $x = 2$.

b **i** $y = \dfrac{x-1}{x}$ from $x = 1$ to $x = 3$.
   ii $y = \dfrac{x-1}{x+1}$ from $x = 0$ to $x = 1$.

c **i** $x = 3t^2 - 1$, $y = t^3$ from $t = 0$ to $t = 2$.
   ii $x = t^3 + 1$, $y = t(t-1)$ from $t = 2$ to $t = 4$.

d **i** $x = \sinh 2t$, $y = 4\cosh t$ from $t = 0$ to $t = 1$.
   ii $x = \tanh t$, $y = \operatorname{sech} t$ from $t = 0$ to $t = \ln 2$.

2 The arc of the curve $y = \sqrt{9 - x^2}$ between $x = -3$ and $x = 3$ is rotated 2π radians about the x-axis. Find the exact value of the area of the surface of revolution.

3 The arc of the curve $y = \sqrt{8x}$ between $x = 2$ and $x = 7$ is rotated 2π radians about the x-axis. Find the exact area of the resulting surface of revolution.

4 Find the area of the surface of revolution formed when the arc of the curve $y = x^3$ for $0 \leqslant x \leqslant 1$ is rotated through a full turn about the x-axis.

5 A frustum is formed by rotating the line segment connecting points $(0, 3)$ and $(4, 11)$ about the x-axis. Find the surface area of the frustum, including the two bases.

6 A curve is defined parametrically by $x = \dfrac{1}{2}\cosh 2t$, $y = 2\sinh t$.

a Show that $\left(\dfrac{dx}{dt}\right)^2 + \left(\dfrac{dy}{dt}\right)^2 = 4\cosh^4 t$.

The arc of the curve between $t = 0$ and $t = \ln 2$ is rotated through a full turn about the x-axis.

b Show that the exact area of the resulting surface of revolution is $k\pi$, where k is a rational number to be found.

7 An ellipse has parametric equations $x = 2\cos\theta$, $y = \sin\theta$. The arc of the ellipse between $\theta = 0$ and $\theta = \pi$ is rotated fully about the x-axis. Let S be the area of the resulting surface of revolution.

a Show that $S = \dfrac{2\pi}{\sqrt{3}}\displaystyle\int_{-\sqrt{3}}^{\sqrt{3}} \sqrt{4 - u^2}\, du$.

b Use a suitable trigonometric substitution to show that $S = \dfrac{8\sqrt{3}\pi^2}{9} + 2\pi$.

225

8 The arc of the curve $y = \sin 2x$ between $x = 0$ and $x = \frac{\pi}{2}$ is rotated 2π radians about the x-axis. The resulting surface of revolution has area S.

   a Show that $S = \int_{-1}^{1} \pi\sqrt{1 + 4u^2}\, du$.

   b Use an appropriate hyperbolic substitution to find the exact value of S.

Checklist of learning and understanding

- Derivatives of inverse trigonometric functions:
  - $\frac{d}{dx}(\sin^{-1} x) = \frac{1}{\sqrt{1-x^2}}$
  - $\frac{d}{dx}(\cos^{-1} x) = \frac{-1}{\sqrt{1-x^2}}$
  - $\frac{d}{dx}(\tan^{-1} x) = \frac{1}{1+x^2}$
- Derivatives of inverse hyperbolic functions:
  - $\frac{d}{dx}(\sinh^{-1} x) = \frac{1}{\sqrt{x^2+1}}$
  - $\frac{d}{dx}(\cosh^{-1} x) = \frac{1}{\sqrt{x^2-1}},\ x > 1$
  - $\frac{d}{dx}(\tanh^{-1} x) = \frac{1}{1-x^2},\ |x| < 1$
- You can derive the corresponding integrals using a trigonometric substitution ($x = a \sin u$ or $x = a \tan u$) or a hyperbolic substitution ($x = a \sinh u$ or $x = a \cosh u$):
  - $\int \frac{1}{\sqrt{a^2 - x^2}}\, dx = \sin^{-1}\left(\frac{x}{a}\right) + c,\ |x| < a$
  - $\int \frac{1}{a^2 + x^2}\, dx = \frac{1}{a}\tan^{-1}\left(\frac{x}{a}\right) + c$
  - $\int \frac{1}{\sqrt{a^2 + x^2}}\, dx = \sinh^{-1}\left(\frac{x}{a}\right) + c$
  - $\int \frac{1}{\sqrt{x^2 - a^2}}\, dx = \cosh^{-1}\left(\frac{x}{a}\right) + c,\ x > a$
- You might need to write a quadratic expression in completed square form in order to apply one of the results shown.
- When splitting an expression into partial fractions, if the denominator has an **irreducible quadratic** factor $x^2 + px + q$ then the corresponding partial fraction is $\frac{Ax + B}{x^2 + px + q}$.
- A reduction formula relates an integral to a similar but simpler one, by reducing the power of one of the expressions. You can derive a reduction formula by using integration by parts or a trigonometric or algebraic identity.
- Length of an arc of a curve in Cartesian and parametric form:
  - $s = \int_a^b \sqrt{1 + \left(\frac{dy}{dx}\right)^2}\, dx = \int_{t_1}^{t_2} \sqrt{\left(\frac{dx}{dt}\right)^2 + \left(\frac{dy}{dt}\right)^2}\, dt$
- Surface area when a curve is rotated about the x-axis:
  - $S_x = \int_a^b 2\pi y \sqrt{1 + \left(\frac{dy}{dx}\right)^2}\, dx = \int_{t_1}^{t_2} 2\pi y \sqrt{\left(\frac{dx}{dt}\right)^2 + \left(\frac{dy}{dt}\right)^2}\, dt$

Mixed practice 9

1 Differentiate f(x) = arctan (e^x).

Choose from these options.

A $\dfrac{1}{1+e^x}$ B $\dfrac{1}{1+(e^x)^2}$ C $\dfrac{x}{1+2e^x}$ D $\dfrac{e^x}{1+e^{2x}}$

2 Find $\dfrac{dy}{dx}$ when $y = x^2 \sin^{-1} x$.

3 Differentiate f(x) = cos^{-1} (1 − x^2).

4 Find the x-coordinates of the points on the curve $y = \tanh^{-1}\left(\dfrac{x}{2}\right)$ where the gradient is 2.

5 A curve C is defined parametrically by

$$x = \dfrac{t^2+1}{t},\ y = 2\ln t$$

    a Show that $\left(\dfrac{dx}{dt}\right)^2 + \left(\dfrac{dy}{dt}\right)^2 = \left(1 + \dfrac{1}{t^2}\right)^2$.

    b The arc of C from $t = 1$ to $t = 2$ is rotated through 2π radians about the x-axis.

       Find the area of the surface generated, giving your answer in the form $\pi(m\ln 2 + n)$, where m and n are integers.

[© AQA 2015]

6 Given that $y = \tan^{-1}(x^2)$, find $\dfrac{d^2y}{dx^2}$.

7 Show that $y = (\text{arsinh } x)^2$ satisfies $(1 + x^2)\dfrac{d^2y}{dx^2} + x\dfrac{dy}{dx} - 2 = 0$.

8 Find $\displaystyle\int \dfrac{1}{2 - 2x + x^2}\,dx$.

9 An ellipse has parametric equations $x = 5\cos\theta$, $y = 3\sin\theta$.

    a Show that the perimeter of the ellipse is given by

$$s = \int_0^{2\pi} \sqrt{25 - 16\cos^2\theta}\,d\theta.$$

    b Show that this perimeter is equal to the length of one complete wave of the curve $y = 4\cos\dfrac{x}{3}$.

10 Find $\displaystyle\int \dfrac{6x+4}{x^2+4}\,dx$.

11 Using integration by parts, or otherwise, show that $\displaystyle\int_0^{\frac{1}{2}} \arctan 2x\,dx = \dfrac{\pi - \ln 4}{8}$.

12 The function f, where f(x) = sec x, has domain $0 \leqslant x \leqslant \dfrac{\pi}{2}$ and has inverse function f^{-1}, where f^{-1}(x) = sec$^{-1} x$.

    a Show that sec$^{-1} x = \cos^{-1}\dfrac{1}{x}$.

    b Hence show that $\dfrac{d}{dx}(\sec^{-1} x) = \dfrac{1}{\sqrt{x^4 - x^2}}$.

[© AQA 2012]

13 A curve is defined parametrically by $x = t^3 + 5$, $y = 6t^2 - 1$.

The arc length between the points where $t = 0$ and $t = 3$ on the curve is s.

a Show that $s = \int_0^3 3t\sqrt{t^2 + A}\,dt$, stating the value of the constant A.

b Hence show that $s = 61$.

[© AQA 2013]

14 a Show that $\sqrt{\dfrac{1-3x}{1+3x}} = \dfrac{1-3x}{\sqrt{1-9x^2}}$.

b Hence find $\int \sqrt{\dfrac{1-3x}{1+3x}}\,dx$.

15 a Express $\dfrac{4-3x}{(x+2)(x^2+1)}$ in partial fractions.

b Hence find $\int \dfrac{4-3x}{(x+2)(x^2+1)}\,dx$.

c Show that $\int_0^{\frac{\sqrt{3}}{2}} \dfrac{4-3x}{\sqrt{1-x^2}}\,dx = \dfrac{8\pi - 9}{6}$.

16 a Using an appropriate substitution, show that $\int \dfrac{2x^2}{\sqrt{1+x^2}}\,dx = x\sqrt{1+x^2} - \sinh^{-1} x + c$.

b Hence show that $\int_0^{\sqrt{3}} 4x \sinh^{-1} x\,dx = 7\ln(\sqrt{3} + 2) - 2\sqrt{3}$.

17 a Show that $\int \sqrt{k^2 - x^2}\,dx = \dfrac{k^2}{2}\arcsin\left(\dfrac{x}{k}\right) + \dfrac{x}{2}\sqrt{k^2 - x^2} + c$

b Hence show that the area enclosed by the ellipse with equation $\dfrac{x^2}{a^2} + \dfrac{y^2}{b^2} = 1$ is πab.

18 a Show that $x^2(1+x^2)^{n-1} = (1+x^2)^n - (1+x^2)^{n-1}$.

b Let $I_n = \int_0^1 (1+x^2)^n\,dx$. Show that $(2n+1)I_n = 2^n + 2nI_{n-1}$ for all $n \in \mathbb{R}$.

c Hence show that $\int_0^1 (1+x^2)^{\frac{-3}{2}}\,dx = \dfrac{1}{\sqrt{2}}$.

19 A curve has Cartesian equation $y = \dfrac{1}{2}\ln(\tanh x)$.

a Show that $\dfrac{dy}{dx} = \dfrac{1}{\sinh 2x}$

b The points A and B on the curve have x-coordinates $\ln 2$ and $\ln 4$ respectively. Find the arc length AB, giving your answer in the form $p \ln q$, where p and q are rational numbers.

[© AQA 2012]

20 a The arc of the curve $y^2 = x^2 + 8$ between the points where $x = 0$ and $x = 6$ is rotated through 2π radians about the x-axis. Show that the area S of the curved surface formed is given by

$$S = 2\sqrt{2}\pi \int_0^6 \sqrt{x^2 + 4}\,dx.$$

b By means of the substitution $x = 2\sinh\theta$, show that

$$S = \pi(24\sqrt{5} + 4\sqrt{2}\sinh^{-1} 3).$$

[© AQA 2011]

228

10 Maclaurin series and limits

In this chapter you will learn how to:

- find Maclaurin series for functions without using any standard results
- use Maclaurin series to approximate particular values of functions or definite integrals
- find limits of functions in certain circumstances, using Maclaurin series or using an alternative method called l'Hôpital's rule
- find the value of definite integrals in certain cases where a limiting process is required (improper integrals).

Before you start…

A Level Mathematics Student Book 2, Chapter 10	You should know how to differentiate functions, using the chain rule.	1 For $f(x) = (x^2 + 3)^5$, find $f'(x)$.

A Level Mathematics Student Book 2, Chapter 9	You should know how to differentiate exponential, logarithmic and trigonometric functions.	2 For each function, find:
		  i $f'(x)$ ii $f''(x)$.
		  a $f(x) = e^{-2x}$
		  b $f(x) = \ln x$
		  c $f(x) = \cos 3x$

Chapter 8	You should know how to differentiate hyperbolic functions.	3 For $f(x) = \tanh x$, find: a $f'(x)$ b $f''(x)$.
Chapter 8	You should know how to differentiate inverse hyperbolic functions.	4 For $f(x) = \cosh^{-1} x$, find: a $f'(x)$ b $f''(x)$.
Chapter 9	You should know how to differentiate inverse trigonometric functions.	5 For $f(x) = \sin^{-1} x$, find: a $f'(x)$ b $f''(x)$.

Analysis of functions

In Further Mathematics Student Book 1, Chapter 11, you were given the Maclaurin series for some common functions. In the first part of this chapter you will see where these results come from and use this method to find Maclaurin series for other functions.

In the second part of the chapter you will use both Maclaurin series and an alternative rule for evaluating some awkward limits of functions.

Finally, you will look at definite integrals where either the integrand is not defined at point(s) in the range of integration, or where the range of integration extends to infinity. These are known as improper integrals.

> **Did you know?**
>
> Analysis is a branch of mathematics that deals with infinite series, limits and calculus among other ideas. It forms a significant component of most mathematics degrees.

Section 1: Maclaurin series

You know from Further Mathematics Student Book 1, Chapter 11, that many functions can be written as infinite series. In general, for some function f(x) such a series will be of the form

f(x) = $a_0 + a_1 x + a_2 x^2 + a_3 x^3 + \ldots$ where a_0, a_1, a_2 etc. are real constants.

Differentiating this series several times:
f'(x) = $a_1 + 2a_2 x + 3a_3 x^2 + 4a_4 x^3 + \ldots$
f''(x) = $2a_2 + (3 \times 2)a_3 x + (4 \times 3)a_4 x^2 + \ldots$
f'''(x) = $(3 \times 2)a_3 + (4 \times 3 \times 2)a_4 x + \ldots$
$\vdots$

> **Did you know?**
>
> You are assuming here that you can differentiate an infinite series term by term in the same way as a finite series. In fact, this is only possible for values of x within the interval of convergence of the series.

> **Rewind**
>
> You met the interval of convergence in Further Mathematics Student Book 1, Chapter 11.

Substituting $x = 0$ into f(x) and each of its derivatives to find expressions for a_0, a_1, a_2, etc:
f(0) = a_0
f'(0) = a_1
f''(0) = $2!a_2$
f'''(0) = $3!a_3$
$\vdots$

Substituting these expressions for a_0, a_1, a_2, etc. back into the expression for f(x) gives the Maclaurin series formula for any function.

> **Key point 10.1**
>
> The Maclaurin series of a function f(x) is given by:
>
> $$f(x) = f(0) + f'(0)x + \frac{f''(0)}{2!}x^2 + \ldots + \frac{f^{(r)}(0)}{r!}x^r + \ldots$$

> **Tip**
>
> Different but equivalent forms of the general term can be given, depending on whether r starts from 0 or 1.

You can use Key point 10.1 to find the first few terms of the Maclaurin series. You can sometimes spot a pattern in the derivatives, which enables you also to write down the **general term**, $\frac{f^{(r)}(0)}{r!}x^r$.

WORKED EXAMPLE 10.1

a Find the first three non-zero terms in the Maclaurin series of sin x.

b Write down a conjecture for the general term (you need not prove your conjecture).

Continues on next page

a $f(x) = \sin x \Rightarrow f(0) = 0$ — Find f(0).

$f'(x) = \cos x \Rightarrow f'(0) = 1$
$f''(x) = -\sin x \Rightarrow f''(0) = 0$
$f'''(x) = -\cos x \Rightarrow f'''(0) = -1$
$f^{(4)}(x) = \sin x \Rightarrow f^{(4)}(0) = 0$
$f^{(5)}(x) = \cos x \Rightarrow f^{(5)}(0) = 1$

Then differentiate and evaluate each derivative at $x = 0$.

Notice that you need to go as far as the fifth derivative to get three non-zero terms.

So

$f(x) = 0 + 1x + \dfrac{0}{2!}x^2 + \dfrac{-1}{3!}x^3 + \dfrac{0}{4!}x^4 + \dfrac{1}{5!}x^5 \ldots$

$= x - \dfrac{x^3}{3!} + \dfrac{x^5}{5!} + \ldots$

Substitute these values into the Maclaurin series formula:

$f(x) = f(0) + f'(0)x + \dfrac{f''(0)}{2!}x^2 + \ldots$

b The general term is

$\dfrac{(-1)^n \cos(0)}{(2n+1)!} x^{2n+1} = \dfrac{(-1)^n}{(2n+1)!} x^{2n+1}$

for $n = 0, 1, 2, \ldots$

$(-1)^n$ ensures that the sign alternates. $2n + 1$ ensures that only odd terms are present. Note that you could also give the general term as, for example, $\dfrac{(-1)^{n-1}}{(2n-1)!} x^{2n-1}$ for $n = 1, 2, \ldots$

Not every function has a Maclaurin series. For example, for $f(x) = \ln x$, f(0) doesn't exist (nor do any of the derivatives of $\ln x$ at $x = 0$). However, $f(x) = \ln(1 + x)$ does have a Maclaurin series, as now f(0) and all the derivatives at $x = 0$ do exist.

WORKED EXAMPLE 10.2

a Find the Maclaurin series of $\ln(1 + x)$ up to and including the term in x^4.

b Prove by induction that the general term is $\dfrac{(-1)^{n-1}}{n} x^n$, for $n = 1, 2, 3, \ldots$

a $f(x) = \ln(1 + x) \Rightarrow f(0) = 0$ — Find f(0)…

$f'(x) = (1 + x)^{-1} \Rightarrow f'(0) = 1$
$f''(x) = -(1 + x)^{-2} \Rightarrow f''(0) = -1$
$f'''(x) = 2(1 + x)^{-3} \Rightarrow f'''(0) = 2$
$f^{(4)}(x) = -6(1 + x)^{-4} \Rightarrow f^{(4)}(0) = -6$

… then differentiate and evaluate each derivative at $x = 0$.

So

$f(x) = 0 + 1x - \dfrac{1}{2!}x^2 + \dfrac{2}{3!}x^3 - \dfrac{6}{4!}x^4 + \ldots$

$= x - \dfrac{x^2}{2} + \dfrac{x^3}{3} - \dfrac{x^4}{4} + \ldots$

Substitute these values into the Maclaurin series formula:

$f(x) = f(0) + f'(0)x + \dfrac{f''(0)}{2!}x^2 + \ldots$

b To prove:
$f^{(n)}(x) = (-1)^{n-1}(n-1)!(1+x)^{-n}$

To find the general term you need an expression for the nth derivative, which you then divide by n to get the coefficient of x^n. You can conjecture the expression by looking at the first four derivatives you found in part **a**.

Continues on next page

When $n = 1$: $f'(x) = (1+x)^{-1}$ .... Show that the expression is correct when $n = 1$.

$\qquad = (-1)^0 (0!)(1+x)^{-1}$

Hence the expression is correct for $n = 1$.

Suppose that the expression is correct for the kth derivative: .... Now suppose that the expression is correct for some k and show that it is still correct for $k + 1$.
$f^{(k)}(x) = (-1)^{k-1}(k-1)!(1+x)^{-k}$

Then the $(k+1)$st derivative is:

$f^{(k+1)}(x) = (-1)^{k-1}(k-1)!(-k)(1+x)^{-(k+1)}$ .... Differentiate $f^{(k)}$ to get $f^{(k+1)}$.

$\qquad = (-1)^k k!(1+x)^{-(k+1)}$ .... $(k-1)! \, k = k!$

Hence the expression is correct for the $(k+1)$st derivative.

The expression is correct for $n = 1$ and, if it is correct for $n = k$ .... Write a conclusion.
then it is also correct for $n = k + 1$. It is therefore true for all $n \geq 1$, by induction.

One use of Maclaurin series is to approximate definite integrals of functions that can't be integrated by standard methods.

💡 Tip

The question will make it clear whether you are required to find the Maclaurin series of a function from first principles or whether you can use one of the standard results in the formula book to find the series you need.

⏪ Rewind

In Further Mathematics Student Book 1, Chapter 11, you saw how to use the Maclaurin series of certain standard functions to find the series of more complicated functions.

WORKED EXAMPLE 10.3

a Use the Maclaurin series of $\sin x$ to find the first three non-zero terms in the Maclaurin series of $\sin(x^2)$.

b Hence find an approximate value for $\int_0^{\frac{\pi}{3}} \sin(x^2) \, dx$, giving your answer to three decimal places.

a $\sin(x^2) = (x^2) - \dfrac{(x^2)^3}{3!} + \dfrac{(x^2)^5}{5!} - \ldots$ .... Substitute x^2 into the series for $\sin x$.

$\qquad = x^2 - \dfrac{x^6}{3!} + \dfrac{x^{10}}{5!} - \ldots$

b $\int_0^{\frac{\pi}{3}} \sin(x^2) \, dx \approx \int_0^{\frac{\pi}{3}} \left(x^2 - \dfrac{x^6}{3!} + \dfrac{x^{10}}{5!} \right) dx$ .... Integrate the polynomial as usual.

$\qquad \approx \left[\dfrac{x^3}{3} - \dfrac{x^7}{7 \times 3!} + \dfrac{x^{11}}{11 \times 5!} \right]_0^{\frac{\pi}{3}}$

$\qquad \approx 0.351$

10 Maclaurin series and limits

EXERCISE 10A

1 Using Key point 10.1, find the first four non-zero terms of the Maclaurin series of these functions. Also conjecture the general term (you need not prove your conjecture).

  a i e^x ii e^{-3x}

  b i $\sin(-x)$ ii $\sin 2x$

  c i $\cos x$ ii $\cos 3x$

  d i $\ln(1-x)$ ii $\ln(1+2x)$

  e i $\sinh x$ ii $\sinh 2x$

  f i $\cosh x$ ii $\cosh(-x)$

2 By differentiating an appropriate number of times, find the Maclaurin series of $f(x) = \sqrt{3 + e^x}$ up to and including the term in x^2.

3 **a** Show that the first two non-zero terms in the Maclaurin series of $\tan x$ are $x + \frac{1}{3}x^3$.

  b Hence find, correct to three decimal places, an approximation to $\tan\frac{\pi}{10}$.

4 It is given that $f(x) = e^{-x^2}$.

  a i Find the first four derivatives of $f(x)$.

  ii Hence find the Maclaurin series of $f(x)$, up to and including the term in x^4.

  b Use your result from part **a ii** to find an approximation to $\int_0^1 e^{-x^2}\,dx$.

  Give your answer in the form $\frac{a}{b}$ where a and b are integers.

5 **a** Find the Maclaurin series of $\cos^2 x$ up to and including the term in x^6.

  b Hence state the Maclaurin series of $\sin^2 x$ up to and including the term in x^6.

6 It is given that $f(x) = \ln(1 + \sin x)$, $-\frac{\pi}{2} < x < \frac{3\pi}{2}$.

  a i Show that $f'(x) = \frac{\cos x}{1 + \sin x}$ and $f''(x) = -\frac{1}{1 + \sin x}$.

  ii Find the third and fourth derivatives of $f(x)$.

  b Hence find the Maclauin series of $\ln(1 + \sin x)$ up to and including the term in x^4.

  c Use your series from part **b** to find an approximation to $\int_0^{\frac{\pi}{6}} \ln(1 + \sin x)\,dx$, giving your answer correct to three decimal places.

7 A function is defined as $f(x) = \ln\left(\frac{1}{1-x}\right)$, $-1 < x < 1$.

  a i Find the first three derivatives of $f(x)$.

  ii Hence show that the Maclaurin series for $f(x)$ up to and including the x^3 term is $x + \frac{x^2}{2} + \frac{x^3}{3}$.

  b Use the series from part **a ii** to find an approximate value for $\ln 3$. Give your answer in the form $\frac{a}{b}$, where a and b are integers.

233

8 **a** Given that f(x) = xe^x, use induction to show that $f^{(n)}(x) = (n+x)e^x$.

   b Hence find the general term in the Maclaurin series for f(x).

9 **a** Given that $f(x) = \dfrac{1}{1-5x}$, prove by induction that $f^{(n)}(x) = \dfrac{5^n n!}{(1-5x)^{n+1}}$.

   b Hence find the general term in the Maclaurin series for $\dfrac{1}{1-5x}$.

10 **a** Find the first three non-zero terms in the Maclaurin series for arcsin x.

   b **i** Let f(x) = arcsin x and g(x) = arccos x.

       State the relationship between $f^{(n)}(x)$, the nth derivative of f(x), and $g^{(n)}(x)$, the nth derivative of g(x), for any integer $n > 0$.

   ii Hence show that arcsin x + arccos x = k, where k is a constant to be determined.

11 The diagram shows part of the graph of y = f(x).

Explain why neither of these can be the Maclaurin series of the function f(x):

a $\dfrac{1}{2} + \dfrac{x}{2} + \dfrac{x^2}{8} + \ldots$

b $1 - 3x - \dfrac{x^2}{4} + \ldots$

Section 2: Limits

You are already familiar with the idea of taking limits, from the process of differentiation from first principles: $\lim\limits_{h \to \infty} \dfrac{f(x+h) - f(x)}{h}$.

In that case you took the limit as $h \to 0$ but found that, to avoid getting $\dfrac{0}{0}$, you first needed to cancel h throughout the expression.

You can apply a similar idea to any rational function where the limit is of the form $\dfrac{\infty}{\infty}$.

> **Rewind**
>
> You met differentiation from first principles in A Level Mathematics Student Book 1, Chapter 12.

234

10 Maclaurin series and limits

WORKED EXAMPLE 10.4

Find $\lim\limits_{x \to \infty} \dfrac{3x^2 - 5}{2x^2 + x}$.

$\lim\limits_{x \to \infty} \dfrac{3x^2 - 5}{2x^2 + x} = \lim\limits_{x \to \infty} \dfrac{\left(\dfrac{3x^2}{x^2} - \dfrac{5}{x^2}\right)}{\left(\dfrac{2x^2}{x^2} + \dfrac{x}{x^2}\right)}$

Just allowing $x \to \infty$ straight away would give $\dfrac{\infty}{\infty}$, so instead start by dividing through the expression by the highest power of x, which is x^2.

$= \lim\limits_{x \to \infty} \dfrac{\left(3 - \dfrac{5}{x^2}\right)}{\left(2 + \dfrac{1}{x}\right)}$

Simplify and then let $x \to \infty$.

$= \dfrac{3 - 0}{2 + 0}$

As $x \to \infty$, $\dfrac{5}{x^2} \to 0$ and $\dfrac{1}{x} \to 0$

$= \dfrac{3}{2}$

Using Maclaurin series to find limits

If you don't have a rational function, then you can't directly use the method in Worked example 10.4 when faced with limits such as $\dfrac{0}{0}$ and $\dfrac{\infty}{\infty}$. However, if you can find the Maclaurin series of any non-polynomial elements of the function, then you can use the method in Worked example 10.4 and again divide through by the highest power of x.

WORKED EXAMPLE 10.5

Using the Maclaurin series for $\ln(1 + x)$ and $\cos x$, evaluate $\lim\limits_{x \to 0} \dfrac{x \ln(1 + x)}{1 - \cos x}$.

$\lim\limits_{x \to 0} \dfrac{x \ln(1 + x)}{1 - \cos x} = \lim\limits_{x \to 0} \dfrac{x\left(x - \dfrac{x^2}{2} + \dfrac{x^3}{3} + \ldots\right)}{1 - \left(1 - \dfrac{x^2}{2!} - \dfrac{x^4}{4!} + \ldots\right)}$

Use $\ln(1 + x) = x - \dfrac{x^2}{2} + \dfrac{x^3}{3} + \ldots$ and $\cos x = 1 - \dfrac{x^2}{2!} + \dfrac{x^4}{4!} + \ldots$

$= \lim\limits_{x \to 0} \dfrac{\left(x^2 - \dfrac{x^3}{2} + \dfrac{x^4}{3} + \ldots\right)}{\left(\dfrac{x^2}{2} - \dfrac{x^4}{24} + \ldots\right)}$

Simplify and then cancel x^2 throughout the expression.

$= \lim\limits_{x \to 0} \dfrac{\left(1 - \dfrac{x}{2} + \dfrac{x^2}{3} + \ldots\right)}{\left(\dfrac{1}{2} - \dfrac{x^2}{24} + \ldots\right)}$

$= \dfrac{1 + 0}{\left(\dfrac{1}{2} + 0\right)} = 2$

Now let $x \to 0$.

A Level Further Mathematics for AQA Student Book 2

You need to be able to recognise two important limits that often occur.

Key point 10.2

- $\lim_{x \to \infty}(x^k e^{-x}) = 0$
- $\lim_{x \to 0}(x^k \ln x) = 0, k > 0$

Fast forward

You will use both of these limits in Section 3.

You can prove the first result in Key point 10.2 using Maclaurin series.

Fast forward

The second result in Key point 10.2 is proved in Worked example 10.9 later in this section.

WORKED EXAMPLE 10.6

Prove that $\lim_{x \to \infty} x^k e^{-x} = 0$.

$\lim_{x \to \infty} x^k e^{-x} = \lim_{x \to \infty} \dfrac{x^k}{e^x}$ Use the Maclaurin series for e^x.

$= \lim_{x \to \infty} \dfrac{x^k}{1 + x + \dfrac{x^2}{2!} + \ldots + \dfrac{x^{k-1}}{(k-1)!} + \dfrac{x^k}{k!} + \dfrac{x^{k+1}}{(k+1)!} + \dfrac{x^{k+2}}{(k+2)!} + \ldots}$

$= \lim_{x \to \infty} \dfrac{1}{x^{-k} + x^{1-k} + \dfrac{x^{2-k}}{2!} + \ldots + \dfrac{x^{-1}}{(k-1)!} + \dfrac{1}{k!} + \dfrac{x}{(k+1)!} + \dfrac{x^2}{(k+2)!} + \ldots}$ Divide through by x^k.

$= 0$ All the terms in the denominator from $\dfrac{x}{(k+1)!}$ onwards will tend to ∞, so the fraction tends to 0.

L'Hôpital's rule

An alternative to using Macaurin series to evaluate limits of the form $\dfrac{0}{0}$ or $\dfrac{\infty}{\infty}$ is given by **l'Hôpital's rule.**

Key point 10.3

L'Hôpital's rule

Given functions $f(x)$ and $g(x)$ such that either

$$\lim_{x \to c} f(x) = \lim_{x \to c} g(x) = 0 \quad \text{or} \quad \lim_{x \to c} f(x) = \lim_{x \to c} g(x) = \infty,$$

then

$$\lim_{x \to c} \dfrac{f(x)}{g(x)} = \lim_{x \to c} \dfrac{f'(x)}{g'(x)}$$

provided that $\lim_{x \to c} \dfrac{f'(x)}{g'(x)}$ exists.

Common error

It is important not to try applying l'Hôpital's rule to a quotient that is not of the form $\dfrac{0}{0}$ or $\dfrac{\infty}{\infty}$. It is only valid in these cases.

WORKED EXAMPLE 10.7

Find $\lim\limits_{x \to e} \dfrac{\ln x - 1}{x - e}$.

$\lim\limits_{x \to e}(\ln x - 1) = 0$

and

$\lim\limits_{x \to e}(x - e) = 0$

⋯⋯ Check the limits of the numerator and denominator of the function.

Using l'Hôpital's rule:

$\lim\limits_{x \to e} \dfrac{\ln x - 1}{x - e} = \lim\limits_{x \to e} \dfrac{\frac{d}{dx}(\ln x - 1)}{\frac{d}{dx}(x - e)}$

⋯⋯ Since the limit of the function is of the form $\dfrac{0}{0}$, use l'Hôpital's rule.

$= \lim\limits_{x \to e} \dfrac{\left(\frac{1}{x}\right)}{1}$

$= \lim\limits_{x \to e} \dfrac{\left(\frac{1}{x}\right)}{1}$

$= \dfrac{\left(\frac{1}{e}\right)}{1}$

⋯⋯ This limit exists, so by l'Hôpital's rule this is the limit of the original function.

$= \dfrac{1}{e}$

Sometimes it may be necessary to use l'Hôpital's rule more than once.

WORKED EXAMPLE 10.8

Evaluate $\lim\limits_{x \to 0} \dfrac{1 - \cos x}{x^2}$.

$\lim\limits_{x \to 0}(1 - \cos x) = 0$

and

$\lim\limits_{x \to 0} x^2 = 0$

⋯⋯ Check the limits of the numerator and denominator of the function.

Using l'Hôpital's rule:

$\lim\limits_{x \to 0} \dfrac{1 - \cos x}{x^2} = \lim\limits_{x \to 0} \dfrac{\frac{d}{dx}(1 - \cos x)}{\frac{d}{dx}(x^2)}$

⋯⋯ Since the limit of the function is of the form $\dfrac{0}{0}$, use l'Hôpital's rule.

$= \lim\limits_{x \to 0} \dfrac{\sin x}{2x}$

⋯⋯ Since $\lim\limits_{x \to 0} \sin x = 0$ and $\lim\limits_{x \to 0} 2x = 0$, the limit of the rational function is again of the form $\dfrac{0}{0}$ ...

Continues on next page

Using l'Hôpital's rule again:

$$\lim_{x \to 0} \frac{\sin x}{2x} = \lim_{x \to 0} \frac{\frac{d}{dx}(\sin x)}{\frac{d}{dx}(2x)}$$

...so use l'Hôpital's rule again.

$$= \lim_{x \to 0} \frac{\cos x}{2}$$

$$= \frac{1}{2}$$

$$\therefore \lim_{x \to 0} \frac{1 - \cos x}{x^2} = \frac{1}{2}$$

WORK IT OUT 10.1

Find $\lim_{x \to 0} \frac{x^3 + x^2}{e^x - 1}$.

Which is the correct solution? Identify the errors made in the incorrect solutions.

Solution 1	Solution 2	Solution 3
$\lim_{x \to 0} \frac{x^3 + x^2}{e^x - 1} = \frac{0 + 0}{1 - 1}$ $= \frac{0}{0}$ $= 1$	Using l'Hôpital's rule: $\lim_{x \to 0} \frac{x^3 + x^2}{e^x - 1} = \lim_{x \to 0} \frac{3x^2 + 2x}{e^x}$ $= \frac{0}{1}$ $= 0$	Using l'Hôpital's rule twice: $\lim_{x \to 0} \frac{x^3 + x^2}{e^x - 1} = \lim_{x \to 0} \frac{3x^2 + 2x}{e^x}$ $= \lim_{x \to 0} \frac{6x + 2}{e^x}$ $= \frac{2}{1}$ $= 2$

You can also use l'Hôpital's rule to find limits of the form $0 \times \infty$ or $\infty - \infty$. First you need to rearrange these expressions into a quotient that is of the form $\frac{0}{0}$ or $\frac{\infty}{\infty}$.

You can use this idea to prove the second result in Key point 10.2.

WORKED EXAMPLE 10.9

Prove that $\lim_{x \to 0}(x^k \ln x)$, for $k > 0$.

$x^k \ln x = \frac{\ln x}{x^{-k}}$

This is a limit of the form $0 \times \infty$, but rewriting x^k as $\frac{1}{x^{-k}}$, the limit becomes of the form $\frac{\infty}{\infty}$.

Continues on next page

10 Maclaurin series and limits

Using l'Hôpital's rule:

$$\lim_{x \to 0}\left(\frac{\ln x}{x^{-k}}\right) = \lim_{x \to 0}\left(\frac{x^{-1}}{-kx^{-k-1}}\right)$$

$$= \lim_{x \to 0}\left(-\frac{x^k}{k}\right)$$

$$= 0$$

$$\therefore \lim_{x \to 0}(x^k \ln x) = 0$$

Apply l'Hôpital's rule:

$\frac{d}{dx}(\ln x) = x^{-1}$ and $\frac{d}{dx}(x^{-k}) = -kx^{-k-1}$

Tidy up the expression and then let $x \to 0$.

EXERCISE 10B

1 Find the limit of each function, where the limit exists.

a **i** $\lim_{x \to \infty} \frac{2x-3}{x+1}$ **ii** $\lim_{x \to \infty} \frac{x-2}{3x+4}$ **b** **i** $\lim_{x \to \infty} \frac{x-5}{2x^2+1}$ **ii** $\lim_{x \to \infty} \frac{3x+1}{3x^2-4}$

c **i** $\lim_{x \to \infty} \frac{x^3+x}{x^2-2x+7}$ **ii** $\lim_{x \to \infty} \frac{2x^3+x^2-3}{5x^2+x-4}$ **d** **i** $\lim_{x \to \infty} \frac{3x^2-2x-6}{4x^2+x-1}$ **ii** $\lim_{x \to \infty} \frac{x^2+5x-3}{x^2+2x-9}$

2 Use standard results to form the Maclaurin series of each function, and use this to find the limit in each case.

a $\lim_{x \to 0} \frac{e^x - 1}{x}$ **b** $\lim_{x \to 0} \frac{\ln(1+x) - x}{x^2}$ **c** $\lim_{x \to 0} \frac{1 - \cos x}{x^2}$

d $\lim_{x \to 0} \frac{\sin x - x}{x^3}$ **e** $\lim_{x \to 0} \frac{x \cos x - \sin x}{x^3}$ **f** $\lim_{x \to 0} \frac{3 \sin x - 4x \cos x + x}{x^3}$

3 Use l'Hôpital's rule to find each limit.

a $\lim_{x \to 0} \frac{e^x - e^{-x}}{\sin x}$ **b** $\lim_{x \to 0} \frac{x^2 + x}{\tan x}$ **c** $\lim_{x \to 2} \frac{\ln(x-1)}{x-2}$

d $\lim_{x \to \pi} \frac{\pi^2 - x^2}{\cos \frac{x}{2}}$ **e** $\lim_{x \to 3} \frac{x^2 - 9}{\sin(x-3)}$ **f** $\lim_{x \to 1} \frac{\sqrt[4]{x} - 1}{\sqrt[3]{x} - 1}$

4 **a** Write down the expansion of $\sin 3x$ in ascending powers of x up to and including the term in x^5.

b Hence evaluate $\lim_{x \to 0} \frac{3x \cos 2x - \sin 3x}{7x^3}$.

5 In each case find the limit if it exists.

a $\lim_{x \to 0} \frac{x - \cos x}{x + \cos x}$ **b** $\lim_{x \to 0} \frac{x + \sin x}{x - \sin x}$ **c** $\lim_{x \to 0} \frac{x - \cos x}{x + \sin x}$

6 Use l'Hôpital's rule to find $\lim_{x \to 4} \left(\frac{x - \sqrt{3x+4}}{4-x}\right)$.

7 Find $\lim_{x \to 1} \frac{(\ln x)^2}{x^3 + x^2 - 5x + 3}$.

239

8 Show that $\lim_{x \to \frac{\pi}{2}} \frac{\cos^2 3x}{\cos^2 x} = 9$.

9 Show that $\lim_{x \to 0} \left(\frac{1}{x} - \frac{1}{\sin x} \right) = 0$.

10 a By using the Maclaurin series for $\ln(1 + x)$, or otherwise, find the first three non-zero terms of the series expansion of $\ln\left(\frac{1}{1 - 2x^3}\right)$.

  b Hence find $\lim_{x \to 0} \frac{\ln\left(\frac{1}{1 - 2x^3}\right)}{x^3}$.

11 Find $\lim_{x \to 1} \left(\frac{1}{x - 1} - \frac{1}{\ln x} \right)$.

12 a State the function f for which $\arctan x = \int_0^x f(t) \, dt$.

  b By integrating an appropriate series, find the Maclaurin series of $\arctan x$ up to and including the term in x^7.

  c Hence evaluate $\lim_{x \to 0} \frac{x - \arctan x}{x^3}$.

  d Use your series for $\arctan x$ from part **b** to estimate π.

Section 3: Improper integrals

Integrals where the range of integration extends to infinity

You are by now very familiar with evaluating definite integrals

$$\int_a^b f(x) \, dx = g(b) - g(a) \text{ where } g'(x) = f(x).$$

In the examples you have encountered so far the limits were often convenient, relatively small numbers such as 0, 1, π. However, there is nothing to stop them from being very large numbers; this would make no difference to the method for evaluating the integral.

If you continue along this line and let $b \to \infty$, you can still find a finite value for the integral in certain cases. In much the same way that you have seen that a sequence can either converge to a finite limit or diverge to infinity, so can an integral. Integrals of the form $\int_a^\infty f(x) \, dx$ are known as **improper integrals**.

To evaluate an improper integral you need to replace the infinite limit by b, find the value of the integral in terms of b and then consider what happens when $b \to \infty$.

10 Maclaurin series and limits

> 🔑 **Key point 10.4**
>
> The value of the improper integral $\int_a^\infty f(x)\,dx$ is
>
> $\lim_{b\to\infty} \int_a^b f(x)\,dx = \lim_{b\to\infty} \{I(b) - I(a)\}$, if this limit exists and is finite.
>
> If this limit is infinite you say that the improper integral diverges (does not have a value).

WORKED EXAMPLE 10.10

a Explain why $\int_0^\infty e^{-3x}\,dx$ is an improper integral.

b Evaluate $\int_0^\infty e^{-3x}\,dx$.

a The integral is improper because the range of integration extends to infinity.

b $\int_0^\infty e^{-3x}\,dx = \lim_{b\to\infty} \int_0^b e^{-3x}\,dx$ *Integrate as normal, but replace the upper limit with b and take the limit as $b \to \infty$ after you have completed the integration.*

$= \lim_{b\to\infty} \left[-\frac{1}{3}e^{-3x}\right]_0^b$

$= \lim_{b\to\infty} \left(-\frac{1}{3}e^{-3b} + \frac{1}{3}\right)$

$= \lim_{b\to\infty} \left(-\frac{1}{3}e^{-3b}\right) + \frac{1}{3}$

$= \frac{1}{3}$ *As $b \to \infty$, $e^{-3b} \to 0$. Therefore the integral converges.*

WORKED EXAMPLE 10.11

Explain why the improper integral $\int_2^\infty \frac{1}{x}\,dx$ diverges.

$\int_2^\infty \frac{1}{x}\,dx = \lim_{b\to\infty} \int_2^b \frac{1}{x}\,dx$ *Integrate as normal, but replace the upper limit with b and consider the limit as $b \to \infty$ after you have completed the integration.*

$= \lim_{b\to\infty} [\ln x]_2^b$

When $b \to \infty$, $\ln x$ tends to infinity.
Therefore the integral diverges.

When evaluating improper integrals, you might need to use some of the limits you met in Section 2.

241

WORKED EXAMPLE 10.12

Evaluate $\int_0^\infty xe^{-x}\,dx$, showing clearly the limiting process used.

$\int_0^\infty xe^{-x}\,dx = \lim_{b\to\infty}\int_0^b xe^{-x}\,dx$ …… Integrate as normal, but replace the upper limit with b and consider the limit as $b \to \infty$ after you have completed the integration.

$u = x,\ \dfrac{dv}{dx} = e^{-x}$

$\Rightarrow \dfrac{du}{dx} = 1,\ v = -e^{-x}$ …… Use integration by parts.

$\int_0^b xe^{-x}\,dx = [-xe^{-x}]_0^b - \int_0^b -e^{-x}\,dx$

$\qquad = [-xe^{-x} - e^{-x}]_0^b$

$\qquad = (-be^{-b} - e^{-b}) - (0 - 1)$

$\qquad = -be^{-b} - e^{-b} + 1$

$\lim_{b\to\infty}\int_0^b xe^{-x}\,dx = \lim_{b\to\infty}(-be^{-b} - e^{-b} + 1)$ …… Now take the limit as $b \to \infty$.

$\qquad = 0 + 0 + 1$ …… Use the result from Key point 10.2:
$\qquad = 1$ $\lim_{x\to\infty} x^k e^{-x} = 0$, with $k = 1$.

$\therefore \int_0^\infty xe^{-x}\,dx = 1$

Integrals where the integrand is undefined at a point within the range of integration

There is another type of improper integral, where the range of integration is finite but the integrand is not defined at some point(s) within the range of integration (which could be at an end point or inside the range).

Examples of such integrals are $\int_0^2 x^3 \ln x\,dx$, which isn't defined at $x = 0$, and $\int_0^5 \dfrac{1}{\sqrt{x-3}}\,dx$, which isn't defined at $x = 3$.

To evaluate the first of these integrals, you need to replace 0 by b as the lower limit, find the value of the integral in terms of b and then consider the limit $b \to 0$.

Key point 10.5

If $f(x)$ is not defined at $x = k$, then

$$\int_a^k f(x)\,dx = \lim_{b\to k}\int_a^b f(x)\,dx$$

and

$$\int_k^c f(x)\,dx = \lim_{b\to k}\int_b^c f(x)\,dx.$$

If the limit is not finite, then the improper integral diverges (does not have a value).

10 Maclaurin series and limits

WORKED EXAMPLE 10.13

Evaluate $\int_0^2 x^3 \ln x \, dx$, showing clearly the limiting process used.

$\int_0^2 x^3 \ln x \, dx = \lim_{b \to 0} \int_b^2 x^3 \ln x \, dx$ — $\ln x$ is not defined at $x = 0$. Integrate as normal, but replace the lower limit with b and consider the limit as $b \to 0$ after you have completed the integration.

$u = \ln x, \dfrac{dv}{dx} = x^3$

$\Rightarrow \dfrac{du}{dx} = \dfrac{1}{x}, v = \dfrac{1}{4}x^4$ — Use integration by parts.

Remember that integrals with ln are an exception where you take $\ln x = u$.

$\int_b^2 x^3 \ln x \, dx = \left[\dfrac{1}{4}x^4 \ln x\right]_b^2 - \int_b^2 \dfrac{1}{4}x^3 \, dx$

$= \left[\dfrac{1}{4}x^4 \ln x - \dfrac{1}{16}x^4\right]_b^2$

$= (4 \ln 2 - 1) - \left(\dfrac{1}{4}b^4 \ln b - \dfrac{1}{16}b^4\right)$

$\lim_{b \to 0} \int_b^2 x^3 \ln x \, dx = \lim_{b \to 0}\left(4 \ln 2 - 1 - \dfrac{1}{4}b^4 \ln b + \dfrac{1}{16}b^4\right)$ — Now take the limit as $b \to 0$.

$= 4 \ln 2 - 1 - 0 + 0$ — Use the result from Key point 10.2:

$= 4 \ln 2 - 1$ — $\lim_{x \to 0} x^k \ln x = 0$, with $k = 4$.

$\therefore \int_0^2 x^3 \ln x \, dx = 4 \ln 2 - 1$

If the point where the integrand is not defined is not an end point, you need to split the integral into two parts.

Key point 10.6

If $f(x)$ is undefined at $x = k \in (a, c)$, then

$\int_a^c f(x) \, dx = \lim_{b \to k} \int_a^b f(x) \, dx + \lim_{b \to k} \int_b^c f(x) \, dx.$

If either limit is not finite, then the improper integral diverges (does not have a value).

WORKED EXAMPLE 10.14

Find the exact value of $\int_0^5 \dfrac{1}{\sqrt[3]{x-3}} \, dx$.

$\int_0^5 \dfrac{1}{\sqrt[3]{x-3}} \, dx = \int_0^3 \dfrac{1}{\sqrt[3]{x-3}} \, dx + \int_3^5 \dfrac{1}{\sqrt[3]{x-3}} \, dx$ — The integrand is not defined at $x = 3$, so you need to split the integral in two.

Continues on next page

$$\int_0^3 \frac{1}{\sqrt[3]{x-3}}\,dx = \lim_{b\to 3}\int_0^b \frac{1}{\sqrt[3]{x-3}}\,dx$$

For each integral replace 3 by b, evaluate the integral and then find the limit when $b \to 3$.

$$= \lim_{b\to 3}\int_0^b (x-3)^{-\frac{1}{3}}\,dx$$

Integrate as usual.

$$= \lim_{b\to 3}\left[\frac{3}{2}(x-3)^{\frac{2}{3}}\right]_0^b$$

$$= \lim_{b\to 3}\left[\frac{3}{2}(b-3)^{\frac{2}{3}} - \frac{3}{2}(0-3)^{\frac{2}{3}}\right]$$

$$= -\frac{3}{2}\sqrt[3]{9}$$

As $b \to 3$, $(b-3)^{\frac{2}{3}} \to 0$.

$$\int_3^5 \frac{1}{\sqrt[3]{x-3}}\,dx = \lim_{b\to 3}\int_b^5 \frac{1}{\sqrt[3]{x-3}}\,dx$$

Repeat the same process for the second integral.

$$= \lim_{b\to 3}\left[\frac{3}{2}(5-3)^{\frac{2}{3}} - \frac{3}{2}(b-3)^{\frac{2}{3}}\right]$$

$$= \frac{3}{2}\sqrt[3]{4}$$

$$\therefore \int_0^5 \frac{1}{\sqrt[3]{x-3}}\,dx = \frac{3}{2}(\sqrt[3]{4} - \sqrt[3]{9})$$

EXERCISE 10C

1 Determine which of these improper integrals converge. Evaluate those that do converge.

  a $\displaystyle\int_0^\infty \frac{1}{(1+x)^2}\,dx$

  b $\displaystyle\int_0^\infty e^{-\frac{x}{4}}\,dx$

  c $\displaystyle\int_0^\infty \frac{1}{\sqrt{1+x}}\,dx$

  d $\displaystyle\int_0^\infty x e^{-x^2}\,dx$

2 For what values of p do each of these improper integrals converge?

  a $\displaystyle\int_0^\infty e^{px}\,dx$

  b $\displaystyle\int_1^\infty \frac{\ln x}{x^p}\,dx$

3 Explain why $\displaystyle\int_0^4 \frac{1}{\sqrt{x}}\,dx$ is an improper integral and find its value.

4 Evaluate $\displaystyle\int_0^\infty e^{-x}\,dx$.

5 Evaluate $\displaystyle\int_0^\infty \frac{1}{x^2+1}\,dx$.

10 Maclaurin series and limits

6 Evaluate the improper integral

$$\int_0^\infty \left(\frac{2x}{x^2+4} - \frac{4}{2x+3} \right) dx$$

showing the limiting process used and giving your answer in the form $\ln k$, where k is a constant.

[©AQA 2013]

Checklist of learning and understanding

- The Maclaurin series for a function $f(x)$ is given by $f(x) = f(0) + f'(0)x + \frac{f''(0)}{2!}x^2 + \ldots + \frac{f^{(r)}(0)}{r!}x^r + \ldots$

- Two common applications of Maclaurin series are:
  - to find limits
  - to approximate integrals.

- L'Hôpital's rule can often be used to find limits of the form $\frac{0}{0}$ or $\frac{\infty}{\infty}$:

  Given functions $f(x)$ and $g(x)$ such that either
  $$\lim_{x \to c} f(x) = \lim_{x \to c} g(x) = 0 \text{ or } \lim_{x \to c} f(x) = \lim_{x \to c} g(x) = \infty,$$
  then
  $$\lim_{x \to c} \frac{f(x)}{g(x)} = \lim_{x \to c} \frac{f'(x)}{g'(x)}$$
  provided that $\lim_{x \to c} \frac{f'(x)}{g'(x)}$ exists.

- Two useful limits that arise often are:
  - $\lim_{x \to \infty}(x^k e^{-x}) = 0$, where $k > 0$
  - $\lim_{x \to 0}(x^k \ln x) = 0$, where $k > 0$.

- Improper integrals are definite integrals where either:
  - the range of integration is infinite or
  - the integrand isn't defined at every point in the range of integration.

- The value of the improper integral $\int_a^\infty f(x) \, dx$ is
  $$\lim_{b \to \infty} \int_a^b f(x) \, dx = \lim_{b \to \infty} \{ I(b) - I(a) \}$$
  if this limit exists and is finite.

- If $f(x)$ is not defined at $x = k$, then
  $$\int_a^k f(x) \, dx = \lim_{b \to k} \int_a^b f(x) \, dx \text{ and } \int_k^c f(x) \, dx = \lim_{b \to k} \int_b^c f(x) \, dx$$
  if the limits exist and are finite.

- If $f(x)$ is undefined at $x = k \in (a, c)$, then
  $$\int_a^c f(x) \, dx = \lim_{b \to k} \int_a^b f(x) \, dx + \lim_{b \to k} \int_b^c f(x) \, dx$$
  if the limits exist and are finite.

Mixed practice 10

1 Which is an example of an improper integral?

Choose from these options.

A $\int_1^3 \frac{1}{x+2}\,dx$ B $\int_{-2}^{-4} \frac{1}{x-2}\,dx$ C $\int_{-1}^1 \ln(x+2)\,dx$ D $\int_2^3 \ln(x-2)\,dx$

2 a Show that the first four terms in the Maclaurin series of e^x are $1 + x + \frac{x^2}{2} + \frac{x^3}{6}$.

   b Use the series in part **a** to show that $\sqrt{e} \approx \frac{79}{48}$.

3 Use the Maclaurin series for $\sin x$ and $\cos x$ to find $\lim_{x \to 0}\left(\frac{\cos x - 1}{x \sin x}\right)$.

4 a Find the first four derivatives of $f(x) = \ln(1+x)$.

   b Hence find the first four non-zero terms of the Maclaurin series of $f(x)$.

   c Using this expansion, find the exact value of the infinite series $1 - \frac{1}{2} + \frac{1}{3} - \frac{1}{4} + \ldots$

5 a Explain why $\int_0^4 \frac{x-4}{x^{1.5}}\,dx$ is an improper integral.

   b Either find the value of the integral $\int_0^4 \frac{x-4}{x^{1.5}}\,dx$, or explain why it does not have a finite value.

[© AQA 2015]

6 a Find the Maclaurin series of $\ln(\cos x)$ up to and including the term in x^4.

   b Hence show that $\ln 2 \approx \frac{\pi^2}{16}\left(1 + \frac{\pi^2}{96}\right)$.

7 Find $\lim_{x \to 0} \frac{2^x - 1}{3^x - 1}$, clearly showing your working.

8 It is given that $f(x) = \ln(1 + \sin x)$, $-\frac{\pi}{2} < x < \frac{3\pi}{2}$.

   a Find the first three derivatives of $f(x)$.

   b Hence find the Maclaurin series of $f(x)$ up to and including the term in x^3.

   c Hence find $\lim_{x \to 0} \frac{\ln(1 + \sin x) - x}{x^2}$.

9 a Write down the expansion of $\cos 4x$ in ascending powers of x up to and including the term in x^4. Give your answer in its simplest form.

   b i Given that $y = \ln(2 - e^x)$, find $\frac{dy}{dx}$, $\frac{d^2y}{dx^2}$ and $\frac{d^3y}{dx^3}$.

      (You may leave your expression for $\frac{d^3y}{dx^3}$ unsimplified)

    ii Hence, by using Maclaurin's theorem, show that the first three non-zero terms in the expansion, in ascending powers of x, of $\ln(2 - e^x)$ are $-x - x^2 - x^3$.

   c Find

$$\lim_{x \to 0}\left(\frac{x \ln(2 - e^x)}{1 - \cos 4x}\right).$$

[© AQA 2010]

10 Macluarin series and limits

10 Find $\lim_{x \to \frac{\pi}{2}}(\sec x - \tan x)$.

11 Using l'Hôpital's rule, show that $\lim_{x \to 1}\left(\dfrac{1}{\ln x} - \dfrac{1}{x-1}\right) = \dfrac{1}{2}$.

12 a Using the series for e^x, or otherwise, find the Maclaurin series of xe^x, stating the first four non-zero terms and the general term.

   b Hence find a series expansion of $\int_0^x te^t \, dt$.

   c Hence show that $\dfrac{1}{2} + \dfrac{1}{3} + \dfrac{1}{4(2!)} + \dfrac{1}{5(3!)} + \dfrac{1}{6(4!)} + \ldots = 1$.

13 a It is given that $y = \ln(e^{3x}\cos x)$.

   i Show that $\dfrac{dy}{dx} = 3 - \tan x$.   **ii** Find $\dfrac{d^4y}{dx^4}$.

   b Hence use Maclaurin's theorem to show that the first three non-zero terms in the expansion, in ascending powers of x, of $\ln(e^{3x}\cos x)$ are $3x - \dfrac{1}{2}x^2 - \dfrac{1}{12}x^4$.

   c Write down the expansion of $\ln(1 + px)$, where p is a constant, in ascending powers of x up to and including the term in x^2.

   d i Find the value of p for which $\lim_{x \to 0}\left(\dfrac{1}{x^2}\ln\left(\dfrac{e^{3x}\cos x}{1 + px}\right)\right)$ exists.

   ii Hence find the value of $\lim_{x \to 0}\left(\dfrac{1}{x^2}\ln\left(\dfrac{e^{3x}\cos x}{1 + px}\right)\right)$ when p takes the value found in part **d i**.

[© AQA 2013]

14 a It is given that $y = \ln(\cos x + \sin x)$.

   i Show that $\dfrac{d^2y}{dx^2} = -\dfrac{2}{1 + \sin 2x}$.

   ii Find $\dfrac{d^3y}{dx^3}$.

   b i Hence use Maclaurin's theorem to show that the first three non-zero terms in the expansion, in ascending powers of x, of $\ln(\cos x + \sin x)$ are $x - x^2 + \dfrac{2}{3}x^3$.

   ii Write down the first three non-zero terms in the expansion, in ascending powers of x, of $\ln(\cos x - \sin x)$.

   c Hence find the first three non-zero terms in the expansion, in ascending powers of x, of $\ln\left(\dfrac{\cos 2x}{e^{3x-1}}\right)$.

[© AQA 2014]

247

11 Differential equations

In this chapter you will learn how to:

- understand and use the language associated with differential equations
- solve differential equations of the form $\dfrac{dy}{dx} + P(x)y = Q(x)$
- solve differential equations of the form $a\dfrac{d^2y}{dx^2} + b\dfrac{dy}{dx} + cy = f(x)$
- use substitutions to turn differential equations into the required form.

Before you start…

A Level Mathematics Student Book 2, Chapter 13	You should know how to solve separable differential equations.	1	Solve $\dfrac{dy}{dx} = xy$.
A Level Mathematics Student Book 2, Chapter 10	You should know how to differentiate expressions, including using the product and chain rules.	2	Differentiate $y = xe^{3x}$ with respect to x.
A Level Mathematics Student Book 2, Chapter 11	You should be able to integrate complicated expressions.	3	Integrate xe^x with respect to x.

Rates of change

In many academic areas such as physics and economics it is easier to describe situations in terms of rates of change. This produces differential equations. In this chapter you will extend the types of differential equations you can solve. You will then see in Chapter 12 how these methods can be applied in many real-life situations.

> **Rewind**
>
> You met differential equations in A Level Mathematics Student Book 2, Chapter 13.

Section 1: Terminology of differential equations

Differential equations usually have an **independent variable** (which is the variable on the bottom of the derivatives) and at least one **dependent variable** (which is the variable on the top of the derivatives). For example, in $\dfrac{dy}{dx} = x^2 + y$ the independent variable is x and the dependent variable is y.

> **Did you know?**
>
> If you read other books about differential equations, you will see that the equations covered in this book are referred to as ordinary differential equations (ODEs). This is in contrast to another type of differential equation called partial differential equations (PDEs) which use a different type of differentiation.

248

11 Differential equations

There are many different types of differential equation. To decide which technique to use when solving differential equations you need to be able to categorise them.

- The **order of a differential equation** is the largest number of times the dependent variable (y in these examples) is differentiated. For example: $\frac{d^3y}{dx^3} + 3\frac{dy}{dx} + y = x^3$ is a third order differential equation.

- A **linear differential equation** is one in which the dependent variable (or any of its derivatives) only appears to the power of 1 or 0 in any term. For example: $3\frac{d^2y}{dx^2} + x^2 y + \sin x = 0$ is a linear differential equation, but any differential equation involving ay^2, $\sin y$ or even a $y\frac{dy}{dx}$ is non-linear.

- A **homogeneous differential equation** is one in which every term involves the dependent variable. For example: $\frac{d^2y}{dx^2} + x\frac{dy}{dx} + y^2 = 0$ is homogeneous, but $\frac{dy}{dx} = 2$ is a **non-homogeneous differential equation**. Every non-homogeneous differential equation has a homogeneous differential equation associated with it, formed by removing all the terms not involving the dependent variable.

> **Tip**
>
> In some books homogeneous is used to refer to a different property of differential equations. The definition given here is the only one relevant to this course.

To solve a differential equation you need to find y as a function of x (if y is the dependent variable and x is the independent variable). When solving a differential equation, because the process is effectively integration there will be arbitrary constants involved. The solution containing all the arbitrary constants is called the **general solution**.

Key point 11.1

The general solution to an nth order differential equation has n arbitrary constants.

To fix the arbitrary constants you either use initial conditions (values of y, $\frac{dy}{dx}$, etc. at one value of x) or boundary conditions (values of y, $\frac{dy}{dx}$, etc. at several values of x). You need one piece of information for each arbitrary constant, and then you normally use simultaneous equation techniques to find the values of each constant. When the constants in the general solution have the values required to fit the conditions, the result is called the **particular solution**.

Any solution to a differential equation is called a **particular integral**. The solution to the associated homogeneous differential equation is called the **complementary function** – and this is usually where the arbitrary constants are found. If the differential equation is linear, these are combined to give the general solution of the differential equation.

249

A Level Further Mathematics for AQA Student Book 2

🔑 Key point 11.2

For a linear differential equation, the general solution is given by

$$y = y_c + y_p$$

where y_c is the complementary function and y_p is the particular integral.

$L[y] = f(x)$ is a differential equation where L is called a linear differential operator. For example: if $\dfrac{d^2y}{dx} + x\dfrac{dy}{dx} + 3y = x^3$, then L is $\dfrac{d^2}{dx^2} + x\dfrac{d}{dx} + 3$ and $f(x) = x^3$.

In Proof 5, you can use the fact that for a linear differential operator $L[y_1 + y_2] = L[y_1] + L[y_2]$.

PROOF 5

If y_c is the complementary function and y_p is the particular integral, then $y = y_c + y_p$ will be a solution to the differential equation.

The complementary function, y_c, is defined by:

$L[y_c] = 0$ (1)

The particular integral is any function, y_p, satisfying

$L[y_p] = f(x)$ (2)

Then if $y_t = y_c + y_p$,

$L[y_t] = L[y_c + y_p]$ *Use the given fact about linear differential operators.*

$= L[y_c] + L[y_p]$

$= 0 + f(x)$ *Use properties (1) and (2).*

So y_t also satisfies $L[y] = f(x)$.

WORKED EXAMPLE 11.1

The differential equation $x\dfrac{dy}{dx} + y = \ln x$ is defined for $x > 0$.

a Find the complementary function.
b A particular integral has the form $y = a \ln x + b$. Find the values of a and b.
c Hence find the particular solution with initial condition $y = 3$ when $x = 1$.

a The associated homogenous differential equation is   *The complementary function is the solution of the associated homogeneous equation.*

$x\dfrac{dy}{dx} + y = 0$

Continues on next page

$$\frac{dy}{dx} = -\frac{y}{x}$$ ⋯ The differential equation is separable.

$$\frac{1}{y}\frac{dy}{dx} = -\frac{1}{x}$$

$$\int \frac{1}{y}\,dy = \int -\frac{1}{x}\,dx$$

$$\ln y = -\ln x + c$$

$$\qquad = \ln\left(\frac{1}{x}\right) + \ln A$$

$$\qquad = \ln\left(\frac{A}{x}\right)$$

$$\therefore y = \frac{A}{x}$$

b If $y = a \ln x + b$, then $\dfrac{dy}{dx} = \dfrac{a}{x}$.

Substituting:

$$x \times \frac{a}{x} + a\ln x + b = \ln x$$

$$a + b + a\ln x = \ln x$$

Comparing coefficients of $\ln x$: ⋯ Frequently when finding the particular integral you look at the coefficients on both sides of the equation.

$a = 1$

Comparing coefficients of the constant term and using the fact that $a = 1$:

$a + b = 0$

$b = -1$

So the particular integral is $\ln x - 1$.

c The general solution is $y = \dfrac{A}{x} + \ln x - 1$. ⋯ Use Key point 11.1. The general solution is the sum of the complementary function and the particular integral.

Using the initial condition, substituting in $x = 1$ when $y = 3$:

$3 = A + \ln 1 - 1$

$A = 4$

Therefore the particular solution is $y = \dfrac{4}{x} + \ln x - 1$.

EXERCISE 11A

1 Write an example of each differential equation.

- **a** **i** Linear
- **ii** Non-linear
- **b** **i** Second order
- **ii** Third order
- **c** **i** Homogeneous
- **ii** Non-homogeneous

2 Classify each differential equation.

a i $\dfrac{d^2y}{dx^2} + 3\dfrac{dy}{dx} + 4y = \sin x$ **ii** $\dfrac{d^2y}{dx^2} + 3\dfrac{dy}{dx} + 4x = 0$

b i $\dfrac{d^2y}{dx^2} + 3y\dfrac{dy}{dx} + 4y = 0$ **ii** $\left(\dfrac{dy}{dx}\right)^2 + 4y = x^2$

c i $5\dfrac{d^2z}{dt^2} + \dfrac{dz}{dt} + \sin z + e^t = 0$ **ii** $t^3\dfrac{d^3z}{dt^3} + t^2\dfrac{d^2z}{dt^2} + t\dfrac{dz}{dt} + z = 0$

d i $\dfrac{d}{dx}\left(x\dfrac{dy}{dx}\right) = y$ **ii** $\dfrac{d}{dx}(x+y) = y^2$

3 Given these solutions to differential equations and the initial or boundary conditions, find the particular solution to each differential equation.

a i $y = Ax^2 + 4$; $y = 12$ when $x = 2$ **ii** $y = A\cos x - 2$; $y = 6$ when $x = 0$

b i $y = Ae^{-x} + 3x$; $\dfrac{dy}{dx} = 2$ when $x = 0$ **ii** $y = A\ln x - 2x^2$; $\dfrac{dy}{dx} = 2$ when $x = 1$

c i $y = Ax^2 + Bx$; $y = 1$ when $x = 1$; $y = 8$ when $x = 2$

ii $y = A\sin x + B\cos x$; $y = 5$ when $x = 0$; $y = 10$ when $x = \dfrac{\pi}{2}$

d i $y = Ae^{2x} + Be^x$; $y = 2$ and $\dfrac{dy}{dx} = 5$ when $x = 0$

ii $y = A\sin x + B\cos 2x$; $y = -2$ and $\dfrac{dy}{dx} = 10$ when $x = 0$

4 The differential equation $2x\dfrac{dy}{dx} + y = \ln x$ is defined for $x > 0$.

a Find the complementary function.

b A particular integral has the form $y = a\ln x + b$. Find the values of a and b.

c Hence find the particular solution with initial condition $y = 3$ when $x = 1$.

5 The differential equation $\cos x\dfrac{dy}{dx} + 2\sin 2x = y\sin x$ is defined for $-\dfrac{\pi}{2} < x < \dfrac{\pi}{2}$.

a Find the complementary function.

b A particular integral exists of the form $y = a\sin x + b\cos x$. Find the values of a and b.

c Hence find the general solution to the differential equation $\cos x\dfrac{dy}{dx} + 2\sin x = y\sin x$ defined for $-\dfrac{\pi}{2} < x < \dfrac{\pi}{2}$.

6 a Find the values of the constants a, b and c for which $a + b\sin 2x + c\cos 2x$ is a particular integral of the differential equation

$$\dfrac{dy}{dx} + 4y = 20 - 20\cos 2x.$$

b Hence find the solution of this differential equation, given that $y = 4$ when $x = 0$.

[©AQA 2014]

7 The differential equation $e^x\dfrac{dy}{dx} + y = 2$ is defined for all x.

a Find the complementary function. **b** Find a particular integral.

c Hence find the general solution.

Section 2: The integrating factor

You already have the necessary tools to solve a differential equation such as:

$$x^2 \frac{dy}{dx} + 2xy = e^x$$

because the left-hand side is of a convenient form. Notice that $2x$ is the derivative of x^2 and that $\frac{dy}{dx}$ is the derivative of y, which means you have an expression that has resulted from the differentiation of a product ($x^2 y$) using the product rule. Therefore you can write the equation equivalently as

$$\frac{d}{dx}(x^2 y) = e^x$$

Now, integrating both sides and rearranging:

$$x^2 y = \int e^x \, dx$$

$$y = \frac{e^x + c}{x^2}$$

When faced with a differential equation like this where you cannot separate the variables, it will not often be the case that the left-hand side is quite so convenient. However, this method does suggest a way forward in such cases.

Consider, in general, a similar linear first order differential equation:

$$\frac{dy}{dx} + P(x)y = Q(x)$$

where $P(x)$ and $Q(x)$ are just functions of x. Note that if there is a function in front of $\frac{dy}{dx}$, you can divide through the equation by that function to get it in this form.

To make the left-hand side the derivative of a product as before, you can multiply through the equation by a function $I(x)$:

$$I(x)\frac{dy}{dx} + I(x)P(x)y = I(x)Q(x)$$

and then notice that if $I(x)$ is chosen such that $I'(x) = I(x)P(x)$, you have the left-hand side in the required form. From here you can proceed exactly as before:

$$\frac{d}{dx}(I(x)y) = I(x)Q(x)$$

$$y = \frac{1}{I(x)} \int I(x)Q(x) \, dx$$

The only remaining question is to decide on the function $I(x)$ to make this work.

A Level Further Mathematics for AQA Student Book 2

You need

$$I'(x) = I(x)P(x)$$
$$\frac{I'(x)}{I'(x)} = P(x)$$
$$\int \frac{I'(x)}{I(x)} dx = \int P(x) dx$$
$$\ln|I(x)| = \int P(x) dx$$
$$I(x) = e^{\int P(x) dx}$$

This function $I(x)$ is known as the **integrating factor**.

Key point 11.3

Given a first order linear differential equation

$$\frac{dy}{dx} + P(x)y = Q(x)$$

multiply through by the integrating factor:

$$I(x) = e^{\int P(x) dx}$$

The solution will be:

$$y = \frac{1}{I(x)} \int I(x) Q(x) dx$$

Tip

When calculating $\int P(x) dx$ you do not actually need to include the '$+c$'. It turns out that it does not actually matter whether there is a constant as it would cancel later in the process.

WORKED EXAMPLE 11.2

Solve the differential equation

$$\cos x \frac{dy}{dx} - 2y \sin x = 3 \text{ for } -\frac{\pi}{2} < x < \frac{\pi}{2}$$

given that $y = 1$ when $x = 0$.

$\cos x \dfrac{dy}{dx} - 2y \sin x = 3$

$\dfrac{dy}{dx} - 2y \dfrac{\sin x}{\cos x} = \dfrac{3}{\cos x}$

$\dfrac{dy}{dx} - (2 \tan x)y = 3 \sec x$

You can't write the LHS as the derivative of a product – always check for this first.

Note that if the LHS had been $\cos x \dfrac{dy}{dx} - y \sin x$ (i.e. without the 2) you could have written it as $\dfrac{d}{dx}(y \cos x)$.

Therefore, start by dividing through by $\cos x$ to get the equation in the correct form for applying the integrating factor.

$I(x) = e^{\int -2 \tan x \, dx}$

$= e^{-2 \ln |\sec x|}$

$= e^{\ln (\sec x)^{-2}}$

$= e^{\ln \cos^2 x}$

$= \cos^2 x$

Find the integrating factor $I(x) = e^{\int P(x) dx}$ making sure not to miss the – sign on $P(x)$.

Continues on next page

254

11 Differential equations

So
$$\cos^2 x \frac{dy}{dx} - (2\cos^2 x \tan x)y = 3\cos^2 x \sec x$$
$$\cos^2 x \frac{dy}{dx} - (2\cos x \sin x)y = 3\cos x$$
$$\frac{d}{dx}(y\cos^2 x) = 3\cos x$$

> Now multiply through by $\cos^2 x$ and check that the LHS is of the form
> $$\frac{d}{dx}(y\cos^2 x) = \cos^2 x \frac{dy}{dx} - 2\cos x \sin x.$$

$$y\cos^2 x = \int 3\cos x \, dx$$
$$= 3\sin x + c$$

> You can now integrate both sides.

Since $x = 0$, $y = 1$:

$$1\cos^2 0 = 3\sin 0 + c$$
$$c = 1$$

> Finally, you need to find the constant c and rearrange into the form $y = f(x)$.

$$\therefore y\cos^2 x = 3\sin x + 1$$
$$y = \sec^2 x(3\sin x + 1)$$

You can transform some differential equations into the required form by using a substitution. In an examination, you would generally be given the required substitution.

WORKED EXAMPLE 11.3

Show that the substitution $z = y^3$ transforms the differential equation
$$3y^2 \frac{dy}{dx} + \frac{y^3}{x} = \frac{e^x}{x}$$
into a linear differential equation. Hence find the general solution of the given differential equation.

If $z = y^3$, then $\frac{dz}{dx} = 3y^2 \frac{dy}{dx}$.

Substituting this in turns the given differential equation into:

$$\frac{dz}{dx} + \frac{z}{x} = \frac{e^x}{x}$$

which is a linear differential equation.

The integrating factor is $e^{\int (1/x)dx} = e^{\ln x} = x.$

> Use Key point 11.3.

Therefore $z = \frac{1}{x}\int x \times \frac{e^x}{x} dx$

> Use Key point 11.3 again.

$$= \frac{1}{x}(e^x + c)$$

> Notice that the $+c$ is in the brackets.

Therefore $y^3 = \frac{1}{x}(e^x + c)$ or $y = \sqrt[3]{\frac{1}{x}(e^x + c)}$

> You need to give the solution in terms of y and x. If you can easily rewrite it to make y the subject, this is the conventional thing to do.

255

EXERCISE 11B

1 Use an integrating factor to find the general solution to each linear differential equation.

a i $\dfrac{dy}{dx} + 2y = e^x$ ii $\dfrac{dy}{dx} - 4y = e^x$

b i $\dfrac{dy}{dx} + y\cot x = 1$ ii $\dfrac{dy}{dx} - (\tan x)y = \sec x$

c i $\dfrac{dy}{dx} + \dfrac{y}{x} = \dfrac{1}{x^2}$ ii $\dfrac{dy}{dx} + \dfrac{y}{x} = \dfrac{1}{x^3}$

2 Find the particular solution of the linear differential equation $\dfrac{dy}{dx} + y = e^x$ for which $y = e$ when $x = 1$.

3 Find the general solution to the differential equation $x^2 \dfrac{dy}{dx} - 2xy = \dfrac{x^4}{x-3}$.

4 Find the general solution of the differential equation $\dfrac{dy}{dx} + y\sin x = e^{\cos x}$.

5 Find the particular solution of the linear differential equation $x^2\dfrac{dy}{dx} + xy = \dfrac{2}{x}$ that passes through the point $(1, 1)$.

6 Given that $\cos x \dfrac{dy}{dx} + y\sin x = \cos^2 x$ and that $y = 2$ when $x = 0$, find y in terms of x.

7 Prove that when finding $\int P(x)\,dx$ in Key point 11.3, it does not matter whether or not the constant of integration is included.

8 Find the general solution to the differential equation $x\dfrac{dy}{dx} + 2y = 1 + \dfrac{1}{x}\dfrac{dy}{dx}$.

9 a Use the substitution $z = \dfrac{1}{y}$ to transform the equation $\dfrac{dy}{dx} + xy = xy^2$ into a linear differential equation in x and z.

b Solve the resulting equation, writing z in terms of x.

c Find the particular solution to the original equation that has $y = 1$ when $x = 1$.

10 a Using the substitution $z = y^2$, or otherwise, solve the equation:

$2y\dfrac{dy}{dx} + \dfrac{y^2}{x} = x^2$ given that when $x = 4$, $y = -5$. Give your answer in the form $y = f(x)$.

b Use another substitution to find the general solution to the equation $\cos y \dfrac{dy}{dx} + \tan x \sin y = \sin x$.

11 A differential equation is given by

$$(x^3 + 1)\dfrac{d^2y}{dx^2} - 3x^2\dfrac{dy}{dx} = 2 - 4x^3.$$

a Show that the substitution

$$u = \dfrac{dy}{dx} - 2x$$

transforms this differential equation into

$$(x^3 + 1)\dfrac{du}{dx} = 3x^2 u.$$

b Hence find the general solution of the differential equation

$$(x^3 + 1)\dfrac{d^2y}{dx^2} - 3x^2\dfrac{dy}{dx} = 2 - 4x^3$$

giving your answer in the form $y = f(x)$.

[©AQA 2011]

Section 3: Homogeneous second order linear differential equations with constant coefficients

A differential equation of the form

$$a\frac{d^2y}{dx^2} + b\frac{dy}{dx} + cy = 0$$

is called a homogeneous second order linear differential equation with constant coefficients.

To find the solution to this type of differential equation, you need to create an **auxiliary equation**.

> **Key point 11.4**
>
> The auxiliary equation to
> $$a\frac{d^2y}{dx^2} + b\frac{dy}{dx} + cy = 0$$
> is
> $$a\lambda^2 + b\lambda + c = 0$$

Solving the auxiliary equation gives you important information about the solution of the differential equation, as set out in Proofs 6, 7 and 8. However, in most instances you will be able to just quote the results set out in Key point 11.5.

If the auxiliary equation has real, distinct roots, λ_1 and λ_2, then the solution to the differential equation is $y = Ae^{\lambda_1 x} + Be^{\lambda_2 x}$.

PROOF 6

If $b^2 - 4ac > 0$ and $a\frac{d^2y}{dx^2} + b\frac{dy}{dx} + cy = 0$,

then $y = Ae^{\lambda_1 x} + Be^{\lambda_2 x}$, where λ_1 and λ_2 are the roots of the associated auxiliary equation.

If $y = e^{\lambda x}$

Then

$\frac{dy}{dx} = \lambda e^{\lambda x}$

and

$\frac{d^2y}{dx^2} = \lambda^2 e^{\lambda x}$.

> One possible solution to the differential equation could occur if you had a function of which the derivative and second derivative are proportional to the original function, allowing everything to 'cancel' and result in zero.
> $e^{\lambda x}$ is one example of a function that has this property (although you will see later that there are others).

Continues on next page

Substituting this into the differential equation:
$a\lambda^2 e^{\lambda x} + b\lambda e^{\lambda x} + c e^{\lambda x} = 0$

$e^{\lambda x}(a\lambda^2 + b\lambda + c) = 0$ .... Take out a factor of $e^{\lambda x}$.

$a\lambda^2 + b\lambda + c = 0$ .... Since $e^{\lambda x}$ can never be zero. This is the auxiliary equation.

If $b^2 - 4ac > 0$, then it will have two real solutions. Call these λ_1 and λ_2.

Therefore two possible solutions to the differential equation are $y = e^{\lambda_1 x}$ and $y = e^{\lambda_2 x}$.

$y = Ae^{\lambda_1 x} + Be^{\lambda_2 x}$ will also be a solution, since any linear combination of solutions is also a solution. .... This was proved in Proof 5.

This is a solution with two arbitrary constants, therefore it is the general solution. .... Use Key point 11.1 to justify that your 'guess' gives the complete solution.

If the roots of the auxiliary equation are complex, you could still write the solution as $y = Ae^{\lambda_1 x} + Be^{\lambda_2 x}$. However, you can use the work from Chapter 1, Section 2, to rewrite this in terms of trigonometric functions. If the solutions are $\alpha \pm \beta i$, then you can write the solution as

$$y = e^{\alpha x}(A\sin(\beta x) + B\cos(\beta x)).$$

PROOF 7

Given that $y = Ce^{\lambda_1 x} + De^{\lambda_2 x}$ with $\lambda_1 = \alpha + \beta i$ and $\lambda_2 = \alpha - \beta i$, then y can be written in the form $y = e^{\alpha x}(A\sin(\beta x) + B\cos(\beta x))$.

Substituting in the given information:
$y = Ce^{\alpha + \beta i} + De^{\alpha - \beta i}$

$= e^{\alpha}(Ce^{\beta i} + De^{-\beta i})$ .... Take out a factor of e^{α}.

$= e^{\alpha}(C(\cos\beta + i\sin\beta) + D(\cos\beta - i\sin\beta))$ .... Rewrite the complex exponential into modulus-argument form.

$= e^{\alpha}((C+D)\cos\beta + i(C-D)\sin\beta)$

$= e^{\alpha}(A\cos\beta + B\sin\beta)$ .... Separate out the cosine and sine terms.

with $A = C + D$ and $B = i(C - D)$

If the roots of the auxiliary equation are equal, then you need to try another possible complementary function $-xe^{\lambda x}$.

11 Differential equations

PROOF 8

Given that $b^2 - 4ac = 0$ and $a\dfrac{d^2y}{dx^2} + b\dfrac{dy}{dx} + cy = 0$, then $y = xe^{\lambda x}$ is a possible solution for a suitably chosen λ.

If $y = xe^{\lambda x}$

then

$\dfrac{dy}{dx} = (1 + \lambda x)e^{\lambda x}$

and

$\dfrac{d^2y}{dx^2} = \lambda(2 + \lambda x)e^{\lambda x}$.

Substituting into the differential equation:
$a\lambda(2 + \lambda x)e^{\lambda x} + b(1 + \lambda x)e^{\lambda x} + cxe^{\lambda x} = 0$
$\qquad 2a\lambda + a\lambda^2 x + b + b\lambda x + cx = 0$ .... Divide through by $e^{\lambda x}$ (which can never be 0) and tidy up.
$\qquad 2a\lambda + b + x(a\lambda^2 + b\lambda + c) = 0$

Comparing coefficients:

x^0: $2a\lambda + b = 0$

$\qquad \lambda = -\dfrac{b}{2a}$

x^1: $a\lambda^2 + b\lambda + c = 0$

Substituting $\lambda = -\dfrac{b}{2a}$ into the second equation:

$a\left(-\dfrac{b}{2a}\right)^2 + b\left(-\dfrac{b}{2a}\right) + c = 0$

$\qquad \dfrac{b^2}{4a} - \dfrac{b^2}{2a} + c = 0$

$\qquad \dfrac{-b^2 + 4ac}{4a} = 0$

$\qquad b^2 - 4ac = 0$ .... This is the given condition.

So $y = xe^{\left(-\frac{b}{2a}x\right)}$ is a solution to the differential equation in this case.

To get to the general solution a linear combination of the two possible values is required, leading to $y = Ae^{\lambda x} + Bxe^{\lambda x}$.

When solving differential equations, normally you will be able to just write down the solution without going through Proofs 6, 7 and 8.

🔑 Key point 11.5

Solution to auxiliary equation	General solution to differential equation
Two distinct roots, λ_1 and λ_2	$y = Ae^{\lambda_1 x} + Be^{\lambda_2 x}$
Repeated root, λ	$y = (A + Bx)e^{\lambda x}$
Complex roots, $\alpha + i\beta$	$y = e^{\alpha x}(A \sin(\beta x) + B \cos(\beta x))$

WORKED EXAMPLE 11.4

Solve the differential equation $\dfrac{d^2y}{dx^2} - 3\dfrac{dy}{dx} + 2y = 0$
given that $y = 1$ and $\dfrac{dy}{dx} = 0$ when $x = 0$.

The auxiliary equation is $\lambda^2 - 3\lambda + 2 = 0$.

This has roots $\lambda = 1$ and $\lambda = 2$, so the general solution to the differential equation is
$y = Ae^x + Be^{2x}$.

> Since the roots are real and distinct you can write the solution to the differential equation in exponential form using Key point 11.5.

$\dfrac{dy}{dx} = Ae^x + 2Be^{2x}$

> You need to differentiate the expression to make use of the initial conditions.

Using the initial conditions, when $x = 0$:
$y = 1 = A + B$
$\dfrac{dy}{dx} = 0 = A + 2B$

Solving gives $A = 2$ and $B = -1$.

> You can use technology to solve these types of simultaneous equation.

So the particular solution is $y = 2e^x - e^{2x}$.

EXERCISE 11C

1 a Write the auxiliary equation associated with the differential equation $\dfrac{d^2y}{dx^2} + 5\dfrac{dy}{dx} + 6y = 0$.

  b Hence find the general solution of the differential equation.

2 a Write the auxiliary equation associated with the differential equation $\dfrac{d^2y}{dx^2} + 4y = 0$.

  b Hence find the general solution of the differential equation.

3 a Write the auxiliary equation associated with the differential equation $\dfrac{d^2y}{dx^2} + 2\dfrac{dy}{dx} + y = 0$.

  b Hence find the general solution of the differential equation.

4 a Find the general solution of the differential equation $\dfrac{d^2y}{dx^2} + 8y = 6\dfrac{dy}{dx}$.

  b Find the particular solution that satisfies $y = 5$ and $\dfrac{dy}{dx} = 12$ when $x = 0$.

5 a Find the general solution of the differential equation $\dfrac{d^2y}{dx^2} + 4\dfrac{dy}{dx} + 4y = 0$.

  b Find the particular solution that satisfies $y(0) = 1$ and $y'(0) = 0$.

6 a Find the general solution of the differential equation $\dfrac{d^2x}{dt^2} - 2\dfrac{dx}{dt} + 2x = 0$.

  b Find the particular solution that satisfies $x(0) = 1$ and $x'(0) = 0$.

7 a Find the general solution of the differential equation $\dfrac{d^2x}{dt^2} + 3x = 4\dfrac{dx}{dt}$.

b Given that $x(0) = 1$ and $x(1) = e$, find $x(2)$.

8 a Find the general solution of the differential equation $\dfrac{d^2y}{dt^2} - 6\dfrac{dy}{dt} + 9y = 0$.

b Find the particular solution that satisfies $y(0) = 0$ and $y(1) = p$, writing your answer in terms of p.

9 Find the general solution of the differential equation $y''' - 5y'' + 9y' = 5y$.

10 Find the general solution of the differential equation $y''' + 3y'' + 3y' + y = 0$.

11 By trying the function $y = x^n$, find the general solution of the differential equation $x^2\dfrac{d^2y}{dx^2} + x\dfrac{dy}{dx} - 9y = 0$.

12 a Use the substitution $y = x^2$ to turn the differential equation

$$x\dfrac{d^2x}{dt^2} + \left(\dfrac{dx}{dt}\right)^2 + x\dfrac{dx}{dt} = 0$$

into a second order differential equation with constant coefficients involving y and t.

b Solve the differential equation to find y as a function of t.

c Hence solve the original differential equation, given that when $t = 0$, $x = 2$ and $\dfrac{dx}{dt} = \dfrac{1}{4}$.

Section 4: Inhomogeneous second order linear differential equations with constant coefficients

The second order differential equations you need to solve can all be written in the form

$$a\dfrac{d^2y}{dx^2} + b\dfrac{dy}{dx} + cy = f(x).$$

To solve these differential equations you use the method in Key point 11.2. You first of all solve the associated homogeneous equation to find a complementary function (using Key point 11.5) and then find a particular integral. The form of the particular integral will depend on $f(x)$.

Key point 11.6

$f(x)$	Trial function
$ax + b$	$px + q$
Polynomial	General polynomial of the same order
ae^{bx}	pe^{bx}
$a\cos bx$ $a\sin bx$	$p\sin bx + q\sin bx$

WORKED EXAMPLE 11.5

Find the general solution of the differential equation
$\frac{d^2y}{dx^2} + 7\frac{dy}{dx} + 12y = 24x + 60e^{2x}$.

The associated homogenous equation is $\frac{d^2y}{dx^2} + 7\frac{dy}{dx} + 12y = 0$. This has auxiliary equation $\lambda^2 + 7\lambda + 12 = 0$, which has roots -3 and -4. Therefore, the complementary function is $y = Ae^{-3x} + Be^{-4x}$.	First solve the associated homogenous equation to find the complementary function.
The trial function associated with $60e^{2x}$ is $y = pe^{2x}$.	You can find the particular integral in two stages. Notice that the coefficient of x in the power of the trial function mirrors the original function.

Differentiating twice:

$\frac{dy}{dx} = 2pe^{2x}$

$\frac{d^2y}{dx^2} = 4pe^{2x}$.

Substituting into the left-hand side of the differential equation and comparing to the exponential part of the right-hand side:

$4pe^{2x} + 7 \times 2pe^{2x} + 12 \times pe^{2x} = 60e^{2x}$
$30pe^{2x} = 60e^{2x}$
$p = 2$

The trial function associated with $24x$ is $y = px + q$.	Notice that although the expression on the right only involves a term in x, you need the general linear expression in the trial function.

Differentiating twice:

$\frac{dy}{dx} = p$

$\frac{d^2y}{dx^2} = 0$.

Substituting this into the left-hand side of the differential equation and comparing to the linear part of the right-hand side: $0 + 7 \times p + 12(px + q) = 24x$

$12px + 7p + 12q = 24x$ Comparing the coefficient of x:	Compare coefficients to find p and q.

$12p = 24$
$p = 2$

Continues on next page

11 Differential equations

Comparing the constant term:

$7p + 12q = 0$
$14 + 12q = 0$
$q = -\dfrac{7}{6}$

> You can use the fact that $p = 2$ to solve for q.

The particular integral is $2e^{2x} + 2x - \dfrac{7}{6}$.

The general solution is

$y = Ae^{-3x} + Be^{-4x} + 2e^{2x} + 2x - \dfrac{7}{6}$.

> The general solution is the sum of the complementary function and the particular integral, from Key point 11.2.

Sometimes the trial function given in Key point 11.6 already appears as a part of the complementary function. In that case, you need to modify the particular integral.

Key point 11.7

If your trial function is already part of the complementary function, try multiplying the trial function by x.

WORKED EXAMPLE 11.6

Find the general solution of the differential equation
$\dfrac{d^2y}{dx^2} + y = 16\sin x$.

The associated homogenous equation is

$\dfrac{d^2y}{dx^2} + y = 0$.

> First solve the associated homogenous equation to find the complementary function.

This has auxiliary equation

$\lambda^2 + 1 = 0$
$\lambda = i \text{ or } -i$

Therefore, the complementary function is $y = A\sin x + B\cos x$.

The trial function associated with $16\sin x$ is
$y = p\sin x + q\cos x$.

> Although the right-hand side of the equation involves only $\sin x$, you need to include both sin and cos in the trial function.

This already appears the complementary function, so try
$y = x(p\sin x + q\cos x)$.

> You need to adjust the trial function according to Key point 11.7.

Continues on next page

Differentiating twice:

$\frac{dy}{dx} = p \sin x + q \cos x + x(p \cos x - q \sin x)$

$\frac{d^2y}{dx^2} = p \cos x - q \sin x + p \cos x - q \sin x + x(-p \sin x - q \cos x).$

> You need to use the product rule to differentiate.

Substituting into the left-hand side of the differential equation:
$2p \cos x - 2q \sin x = 16 \sin x$
$p = 0, q = -8$

> Notice that the terms containing $x \sin x$ and $x \cos x$ all cancel. This will always happen in the situation described in Key point 11.7.

The particular integral is $-8x \cos x$.

The general solution is
$y = A \sin x + B \cos x - 8x \cos x.$

> The general solution is the sum of the complementary function and the particular integral, from Key point 11.2.

EXERCISE 11D

1 For the differential equation $\frac{d^2y}{dx^2} - 4\frac{dy}{dx} - 5y = e^{2x}$:

  a find the complementary function

  b find the particular integral

  c hence write down the general solution.

2 For the differential equation $\frac{d^2y}{dx^2} + 9\frac{dy}{dx} + 20y = 60x$:

  a find the complementary function

  b find the particular integral

  c hence write down the general solution.

3 For the differential equation $\frac{d^2y}{dx^2} + \frac{dy}{dx} + \sin x = 0$:

  a find the complementary function

  b find the particular integral

  c hence find the general solution.

4 For the differential equation $\frac{d^2y}{dx^2} + 9y = 20e^{-x}$:

  a find the complementary function

  b hence find the general solution

  c find the particular solution for which $y = 7$ and $y' = 10$ when $x = 0$.

5 For the differential equation $\dfrac{d^2y}{dx^2} + 4\dfrac{dy}{dx} + 4y = 12x + 25\sin x$, find:

   a the general solution

   b the particular solution for which $y = 0$ and $y' = 10$ when $x = 0$.

6 For the differential equation $\dfrac{d^2y}{dt^2} - 4\dfrac{dy}{dt} + 8y = 32t^2$, find:

   a the general solution

   b the particular solution for which $y = 0$ and $y' = 0$ when $t = 0$.

7 For the differential equation $\dfrac{d^2y}{dx^2} - 10\dfrac{dy}{dx} + 25y = e^{5x}$:

   a find the complementary function

   b show that there is a particular integral of the form qx^2e^{5x}

   c hence find the general solution

   d find the particular solution for which $y = 4$ and $y' = 2$ when $t = 0$.

8 Find the solution of the differential equation

$$\dfrac{d^2y}{dx^2} + 4y = 10e^{4x} + 8\sin 2x + 4\cos 2x$$

given that $y = 2.5$ when $x = 0$ and $y = \dfrac{\pi}{4}$ when $x = \dfrac{\pi}{4}$.

[©AQA 2016]

9 A differential equation is given by

$$\sin^2 x \dfrac{d^2y}{dx^2} - 2\sin x \cos x \dfrac{dy}{dx} + 2y = 2\sin^4 x \cos x, \ 0 < x < \pi.$$

   a Show that the substitution

$$y = u \sin x$$

where u is a function of x, transforms this differential equation into

$$\dfrac{d^2u}{dx^2} + u = \sin 2x.$$

   b Hence find the general solution of the differential equation

$$\sin^2 x \dfrac{d^2y}{dx^2} - 2\sin x \cos x \dfrac{dy}{dx} + 2y = 2\sin^4 x \cos x$$

giving your answer in the form $y = f(x)$.

[©AQA 2013]

Checklist of learning and understanding

- The general solution to an nth order differential equation has n arbitrary constants.
- For a linear differential equation, the general solution is given by $y = y_c + y_p$, where y_c is the complementary function and y_p is the particular integral.
    - The complementary function is the solution of the associated homogeneous equation.
    - The particular integral is any solution of the differential equation.
- Given a first order linear differential equation $\dfrac{dy}{dx} + P(x)y = Q(x)$, multiply through by the integrating factor $I(x) = e^{\int P(x)\,dx}$. The solution will be $y = \dfrac{1}{I(x)} \int I(x) Q(x)\, dx$.
- The auxiliary equation to the homogeneous differential equation $a\dfrac{d^2y}{dx^2} + b\dfrac{dy}{dx} + cy = 0$ is $a\lambda^2 + b\lambda + c = 0$.
- The solution to the auxiliary equation gives the general solution of the homogeneous equation:

Solution to auxiliary equation	General solution to differential equation
Two distinct roots, λ_1 and λ_2	$y = Ae^{\lambda_1 x} + Be^{\lambda_2 x}$
Repeated root, λ	$y = (A + Bx)e^{\lambda x}$
Complex roots, $\alpha + i\beta$	$y = e^{\alpha x}(A \sin(\beta x) + B \cos(\beta x))$

- The form of the particular integral for the homogeneous differential equation $a\dfrac{d^2y}{dx^2} + b\dfrac{dy}{dx} + cy = f(x)$ depends on $f(x)$:

$f(x)$	Trial function
$ax + b$	$px + q$
Polynomial	General polynomial of the same order
ae^{bx}	pe^{bx}
$a \cos bx$ $a \sin bx$	$p \sin bx + q \sin bx$

- If the trial function is already part of the complementary function, multiply the trial function by x.

Mixed practice 11

1 What is the complementary function of the differential equation $4\dfrac{d^2y}{dx^2} + 9y = \sin 3x$?

Choose from these options.

A $A\cos\left(\dfrac{3}{2}x\right) + B\sin\left(\dfrac{3}{2}x\right)$

B $A\cos(3x) + B\sin(3x)$

C $Ae^{\frac{3}{2}x} + Be^{-\frac{3}{2}x}$

D $Ae^{3x} + Be^{-3x}$

2 What is the integrating factor for the differential equation $\dfrac{dy}{dx} - \dfrac{3}{x}y = x^2$?

Choose from these options.

A $-3\ln x$
B $\dfrac{1}{x^3}$
C $\dfrac{3}{x}$
D x^3

3 a Solve the quadratic equation $\lambda^2 + 6\lambda + 5 = 0$.

b Hence write down the general solution of the differential equation $\dfrac{d^2y}{dx^2} + 6\dfrac{dy}{dx} + 5y = 0$.

4 a Show that the integrating factor for the differential equation $\dfrac{dy}{dx} + 2xy = xe^{-x^2}$ is e^{x^2}.

b Hence find the general solution of the differential equation.

5 The differential equation $\dfrac{d^2y}{dx^2} + 7\dfrac{dy}{dx} + 10y = e^x$ is defined for all x.

a By considering the associated homogeneous differential equation, find the complementary function.

b Show that a function of the form qe^x forms a particular integral, and find the value of q.

c Hence write down the general solution of the differential equation.

d Find the particular solution for which $y(0) = 0$ and $y'(0) = 6$.

6 a Find the value of the constant q for which $q\cos x$ is a particular integral of the differential equation $\dfrac{d^2y}{dx^2} + 4y = \cos x$.

b Hence find the general solution of the differential equation.

7 The differential equation $\dfrac{d^2y}{dx^2} + 6\dfrac{dy}{dx} + 25y = 50x$ is defined for all x.

a By considering the associated homogeneous differential equation, find the complementary function.

b Show that a function of the form $px + q$ forms a particular integral, and find the values of p and q.

c Hence write down the general solution of the differential equation.

d Find the particular solution for which $y = -\dfrac{12}{25}$ and $y' = 6$ when $x = 0$.

8 Solve the differential equation
$$\frac{d^2y}{dx^2} - 2\frac{dy}{dx} - 3y = 2e^{-x}$$
given that $y \to 0$ as $x \to \infty$ and that $\frac{dy}{dx} = -3$ when $x = 0$.

[©AQA 2014]

9 Find the general solution of the differential equation
$$\frac{d^2y}{dx^2} + 4y = 8x^2 + 9\sin x.$$

[©AQA 2010]

10 **a** Find the general solution of $x\frac{du}{dx} + 3u = x$ for $x > 0$.

b Show that the substitution $u = \frac{dy}{dx}$ transforms the differential equation $x\frac{d^2y}{dx^2} + 3\frac{dy}{dx} = x$ into
$$x\frac{du}{dx} + 3u = x.$$

c Hence find the general solution of the differential equation $x\frac{d^2y}{dx^2} + 3\frac{dy}{dx} = x$ for $x > 0$.

11 **a** Find the general solution of the differential equation $\cos x \frac{dy}{dx} + y\sin x = \sin 2x$.

b Find the particular solution if $y(0) = 5$.

12 It is given that, for $x \neq 0$, y satisfies the differential equation
$$x\frac{d^2y}{dx^2} + 2(3x+1)\frac{dy}{dx} + 3y(3x+2) = 18x.$$

a Show that the substitution $u = xy$ transforms this differential equation into
$$\frac{d^2u}{dx^2} + 6\frac{du}{dx} + 9u = 18x.$$

b Hence find the general solution of the differential equation
$$x\frac{d^2y}{dx^2} + 2(3x+1)\frac{dy}{dx} + 3y(3x+2) = 18x$$
giving your answer in the form $y = f(x)$.

[©AQA 2012]

11 Differential equations

13 a By using an integrating factor, find the general solution of the differential equation

$$\frac{du}{dx} - \frac{2x}{x^2+4}u = 3(x^2+4)$$

giving your answer in the form $u = f(x)$.

b Show that the substitution $u = x^2\frac{dy}{dx}$ transforms the differential equation

$$x^2(x^2+4)\frac{d^2y}{dx^2} + 8x\frac{dy}{dx} = 3(x^2+4)^2$$

into

$$\frac{du}{dx} - \frac{2x}{x^2+4}u = 3(x^2+4)$$

c Hence, given that $x > 0$, find the general solution of the differential equation

$$x^2(x^2+4)\frac{d^2y}{dx^2} + 8x\frac{dy}{dx} = 3(x^2+4)^2.$$

[©AQA 2014]

14 a Express $\frac{1}{(1+x)(2+x)}$ in the form $\frac{A}{1+x} + \frac{B}{2+x}$, where A and B are integers.

b Use the substitution $u = \frac{dy}{dx}$ to solve the differential equation

$$\frac{d^2y}{dx^2} + \frac{1}{(1+x)(2+x)}\frac{dy}{dx} = \frac{2+x}{1+x}$$

given that $y = 1$ and $\frac{dy}{dx} = 4$ when $x = 0$. Give your answer in the form $y = f(x)$.

[©AQA 2016]

12 Applications of differential equations

In this chapter you will learn how to:

- use differential equations in modelling, in kinematics and in other contexts
- solve the equation for simple harmonic motion and relate the solution to the motion
- use Hooke's law
- model damped oscillations using second order differential equations and interpret their solution
- solve coupled first order differential equations.

Before you start…

Chapter 11	You should know how to solve second order differential equations.	1 Find the general solution to $y'' + 5y' + 4y = x$.
A Level Mathematics Student Book 1, Chapter 18	You should be able to use Newton's second law.	2 A falling object of mass 10 kg is subjected to a constant air resistance of 50 N. Find the acceleration of the object when $g = 9.8 \text{ m s}^{-2}$.

Real world modelling

In reality nearly everything of interest – be it the effect of a medicine or the price of a share – changes over time. The tool that mathematicians use to model these situations is differential equations, and in this chapter you will look at some common situations modelled by differential equations and how you can use the methods from Chapter 11 to solve them and interpret their solutions in context.

Section 1: Forming differential equations

When modelling real-life situations, it is often the case that the description can be interpreted in terms of differential equations.

You have already met many examples of setting up differential equations in A Level Mathematics Student Book 2, Chapter 13. In this section you will see further types of situations in which differential equations arise, but this time you will often need to use methods from Chapters 9 and 11 to solve them. You will also look at the types of assumptions that are made when writing these differential equations.

> ⏮ **Rewind**
>
> See A Level Mathematics Student Book 1, Chapter 18, for a reminder of using $F = ma$, and A Level Mathematics Student Book 2, Chapter 13, for its use in setting up differential equations.

12 Applications of differential equations

WORKED EXAMPLE 12.1

A car, of mass m kg, is moving along a straight horizontal road. At time t seconds, the car has speed v m s^{-1}. The only force acting is a resistance proportional to $m(u^2 + v^2)$ newtons, where u is the initial speed of the car.

Find the time taken for the car to come to rest.

	The resistance force is $mk(u^2 + v^2)$ for some constant k.
Using $F = ma$ and $a = \dfrac{dv}{dt}$:	The resistance force is negative as the car is moving in the opposite direction to that in which this force acts.
$-mk(u^2 + v^2) = m\dfrac{dv}{dt}$	
$-k(u^2 + v^2) = \dfrac{dv}{dt}$	
Separating the variables:	
$\displaystyle\int \dfrac{1}{u^2 + v^2}\, dv = -\int k\, dt$	
$\dfrac{1}{u}\arctan\left(\dfrac{v}{u}\right) = -kt + c$	This is a standard arctan integral.
When $t = 0$, $v = u$:	Use the initial condition to find c.
$\dfrac{1}{u}\arctan\left(\dfrac{u}{u}\right) = 0 + c$	
$c = \dfrac{\pi}{4u}$	
$\therefore \dfrac{1}{u}\arctan\left(\dfrac{v}{u}\right) = -kt + \dfrac{\pi}{4u}$	
When $v = 0$:	The car will come to rest when $v = 0$.
$\dfrac{1}{u}\arctan 0 = -kt + \dfrac{\pi}{4u}$	
$kt = \dfrac{\pi}{4u}$	
$t = \dfrac{\pi}{4uk}$	

EXERCISE 12A

1 A stone, of mass m, falls vertically downwards under gravity through still water. At time t, the stone has speed v and it experiences a resistance force of magnitude λmv, where λ is a constant.

  a Show that $\dfrac{dv}{dt} = g - \lambda v$.

  b The initial speed of the stone is u.
  Find an expression for v at time t.

[©AQA 2016]

A Level Further Mathematics for AQA Student Book 2

2 A car, of mass m kg, is moving along a straight horizontal road. At time t seconds, the car has speed $v\,\text{m s}^{-1}$. As the car moves, it experiences a resistance force of magnitude $2mv^{\frac{5}{4}}$ newtons. No other horizontal force acts on the car.

  a Show that $\dfrac{\mathrm{d}v}{\mathrm{d}t} = -2v^{\frac{5}{4}}$.

  b The initial speed of the car is $16\,\text{m s}^{-1}$.
  Show that $v = \left(\dfrac{2}{t+1}\right)^4$.

[©AQA 2011]

3 The current I in a circuit with resistance $2R$, capacitance C and inductance L is modelled by:
$$L\frac{\mathrm{d}^2 I}{\mathrm{d}t^2} + 2R\frac{\mathrm{d}I}{\mathrm{d}t} + \frac{1}{C}I = 0.$$
Sketch the solution in each situation.

  a $R = 0$ **b** $R^2 < \dfrac{L}{C}$ **c** $R^2 > \dfrac{L}{C}$

4 The rate of immigration into a country is modelled as being exponentially decreasing. The initial rate is 200 000 per year. One year later the rate is 50 000 per year.

  a Write a differential equation for the population, Y, assuming that changes in the population are due only to immigration.

  b Given that the initial population is 12 million, find the long-term population predicted by the model.

  c The model is refined by adding the term $0.02Y$. Suggest what this term represents.

5 A chicken is placed into an oven. The temperature of the oven, $T_{\text{oven}}\,°\text{C}$, follows the rule $T_{\text{oven}} = 25 + 20t$, where t is the time in minutes after the chicken is put into the oven. The rate of increase of the temperature of the chicken, $T\,°\text{C}$, is modelled as proportional to the difference between the chicken's temperature and the oven's temperature.

  a Write a differential equation for the temperature of the chicken.

  b If the temperature of the chicken is originally $5\,°\text{C}$ and it is increasing at a rate of $10\,°\text{C s}^{-1}$, find the particular solution of the differential equation.

  c Find an estimate of the chicken's temperature after 10 minutes, giving your answer to an appropriate degree of accuracy.

  d Describe one way in which the model is a simplification of the chicken's temperature.

6 A school has N students. The rate of spread of a rumour in the school is thought to be proportional to both the number of students who know the rumour, R, and the number who do not know the rumour.

  a Write this information as a differential equation.

  b Find the number of students who know the rumour when the rumour is spreading fastest.

  c Write down two assumptions that are being made in this situation.

7 A bacterium is modelled as a sphere. According to one biological model the volume of the bacterium, V, follows this differential equation:

$$\frac{dV}{dt} = 2V^{\frac{2}{3}} - V$$

a Explain the biological significance of the $V^{\frac{2}{3}}$ term.

b By using the substitution $u = V^{\frac{1}{3}}$, solve the differential equation given that initially $V = 1$.

c Sketch the solution and hence find the long-term volume of the bacterium.

> **Did you know?**
>
> The model in Question 7 is called Von Bertalanffy growth. It is very important in mathematical biology.

Section 2: Simple harmonic motion and Hooke's law

In Chapter 11, Section 3, you saw that some second order differential equations have solutions involving sines and cosines. These describe **oscillating behaviour**.

The differential equation which has pure sinusoidal behaviour is called **simple harmonic motion**. It occurs in a surprisingly wide range of physical situations.

> **Tip**
>
> Simple harmonic motion is often abbreviated to SHM.

> **Key point 12.1**
>
> The differential equation for simple harmonic motion is
>
> $$\frac{d^2 x}{dt^2} = -\omega^2 x$$
>
> where ω is a constant with units rad s^{-1}.

> **Tip**
>
> The constant ω is sometimes referred to as the **angular frequency**.

In the equation in Key point 12.1, x represents the displacement of an object and t is the time.

To solve this differential equation you find the auxiliary equation:

$$\lambda^2 = -\omega^2$$

This has solutions $\lambda = \pm i\omega$, which lead to the general solution to the differential equation.

> **Key point 12.2**
>
> The general solution to the simple harmonic motion differential equation is
>
> $$x = A \sin \omega t + B \cos \omega t.$$

You need to know some pieces of terminology that are useful in describing these solutions.

- The average position around which the object oscillates is called the **central line**.
- The maximum distance from the central line is called the **amplitude**.
- The motion repeats itself after time, T, which is called the **period**.

If initially the object is:

- on the central line, then the solution will be $x = a \sin \omega t$
- at the maximum displacement from the central line, then the solution will be $x = a \cos \omega t$.

In both of these cases the amplitude is given by a.

Since $\sin \theta$ and $\cos \theta$ repeat when θ gets to 2π, one full period, T, occurs when $\omega T = 2\pi$.

> **Key point 12.3**
>
> The period, T, of a particle moving with simple harmonic oscillation is
> $$T = \frac{2\pi}{\omega}.$$

The object has its maximum speed as it is going through the central line, and it is instantaneously at rest when it reaches the maximum displacement.

> **Key point 12.4**
>
> The relationship between velocity and displacement for a particle moving with simple harmonic oscillation is
> $$v^2 = \omega^2(a^2 - x^2).$$

PROOF 9

Prove that $v^2 = \omega^2(a^2 - x^2)$.

If $x = 0$ when $t = 0$, then $x = a \sin \omega t$.	Since you are only looking for a relationship between v and x, choose to start the time when the object moves through the central line.
$v = \dfrac{dx}{dt} = a\omega \cos \omega t$	Use $v = \dfrac{dx}{dt}$.

Continues on next page

$v^2 = \omega^2 a^2 \cos^2 \omega t$
$= \omega^2 a^2 (1 - \sin^2 \omega t)$
$= \omega^2 (a^2 - (a \sin \omega t)^2)$
$= \omega^2 (a^2 - x^2)$

Use $\cos^2 \theta \equiv 1 - \sin^2 \theta$.

Group the terms together to make a link with the expression for displacement.

One common context for simple harmonic motion is situations with springs. You can use a standard model from physics for the force from a spring. This says that the tension, T, in the spring is proportional to the extension, x, from the spring's natural length. The tension is always directed back towards the equilibrium position.

Key point 12.5

Hooke's law:

$$T = kx$$

The value k is sometimes referred to as the **spring constant** or the **stiffness** of the spring.

Fast forward

If you are taking the Mechanics option of Further Mathematics, you will meet Hooke's Law again in Chapter 5 of the Further Mechanics Student Book.

WORKED EXAMPLE 12.2

A spring of natural length 10 cm and spring constant 100 N m⁻¹ is attached to a hook in the ceiling. A mass 0.5 kg is attached to the other end of the spring.

Use $g = 10$ m s⁻², giving your final answers to an appropriate degree of accuracy.

a Show that the equilibrium length of the spring is 15 cm.
b Show that if the spring is displaced from the equilibrium it will undergo simple harmonic motion and find the time period of oscillations about this equilibrium.
c Given that the spring is stretched an additional 2 cm and then released, find its maximum speed.

a

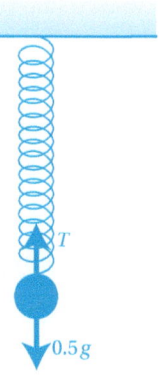

Draw a diagram to help visualise the situation.

Only tension and weight are acting on the mass. These must balance.

When the spring is in equilibrium:
$T = 0.5g$
$kx = 0.5g$

Continues on next page

Substituting $k = 100$ and $g = 10$:

$$100x = 5$$
$$x = \frac{5}{100}$$

So the extension is 5 cm and the equilibrium length is 15 cm.

b

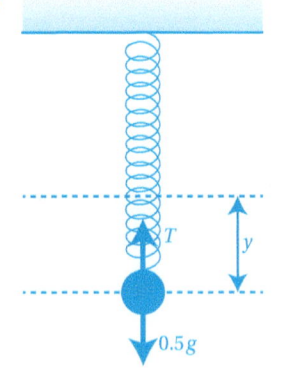

> This is Newton's second law vertically. The acceleration is $\frac{d^2y}{dt^2}$. If y is positive when below the equilibrium position, then you need to use down as positive, so the resultant force is weight – tension.

If y is the extension below the equilibrium position, then:

$$m\frac{d^2y}{dt^2} = mg - k(0.05 + y)$$
$$= 0.5 \times 10 - 100 \times 0.05 - ky$$
$$= -ky$$

$$\therefore \frac{d^2y}{dt^2} = -\frac{k}{m}y$$

> Rearrange into the standard form for simple harmonic motion.

So, $\frac{d^2y}{dt^2} = -\omega^2 y$, where $\omega^2 = \frac{k}{m}$.

This is the equation for simple harmonic motion.

Then

> Use $T = \frac{2\pi}{\omega}$ from Key point 12.3.

$$T = 2\pi\sqrt{\frac{m}{k}}$$

$$= 2\pi\sqrt{\frac{0.5}{100}}$$

$$\approx 0.44\,s$$

So $T = 0.4\,s$ (1 s.f.)

c If the spring is stretched an additional 2 cm, then the amplitude is 0.02 m.

> It is important to be consistent with units – in this case working only in metres.

$$v^2 = \omega^2(a^2 - x^2) = \frac{100}{0.5}(0.02^2 - x^2).$$

> Use $v^2 = \omega(a^2 - x^2)$ from Key point 12.4.

This is maximised when $x = 0$, so the maximum speed is

$$\sqrt{\frac{100}{0.5} \times 0.02^2} \approx 0.28\,m\,s^{-1}.$$

So, maximum speed = $0.3\,m\,s^{-1}$ (1 s.f.)

12 Applications of differential equations

EXERCISE 12B

In this exercise, unless otherwise instructed, use $g = 9.8 \text{ m s}^{-2}$, giving your final answers to an appropriate degree of accuracy.

1 State the amplitude and the period of the simple harmonic motion described by each equation. Also state whether the particle is at rest or passing through the equilibrium point when $t = 0$.

   a   **i** $x = 4.5 \cos 3t$ **ii** $x = 3 \sin 4t$

   b   **i** $x = 2.6 \sin \dfrac{t}{3}$ **ii** $x = 5 \cos \dfrac{t}{4}$

   c   **i** $x = 3.2 \sin \dfrac{2\pi t}{3}$ **ii** $x = 10.4 \cos \dfrac{3\pi t}{5}$

2 For each description of simple harmonic motion, write an equation for x in terms of t (where x is in metres and t is in seconds).

   a   **i**   Amplitude 0.6 m, period $\dfrac{\pi}{5}$ seconds; at rest when $t = 0$.

        ii   Amplitude 3.4 m, period $\dfrac{\pi}{7}$ seconds; at rest when $t = 0$.

   b   **i**   Amplitude 0.7 m, period 6π seconds; in equilibrium when $t = 0$.

        ii   Amplitude 1.3 m, period 10π seconds; in equilibrium when $t = 0$.

   c   **i**   Amplitude 12.1 m, period 2.5 seconds; in equilibrium when $t = 0$.

        ii   Amplitude 0.3 m, period 0.6 seconds; at rest when $t = 0$.

3 Each differential equation models a particle performing simple harmonic motion. Find the period of the motion.

> **Tip**
>
> $\ddot{x}$ is an alternative notation for $\dfrac{d^2x}{dt^2}$.

   a   **i** $\dfrac{d^2x}{dt^2} + 25x = 0$ **ii** $\dfrac{d^2x}{dt^2} + 9x = 0$

   b   **i** $\ddot{x} + 2x = 0$ **ii** $\ddot{x} + 8x = 0$

   c   **i** $3\dfrac{d^2x}{dt^2} + 9x = 0$ **ii** $5\dfrac{d^2x}{dt^2} + 45x = 0$

   d   **i** $4\ddot{x} = -4x$ **ii** $3\ddot{x} = -15x$

4 A particle performs simple harmonic motion with amplitude 0.2 m and angular frequency 5 rad s^{-1}. The particle passes through the equilibrium position when $t = 0$.

   a   Find the distance of the particle from the equilibrium position when $t = 4$ s.

   b   Find the maximum speed of the particle.

5 A small ball is attached to one end of an elastic spring. When $t = 0$ the ball is released from rest 0.6 m from the equilibrium position and performs simple harmonic motion with period $\dfrac{\pi}{6}$ s.

   a   Find the displacement of the ball from the equilibrium position after 3 seconds.

   b   Find the time when the ball first passes through the equilibrium position, and the speed of the ball at this time.

A Level Further Mathematics for AQA Student Book 2

6 A small ball attached to the end of a spring performs simple harmonic motion with amplitude 8 cm and angular frequency 15 rad s^{-1}.

   a Find the maximum speed of the ball.

   b The ball is at rest when $t = 0$. Find the speed of the ball 5 seconds later. Find also the magnitude of the acceleration of the ball at this time.

7 A particle performs simple harmonic motion with amplitude 12 cm. Its speed as it passes through the equilibrium point is 0.08 m s^{-1}.

   a Find the period of the simple harmonic motion.

   b Find the speed of the particle when its displacement from the equilibrium position is 8 cm.

8 A particle performs simple harmonic motion with amplitude 0.6 m and period $\frac{\pi}{5}$ s. The particle passes through the equilibrium position when $t = 0$ with positive displacement immediately after $t = 0$.

   a Find the displacement of the particle when $t = 3.6$ s.

   b Find the first time when the particle is 0.3 m from the equilibrium position.

   c Find the speed of the particle at that point. Is it moving towards or away from the equilibrium position?

9 A particle is attached to one end of an elastic spring. It is displaced from its equilibrium position and performs simple harmonic motion with amplitude 0.5 m. When its displacement from the equilibrium position is 0.2 m the speed of the particle is 0.4 m s^{-1}.

   a Find the period of the simple harmonic motion.

   b Hence find the distance from the equilibrium position when the speed of the particle is 0.05 m s^{-1}.

10 A particle moves in a straight line between points A and B, which are 0.6 m apart. The midpoint of AB is O and the displacement of the particle from O at time t seconds is x metres.

   The motion of the particle is described by the equation $\frac{d^2x}{dt^2} + 0.16x = 0$. When $t = 0$ the particle is at A.

   a Write down the amplitude and the period of the simple harmonic motion.

   b Write down an expression for x in terms of t.

   c Point C is between A and B, and $AC = 0.4$ m. Find the first time when the particle passes through C.

   d The mass of the particle is 0.2 kg. Find the magnitude of the force acting on the particle when it passes through C.

11 A particle of mass m kg is attached to one end of a light spring and rests on a smooth horizontal table. The string is horizontal and its other end is attached to a fixed wall.

   The particle is displaced away from the wall so that the extension of the spring is 0.6 m and then released. When the extension of the spring is e the elastic force in the spring is $T = mq^2e$, where q is a constant. All other forces on the particle can be ignored.

   a Show that the particle performs simple harmonic motion and find, in terms of q, the period of the motion.

   b Find the maximum speed and the maximum acceleration of the particle.

   c Find the extension of the spring at the moment when the speed of the particle equals half of its maximum speed.

12 Applications of differential equations

12 A cart of mass 300 kg is moving in a straight line with a speed of $12\,\text{m s}^{-1}$ when it hits a buffer that is attached to a fixed wall by a light spring.

At time t seconds after the impact the compression of the spring is x metres and the force in the spring is given by $T = 192x$ newtons. Any other forces acting on the cart can be ignored.

   a Show that the cart performs simple harmonic motion as long as it remains in contact with the buffer.

   b Find the maximum compression of the spring and the magnitude of the force acing on the cart at that point.

   c Find the time taken to reach the point of maximum compression.

13 A particle of mass 0.5 kg rests on a smooth horizontal table. The particle is attached to two light springs and the other ends of the springs are attached to fixed points A and B, which are 0.8 m apart. The natural length of each spring is 0.3 m and the magnitude of the tension in the spring is given by $1.2e$, where e is the extension of the spring.

The particle is released from rest 0.04 m from O, the midpoint of AB.

At time t the displacement of the particle from O is x.

   a Find the magnitude of the resultant force on the particle at time t.

   b Hence show that the particle performs simple harmonic motion.

   c Find an expression for x in terms of t.

14 A light spring is attached to a fixed point A. A particle of mass 0.2 kg is attached to the other end of the spring and hangs vertically below A.

When the extension of the spring is e metres, the magnitude of the tension in the spring is $T = 2ge$ newtons.

   a The particle hangs in equilibrium at point B. Find the extension of the spring.

The particle is displaced x m downward from the equilibrium position.

   b Write down the extension of the spring. Hence show that, as long as $|x| < 0.1$, the magnitude of the resultant force on the particle is $2gx$.

   c Hence show that the particle performs simple harmonic motion and find the period of the motion.

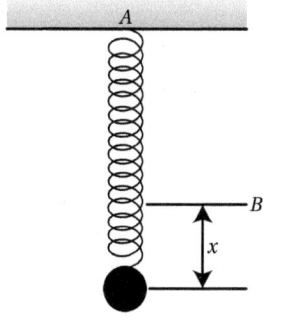

15 A particle P, of mass 0.4 kg, is attached to one end of a light elastic string, and the other end of the string is attached to a fixed point A.

   a The particle P hangs in equilibrium at a point E, vertically below A, where the extension of the string is 0.2 metres. Calculate the stiffness of the string.

   b The particle P is pulled vertically downwards from the point E by a distance of 0.1 metres, and released from rest. The displacement of P from E at time t seconds after being released is x metres.

      i Given that the string does not become slack during the subsequent motion, show that $\ddot{x} = hx$ where h is a constant to be determined.

      ii Hence deduce that the motion of P is simple harmonic.

      iii Show that the period of this motion is 0.898 seconds, correct to three significant figures.

      iv Calculate the maximum speed of P during its motion.

[©AQA 2012]

16 A particle moves along a straight line between the points A and B with simple harmonic motion. The point O is the midpoint of AB. At time t seconds, the particle is x metres from O and moving with speed $v\,\text{m s}^{-1}$.

The motion of the particle satisfies the equation $\dfrac{d^2x}{dt^2} + \omega^2 x = 0$.

a The particle completes one oscillation in 7.5 seconds.

Show that $\omega = \dfrac{4\pi}{15}$.

b When the particle passes through the point C, as shown in the diagram, $x = 1$ and $v = 2$.

i Show that the amplitude of the motion is 2.59 metres, correct to three significant figures.

ii When the particle first passes through C, it is heading away from O towards B.

Find the time that it takes to move from C to B and back to C, giving your answer to two significant figures.

iii Find the maximum speed of the particle during the oscillations.

[©AQA 2010]

17 A particle, of mass 9 kg, is attached to two identical springs. The other ends of the springs are attached to fixed points, A and B, which are 1.2 metres apart on a smooth horizontal surface. Each spring has a natural length 0.4 m and stiffness 112.5 N m^{-1}.

The particle is released from rest at a distance of 0.5 metres from B and moves on the line AB. The midpoint of AB is C. At time t seconds after release, the displacement of the particle from C is x metres, where the direction from A to B is taken to be positive.

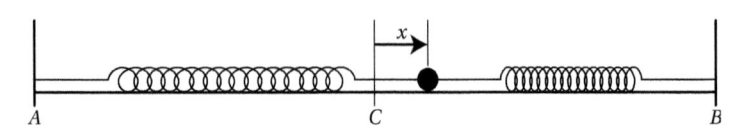

a Show that the resultant force on the particle, at time t, is $-225x$ newtons.

b Hence show that the particle moves with simple harmonic motion.

c State the period of this motion.

d Find the speed of the particle when it is 0.05 metres from C.

e Write down an expression for x in terms of t.

[©AQA 2013]

18 A spring has natural length 0.2 m and stiffness $5\,mg\,\text{N}\,\text{m}^{-1}$. A particle of mass m kg is attached to one end of the spring. The other end of the spring is attached to a peg which moves up and down between two points, A and B. The midpoint of AB is O. The point A is 0.1 metres above O, and B is 0.1 metres below O. At time t seconds, the displacement of the peg from the point O is $0.1 \sin 4t$ metres, where the downward direction is taken as positive. The displacement of the particle from O at time t is x metres, as shown in the diagram.

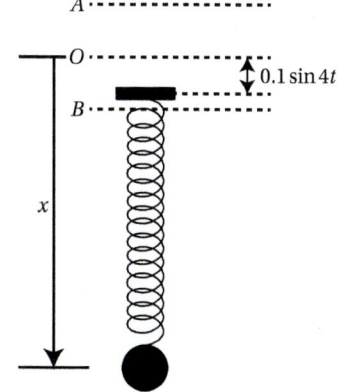

Assume that there is no air resistance.

a Show that

$$\frac{d^2 x}{dt^2} + 49x = 19.6 + 4.9 \sin 4t.$$

b At time $t = 0$, the particle is at rest with $x = 0.4$. Find an expression for x at time t.

[©AQA 2014]

Section 3: Damping and damped oscillations

When bodies are moving they are usually subjected to resistive forces such as air resistance or drag in water. There are several ways in which you can model this situation. One common model is to assume that the drag force, D, is proportional to the speed, acting in the opposite direction.

Key point 12.6

The drag force is given by
$$D = -Kv.$$

If you add this to the standard equation for simple harmonic motion, the differential equation becomes:

$$\frac{d^2 x}{dt^2} + k\frac{dx}{dt} + \omega^2 x = 0$$

where $k = \frac{K}{m}$ is a positive constant. This is called **damped simple harmonic motion**.

As you saw in Chapter 11, the solutions to this differential equation depend upon how many solutions there are to the auxiliary equation, and each is given a different name.

281

Key point 12.7

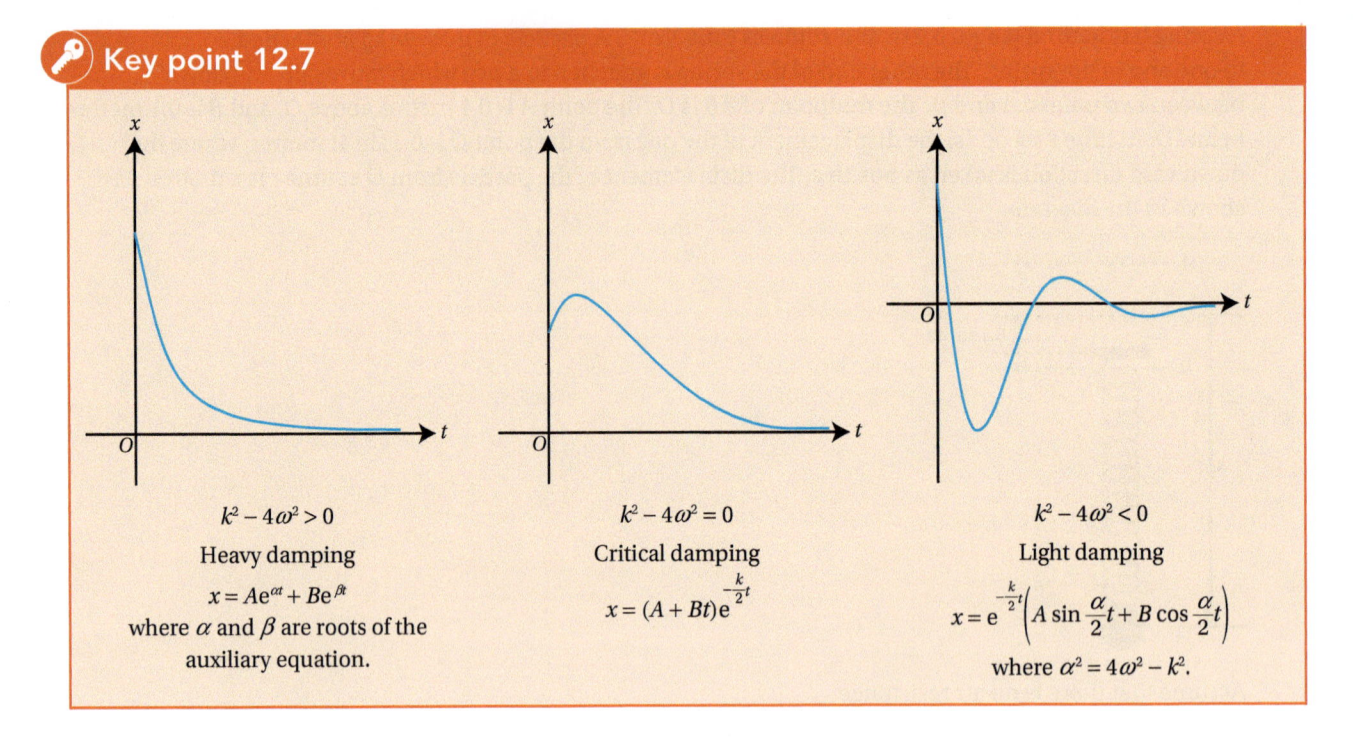

$k^2 - 4\omega^2 > 0$	$k^2 - 4\omega^2 = 0$	$k^2 - 4\omega^2 < 0$
Heavy damping	Critical damping	Light damping
$x = Ae^{\alpha t} + Be^{\beta t}$ where α and β are roots of the auxiliary equation.	$x = (A + Bt)e^{-\frac{k}{2}t}$	$x = e^{-\frac{k}{2}t}\left(A \sin \frac{\alpha}{2}t + B \cos \frac{\alpha}{2}t\right)$ where $\alpha^2 = 4\omega^2 - k^2$.

In physical situations, such as the suspension of a car, critical damping is often desirable as it minimises vibrations without too much jerkiness.

WORKED EXAMPLE 12.3

A bob of mass 0.1 kg is connected to a spring. In air the bob is found to follow simple harmonic motion with period π seconds. The bob is then placed into oil where there is a drag force of magnitude Kv. Find the value of K that produces critical damping.

As the time period is π, the value of ω is given by $\omega = \dfrac{2\pi}{T} = 2$.	Rearrange the formula in Key point 12.3 to express ω in terms of T.
Therefore, in air the differential equation is $\dfrac{d^2x}{dt^2} + 4x = 0$	
The force is therefore given by $F = ma = m\dfrac{d^2x}{dt^2} = -4mx$	
In oil, there must be the additional drag force: $-4mx - K\dfrac{dx}{dt} = m\dfrac{d^2x}{dt^2}$ $\therefore \dfrac{d^2x}{dt^2} + \dfrac{K}{m}\dfrac{dx}{dt} + 4x = 0$	Now $F = -4mx - K\dfrac{dx}{dt}$.
$\dfrac{d^2x}{dt^2} + 10K\dfrac{dx}{dt} + 4x = 0$	Since $m = 0.1$.
Critical damping occurs when $(10K)^2 - 4 \times 4 = 0$ $\therefore K = 0.4$	Only the positive solution to the equation is required, since from the context you need $K > 0$.

12 Applications of differential equations

EXERCISE 12C

1 Each differential equation describes damped harmonic motion. In each case determine whether the damping is light, heavy or critical.

   a   **i** $\dfrac{d^2x}{dt^2} + 2\dfrac{dx}{dt} + 5x = 0$ **ii** $\dfrac{d^2x}{dt^2} + 8\dfrac{dx}{dt} + 3x = 0$

   b   **i** $\ddot{x} + 4\dot{x} + 4x = 0$ **ii** $\ddot{x} + 3\dot{y} + 4x = 0$

   c   **i** $3\dfrac{d^2x}{dt^2} + 9\dfrac{dx}{dt} + 3x = 0$ **ii** $5\dfrac{d^2x}{dt^2} + 30\dfrac{dx}{dt} + 45x = 0$

   d   **i** $4\ddot{x} = -8\dot{x} - 4x$ **ii** $3\ddot{x} = -6\dot{x} - 15x$

2 A particle performs damped harmonic motion described by the differential equation $\dfrac{d^2x}{dt^2} + 3n\dfrac{dx}{dt} + 6nx = 0$. Given that the damping is critical, find the value of n.

3 A particle of mass 0.2 kg is attached to one end of a light spring and rests on a horizontal table, with the spring horizontal. When the extension of the spring is x metres the tension in the spring has magnitude $3.6x$ newtons. The resistance force acting on the particle has magnitude kv newtons, where $v\,\text{m s}^{-1}$ is the speed of the particle.

   a Show that the equation of motion of the particle is $\ddot{x} + 5k\dot{x} + 18x = 0$.

   b Given that the motion of the particle is critically damped, find the exact value of k.

   c Name the type of damping that occurs when $k = 1.8$.

4 A particle P of mass m kg is attached to one end of a spring. When the displacement of P from its equilibrium position is x metres the magnitude of the tension in the spring is $4nx$ newtons and the resistance force on P has magnitude $5c\dot{x}$ newtons.

   a Write down a differential equation which models the motion of the particle.

   b Given that the motion of the particle is critically damped, express n in terms of m and c.

5 A particle is attached to one end of a spring and moves under the action of a tension and a resistance force. The motion of the particle is described by the differential equation $\dfrac{d^2x}{dt^2} + 4\dfrac{dx}{dt} + 13x = 0$. When $t = 0$, $x = 0$ and $\dfrac{dx}{dt} = 2.7$.

   a Find an expression for x in terms of t.

   b Name the type of damping that occurs and sketch the graph of x as a function of t.

6 A particle of mass 0.2 kg is attached to one end of a spring and moves in a straight line on a horizontal table. When the displacement of the particle from a fixed point O is x m the tension in the spring has magnitude $1.2x$ N. The resistance force acting on the particle has magnitude $1.4v$ N, where $v\,\text{m s}^{-1}$ is the speed of the particle.

   a Show that the equation of motion for the particle is $\dfrac{d^2x}{dt^2} + 7\dfrac{dx}{dt} + 6x = 0$.

When $t = 0$ the particle is at rest, 1 m from O.

   b Find x in terms of t.

   c Show that the particle never reaches O.

   d Name the type of damping that occurs in this case.

7. A particle of mass 3 kg moves in a straight line under the action of two forces. When the particle's displacement from a fixed point O is x m there is a force towards O of magnitude $2.43x$ N as well as a resistance force of magnitude $12kv$ N (where v is the speed of the particle). When $t = 0$ the particle is at rest 0.8 m from O.

   a Show that the motion of the particle is described by the equation $\ddot{x} + 4k\dot{x} + 0.81x = 0$.

   b Given that the motion of the particle is critically damped, find the value of k.

   c In this case, find an expression for x in terms of t.

8. **In this question use $g = 10\,\text{m s}^{-2}$, giving your final answers to an appropriate degree of accuracy.**

   A particle P of mass 0.16 kg is suspended by a light elastic string, and the other end of the string is attached to a fixed point A vertically above P. The natural length of the string is 1.2 m. When the extension of the string is d metres the magnitude of the tension in the string is $T = 4d$ newtons.

   a P hangs in equilibrium at the point B. Find the extension of the string at this point.

   P is held at rest with the string at its natural length, and then released. When the speed of P is $v\,\text{m s}^{-1}$ the resistance force acting on P has magnitude $1.28v$ newtons.

   b Show that the subsequent motion of P can be modelled by the differential equation $\ddot{x} + 8\dot{x} + 25x = 0$.

   c Name the type of damping that occurs in this case and find an expression for x in terms of t.

   d According to this model, what will the length of the string be in the long term?

   e Find the speed of P when it passes through B for the first time.

9. A particle is attached to one end of a light spring and performs damped oscillations described by the differential equation $\ddot{x} + k\dot{x} + c^2 x = 0$, where x is the extension of the spring beyond the equilibrium position.

   It is given that $k = \dfrac{8c}{5}$.

   a Determine whether the type of damping is light, heavy or critical.

   At $t = 0$, $x = 0$ and $\dot{x} = u$.

   b Find an expression for x in terms of t.

   c Show that the maximum extension of the spring is approximately $\dfrac{0.424u}{c}$.

10. **In this question use $g = 10\,\text{m s}^{-2}$, giving your final answers to an appropriate degree of accuracy.**

    A bungee jumper has mass 75 kg. He uses an elastic rope of natural length 12 m and stiffness $37.5\,\text{N m}^{-1}$. He falls vertically and, when the rope becomes taut for the first time, he is travelling at $12.5\,\text{m s}^{-1}$. Assume that, once the rope is taut, the bungee jumper experiences an air resistance force that has magnitude $15v$ newtons, where $v\,\text{m s}^{-1}$ is his speed.

    At time t seconds after the rope has become taut, the extension of the rope is x metres.

    a Show that
    $$10\dfrac{d^2 x}{dt^2} + 2\dfrac{dx}{dt} + 5x = 100.$$

    b Find x in terms of t.

    c Find the value of t when the bungee jumper first comes instantaneously to rest.

[©AQA 2013, adapted]

12 Applications of differential equations

11 A light spring *AB* lies at rest and unstretched on a smooth horizontal surface. A particle, *P*, of mass *m* is attached to the end *A* of the spring.

The spring has stiffness $2mn^2$, where n is a positive constant. The end *B* of the spring is set in motion and moves with constant acceleration of magnitude f in the direction *AB*, as shown in the diagram. The particle *P* is consequently forced into motion.

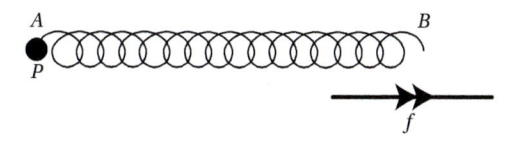

At time t after the motion begins, *P* is moving with speed v and experiences a resistant force of magnitude $3mnv$. The extension of the spring is x and the displacement of *P* from its initial position in the direction *AB* is y.

a Show that
$$y = \tfrac{1}{2}ft^2 - x.$$

b Hence show that *P* has velocity
$$ft - \frac{dx}{dt}.$$

c Hence show that
$$\frac{d^2x}{dt^2} + 3n\frac{dx}{dt} + 2n^2 x = f + 3nft.$$

d Given that $n = 1$, and that a particular integral for this differential equation is
$$x = \frac{f}{4}(6t - 7)$$
find an expression for x, in terms of f and t.

[©AQA 2010]

Section 4: Coupled first order differential equations

There are many situations in which two variables are linked by differential equations. If both of these differential equations are linear and first order, then you can eliminate one of the variables to form a second order differential equation.

WORKED EXAMPLE 12.4

In a population of foxes (f thousands) and rabbits (r thousands) the foxes have a birth rate of $12r$ and a death rate of $6f$. The rabbits have a birth rate of $4r$ and a death rate of $2f$.

a Write this information in the form of a pair of differential equations.
b Rewrite these differential equations as a second order differential equation for f.
c Solve this second order differential equation, given that initially $f = 2$ and $\frac{df}{dt} = 2$.
d Hence find the solution for r, given that the initial population of rabbits is three thousand.
e What is the long-term population of foxes and rabbits?

Continues on next page

a $\dfrac{df}{dt} = 12r - 6f$ (1)

$\dfrac{dr}{dt} = 4r - 2f$ (2)

> The rate of change of the fox population will be birth rate – death rate, and likewise for the rabbit population.

b Differentiating (1) with respect to t:

$\dfrac{d^2 f}{dt^2} = 12 \dfrac{dr}{dt} - 6 \dfrac{df}{dt}$

Substituting in the expression for $\dfrac{dr}{dt}$ from (2):

$\dfrac{d^2 f}{dt^2} = 12(4r - 2f) - 6\dfrac{df}{dt}$

$= 4 \times 12r - 24f - 6\dfrac{df}{dt}$

Rearranging (1):

$12r = \dfrac{df}{dt} + 6f$

Substituting this in:

$\dfrac{d^2 f}{dt^2} = 4 \times \left(\dfrac{df}{dt} + 6f \right) - 24f - 6\dfrac{df}{dt}$

$= -2\dfrac{df}{dt}$

So $\dfrac{d^2 f}{dt^2} + 2 \dfrac{df}{dt} = 0$.

c Auxiliary equation is:

$\lambda^2 + 2\lambda = 0$

$\lambda(\lambda + 2) = 0$

$\lambda = 0$ or -2

$\therefore f = A + Be^{-2t}$

$\dfrac{df}{dt} = -2Be^{-2t}$

When $t = 0$, $\dfrac{df}{dt} = 2$ so $B = -1$.

When $t = 0$, $f = 2$ so $A = 3$.

So the solution is $f = 3 - e^{-2t}$.

d Substituting the solution from part **c** into (2):

$\dfrac{dr}{dt} = 4r - 2(3 - e^{-2t})$

$\dfrac{dr}{dt} - 4r = 2e^{-2t} - 6$

> This is a first order linear differential equation, so you can write it into an appropriate form to use integrating factors.

The integrating factor is e^{-4t}, so:

$re^{-4t} = \displaystyle\int e^{-4t}(2e^{-2t} - 6)\,dt$

$= \displaystyle\int 2e^{-6t} - 6e^{-4t}\,dt$

$= -\dfrac{1}{3} e^{-6t} + \dfrac{3}{2} e^{-4t} + c$

Continues on next page

12 Applications of differential equations

$$\therefore r = -\frac{1}{3}e^{-2t} + \frac{3}{2} + ce^{4t}$$

When $t = 0$, $r = 3$ so $c = \frac{11}{6}$.

$$\therefore r = -\frac{1}{3}e^{-2t} + \frac{3}{2} + \frac{11}{6}e^{4t}.$$

e As t gets very large e^{-2t} gets very small, but e^{4t} gets very large, so the population of foxes tends towards 3000, but the population of rabbits grows without limit.

EXERCISE 12D

1 Write each pair of differential equations as a single second order equation for x. Hence find the general solution for x and y in terms of t.

  a **i** $\dfrac{dx}{dt} = 5x - 2y$, $\dfrac{dy}{dt} = x + 2y$ **ii** $\dfrac{dx}{dt} = x + 2y$, $\dfrac{dy}{dt} = 2x + y$

  b **i** $\dot{x} = 4y - 3x$, $\dot{y} = y - 2x$ **ii** $\dot{x} = 3x - y$, $\dot{y} = 8x - y$

  c **i** $\dot{x} = 4y - 5x + e^{-3t}$, $\dot{y} = 2y - 3x + 2e^{-3t}$ **ii** $\dot{x} = 2y - 3x + 5$, $\dot{y} = 2y - 2x - 8$

2 Find the general solution of $\dfrac{dy}{dt} = x + \cos t$, $\dfrac{dx}{dt} = y + \sin t$.

3 Find the general solution for x and y in terms of t for this system of differential equations:

$$\dfrac{dx}{dt} = -2y, \quad \dfrac{dy}{dt} = -8x.$$

4 The variables x and y satisfy the differential equations

$$\dfrac{dx}{dt} = 35 - 5y, \quad 5\dfrac{dy}{dt} = 16x - 192.$$

When $t = 0$, $x = 17$ and $y = 7$.

Find expressions for x and y in terms of t.

5 Consider the system of differential equations

$$\dfrac{dx}{dt} = 3x + y, \quad \dfrac{dy}{dt} = 6x - 2y.$$

  a Form a second order differential equation for x.

When $t = 0$, $x = 1$ and $y = 15$.

  b Find expressions for x and y in terms of t.

6. Three identical cylindrical cans, each with cross-sectional area 0.25 m² are placed vertically one above another. A hole is drilled in the base of each of the top two cans so that water can flow from the top can to the middle one and from the middle to the bottom one.

   For each of the top two cans, when the height of water in the can is h m, the rate of flow of water out of the can is $0.5h$ m³s⁻¹. Initially, the height of water in the top can is 30 cm and the middle can is empty.

   Let x be the height of water in the top can and y the height of water in the middle can at time t.

   The time taken for water to fall between cans can be ignored.

   a Show that $x = 0.3e^{-2t}$ and write a differential equation for y in terms of t.

   b Find an expression for y in terms of t and show that this model predicts that the second can never empties.

   c Find the maximum height of water in the second can.

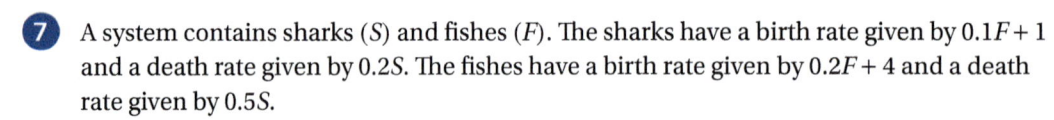

7. A system contains sharks (S) and fishes (F). The sharks have a birth rate given by $0.1F + 1$ and a death rate given by $0.2S$. The fishes have a birth rate given by $0.2F + 4$ and a death rate given by $0.5S$.

   a Write this information in the form of a pair of differential equations.

   b Rewrite these differential equations as a second order differential equation for S.

   c Solve this second order differential equation given that initially $S = 17$ and $F = 28$.

   d By writing the solution for S in the form $S = A + B\cos(kt - \alpha)$, where $\alpha \in (0, \pi)$, find the time of the first peak in the shark population. Find the equivalent time at which the fish population first peaks.

   e Describe the long-term behaviour of the two populations.

   Focus on...

   See Focus on... Modelling 2 for an improved version of the model in Question 7.

8. A predator prey system is of the form $\dfrac{dx}{dt} = ax + by$, $\dfrac{dy}{dt} = cx + dy$.

   Prove that the system will only oscillate if $(a + d)^2 < 4(ad - bc)$.

Checklist of learning and understanding

- The differential equation for simple harmonic motion is $\dfrac{d^2x}{dt^2} = -\omega^2 x$.
- The general solution to the simple harmonic motion differential equation is $x = A\sin\omega t + B\cos\omega t$.
- Time period of the solution: $T = \dfrac{2\pi}{\omega}$
- Speed, v, is given by: $v^2 = \omega^2(a^2 - x^2)$
- Hooke's law: $T = kx$
- The drag force is given by: $D = -Kv$.
- If there is a drag force there can be light damping, heavy damping or critical damping, depending on the number of solutions to the auxiliary equation.
- You can rewrite coupled pairs of linear first order differential equations as a second order differential equation in one variable.

Mixed practice 12

1. Find the period of the oscillations of a particle modelled by:
$$\frac{d^2y}{dt^2} + 4y = 0.$$

   Choose from these options.

   A $\frac{\pi}{2}$ B 2 C π D 4

2. Find the value of q which would result in critical damping in the system modelled by:
$$\frac{d^2x}{dt^2} + 16\frac{dx}{dt} + qx = 0.$$

   Choose from these options.

   A 4 B 16 C 32 D 64

3. A particle of mass 5 kg is acted on by a force $F = 10 \sin t$ newtons, where t is the time measured in seconds.

   a Write down a differential equation satisfied by the displacement, x metres, of the particle from its initial position.

   b Given that the particle is initially at rest, find its displacement after 3 seconds.

4. A ball is attached to one end of an elastic string and performs simple harmonic motion with amplitude 0.3 m and angular frequency 6 rad s^{-1}.

   a Find the maximum speed of the ball.

   b Find the speed of the ball when its displacement from the equilibrium position is 0.2 m.

   c The mass of the ball is 0.3 kg. Find the magnitude of the maximum force acting on the ball during the motion.

5. A particle of mass 2 kg moves in a straight line so that, when the displacement of the particle from the origin is x metres, the force acting on the particle is directed towards the origin and has magnitude $18x$ newtons.

   a Show that the displacement of the particle satisfies the differential equation $\frac{d^2x}{dt^2} = -9x$.

   b Verify that, for some value of ω, which you should state, $x = A \cos \omega t + B \sin \omega t$, where A and B are constants, satisfies this differential equation.

   c The particle is initially at rest 0.3 metres from the origin. Find the value of the constants A and B.

   d Hence find the maximum speed of the particle.

6. A particle moves along a straight line AB with simple harmonic motion. The point O is the midpoint of AB. When the displacement of the particle relative to O is x metres, its speed is v m s^{-1}.

   When $x = 3$, $v = 5$ and when $x = 6$, $v = 2.5$.

   a Show that the amplitude of the motion is $3\sqrt{5}$ metres.

   b Find the maximum speed of the particle during the motion.

   [©AQA 2011]

A Level Further Mathematics for AQA Student Book 2

7 One end of a light elastic spring is attached to a fixed wall and a small ball is attached to the other end. The ball rests on a smooth horizontal table.

At $t = 0$ the ball is given the velocity of $15\,\text{m s}^{-1}$ away from the equilibrium position. When the displacement of the ball from the equilibrium position is x metres the force acting on the particle is $5x$ newtons.

a Given that the mass of the ball is $0.2\,\text{kg}$, show that the equation of motion of the ball is $\dfrac{d^2x}{dt^2} = -25x$.

b Show that $x = A\cos 5t + B\sin 5t$ satisfies the equation and find the value of the constants A and B.

c Find the time when the particle first returns to the equilibrium position.

8 The spread of a disease through a population is modelled using these differential equations:

$$\begin{cases} \dfrac{dS}{dt} = -2I \\ \dfrac{dI}{dt} = 2I \end{cases}$$

where S is the number of uninfected individuals and I is the number of infected individuals in the population at time t months.

Initially there are 199 uninfected individuals and 1 infected individual. According to this model, how long will it take for half the population to become infected?

9 Solve this system of differential equations:

$$\begin{cases} \dot{x} = 3x - 5y \\ \dot{y} = 5x - 3y \end{cases}$$

given that $x(0) = 1$ and $y(0) = 1$.

10 Two particles, P and Q, each have a mass of $1\,\text{kg}$ and are initially at rest. P moves under the action of a force F_P newtons, modelled by $F_P(t) = t + 1$, where t is the time measured in seconds. Q moves under the action of a force F_Q newtons, modelled by $F_Q(x) = x + 1$, where x metres is the displacement from the initial position. Which particle travels further in the first 5 seconds?

11 A particle moves with simple harmonic motion in a straight line between points A and B, which are $1.2\,\text{m}$ apart. The midpoint of AB is O.

The motion of the particle satisfies the differential equation $\dfrac{d^2x}{dt^2} = -\omega^2 x$, where x is the displacement of the particle from O.

a By writing $\dfrac{d^2x}{dt^2}$ as $v\dfrac{dv}{dx}$, show that $v^2 = \omega^2(0.36 - x^2)$.

b Given that the particle takes 4 seconds to travel from A to B, find the value of ω.

c Given that the mass of the particle is 400 grams, find the maximum force acting on the particle.

12 One end of a light spring is attached to a fixed wall. A ball of mass $0.25\,\text{kg}$ is attached to the other end and rests on a smooth horizontal table. The ball is displaced $0.2\,\text{m}$ from the equilibrium position and then released. When the extension of the spring is $x\,\text{m}$, the magnitude of the tension in the spring is given by $T = 64x\,\text{N}$.

a Show that the equation of motion of the ball can be written as $\dfrac{d^2x}{dt^2} = -256x$.

b By writing $a = v\dfrac{dv}{dx}$ and integrating, show that $v = 16\sqrt{0.04 - x^2}$. Hence find the maximum speed of the ball.

12 Applications of differential equations

13 One end of a light spring is attached to a fixed wall. A particle P of mass m kg is attached to the other end and rests on a smooth horizontal table with the spring horizontal. P is displaced 30 cm from its equilibrium position and released from rest. When the displacement of P from equilibrium is x m the tension in the spring has magnitude 6.25m N.

  a Show that $\dfrac{d^2x}{dt^2} + 6.25x = 0$.

  b By writing $\dfrac{d^2x}{dt^2}$ as $v\dfrac{dv}{dx}$, show that $v^2 = 6.25(0.09 - x^2)$.

  c Hence find the maximum speed of the particle.

14 A cart of mass 13 kg is attached to one end of a horizontal spring. When the extension of the spring is x m the tension in the spring is $13x$ N. Initially the cart is displaced 5 m from its equilibrium position along the axis of the spring. It is held at rest and then released.

In a simple model the only force acting on the cart is the tension in the spring.

  a Find an expression for x in terms of time.

  b How long does it take for the cart to reach the equilibrium position for the first time?

  c In an improved model there is also a resistance force on the cart of magnitude $10v$ N, where v m s^{-1} is the speed of the cart.
  Find an expression for x is terms of t for the second model.

  d Which model predicts the cart reaching the equilibrium position later?

15 Find the general solution of this system of differential equations:

$$\dfrac{dx}{dt} = x - y, \quad \dfrac{dy}{dt} = 2x + y$$

16 Snakes and badgers are in competition for resources on a plain. There are no other types of animals on this plain. The populations of snakes (S) and badgers (B) at time t years are modelled by these differential equations:

$$\dfrac{dB}{dt} = B - S, \quad \dfrac{dS}{dt} = S - B$$

Initially there are 1000 badgers and 3000 snakes on the plain. Find the total number of animals on the plain after 3 months.

17 A particle of mass 3 kg is attached to two identical springs, each of natural length 1 m. The magnitude of the tension in each spring is $24e$, where e is the extension of the spring.

The other ends of the springs are attached to points A and B, which are 2.6 m apart on a smooth horizontal surface. The midpoint of AB is C.

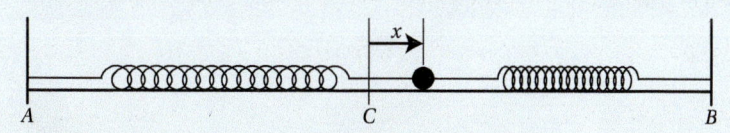

The particle is released from rest 0.15 m from C.

  a Show that, when the displacement of the particle from C is x, the magnitude of the force acting on the particle is $48x$.

  b Hence show that the particle performs simple harmonic motion, and find the period of the motion.

  c Find the speed of the particle when it is 0.05 m from C.

291

18. A railway truck, of mass m, is travelling in a straight line along a horizontal track. At time $t = 0$, the truck strikes one end of a buffer which is fixed at its other end. The buffer may be modelled as a light spring of natural length a and stiffness mn^2, where n is a positive constant. At time t, the compression of the buffer is x.

   a In a simple model of the motion, the only force affecting the truck during this motion is the thrust from the buffer.

   i Show that, while the truck is in contact with the buffer, the truck performs simple harmonic motion.

   ii Find, in terms of n, the period of this motion.

   b In a more realistic model, the motion of the truck is affected by a resistance force of magnitude mkv, where v is the speed of the truck and k is a positive constant.

   i Show that, while the buffer is being compressed, x satisfies the equation
   $$\ddot{x} + k\dot{x} + n^2 x = 0.$$

   ii At time $t = 0$, the truck is travelling with speed U. Given that $k = \dfrac{5n}{2}$, find x in terms of n, U and t.

   iii By means of a sketch, or otherwise, explain whether the type of damping is light, critical or heavy.

   [©AQA 2011]

19. A uniform metal bar, of mass m, is held at rest in a horizontal position. The ends of the bar are attached to identical light elastic strings, which each have stiffness $2m$. The strings are also attached to fixed points that are directly above the ends of the bar. A damping device is also connected to the bar.

   The bar is released from rest with the strings vertical and at their natural length. As the bar falls, it remains horizontal and the damping device exerts an upward force of magnitude cmv on the centre of the bar, where c is a constant, in appropriate units, and v is the speed of the bar.

   The motion of the bar is critically damped.

   At time t after the bar has been released, the displacement of the bar below its initial position is x.

   a Show that $c = 4$.

   b Find an expression for x in terms of g and t.

   c Find the value of x as t tends to infinity.

   d Find the maximum speed of the bar.

   [©AQA 2016]

20 In a strongman competition the competitors pull a truck (initially at rest) for 20 seconds. The winner is the person who pulls the truck furthest.

The truck has a mass of 2000 kg and is subject to a constant resistance force of 2000 N. Brawny Bill initially pulls with a force of 3000 N, but by the end of the 20 seconds he is pulling with a force of 1000 N.

   a State one assumption needed to model this force as a linear function of time. Comment on the appropriateness of this assumption.

   b Given that the assumption from part **a** is satisfied, write down a differential equation satisfied by the displacement, x, of the truck from its initial position.

   c Solve your differential equation and hence find the displacement of the truck at the end of the 20 seconds.

   d Muscly Mike models his force, F newtons, at time t seconds as $F = 3000 \times \left(\dfrac{1}{3}\right)^{\frac{t}{20}}$. Determine who wins.

13 Numerical methods

In this chapter you will learn how to:

- approximate definite integrals, using the mid-ordinate rule
- approximate definite integrals, using Simpson's rule
- find approximate numerical solutions to differential equations, using Euler's method and the improved Euler method.

Before you start…

A Level Mathematics Student Book 2, Chapter 15	You should know how to use the trapezium rule.	1	Use the trapezium rule with four strips to estimate $\int_0^2 2^{\sin x} \, dx$ correct to three significant figures.
A Level Mathematics Student Book 2, Chapter 4	You should know how to use an iterative formula.	2	If $u_{r+1} = \sqrt{u_r^2 + 2u_{r-1} - 1}$, $u_0 = 0$ and $u_1 = 1.2$, find u_4, correct to four decimal places.
A Level Mathematics Student Book 2, Chapter 13	You should be able to recognise and solve a separable differential equation.	3	Find the particular solution to the differential equation $\frac{dy}{dx} = 2xy$, where $y = 3$ when $x = 1$.
Chapter 11	You should know how to use the method of integrating factors for solving differential equations.	4	Find the particular solution to the differential equation $\frac{dy}{dx} = 6x - 2y$, where $y = 3$ when $x = 0$.
A Level Mathematics Student Book 2, Chapter 10	You should be able to use implicit differentiation.	5	Given that $\frac{dy}{dx} = 3xy - x^2$, use implicit differentiation to find an expression for $\frac{d^2y}{dx^2}$ in terms of x and y.

Approximating integrals

In integral problems you have met so far, you have been aiming either to calculate the area enclosed by the curve of a function over a given interval (definite integration) or to find the equation of the curve of which the derivative is that function (indefinite integration).

In A Level Mathematics Student Book 2, Chapter 15, you met the trapezium rule as a means of approximating the area under a curve where the function is either not explicitly known or cannot be integrated. You also learned methods for giving upper and lower bounds on the area, using rectangular strips anchored to the curve at either their upper left or upper right corners.

> ⏮ **Rewind**
>
> See A Level Mathematics Student Book 2, Chapter 15, for a reminder of upper and lower bounds for definite integrals.

13 Numerical methods

In both cases, you can generally improve the approximation by taking increasing numbers of strips. In the pre-computer era, doubling the number of strips would at least double the amount of calculation effort, and beyond a certain level the improvement in accuracy would not justify the additional effort involved. So alternative, more efficient methods were devised, which would improve accuracy with less additional effort; two such methods are the mid-ordinate rule and Simpson's rule.

Section 1: Mid-ordinate rule

The simplest way to approximate an area under a curve is to split it into vertical strips, each of which is approximated as being rectangular.

Rather than taking the end points of the intervals to form the rectangles, as you did when finding the upper and lower bounds, the **mid-ordinate rule** uses the midpoint of each interval to fit the rectangles.

With an expected error approximately half that of the trapezium rule, this method also uses fewer calculations and is therefore preferable where the number of calculations is a relevant cost.

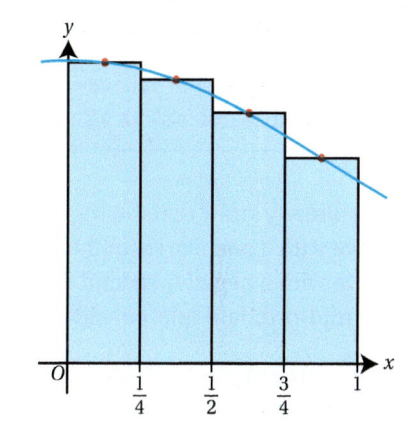

Key point 13.1

The **mid-ordinate rule** using n equal-sized intervals with end-points $a = x_0, x_1, \ldots, x_n = b$ is given by

$$\int_a^b f(x)\,dx \approx h\left[y_{\frac{1}{2}} + y_{\frac{3}{2}} + \ldots y_{n-\frac{1}{2}}\right]$$

where $h = \dfrac{b-a}{n}$.

This will be given in your formula book.

Tip

As with other numerical methods, it can be useful to lay out all the values in a table when showing your working.

WORKED EXAMPLE 13.1

Using the mid-ordinate rule with four strips, approximate $\int_1^3 2^{-x}\,dx$ to three decimal places.

$h = 0.5$ — Divide the interval from 1 to 3 into four strips.

$x_0 = 1.0$		
	$x_{0.5} = 1.25$	$y_{0.5} = 0.4204$
$x_1 = 1.5$		
	$x_{1.5} = 1.75$	$y_{1.5} = 0.2973$
$x_2 = 2.0$		
	$x_{2.5} = 2.25$	$y_{2.5} = 0.2102$
$x_3 = 2.5$		
	$x_{3.5} = 2.75$	$y_{3.5} = 0.1487$
$x_4 = 3.0$		

The x-values start at 1 and go up to 3 in increments of 0.5.

The mid-values therefore start at 1.25 and also rise in increments of 0.5.

Calculate the y-values, using $y = 2^{-x}$.

Since you want a final result accurate to three decimal places, you should either hold values in your calculator or record them to at least four decimal places of accuracy and round at the end of the calculation.

Continues on next page

295

Using the formula:

area = 0.5 [0.4204 + 0.2973 + 0.2102 + 0.1487]
     = 0.5383

So $\int_1^3 2^{-x}\,dx = 0.538$ (3 d.p.).

> You should show the values used in the calculation.

Tip

Remember that your calculator might have a TABLE function that will produce the table of values for you.

You already know that the trapezium rule will overestimate the area for a curve with a positive second derivative and underestimate the area for a curve with a negative second derivative. To see the equivalent criteria for the mid-ordinate rule, consider a single strip.

The area of the rectangular strip will be the same as the area of any trapezium with the same width and base with slanting edge that passes through the same midpoint. In particular, it will be the same as the trapezium that is tangent to the curve at the midpoint.

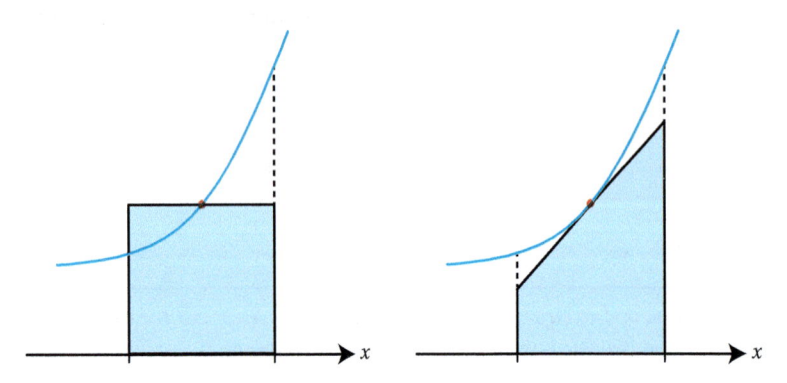

It is clear that for a convex curve like this (having a positive second derivative throughout the interval considered), the mid-ordinate rule will give an underestimate. Similarly, for a concave curve (having a negative second derivative), the mid-ordinate rule will give an overestimate. Again, it should be clear from the graph that the error will be in the opposite direction to the error from the trapezium rule in the same interval.

Rewind

For a reminder of convex and concave, see A Level Mathematics Student Book 2, Chapter 12. For a reminder of how this affects the trapezium rule, see A Level Student Book 2, Chapter 15.

Key point 13.2

The mid-ordinate rule:
- underestimates the area when the curve is convex
- overestimates the area when the curve is concave.

13 Numerical methods

EXERCISE 13A

1 For each of these curves, use the mid-ordinate rule to estimate the area beneath the curve for the given interval to three decimal places with:

  i four strips **ii** six strips.

  a $y = \ln(1+x^2)$ for $0 \leq x \leq 2$
  b $y = x^x$ for $1 \leq x \leq 3$
  c $y = 2^{\sin x}$ for $0 \leq x \leq 2\pi$
  d $y = (1+x)^{\cos x}$ for $0 \leq x \leq \pi$

2 Use the mid-ordinate rule, with:

  i four intervals **ii** five intervals

  to find the approximate value of each of these integrals, giving your answers to three significant figures.

  a $\int_0^1 e^{\sqrt{x}}\,dx$
  b $\int_0^2 e^{-x^2}\,dx$
  c $\int_0^\pi \dfrac{1}{x^2+1}\,dx$
  d $\int_2^3 \ln(x^2-2)\,dx$

3 For each integral in Question **2**:

  i use technology to find the value correct to eight decimal places
  ii use a spreadsheet to calculate mid-ordinate approximations, using 2, 4, 8 and 16 intervals
  iii find the percentage errors in each approximation and assess how the error changes as the number of intervals is doubled.

4 **a** Sketch the graph of $y = 4\ln(x-1)$.

  b Use the mid-ordinate rule with five strips to estimate the value of $\int_2^4 4\ln(x-1)\,dx$, giving your answer to two decimal places.

  c Explain whether your answer is an overestimate or an underestimate.

5 **a** Use the mid-ordinate rule with four intervals to find an approximate value for $\int_3^4 e^{\sqrt{4-x}}\,dx$ to three decimal places.

  b Describe how you could use the mid-ordinate rule to obtain a more accurate approximation.

6 The diagram shows a part of the graph of $y = \cos x^3$.

  a is the first positive root of the equation $\cos x^3 = 0$.

  a Find the exact value of a.

  b Use the mid-ordinate rule with four intervals to find an approximation to four decimal places for $\int_0^a \cos x^3\,dx$.

  c Is your approximation an overestimate or an underestimate? Explain your answer.

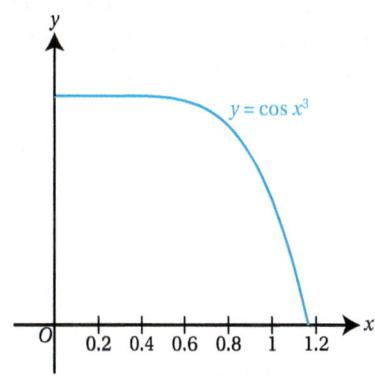

7. The velocity $v\,\text{m s}^{-1}$ of a particle moving in a straight line is given by $v = \dfrac{1}{t+1}\sin(\sqrt{t})$. The diagram shows the velocity–time graph for the particle.

   a The particle changes direction at $t = a$ and $t = b$ $(0 < a < b)$. Find the values a and b.

   b Use the mid-ordinate rule, with eight intervals, to estimate the total distance travelled by the particle during the first b seconds of movement.

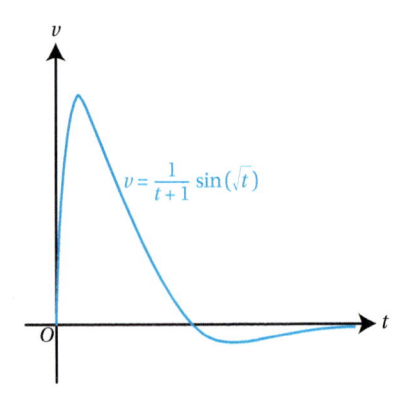

Section 2: Simpson's rule

When applying the trapezium rule or the mid-ordinate rule, you are using a straight line to approximate the curve for each strip; the trapezium rule uses the chord that connects the two end-points of the curve in the strip interval and the mid-ordinate rule uses a rectangle at the midpoint of the strip.

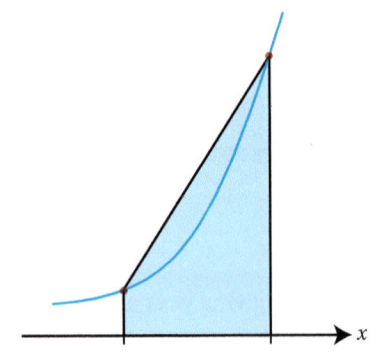

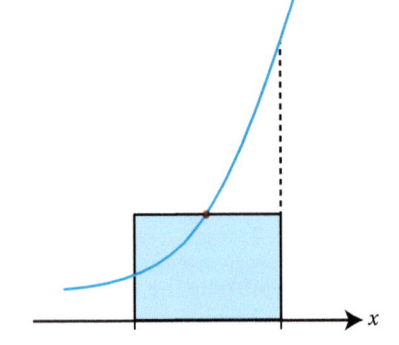

For a more accurate approximation of the curve in the strips, it is possible to fit a quadratic instead of a straight line. While a straight line is defined by any two points on it, a quadratic is defined by any three points on the curve. Conventionally, the area to be approximated is divided into an even number of strips, and a quadratic curve fitted to each pair of strips so that it passes through the three points defined on the curve by the strip boundaries.

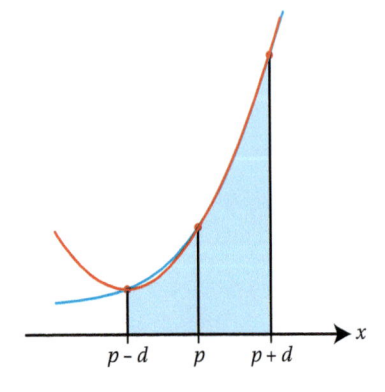

13 Numerical methods

PROOF 10

A quadratic curve passing through points $(p-d, y_0)$, (p, y_1) and $(p+d, y_2)$ will have area $\frac{d}{3}(4y_1 + y_0 + y_2)$ over that interval.

The general equation for a quadratic is $y = ax^2 + bx + c$.

Substituting the values of the coordinates:
$$y_0 = a(p^2 - 2pd + d^2) + b(p - d) + c \quad (1)$$
$$y_1 = ap^2 + bp + c \quad (2)$$
$$y_2 = a(p^2 + 2pd + d^2) + b(p + d) + c \quad (3)$$

Substitute $(p-d, y_0)$, (p, y_1) and $(p+d, y_2)$ into the quadratic.

$(1) + (3)$: $y_0 + y_2 = 2ap^2 + 2ad^2 + 2bp \quad (4)$

The area under the curve between $p - d$ and $p + d$ is:

$$\int_{p-d}^{p+d} ax^2 + bx + c \, dx = \left[\frac{1}{3}ax^3 + \frac{1}{2}bx^2 + cx\right]_{p-d}^{p+d}$$

$$= 2adp^2 + \frac{2}{3}ad^3 + 2bdp + 2cd$$

$$= \frac{d}{3}[6ap^2 + 2ad^2 + 6bp + 4c]$$

$$= \frac{d}{3}[4ap^2 + 4bp + 4c + 2ap^2 + 2ad^2 + 2bp]$$

$$= \frac{d}{3}(4y_1 + y_0 + y_2)$$

Use equations (2) and (4).

Using the fact in Proof 10, you can approximate the area beneath a curve of several pairs of strips.

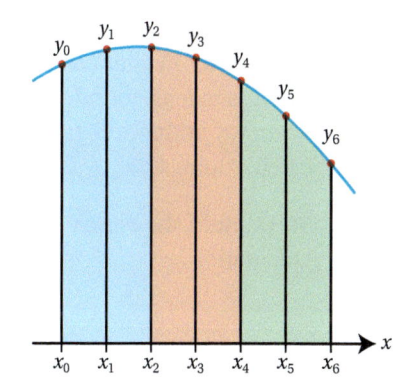

The first pair has area $\frac{d}{3}(y_0 + 4y_1 + y_2)$.

The second pair has area $\frac{d}{3}(y_2 + 4y_3 + y_4)$.

The third pair has area $\frac{d}{3}(y_4 + 4y_5 + y_6)$.

Adding these up: the end points y_0 and y_6 are seen once; the odd-numbered values y_1, y_3 and y_5, which are the heights at the centre of each pair of strips, are each seen once with a multiple of 4; the even numbered values y_2 and y_4 at the junctions between pairs are each seen twice with a multiple of 1.

This can be generalised to give **Simpson's rule**.

> **Key point 13.3**
>
> Simpson's rule using an even number n of equal-sized intervals with end points $a = x_0, x_1, \ldots, x_n = b$ is given by:
>
> $$\int_a^b f(x)\,dx \approx \frac{h}{3}[y_0 + y_n + 2(y_2 + y_4 + \ldots + y_{n-2}) + 4(y_1 + y_3 + \ldots + y_{n-1})]$$
>
> where $h = \frac{b-a}{n}$.
>
> **This will be given in your formula book.**

> **Tip**
>
> As with other numerical methods, it can be useful to lay out all the values in a table when showing your working.

WORKED EXAMPLE 13.2

Using Simpson's rule with four strips, approximate $\int_1^3 2^{-x}\,dx$ to three decimal places.

$h = 0.5$ — Divide the interval from 1 to 3 into 4 strips.

		Multiple	
$x_0 = 1.0$	$y_0 = 0.5$	1	0.5
$x_1 = 1.5$	$y_1 = 0.3536$	4	1.4142
$x_2 = 2.0$	$y_2 = 0.25$	2	0.5
$x_3 = 2.5$	$y_3 = 0.1768$	4	0.7071
$x_4 = 3.0$	$y_4 = 0.125$	1	0.125
	Sum		3.2463

The x-values start at 1 and go up to 3 in increments of 0.5.

Calculate the y-values, using $y = 2^{-x}$.

Since you want a final result accurate to three decimal places, you should either hold values in your calculator or record them to at least four decimal places of accuracy and round at the end of the calculation.

Using the formula:

Area $= \frac{0.5}{3} \times 3.2463 = 0.5411$.

So $\int_1^3 2^{-x}\,dx = 0.541$ (3 s.f.).

You should show the values used in the calculation.

Since the true value of the integral in Worked example 13.2 is

$$\left[-\frac{1}{\ln 2} \times 2^{-x}\right]_1^3 = \frac{3}{8 \ln 2} = 0.541\,011,$$ the Simpson's rule approximation shown

is an improvement on the mid-ordinate rule approximation of 0.538 from Worked example 13.1, and in general you can expect Simpson's rule, for the same number of strips, to give a better approximation than any of the linear methods.

13 Numerical methods

ⓘ Did you know?

Since the error for the mid-ordinate rule is approximately half that of the trapezium rule, and in the opposite direction (one will overestimate and the other will underestimate, depending on whether the curve is convex or concave), taking a weighted average of the two in an attempt to cancel out the bulk of the error might seem a sensible step. If M represents the approximation by the mid-ordinate rule and T the approximation by the trapezium rule, then $S = \dfrac{2M + T}{3}$ should be an improvement on both, and is an alternative representation of Simpson's rule.

EXERCISE 13B

1 For each of these curves, use Simpson's rule to estimate the area beneath the curve for the given interval to three decimal places with:

  i four strips **ii** six strips.

  a $y = \ln(1 + x^2)$ for $0 \leqslant x \leqslant 2$ **b** $y = x^x$ for $1 \leqslant x \leqslant 3$

  c $y = 2^{\sin x}$ for $0 \leqslant x \leqslant 2\pi$ **d** $y = (1 + x)^{\cos x}$ for $0 \leqslant x \leqslant \pi$

2 Use Simpson's rule, with:

  i five ordinates **ii** seven ordinates

  to find the approximate value of each of these integrals, giving your answers to four significant figures.

  a $\displaystyle\int_0^1 e^{\sqrt{x}}\,dx$ **b** $\displaystyle\int_0^2 e^{-x^2}\,dx$

  c $\displaystyle\int_0^\pi \dfrac{1}{x^2 + 1}\,dx$ **d** $\displaystyle\int_2^3 \ln(x^2 - 2)\,dx$

> **! Common error**
>
> A question might specify the number of strips, intervals or ordinates when using Simpson's rule. Remember that the number of ordinates means the number of x-values, so five ordinates means $x_0, x_1, ..., x_4$, the boundary values for four strips.

3 For each integral in Question **2**:

  i use technology to find the value, correct to six decimal places

  ii use a spreadsheet to calculate Simpson's rule approximations, using 2, 4, 8 and 16 intervals

  iii find the percentage errors in each approximation and assess how the error changes as the number of intervals is doubled.

4 a Sketch the graph of $y = 2\ln(x^2 + 1)$ for $0 \leqslant x \leqslant 4$.

  b Use Simpson's rule with six strips to estimate the value of $\displaystyle\int_1^4 2\ln(x^2 + 1)\,dx$, giving your answer to three decimal places.

5 a Use Simpson's rule with five ordinates to find an approximate value for $\displaystyle\int_2^4 e^{\cos 2x}\,dx$.

  b Describe how you could use Simpson's rule to obtain a more accurate approximation.

301

6 The diagram shows a part of the graph of $y = 1 - \sin \sqrt{x}$.

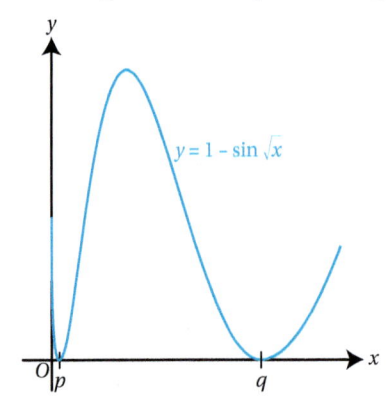

p and q are, respectively, the first and second positive roots of the equation $1 - \sin \sqrt{x} = 0$.

  a Find the exact values of p and q.
  b Use Simpson's rule with six intervals to find an approximation for $\int_p^q 1 - \sin \sqrt{x} \, dx$ to three decimal places.

7 a Write down the exact area A of the semicircle with curved edge defined by $y = \sqrt{1 - x^2}$.

  b i Explain why, when estimating the value of $\int_{-1}^{1} \sqrt{1 - x^2} \, dx$, using Simpson's rule with seven ordinates, it is preferable to use ordinates from 0 to 1 than from -1 to 1.

     ii Use Simpson's rule with seven ordinates to find the approximate value of $\int_{-1}^{1} \sqrt{1 - x^2} \, dx$, giving your answer correct to three decimal places.

  c Hence find an approximation to the value of π.

Section 3: Euler's method

In Sections 1 and 2, you met two new methods for approximating the definite integral for a function given solely in terms of x.

However, in many mathematical models, a differential equation is formed where $\dfrac{dy}{dx}$ is a function of both x and y. You already know how to approach some such problems if they are separable or can be rearranged as linear differential equations, but there are many differential equations that cannot be solved analytically.

> ⏮ **Rewind**
>
> See Chapter 11 for a reminder of how to solve linear differential equations.

If you know a point on the required solution curve, then you can use the principles encountered in Chapter 10, Section 1, on Maclaurin series:

The Maclaurin series of a function is $g(x) = g(0) + xg'(0) + \dfrac{x^2}{2}g''(0) + \ldots$

If you apply a translation to this expansion such that $f(x + a) = g(x)$, you obtain the expansion about an arbitrary value a rather than about 0.

$$f(a + x) = f(a) + xf'(a) + \frac{1}{2}x^2 f''(a) + \ldots$$

The simplest approximation to track the curve uses the first two terms of this expansion:

$$y(a+h) \approx y(a) + hy'(a).$$

> **Tip**
>
> Notice that this formula is a rearrangement of $y'(a) \approx \dfrac{y(a+h) - y(a)}{h}$; in the limit as $h \to 0$ you know this as the first principles definition of the derivative.

> **Did you know?**
>
> This generalisation of Maclaurin series is called a Taylor series after the English mathematician Brook Taylor who formalised this idea. The Scottish mathematician Colin Maclaurin then made use of the particular case where $a = 0$.

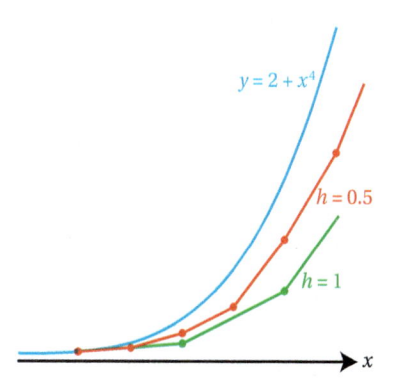

Geometrically, this means that if you know a point on the curve and the gradient at that point, you can estimate the position of another point on the curve by extending the tangent.

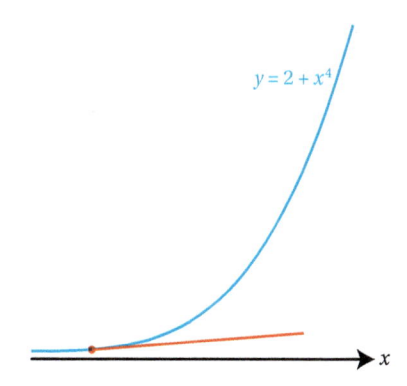

For values of x far from the known point, the approximation gets increasingly unreliable. To keep the approximated path close to the curve, you can recalculate the gradient according to the formula for the derivative. As in all the approximations encountered so far, the smaller the value of h, the more accurate you can expect the approximation to be.

The diagram shows the curve $y = 2 + x^4$ along with two approximations that both begin at the point on the curve with $x = 0.5$. You can see that the approximation error is approximately halved by halving the distance h.

You can take this principle a step further for the general case where the derivative is a function of both x and y. To track the series of tangents you use the general formula for **Euler's method**.

> **Did you know?**
>
> A plot of tangents at regular points (x, y) in the plane is called a slope field diagram and can be used to sketch curves. Try plotting slope field diagrams for Worked example 13.3 and for part **a** of Question 1 in Exercise 13C and use them to sketch curves.

> **Key point 13.4**
>
> **Euler's method**: for $\dfrac{dy}{dx} = f(x, y)$ and known point $y(x_0) = y_0$,
>
> $y_{r+1} = y_r + hf(x_r, y_r)$, where $x_{r+1} = x_r + h$.
>
> **This will be given in your formula book.**

Notice that in the approximation to the curve $y = 2 + x^4$ shown, each line section was parallel to the tangent to the curve vertically above it (because the gradient is a function solely in x). This will not be the case when the gradient is a function of both x and y.

WORKED EXAMPLE 13.3

The function $y(x)$ satisfies the differential equation $\frac{dy}{dx} = f(x, y)$ where $f(x, y) = x + y$ and $y(1) = 2$.

Use the Euler formula $y_{r+1} = y_r + h f(x_r, y_r)$, with $h = 0.1$, to obtain an approximation to $y(1.3)$, giving your answer to three decimal places.

$y(1) = 2, h = 0.1$	State the start value and the interval h.
Using the Euler formula:	At each step, apply the Euler formula $y_{r+1} = y_r + h f(x_r, y_r)$, using the previous value of x and y as x_r and y_r.
$y(1.1) \approx 2 + 0.1(1 + 2) = 2.3$	
$y(1.2) \approx 2.3 + 0.1(1.1 + 2.3) = 2.64$	
$y(1.3) \approx 2.64 + 0.1(1.2 + 2.64) = 3.024$	

You should recognise that the differential equation in Worked example 13.3 is solvable using the method of integrating factors, with solution $y = 4e^{x-1} - x - 1$.

Plotting the solution from Worked example 13.3 against the actual curve shows the approximation accumulating errors with each step.

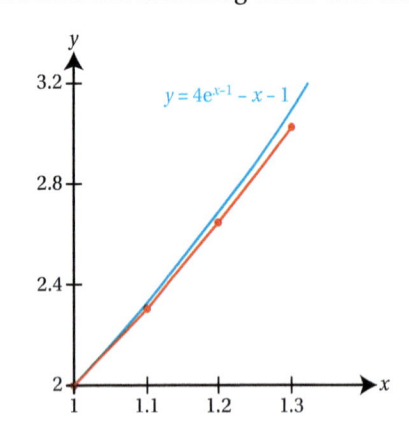

> **Rewind**
>
> See Chapter 11, Section 2, for the method of solving a first order linear differential equation using the integrating factor.

EXERCISE 13C

1 Use Euler's method with step length $h = 0.1$ to find an approximate value of $y(0.4)$ for these differential equations.

    a i $\frac{dy}{dx} = x^2 - y^2,\ y(0) = 1$ **ii** $\frac{dy}{dx} = \ln(x + y),\ y(0) = 2$

    b i $\frac{dy}{dx} - y^2 = \sin(x^2),\ y(0) = 1$ **ii** $\frac{dy}{dx} - y = 2e^x,\ y(0) = 0$

    c i $(x + y)\frac{dy}{dx} = 3x^2 + y^2,\ y(0) = 2$ **ii** $(x + y)\frac{dy}{dx} = e^{x + 0.2y},\ y(0) = 1$

13 Numerical methods

2 For the differential equation $\dfrac{dy}{dx} = \dfrac{x+y}{xy+2}$ with $y(0) = 1$, use Euler's method with step length $h = 0.2$ to find an approximate value of $y(1)$. Give your answer correct to three decimal places.

3 Consider the differential equation $\dfrac{dy}{dx} = xe^x$ with the boundary condition $y(1) = 0.3$.

  a Use Euler's method with $h = 0.1$ to find an approximate value of $y(1.3)$.

  b Solve the differential equation.

  c **i** Find the percentage error in your approximation from part **a**.

     ii How can this error be decreased?

4 The function $y = g(x)$ satisfies the differential equation $g'(x) = x^2 y$ with $g(0) = 0.5$.

  a **i** Use Euler's method with step length $h = 0.25$ to find an approximate value of $g(1)$.

     ii How can your approximation be made more accurate?

  b Solve the differential equation and hence find the actual value of $g(1)$.

  c Sketch the graph of your solution and use it to explain why your approximation from part **a** is smaller than the actual value of $g(1)$.

5 Consider the differential equation $\dfrac{d^2 y}{dx^2} = 6xe^{-x^2}$ where $y = 1$ and $\dfrac{dy}{dx} = 1$ when $x = 0$.

  a Find an expression for $\dfrac{dy}{dx}$ in terms of x.

  b Use Euler's method with step length $h = 0.2$ to find the approximate value of y when $x = 1$.

Section 4: Improved Euler's method

As seen in Section 3, when making the second approximation using Euler's method, if the curve continues convex or concave then you will compound any error from the first approximation.

If $P_0(x_0, y_0)$ is the known point on the curve, you obtain point P_1, using Euler's method, taking the tangent at P_0 over the interval distance h, so that $x_1 = x_0 + h$ and $y_1 = y_0 + f(x_0, y_0)$.

Just using the original Euler method, you would obtain the second approximation point P_2 by taking a tangent at point P_1 over interval h. If the curve continues concave or convex, this tangent at P_1 will be at a distance from the curve.

However, translating the tangent at P_1 so that it passes through P_0 will give a better estimate Q_2; this leads to an amended approximation when iterating.

> 🔑 **Key point 13.5**
>
> The **improved Euler method**: for $\dfrac{dy}{dx} = f(x, y)$ and known point $y(x_0) = y_0$,
>
> $$y_{r+1} = y_{r-1} + 2h f(x_r, y_r), \text{ where } x_{r+1} = x_r + h.$$
>
> **This will be given in your formula book.**

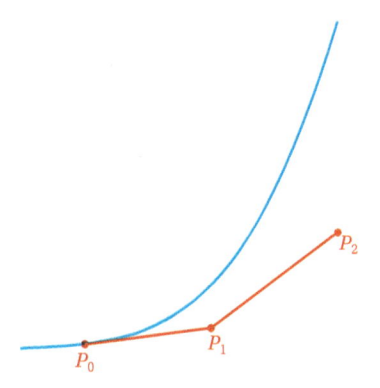

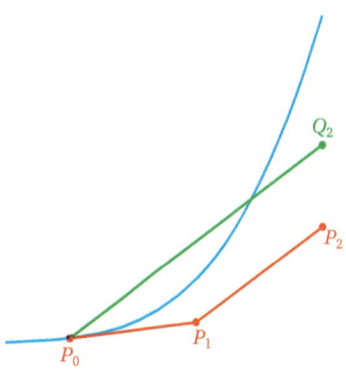

305

A Level Further Mathematics for AQA Student Book 2

WORKED EXAMPLE 13.4

It is given that $y(x)$ satisfies the differential equation $\dfrac{dy}{dx} = f(x, y)$, where $f(x, y) = \dfrac{x - y^2}{2x}$ and $y(2) = 3$.

a Use the Euler formula $y_{r+1} = y_r + hf(x_r, y_r)$, with $h = 0.1$, to obtain an approximation to $y(2.1)$.

b Use the improved Euler formula $y_{r+1} = y_{r-1} + 2hf(x_r, y_r)$ with your answer to part **a** to obtain an approximation to $y(2.2)$, giving your answer to three significant figures.

a $y(2) = 3, h = 0.1$ — State the start value and the interval h.

Using the Euler formula: — Apply the Euler formula $y_{r+1} = y_r + hf(x_r, y_r)$.

$y(2.1) \approx 3 + 0.1 \times \dfrac{(2 - 3^2)}{2 \times 2} = 2.825$

b $f(2.1, 2.825) = -1.40$ — Calculate the gradient at the approximated point (x_1, y_1).

$y(2.2) \approx 3 + 2 \times 0.1 \times (-1.40) = 2.72$ — Apply the improved Euler formula $y_{r+1} = y_{r-1} + 2hf(x_r, y_r)$.

EXERCISE 13D

1 In each part of this question, $y(x)$ satisfies the differential equation $\dfrac{dy}{dx} = f(x, y)$ for the given function $f(x)$ and known value $y(a)$.

Use the Euler formula $y_{r+1} = y_r + hf(x_r, y_r)$ to find $y(a + h)$ and then use the improved Euler formula $y_{r+1} = y_{r-1} + 2hf(x_r, y_r)$ to find $y(a + 2h)$, giving each answer correct to three significant figures.

a i $f(x, y) = \sqrt{x^2 + y^2}$, $y(1) = 3$, $h = 0.1$
   ii $f(x, y) = \sqrt{x + 2y}$, $y(1) = 2$, $h = 1$

b i $f(x, y) = x + \sin y$, $y(2) = 0$, $h = 0.1$
   ii $f(x, y) = \cos(xy)$, $y(\pi) = 1$, $h = 0.2$

c i $f(x, y) = \dfrac{x + 3y}{y^2}$, $y(0) = 1$, $h = 0.01$
   ii $f(x, y) = \dfrac{2x^2 - y}{xy^2}$, $y(2) = 1$, $h = 0.1$

d i $f(x, y) = 2^{-xy}$, $y(1) = 0$, $h = 0.01$
   ii $f(x, y) = 2^{\cos(xy)}$, $y(0) = 1$, $h = 0.1$

2 It is given that $y(x)$ satisfies the differential equation $\dfrac{dy}{dx} = f(x, y)$, where $f(x, y) = \dfrac{2x + \sqrt{y}}{2x}$ and $y(1) = 1$.

a Use the Euler formula $y_{r+1} = y_r + hf(x_r, y_r)$, with $h = 0.1$, to obtain an approximation to $y(1.1)$.

b Use the improved Euler formula $y_{r+1} = y_{r-1} + 2hf(x_r, y_r)$ with your answer to part **a**, to obtain an approximation to $y(1.2)$, giving your answer to three significant figures.

3 It is given that $y(x)$ satisfies the differential equation $\dfrac{dy}{dx} = f(x, y)$, where $f(x, y) = 2\sqrt{xy} + \dfrac{1}{x}$ and $y(1) = 1$.

a Use the Euler formula $y_{r+1} = y_r + hf(x_r, y_r)$, with $h = 0.1$, to obtain an approximation to $y(1.1)$.

b Use the Euler formula with $h = 0.05$ followed by the improved Euler formula $y_{r+1} = y_{r-1} + 2hf(x_r, y_r)$ to obtain an alternative approximation to $y(1.1)$, giving your answer to three decimal places.

c Without further calculation, state, with reasoning, which approximation you consider likely to be more accurate.

13 Numerical methods

4 It is given that $y(x)$ satisfies the differential equation $\dfrac{dy}{dx} = f(x, y)$, where $f(x, y) = x + y$ and $y(3) = c$.

  a Use the Euler formula $y_{r+1} = y_r + h\,f(x_r, y_r)$, with $h = 0.1$, to obtain an approximation to $y(3.1)$, in terms of c.

  b The improved Euler formula $y_{r+1} = y_{r-1} + 2h\,f(x_r, y_r)$ is used in conjunction with the Euler formula in part **a** to obtain an approximation $y(3.2) = 1.656$. Find c.

5 It is given that $y(x)$ satisfies the differential equation $\dfrac{dy}{dx} = f(x, y)$, where $f(x, y) = \dfrac{2}{1 + xy} - \dfrac{y}{x}$ and $y(1) = 2$.

  a Use the Euler formula $y_{r+1} = y_r + h\,f(x_r, y_r)$, with $h = 0.1$, to obtain an approximation to $y(1.1)$.

  b Use the improved Euler formula $y_{r+1} = y_{r-1} + 2h\,f(x_r, y_r)$, with your answer to part **a**, to obtain an approximation to $y(1.2)$, giving your answer to four decimal places.

  c **i** Using the substitution $u = xy$, or otherwise, solve the differential equation, giving your answer in the form $y = \dfrac{\sqrt{a + bx^2} - c}{x}$.

   ii Find the percentage error in the approximation from part **b**.

Checklist of learning and understanding

- The mid-ordinate rule and Simpson's rule are more sophisticated methods of approximating a definite integral than the trapezium rule.
- The **mid-ordinate rule** using n equal-sized intervals with end points $a = x_0, x_1, \ldots, x_n = b$ is given by

$$\int_a^b f(x)\,dx \approx h\left[y_{\frac{1}{2}} + y_{\frac{3}{2}} + \ldots y_{n-\frac{1}{2}}\right],$$

 where $h = \dfrac{b-a}{n}$.

- The mid-ordinate rule:
  - underestimates the area when the curve is convex
  - overestimates the area when the curve is concave.
- **Simpson's rule** using an even number n of equal-sized intervals with end points $a = x_0, x_1, \ldots, x_n = b$ is given by

$$\int_a^b f(x)\,dx \approx \dfrac{h}{3}[y_0 + y_n + 2(y_2 + y_4 \ldots + y_{n-2}) + 4(y_1 + y_3 \ldots + y_{n-1})],$$

 where $h = \dfrac{b-a}{n}$.

- Euler's method and associated variations are methods of approximating the path of a curve from a formula for the first derivative.
- **Euler's method**: for $\dfrac{dy}{dx} = f(x, y)$ and known point $y(x_0) = y_0$.

$$y_{r+1} = y_r + h\,f(x_r, y_r), \text{ where } x_{r+1} = x_r + h.$$

- **Improved Euler method**: for $\dfrac{dy}{dx} = f(x, y)$ and known point $y(x_0) = y_0$.

$$y_{r+1} = y_{r-1} + 2h\,f(x_r, y_r), \text{ where } x_{r+1} = x_r + h.$$

Mixed practice 13

1. Simpson's rule with nine ordinates is used to find an estimate for $\int_1^7 f(x)\,dx$.

   What is the width of each interval?

   Choose from these options.

   A $\dfrac{1}{6}$ **B** $\dfrac{3}{5}$ **C** $\dfrac{2}{3}$ **D** $\dfrac{3}{4}$

2. Use the mid-ordinate rule with four strips to estimate $\int_1^3 \sqrt{2+x}\,dx$, giving your answer correct to three decimal places.

3. Use the mid-ordinate rule with five strips to estimate
   $$\int_2^4 2^{5-x^2}\,dx,$$
   giving your answer correct to four decimal places.

4. The function $f(x) = 5 - \dfrac{1}{2}x^2$.

   Use Simpson's rule with seven ordinates to find the approximate value of $\int_3^4 e^{f(x)}\,dx$, giving your answer correct to three decimal places.

5. Use Simpson's rule with seven ordinates (six strips) to estimate
   $$\int_2^8 \dfrac{x^2 - \sqrt{1+x}}{1 + x\sqrt{1+x}}\,dx$$
   giving your answer correct to three decimal places.

6. The function $y(x)$ satisfies the differential equation $\dfrac{dy}{dx} = f(x, y)$,

   where $f(x, y) = x + \sqrt{y}$ and $y(2) = 4$.

   Use the Euler formula $y_{r+1} = y_r + h f(x_r, y_r)$ with $h = 0.1$, to obtain an approximation to $y(2.2)$, giving your answer to three decimal places.

7. The function $y(x)$ satisfies the differential equation $\dfrac{dy}{dx} = f(x, y)$,

   where $f(x, y) = x^3 y - x$ and $y(1) = 2$.

   a Use the Euler formula $y_{r+1} = y_r + h f(x_r, y_r)$, with $h = 0.1$, to find the approximate value of $y(1.1)$.

   b Use the improved Euler formula $y_{r+1} = y_{r-1} + 2h f(x_r, y_r)$ to find $y(1.2)$, correct to three significant figures.

8 The function $y(x)$ satisfies the differential equation

$$\frac{dy}{dx} = f(x, y),$$

where $f(x, y) = x \ln(2x + y)$ and $y(3) = 2$.

a Use the Euler formula,

$$y_{r+1} = y_r + h f(x_r, y_r)$$

with $h = 0.1$, to obtain an approximation to $y(3.1)$, giving your answer to four decimal places.

b Use the improved Euler formula

$$y_{r+1} = y_{r-1} + 2h f(x_r, y_r),$$

with $h = 0.1$, to obtain an approximation to $y(3.1)$, giving your answer to four decimal places.

[©AQA 2010]

9 The function $y(x)$ satisfies the differential equation

$$\frac{dy}{dx} = f(x, y),$$

where $f(x, y) = x + 3 + \sin y$ and $y(1) = 1$.

a Use the Euler formula

$$y_{r+1} = y_r + h f(x_r, y_r),$$

with $h = 0.1$, to obtain an approximation to $y(1.1)$, giving your answer to four decimal places.

b Use the improved Euler formula

$$y_{r+1} = y_{r-1} + 2h f(x_r, y_r),$$

with your answer to part **a**, to obtain an approximation to $y(1.2)$, giving your answer to three decimal places.

[©AQA 2010]

10 The mid-ordinate rule with n equal intervals is used to find an estimate for $\int_a^b f(x)\,dx$, where for $x \in (a, b)$, $f(x) > 0$ and $f'(x) < 0$.

What will happen to the value obtained by the mid-ordinate rule if $n + 1$ equal intervals are now used?

Choose from these options.

A Increase

B Decrease

C Stay the same

D It depends on the particular function f.

11 a Use the mid-ordinate rule with six strips to estimate $\int_3^6 \frac{4\sqrt{x} + 2x}{x - 1}\,dx$, correct to three decimal places.

b Using the substitution $x = u^2$, calculate the true value of the integral to three decimal places.

c Calculate the percentage error of the approximation.

d How might the approximation with the mid-ordinate rule be improved?

A Level Further Mathematics for AQA Student Book 2

12 A class is asked to use Simpson's rule with five ordinates (four strips) to estimate $\int_{-1}^{1} e^{-\frac{1}{2}x^2} dx$.

  a Most of the students used $h = 0.5$. Show that the approximate value the students calculated is 1.712, correct to three decimal places.

  Some of the students answered the question using $h = 0.25$ instead.

  b Explain their reasoning and, without further working, suggest whether they will get a more or less accurate estimate.

13 Simpson's rule, with two pairs of strips, is used to approximate $\int_0^k x^3 dx$.

  a Show that the value obtained by Simpson's rule is exactly accurate.

  b Without further calculation, explain why this result can be generalised to the approximation of any integral of a cubic equation

  $$\int_{k_1}^{k_2} ax^3 + bx^2 + cx + d \, dx$$

  using Simpson's rule with two pairs of strips.

14 The function $y(x)$ satisfies the differential equation $\dfrac{dy}{dx} = f(x, y)$, where $f(x, y) = 2x + \sqrt{y}$ and $y(0) = 1$.

  a Use the Euler formula $y_{r+1} = y_r + h f(x_r, y_r)$ to estimate $y(0.2)$ to four decimal places, using a step size:

   i $h = 0.1$ **ii** $h = 0.2$.

  b Which of your answers to part **a** do you expect to be more accurate? Justify your answer.

15 a Use the mid-ordinate rule with four strips to find an estimate for $\int_{1.5}^{5.5} e^{2-x} \ln(3x - 2) \, dx$, giving your answer to three decimal places.

  b Find the exact value of the gradient of the curve $y = e^{2-x} \ln(3x - 2)$ at the point on the curve where $x = 2$.

[©AQA 2015]

16 a Use Simpson's rule with seven ordinates (six strips) to find an approximation to

  $$\int_{0.5}^{1.7} (5 - x^x) \, dx,$$

  giving your answer to three significant figures.

  b Hence find an approximation to $\int_{0.5}^{1.7} x^x \, dx$.

[©AQA 2016, adapted]

17 Use Simpson's rule, with five ordinates (four strips), to calculate an estimate for $\int_0^\pi x^{\frac{1}{2}} \sin x \, dx$.

Give your answer to four significant figures.

[©AQA 2014]

18 The mid-ordinate rule with two strips is used to estimate $\int_0^{2a} 16x^4 \, dx$.

What is the percentage error in the estimate?

19 The function $y(x)$ satisfies the differential equation $\frac{dy}{dx} = f(x, y)$, where $f(x, y) = 3x - 2y$ and $y(0) = c$, where c is a constant.

   a The Euler formula $y_{r+1} = y_r + h f(x_r, y_r)$ is used with a step size $h = 0.1$ to give the approximation $y(0.2) = 0.99$. Find c.

   b Using the method of integrating factors, or otherwise, find the particular solution to the differential equation.

   c Calculate the percentage error in the approximation $y(0.2) = 0.99$.

20 a It is given that $y(x)$ satisfies the differential equation
   $$\frac{dy}{dx} = f(x, y),$$
   where $f(x, y) = (2x + 1) \ln(x + y)$ and $y(0) = 2$.

   Use the Euler formula $y_{r+1} = y_r + h f(x_r, y_r)$, with a step size $h = 0.1$, to obtain an approximation to $y(0.1)$, giving your answer to three decimal places.

   b It is given that $y(x)$ satisfies the differential equation
   $$\frac{dy}{dx} = (2x + 1) \ln(x + y)$$
   and $y = 2$ when $x = 0$.

   i Use implicit differentiation to find $\frac{d^2 y}{dx^2}$, giving your answer in terms of x and y.

   ii Hence find the first three non-zero terms in the expansion, in ascending powers of x, of $y(x)$. Give your answer in an exact form.

   iii Use your answer to part **b ii** to obtain an approximation to $y(0.1)$, giving your answer to three decimal places.

[©AQA 2016, adapted]

FOCUS ON ... PROOF 2

Elements of area and Gaussian integrals

You have seen that you can find areas under a curve, using an integral, which you thought of as summing up lots of little rectangles. In more advanced work it is useful to sum up lots of little elements of area instead and do a double sum over all coordinates. You can write this as:

$$A = \iint dA$$

where, in Cartesian coordinates, $dA = dy\,dx$.

The double integrals become

$$A = \int_{x=a}^{x=b} \left(\int_{y=c}^{y=d} dy \right) dx.$$

> **Tip**
>
> This Focus on section extends significantly beyond the scope of the specification, but it will be of interest to anyone wanting to go on to study Mathematics, Physics, Chemistry, Engineering or Theoretical Economics.

If you are looking for the area between a curve and the x-axis, then the limits on y are from 0 to $f(x)$ so the area is:

$$A = \int_{x=a}^{x=b} \left(\int_{y=0}^{y=f(x)} dy \right) dx$$

$$= \int_{x=a}^{x=b} \left[y \right]_0^{f(x)} dx$$

$$= \int_{x=a}^{x=b} f(x)\,dx$$

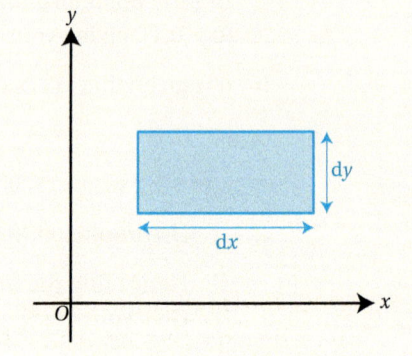

which is the formula you are used to using.

In Chapter 7 you found that the area between two half lines in polar coordinates is given by

$$A = \int_\alpha^\beta \frac{1}{2} r^2 \, d\theta.$$

You can derive this, using a similar method to the one shown for Cartesian coordinates. In the diagram the shaded area is approximately a rectangle with one dimension $r\,d\theta$ (using the formula for arc length in radians) and the other dr.

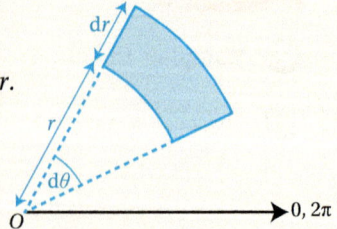

The area element in polar coordinates is therefore:

$$dA = r\,dr\,d\theta$$

QUESTION

1 Prove that the area bounded by the lines $\theta = \alpha$, $\theta = \beta$ and $r = r(\theta)$ is given by the formula

$$A = \int_\alpha^\beta \frac{1}{2} r^2 \, d\theta.$$

These area elements have some lovely consequences, including allowing you to evaluate otherwise impossible integrals.

Consider the integral $I = \int_{x=-\infty}^{x=\infty} e^{-x^2}\,dx$.

> **Rewind**
>
> This is an example of an improper integral, which you met in Chapter 10.

You cannot find the indefinite integral of e^{-x^2}, using standard functions, however you can evaluate this definite integral exactly. The x in the integral is just a dummy variable. You could also write

$$I = \int_{y=-\infty}^{y=\infty} e^{-y^2}\,dy$$

Multiplying the two expressions together:

$$I^2 = \int_{x=-\infty}^{x=\infty} e^{-x^2}\,dx \int_{y=-\infty}^{y=\infty} e^{-y^2}\,dy$$

It turns out that you can combine these two integrals into one double integral:

$$I^2 = \int_{x=-\infty}^{x=\infty} \int_{y=-\infty}^{y=\infty} e^{-y^2} e^{-x^2}\,dy\,dx$$

$$= \int_{x=-\infty}^{x=\infty} \int_{y=-\infty}^{y=\infty} e^{-y^2-x^2}\,dy\,dx$$

But $dx\,dy = dA$ is just an element of area, so you could rewrite it as $r\,dr\,d\theta$. You can recast the whole expression in terms of polar coordinates, noting that $x^2 + y^2 = r^2$ and that the limits represent the whole plane:

$$I^2 = \int_{\theta=0}^{\theta=2\pi} \left(\int_{r=0}^{r=\infty} e^{-r^2} r\,dr \right) d\theta$$

QUESTIONS

2 Complete the proof to evaluate I.

3 Hence evaluate $\int_{-\infty}^{\infty} e^{-\frac{x^2}{2\sigma^2}}\,dx$, where σ is a constant.

> **Rewind**
>
> The integral in Question 3 is of vital importance in working with the normal distribution, which you met in A Level Mathematics Student Book 2, Chapter 21.

FOCUS ON ... PROBLEM SOLVING 2

Finding the shape of a hanging chain

Consider this problem:

> A uniform chain is suspended from two fixed points at the same height and hangs under its own weight. Find the shape of the chain.

The first step is to express the question in a mathematical form. If you set up the coordinate axes so that the two end points have the same y-coordinate, then you can describe the shape of the chain by a function $y = f(x)$. The question then becomes to find an expression for $f(x)$.

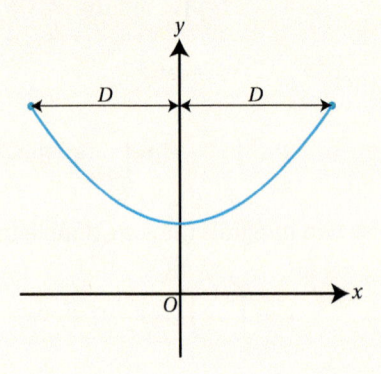

It is clear that the shape of the chain will be symmetrical, with the lowest point half-way between the end points. Note that the position of the x-axis is irrelevant, since the shape of the chain does not change if the end points are moved vertically.

Next you need to introduce some parameters: what could the exact shape of the chain depend on? It seems reasonable to consider these factors:

- the mass of the chain (M)
- the length of the chain (L)
- the distance between the end points ($2D$).

As already noted, the height of the end points does not affect the shape of the chain.

The shape of the chain is determined by the forces acing on it. As well as the mass of the chain, there is a tension force acting along the chain. At each point the tension acts along the tangent to the chain. So, if you can determine the direction of the tension at each point, you will know the gradient of the tangent, which is $\dfrac{dy}{dx}$. Knowing the gradient will enable you to find the equation for y in terms of x.

Consider the part of the chain between the lowest point and another point with a variable x-coordinate. The forces acting on this part of the chain are shown in the diagram (m is the mass of this part of the chain). The force T_0 is fixed, but T changes with x.

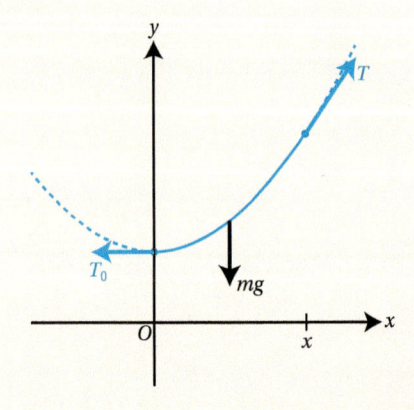

Resolving forces horizontally and vertically gives:

$$T\cos\theta = T_0, \quad T\sin\theta = mg$$

and therefore $\tan\theta = \dfrac{mg}{T_0}$. But, since the force T is directed along the tangent to the curve, $\tan\theta$ equals the gradient of the curve at that point. Hence $\dfrac{dy}{dx} = \dfrac{mg}{T_0}$.

⏮ Rewind

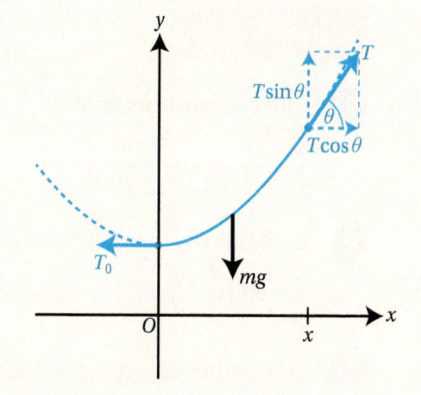

For a reminder about resolving forces, see A Level Mathematics Student Book 2, Chapter 18.

In the expression for the gradient, g and T_0 are constants, but m (the mass of this part of the chain) depends on the x-coordinate. If you can express m in terms of x, you can then integrate $\dfrac{dy}{dx}$ to obtain your required equation for the shape of the chain.

Since the chain is uniform, the mass of a part of the chain is proportional to the length of that part. The whole chain has length L and mass M, so $m = \dfrac{Ms}{L}$ where s is the length of the section of the chain between x-coordinates 0 and x.

The length of a curve is given by $s = \displaystyle\int_0^x \sqrt{1 + \left(\dfrac{dy}{dx}\right)^2}\,dx$ and so $m = \dfrac{M}{L}\displaystyle\int_0^x \sqrt{1 + \left(\dfrac{dy}{dx}\right)^2}\,dx$.

Substituting this into $\dfrac{dy}{dx} = \dfrac{mg}{T_0}$ results in an equation involving both a derivative and an integral. You don't know how to solve such equations. However, differentiating it gives

$$\dfrac{d^2y}{dx^2} = \dfrac{d}{dx}\left(\dfrac{mg}{T_0}\right)$$
$$= \dfrac{gM}{T_0 L}\dfrac{ds}{dx}$$

$$\therefore \dfrac{d^2y}{dx^2} = \dfrac{gM}{T_0 L}\sqrt{1 + \left(\dfrac{dy}{dx}\right)^2}$$

⏮ Rewind

You met the expression for the length of the curve in Chapter 9, Section 6.

You can now proceed to solve this differential equation.

QUESTIONS

1 Make a substitution $u = \dfrac{dy}{dx}$ and show that
$$\int \frac{1}{\sqrt{1+u^2}}\, du = \frac{gM}{T_0 L}\int 1\, dx.$$

> **Rewind**
>
> You met integrals of this type in Chapter 9, Section 3.

2 Explain why the constant of integration is zero. Hence show that $u = \sinh\left(\dfrac{gm}{T_0 L}x\right).$

3 Hence find an expression for y in terms of x. Explain why the constant of integration can be taken to be zero.

> **Did you know?**
>
> The cosh curve is called a catenary, meaning 'relating to a chain'.

In the expression you found in Question 3, g is a constant and M and L are fixed properties of the chain. However, you don't yet know what T_0 is; you defined it as the magnitude of the tension acting at the lowest point of the chain. You should also notice that you have not yet used the condition that the end points of the chain are a distance $2D$ apart. It seems reasonable that the tension in the chain will depend on how far apart the end points are.

QUESTIONS

4 Show that the length of the curve $y = k\cosh\left(\dfrac{x}{k}\right)$ between points with coordinates $x = a$ and $x = b$ is $k\left(\sinh\left(\dfrac{b}{k}\right) - \sinh\left(\dfrac{a}{k}\right)\right).$

5 Use the fact that the total length of the chain is L, and that the end points are at $x = -D$ and $x = D$, to show that $\dfrac{2T_0}{gM}\sinh\left(\dfrac{gMD}{LT_0}\right) = 1.$

6 Use technology to show that the equation in Question 5 has a solution for T_0 whenever $\dfrac{D}{L} < \dfrac{1}{2}$. Explain why this condition always holds in this problem.

In summary, you have found that a chain suspended freely from two fixed points hangs in the shape of a catenary, $y = k\cosh\left(\dfrac{x}{k}\right)$, where k is a constant depending on the mass and the length of the chain and the distance between the end points.

Focus on ... Modelling 2

The Lotka-Volterra model and phase planes

During World War 1 the marine biologist Umberto D'Ancona noticed something puzzling about fish in the Adriatic Sea. Although they were being fished less (and so their natural death rate decreased), the numbers of small fish were actually decreasing while the numbers of predator fish were increasing. His father-in-law, Vito Volterra, applied the work of Alfred Lotka to try to explain this observation.

Consider a population of a species of fish (F million) and sharks (S thousand).

The natural net birth rate of the fish (i.e. the birth rate minus the death rate) is proportional to the number of fish with constant of proportionality a. There is also a death rate due to predation which is proportional to both the number of fish and the number of sharks with constant of proportionality b. This means that:

$$\frac{dF}{dt} = aF - bFS.$$

A similar differential equation governs the population of sharks:

$$\frac{dS}{dt} = cFS - kS$$

where the cFS term represents the growth in the shark population due to their predation on the fish and the $-kS$ term is the natural net death rate of the sharks.

These differential equations comprise the Lotka-Volterra model.

QUESTION

1 Describe some modelling assumptions that have been made in creating this model.

When analysing systems like this it is often the case that solving the differential equation is less important than finding fixed points of the system – values of the population where there is no change in the population i.e. places where $\frac{dF}{dt} = 0$ and $\frac{dS}{dt} = 0$.

QUESTIONS

2 Find all fixed points of the differential equations in the Lotka-Volterra model. Which corresponds to the biological equilibrium values if the populations do not go extinct?

3 When trawler fishing is reduced, the net birth rate of the fish will increase and the net death rate of the sharks will decrease. Use the Lokta-Volterra model to explain this.

A common way to visualise these systems of equations is to use a phase plane. These plot the 'flow' of the system at each value of F and S. You can find phase plane plotters online. Assuming that $a = b = c = k = 1$, the phase plane for Lotka-Voltera is shown in the diagram.

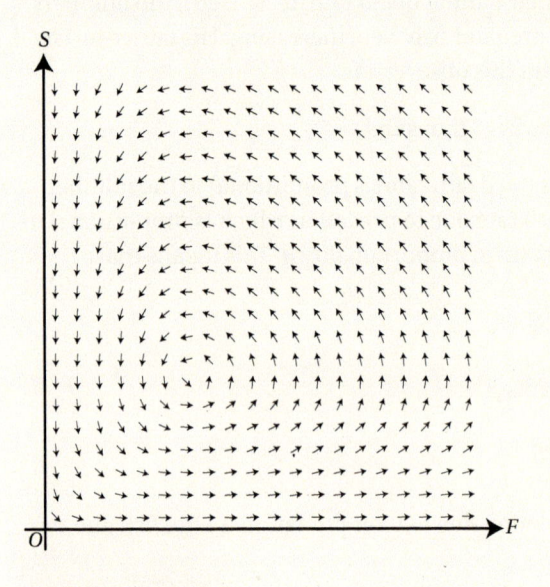

QUESTIONS

4 If the original value is $F = 0.5$ and $S = 1$, sketch the trajectory of the system over time. Hence estimate the maximum fish population.

5 Hence sketch the behaviour of S against t and of F against t for these initial conditions.

6 The effect of competition amongst the fish can be included in the model by adding another term in F^2 to the original differential equation:

$$\frac{dF}{dt} = aF - eF^2 - bFS$$

$$\frac{dS}{dt} = cFS - kS$$

Assuming that all parameters are positive, explain why this adaptation introduces a competition effect into the differential equations.

7 By using online technology, investigate the system in Question 6 with $a = b = c = k = 1$ and $e = 0.5$. How has the introduction of competition changed the behaviour of the system?

CROSS-TOPIC REVIEW EXERCISE 2

1 The curve C has polar equation $r^2 = a\sin 4\theta$, where $0 \leq \theta < 2\pi$ and $a > 0$.

    a Sketch C, including the equations of any tangents at the pole.

    b Find the total area enclosed by C.

2 **a** Sketch the graph of $y = \tanh x$ and state the equations of its asymptotes.

    b Use the definitions of $\sinh x$ and $\cosh x$ in terms of e^x and e^{-x} to show that
$$\text{sech}^2 x + \tanh^2 x = 1.$$

    c Solve the equation $6\,\text{sech}^2 x = 4 + \tanh x$, giving your answers in terms of natural logarithms.

[©AQA 2015]

3 Use l'Hôpital's rule to evaluate each limit.

    a $\displaystyle\lim_{x \to 0} \frac{\sin 3x}{\sinh x}$
    b $\displaystyle\lim_{x \to 0} \frac{\cos x - \cos 3x}{x^2}$

4 **a** Find, in terms of p and q, the value of the integral $\displaystyle\int_p^q \frac{2}{x^3}\,dx$.

    b Show that only one of the following improper integrals has a finite value, and find that value:

        i $\displaystyle\int_0^2 \frac{2}{x^3}\,dx$
        ii $\displaystyle\int_2^\infty \frac{2}{x^3}\,dx.$

[©AQA 2011]

5 The length of the arc of the curve $y = \cosh x$ between $x = 0$ and $x = a$ is 3.

Find the exact positive value of a.

6 A particle, of mass 12 kg, is moving along a straight horizontal line. At time t seconds, the particle has speed $v\,\text{m s}^{-1}$. As the particle moves, it experiences a resistance force of magnitude $4v^{\frac{1}{3}}$. No other horizontal force acts on the particle.

The initial speed of the particle is $8\,\text{m s}^{-1}$.

    a Show that
$$v = \left(4 - \frac{2}{9}t\right)^{\frac{3}{2}}$$

    b Find the value of t when the particle comes to rest.

[©AQA 2013]

7 **a** Write down the expansion of $\sin 3x$ in ascending powers of x up to and including the term in x^3.

    b Find
$$\lim_{x \to 0}\left(\frac{3x\cos 2x - \sin 3x}{5x^3}\right).$$

[©AQA 2010]

8 The diagram shows a sketch of the graph of $y = \sqrt{27 + x^3}$.

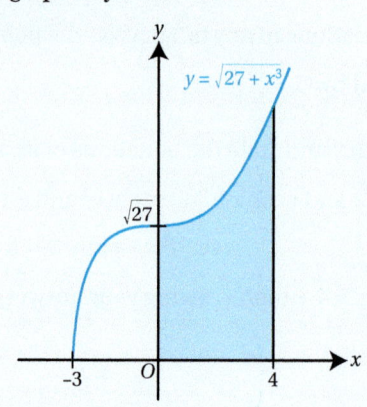

a The area of the shaded region, bounded by the curve, the x-axis and the lines $x = 0$ and $x = 4$, is given by $\int_0^4 \sqrt{27 + x^3}\, dx$.

Use the mid-ordinate rule with **five** strips to find an estimate for this area. Give your answer to three significant figures.

b With the aid of a diagram, explain whether the mid-ordinate rule applied in part **a** gives an estimate which is smaller than or greater than the area of the shaded region.

[©AQA 2013]

9 It is given that the function $y(x)$ satisfies the differential equation
$$\frac{dy}{dx} = f(x, y)$$
where
$$f(x, y) = (x - y)\sqrt{x + y}$$
and
$$y(2) = 1.$$

a Use the Euler formula $y_{r+1} = y_r + h f(x_r, y_r)$ with $h = 0.1$ to obtain an approximation to $y(2.1)$, giving your answer to three decimal places.

b Use your answer to part **a** and the improved Euler formula $y_{r+1} = y_{r-1} + 2h f(x_r, y_r)$, with $h = 0.1$, to obtain an approximation to $y(2.2)$, giving your answer to three decimal places.

[©AQA 2013]

Cross-topic review exercise 2

10 The polar equation of a curve C_1 is
$$r = 2(\cos\theta - \sin\theta), 0 \leq \theta \leq 2\pi$$

a **i** Find the Cartesian equation of C_1.

ii Deduce that C_1 is a circle and find its radius and the Cartesian coordinates of its centre.

b The diagram shows the curve C_2 with polar equation
$$r = 4 + \sin\theta, 0 \leq \theta \leq 2\pi$$

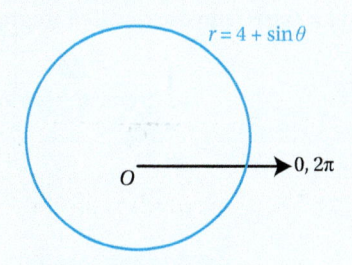

i Find the area of the region that is bounded by C_2.

ii Prove that the curves C_1 and C_2 do not intersect.

iii Find the area of the region that is outside C_1 but inside C_2.

[©AQA 2010]

11 **a** By using the substitution $u = \sinh x$, show that
$$\int \operatorname{sech} x \, dx = \arctan(\sinh x) + c$$

The part of the curve $y = \sqrt{\operatorname{sech} x}$ between $x = 0$ and $x = k$, where k is a positive constant, is rotated through 360° about the x-axis. The volume of the solid formed is $\dfrac{\pi^2}{6}$.

b Find the exact value of k.

12 Given that $I_n = \int x^n \cosh x \, dx, n \in \mathbb{Z}^+$:

a show that, for $n \geq 2$, $I_n = x^n \sinh x - nx^{n-1}\cosh x + n(n-1)I_{n-2}$

b hence evaluate $\int_0^1 x^4 \cosh x \, dx$, giving your answer in terms of e.

13 A curve is defined parametrically by $x = 4\sinh t$, $y = \cosh 2t$. The length of the arc of the curve between $t = 0$ and $t = 1$ is s.

a Show that $s = \int_0^1 4\cosh^2 t \, dt$.

b Find the exact value of s.

321

14 a Explain why $\int_2^\infty (x-2)e^{-2x}\,dx$ is an improper integral.

b Evaluate $\int_2^\infty (x-2)e^{-2x}\,dx$, showing the limiting process used.

[©AQA 2015]

15 a Show that the substitution $t = \tan\theta$ transforms the integral

$$\int \frac{d\theta}{9\cos^2\theta + \sin^2\theta}$$

into $\int \frac{dt}{9+t^2}$.

b Hence show that

$$\int_0^{\frac{\pi}{3}} \frac{d\theta}{9\cos^2\theta + \sin^2\theta} = \frac{\pi}{18}.$$

[©AQA 2010]

16 a Express $7 + 4x - 2x^2$ in the form $a - b(x-c)^2$, where a, b and c are integers.

b By means of a suitable substitution, or otherwise, find the exact value of

$$\int_1^{\frac{5}{2}} \frac{dx}{\sqrt{7+4x-2x^2}}.$$

[©AQA 2012]

17 a Given that $y = (x-2)\sqrt{5+4x-x^2} + 9\sin^{-1}\frac{x-2}{3}$, show that

$$\frac{dy}{dx} = k\sqrt{5+4x-x^2}$$

where k is an integer.

b Hence show that

$$\int_2^{\frac{7}{2}} \sqrt{5+4x-x^2}\,dx = p\sqrt{3} + q\pi$$

where p and q are rational numbers.

[©AQA 2015]

Cross-topic review exercise 2

18 a Given that $y = \ln(1 + 2\tan x)$, find $\dfrac{dy}{dx}$ and $\dfrac{d^2y}{dx^2}$.

(You may leave your expression for $\dfrac{d^2y}{dx^2}$ unsimplified.)

b Hence, using Maclaurin's theorem, find the first two non-zero terms in the expansion, in ascending powers of x, of $\ln(1 + 2\tan x)$.

c Find
$$\lim_{x \to 0}\left(\frac{\ln(1 + 2\tan x)}{\ln(1 - x)}\right).$$

[©AQA 2011]

19 Solve the differential equation
$$\frac{d^2y}{dx^2} + 2\frac{dy}{dx} + 10y = 26\,e^x$$
given that $y = 5$ and $\dfrac{dy}{dx} = 11$ when $x = 0$. Give your answer in the form $y = f(x)$.

[©AQA 2012]

20 a Given that $x = t^{\frac{1}{2}}$, $x > 0$, $t > 0$ and y is a function of x, show that:

i $\dfrac{dy}{dx} = 2t^{\frac{1}{2}}\dfrac{dy}{dt}$ 　　**ii** $\dfrac{d^2y}{dx^2} = 4t\dfrac{d^2y}{dt^2} + 2\dfrac{dy}{dt}$.

b Hence show that the substitution $x = t^{\frac{1}{2}}$ transforms the differential equation
$$x\frac{d^2y}{dx^2} - (8x^2 + 1)\frac{dy}{dx} + 12x^3y = 12x^5$$
into
$$\frac{d^2y}{dt^2} - 4\frac{dy}{dt} + 3y = 3t$$

c Hence find the general solution of the differential equation
$$x\frac{d^2y}{dx^2} - (8x^2 - 1)\frac{dy}{dx} + 12x^3y = 12x^5$$
giving your answer in the form $y = f(x)$.

[©AQA 2010]

21 A particle moves with simple harmonic motion on a line between two points A and B, which are 0.4 metres apart. The maximum speed of the particle is $0.8\,\text{m s}^{-1}$. The particle passes through a point C that is 0.1 metres from A.

a Find the period of the motion.

b Find the speed of the particle when it is at C.

c Given that the particle is at rest at A at time $t = 0$, find an expression for the displacement of the particle from A at time t seconds.

d Find the time that it takes for the particle to move from A to C.

[©AQA 2015]

323

22. The diagram shows a sketch of a curve and a circle.

    The polar equation of the curve is
    $$r = 3 + 2\sin\theta, \ 0 \leq \theta \leq 2\pi.$$

    The circle, whose polar equation is $r = 2$, intersects the curve at the points P and Q, as shown in the diagram.

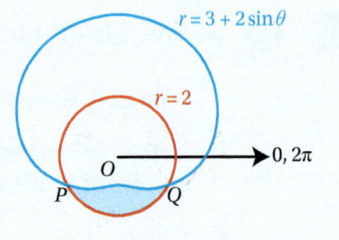

    a Find the polar coordinates of P and the polar coordinates of Q.

    b A straight line, drawn from the point P through the pole O, intersects the curve again at the point A.

       i   Find the polar coordinates of A.
       ii Find, in surd form, the length of AQ.
       iii Hence, or otherwise, explain why the line AQ is a tangent to the circle $r = 2$.

    c Find the area of the shaded region which lies inside the circle $r = 2$ but outside the curve $r = 3 + 2\sin\theta$. Give your answer in the form $\frac{1}{6}(m\sqrt{3} + n\pi)$, where m and n are integers.

    [©AQA 2013]

23. The hyperbola H has parametric equations $x = a\cosh t$, $y = b\sinh t$.

    a Show that the equation of a normal to H is $(a\tanh t)x + by = (a^2 + b^2)\sinh t$.

    The normal to the point P on H intersects the x-axis at the point Q.

    b Show that as P varies, the locus of the mid-point of PQ is part of another hyperbola.

24. Prove that if $y = \ln(\tan x)$, then $\tanh y = -\cos 2x$.

25. a Use the substitution $x = \sinh\theta$ to show that
    $$\int \frac{1}{x^2\sqrt{1+x^2}}\,dx = -\frac{\sqrt{1+x^2}}{x} + c.$$

    b Hence find $\int \frac{\sqrt{1+x^2}}{x^2}\,dx$.

26. a Find $\int \arcsin x\,dx$.

    b Show that $\int \sin^2 x\,dx = \frac{1}{2}(x - \sin x \cos x) + c$.

    The area A is bounded by the curve with equation $y = \sin^2 x$, the y-axis and the line $y = p$ as shown.

    c i   Find the area A in terms of p.
       ii Hence state $\int \arcsin\sqrt{x}\,dx$, $0 < x < 1$.

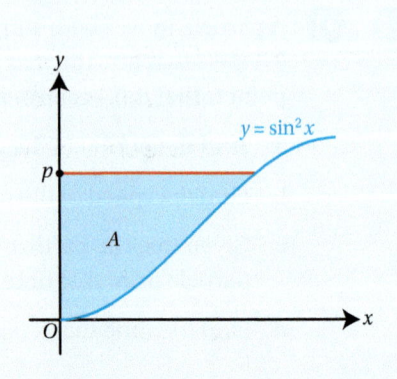

27 Evaluate the improper integral $\int_0^\infty \dfrac{6x-4}{(3x^2+2)(x+1)}\,dx$, clearly showing the limiting process used.

28 A curve has equation $y = f(x)$ for all $x \in \mathbb{R}$. The arc from the point $(0, f(0))$ to the point $(a, f(a))$ has length $s(a)$.

   a Write down an expression for $\dfrac{ds}{da}$.

   It is given that, for all a, $s(a)$ is proportional to a.

   b Show that the only curve with this property is a straight line.

29 A differential equation is given by
$$4\sqrt{x^5}\,\frac{d^2y}{dx^2} + (2\sqrt{x})y = \sqrt{x}(\ln x)^2 + 5,\ x > 0$$

   a Show that the substitution $x = e^{2t}$ transforms this differential equation into
$$\frac{d^2y}{dt^2} - 2\frac{dy}{dt} + 2y = 4t^2 + 5e^{-t}$$

   b Hence find the general solution of the differential equation
$$4\sqrt{x^5}\,\frac{d^2y}{dx^2} + (2\sqrt{x})y = \sqrt{x}(\ln x)^2 + 5,\ x > 0$$

[© AQA 2015]

30 A particle, P, of mass m kg, moves in a straight horizontal line. At time t seconds, the displacement of P from a fixed point O on the line is x metres, and P is moving with velocity $\dot{x}$ m s^{-1}. Throughout the motion, two horizontal forces act on P: a force of magnitude $4mn^2|x|$ newtons directed towards O, and a resistance force of magnitude $2mk|\dot{x}|$ newtons, where n and k are positive constants.

   a Show that $\ddot{x} + 2k\dot{x} + 4n^2x = 0$

   b In one case, $k = n$. When $t = 0$, $x = a$ and $\dot{x} = 0$

      i Show that $x = e^{-nt}\left(a\cos\sqrt{3}nt + \dfrac{\sqrt{3}a}{3}\sin\sqrt{3}nt\right)$.

      ii Show that P passes through O when $\tan\sqrt{3}nt = -\sqrt{3}$.

   c In a different case, $k = 2n$.

      i Find a general solution for x at time t seconds.

      ii Hence state the type of damping which occurs.

[©AQA 2012]

31 A curve C is given parametrically by the equations

$$x = \frac{1}{2}\cosh 2t, \ y = 2\sinh t$$

a Express

$$\left(\frac{dx}{dt}\right)^2 + \left(\frac{dy}{dt}\right)^2$$

in terms of $\cosh t$.

b The arc of C from $t = 0$ to $t = 1$ is rotated through 2π radians about the x-axis.

   i Show that S, the area of the curved surface generated, is given by

$$S = 8\pi \int_0^1 \sinh t \cosh^2 t \ dt.$$

   ii Find the exact value of S.

[©AQA 2010]

32 a i Show that

$$\frac{d}{du}(2u\sqrt{1 + 4u^2} + \sinh^{-1} 2u) = k\sqrt{1 + 4u^2}$$

where k is an integer.

   ii Hence show that

$$\int_0^1 \sqrt{1 + 4u^2} \ du = p\sqrt{5} + q \sinh^{-1} 2$$

where p and q are rational numbers.

b The arc of the curve with equation $y = \frac{1}{2}\cos 4x$ between the points where $x = 0$ and $x = \frac{\pi}{8}$ is rotated through 2π radians about the x-axis.

   i Show that the area S of the curved surface formed is given by

$$S = \pi \int_0^{\frac{\pi}{8}} \cos 4x \sqrt{1 + 4\sin^2 4x} \ dx.$$

   ii Use the substitution $u = \sin 4x$ to find the exact value of S.

[© AQA 2013]

Practice paper

2 hours, 100 marks

1. Find the value of k for which the matrix $\begin{pmatrix} 2k & -1 & 5 \\ 1 & k & -1 \\ k+1 & 0 & 3 \end{pmatrix}$ is singular.

   Choose from these options.

   A $k=0$ **B** $k=-1$ **C** $k=1$ **D** $k=2$

   [1 mark]

2. Find the Cartesian equation of the curve with polar equation $r^3 = 8\cos\theta$.

   Choose from these options.

   A $x^2+y^2 = 2\sqrt[3]{x}$ **B** $x^2+y^2 = 2\sqrt[3]{y}$ **C** $(x^2+y^2)^2 = 8x$ **D** $(x^2+y^2)^2 = 8y$

   [1 mark]

3. Let $\mathbf{a} = \begin{pmatrix} 3 \\ -1 \\ 2 \end{pmatrix}$, $\mathbf{b} = \begin{pmatrix} 1 \\ 1 \\ k \end{pmatrix}$ and $\mathbf{c} = \begin{pmatrix} 2 \\ 22 \\ 8 \end{pmatrix}$.

   Find the value of k such that $\mathbf{c}$ is perpendicular to $\mathbf{a}$ and $\mathbf{b}$.

   [3 marks]

4. Use the definitions of $\sinh x$ and $\cosh x$ to prove that
   $\cosh(x+y) \equiv \cosh x \cosh y + \sinh x \sinh y$.

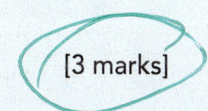

   [3 marks]

5. Given that $y=1$ when $x=0$, solve the differential equation
   $(1-x^2)\dfrac{dy}{dx} - xy = 2$, $|x| < 1$.

   Give your answer in the form $y = f(x)$.

   [6 marks]

6. Show that the mean value of the function $f(x) = \dfrac{3x^2 + 2x - 5}{(2x+1)(x^2+5)}$ between 0 and 4 is $a \ln b$, where a and b are constants to be found.

   [7 marks]

7. The function f is defined by $f(x) = \dfrac{ax - a^2 + 1}{x-a}$, $a > 1$.

   a Show that $f(x) = p + \dfrac{q}{x-a}$, where p and q are constants in terms of a.

   b Hence state a transformation that maps the graph of $y = \dfrac{1}{x}$ onto the graph of $y = f(x)$.

   c **i** Sketch the graph of $y = |f(|x|)|$

   ii Find, in terms of a, the range of values of k for which the equation $|f(|x|)| = k$ has exactly two solutions.

   [10 marks]

8. **a** If $z = \cos\theta + i\sin\theta$, show that $\dfrac{1}{z} = \cos\theta - i\sin\theta$.

   b Show that $\cos(n\theta) = \dfrac{1}{2}\left(z^n + \dfrac{1}{z^n}\right)$, for integer n.

   c Hence solve $z^4 - 3z^3 + 4z^2 - 3z + 1 = 0$.

   [8 marks]

9. Given that $I_n = \int \sinh^n x \, dx$, $n \in \mathbb{Z}^+$,

   a show that, for $n \geq 2$, $nI_n = \sinh^{n-1} x \cosh x - (n-1)I_{n-2}$.

   b Hence evaluate $\int_0^{\ln 3} \sinh^5 x \, dx$. [8 marks]

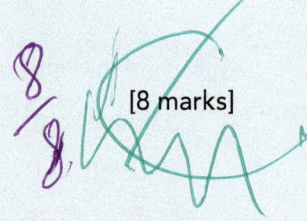

10. Three planes have equations $\Pi_1: x - 2y + z = 0$, $\Pi_2: 3x - z = 4$, $\Pi_3: x + y - z = k$.

    a Show that for all values of k, the planes do not intersect at a unique point.

    b Find the value of k for which the intersection of the three planes is a line, and find the vector equation of this line. [9 marks]

11. Given the matrix $\mathbf{M} = \begin{pmatrix} 3 & 2 & 1 \\ 1 & 4 & 0 \\ 0 & 0 & 1 \end{pmatrix}$:

    a i show that 1 is an eigenvalue of $\mathbf{M}$ and find the other two eigenvalues

    ii find eigenvectors corresponding to these three eigenvalues.

    The transformation T has matrix $\mathbf{M}$.

    b Describe the geometrical significance of the eigenvectors of $\mathbf{M}$ in relation to T. [14 marks]

12. a i Find the first four derivatives of $\tanh x$.

    ii Hence find the Maclaurin series for $\tanh x$ up to and including the term in x^3.

    b Use your result to part a ii and the series for e^x to find the Maclaurin series for $e^{\tanh x}$, up to and including the term in x^4.

    c Evaluate $\lim_{x \to 0} \dfrac{e^{\tanh x} - 1 - x}{x^2}$, clearly showing your working. [12 marks]

13. a Prove by induction that, for $n \in \mathbb{Z}^+$,
    $$\cos\theta + \cos(3\theta) + \cos(5\theta) + \ldots + \cos((2n-1)\theta) = \frac{\sin(2n\theta)}{2\sin\theta}.$$

    b Hence find the exact value of $\cos\dfrac{\pi}{7} + \cos\dfrac{3\pi}{7} + \ldots + \cos\dfrac{13\pi}{7}$. [8 marks]

14. A particle P of mass m is attached to one end of a light horizontal spring. The other end of the spring is attached to a fixed point.

    The magnitude of the tension in the spring is given by $2mk^2x$, where x is the extension in the spring at time t seconds and $k > 0$ is a constant.

    The particle experiences a resistance to motion of magnitude $3kmv$, where v is the speed of the particle at time t seconds.

    a Show that $\dfrac{d^2x}{dt^2} + 3k\dfrac{dx}{dt} + 2k^2x = 0$.

    b Given that when $t = 0$, $x = 4$ and $v = -3k$:

       i find x in terms of t and k

       ii state whether the damping is light, heavy or critical. [10 marks]

FORMULAE

Further Pure Mathematics

Differentiation

$f(x)$	$f'(x)$
$\sin^{-1} x$	$\dfrac{1}{\sqrt{1-x^2}}$
$\cos^{-1} x$	$-\dfrac{1}{\sqrt{1-x^2}}$
$\tan^{-1} x$	$\dfrac{1}{1+x^2}$
$\tanh x$	$\operatorname{sech}^2 x$
$\sinh^{-1} x$	$\dfrac{1}{\sqrt{1+x^2}}$
$\cosh^{-1} x$	$\dfrac{1}{\sqrt{x^2-1}}$
$\tanh^{-1} x$	$\dfrac{1}{1-x^2}$

Integration

$f(x)$	$\int f(x)\,dx$
$\tanh x$	$\ln \cosh x$
$\dfrac{1}{\sqrt{a^2-x^2}}$	$\sin^{-1}\left(\dfrac{x}{a}\right)\quad (|x|<a)$
$\dfrac{1}{a^2+x^2}$	$\dfrac{1}{a}\tan^{-1}\left(\dfrac{x}{a}\right)$
$\dfrac{1}{\sqrt{x^2-a^2}}$	$\cosh^{-1}\left(\dfrac{x}{a}\right)$ or $\ln\left\{x+\sqrt{x^2-a^2}\right\}\quad (x>a)$
$\dfrac{1}{\sqrt{a^2+x^2}}$	$\sinh^{-1}\left(\dfrac{x}{a}\right)$ or $\ln\left\{x+\sqrt{x^2+a^2}\right\}$
$\dfrac{1}{a^2-x^2}$	$\dfrac{1}{2a}\ln\left|\dfrac{a+x}{a-x}\right| = \dfrac{1}{a}\tanh^{-1}\dfrac{x}{a}\quad (|x|<a)$
$\dfrac{1}{x^2-a^2}$	$\dfrac{1}{2a}\ln\left|\dfrac{x-a}{x+a}\right|$

Complex numbers

$[r(\cos\theta + i\sin\theta)]^n = r^n(\cos n\theta + i\sin n\theta)$

The roots of $z^n = 1$ are given by $z = e^{\frac{2\pi ki}{n}}$ for $k = 0, 1, 2, \ldots, n-1$

Matrix transformations

Anticlockwise rotation through θ about O: $\begin{bmatrix} \cos\theta & -\sin\theta \\ \sin\theta & \cos\theta \end{bmatrix}$

Reflection in the line $y = (\tan\theta)x$: $\begin{bmatrix} \cos 2\theta & \sin 2\theta \\ \sin 2\theta & -\cos 2\theta \end{bmatrix}$

The matrices for rotations (in three dimensions) through an angle θ about one of the axes are:

$\begin{bmatrix} 1 & 0 & 0 \\ 0 & \cos\theta & -\sin\theta \\ 0 & \sin\theta & \cos\theta \end{bmatrix}$ for the x-axis

$\begin{bmatrix} \cos\theta & 0 & \sin\theta \\ 0 & 1 & 0 \\ -\sin\theta & 0 & \cos\theta \end{bmatrix}$ for the y-axis

$\begin{bmatrix} \cos\theta & -\sin\theta & 0 \\ \sin\theta & \cos\theta & 0 \\ 0 & 0 & 1 \end{bmatrix}$ for the z-axis

Summations

$$\sum_{r=1}^{n} r^2 = \frac{1}{6}n(n+1)(2n+1)$$

$$\sum_{r=1}^{n} r^3 = \frac{1}{4}n^2(n+1)^2$$

Maclaurin's series

$f(x) = f(0) + x\,f'(0) + \frac{x^2}{2!}f''(0) + \ldots + \frac{x^r}{r!}f^{(r)}(0) + \ldots$

$e^x = \exp(x) = 1 + x + \frac{x^2}{2!} + \ldots + \frac{x^r}{r!} + \ldots$ for all x

$\ln(1+x) = x - \frac{x^2}{2} + \frac{x^3}{3} - \ldots + (-1)^{r+1}\frac{x^r}{r} + \ldots \quad (-1 < x_n \leq 1)$

$\sin x = x - \frac{x^3}{3!} + \frac{x^5}{5!} - \ldots + (-1)^r \frac{x^{2r+1}}{(2r+1)!} + \ldots$ for all x

$\cos x = 1 - \frac{x^2}{2!} + \frac{x^4}{4!} - \ldots + (-1)^r \frac{x^{2r}}{(2r)!} + \ldots$ for all x

Formulae

Vectors

The resolved part of **a** in the direction of **b** is $\dfrac{\mathbf{a} \cdot \mathbf{b}}{|\mathbf{b}|}$

The vector product $\mathbf{a} \times \mathbf{b} = |\mathbf{a}||\mathbf{b}|\sin\theta\,\hat{\mathbf{n}} = \begin{vmatrix} \mathbf{i} & a_1 & b_1 \\ \mathbf{j} & a_2 & b_2 \\ \mathbf{k} & a_3 & b_3 \end{vmatrix} = \begin{bmatrix} a_2 b_3 - a_3 b_2 \\ a_3 b_1 - a_1 b_3 \\ a_1 b_2 - a_2 b_1 \end{bmatrix}$

If A is the point with position vector $\mathbf{a} = a_1 \mathbf{i} + a_2 \mathbf{j} + a_3 \mathbf{k}$, then

- the straight line through A with direction vector $\mathbf{b} = b_1 \mathbf{i} + b_2 \mathbf{j} + b_3 \mathbf{k}$ has equation $\dfrac{x - a_1}{b_1} = \dfrac{y - a_2}{b_2} = \dfrac{z - a_3}{b_3} = \lambda$ (Cartesian form) or $(\mathbf{r} - \mathbf{a}) \times \mathbf{b} = 0$ (vector product form)

- the plane through A and parallel to **b** and **c** has vector equation $\mathbf{r} = \mathbf{a} + s\mathbf{b} + t\mathbf{c}$

Area of a sector

$A = \dfrac{1}{2} \int r^2 \, d\theta$ (polar coordinates)

Hyperbolic functions

$\cosh^2 x - \sinh^2 x \equiv 1$

$\sinh 2x \equiv 2 \sinh x \cosh x$

$\cosh 2x \equiv \cosh^2 x + \sinh^2 x$

$\cosh^{-1} x = \operatorname{arcosh} x = \ln\left\{x + \sqrt{x^2 - 1}\right\} \quad (x \geqslant 1)$

$\sinh^{-1} x = \operatorname{arsinh} x = \ln\left\{x + \sqrt{x^2 + 1}\right\}$

$\tanh^{-1} x = \operatorname{artanh} x = \dfrac{1}{2} \ln\left\{\dfrac{1 + x}{1 - x}\right\} \quad (|x| < 1)$

Conics

	Ellipse	Parabola	Hyperbola
Standard form	$\dfrac{x^2}{a^2} + \dfrac{y^2}{b^2} = 1$	$y^2 = 4ax$	$\dfrac{x^2}{a^2} - \dfrac{y^2}{b^2} = 1$
Parametric form	$x = a \cos\theta$ $y = b \sin\theta$	$x = at^2$ $y = 2at$	$x = a \sec\theta$ $y = b \tan\theta$
Asymptotes	none	none	$\dfrac{x}{a} = \pm \dfrac{y}{b}$

Further numerical integration

The mid-ordinate rule: $\int_a^b y \, dx \approx h\left(y_{\frac{1}{2}} + y_{\frac{3}{2}} + \ldots + y_{n-\frac{3}{2}} + y_{n-\frac{1}{2}}\right)$

where $h = \dfrac{b-a}{n}$

Simpson's rule: $\int_a^b y \, dx \approx \dfrac{1}{3} h \left\{ (y_0 + y_n) + 4(y_1 + y_3 + \ldots + y_{n-1}) + 2(y_2 + y_4 + \ldots + y_{n-2}) \right\}$

where $h = \dfrac{b-a}{n}$ and n is even

Numerical solution of differential equations

For $\dfrac{dy}{dx} = f(x)$ and small h, recurrence relations are:

   Euler's method: $y_{n+1} = y_n + h\, f(x_n)$, $x_{n+1} = x_n + h$

For $\dfrac{dy}{dx} = f(x, y)$:

   Euler's method: $y_{r+1} = y_r + h\, f(x_r, y_r)$, $x_{r+1} = x_r + h$

   Improved Euler method: $y_{r+1} = y_{r-1} + 2h\, f(x_r, y_r)$, $x_{r+1} = x_r + h$

Arc length

$s = \int \sqrt{1 + \left(\dfrac{dy}{dx}\right)^2} \, dx$ (Cartesian coordinates)

$s = \int \sqrt{\left(\dfrac{dx}{dt}\right)^2 + \left(\dfrac{dy}{dt}\right)^2} \, dt$ (parametric form)

Surface area of revolution

$S_x = 2\pi \int y \sqrt{1 + \left(\dfrac{dy}{dx}\right)^2} \, dx$ (Cartesian coordinates)

$S_x = 2\pi \int y \sqrt{\left(\dfrac{dx}{dt}\right)^2 + \left(\dfrac{dy}{dt}\right)^2} \, dt$ (parametric form)

Pure mathematics

Binomial series

$(a+b)^n = a^n + \binom{n}{1} a^{n-1} b + \binom{n}{2} a^{n-2} b^2 + \ldots + \binom{n}{r} a^{n-r} b^r + \ldots + b^n \quad (n \in \mathbb{Z}^+)$

where $\binom{n}{r} = {}^nC_r = \dfrac{n!}{r!(n-r)!}$

$(1+x)^n = 1 + nx + \dfrac{n(n-1)}{1.2} x^2 + \ldots + \dfrac{n(n-1)\ldots(n-r+1)}{1.2\ldots r} x^r + \ldots \quad (|x| < 1, n \in \mathbb{Q})$

Formulae

Arithmetic series

$$S_n = \tfrac{1}{2}n(a+l) = \tfrac{1}{2}n[2a+(n-1)d]$$

Geometic series

$$S_n = \frac{a(1-r^n)}{1-r}$$

$$S_\infty = \frac{a}{1-r} \quad \text{for} \quad |r|<1$$

Trigonometry: small angles

For small angle θ,

$\sin \theta \approx \theta$

$\cos \theta \approx 1 - \dfrac{\theta^2}{2}$

$\tan \theta \approx \theta$

Trigonometric identities

$\sin(A \pm B) \equiv \sin A \cos B \pm \cos A \sin B$

$\cos(A \pm B) \equiv \cos A \cos B \mp \sin A \sin B$

$\tan(A \pm B) \equiv \dfrac{\tan A \pm \tan B}{1 \mp \tan A \tan B} \quad \left(A \pm B \neq \left(k+\tfrac{1}{2}\right)\pi\right)$

$\sin A + \sin B \equiv 2 \sin \dfrac{A+B}{2} \cos \dfrac{A-B}{2}$

$\sin A - \sin B \equiv 2 \cos \dfrac{A+B}{2} \sin \dfrac{A-B}{2}$

$\cos A + \cos B \equiv 2 \cos \dfrac{A+B}{2} \cos \dfrac{A-B}{2}$

$\cos A - \cos B \equiv 2 \sin \dfrac{A+B}{2} \sin \dfrac{A-B}{2}$

Differentiation

$f(x)$	$f'(x)$
$\tan kx$	$k \sec^2 kx$
$\operatorname{cosec} x$	$-\operatorname{cosec} x \cot x$
$\sec x$	$\sec x \tan x$
$\cot x$	$-\operatorname{cosec}^2 x$
$\dfrac{f(x)}{g(x)}$	$\dfrac{f'(x)g(x) - f(x)g'(x)}{(g(x))^2}$

Differentiation from first principles

$$f'(x) = \lim_{h \to 0} \frac{f(x+h) - f(x)}{h}$$

Integration

$$\int u \frac{dv}{dx} \, dx = uv - \int v \frac{du}{dx} \, dx$$

(+ constant; $a > 0$ where relevant)

$f(x)$	$\int f(x) \, dx$
$\tan x$	$\ln \|\sec x\|$
$\cot x$	$\ln \|\sin x\|$
$\csc x$	$-\ln \|\csc x + \cot x\| = \ln \left\| \tan\left(\frac{1}{2}x\right) \right\|$
$\sec x$	$\ln \|\sec x + \tan x\| = \ln \left\| \tan\left(\frac{1}{2}x + \frac{1}{4}\pi\right) \right\|$
$\sec^2 kx$	$\frac{1}{k} \tan kx$

Numerical solution of equations

The Newton-Raphson iteration for solving $f(x) = 0$: $x_{n+1} = x_n - \frac{f(x_n)}{f'(x_n)}$

Numerical integration

The trapezium rule: $\int_a^b y \, dx \approx \frac{1}{2} h \{(y_0 + y_n) + 2(y_1 + y_2 + \ldots + y_{n-1})\}$, where $h = \frac{b-a}{n}$

Answers to exercises

1 Further complex numbers: powers and roots

BEFORE YOU START

1. 5; 2.21 radians
2. $-3 + 2i$; $-3i$
3. **a** $1 - 3i$ **b** $\frac{4}{5} - \frac{7}{5}i$
4. **a** $20\left(\cos\left(-\frac{7\pi}{12}\right) + i\sin\left(-\frac{7\pi}{12}\right)\right)$
   b $5\left(\cos\frac{\pi}{12} + i\sin\frac{\pi}{12}\right)$
5. **a** $-3 - 5i$
   b $3\left(\cos\left(-\frac{\pi}{4}\right) + i\sin\left(-\frac{\pi}{4}\right)\right)$
6. **a** Reflection in the real axis.
   b Translation by $\binom{2}{1}$.

WORK IT OUT 1.1

Solution 1 is correct.

EXERCISE 1A

1. **a i** $64\left(\cos\left(-\frac{4\pi}{5}\right) + i\sin\left(-\frac{4\pi}{5}\right)\right)$
   ii $81\left(\cos\frac{2\pi}{3} + i\sin\frac{2\pi}{3}\right)$
   b i $\cos\left(-\frac{11\pi}{12}\right) + i\sin\left(-\frac{11\pi}{12}\right)$
   ii $\cos\left(-\frac{5\pi}{6}\right) + i\sin\left(-\frac{5\pi}{6}\right)$
   c i $\cos\left(-\frac{\pi}{2}\right) + i\sin\left(-\frac{\pi}{2}\right)$
   ii $\cos\frac{\pi}{2} + i\sin\frac{\pi}{2}$

2. **a** $z^2 = \cos\frac{\pi}{3} + i\sin\frac{\pi}{3}$, $z^3 = \cos\frac{\pi}{2} + i\sin\frac{\pi}{2}$,
   $z^4 = \cos\frac{2\pi}{3} + i\sin\frac{2\pi}{3}$

b

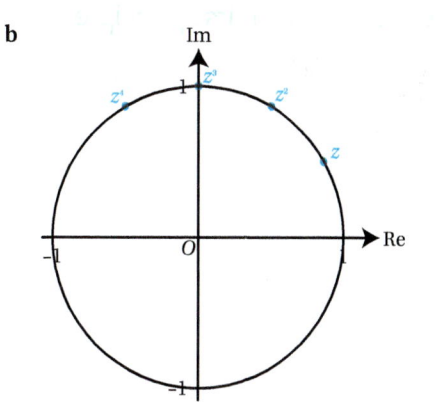

3. **a i** $z^2 = \cos\left(-\frac{2\pi}{3}\right) + i\sin\left(-\frac{2\pi}{3}\right)$, $z^3 = 1$,
   $z^4 = \cos\frac{2\pi}{3} + i\sin\frac{2\pi}{3}$
   ii

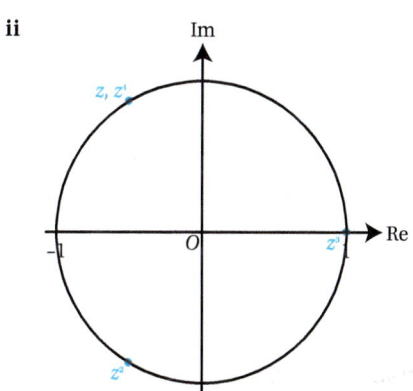

   b $n = 1 + 3k$, $k \in \mathbb{Z}^+$

4. **a** $2; \frac{\pi}{3}$ **b** $32\left(\cos\frac{5\pi}{3} + i\sin\frac{5\pi}{3}\right)$
   c $16 - 16i\sqrt{3}$

5. **a** $2\left(\cos\frac{3\pi}{4} + i\sin\frac{3\pi}{4}\right)$ **b** $64i$

6. 12   7. 14

EXERCISE 1B

1. **a i** $\frac{3\sqrt{3}}{2} + \frac{3}{2}i$ **ii** $2\sqrt{2} + 2\sqrt{2}i$
   b i -4 **ii** 5
   c i $-\frac{1}{2} + \frac{\sqrt{3}}{2}i$ **ii** $-2i$

335

2 a i $5\sqrt{2}e^{i\frac{\pi}{4}}$ **ii** $4e^{-i\frac{\pi}{6}}$

b i $\frac{1}{\sqrt{2}}e^{i\frac{3\pi}{4}}$ **ii** $2e^{-i\frac{\pi}{3}}$

c i $4e^{-i\frac{\pi}{2}}$ **ii** $5e^{i\pi}$

3 a i $20e^{i\frac{5\pi}{12}}$ **ii** $\frac{1}{2}e^{i\frac{\pi}{2}}$

b i $\frac{8}{25}e^{i\frac{\pi}{12}}$ **ii** $2e^{-i\frac{\pi}{2}}$

4

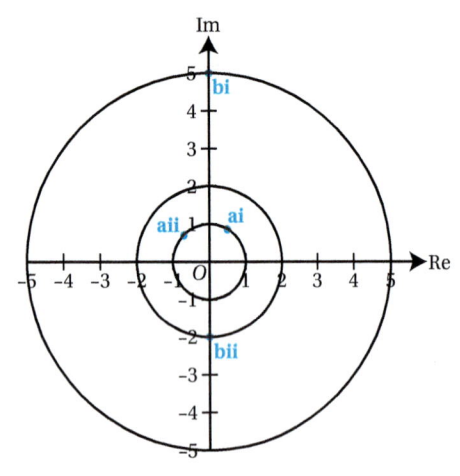

5 Proof.

6 a $\frac{2}{3}i$ **b** $-432\sqrt{3} - 432i$

7 $-54.1 + 7.70i$ (3 s.f.)   **8** $\frac{e^2}{2} - \frac{e^2\sqrt{3}}{2}i$

9 $a = -3, b = 3, c = -2$

10 $x^4 - (2 + \sqrt{3})x^3 + (5 + 2\sqrt{3})x^2 - (2 + 4\sqrt{3})x + 4 = 0$

11 $\cos(\ln 5) + i\sin(\ln 5)$

12 $9\cos(\ln 3) - 9i\sin(\ln 3)$

EXERCISE 1C

1 a i $3, 3e^{\frac{2\pi i}{3}}, 3e^{-\frac{2\pi i}{3}}$

    ii $\sqrt[3]{100}, \sqrt[3]{100}e^{\frac{2\pi i}{3}}, \sqrt[3]{100}e^{-\frac{2\pi i}{3}}$

b i $2e^{\frac{\pi i}{6}}, 2e^{\frac{5\pi i}{6}}, 2e^{\frac{3\pi i}{2}}$ **ii** $e^{\frac{\pi i}{6}}, e^{\frac{5\pi i}{6}}, e^{\frac{3\pi i}{2}}$

c i $2^{\frac{1}{6}}e^{\frac{\pi i}{12}}, 2^{\frac{1}{6}}e^{\frac{3\pi i}{4}}, 2^{\frac{1}{6}}e^{\frac{17\pi i}{12}}$

  ii $7^{\frac{1}{6}}e^{-0.238i}, 7^{\frac{1}{6}}e^{1.86i}, 7^{\frac{1}{6}}e^{-2.33i}$

2 a i $2\left(\cos\frac{\pi}{4} + i\sin\frac{\pi}{4}\right)$,

$2\left(\cos\frac{3\pi}{4} + i\sin\frac{3\pi}{4}\right)$,

$2\left(\cos\frac{5\pi}{4} + i\sin\frac{5\pi}{4}\right)$,

$2\left(\cos\frac{7\pi}{4} + i\sin\frac{7\pi}{4}\right)$;

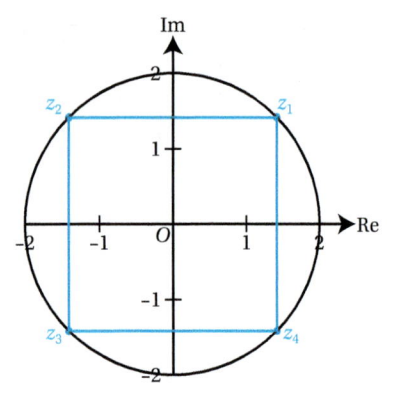

ii $3\left(\cos\frac{\pi}{8} + i\sin\frac{\pi}{8}\right)$,

$3\left(\cos\frac{5\pi}{8} + i\sin\frac{5\pi}{8}\right)$,

$3\left(\cos\frac{9\pi}{8} + i\sin\frac{9\pi}{8}\right)$,

$3\left(\cos\frac{13\pi}{8} + i\sin\frac{13\pi}{8}\right)$;

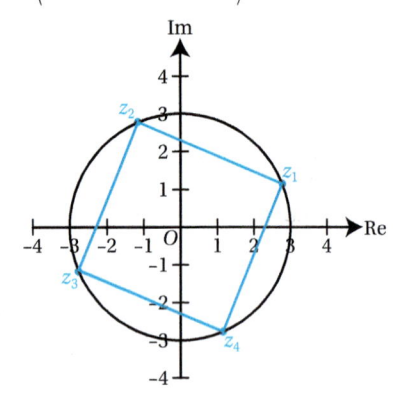

b i $4\left(\cos\frac{\pi}{16} + i\sin\frac{\pi}{16}\right)$,

$4\left(\cos\frac{9\pi}{16} + i\sin\frac{9\pi}{16}\right)$,

$4\left(\cos\frac{17\pi}{16} + i\sin\frac{17\pi}{16}\right)$,

$4\left(\cos\frac{25\pi}{16} + i\sin\frac{25\pi}{16}\right)$;

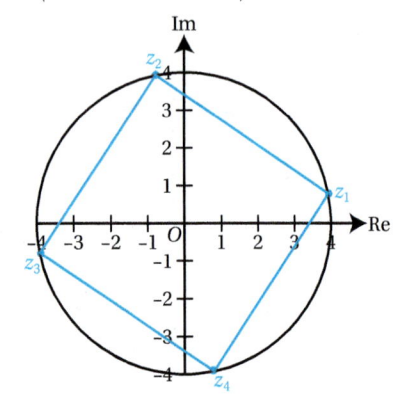

Answers to exercises

  ii $\cos\frac{\pi}{6}+i\sin\frac{\pi}{6}, \cos\frac{2\pi}{3}+i\sin\frac{2\pi}{3},$
  $\cos\frac{7\pi}{6}+i\sin\frac{7\pi}{6},$
  $\cos\frac{5\pi}{3}+i\sin\frac{5\pi}{3};$

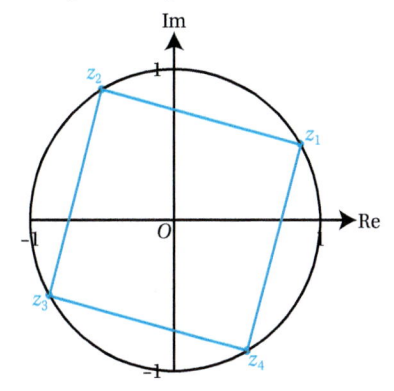

3 $-2, 1+i\sqrt{3}, 1-i\sqrt{3}$

4 a $16; -\frac{\pi}{6}$

  b $2\left(\cos\left(-\frac{\pi}{24}\right)+i\sin\left(-\frac{\pi}{24}\right)\right),$
  $2\left(\cos\frac{11\pi}{24}+i\sin\frac{11\pi}{24}\right),$
  $2\left(\cos\frac{23\pi}{24}+i\sin\frac{23\pi}{24}\right),$
  $2\left(\cos\left(-\frac{13\pi}{24}\right)+i\sin\left(-\frac{13\pi}{24}\right)\right)$

5 $\frac{\sqrt{2}+\sqrt{6}}{2}+\left(\frac{\sqrt{2}-\sqrt{6}}{2}\right)i, \frac{\sqrt{2}-\sqrt{6}}{2}+\left(\frac{\sqrt{2}+\sqrt{6}}{2}\right)i,$
$-\sqrt{2}-i\sqrt{2}$

6 $3\left(\cos\frac{3\pi}{8}+i\sin\frac{3\pi}{8}\right), 3\left(\cos\frac{7\pi}{8}+i\sin\frac{7\pi}{8}\right),$
$3\left(\cos\left(-\frac{\pi}{8}\right)+i\sin\left(-\frac{\pi}{8}\right)\right),$
$3\left(\cos\left(-\frac{5\pi}{8}\right)+i\sin\left(-\frac{5\pi}{8}\right)\right)$

7 a $8e^{i\frac{\pi}{3}}$ **b** $8^{\frac{1}{4}}e^{i\frac{\pi}{12}}, 8^{\frac{1}{4}}e^{i\frac{7\pi}{12}}, 8^{\frac{1}{4}}e^{i\frac{13\pi}{12}}, 8^{\frac{1}{4}}e^{i\frac{19\pi}{12}}$
  c

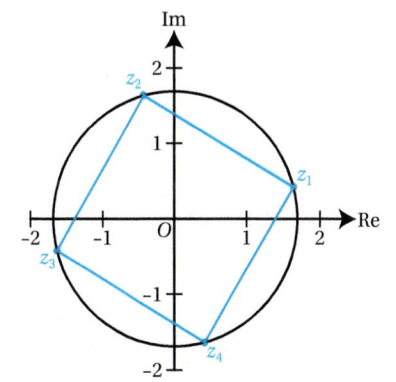

8 $n=4, w=-64$

9 a $\sqrt{2}\pm i\sqrt{2}, -\sqrt{2}\pm i\sqrt{2}$
  b $(z^2+2\sqrt{2}z+4)(z^2-2\sqrt{2}z+4)$

10 a $2i, -\sqrt{3}-i, \sqrt{3}-i$
  b $\frac{4}{5}-\frac{2}{5}i, \frac{14-3\sqrt{3}}{13}+\frac{(5-2\sqrt{3})}{13}i,$
  $\frac{14+3\sqrt{3}}{13}+\frac{(5+2\sqrt{3})}{13}i$

11 a $2\left(\cos\frac{\pi}{4}+i\sin\frac{\pi}{4}\right), 2\left(\cos\frac{11\pi}{12}+i\sin\frac{11\pi}{12}\right),$
  $2\left(\cos\frac{19\pi}{12}+i\sin\frac{19\pi}{12}\right)$
  b $1; \frac{7\pi}{12}$ **c** $\frac{\sqrt{2}}{2}-\frac{\sqrt{2}}{2}i$

12 a $-1, e^{\frac{i\pi}{3}}, e^{-\frac{i\pi}{3}}$ **b** $x^3+6x^2+12x+8$
  c $-3, -\frac{3}{2}+\frac{\sqrt{3}}{2}i, -\frac{3}{2}-\frac{\sqrt{3}}{2}i$

EXERCISE 1D

1 a i $\cos 0+i\sin 0, \cos\frac{2\pi}{3}+i\sin\frac{2\pi}{3},$
    $\cos\frac{4\pi}{3}+i\sin\frac{4\pi}{3}$
  ii $\cos 0+i\sin 0, \cos\pi+i\sin\pi$

  b i $\cos 0+i\sin 0, \cos\frac{\pi}{3}+i\sin\frac{\pi}{3},$
    $\cos\frac{2\pi}{3}+i\sin\frac{2\pi}{3}, \cos\pi+i\sin\pi,$
    $\cos\frac{4\pi}{3}+i\sin\frac{4\pi}{3}, \cos\frac{5\pi}{3}+i\sin\frac{5\pi}{3}$
  ii $\cos 0+i\sin 0, \cos\frac{\pi}{2}+i\sin\frac{\pi}{2},$
    $\cos\pi+i\sin\pi, \cos\frac{3\pi}{2}+i\sin\frac{3\pi}{2}$

2 a i $1, -\frac{1}{2}\pm i\frac{\sqrt{3}}{2}$ **ii** ± 1
  b i $\pm 1, \frac{1}{2}\pm i\frac{\sqrt{3}}{2}, -\frac{1}{2}\pm i\frac{\sqrt{3}}{2}$
  ii $\pm 1, \pm i$

3 a $1, e^{\frac{2\pi i}{5}}, e^{\frac{4\pi i}{5}}, e^{\frac{6\pi i}{5}}, e^{\frac{8\pi i}{5}}$
  b

4 a 5   b −1   c A, B, C

5 a 1 (or ω^0), $\omega, \omega^2, \omega^3, \omega^4, \omega^5, \omega^6$

   b No. Consider $\omega^7 = 1$, or an Argand diagram.

   c 3   d 5

6 a, b Proof.

7 a $1, \dfrac{1}{2} \pm \dfrac{\sqrt{3}}{2}i$ b $\dfrac{-1 \pm 3\sqrt{3}i}{2}$

8 $a^2 + b^2 + ab$

9 a (1), $\omega, \omega^2, \omega^3, \omega^4$

   b $\dfrac{1+\omega^k}{1-\omega^k}$ for $k = 1, 2, 3, 4$

   c–e Proof.

10 a

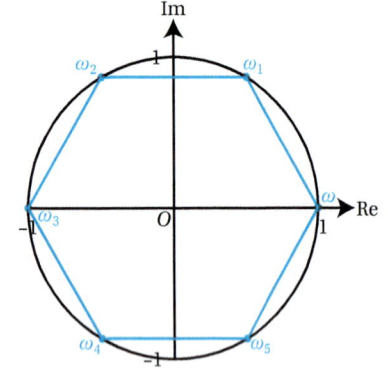

   b i $\dfrac{\sqrt{3}}{2}e^{i\frac{\pi}{6}}$ ii $\dfrac{\sqrt{3}}{2}e^{i\frac{7\pi}{6}}$

11 a Proof.

   b i Proof.   ii $-\dfrac{1}{2}$

   c Proof.

EXERCISE 1E

1 a $2e^{i\frac{\pi}{4}}, 2e^{i\frac{3\pi}{4}}, 2e^{i\frac{5\pi}{4}}, 2e^{i\frac{7\pi}{4}}$

   b $\sqrt{2} + i\sqrt{2}, \sqrt{2} - i\sqrt{2}, -\sqrt{2} + i\sqrt{2}, -\sqrt{2} - i\sqrt{2}$

   c $(z^2 + 2\sqrt{2}z + 4)(z^2 - 2\sqrt{2}z + 4)$

2 $(z^2 - 2)(z^2 + 2)(z^2 - 2z + 2)(z^2 + 2z + 2)$

3 Proof; $\theta = \dfrac{2\pi}{5}, \phi = \dfrac{4\pi}{5}$

4 a $1, \omega, \omega^2, \omega^3, \omega^4$ b 31

5 a Proof.

   b $e^{\frac{i\pi}{6}}, e^{\frac{2i\pi}{3}}, e^{\frac{7i\pi}{6}}, e^{\frac{5i\pi}{3}}$

   c $(z^2 + z + 1)(z^2 - z + 1)(z^2 + \sqrt{3}z + 1)(z^2 - \sqrt{3}z + 1)$

6 a $\omega, \omega^2, \omega^3, \omega^4, \omega^5, \omega^6$ (or $\omega, \omega^2, \omega^3, \omega^*, \omega^{*2}, \omega^{*3}$)

   b, c Proof.

EXERCISE 1F

1 a $\sqrt{17}, 0.245; \sqrt{34}, 0.540$ (3 s.f.)

   b $\sqrt{2}, 0.295$ (16.9°) (3 s.f.)

2 a Proof.

   b Rotation through 1.76 radians (101°) about the origin.

3 $\dfrac{3\sqrt{3}-2}{2} + i\dfrac{3+2\sqrt{3}}{2}$

4 (7, −3), (2, −5)

5 a $\sqrt{60}$ b $(6 - \sqrt{3}, 3 + 2\sqrt{3})$

6 a

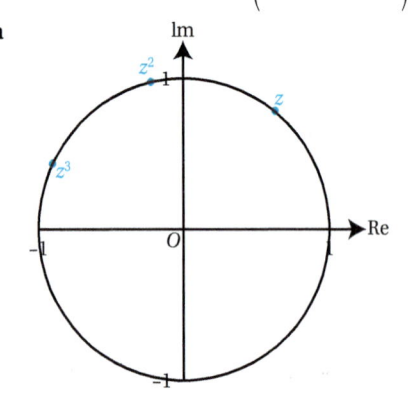

   b Rotation through 1.85 radians (106°) (3 s.f.) about the origin.

7 a $4 - i$

   b $B\left(\dfrac{\sqrt{3}-4}{2}, \dfrac{4\sqrt{3}+1}{2}\right), C\left(-\dfrac{4+\sqrt{3}}{2}, -\dfrac{4\sqrt{3}-1}{2}\right)$

8 a $\dfrac{\pi}{3}$ b $\dfrac{\pi}{6}$ c $\left(\dfrac{\sqrt{6}-\sqrt{2}}{2}, \dfrac{\sqrt{6}+\sqrt{2}}{2}\right)$

9 a iz^* b Proof.

10 a Proof.   b $\left(\dfrac{3-4\sqrt{3}}{2}, \dfrac{2-\sqrt{3}}{2}\right)$

11 a $c - a = (b - a)e^{i\theta}$

   b (0.935, 4.89)

12 $\dfrac{1-\sqrt{3}}{4} + \dfrac{1+\sqrt{3}}{4}i$

MIXED PRACTICE 1

1 A

2 a $2; \dfrac{2\pi}{3}$ b $-16 - 16i\sqrt{3}$

338

Answers to exercises

3 **a** $e^{\frac{2k\pi i}{5}}$ for $k = 0, 1, 2, 3, 4$

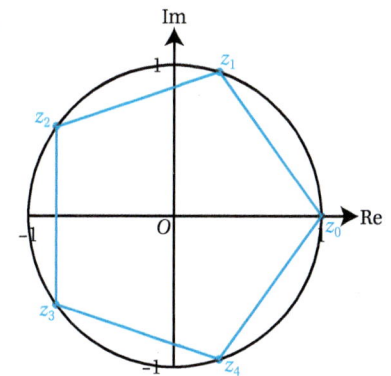

   b [diagram of unit circle with points z_0, z_1, z_2, z_3, z_4 forming a regular pentagon]

4 $e^{\frac{7\pi i}{12}}$

5 **a** $8\sqrt{2}; -\frac{\pi}{4}$

   b $z = 2^{\frac{7}{8}}\left(\cos\left(\frac{(8k-1)\pi}{16}\right) + i\sin\left(\frac{(8k-1)\pi}{16}\right)\right)$
   for $k = 0, 1, 2, 3$

6 **a** $\sqrt{2}, \frac{\pi}{4}$ **b** $z^6 = -8i$

7 **a** $9e^{-\frac{\pi i}{2}}$

   b $z = \sqrt{3}e^{\frac{k\pi i}{8}}$ for $k = -5, -1, 3, 7$

8 C

9 $-\frac{1}{64}$

10 **a** $\cos\left(-\frac{\pi}{6}\right) + i\sin\left(-\frac{\pi}{6}\right)$

   b Proof; $c = 1$.

   c For example, $m = 6, n = 4$

11 **a, b** Proof.

12 θ

13 Proof.

14 **a** $e^{i\frac{\pi}{2}}$ **b** $e^{-\frac{\pi}{2}}$

15 **a** $\omega^2 = e^{\frac{4\pi i}{5}}, \omega^3 = e^{\frac{6\pi i}{5}}, \omega^4 = e^{\frac{8\pi i}{5}}$

   b–d Proof.

16 **a** Proof.

   b **i** 1   **ii** 1

   c $z^3 - 4z^2 + 4z - 3 = 0$

17 Proof; it equals $2|a|\cos\frac{\theta}{2}$.

18 **a** $8e^{\frac{2\pi i}{3}}$

   b **i** $2e^{\frac{k\pi i}{9}}$ for $k = -4, 2, 8$

        ii $3\sqrt{3}$

   c Proof.

19 **a** $\frac{3-\sqrt{3}}{2} + \frac{1+3\sqrt{3}}{2}i$ **b** 5.35 (3 s.f.)

20 **a** Proof.

   b **i** a **ii** $b(\cos\theta + i\sin\theta)$

        iii $AB = \sqrt{a^2 + b^2 - 2ab\cos\theta}$

        iv Proof.

2 Further complex numbers: trigonometry

BEFORE YOU START

1 $32\left(\cos\frac{5\pi}{7} + i\sin\frac{5\pi}{7}\right)$

2 **a** $2 - i2\sqrt{3}$ **b** $2 + e^{-3i}$

3 $x^5 - 10x^4y + 40x^3y^2 - 80x^2y^3 + 80xy^4 - 32y^5$

4 Re = 0; Im = $-\frac{\sin x}{1 + \cos x}$

5 **a** $\frac{e^x(1 - e^{nx})}{1 - e^x}$ **b** $x < 0$

WORK IT OUT 2.1

Solution 2 is correct.

EXERCISE 2A

1 **a** $4\cos^3\theta\sin\theta - 4\cos\theta\sin^3\theta$

   b Proof.

2 $\sin 3\theta = 3\sin\theta - 4\sin^3\theta$

3 **a** $\cos^5\theta + 5i\cos^4\theta\sin\theta - 10\cos^3\theta\sin^2\theta$
   $- 10i\cos^2\theta\sin^3\theta + 5\cos\theta\sin^4\theta + i\sin^5\theta$

   b $\sin 5\theta = 16\sin^5\theta - 20\sin^3\theta + 5\sin\theta$

4 **a** Proof.   **b** $\frac{\pi}{2}, \frac{3\pi}{2}$

5 **a** $A = 16, B = 20, C = 5$

   b $0, \pm\frac{\sqrt{2}}{2}$

6 **a** Re: $\cos^4\theta - 6\sin^2\theta\cos^2\theta + \sin^4\theta$;
   Im: $4\cos^3\theta\sin\theta - 4\cos\theta\sin^3\theta$

   b $\tan 4\theta = \frac{4\tan\theta - 4\tan^3\theta}{1 - 6\tan^2\theta + \tan^4\theta}$

7 **a** Proof.   **b** $\frac{\pi}{24}, \frac{5\pi}{24}, \frac{3\pi}{8}$

8 **a** Re: $\cos^5\theta - 10\cos^3\theta\sin^2\theta + 5\cos\theta\sin^4\theta$;
   Im: $5\cos^4\theta\sin\theta - 10\cos^2\theta\sin^3\theta + \sin^5\theta$

   b Proof.   **c** $5 - 20\theta^2 + \ldots$

EXERCISE 2B

1 **a** $\cos 2\theta = 2\cos^2\theta - 1$

   b $2c^2 - \left(1 + \frac{\sqrt{3}}{2}\right) = 0$ **c** $\frac{\sqrt{2+\sqrt{3}}}{2}$

2 **a** Proof.   **b** $\frac{\pi}{8}, \frac{5\pi}{8}$ **c** $-1 - \sqrt{2}$

339

3 a $\frac{\pi}{10}, \frac{3\pi}{10}, \frac{7\pi}{10}, \frac{9\pi}{10}$ b Proof.

4 a Proof.

  b $\frac{\pi}{18}, \frac{5\pi}{18}, \frac{13\pi}{18}, \frac{17\pi}{18}, \frac{25\pi}{18}, \frac{29\pi}{18}$

  c Proof; $\sin\frac{5\pi}{18}, \sin\frac{25\pi}{18}$

5 a Proof.

  b $\tan 3\theta = \frac{3t - t^3}{1 - 3t^2}$; $\tan 4\theta = \frac{4t - 4t^3}{1 - 6t^2 + t^4}$; proof.

6 a Proof.   b $\frac{\sqrt{7}}{8}$

EXERCISE 2C

1 a i $2\cos 3\theta + 6\cos\theta$

   ii $\cos 4\theta + 4\cos 2\theta + 6$

  b i $2\cos 4\theta - 8\cos 2\theta + 6$

   ii $\sin 5\theta - 5\sin 3\theta + 10\sin\theta$

2 a Proof.

  b Proof; $A = 2$, $B = 10$, $C = 20$

3 a Proof.

  b $\frac{5\pi}{48} - \frac{9\sqrt{3}}{64}$

4 a i, ii Proof.

  b i $z^5 - 5z^3 + 10z - \frac{10}{z} + \frac{5}{z^3} - \frac{1}{z^5}$

   ii $a = 1$, $b = -5$, $c = 10$

  c $\frac{1}{16}\left(-\frac{1}{10}\cos 10x + \frac{5}{6}\cos 6x - 5\cos 2x\right) + c$

5 a Proof.

  b $(z + z^{-1})^6 = z^6 + 6z^4 + 15z^2 + 20 + 15z^{-2}$
       $+ 6z^{-4} + z^{-6}$

   $(z - z^{-1})^6 = z^6 - 6z^4 + 15z^2 - 20 + 15z^{-2}$
       $- 6z^{-4} + z^{-6}$

  c Proof.

6 a $\sin x = \frac{e^{ix} - e^{-ix}}{2i}$, $\cos x = \frac{e^{ix} + e^{-ix}}{2}$

  b $\frac{4}{35}$

EXERCISE 2D

1 a $\frac{3}{3 - e^{i\theta}}$ or, alternatively, $\frac{3(3 - e^{-i\theta})}{10 - 6\cos\theta}$

  b $\frac{9 - 3\cos 1}{10 - 6\cos 1}$ (≈ 1.09)

2 a Proof; $\frac{2}{2 - e^{i\theta}}$ or, alternatively, $\frac{2(2 - e^{-i\theta})}{5 - 4\cos\theta}$

  b Proof.

3 $\frac{2\sin 1}{5 + 4\cos 2}$ (≈ 0.505)

4 Proof.

5 Proof.

6 a $\frac{e^{i\theta}(1 - e^{2ni\theta})}{1 - e^{2i\theta}}$ b Proof.

  c $\theta = \frac{\pi}{6}, \frac{2\pi}{6}, \frac{3\pi}{6}, \frac{4\pi}{6}, \frac{5\pi}{6}$

MIXED PRACTICE 2

1 a $\cos^4\theta + 4i\cos^3\theta\sin\theta - 6\cos^2\theta\sin^2\theta$
     $- 4i\cos\theta\sin^3\theta + \sin^4\theta$

  b $A = 4$, $B = 8$

2 Proof; $\frac{1}{5}, -\frac{1}{5}$

3 a $A = \frac{1}{16}$, $B = \frac{5}{16}$, $C = \frac{5}{8}$

  b $\frac{8}{15}$

4 Proof.   5 Proof.   6 Proof.

7 a, b Proof.

  c i Proof.

   ii $\frac{2}{3} \pm \frac{\sqrt{5}}{3}i$, $-\frac{1}{2} \pm \frac{\sqrt{3}}{2}i$

8 a $\cos 3\theta = \cos^3\theta - 3\sin^2\theta\cos\theta$
     $\sin 3\theta = 3\sin\theta\cos^2\theta - \sin^3\theta$

  b, c Proof.

  d Proof; -1, $2 \pm \sqrt{3}$

  e Proof.

  f $2 - \sqrt{3}$

9 a i Proof; $\sin 5\theta = 5\cos^4\theta\sin\theta$
         $- 10\cos^2\theta\sin^3\theta + \sin^5\theta$

   ii Proof.

  b Proof; $\tan\frac{2\pi}{5}$, $\tan\frac{3\pi}{5}$, $\tan\frac{4\pi}{5}$

  c Proof.

10 a Proof.

  b i $z^8 + 4z^4 + 6 + 4z^{-4} + z^{-8}$

   ii Proof; $A = \frac{1}{8}$, $B = \frac{1}{2}$, $C = \frac{3}{8}$.

  c $\theta = \frac{\pi}{12}, \frac{5\pi}{12}, \frac{7\pi}{12}, \frac{11\pi}{12}$

  d Proof.

3 Further transformations of the ellipse, hyperbola and parabola

BEFORE YOU START

1 Hyperbola; asymptotes $\frac{y}{3} = \pm\frac{x}{4}$; axis intercepts $(\pm 4, 0)$.

2 **a** $(y+2)^2 = 6(x-5)$

   b $x^2 = -6y$

3 Reflection in the x-axis, horizontal stretch with scale factor $\frac{1}{3}$.

EXERCISE 3A

1 Proof; $y^2 = 12x$

2 Proof; $(1, -2)$

3 $\frac{x^2}{16} + \frac{y^2}{25} = 1$;

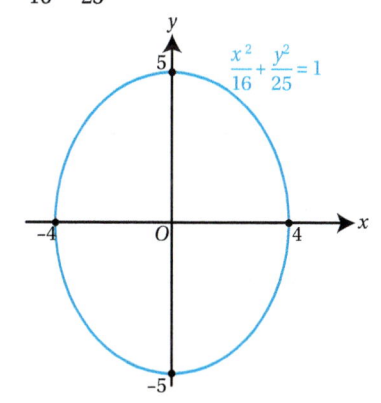

4 Proof; $y = \pm\frac{3}{7}x$

5

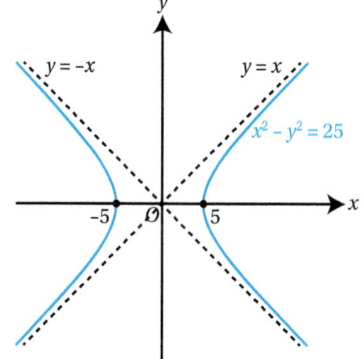

6 Proof; $x = 3$, $y = 1$

7 Proof; $(-1, 0)$

8 $x^2 - y^2 = 5$; (rectangular) hyperbola.

9 $x^2 + 4y^2 = 2$; ellipse.

10 **a** $\frac{(x-6)^2}{9} - \frac{y^2}{27} = 1$

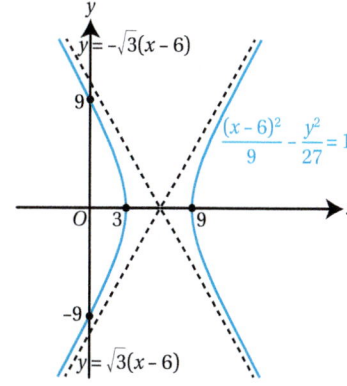

   b

11 $\frac{x^2}{200} + \frac{(y-5)^2}{225} = 1$; ellipse; $x = 0$, $y = 5$.

12 **a** $5x + 6y = 16$

   b Translation with vector $\begin{pmatrix} 3 \\ -2 \end{pmatrix}$.

   c $5x + 6y = 19$

13 **a** $\frac{x^2}{25} + y^2 = 18$

   b $x + y = 6$

   c $x + 5y = 30$

14 **a** $y = \pm\sqrt{2}x$

   b Horizontal stretch with scale factor 4.

   c $y = \pm\frac{\sqrt{2}}{4}x$

EXERCISE 3B

1

	90°	180°	270°	unchanged under rotations
a	$\frac{y^2}{4} + \frac{x^2}{7} = 1$	$\frac{x^2}{4} + \frac{y^2}{7} = 1$	$\frac{y^2}{4} + \frac{x^2}{7} = 1$	180°
b	$\frac{y^2}{4} - \frac{x^2}{7} = 1$	$\frac{x^2}{4} - \frac{y^2}{7} = 1$	$\frac{y^2}{4} - \frac{x^2}{7} = 1$	180°
c	$x^2 = 8y$	$y^2 = -8x$	$x^2 = -8y$	–

2 **a** $\frac{x^2}{2} + \frac{y^2}{5} = 1$; reflections in $y = \pm x$.

   b $\frac{y^2}{12} - \frac{x^2}{5} = 1$; reflections in $y = \pm x$.

   c $y = \frac{1}{5}x^2$; reflection in $y = x$.

3 $\frac{y^2}{5} - \frac{x^2}{12} = 1$

4 $y = \frac{1}{6}x^2$

5 $\frac{x^2}{9} - \frac{2y^2}{9} = 1$

341

6 a

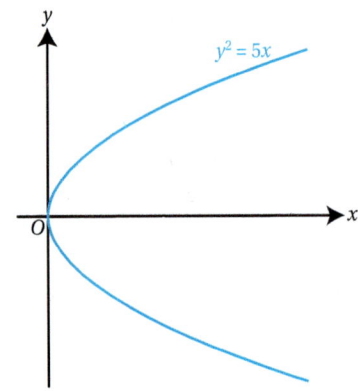

[Graph of $y^2 = 5x$]

  b $y^2 = 15x$

  c Horizontal stretch with scale factor 3.

7 Enlargement, centre at the origin, scale factor $\sqrt{7}$.

8 Rotation through 90° (in either direction) about the origin or reflection in $y = x$; $y = \pm\sqrt{3}\,x$.

9 a

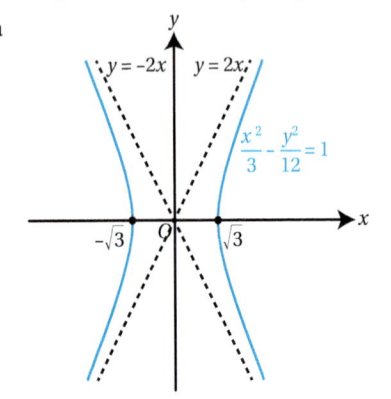

[Graph of $\frac{x^2}{3} - \frac{y^2}{12} = 1$ with asymptotes $y = \pm 2x$ and vertices at $\pm\sqrt{3}$]

  b Proof.

10 Proof; $y = \pm\frac{3}{4}x$

WORK IT OUT 3.1

Solution 3 is correct.

EXERCISE 3C

1 a i $\dfrac{(y+1)^2}{3} + \dfrac{(x-3)^2}{5} = 1$

  ii $\dfrac{(y-5)^2}{4} - \dfrac{(x+2)^2}{3} = 1$

  b i $x^2 = -6(y+3)$

  ii $(x-5)^2 = -10y$

  c i $\dfrac{x^2}{25} - \dfrac{(y-3)^2}{4} = 16$

  ii $\dfrac{(x+2)^2}{4} + \dfrac{y^2}{9} = 12$

  d i $y^2 = 4(x-3)$

  ii $y^2 = 16(x+3)$

2 a i Translation with vector $\begin{pmatrix} 1 \\ -5 \end{pmatrix}$ and enlargement with scale factor 3.

  ii Translation with vector $\begin{pmatrix} 3 \\ 2 \end{pmatrix}$ and enlargement with scale factor 4.

  b i Horizontal stretch with scale factor $\frac{1}{3}$, vertical stretch with scale factor $\frac{1}{2}$ and translation with vector $\begin{pmatrix} 2 \\ 0 \end{pmatrix}$.

  ii Enlargement with scale factor $\sqrt{3}$ and translation with vector $\begin{pmatrix} -5 \\ 3 \end{pmatrix}$.

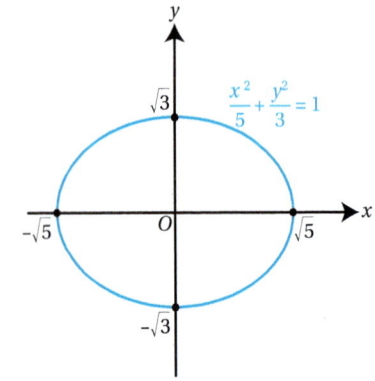

  c i Translation with vector $\begin{pmatrix} 4 \\ 2 \end{pmatrix}$ and reflection in the line $y = x$.

    (Or reflection in $y = x$ followed by translation $\begin{pmatrix} 2 \\ 4 \end{pmatrix}$; or 90° rotation instead of the reflection.)

  ii Translation with vector $\begin{pmatrix} -3 \\ 4 \end{pmatrix}$ and reflection in the line $y = x$.

    (Or reflection in $y = x$ followed by translation $\begin{pmatrix} 4 \\ -3 \end{pmatrix}$.)

  d i Reflection in $y = x$, vertical stretch with scale factor $\frac{1}{2}$ and translation 3 units in the positive x-direction.

  ii Reflection in $y = x$, vertical stretch with scale factor 4 and translation 1 unit in the positive y-direction.

3 $y^2 = 12(x-15)$; $(15, 0)$

4 $p = 8$

5 $\begin{pmatrix} 3 \\ -1 \end{pmatrix}$

6 $\begin{pmatrix} 5 \\ -3 \end{pmatrix}$

7 a

[Graph of ellipse $\frac{x^2}{5} + \frac{y^2}{3} = 1$ with intercepts $\pm\sqrt{5}$ and $\pm\sqrt{3}$]

Answers to exercises

b $\dfrac{(2y-3)^2}{5} + \dfrac{4x^2}{3} = 1$

8 a Hyperbola; $y = \pm\sqrt{\dfrac{7}{12}}x$

b $\dfrac{9y^2}{12} - \dfrac{(-3x-5)^2}{7} = 1$

(or $\dfrac{9y^2}{12} - \dfrac{(3x+5)^2}{7} = 1$)

c $y = \pm\dfrac{6x+10}{\sqrt{21}}$

(or, for example: $6x = -10 \pm \sqrt{21}y$)

9 a $x = -4, y = 7$

b Enlargement with scale factor 2, centre origin.

10 a Stretch scale factor a in the x-direction and scale factor b in the y-direction.

b πab

11 a $y^2 = 32(x+1)$

b Translation 1 unit to the left; vertical stretch with scale factor $2\sqrt{2}$.

12 $\dfrac{(x-2)^2}{4} - \dfrac{y^2}{36} = 1$; $y = 3x - 6$, $y = -3x + 6$

13 a Proof.

b $y = 3x - 3$, $y = -3x + 3$

14 $\begin{pmatrix} -1 \\ -3 \end{pmatrix}$

15 Translation with vector $\begin{pmatrix} 1 \\ 1 \end{pmatrix}$; horizontal stretch with scale factor $\dfrac{1}{3}$; vertical stretch with scale factor 2.

MIXED PRACTICE 3

1 C

2 a

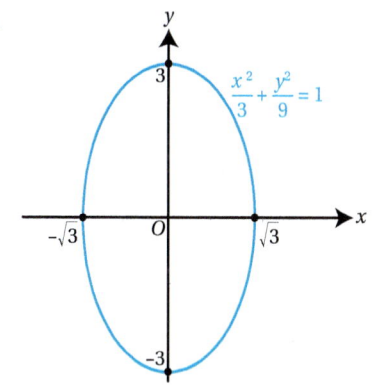

[Graph of ellipse $\dfrac{x^2}{3} + \dfrac{y^2}{9} = 1$ with intercepts at $\pm\sqrt{3}$ on x-axis and ± 3 on y-axis]

b $x^2 + \dfrac{y^2}{3} = 1$

3 $(y-4)^2 = 15(x+1)$; $(-1, 4)$

4 $(x+2)^2 - (y-2)^2 = 45$; $y = x + 4$ and $y = -x$

5 $(0, 0)$ and $(26.0, 12.5)$

6 a $(4, 4)$ and $(-4, -4)$.

b Translation 3 units in the positive x-direction, vertical stretch with scale factor $\dfrac{1}{2}$.

c $(7, 2)$ and $(-1, -2)$.

7 A

8 $(-y-5)^2 = 7(-x-3)$ (or $(y+5)^2 = -7(x+3)$); $(-3, -5)$

9 a Proof.

b $k = \dfrac{\sqrt{3}}{3}$

10 a $k = \pm\sqrt{13}$

b $(x+1)^2 + \dfrac{(3y-2)^2}{4} = 1$

c $c = \dfrac{-1 \pm \sqrt{13}}{3}$

11 a $c = 36, d = 20$

b Translation $\begin{pmatrix} 4 \\ 0 \end{pmatrix}$.

12 B

13 $\dfrac{4a^2b^2}{a^2+b^2}$

14 a $\dfrac{(y-2)^2}{25} - \dfrac{(x-1)^2}{16} = 1$

b For example, reflection in $y = x$; translation $\begin{pmatrix} 1 \\ 2 \end{pmatrix}$.

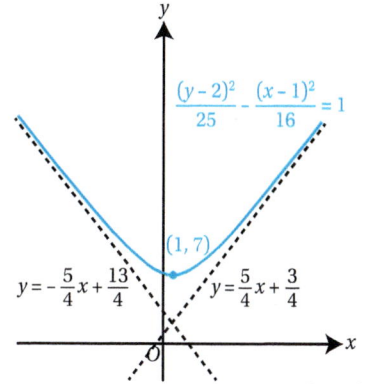

c

[Graph of hyperbola $\dfrac{(y-2)^2}{25} - \dfrac{(x-1)^2}{16} = 1$ with vertex $(1, 7)$ and asymptotes $y = -\dfrac{5}{4}x + \dfrac{13}{4}$ and $y = \dfrac{5}{4}x + \dfrac{3}{4}$]

vertex $(1, 7)$; asymptotes $y = \dfrac{5}{4}x + \dfrac{3}{4}$ and $y = -\dfrac{5}{4}x + \dfrac{13}{4}$.

15 a $\dfrac{(x+6)^2}{45} + \dfrac{y^2}{9} = 1$

b Translation 6 units to the right; vertical stretch with scale factor $\sqrt{5}$.

c $9\sqrt{5}\pi$

343

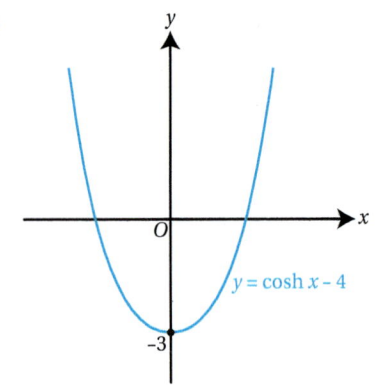

4 Further graphs and inequalities

BEFORE YOU START

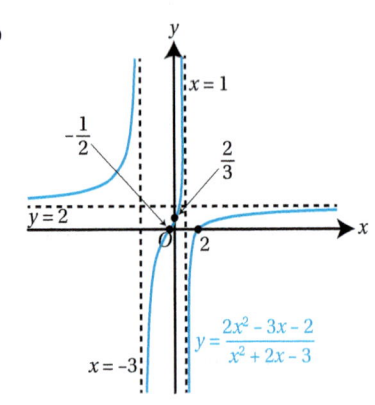

1 a Graph of $y = \dfrac{x+3}{x-2}$ with asymptotes $y = 1$ and $x = 2$; intercepts at -3 and $-\dfrac{3}{2}$.

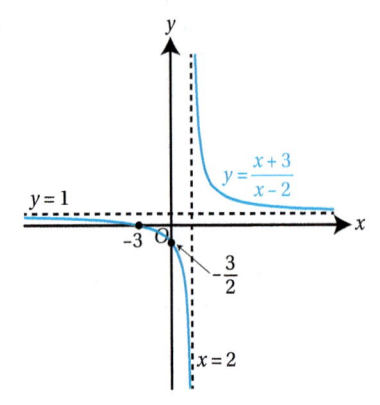

b Graph of $y = \dfrac{2x^2 - 3x - 2}{x^2 + 2x - 3}$ with asymptotes $x = 1$, $x = -3$, $y = 2$; intercepts $-\dfrac{1}{2}$ and $\dfrac{2}{3}$.

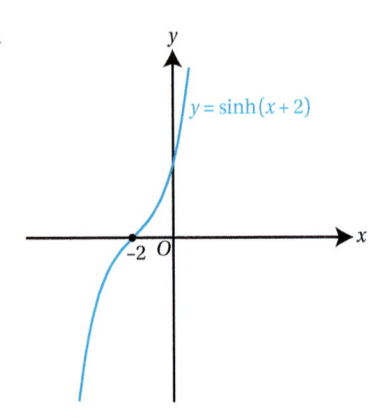

2 a Graph of $y = \sinh(x+2)$ passing through -2 on the x-axis.

b Graph of $y = \cosh x - 4$ with minimum at -3.

3 Graphs of $y = |2x - 3|$ and $y = |x + 1|$ intersecting; key points -1, 1, $\dfrac{3}{2}$, 3.

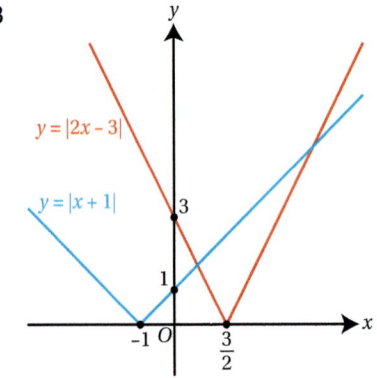

4 $\dfrac{2}{3} < x < 4$

EXERCISE 4A

1 a i Graph with vertical asymptote $x = 3$, horizontal asymptote $y = 0$, intercept $\left(0, -\dfrac{1}{3}\right)$.

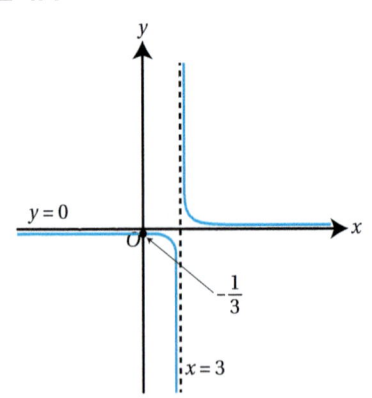

vertical asymptote: $x = 3$; horizontal asymptote: $y = 0$; axis intercept $\left(0, -\dfrac{1}{3}\right)$.

ii

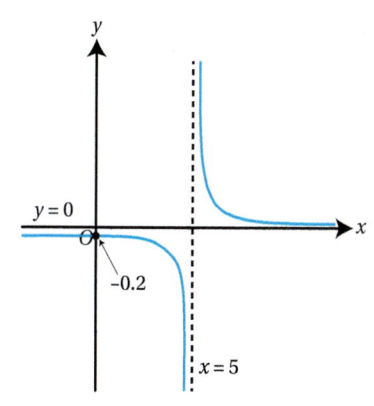

vertical asymptote: $x = 5$; horizontal asymptote: $y = 0$; axis intercept $(0, -0.2)$.

b i

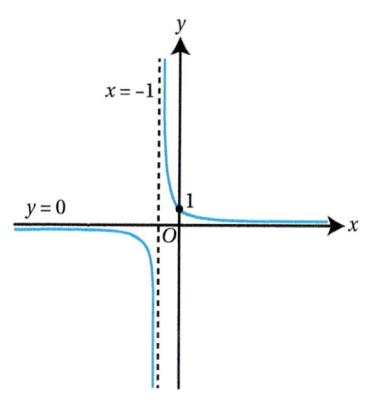

vertical asymptote: $x = -1$; horizontal asymptote: $y = 0$; axis intercept $(0, 1)$.

ii

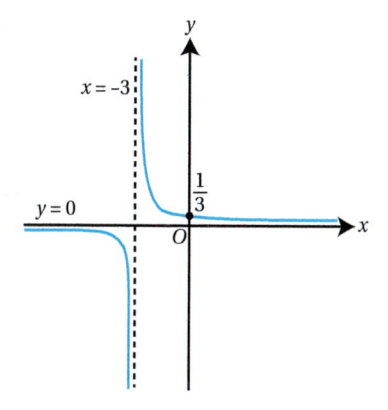

vertical asymptote: $x = -3$; horizontal asymptote: $y = 0$; axis intercept $\left(0, \dfrac{1}{3}\right)$.

c i

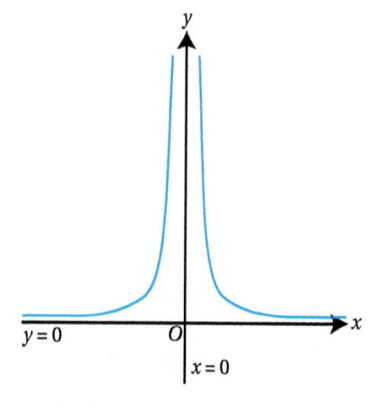

vertical asymptote: $x = 0$; horizontal asymptote: $y = 0$; no axis intercepts.

ii

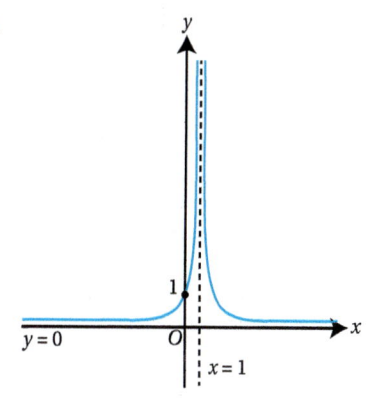

vertical asymptote: $x = 1$; horizontal asymptote: $y = 0$; axis intercept $(0, 1)$.

d i

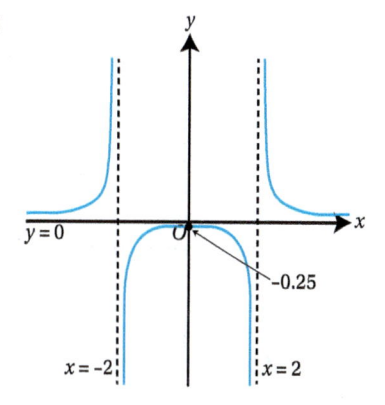

vertical asymptotes: $x = \pm 2$; horizontal asymptote: $y = 0$; axis intercept $(0, -0.25)$.

ii

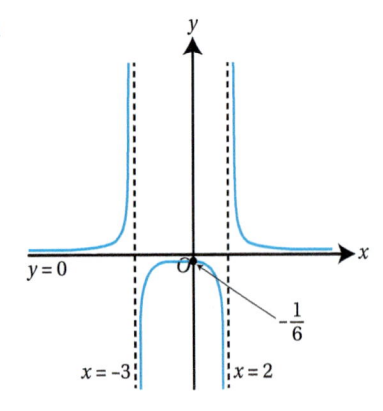

vertical asymptotes: $x = 2$, $x = -3$; horizontal asymptote: $y = 0$; axis intercept $\left(0, -\dfrac{1}{6}\right)$.

e i

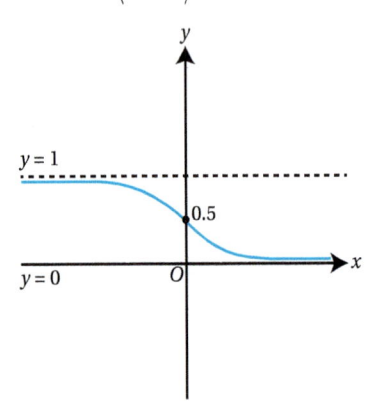

horizontal asymptotes: $y = 1$, $y = 0$; axis intercept $(0, 0.5)$.

ii

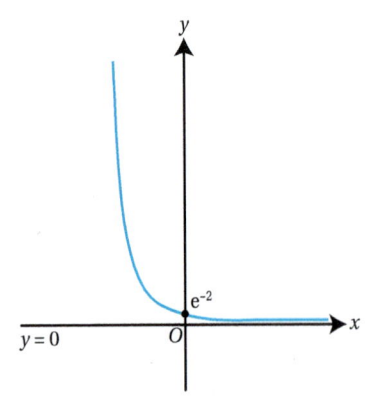

horizontal asymptote: $y = 0$; axis intercept $(0, e^{-2})$.

f i

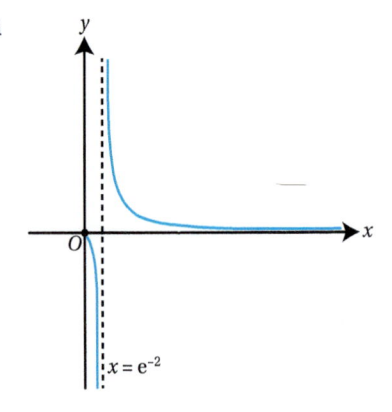

vertical asymptote: $x = e^{-2}$; axis intercept $(0, 0)$.

ii

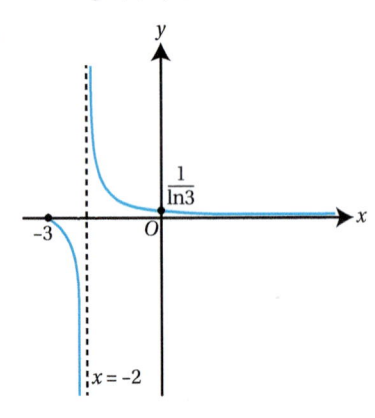

vertical asymptote: $x = -2$; axis intercepts $(-3, 0)$, $\left(0, \dfrac{1}{\ln 3}\right)$.

g i

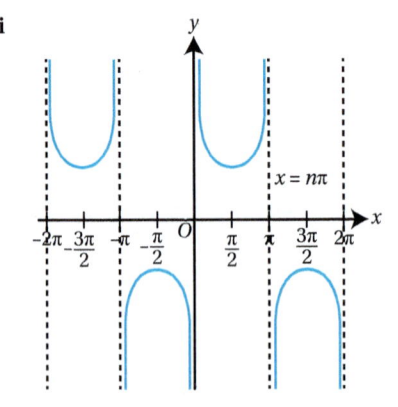

vertical asymptotes: $x = n\pi$ for integer n; no axis intercepts.

Answers to exercises

ii vertical asymptotes: $x = n\pi$ for integer n; axis intercepts $\left(\dfrac{2n+1}{2}\pi, 0\right)$.

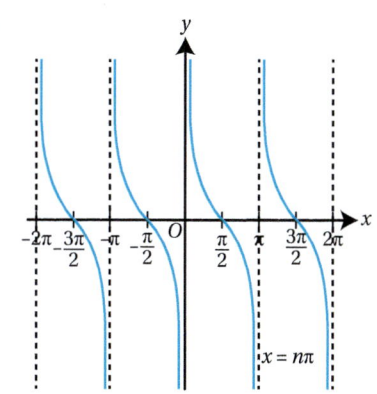

2 a i **A:** $(2, 0), (0, -0.4); x = \pm\sqrt{5}$
B: $(\pm\sqrt{5}, 0)(0, -2.5); x = 2$

ii **A:** $(\pm 2, 0), (0, -4); x = -1, x = -0.5$
B: $(-1, 0), (-0.5, 0), (0, -0.25); x = \pm 2$

b i **A:** $(0, 0), (\pm 2, 0), (4, 0); x = 1, x = 3$
B: $(1, 0), (3, 0); x = 0, x = \pm 2, x = 4$

ii **A:** $(1, 0), (-3, 0), (0, 1); x = -1, x = 3$
B: $(-1, 0), (3, 0), (0, 1); x = 1, x = -3$

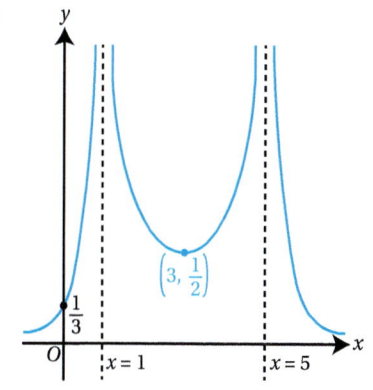

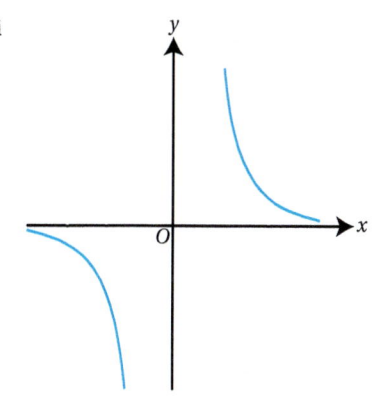

3 a i [graph: parabola-like curve with minimum at $(0, 2)$]

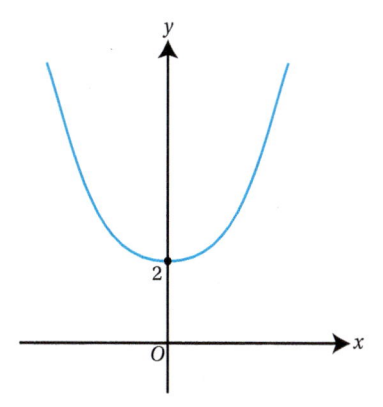

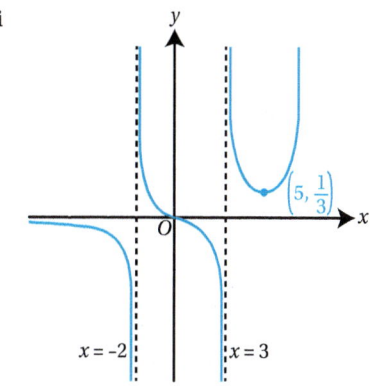

ii [graph with asymptotes $x = -1$ and $x = 3$, horizontal asymptote $y = \tfrac{1}{5}$, passing through $-\tfrac{1}{2}$]

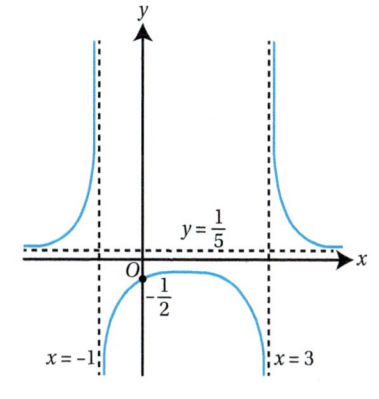

b i [graph with asymptotes $x = 1$ and $x = 5$, point $\left(3, \tfrac{1}{2}\right)$, y-intercept $\tfrac{1}{3}$]

ii [graph of hyperbola-like curve in first and third quadrants]

c i [graph with asymptotes $x = -2$ and $x = 3$, point $\left(5, \tfrac{1}{3}\right)$]

ii [graph with asymptotes $x = -3$ and $x = 4$, points $\left(-2, \tfrac{1}{4}\right)$ and $\left(2, -\tfrac{1}{5}\right)$]

347

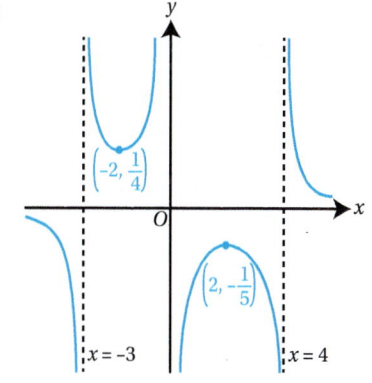

d i

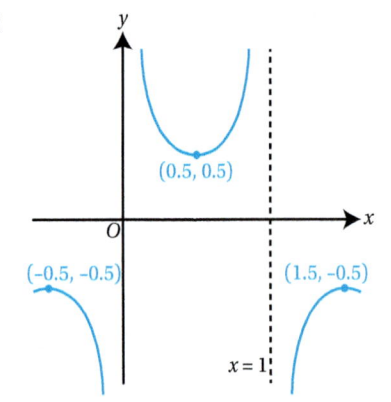

ii

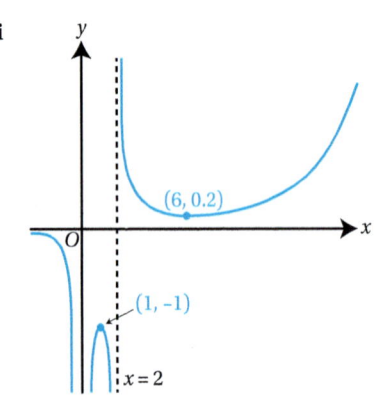

e i

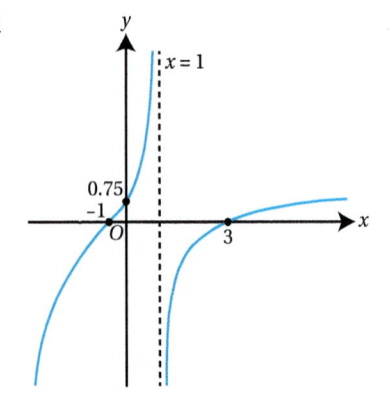

ii

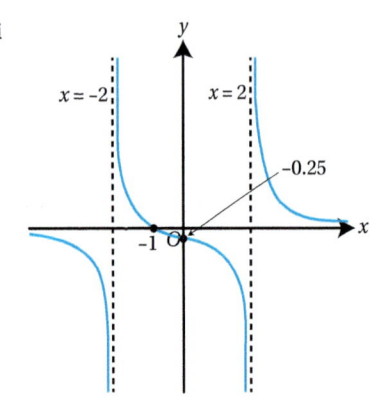

4

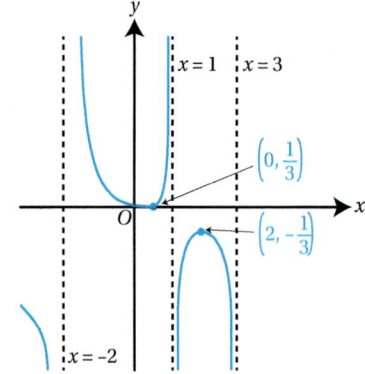

5

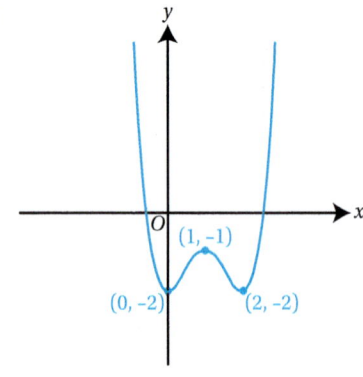

6 $a = 2$, $b = -12$, $c = 18$, $d = -2$, $e = 1$

7

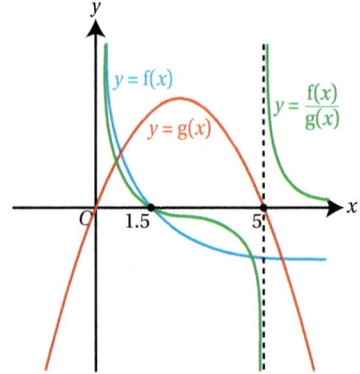

EXERCISE 4B

1 a i

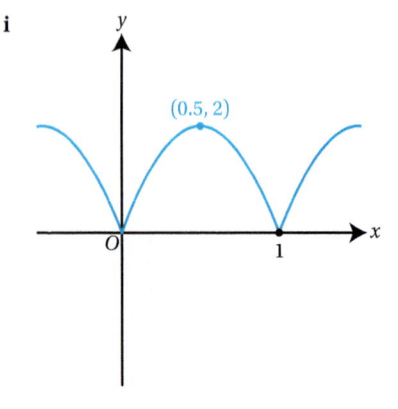

Answers to exercises

ii

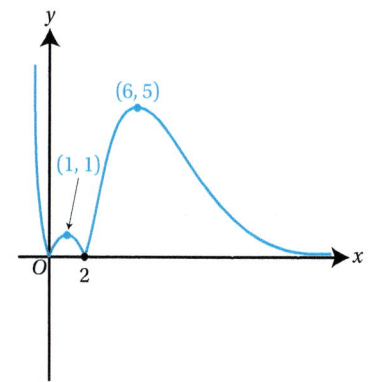

b i

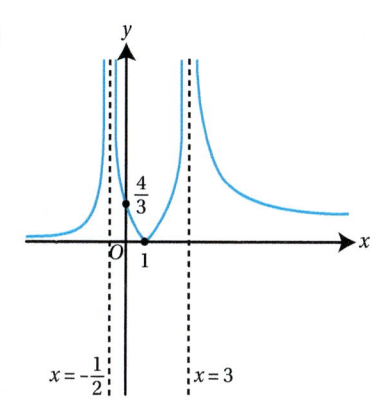

ii

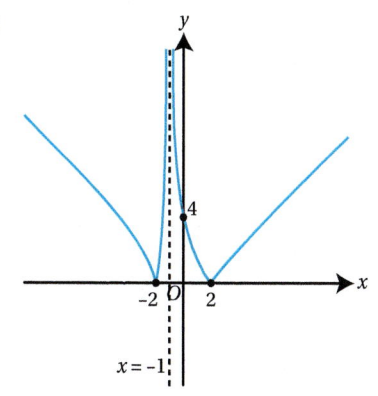

2 a i

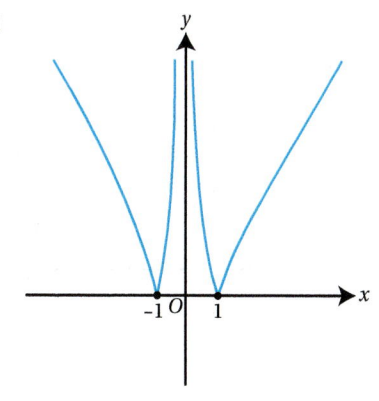

ii

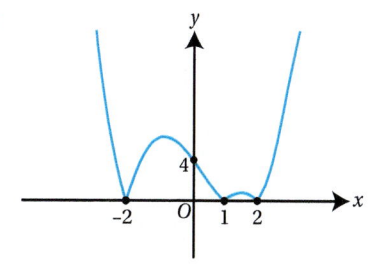

b i

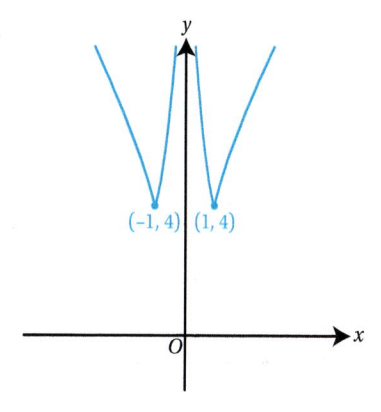

ii

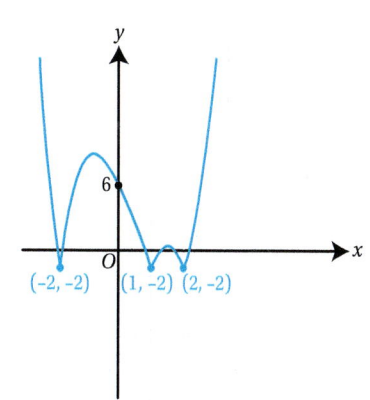

c i

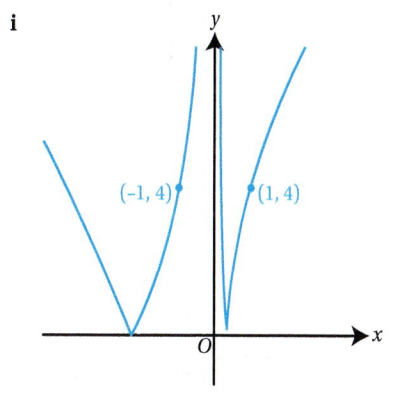

349

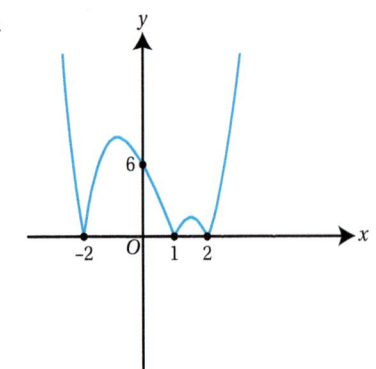

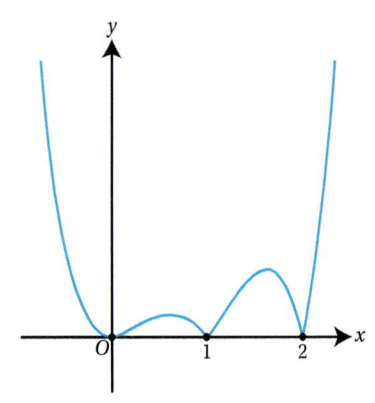

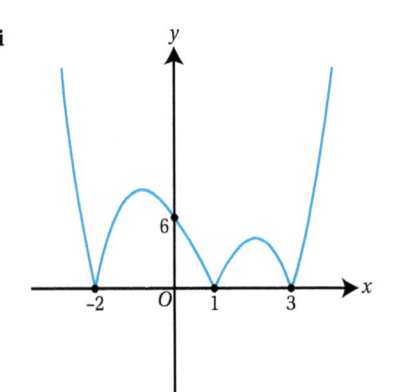

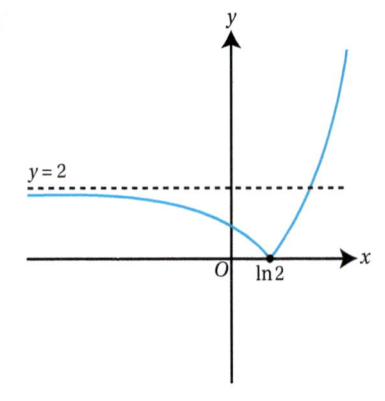

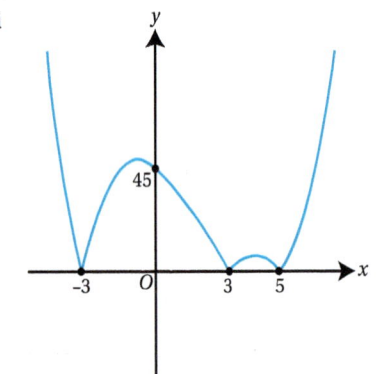

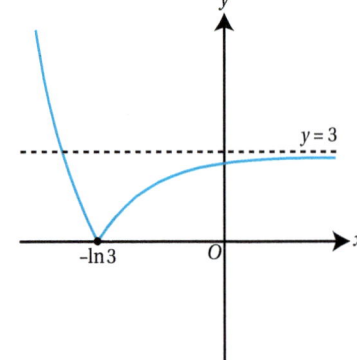

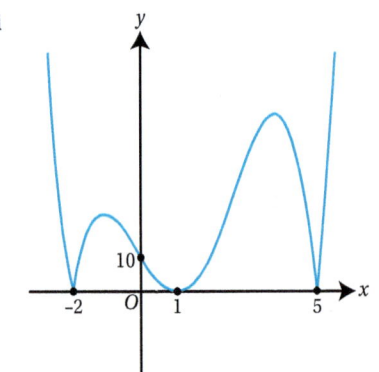

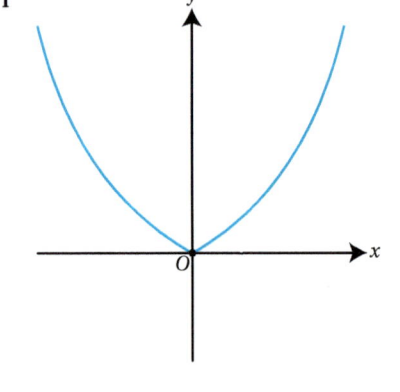

ii

3 a i

ii

b i

c i

ii

d i

Answers to exercises

ii

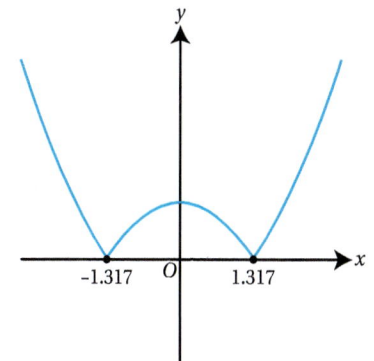

[Graph: parabola-like curve with minima at -1.317 and 1.317]

e i

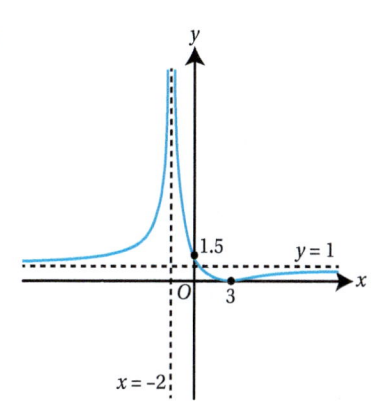

[Graph with asymptotes $x=-2$ and $y=1$, passing through 1.5 and 3]

ii

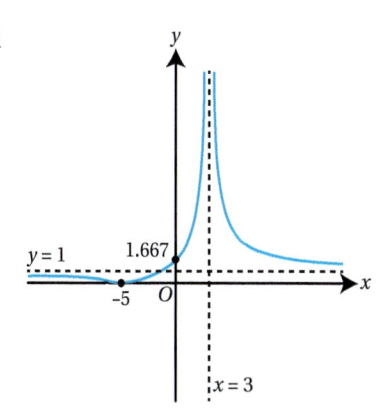

[Graph with asymptotes $x=3$ and $y=1$, passing through -5 and 1.667]

4

[Graph: W-shaped curve with minima at a and b, local max at $-ab$]

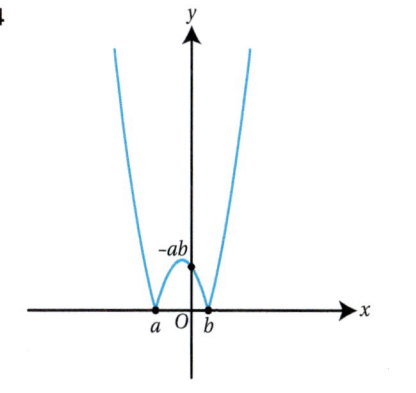

5 Three.

6 Four.

7 a -4 **b** $k=0$ or $k>4$

8 a

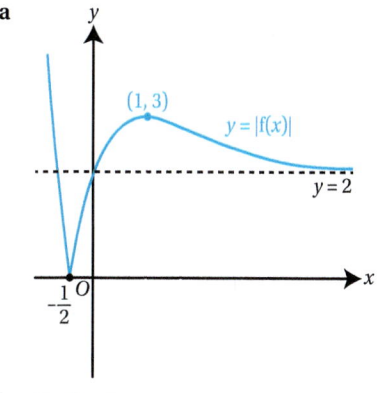

[Graph of $y=|f(x)|$ with point $(1,3)$, asymptote $y=2$, minimum at $-\frac{1}{2}$]

b $2<k<3$

9 $2 \leqslant x \leqslant 5$

10 $0 \leqslant f(x) < 5$

11

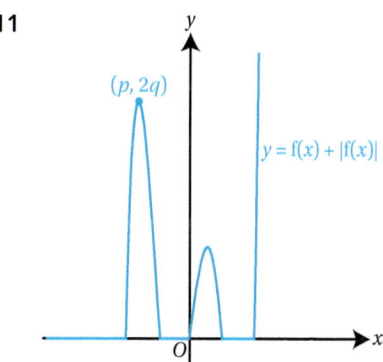

[Graph of $y=f(x)+|f(x)|$ with point $(p, 2q)$]

12 a

[Graph of $y=\frac{1}{2}(f(x)+|f(x)|)$ with points a, $(p, f(p))$, d, b, c]

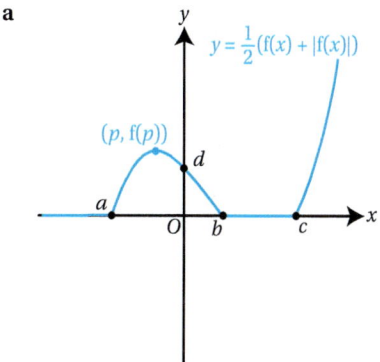

b $x \in [a, b] \cup [c, \infty[$

WORK IT OUT 4.1

Solution 2 is correct.

EXERCISE 4C

1 $x = \pm 3$

2 $-3 < x < -1$

3 $x<-3, -1<x<4, x>4$

351

4   0.472, 8.47 (3 s.f.)

5    $x = \alpha + 2n\pi$ for integer n and $\alpha \in \left[\dfrac{\pi}{6}, \dfrac{5\pi}{6}\right] \cup \left[\dfrac{7\pi}{6}, \dfrac{11\pi}{6}\right]$

6    $x \leq \ln \dfrac{7}{6}, x \geq \ln \dfrac{7}{4}$

7    $-4 < x < \dfrac{2}{3}$

8    $x \leq \dfrac{5}{7}, x \geq 3$

9    $x = 0, 4, -4$

10    $x = 4, -\dfrac{4}{3}$

11    $-1 < x < -\dfrac{\sqrt{2}}{2}$ or $\dfrac{\sqrt{2}}{2} < x < 1$

12    $x \in [-2.06, -1.32] \cup [1.32, 2.06]$ (3 s.f.)

13    $x = \dfrac{q^2}{2}$

14    $xy \geq 0$

MIXED PRACTICE 4

1   D

2   a   [graph of $\dfrac{1}{f(x)}$ with asymptotes $x=-5$, $x=5$]

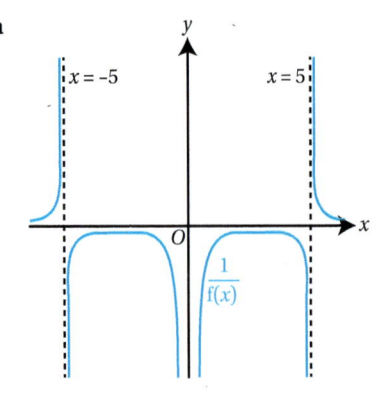

     b $\left(-3, -\dfrac{1}{5}\right), \left(3, -\dfrac{1}{5}\right)$

3    $\dfrac{1}{3} < x < 1$

4    $x = 2, y = x - 2, y = 2 - x$;

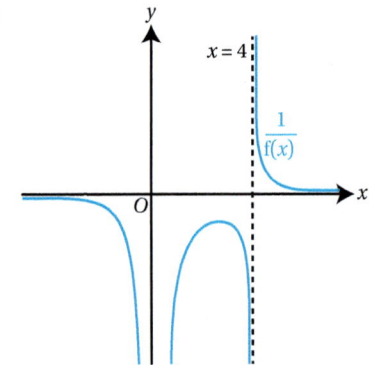

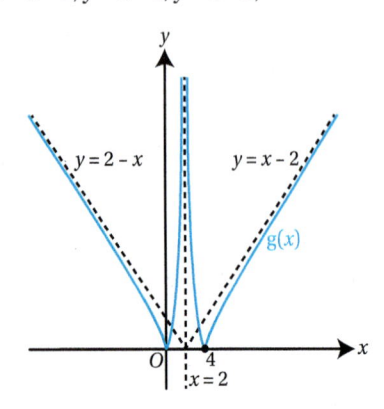

[graph of $g(x)$ with asymptote $x=2$, passing through 4]

5   [graph of $\dfrac{1}{f(x)}$ with asymptote $x=4$]

6   a   [graph of $y = |4\ln(x-e)|$ with asymptote $x=e$, minimum at $1+e$]

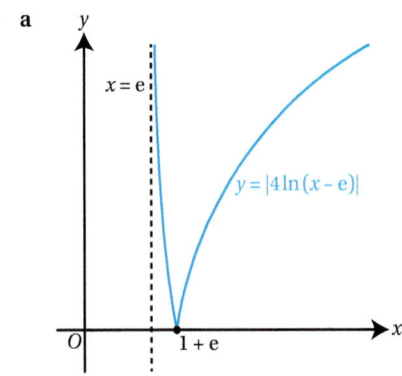

     b   i $x = e + \dfrac{1}{e}$ or $x = 2e$

         ii $e < x \leq e + \dfrac{1}{e}$ or $x \geq 2e$

7   a   i   [graph of $y = |3x+3|$, vertex at -1, y-intercept 3]

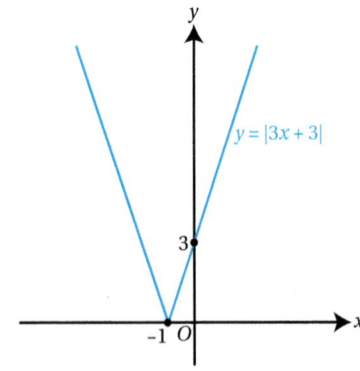

         ii   [graph of $y = |x^2 - 1|$, zeros at $-1, 1$, value 1 at 0]

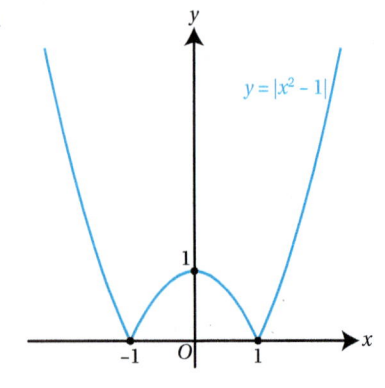

     b   i $x = -2, -1, 4$ ii $x > 4, x < -2$

8   a $x = 1.2, -0.8$

   b $-0.8 \leq x \leq 1.2$

9   $1 \leq x < 2$ or $2 < x \leq 5$

10 $x < -5$ or $x > -2$

11 $x = 0, 1, 5$

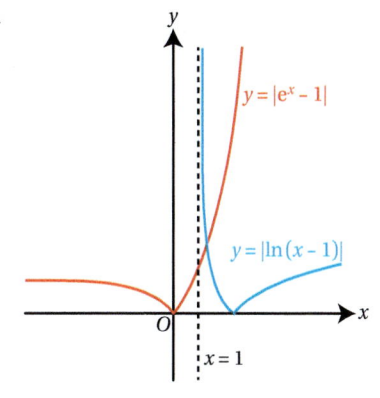

12 a   [graph of $y = |e^x - 1|$ and $y = |\ln(x-1)|$ with asymptote $x = 1$]

   b   One.

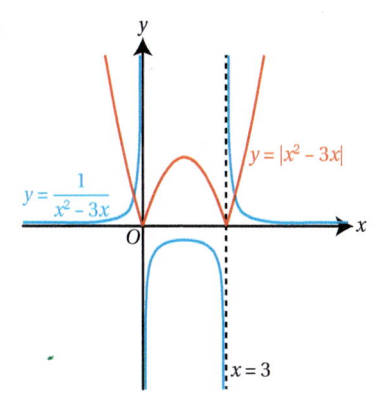

13 a   [graph of $y = \frac{1}{x^2 - 3x}$ and $y = |x^2 - 3x|$ with asymptote $x = 3$]

   b $x < -0.303$, $0 < x < 3$, $x > 3.30$

14 $x \geq 0$

15 a   Proof.

   b $x = 2$

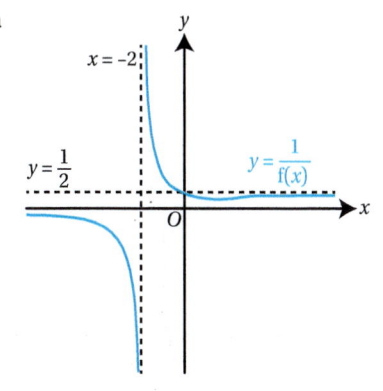

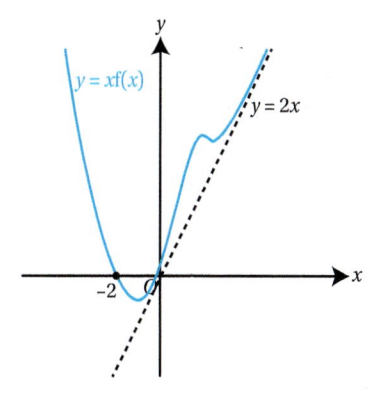

16 a   [graph of $y = \frac{1}{f(x)}$ with asymptotes $x = -2$ and $y = \frac{1}{2}$]

   b   [graph of $y = xf(x)$ with asymptote $y = 2x$, passing through -2]

17 a   Asymptote $y = 0$; [graph of $y = \text{sech}\, x$ through $(0, 1)$]

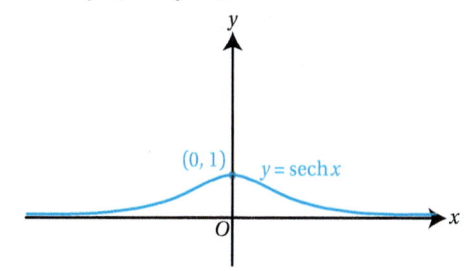

   b $x = \ln(3 \pm 2\sqrt{2})$

18 a $x = -\ln 2$ b $x \geq \ln 2$

5 Further vectors

BEFORE YOU START

1   a $\mathbf{r} = \begin{pmatrix} 3 \\ -1 \\ 2 \end{pmatrix} + \lambda \begin{pmatrix} 1 \\ 1 \\ 3 \end{pmatrix}$

   b $\dfrac{x - 3}{1} = \dfrac{y + 1}{1} = \dfrac{z - 2}{3}$

2   $(4, 0, 5)$ 3 $42.4°$ 4 $\sqrt{14}$

WORK IT OUT 5.1

Solution 3 is correct.

EXERCISE 5A

1   a   i $\mathbf{a} \times \mathbf{b} = \begin{pmatrix} 19 \\ -13 \\ -5 \end{pmatrix}$; $\mathbf{b} \times \mathbf{a} = \begin{pmatrix} -19 \\ 13 \\ 5 \end{pmatrix}$

      ii $\mathbf{a} \times \mathbf{b} = \begin{pmatrix} -14 \\ -5 \\ -6 \end{pmatrix}$; $\mathbf{b} \times \mathbf{a} = \begin{pmatrix} 14 \\ 5 \\ 6 \end{pmatrix}$

   b   i $\mathbf{a} \times \mathbf{b} = 6\mathbf{i} - 8\mathbf{j} - 19\mathbf{k}$;
         $\mathbf{b} \times \mathbf{a} = -6\mathbf{i} + 8\mathbf{j} + 19\mathbf{k}$

      ii $\mathbf{a} \times \mathbf{b} = -2\mathbf{i} - 2\mathbf{j} - 6\mathbf{k}$;
         $\mathbf{b} \times \mathbf{a} = 2\mathbf{i} + 2\mathbf{j} + 6\mathbf{k}$

2 a i $\mathbf{a} \times \mathbf{b} = \begin{pmatrix} 1 \\ -7 \\ 3 \end{pmatrix}$

   ii $\mathbf{a} \times \mathbf{b} = \begin{pmatrix} 16 \\ 1 \\ 5 \end{pmatrix}$

  b i $\mathbf{a} \times \mathbf{b} = -15\mathbf{j} - 5\mathbf{k}$

   ii $\mathbf{a} \times \mathbf{b} = -4\mathbf{i} + 11\mathbf{j} + 3\mathbf{k}$

3 a 0.775 b 0.128
  c 0.630 d 0

4 a $\left(\mathbf{r} - \begin{pmatrix} 4 \\ 3 \\ 7 \end{pmatrix}\right) \times \begin{pmatrix} 2 \\ 8 \\ 7 \end{pmatrix} = \mathbf{0}$

  b $\left(\mathbf{r} - \begin{pmatrix} -3 \\ 0 \\ 1 \end{pmatrix}\right) \times \begin{pmatrix} 1 \\ 1 \\ -9 \end{pmatrix} = \mathbf{0}$

5 a $(\mathbf{r} - (\mathbf{i} + \mathbf{j} - \mathbf{k})) \times (2\mathbf{i} - 3\mathbf{k}) = \mathbf{0}$
  b $(\mathbf{r} - (3\mathbf{i} - 4\mathbf{k})) \times (\mathbf{i} - 5\mathbf{j} + 2\mathbf{k}) = \mathbf{0}$

6 a i $\frac{1}{2}\sqrt{153}$ ii $\sqrt{157}$
  b i $\frac{15\sqrt{3}}{2}$ ii $\frac{9}{2}$

7 $-2\mathbf{i} + 9\mathbf{j} + 3\mathbf{k}$

8 $\mathbf{r} = \begin{pmatrix} -1 \\ 1 \\ 7 \end{pmatrix} + \lambda \begin{pmatrix} 0 \\ 1 \\ 0 \end{pmatrix}$

9 a $(11, -2, 0)$ b 21.9 (3 s.f)

10 $\mathbf{r} = \begin{pmatrix} 3 \\ 1 \\ 6 \end{pmatrix} + \lambda \begin{pmatrix} 6 \\ 4 \\ 3 \end{pmatrix}$

11 $\frac{x-3}{-3} = \frac{y-1}{1} = \frac{z-2}{7}$

12 17.5

13 a Proof. b $13 \mathbf{a} \times \mathbf{b}$

14 a Proof. b 0

15 $\frac{x+3}{7} = \frac{1-y}{6} = \frac{1-z}{3}$

16 Proof.

17 Proof.

18 a Proof.

  b i $\begin{pmatrix} \mu - 2\lambda + 8 \\ \mu + \lambda - 3 \\ -\mu + 8\lambda - 16 \end{pmatrix}$

   ii Proof.
   iii $3\mu - 9\lambda + 21 = 0$
   iv $P(1, 1, 2)$, $Q(4, -1, 3)$
   v $\sqrt{14}$

EXERCISE 5B

1 a i $\mathbf{r} = \begin{pmatrix} 1 \\ 0 \\ 2 \end{pmatrix} + \lambda \begin{pmatrix} -1 \\ 5 \\ 2 \end{pmatrix} + \mu \begin{pmatrix} 1 \\ -2 \\ 3 \end{pmatrix}$

   ii $\mathbf{r} = \begin{pmatrix} 0 \\ 2 \\ 0 \end{pmatrix} + \lambda \begin{pmatrix} 0 \\ 4 \\ -1 \end{pmatrix} + \mu \begin{pmatrix} 5 \\ 3 \\ 0 \end{pmatrix}$

  b i $\mathbf{r} = (\mathbf{j} + \mathbf{k}) + \lambda(3\mathbf{i} + \mathbf{j} - 3\mathbf{k}) + \mu(\mathbf{i} - 3\mathbf{j})$
   ii $\mathbf{r} = (\mathbf{i} - 6\mathbf{j} + 2\mathbf{k}) + \lambda(5\mathbf{i} - 6\mathbf{j})$
       $+ \mu(-\mathbf{i} + 3\mathbf{j} - \mathbf{k})$

2 a i $\mathbf{r} = \begin{pmatrix} 3 \\ -1 \\ 3 \end{pmatrix} + \lambda \begin{pmatrix} -2 \\ 2 \\ -1 \end{pmatrix} + \mu \begin{pmatrix} 1 \\ 0 \\ -1 \end{pmatrix}$

   ii $\mathbf{r} = \begin{pmatrix} -1 \\ -1 \\ 5 \end{pmatrix} + \lambda \begin{pmatrix} 5 \\ 2 \\ -3 \end{pmatrix} + \mu \begin{pmatrix} -6 \\ 2 \\ -4 \end{pmatrix}$

  b i $\mathbf{r} = \begin{pmatrix} 9 \\ 0 \\ 0 \end{pmatrix} + \lambda \begin{pmatrix} -11 \\ 1 \\ 0 \end{pmatrix} + \mu \begin{pmatrix} -8 \\ -1 \\ 2 \end{pmatrix}$

   ii $\mathbf{r} = \begin{pmatrix} 11 \\ -7 \\ 3 \end{pmatrix} + \lambda \begin{pmatrix} -10 \\ 21 \\ -1 \end{pmatrix} + \mu \begin{pmatrix} -16 \\ 17 \\ -3 \end{pmatrix}$

3 a i $\mathbf{r} = \begin{pmatrix} -1 \\ 4 \\ 3 \end{pmatrix} + \lambda \begin{pmatrix} 4 \\ 1 \\ 2 \end{pmatrix} + \mu \begin{pmatrix} 2 \\ -1 \\ 2 \end{pmatrix}$

   ii $\mathbf{r} = \begin{pmatrix} 11 \\ 12 \\ 13 \end{pmatrix} + \lambda \begin{pmatrix} 6 \\ -3 \\ 1 \end{pmatrix} + \mu \begin{pmatrix} 2 \\ 15 \\ 6 \end{pmatrix}$

  b i $\mathbf{r} = \begin{pmatrix} -3 \\ 1 \\ 0 \end{pmatrix} + \lambda \begin{pmatrix} 0 \\ 0 \\ 1 \end{pmatrix} + \mu \begin{pmatrix} -7 \\ -3 \\ -1 \end{pmatrix}$

   ii $\mathbf{r} = \begin{pmatrix} 4 \\ 0 \\ 2 \end{pmatrix} + \lambda \begin{pmatrix} 2 \\ 1 \\ 1 \end{pmatrix} + \mu \begin{pmatrix} 4 \\ 0 \\ 2 \end{pmatrix}$

Answers to exercises

4 a i $\mathbf{r} \cdot \begin{pmatrix} 3 \\ -5 \\ 2 \end{pmatrix} = -4; \; 3x - 5y + 2z = -4$

ii $\mathbf{r} \cdot \begin{pmatrix} 6 \\ -1 \\ 2 \end{pmatrix} = 19; \; 6x - y + 2z = 19$

b i $\mathbf{r} \cdot \begin{pmatrix} 3 \\ -1 \\ 0 \end{pmatrix} = -9; \; 3x - y = -9$

ii $\mathbf{r} \cdot \begin{pmatrix} 4 \\ 0 \\ -5 \end{pmatrix} = -10; \; 4x - 5z = -10$

5 a i $\begin{pmatrix} 10 \\ 13 \\ -12 \end{pmatrix}$ **ii** $\begin{pmatrix} 10 \\ 4 \\ 3 \end{pmatrix}$

b i $\begin{pmatrix} 1 \\ 5 \\ 0 \end{pmatrix}$ **ii** $\begin{pmatrix} 1 \\ 20 \\ 7 \end{pmatrix}$

6 a i $\mathbf{r} \cdot \begin{pmatrix} 10 \\ 13 \\ -12 \end{pmatrix} = 38$ **ii** $\mathbf{r} \cdot \begin{pmatrix} 10 \\ 4 \\ 3 \end{pmatrix} = 3$

b i $\mathbf{r} \cdot \begin{pmatrix} 1 \\ 5 \\ 0 \end{pmatrix} = 22$ **ii** $\mathbf{r} \cdot \begin{pmatrix} 1 \\ 20 \\ 7 \end{pmatrix} = 152$

7 a i $10x + 13y - 12z = 38$
ii $10x + 4y + 3z = 3$

b i $x + 5y = 22$
ii $x + 20y + 7z = 152$

8 a i $x + y + z = 10$
ii $z = 2$

b i $40x + 5y + 8z = 580$
ii $x + y + z = 1$

9 a–c Proof.

10 $6x + y - 3z = 1$

11 For example, $\mathbf{r} = \begin{pmatrix} 5 \\ 1 \\ 5 \end{pmatrix} + \lambda \begin{pmatrix} 8 \\ 0 \\ 3 \end{pmatrix} + \mu \begin{pmatrix} 5 \\ 0 \\ 0 \end{pmatrix}$

12 a $\begin{pmatrix} -1 \\ -4 \\ -17 \end{pmatrix}$ **b** $x + 4y + 17z = 37$

13 a $\mathbf{r} \cdot \begin{pmatrix} -11 \\ 7 \\ 13 \end{pmatrix} = 39$ **b** No.

14 a $\begin{pmatrix} 13 \\ -11 \\ -8 \end{pmatrix}$

b $-13x + 11y + 8z = 38$

15 a $\begin{pmatrix} -2 \\ 3 \\ -1 \end{pmatrix}$

b i Proof. **ii** $(1, -3, 14)$

c $2x - 3y + z = 25$

16 No.

17 a $\begin{pmatrix} 1 \\ -3 \\ 4 \end{pmatrix}$ **b** $p = -\frac{1}{4}, \; q = \frac{3}{4}$

c For example, $\mathbf{r} = \begin{pmatrix} 4 \\ -4 \\ 0 \end{pmatrix} + \lambda \begin{pmatrix} 4 \\ 0 \\ -1 \end{pmatrix} + \mu \begin{pmatrix} 0 \\ 4 \\ 3 \end{pmatrix}$

18 a $8x - 10y + 17z = 75$

b For example, $\mathbf{r} = \begin{pmatrix} 0 \\ 0 \\ 7 \end{pmatrix} + \lambda \begin{pmatrix} 1 \\ 0 \\ -1 \end{pmatrix} + \mu \begin{pmatrix} 3 \\ 1 \\ 0 \end{pmatrix}$

19 For example, $\mathbf{r} = \begin{pmatrix} 0 \\ 0 \\ -5 \end{pmatrix} + \lambda \begin{pmatrix} 1 \\ 0 \\ 0 \end{pmatrix} + \mu \begin{pmatrix} 0 \\ 1 \\ 3 \end{pmatrix}$

EXERCISE 5C

1 a i $(7, 1, 1)$ **ii** $(-19, -5, 7)$
b i $\left(-\frac{4}{3}, -\frac{7}{3}, -4\right)$ **ii** $(8, -3, 2)$

2 a–d Proof.

3 a i $\mathbf{r} = \begin{pmatrix} 1 \\ 1 \\ -1 \end{pmatrix} + \lambda \begin{pmatrix} 2 \\ -13 \\ -7 \end{pmatrix}$

ii $\mathbf{r} = \begin{pmatrix} 4 \\ -1 \\ 0 \end{pmatrix} + \lambda \begin{pmatrix} 0 \\ 0 \\ -2 \end{pmatrix}$

b i $\mathbf{r} = \begin{pmatrix} 2 \\ 0 \\ 5 \end{pmatrix} + \lambda \begin{pmatrix} -1 \\ -2 \\ 4 \end{pmatrix}$

ii $\mathbf{r} = \begin{pmatrix} 2 \\ 2 \\ 0 \end{pmatrix} + \lambda \begin{pmatrix} 2 \\ -1 \\ 0 \end{pmatrix}$

355

4 (15, 5, 8)

5 a $\begin{pmatrix} -1 \\ 2 \\ 1 \end{pmatrix}$ b (0.2, 2.6, 3.8)

6 (5, 3, 0)

7 a $\begin{pmatrix} -7 \\ 3 \\ 8 \end{pmatrix}$ b $\mathbf{r} = \begin{pmatrix} 1 \\ 1 \\ 6 \end{pmatrix} + \lambda \begin{pmatrix} -7 \\ 3 \\ 8 \end{pmatrix}$

8 a $8\mathbf{i} + 13\mathbf{j} + 2\mathbf{k}$
   b $(\mathbf{r} - (\mathbf{i} + \mathbf{j} + 2\mathbf{k})) \times (8\mathbf{i} + 13\mathbf{j} + 2\mathbf{k}) = \mathbf{0}$

9 a $P(5, 0, 0), Q(0, -20, 0), R(0, 0, 12)$
   b $10\sqrt{178}$

10 a For example, $\mathbf{r} = \begin{pmatrix} 0 \\ -3 \\ 11 \end{pmatrix} + \lambda \begin{pmatrix} 1 \\ 5 \\ -8 \end{pmatrix}$
   b $\left(\dfrac{5}{3}, \dfrac{16}{3}, -\dfrac{7}{3} \right)$

11 a For example, $\mathbf{r} = \begin{pmatrix} -0.2 \\ -6.4 \\ 0 \end{pmatrix} + \lambda \begin{pmatrix} -6 \\ -7 \\ 5 \end{pmatrix}$
   b Proof.

12 a For example, $\mathbf{r} = \begin{pmatrix} 0 \\ -0.8 \\ -0.4 \end{pmatrix} + \lambda \begin{pmatrix} 1 \\ 0 \\ 1 \end{pmatrix}$
   b $d = -2$

13 Proof; $2\mathbf{i} - 2\mathbf{j} + 5\mathbf{k}$

14 a $\dfrac{x + 15}{7} = y = \dfrac{z + 13}{5}$
   b $a = 1.6$
   c They form a triangular prism.

EXERCISE 5D

1 a i 46.4°   ii 17.6°
  b i 47.6°   ii 10.8°

2 a 75.8°   b 60°

3 a $\begin{pmatrix} 2 \\ 3 \\ -1 \end{pmatrix}$ b 32.8° (3 s.f.)

4 a $\begin{pmatrix} 3 \\ -1 \\ 1 \end{pmatrix}$ b 57° (to the nearest degree)

5 a $\begin{pmatrix} 4 \\ 2 \\ 3 \end{pmatrix}$ b 28.3° (3 s.f.)

6 a $\begin{pmatrix} 13 \\ 7 \\ -8 \end{pmatrix}$ b 3.46° (3 s.f.)

7 Proof.

8 a $\begin{pmatrix} -5 \\ 0 \\ 1 \end{pmatrix}$ b 64.4° (3 s.f.)

9 a Proof.   b $\dfrac{\sqrt{7}}{3}$
  c $3\sqrt{5}$ d $\sqrt{35}$

EXERCISE 5E

1 a $\begin{pmatrix} 1 \\ -3 \\ 1 \end{pmatrix}$ b (1, -1, 2) c $2\sqrt{11}$

2 a $\mathbf{r} = \begin{pmatrix} -3 \\ -3 \\ 4 \end{pmatrix} + \lambda \begin{pmatrix} 2 \\ 2 \\ -1 \end{pmatrix}$
  b (3, 3, 1)
  c 9

3 a $\left(\dfrac{96}{41}, -\dfrac{32}{41}, \dfrac{16}{41} \right)$ b $\dfrac{16\sqrt{41}}{41}$

4 a $\mathbf{r} = \begin{pmatrix} -3 \\ -4 \\ 8 \end{pmatrix} + \lambda \begin{pmatrix} 4 \\ 6 \\ -3 \end{pmatrix}$
  b (1, 2, 5)
  c (5, 8, 2)

5 a Proof.   b $\mathbf{r} \cdot \begin{pmatrix} -1 \\ 5 \\ 2 \end{pmatrix} = -5$
  c $\sqrt{30}$ d (8, -5, -1)

6 a $\begin{pmatrix} -3 \\ -10 \\ 2 \end{pmatrix}$
  b 5.32 (3 s.f.)
  c $3x + 10y - 2z = 16$
  d $\mathbf{r} = \begin{pmatrix} -7 \\ -28 \\ 11 \end{pmatrix} + \lambda \begin{pmatrix} 3 \\ 10 \\ -2 \end{pmatrix}$
  e (2, 2, 5); 31.9 (3 s.f.)
  f 56.5

7 a, b Proof. c $\mathbf{r} = \lambda \begin{pmatrix} 1 \\ -3 \\ 1 \end{pmatrix}$ d $\dfrac{6\sqrt{11}}{11}$

Answers to exercises

8 a Proof. **b** $r = \lambda \begin{pmatrix} 1 \\ 0 \\ -1 \end{pmatrix}$

  c i $(2, 0, -2)$ **ii** $(-4, 0, 4)$

  d $6\sqrt{2}$

MIXED PRACTICE 5

1 For example, $\mathbf{i} + 3\mathbf{k}$

2 -1

3 a $3x + y - z = 6$ **b** $a = 1.25$

4 a $\mathbf{r} = \begin{pmatrix} 4 \\ -1 \\ 2 \end{pmatrix} + \lambda \begin{pmatrix} 1 \\ -2 \\ 1 \end{pmatrix}$

  b $(6, -5, 4)$ **c** $2\sqrt{6}$

5 a $\begin{pmatrix} 0 \\ 5 \\ 5 \end{pmatrix}$

  b $2x - y + z = 0$

  c Proof.

  d For example, $\mathbf{r} = \begin{pmatrix} 3 \\ 4 \\ -2 \end{pmatrix} + \lambda \begin{pmatrix} 0 \\ 5 \\ 5 \end{pmatrix}$

  e $(3, 6, 0)$

  f $47.1°$ (3 s.f.)

6 a Proof. **b** $\mathbf{r} = \begin{pmatrix} 9 \\ -7 \\ 6 \end{pmatrix} + \lambda \begin{pmatrix} -4 \\ 8 \\ -3 \end{pmatrix}$

  c $\mathbf{r} = \begin{pmatrix} 9 \\ -7 \\ 6 \end{pmatrix} + \mu \begin{pmatrix} 1 \\ -4 \\ 2 \end{pmatrix}$

  d $(7, 1, 2)$ **e** $2\sqrt{21}$

7 a $\left(\mathbf{r} - \begin{pmatrix} 3 \\ -4 \\ 1 \end{pmatrix} \right) \times \begin{pmatrix} 1 \\ -5 \\ 4 \end{pmatrix} = \mathbf{0}$ or

  $\left(\mathbf{r} - \begin{pmatrix} 2 \\ 1 \\ -3 \end{pmatrix} \right) \times \begin{pmatrix} 1 \\ -5 \\ 4 \end{pmatrix} = \mathbf{0}$

  b $\begin{pmatrix} 3t + 5 \\ 3t - 16 \\ 3t - 2 \end{pmatrix}$

  c i Proof; 77
     ii $\mathbf{a}$, $\mathbf{b}$ and $\mathbf{c}$ aren't in the same plane.

8 $p = 4$

9 a $\begin{pmatrix} -2 \\ 7 \\ -3 \end{pmatrix}$ **b** $(3, 3, 8)$

  c $\begin{pmatrix} -2 \\ 7 \\ -3 \end{pmatrix}$ **d** $2x - 7y + 3z = 9$

10 a $9\mathbf{i} + 5\mathbf{j} + 7\mathbf{k}$ **b** $\sqrt{155}$

11 C

12 a $(10, 11, -6)$ **b** $\begin{pmatrix} 7 \\ -9 \\ -5 \end{pmatrix}$

  c $7x - 9y - 5z = 1$

13 a $\dfrac{x-3}{3} = \dfrac{y-1}{-1} = \dfrac{z+4}{-1}$

  b $(0, 2, -3)$ **c** $(-3, 3, -2)$

  d Proof.   **e** $3\sqrt{2}$

14 a $\mathbf{r} = \begin{pmatrix} 0 \\ -8 \\ -11 \end{pmatrix} + \lambda \begin{pmatrix} 1 \\ 5 \\ 7 \end{pmatrix}$

  b i They do not meet; inconsistent.
     ii Triangular prism.

  c i For example, $(0, -15, -25)$, $(3, 0, -4)$

     ii $\mathbf{r} = \begin{pmatrix} 0 \\ -15 \\ -25 \end{pmatrix} + \lambda \begin{pmatrix} 1 \\ 5 \\ 7 \end{pmatrix}$

15 a $\dfrac{1}{2}|\mathbf{a} \times \mathbf{b}|$ **b** $h = |\mathbf{c}| \cos \theta$

  c Proof.   **d** $\dfrac{1}{3}$

16 a $\mathbf{r} = \begin{pmatrix} -1 \\ 1 \\ 4 \end{pmatrix} + \lambda \begin{pmatrix} 6 \\ 1 \\ 5 \end{pmatrix}$ **b** Proof.

  c $\begin{pmatrix} -13 \\ 38 \\ 8 \end{pmatrix}$ **d** $13x - 38y - 8z = -83$

17 $k = 8$

18 $7x + 2y - 3z = 3$

19 a $\begin{pmatrix} -1 \\ 4 \\ 7 \end{pmatrix}$ **b** Proof.

  c Proof.   **d** $\mathbf{r} = \begin{pmatrix} 1 \\ 1 \\ 2 \end{pmatrix} + \lambda \begin{pmatrix} -1 \\ 4 \\ 7 \end{pmatrix}$

20 a $\begin{pmatrix} 2 \\ 5 \\ 2 \end{pmatrix}$

  b i Proof.

  ii $A(1, -17, -5)$, $B(13, 13, 7)$

  iii $6\sqrt{33}$

21 a $\mathbf{r} \cdot \begin{pmatrix} 5 \\ 2 \\ -1 \end{pmatrix} = 11$ **b** Proof; $d = 5$ **c** Proof.

  d i Proof; $k = -1$

  ii $k = 1$: Π_2 and Π_3 are parallel (Π_1 not parallel). $k = -1$: planes form a triangular prism.

6 Further matrices

BEFORE YOU START

1 a $\begin{pmatrix} -2 & 9 \\ 17 & -1 \end{pmatrix}$ **b** $\begin{pmatrix} -3 & 11 \\ -7 & -11 \end{pmatrix}$

2 8

3 $\dfrac{1}{10}\begin{pmatrix} 2 & -1 \\ 4 & 3 \end{pmatrix}$

4 $\mathbf{A}^T = \begin{pmatrix} 1 & 6 \\ 3 & 3 \\ 2 & -4 \end{pmatrix}$

5 $\begin{pmatrix} 2 & -3 \\ 5 & -8 \end{pmatrix}\begin{pmatrix} x \\ y \end{pmatrix} = \begin{pmatrix} 2 \\ 3 \end{pmatrix}$; $\mathbf{M}^{-1} = \begin{pmatrix} 8 & -3 \\ 5 & -2 \end{pmatrix}$; $x = 7, y = 4$

6 a $\mathbf{r} = \begin{pmatrix} 1 \\ 2 \\ 1 \end{pmatrix} + \lambda \begin{pmatrix} 1 \\ 1 \\ -4 \end{pmatrix} + \mu \begin{pmatrix} 1 \\ 1 \\ -1 \end{pmatrix}$

  b $\mathbf{r} \cdot \begin{pmatrix} 1 \\ -1 \\ 0 \end{pmatrix} = -1$ **c** $x - y = -1$

7 $\mathbf{r} = \begin{pmatrix} 1 \\ 2 \\ 1 \end{pmatrix} + \lambda \begin{pmatrix} 1 \\ 1 \\ -4 \end{pmatrix}$

8 a Proof. **b** $f(x) = (x-3)(x+3)(2x-1)$

9 $x - 2y = 0$, $5x + y = 0$. Neither is a line of invariant points.

EXERCISE 6A

1 a i $\begin{pmatrix} 1 & 1 \\ 2 & 3 \end{pmatrix}$ **ii** $\begin{pmatrix} 1 & 2 & 1 \\ 5 & 3 & -3 \end{pmatrix}$

  b i $\begin{pmatrix} 2 & 4 \\ 6 & 1 \\ 0 & 0 \end{pmatrix}$ **ii** $\begin{pmatrix} 1 & 8 & -1 & -5 \\ 2 & -3 & 7 & -2 \\ -4 & 3 & 22 & 0 \end{pmatrix}$

2 a i -52 **ii** 8

  b i 12 **ii** 0

  c i $7a + 1$ **ii** $-5 - 4b$

  d i $3c^2 + 15c + 9$

  ii $-3d^2 - 12d - 4$

3 a i $\dfrac{1}{26}\begin{pmatrix} 0 & 3 & 4 \\ 0 & 5 & -2 \\ 13 & -9 & 1 \end{pmatrix}$

  ii $\dfrac{1}{8}\begin{pmatrix} -12 & 8 & 4 \\ -3 & 2 & -1 \\ -10 & 4 & 2 \end{pmatrix}$

  b i $\dfrac{1}{12}\begin{pmatrix} 6 & 2 & 4 \\ 30 & 22 & 20 \\ 9 & 7 & 8 \end{pmatrix}$

  ii Singular matrix.

  c i $\dfrac{1}{7a+1}\begin{pmatrix} 2 & -2a & a-1 \\ 7 & 1 & -4 \\ -3 & 3a & 2+2a \end{pmatrix}$

  ii $\dfrac{1}{5+4b}\begin{pmatrix} -1 & -2-b & 4+3b \\ 4 & 3 & -1 \\ 4 & 3 & -6-4b \end{pmatrix}$

  d i $\dfrac{1}{3c^2+15c+9}\begin{pmatrix} 14+3c & 1 & 7+c \\ c-4 & 1+2c & -c^2-2 \\ -13 & 1+3c & 7c-2 \end{pmatrix}$

  ii $\dfrac{1}{3d^2+12d+4}\begin{pmatrix} 2+5d & -d^2 & 2d \\ -2 & 2+d & 10+3d \\ 2+3d & 2d & -4 \end{pmatrix}$

4 a, b Proof.

5 $k = -1.5$

6 $x = 3$ or $x = -6$

7 Proof.

8 $a = -\dfrac{2}{7}$, $b = -\dfrac{27}{7}$

9 a $\det \mathbf{A} = 2k - 14$; $\det \mathbf{B} = 4 + 4k - 3k^2$

  b $k = -\dfrac{2}{3}$, 2 or 7

10 a 10

  b i $25\,\text{cm}^3$ **ii** $25\,\text{cm}^3$ **iii** $1\,\text{cm}^3$

11 $(8, -5, 0.5)$

12 a $p = 1, q = -1, r = 10$ **b** $(0, 0, 1)$

13 $a = -2, b = 3$; $(4, 1, -2)$

14 Proof.

WORK IT OUT 6.1

Solution 2 is correct.

358

Answers to exercises

EXERCISE 6B

1. **a** **i** $6x(x-2)(x-3)(x+5)$
   ii $8[a(a-1)(a-2)+b(b-1)(b-2)]$
   b **i** 0
   ii 0
   c **i** $(1-\sin t)(1-\cos t)(\cos t - \sin t)$
   ii $(a-b)(b-c)(c-a)$

2. **a** **i** $\begin{pmatrix} 13 \\ -11 \\ 14 \end{pmatrix}$ **ii** $\begin{pmatrix} 22 \\ 25 \\ -4 \end{pmatrix}$
   b **i** $-\mathbf{i}+\mathbf{j}-2\mathbf{k}$ **ii** $-5\mathbf{i}+17\mathbf{j}-3\mathbf{k}$

3. **a** **i** $R_1+2R_2-R_3=0$ or $38C_1-25C_2+7C_3=0$
   ii $3R_1+4R_2-R_3=0$ or $C_1-3C_2-2C_3=0$
   b **i** $c(C_1+C_2)=(a+b)C_3$
   ii $R_1=xyzR_3$

4. **a** Proof.
   b $2(a-3)(2a-21)$

5. **a** **i-iii** Proof.
   b $2xy(x-2)(y-2)(y-x)$

6. **a** $C_1 \to C_1+kC_2$
   b Proof.

7. $(a-b)[(1-a)(1-b)-(a+b)^2]$

8. **a, b** Proof.

9. $(p-q)(q-r)(r-p)(p+q+r)$

10. **a** **i** $3x+4y-z=0$; proof. **ii** $\sqrt{26}$
    iii $\dfrac{16}{\sqrt{26}}$ **iv** $\dfrac{16}{3}$
    b The volume of tetrahedron $OABC$ equals one sixth of the determinant of the matrix with column vectors **a**, **b** and **c**.
    $$\tfrac{1}{6}\begin{vmatrix} 1 & -1 & 2 \\ 0 & 2 & -5 \\ 3 & 5 & 2 \end{vmatrix} = \tfrac{1}{6}\begin{vmatrix} \mathbf{i} & 1 & -1 \\ \mathbf{j} & 0 & 2 \\ \mathbf{k} & 3 & 5 \end{vmatrix} \cdot \mathbf{c}$$
    $$= \tfrac{1}{3}\left[\tfrac{1}{2}(\mathbf{a}\times\mathbf{b})\right]\cdot\mathbf{c}$$
    $$= \tfrac{1}{3}B\mathbf{n}\cdot\mathbf{c}$$
    $$= \tfrac{1}{3}Bh$$
    where B is the base area and h is the perpendicular height.

EXERCISE 6C

1. **a** **i** $x=3, y=1, z=7$
   ii $x=3, y=-1, z=-2$
   b **i** $x=\tfrac{2}{3}, y=\tfrac{1}{3}, z=\tfrac{5}{3}$
   ii $x=-\tfrac{3}{7}, y=\tfrac{1}{7}, z=\tfrac{4}{7}$
   c **i** $x=1-k, y=3k-2, z=1$
   ii $x=\dfrac{7k-17}{67}, y=\dfrac{5k+7}{67}, z=\dfrac{-9k-26}{67}$

2. Proof.

3. $x=2, y=-3, z=1$

4. $k=2, -3$

5. **a** Proof.
   b $\mathbf{M}^{-1}=\dfrac{1}{a^2+4a+5}\begin{pmatrix} 2+a & 1 & -2-2a \\ -1 & 2+a & 6+2a \\ 3+a & -1-a & a^2-3 \end{pmatrix}$
   c $x=2.1, y=-1.7, z=1.8$

6. **a** Proof. **b** $k=\pm 1, -2$
   c $x=2, y=-1, z=5$

EXERCISE 6D

1. **a** **i** Consistent; unique solution: $x=3, y=2, z=2$.
   ii Consistent; unique solution: $x=1, y=1, z=4$.
   b **i** Consistent; line intersection of two distinct planes.
   ii Consistent; line intersection of three distinct planes (sheaf).
   c **i** Inconsistent; prism.
   ii Inconsistent; two parallel planes with a single intersecting plane.
   d **i** Consistent; unique solution: $x=\tfrac{1}{6}, y=\tfrac{1}{6}, z=\tfrac{7}{6}$.
   ii Consistent; unique solution: $x=0.5, y=0.5, z=4$.

2. **a** Proof; $x=\tfrac{5}{3}, y=\tfrac{16}{3}, z=-\tfrac{7}{3}$
   b The planes intersect at a single point.

3. **a** Proof.
   b The planes intersect at a single point.

4. $\left(\tfrac{3}{2}, -\tfrac{11}{6}, -\tfrac{1}{6}\right)$

5. **a, b** Proof. **c** Triangular prism.

6. **a** Proof.
   b $d=-2$
   c Intersect along a line (sheaf).

359

d $\mathbf{r} = \begin{pmatrix} 0 \\ -0.8 \\ -0.4 \end{pmatrix} + \lambda \begin{pmatrix} 1 \\ 0 \\ 1 \end{pmatrix}$

7 a Proof.

   b Intersect along a line (sheaf).

   c $x = 2t, y = -2t, z = 5t$

8 a $\begin{pmatrix} 0.5 & 0.5 & 0.5 \\ -0.5 & 0.5 & 0.5 \\ 0.5 & 0.5 & -0.5 \end{pmatrix}$

   b $\left(\dfrac{5+d}{2}, \dfrac{d-3}{2}, \dfrac{5-d}{2} \right)$

9 a $a = 2$

   b Inconsistent; triangular prism.

10 a $p = -4$ b $a = 2, -1.4$

   c Intersect in a line (sheaf).

   d $x = 2t, y = 2 + t, z = t$

EXERCISE 6E

1 a i 5 and $\begin{pmatrix} 1 \\ 1 \end{pmatrix}$, −1 and $\begin{pmatrix} 2 \\ -1 \end{pmatrix}$

      ii 2 and $\begin{pmatrix} 1 \\ 2 \end{pmatrix}$, 1 and $\begin{pmatrix} 1 \\ 3 \end{pmatrix}$

   b i 4 and $\begin{pmatrix} 1 \\ 1 \end{pmatrix}$, 2 and $\begin{pmatrix} 1 \\ -1 \end{pmatrix}$

      ii 4 and $\begin{pmatrix} 1 \\ -1 \end{pmatrix}$, 2 and $\begin{pmatrix} 3 \\ -5 \end{pmatrix}$

   c i 3 and $\begin{pmatrix} 1 \\ -1 \end{pmatrix}$

      ii 5 and $\begin{pmatrix} 3 \\ -1 \end{pmatrix}$

   d i i and $\begin{pmatrix} 5 \\ i-2 \end{pmatrix}$, $-i$ and $\begin{pmatrix} 5 \\ -i-2 \end{pmatrix}$

      ii $3i$ and $\begin{pmatrix} 5 \\ 3i-1 \end{pmatrix}$, $-3i$ and $\begin{pmatrix} 5 \\ -i-2 \end{pmatrix}$

2 a i $a = 5; \lambda = 4, \begin{pmatrix} 1 \\ -1 \end{pmatrix}$

      ii $p = 2; \lambda = -2, \begin{pmatrix} 1 \\ -2 \end{pmatrix}$

   b i $b = -\dfrac{1}{2}; \lambda = 4, \begin{pmatrix} 1 \\ 2 \end{pmatrix}$

      ii $q = -1; \lambda = 0, \begin{pmatrix} 2 \\ -1 \end{pmatrix}$

3 3 and $\begin{pmatrix} 1 \\ -1 \end{pmatrix}$, 7 and $\begin{pmatrix} 1 \\ 3 \end{pmatrix}$

4 2 and $\begin{pmatrix} 1 \\ -1 \end{pmatrix}$, −2 and $\begin{pmatrix} 1 \\ -3 \end{pmatrix}$

5 Proof; 2 and $\begin{pmatrix} 28 \\ -11 \\ -1 \end{pmatrix}$, 4 and $\begin{pmatrix} 8 \\ -3 \\ 5 \end{pmatrix}$,

   −2.5 and $\begin{pmatrix} 1 \\ -2 \\ -1 \end{pmatrix}$

6 1 and $\begin{pmatrix} 1 \\ 0 \\ 1 \end{pmatrix}$, −3 and $\begin{pmatrix} 1 \\ 0 \\ -1 \end{pmatrix}$

7 a Proof.   b 3 and $\begin{pmatrix} 1 \\ 1 \\ 2 \end{pmatrix}$, 6 and $\begin{pmatrix} 1 \\ 1 \\ -1 \end{pmatrix}$

8 a $p = 5, q = 6$ b $\lambda = -9, \begin{pmatrix} 1 \\ 0 \\ 2 \end{pmatrix}$

9 2 and $\begin{pmatrix} 1 \\ -1 \\ 0 \end{pmatrix}$, 6 and $\begin{pmatrix} 1 \\ 1 \\ 2 \end{pmatrix}$, −3 and $\begin{pmatrix} 1 \\ 1 \\ -1 \end{pmatrix}$

10 a $(\lambda - 9)^2 (\lambda + 9) = 0$; proof; $k = 9$

   b i For example, 9, $\begin{pmatrix} 1 \\ -2 \\ 2 \end{pmatrix}$ and $\begin{pmatrix} -2 \\ 1 \\ 2 \end{pmatrix}$;

      $-9, \begin{pmatrix} 2 \\ 2 \\ 1 \end{pmatrix}$

      ii Proof.

   c Reflection in the plane $2x + 2y + z = 0$.

11 For example, 2, $\begin{pmatrix} 0 \\ 1 \\ 5 \end{pmatrix}$ and $\begin{pmatrix} 1 \\ 3 \\ 2 \end{pmatrix}$; −1, $\begin{pmatrix} 2 \\ 5 \\ -2 \end{pmatrix}$

EXERCISE 6F

1 a i $\mathbf{U} = \begin{pmatrix} 1 & 1 \\ 1 & -2 \end{pmatrix}$, $\mathbf{D} = \begin{pmatrix} 7 & 0 \\ 0 & -5 \end{pmatrix}$

      ii $\mathbf{U} = \begin{pmatrix} 2 & 1 \\ 3 & -1 \end{pmatrix}$, $\mathbf{D} = \begin{pmatrix} 6 & 0 \\ 0 & 1 \end{pmatrix}$

   b i Not diagonalisable.

      ii Not diagonalisable.

2 a i $\mathbf{U} = \begin{pmatrix} 1 & 4 & 1 \\ 2 & 2 & 1 \\ 1 & -3 & 0 \end{pmatrix}$, $\mathbf{D} = \begin{pmatrix} 1 & 0 & 0 \\ 0 & -2 & 0 \\ 0 & 0 & -1 \end{pmatrix}$

      ii $\mathbf{U} = \begin{pmatrix} 2 & 2 & 1 \\ 3 & 1 & 2 \\ 1 & -2 & 1 \end{pmatrix}$, $\mathbf{D} = \begin{pmatrix} 1 & 0 & 0 \\ 0 & -3 & 0 \\ 0 & 0 & 2 \end{pmatrix}$

b **i** $U = \begin{pmatrix} 5 & 1 & 0 \\ -1 & 0 & 1 \\ 3 & 1 & -3 \end{pmatrix}$, $D = \begin{pmatrix} 1 & 0 & 0 \\ 0 & 2 & 0 \\ 0 & 0 & 2 \end{pmatrix}$

ii $U = \begin{pmatrix} 2 & 1 & 4 \\ 0 & 1 & 1 \\ 1 & -1 & 1 \end{pmatrix}$, $D = \begin{pmatrix} 1 & 0 & 0 \\ 0 & 1 & 0 \\ 0 & 0 & 2 \end{pmatrix}$

3 $\begin{pmatrix} 1 & 1 \\ -1 & -2 \end{pmatrix} \begin{pmatrix} 3 & 0 \\ 0 & 4 \end{pmatrix} \begin{pmatrix} 1 & 1 \\ -1 & -2 \end{pmatrix}^{-1}$

4 Only one eigenvector $\begin{pmatrix} 1 \\ -2 \end{pmatrix}$.

5 a $\begin{pmatrix} 2.5 & -1.5 \\ 4.5 & -3.5 \end{pmatrix}$ and $\begin{pmatrix} -3.5 & 1.5 \\ -4.5 & 2.5 \end{pmatrix}$

b $M_1 M_2 = -2I$. All vectors in the plane can be expressed as $r = a\begin{pmatrix} 1 \\ 3 \end{pmatrix} + b\begin{pmatrix} 1 \\ 1 \end{pmatrix}$, and each of the eigenvectors has eigenvalue $(-2) \times 1$ through $M_1 M_2$.

6 a $U = \begin{pmatrix} 2 & 2 \\ 1 & 3 \end{pmatrix}$, $D = \begin{pmatrix} 2 & 0 \\ 0 & -2 \end{pmatrix}$

b **i** $2^{n-1}\begin{pmatrix} 4 & -4 \\ 3 & -4 \end{pmatrix}$ **ii** $2^n I$

7 a $k = 2$

b 2 and $\begin{pmatrix} \sqrt{3} \\ -1 \end{pmatrix}$, -2 and $\begin{pmatrix} 1 \\ \sqrt{3} \end{pmatrix}$; proof.

c Reflection in the line $x + \sqrt{3}y = 0$.

d $M^{11} = 2^{10}\begin{pmatrix} 1 & -\sqrt{3} \\ -\sqrt{3} & -1 \end{pmatrix}$

8 a $U = \begin{pmatrix} 1 & 3 & 1 \\ 1 & 2 & 2 \\ 1 & -1 & 4 \end{pmatrix}$, $D = \begin{pmatrix} 0 & 0 & 0 \\ 0 & 2 & 0 \\ 0 & 0 & -1 \end{pmatrix}$

b $\begin{pmatrix} 3(1-2^{n+1}) & 9 \times 2^n - 4 & 1 - 3 \times 2^n \\ 6 - 2^{n+2} & 3 \times 2^{n+1} - 8 & 2 - 2^{n+1} \\ 12 + 2^{n+1} & -16 - 3 \times 2^n & 4 + 2^n \end{pmatrix}$

9 a Rotation about the origin through 30° anticlockwise.

b Proof; $e^{i\frac{\pi}{6}}$ and $\begin{pmatrix} 1 \\ -i \end{pmatrix}$, $e^{-i\frac{\pi}{6}}$ and $\begin{pmatrix} 1 \\ i \end{pmatrix}$.

c $U = \begin{pmatrix} 1 & 1 \\ -i & i \end{pmatrix}$, $D = \begin{pmatrix} e^{i\frac{\pi}{6}} & 0 \\ 0 & e^{-i\frac{\pi}{6}} \end{pmatrix}$.

d Proof.

MIXED PRACTICE 6

1 C

2 A

3 3 and $\begin{pmatrix} 2 \\ 1 \end{pmatrix}$, 8 and $\begin{pmatrix} 1 \\ -2 \end{pmatrix}$

4 a $x = 3$ **b** $\lambda_1 = 5$; $\lambda_2 = 1$, $v_2 = \begin{pmatrix} 1 \\ -2 \end{pmatrix}$

5 a Proof. **b** $(x + y + z)(x - 2y + z)$

6 Proof.

7 a $\begin{pmatrix} x^2 + 9 & 7x - 3 \\ 7x - 3 & 50 \end{pmatrix}$

b Proof. **c** $x = -1$

8 a $t = 1, -\frac{1}{8}$ **b** $a + b = c$

9 a Proof. **b** $(x - z)(y + z)(x + y)(xz - xy - yz)$

10 a $k = \frac{5}{3}, -1$ **b** Proof.

11 a $\begin{pmatrix} 32 - 4t & 0 & 0 \\ 98 - 2t^2 & 4t - 24 & 2t - 14 \\ 28 - 4t & 0 & 4 \end{pmatrix}$; $t = 7$

b $A^{-1} = \frac{1}{4}\begin{pmatrix} 15 & -4 & -1 \\ -14 & 4 & 2 \\ 17 & -4 & -3 \end{pmatrix}$

12 $(x - y)(y - z)(z - x)(xy + yz + zx)$

13 a $a = 3, -3$

b $\left(\frac{-9(2a+3)}{a^2 - 9}, \frac{3a}{a^2 - 9}, \frac{4a^2 - 9}{a^2 - 9}\right)$

c $k = 1.5$

14 a Proof.

b $(AB)^{-1} = \frac{1}{3}\begin{pmatrix} 0 & 4 & -1 \\ 0 & -1 & 1 \\ 3 & 8 - 4k & k - 8 \end{pmatrix}$

c $B^{-1} = \begin{pmatrix} 1 & 0 & 0 \\ -1 & 1 & 2 \\ 8 & -2 & -8 \end{pmatrix}$

15 a Proof. **b** $-7(a - 4)(a + 1)(a + 3)$

16 a $p = -1$, $q = 10$ **b** Proof.

c $r = 4$, $s = -2$

d $x = \frac{2k+2}{3}$, $y = \frac{11-k}{6}$, $z = \frac{2-k}{3}$

17 a Proof.

b **i** Consistent.

ii Planes intersect at a single point (3, 1, 1).

18 a Proof.

b $M^{-1} = \frac{1}{12}\begin{pmatrix} -2k & 2k - 4 & 12 - 2k \\ 3 & -3 & 3 \\ k & 8 - k & k - 12 \end{pmatrix}$

c $x = 1 - 4k$, $y = 6$, $z = 2k$

19 a $p = -11$ **b** $\lambda_2 = -2, \lambda_3 = 7$

    c $\mathbf{r} = t\mathbf{v}$ for $\mathbf{v} = \begin{pmatrix} 7 \\ 1 \\ 3 \end{pmatrix}, \begin{pmatrix} -5 \\ 1 \\ 7 \end{pmatrix}$ or $\begin{pmatrix} -1 \\ 2 \\ -4 \end{pmatrix}$.

20 a i 27 and $\begin{pmatrix} 4 \\ 1 \end{pmatrix}$, 1 and $\begin{pmatrix} -1 \\ 3 \end{pmatrix}$

    ii $3x + y = 0$

  b $\mathbf{U}^{-1} = \frac{1}{13}\begin{pmatrix} 3 & 1 \\ -1 & 4 \end{pmatrix}$, $\mathbf{M} = \begin{pmatrix} 25 & 8 \\ 6 & 3 \end{pmatrix}$

  c Proof.

FOCUS ON … PROOF 1

1 Proof.

2 Proof.

FOCUS ON … PROBLEM SOLVING 1

1 $\begin{pmatrix} -\frac{1}{2}x - \frac{\sqrt{3}}{2}y \\ \frac{\sqrt{3}}{2}x - \frac{1}{2}y \end{pmatrix}$

2 The velocity is parallel to $S_2 - S_1$; proof.

3 Proof.

4 Proof.

5 Proof.

6 Proof.

7 Proof.

8 $t = \frac{2}{\sqrt{3}v}$; $\theta \to \infty$

9 Proof; $\frac{dy}{dt} = \frac{dr}{dt}\sin\theta + r\frac{d\theta}{dt}\cos\theta$

10 $\begin{cases} \frac{dr}{dt}\cos\theta - r\frac{d\theta}{dt}\sin\theta = -\frac{v\sqrt{3}}{2}\cos\theta - \frac{v}{2}\sin\theta \\ \frac{dr}{dt}\sin\theta + r\frac{d\theta}{dt}\cos\theta = \frac{v}{2}\cos\theta - \frac{v\sqrt{3}}{2}\sin\theta \end{cases}$; proof.

11 $\frac{dr}{d\theta} = -r\sqrt{3}$; proof.

FOCUS ON … MODELLING 1

1 Proof.

2 $j_{n+1} = 3a_n$

3 $\begin{pmatrix} 0.9 & 0.8 \\ 3 & 0 \end{pmatrix}$

4 a 180   **b** 179 108

5 2.06

6 1.45

7 $\begin{pmatrix} 1 \\ 1.45 \end{pmatrix}$ with $\lambda = 2.06$ and $\begin{pmatrix} 1 \\ -2.58 \end{pmatrix}$ with $\lambda = -1.16$.

The larger eigenvalue is the growth rate and the ratio of the components of the eigenvector is the ratio of juveniles to adults.

8 0.125

9 For example: all adults are the same; there is no reference to gender; the average of 3 might not give a good prediction with small numbers; no randomness; there are no limiting factors such as the size of the island; there are no direct effects of predators.

10 This is the situation described by Fibonacci leading to his eponymous sequence.

CROSS-TOPIC REVIEW EXERCISE 1

1 a Proof.   **b** 3.76 (3 s.f.)

2 a $8e^{-i\frac{\pi}{2}}$

  b $\sqrt{2}e^{-i\frac{\pi}{12}}, \sqrt{2}e^{i\frac{\pi}{4}}, \sqrt{2}e^{i\frac{7\pi}{12}}, \sqrt{2}e^{i\frac{11\pi}{12}}, \sqrt{2}e^{-i\frac{5\pi}{12}}, \sqrt{2}e^{-i\frac{3\pi}{4}}$

3 Translation by $\begin{pmatrix} -2 \\ 0 \end{pmatrix}$, stretch parallel to y-axis with scale factor $\frac{1}{\sqrt{3}}$

4 a

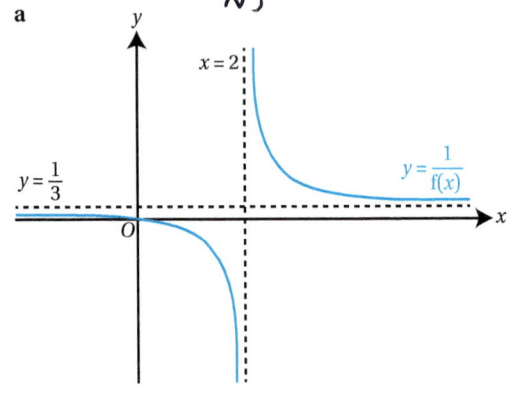

b

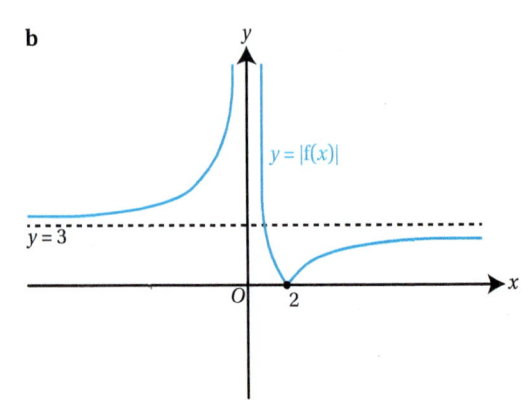

Answers to exercises

5 a

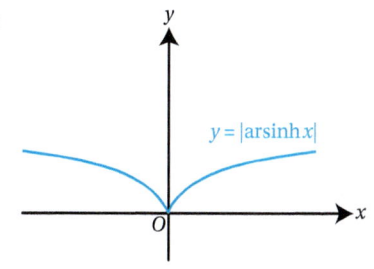

[Graph of $y = |\operatorname{arsinh} x|$]

b $x \in \left(-\infty, -\dfrac{4}{3}\right) \cup \left(\dfrac{4}{3}, \infty\right)$

6 a

[Graph showing $y = |x^2 - x - 12|$ and $y = |3x - 7|$, with key points at -3, $\dfrac{7}{3}$, 4, and y-intercepts 12 and 7.]

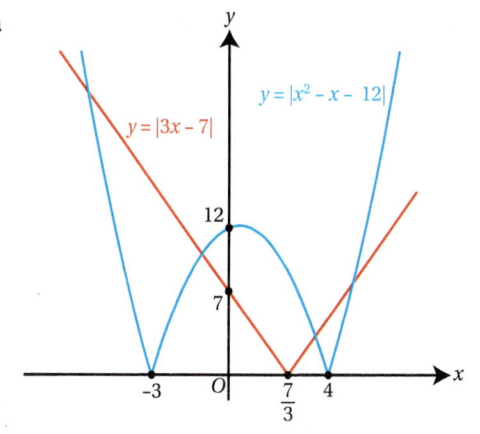

b $x \in \left(-1 - 2\sqrt{5}, -1\right) \cup \left(-1 + 2\sqrt{5}, 5\right)$

7 a $\overrightarrow{AB} \times \overrightarrow{AC} = \begin{pmatrix} 24 \\ -11 \\ -28 \end{pmatrix}$

b $\mathbf{r} = \begin{pmatrix} -3 \\ 1 \\ 1 \end{pmatrix} + \lambda \begin{pmatrix} 24 \\ -11 \\ -28 \end{pmatrix}$

8 a $6x - 2y + 3z = 4$

b $80.8°$ (3 s.f.)

9 a Proof.

b $5 \arctan\left(\dfrac{1}{a}\right)$

c Proof.

10 $p = 2$, $q = 3$

11 a $\mathbf{a} \times \mathbf{b} = \begin{pmatrix} -5 \\ -3p - 1 \\ 15 \end{pmatrix}$ **b** $p = \dfrac{19}{3}$

12 a $7\mathbf{a} \times \mathbf{b}$ **b** Proof; $\lambda = 7$.

13 a $n = 1, -18$

b Inconsistent; form a triangular prism.

14 a $\det \mathbf{M} = 8k^3$

b i $k = \dfrac{1}{8}$; scale factor $\dfrac{1}{4}$.

ii Rotation about the y-axis through $210°$.

15 a i Proof; $k = -\dfrac{2}{3}$, $m = \dfrac{49}{9}$.

ii $\mathbf{A}^{-1} = \dfrac{9}{49} \begin{pmatrix} -\dfrac{2}{3} & 2 & 1 \\ 1 & -\dfrac{2}{3} & 2 \\ 2 & 1 & -\dfrac{2}{3} \end{pmatrix}$

b i $\det \mathbf{A} = k^3 - 6k + 9$

ii $k = -3$; proof.

iii $k = 4$

16 a Proof; 1.

b $\begin{pmatrix} 1 \\ 1 \\ -1 \end{pmatrix}$ and, for example, $\begin{pmatrix} 1 \\ 0 \\ 1 \end{pmatrix}, \begin{pmatrix} 0 \\ 1 \\ 1 \end{pmatrix}$.

c T is an enlargement in the plane

$\mathbf{r} = s \begin{pmatrix} 1 \\ 0 \\ 1 \end{pmatrix} + t \begin{pmatrix} 0 \\ 1 \\ 1 \end{pmatrix}$ (or equivalently

$x + y - z = 0$) with scale factor 4. The line

$\mathbf{r} = t \begin{pmatrix} 1 \\ 1 \\ -1 \end{pmatrix}$, which is normal to the plane,

is a line of invariant points.

17 a $\dfrac{1}{k} e^{kx} + c$

b Proof.

c $\dfrac{3 - e^{\frac{\pi}{2}}}{10}$

18 a Proof.

b $z = -i \ln(2 \pm \sqrt{3}) + 2k\pi$

19 a, b Proof.

20 a $p + q$, $p - q$

b $\begin{pmatrix} 1 \\ 1 \end{pmatrix}, \begin{pmatrix} 1 \\ -1 \end{pmatrix}$

c $\mathbf{D} = \begin{pmatrix} p+q & 0 \\ 0 & p-q \end{pmatrix}$, $\mathbf{U} = \begin{pmatrix} 1 & 1 \\ 1 & -1 \end{pmatrix}$

d Proof.

e $L = \begin{pmatrix} 0.5 & 0.5 \\ 0.5 & 0.5 \end{pmatrix}$

21 a i $k \neq 5$

ii $M^{-1} = \dfrac{1}{3k-15}\begin{pmatrix} -7 & k+2 & 8-3k \\ -4 & k-1 & -4 \\ 3 & -3 & 3 \end{pmatrix}$

b 0.5 cm^3

c Proof.

d $k = 4; \dfrac{x}{4} = \dfrac{y}{2} = -z$

22 a i Proof.

ii $2\cos n\theta$

b i $z^4 - 2 + \dfrac{1}{z^4}$

ii Proof; $A = 1, B = -1$

c $\dfrac{2\pi}{3} + \dfrac{\sqrt{3}}{4}$

23 a $\begin{pmatrix} c & s \\ -s & c \end{pmatrix}$; proof.

b i Proof; $p = c^2 + 6sc - 7s^2$, $r = s^2 - 6sc - 7c^2$.

ii $c = \dfrac{3}{\sqrt{10}}, s = \dfrac{1}{\sqrt{10}}$;

$\dfrac{X^2}{2^2} - \dfrac{Y^2}{1^2} = 1$

iii Since C' is a hyperbola that is just a rotation of C, C must also be a hyperbola.

24 a i $A^{-1} = \dfrac{1}{5}\begin{pmatrix} 1 & 2 \\ -2 & 1 \end{pmatrix}$

ii $x = \dfrac{1}{5}(X + 2Y), y = \dfrac{1}{5}(Y - 2X)$

b Enlargement, scale factor $\sqrt{5}$; Rotation through $\cos^{-1}\dfrac{1}{\sqrt{5}}$.

c i, ii Proof.

iii It's an enlarged rotation of E, so it is still an ellipse.

7 Further polar coordinates

BEFORE YOU START

1 [Graph: $r = 2 - 2\cos\theta$, pointing to $0, 2\pi$]

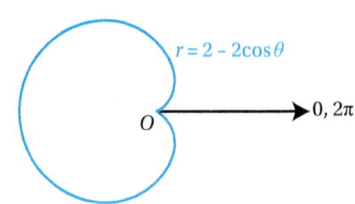

2 $r = 2\sin\theta$

3 a $\dfrac{1}{3}$ b $\dfrac{\pi}{4}$

EXERCISE 7A

1 a i $\dfrac{1}{2}$ ii $\dfrac{1}{3}$

b i $\dfrac{2\pi^3}{3}$ ii $\dfrac{\pi^5}{10}$

c i $e^{4\pi} - 1$ ii $\dfrac{e^{2\pi} - 1}{2}$

d i $\dfrac{\pi}{8}$ ii $\dfrac{2+\pi}{16}$

e i $\dfrac{3\pi}{4}$ ii $\dfrac{3\pi}{2}$

2 a $r = a$ b Proof.

3 $\dfrac{4-\pi}{8}$

4 Proof.

5 27π

6 a [Graph: $r = \theta^{-\frac{1}{2}}$, pointing to $0, 2\pi$]

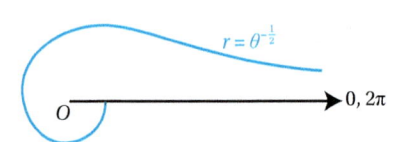

b Proof.

7 a [Graph: $r = 3\sin 2\theta$, four-petal rose]

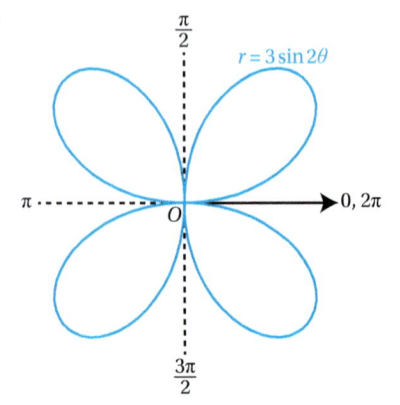

b $\dfrac{9\pi}{2}$

Answers to exercises

8 a

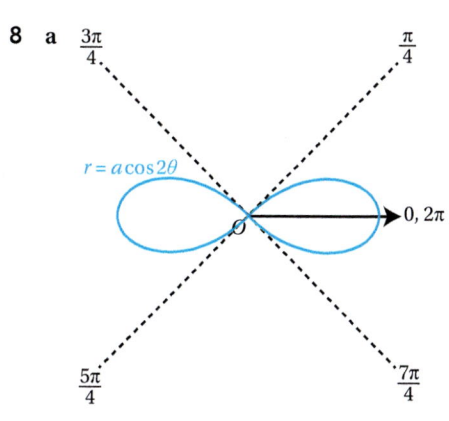

Tangents: $\theta = \dfrac{\pi}{4}, \dfrac{3\pi}{4}, \dfrac{5\pi}{4}, \dfrac{7\pi}{4}$

b $\dfrac{\pi a^2}{4}$

9 $k = \dfrac{\pi}{3}$

10 Proof.

EXERCISE 7B

1 a $\left(2, \dfrac{\pi}{6}\right)$

b i $\dfrac{\sqrt{3}}{2}$ **ii** Proof.

2 $\dfrac{3\pi a^2}{8}$

3 a $\left(a, \dfrac{\pi}{12}\right)$ and $\left(a, \dfrac{5\pi}{12}\right)$

b $\dfrac{a^2}{12}(4\pi - 3\sqrt{3})$

4 a $\left(\dfrac{1}{2}, \dfrac{\pi}{6}\right), \left(\dfrac{1}{2}, \dfrac{5\pi}{6}\right)$ **b** $\dfrac{16\pi - 21\sqrt{3}}{24}$

5 a $\left(3, \dfrac{\pi}{3}\right), \left(3, \dfrac{5\pi}{3}\right)$

b Proof.

6 a

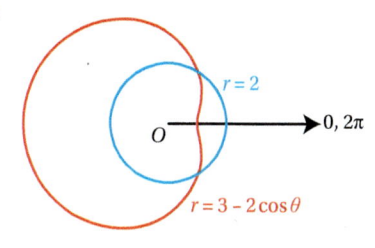

b Proof.

MIXED PRACTICE 7

1 B

2 a

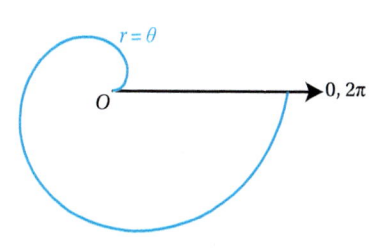

b Proof.

3 a

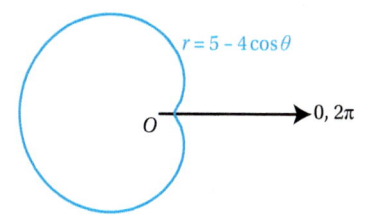

b 33π

4 a Proof.

b $\theta = \dfrac{2\pi}{3}$ or $\dfrac{4\pi}{3}$

c

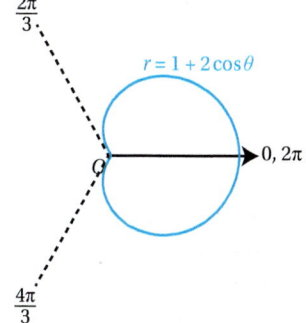

d Proof.

5 Proof.

6 $4\pi - 6\sqrt{3}$

365

7   **a** Proof.

   b $\left(5, \dfrac{\pi}{3}\right)$ and $\left(5, \dfrac{5\pi}{3}\right)$

   c $\dfrac{200\pi}{3} - \dfrac{175\sqrt{3}}{2}$

8   Proof.

9   **a** **i** Proof.

   ii $\theta = \dfrac{\pi}{4}, \dfrac{\pi}{2}, \dfrac{3\pi}{4}, \dfrac{5\pi}{4}, \dfrac{3\pi}{2}, \dfrac{7\pi}{4}$

   b Proof.

10 **a** **i** $\dfrac{3\sqrt{3}}{4}$ **ii** Proof.

   iii $\dfrac{27\sqrt{3}}{128}$

   b **i** $\dfrac{\sin^{n+1}\theta}{n+1} + c$

   ii $\dfrac{\pi}{12} - \dfrac{21\sqrt{3}}{160} + \dfrac{2}{15}$

8 Further hyperbolic functions

BEFORE YOU START

1   Proof.

2   **a** (graph of $y = \cosh x$ and $y = 1 + \tanh x$)

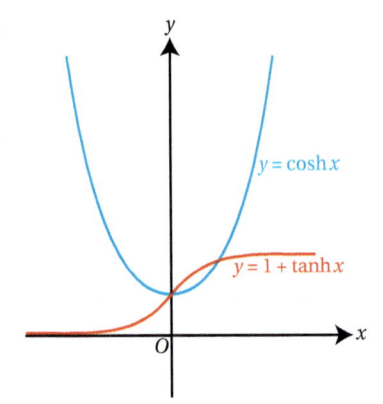

   b 2 solutions.

3   (graph of $y = \sinh x$, $y = x$, $y = \text{arsinh}\,x$)

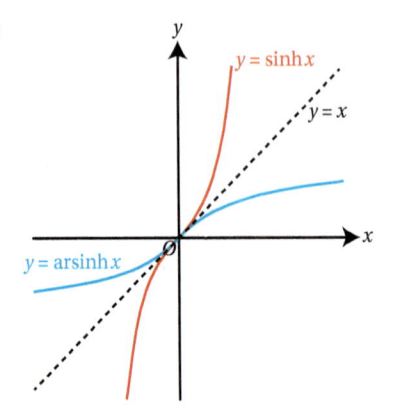

4   **a** $\ln(\sqrt{3}+2)$ **b** $\ln\sqrt{5}$

5   $x = \pm \ln 3$

6   **a** $x \geq 3$ **b** $f(x) \geq 0$

7   (graph with points $(-1, 11)$, $(1, 11)$, $(0, 3)$, $y = 3 - f(2x)$)

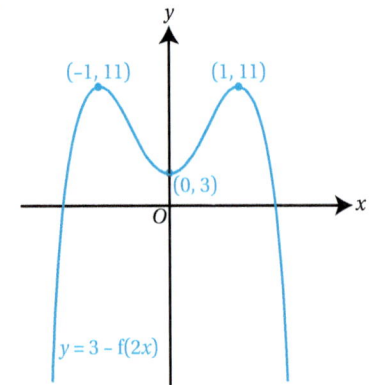

8   **a** $2e^{2x}$ **b** $-e^{-x} + c$

9   **a** $\sec^2 x$ **b** $\sin x + c$

10 **a** $6\sin 3x \cos 3x$ **b** $\cos x - x\sin x$

   c $\dfrac{2x\sec^2 2x - \tan 2x}{x^2}$

11 **a** $\tan x - x + c$

   b $\dfrac{1}{4}\sin^4 x + c$

   c $-x\cos x + \sin x + c$

EXERCISE 8A

1   **a** **i** (graph of $f(x) = 3 - \sinh\left(\dfrac{x}{2}\right)$, passing through 3)

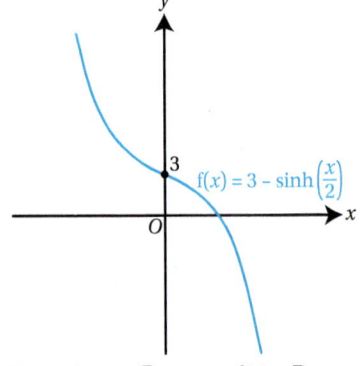

   Domain: $x \in \mathbb{R}$; range: $f(x) \in \mathbb{R}$.

   ii (graph of $f(x) = 2\sinh(x-1)$, passing through 1)

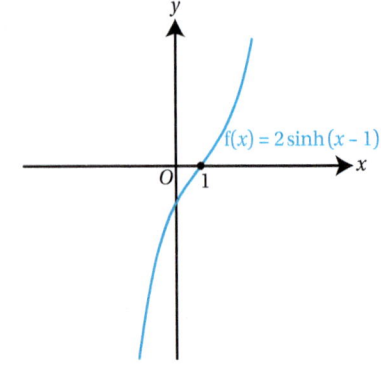

   Domain: $x \in \mathbb{R}$; range: $f(x) \in \mathbb{R}$.

b i

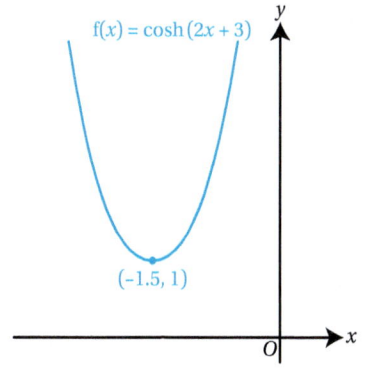

[Graph: $f(x) = \cosh(2x+3)$, minimum at $(-1.5, 1)$]

Domain: $x \in \mathbb{R}$; range: $f(x) \geq 1$.

ii

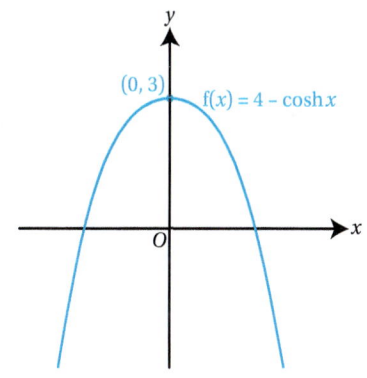

[Graph: $f(x) = 4 - \cosh x$, maximum at $(0, 3)$]

Domain: $x \in \mathbb{R}$; range: $f(x) \leq 3$.

c i

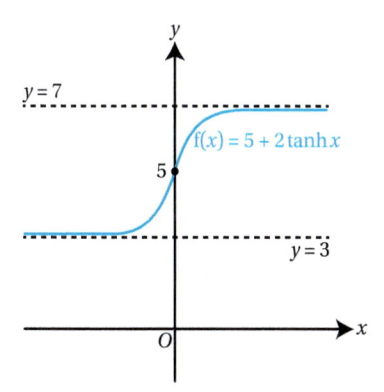

[Graph: $f(x) = 5 + 2\tanh x$, asymptotes $y = 7$ and $y = 3$, passes through 5]

Domain: $x \in \mathbb{R}$; range: $3 < f(x) < 7$.

ii

[Graph: $f(x) = 4\tanh(-x)$, asymptotes $y = 4$ and $y = -4$]

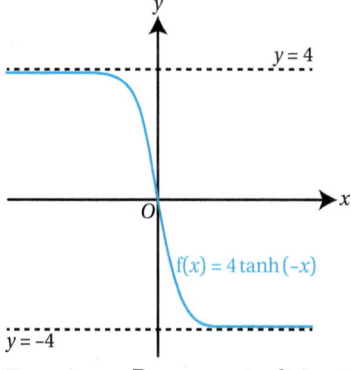

Domain: $x \in \mathbb{R}$; range: $-4 < f(x) < 4$.

2 a i

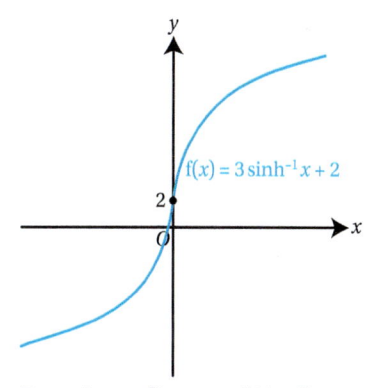

[Graph: $f(x) = 3\sinh^{-1} x + 2$, passes through $(0, 2)$]

Domain: $x \in \mathbb{R}$; range: $f(x) \in \mathbb{R}$.

ii

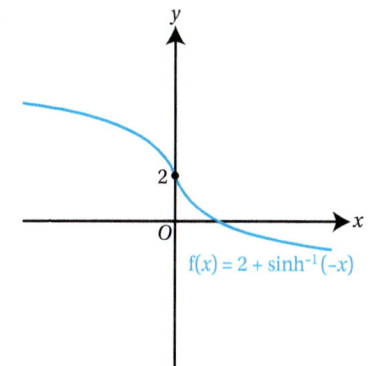

[Graph: $f(x) = 2 + \sinh^{-1}(-x)$, passes through $(0, 2)$]

Domain: $x \in \mathbb{R}$; range: $f(x) \in \mathbb{R}$.

b i

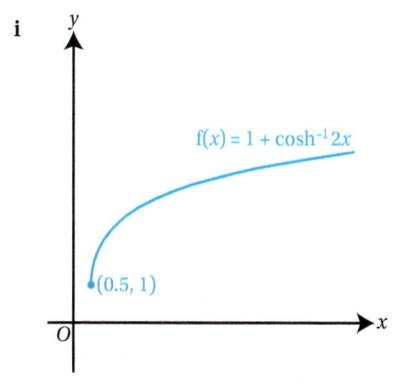

[Graph: $f(x) = 1 + \cosh^{-1} 2x$, starting at $(0.5, 1)$]

Domain: $x \geq 0.5$; range: $f(x) \geq 1$.

ii

[Graph: $f(x) = 2\cosh^{-1}\left(\dfrac{x}{3}\right)$, starting at $(3, 0)$]

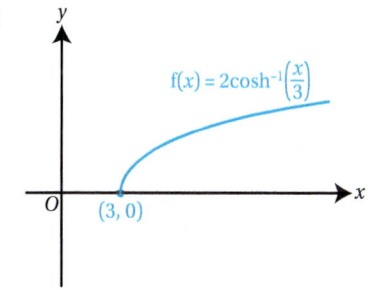

Domain: $x \geq 3$; range: $f(x) \geq 0$.

c i

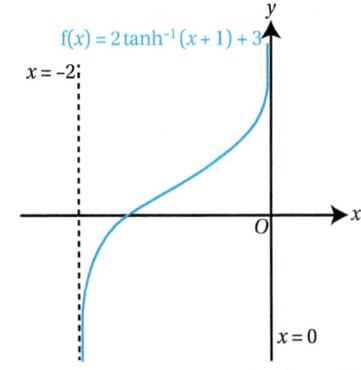

$f(x) = 2\tanh^{-1}(x+1) + 3$

Domain: $-2 < x < 0$; range: $f(x) \in \mathbb{R}$.

ii

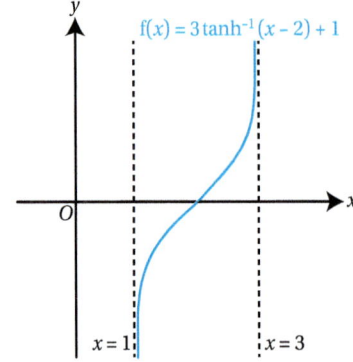

$f(x) = 3\tanh^{-1}(x-2) + 1$

Domain: $1 < x < 3$; range: $f(x) \in \mathbb{R}$.

3 $a = 4, b = -2$ **4** $a = -3, b = 1$

5 $b \leq a - 2$

EXERCISE 8B

1 a i

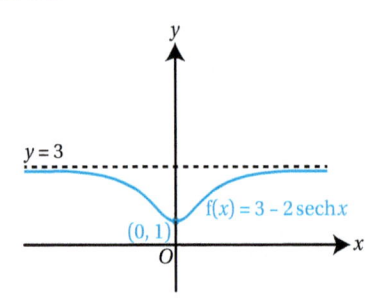

$f(x) = 3 - 2\text{sech}\,x$, $(0, 1)$, $y = 3$

Domain: $x \in \mathbb{R}$, range: $1 \leq f(x) < 3$.

ii

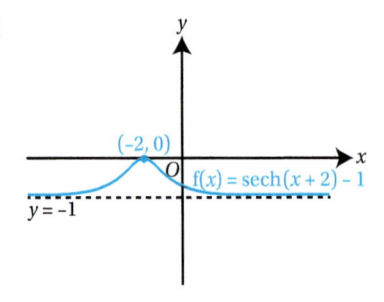

$f(x) = \text{sech}(x+2) - 1$, $(-2, 0)$, $y = -1$

Domain: $x \in \mathbb{R}$; range: $-1 < f(x) \leq 0$.

b i

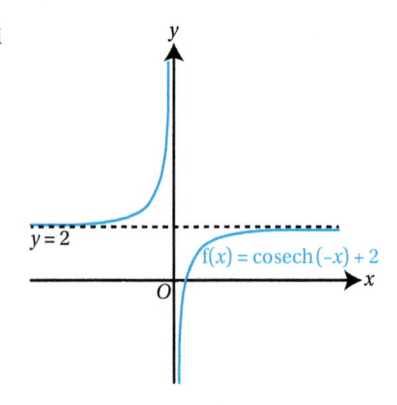

$f(x) = \text{cosech}(-x) + 2$, $y = 2$

Domain: $x \neq 0$; range: $f(x) \neq 2$.

ii

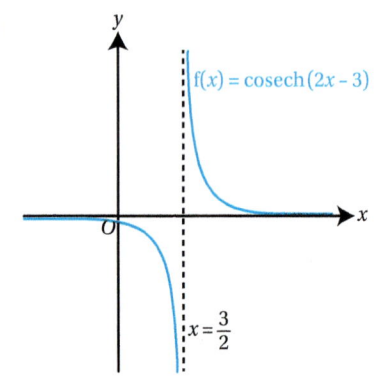

$f(x) = \text{cosech}(2x - 3)$, $x = \frac{3}{2}$

Domain: $x \neq \frac{3}{2}$; range: $f(x) \neq 0$.

c i

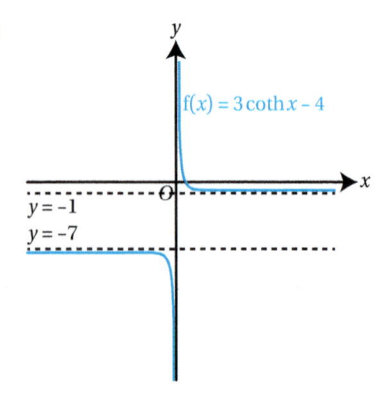

$f(x) = 3\coth x - 4$, $y = -1$, $y = -7$

Domain: $x \neq 0$; range: $f(x) > -1$ or $f(x) < -7$.

ii

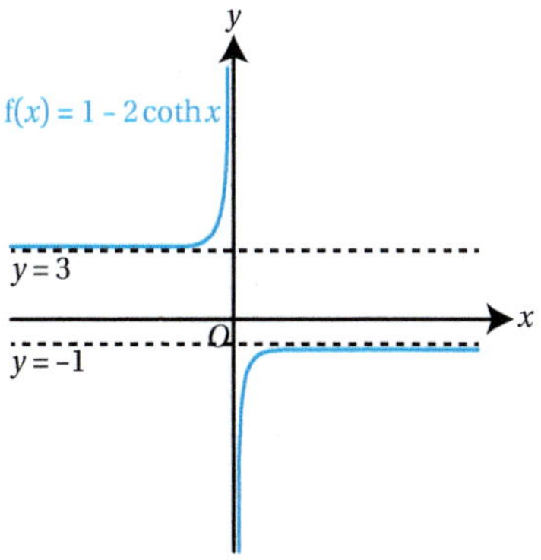

[Graph: $f(x) = 1 - 2\coth x$, with asymptotes $y = 3$ and $y = -1$]

Domain: $x \neq 0$; range: $f(x) > 3$ or $f(x) < -1$.

2 a

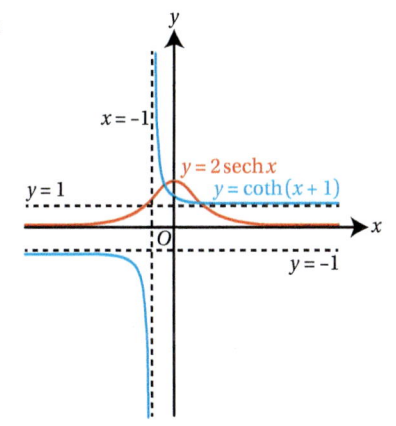

[Graph: $y = 2\,\text{sech}\,x$ and $y = \coth(x+1)$, with asymptotes $x = -1$, $y = 1$, $y = -1$]

b 2 solutions.

3 a

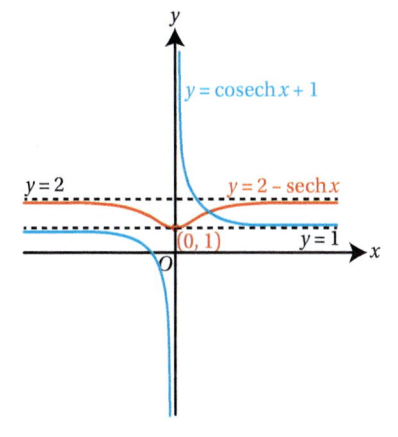

[Graph: $y = \text{cosech}\,x + 1$ and $y = 2 - \text{sech}\,x$, with asymptotes $y = 2$, $y = 1$, point $(0, 1)$]

b 1 solution.

4 Proof.

5 a

[Graph: $y = \text{arcoth}\,x$, $y = \coth x$, $y = x$, with asymptotes $x = -1$, $x = 1$, $y = 1$, $y = -1$]

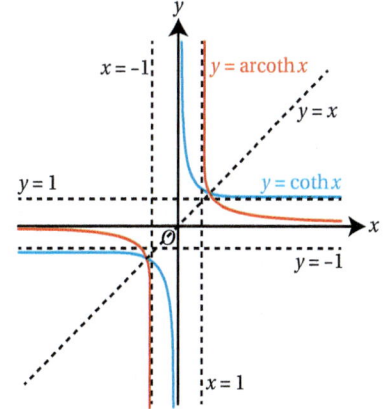

b **i** $x \in (-\infty, -1) \cup (1, \infty)$

  ii $f(x) \neq 0$

c Proof.

6 a, b Proof.

EXERCISE 8C

1 a–c Proof.

2 $x = 0, \pm 1.57$ (3 s.f.)

3 $x = -0.881, 1.19$ (3 s.f.)

4 $x = \ln(3 \pm 2\sqrt{2})$

5 $x = 0, \ln\left(\dfrac{3 \pm \sqrt{5}}{2}\right)$

6 $x = \ln\sqrt{3}$

7 $x = \ln 4$

8 $x = \dfrac{1}{2}\ln 2$

9 $x = \ln(2 \pm \sqrt{3})$

10 Proof.

11 a Proof.

  b $x = \dfrac{1}{2}\ln(1 + \sqrt{2})$

12 a Proof.

  b $x = \dfrac{1}{6}\ln(3 \pm 2\sqrt{2})$

EXERCISE 8D

1 a i $3\cosh 3x$ **ii** $\dfrac{1}{2}\cosh \dfrac{1}{2}x$

  b i $4\sinh(4x+1)$ **ii** $\dfrac{1}{3}\sinh \dfrac{1}{3}x$

  c i $\dfrac{2}{3}\text{sech}^2 \dfrac{2}{3}x$ **ii** $-2\,\text{sech}^2(1-2x)$

d i $\frac{1}{4}\text{sech}\left(-\frac{1}{4}x\right)\tanh\left(-\frac{1}{4}x\right)$

ii $-3\,\text{sech}\,3x\tanh 3x$

e i $-5\,\text{cosech}\,5x\coth 5x$

ii $-\frac{1}{2}\text{cosech}\,\frac{1}{2}x\coth\frac{1}{2}x$

f i $-3\,\text{cosech}^2(3x-1)$

ii $4\,\text{cosech}^2(-4x)$

2 a $2x\tanh 3x + 3x^2\,\text{sech}^2 3x$

b $-10\coth 5x\,\text{cosech}^2 5x$

3 $(0, e-1)$

4 $(-\ln 2, 4)$

5 Proof.

6 $x + 2y - \ln 3 - 2 = 0$

7 a $\pm\frac{1}{2}\ln(\sqrt{2}+1)$

b Proof.

8 $\left(\ln 3, \frac{\sqrt{3}}{9}\right)$

9 Proof; $k = 1 + \sqrt{2}$.

10 a $\pm\ln\left(\frac{3+\sqrt{5}}{2}\right)$

b Proof.

EXERCISE 8E

1 a i $\frac{1}{3}\cosh 3x + c$

ii $2\cosh\frac{x}{2} + c$

b i $\frac{1}{2}\sinh(2x+1) + c$

ii $\frac{1}{4}\sinh 4x + c$

c i $-\frac{1}{2}\ln\cosh(-2x) + c$

ii $\frac{1}{3}\ln\cosh(3x-2) + c$

2 a i $-\frac{1}{4}\tanh(3-4x) + c$

ii $\frac{1}{2}\tanh 2x + c$

b i $-3\,\text{sech}\,\frac{x}{3} + c$

ii $\frac{1}{3}\text{sech}(-3x) + c$

c i $-\frac{1}{4}\text{cosech}\,4x + c$

ii $-2\,\text{cosech}\,\frac{x}{2} + c$

d i $4\coth\left(-\frac{x}{4}\right) + c$

ii $-\frac{1}{2}\coth(2x-3) + c$

3 a i $\frac{1}{8}\sinh 4x - \frac{1}{2}x + c$

ii $\frac{1}{12}\sinh 6x + \frac{1}{2}x + c$

b i $x - 2\tanh\frac{x}{2} + c$

ii $x - \coth x + c$

c i $\frac{1}{4}\cosh 2x + c$

ii $\frac{1}{12}\cosh 6x + c$

4 a i $\frac{1}{5}\cosh^5 x + c$

ii $\frac{1}{4}\tanh^4 x + c$

b i $\ln|2 + \tanh x| + c$

ii $\ln|\sinh x - 3| + c$

c i $-\frac{1}{2}e^{\coth 2x} + c$

ii $e^{-\text{sech}\,x} + c$

5 a i $x\cosh x - \sinh x + c$

ii $\frac{1}{2}x\cosh 2x - \frac{1}{4}\sinh 2x + c$

b i $3x\sinh x - 3\cosh x + c$

ii $2x\sinh\frac{x}{2} - 4\cosh\frac{x}{2} + c$

c i $x^2\cosh x - 2x\sinh x + 2\cosh x + c$

ii $\frac{1}{3}x^2\cosh 3x - \frac{2}{9}x\sinh 3x + \frac{2}{27}\cosh 3x + c$

d i $\frac{1}{2}x^2\sinh 2x - \frac{1}{2}x\cosh 2x + \frac{1}{4}\sinh 2x + c$

ii $3x^2\sinh x - 6x\cosh x + 6\sinh x + c$

6 a i $\frac{1}{6}e^{3x} + \frac{1}{2}e^{-x} + c$

ii $\frac{1}{6}e^{3x} + \frac{1}{2}e^{x} + c$

b i $\frac{1}{20}e^{5x} - \frac{1}{20}e^{-5x} - \frac{1}{12}e^{3x} + \frac{1}{12}e^{-3x} + c$

ii $\frac{1}{20}e^{5x} - \frac{1}{20}e^{-5x} + \frac{1}{4}e^{x} - \frac{1}{4}e^{-x} + c$

7 $\frac{1}{4}(\ln(\cosh x) + x) + c$

8 $1 - e^{-1}$

9 a $\ln(\cosh x) + \frac{1}{2}\text{sech}^2 x + c$

b $\ln(\cosh x) + \frac{1}{2}\text{sech}^2 x + c$

10 Proof.

11   a $\frac{1}{5}\sinh^5 x + \frac{1}{3}\sinh^3 x + c$

    b $\sinh x - \text{cosech}\, x + c$

12   $x \tanh x - \ln(\cosh x) + c$

13   $2\pi(5\ln 2 - 3)$

14   a   Proof.

    b $\frac{3}{4}\ln\left|\frac{e^{4x}-1}{e^{4x}+1}\right| - \frac{1}{12}\cosh^3 4x + c$

15   Proof.

16   Proof.

MIXED PRACTICE 8

1   B

2   a

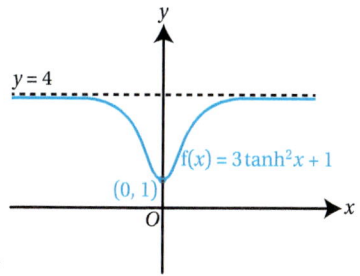

    b $1 \leq f(x) < 4$

3   $x = \frac{1}{2}\ln(2+\sqrt{5})$

4   Proof.

5   Proof.

6   Proof.

7   $-\frac{1}{3}\text{sech}\, 3x + c$

8   Proof.

9   $x = \ln\frac{5}{3}$

10   $x = \ln\sqrt{3},\ -\ln\sqrt{5}$

11   Proof.

12   $\frac{2}{3}\tan^{-1}(3e^x) + c$

13   $7\ln 6 - 10$

14   a

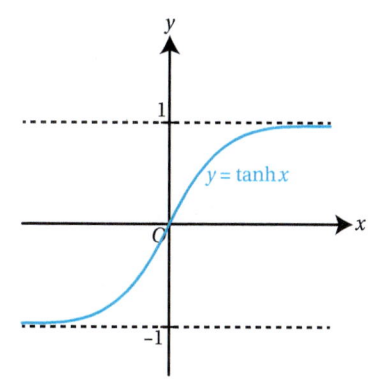

    b   Proof.

    c   i   Proof.   ii   Proof; $x = \frac{1}{2}\ln 2$.

15   a   i

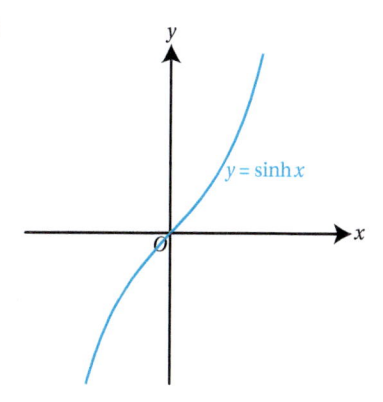

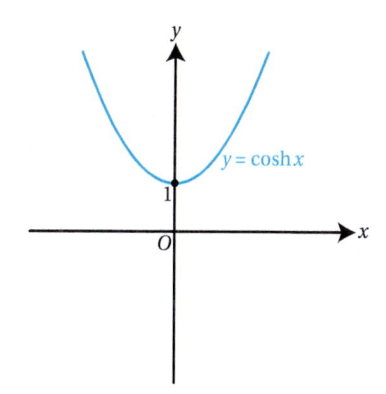

        ii   Proof.

    b   Proof.

16   a, b   Proof.

17   Proof.

18   a   Proof.   b $\ln(\sqrt{2}\pm 1)$

19   a   Proof.

    b   i   Proof; $\ln\frac{2}{3}$.

        ii   Proof; $a = 3, b = 6, c = 5$.

9 Further calculus

BEFORE YOU START

1   $\frac{2x-5}{3y^2}$

2   $\frac{1}{9}(3\sqrt{3}-1)$

3   $\frac{x^4}{16}(4\ln x - 1) + c$

4   $\ln|(x-1)(x-2)| + \frac{2}{x-2} + c$

371

EXERCISE 9A

1. a i $\dfrac{-3}{\sqrt{1-9x^2}}$

   ii $\dfrac{-2}{\sqrt{1-4x^2}}$

   b i $\dfrac{2}{4+x^2}$

   ii $\dfrac{10}{25+4x^2}$

   c i $\arcsin x + \dfrac{x}{\sqrt{1-x^2}}$

   ii $2x\arcsin x + \dfrac{x^2}{\sqrt{1-x^2}}$

   d i $\dfrac{2x}{(2+2x^2+x^4)}$

   ii $-\dfrac{2}{\sqrt{2-x^2}}$

2. $-\dfrac{3}{\sqrt{35}}$

3. $-\dfrac{\pi}{4} - \dfrac{1}{2}$

4. $\dfrac{3}{9x^2+12x+5}$

5. $\dfrac{2x}{\sqrt{-x^4+6x^2-8}}$; $x \in (-2, -\sqrt{2}) \cup (\sqrt{2}, 2)$

6. a Proof.

   b $-\dfrac{1}{x^2+1}$

7. Proof; $|x| < \dfrac{2}{3}$

8. Proof; $a = -1$, $b = -2$.

9. a $\sin^{-1} x + \dfrac{x}{\sqrt{1-x^2}}$

   b $x\sin^{-1} x + \sqrt{1-x^2} + c$

10. Proof.

EXERCISE 9B

1. a i $\dfrac{2}{\sqrt{4x^2+1}}$

   ii $\dfrac{1}{\sqrt{(x+2)^2+1}}$

   b i $\dfrac{-1}{\sqrt{x^2-1}}$

   ii $\dfrac{3}{\sqrt{9x^2-1}}$

   c i $\dfrac{4}{1-16x^2}$

   ii $\dfrac{1}{2x^2-2x}$

2. $\dfrac{\sinh x}{\sqrt{\cosh^2 x + 1}}$

3. $\operatorname{arcosh}(x^2) + \dfrac{2x^2}{\sqrt{x^4-1}}$

4. Proof; $a = 2$, $b = 4$.

5. $25x - 16y + 16\ln 2 - 15 = 0$

6. Proof.

7. $(-1, 0)$

8. Proof.

9. Proof; $a = -\dfrac{1}{2}$.

10. a Proof.

    b $\dfrac{769}{300}\ln 2$

EXERCISE 9C

1. a i $\dfrac{3}{2}\arctan\left(\dfrac{x}{2}\right) + c$

   ii $\dfrac{5}{6}\arctan\left(\dfrac{x}{6}\right) + c$

   b i $\dfrac{1}{6}\arctan\left(\dfrac{3x}{2}\right) + c$

   ii $\dfrac{2}{5}\arctan\left(\dfrac{2x}{5}\right) + c$

   c i $\sqrt{6}\arctan\left(\dfrac{\sqrt{6}x}{3}\right) + c$

   ii $\sqrt{10}\arctan\left(\dfrac{\sqrt{10}x}{2}\right) + c$

   d i $2\arcsin\left(\dfrac{x}{3}\right) + c$

   ii $5\arcsin\left(\dfrac{x}{2}\right) + c$

   e i $\dfrac{1}{2}\arcsin\left(\dfrac{2x}{3}\right) + c$

   ii $\arcsin\left(\dfrac{3x}{5}\right) + c$

   f i $5\sqrt{3}\arcsin\left(\dfrac{\sqrt{15}x}{5}\right) + c$

   ii $\sqrt{3}\arcsin\left(\dfrac{\sqrt{84}x}{7}\right) + c$

Answers to exercises

2 a i $3\sinh^{-1}\left(\dfrac{x}{4}\right)+c$

ii $5\sinh^{-1}\left(\dfrac{x}{5}\right)+c$

b i $\dfrac{10}{3}\sinh^{-1}\left(\dfrac{3x}{5}\right)+c$

ii $\dfrac{3}{2}\sinh^{-1}\left(\dfrac{2x}{3}\right)+c$

c i $2\sqrt{2}\sinh^{-1}\left(\sqrt{\dfrac{2}{3}}x\right)+c$

ii $\dfrac{6\sqrt{7}}{7}\sinh^{-1}\left(\sqrt{\dfrac{7}{5}}x\right)+c$

d i $2\cosh^{-1}\left(\dfrac{x}{7}\right)+c$

ii $7\cosh^{-1}\left(\dfrac{x}{6}\right)+c$

e i $\dfrac{1}{3}\cosh^{-1}\left(\dfrac{3x}{4}\right)+c$

ii $3\cosh^{-1}\left(\dfrac{5x}{6}\right)+c$

f i $\dfrac{4\sqrt{3}}{3}\cosh^{-1}\left(\sqrt{\dfrac{3}{7}}x\right)+c$

ii $\dfrac{2\sqrt{7}}{7}\cosh^{-1}\left(\sqrt{\dfrac{7}{11}}x\right)+c$

3 a i $\arctan(x+2)+c$

ii $\arctan(x-3)+c$

b i $\arcsin(x-4)+c$

ii $\arcsin(x-1)+c$

c i $3\sqrt{2}\arctan\left(\dfrac{x+5}{\sqrt{2}}\right)+c$

ii $\dfrac{5}{2}\arcsin\left(\dfrac{2x+3}{3}\right)+c$

d i $\sinh^{-1}(x+3)+c$

ii $\sinh^{-1}(x+2)+c$

e i $\cosh^{-1}\left(\dfrac{x-2}{4}\right)+c$

ii $\cosh^{-1}(x-1)+c$

f i $3\cosh^{-1}\left(\dfrac{2x-3}{\sqrt{5}}\right)+c$

ii $3\sinh^{-1}\left(\dfrac{x+1}{2}\right)+c$

4 $\ln(1+\sqrt{2})$

5 Proof.

6 Proof.

7 a $\dfrac{1}{3}\arctan 3x+c$

b $4\arctan\dfrac{x}{4}+c$

8 a Proof.   **b** $\dfrac{5\pi}{8}$

9 a Proof.   **b** $2\ln(2+\sqrt{3})$

10 a $2(x+1)^2+9$

b $\dfrac{1}{\sqrt{2}}\arctan\left(\dfrac{\sqrt{2}(x+1)}{3}\right)+c$

11 a $2^2-3(x-1)^2$

b $\dfrac{\sqrt{3}\pi}{9}$

12 a Proof.

b $\dfrac{3}{2}\sin^{-1}\left(\dfrac{2x+1}{3}\right)+c$

13 Proof.

14 $\arctan(x+1)+c$

15 Proof.

16 $-4\sqrt{1-x^2}+5\arcsin x+c$

17 $\sqrt{x^2-1}+\cosh^{-1}x+c$

18 $3\ln(x^2+9)-\dfrac{5}{3}\arctan\left(\dfrac{x}{3}\right)+c$

19 a $2(x-2)^2+9$

b $\dfrac{1}{2}\ln|2x^2-8x+17|$
$+2\sqrt{2}\arctan\left(\dfrac{\sqrt{2}(x-2)}{3}\right)+c$

20 Proof.

21 Proof.

22 a $\cos u=\dfrac{1}{\sqrt{1+x^2}}$, $\sin u=\dfrac{x}{\sqrt{1+x^2}}$

b Proof.

EXERCISE 9D

1. **a** **i** $\frac{1}{\sqrt{2}}\arctan\left(\frac{x}{\sqrt{2}}\right) + 2\ln|x+3| + c$

    ii $2\arctan x - \ln|x-2| + c$

   b **i** $2\ln|x+1| + \arctan(x+3) + c$

    ii $\ln|x-2| - 2\arctan\left(\frac{x+1}{2}\right) + c$

   c **i** $\ln|x^2+1| + \arctan x - 3\ln|x+1| + c$

    ii $\frac{1}{2}\ln|x^2+4| - \arctan\left(\frac{x}{2}\right) - \ln|x-1| + c$

   d **i** $\ln|x+1| - \frac{2}{x+1} - \frac{1}{\sqrt{3}}\arctan\left(\frac{x}{\sqrt{3}}\right) + c$

    ii $\ln|x-2| - \frac{1}{x-2} + 2\arctan x + c$

2. $\frac{\pi}{4} - \ln 4$

3. **a** $\frac{1}{x-2} - \frac{1}{x^2+9}$

   b $y = \ln\left|\frac{x-2}{2}\right| - \frac{1}{3}\arctan\left(\frac{x}{3}\right)$

4. **a** $\ln|x-2| + 2\ln|x+1| - \frac{1}{x+1} + c$

   b $\ln|x-2| + 2\arctan(x+1) + c$

5. **a** $\frac{1}{x-4} + \frac{1}{x+4} + \frac{1}{x^2+4}$

   b $\frac{\pi}{6} - \ln 4$

6. $\ln 2 + 1 + \frac{\pi}{4}$

7. $\ln\left|\frac{x-1}{x+3}\right| - \sqrt{2}\arctan\left(\frac{x+1}{\sqrt{2}}\right) + c$

8. Proof; $P = \frac{3}{2}$, $Q = -\frac{1}{2}$, $R = -1$.

EXERCISE 9E

1. **a–e** Proof.

2. **a** **i** $\frac{1}{8}e^2 + \frac{3}{8}$

    ii $24 - 65e^{-1}$

   b **i** $\frac{1}{2^{11}}\pi^5 - \frac{5}{2^7}\pi^3 + \frac{15\pi}{2^4} - \frac{15}{2^3}$

    ii $-\frac{3}{2}\pi^4 + 18\sqrt{3}\pi^3 + 162\pi^2 - 972\sqrt{3}\pi + 2916$

   c **i** $9e - 24$

    ii $24 - 65e^{-1}$

   d **i** $\frac{1}{8}(e^2 + 3)$

    ii $\frac{1}{32}(5e^4 - 1)$

   e **i** $-\frac{4096\sqrt{2}}{315} + \frac{374\sqrt{3}}{35}$

    ii $-\frac{32}{35}(\sqrt{3} + 1)$

3. **a** Proof.
   b $120 - 44e$

4. **a** $I_n = \frac{x^2}{2}(\ln x)^n - \frac{n}{2}I_{n-1}$

   b $\frac{1}{8}(e^2 + 19e^{-2})$

5. **a** $x\ln x - x + c$
   b Proof.
   c $120 - 44e$

6. **a** Proof.

   b $e^{-2x}\left(-\frac{1}{2}x^4 - x^3 - \frac{3}{2}x^2 - \frac{3}{2}x - \frac{3}{4}\right) + c$

7. **a** Proof.
   b $\frac{\pi}{4} - \frac{2}{3}$

8. **a** Proof.
   b $\frac{120}{a^6}$
   c Proof.

9. **a** Proof.
   b $\frac{16}{15}$

10. **a** Proof.   **b** $\ln 2 - \frac{84}{125}$

11. **a, b** Proof.

12. **a** Proof.   **b** $\frac{3\pi}{16}$ **c** Proof.

13. $\frac{63}{256}\pi$

EXERCISE 9F

1. **a** **i** $s = \int_0^3 \sqrt{1+4x^2}\,dx = 9.75$

    ii $s = \int_1^2 \sqrt{1+x^{-2}}\,dx = 1.22$

   b **i** $s = \int_0^1 \frac{\sqrt{16-4x^2+x^4}}{4-x^2}\,dx = 1.06$

    ii $s = \int_0^{\frac{1}{4}} \sqrt{1 + \frac{64x^2}{(1-4x^2)^2}}\,dx = 0.402$

c i $s = \int_0^2 3t\sqrt{4+t^2}\,dt = 14.6$

ii $s = \int_2^4 \sqrt{9t^4 + (2t-1)^2}\,dt = 56.9$

d i $s = \int_0^1 \sqrt{4\cosh^2 2t + 16\sinh^2 t}\,dt = 4.26$

ii $s = \int_0^{\ln 2} \operatorname{sech} t\sqrt{1+\tanh^2 t}\,dt = 0.402$

2 a i $\dfrac{1}{54}\left(145^{\frac{3}{2}} - 37^{\frac{3}{2}}\right)$ **ii** $\dfrac{1}{3}\left(7^{\frac{3}{2}} - 8\right)$

b i $\dfrac{3}{4}$ **ii** $\dfrac{56}{15}$

c i $\dfrac{61}{3}$ **ii** $\dfrac{98}{3}$

d i $\dfrac{5\pi}{2}$ **ii** $\dfrac{3\pi}{2}$

3 $\dfrac{14}{3}$

4 $\ln(\sqrt{2}+1)$

5 $\dfrac{\pi\sqrt{5}}{2}$

6 a Proof. **b** $\dfrac{3}{2}$

7 8

8 a Proof.

b $\dfrac{\sqrt{5}}{4} + \ln\left(\dfrac{1+\sqrt{5}}{2}\right)$

9 a $\dfrac{\pi}{4}$

b $\left(x - \dfrac{1}{2}\right)^2 + y^2 = \dfrac{1}{4}$;

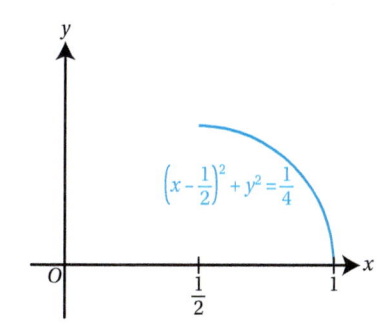

10 a Proof; $k = 4$.

b $16\sqrt{2} - 8$

11 a, b Proof.

12 a Proof. **b** Proof; $A = 10$.

13 Proof; $a = \sqrt{2}$, $b = 1 + \sqrt{2}$.

EXERCISE 9G

1 a i $2\pi\int_0^3 x^2\sqrt{1+4x^2}\,dx = 261$

ii $2\pi\int_1^2 x^{-2}\sqrt{1+4x^{-6}}\,dx = 4.46$

b i $s = 2\pi\int_1^3 (x-1)\sqrt{x^{-2}+x^{-6}}\,dx = 5.88$

ii $s = 2\pi\left|\int_0^1 \left(\dfrac{x-1}{x+1}\right)\sqrt{1 + \dfrac{4}{(x+1)^4}}\,dx\right|$
$= 4.02$

c i $s = 6\pi\int_0^2 t^4\sqrt{4+t^2}\,dt = 315$

ii $s = 2\pi\int_2^4 t(t-1)\sqrt{9t^4 + (2t-1)^2}\,dt = 2646$

d i $s = 8\pi\int_0^1 \cosh t\sqrt{4\cosh^2 2t + 16\sinh^2 t}\,dt$
$= 134$

ii $s = 2\pi\int_0^{\ln 2} \operatorname{sech}^2 t\sqrt{\operatorname{sech}^2 t + \tanh^2 t}\,dt = 3.77$

2 36π

3 $\dfrac{152\sqrt{2}\,\pi}{3}$

4 $\dfrac{\pi}{27}(10\sqrt{10} - 1)$

5 $(130 + 56\sqrt{5})\pi$

6 a Proof. **b** Proof; $k = \dfrac{61}{24}$.

7 a, b Proof.

8 a Proof.

b $\pi\left(\ln\sqrt{2+\sqrt{5}} + \sqrt{5}\right)$

MIXED PRACTICE 9

1 D

2 $2x\sin^{-1}x + \dfrac{x^2}{\sqrt{1-x^2}}$

3 $\dfrac{2x}{\sqrt{1-(1-x^2)^2}}$

4 $\pm\sqrt{3}$

5 a Proof.

b $\pi(6\ln 2 - 2)$

6 $\dfrac{2(1-3x^4)}{(1+x^4)^2}$

7 Proof.

8 $\arctan(x-1) + c$

9 a, b Proof.

10 $3\ln(x^2+4) + 2\arctan\left(\dfrac{x}{2}\right) + c$

11 Proof.

12 a, b Proof.

13 a Proof; $A = 16$.   b Proof.

14 a Proof.

  b $\dfrac{1}{3}\left(\arcsin 3x + \sqrt{1-9x^2}\right) + c$

15 a $\dfrac{2}{x+2} - \dfrac{2x-1}{x^2+1}$

  b $2\ln|x+2| - \ln|x^2+1| + \arctan x + c$

  c Proof.

16 a, b Proof.

17 a, b Proof.

18 a–c Proof.

19 a Proof.

  b $\dfrac{1}{2}\ln\left(\dfrac{17}{4}\right)$

20 a, b Proof.

10 Maclaurin series and limits

BEFORE YOU START

1 $10x(x^2+3)^4$

2 a i $-2e^{-2x}$ ii $4e^{-2x}$

  b i $\dfrac{1}{x}$ ii $-\dfrac{1}{x^2}$

  c i $-3\sin 3x$ ii $-9\cos 3x$

3 a $\operatorname{sech}^2 x$ b $-2\operatorname{sech}^2 x \tanh x$

4 a $\dfrac{1}{\sqrt{x^2-1}}$ b $-x(x^2-1)^{-\frac{3}{2}}$

5 a $\dfrac{1}{\sqrt{1-x^2}}$ b $x(1-x^2)^{-\frac{3}{2}}$

EXERCISE 10A

1 a i $1 + x + \dfrac{x^2}{2!} + \dfrac{x^3}{3!} + \ldots + \dfrac{x^n}{n!} + \ldots$

    ii $1 - 3x + \dfrac{9}{2}x^2 - \dfrac{9}{2}x^3 + \ldots + \dfrac{(-3)^n}{n!}x^n + \ldots$

  b i $-x + \dfrac{x^3}{3!} - \dfrac{x^5}{5!} + \dfrac{x^7}{7!} + \ldots + \dfrac{(-1)^{n+1}x^{2n+1}}{(2n+1)!} + \ldots$

    ii $2x - \dfrac{4}{3}x^3 + \dfrac{4}{15}x^5 - \dfrac{8}{315}x^7 + \ldots$
    $+ \dfrac{(-1)^n 2^{2n+1}}{(2n+1)!}x^{2n+1} + \ldots$

  c i $1 - \dfrac{x^2}{2!} + \dfrac{x^4}{4!} - \dfrac{x^6}{6!} + \ldots + \dfrac{(-1)^n x^{2n}}{(2n)!} + \ldots$

    ii $1 - \dfrac{9}{2}x^2 + \dfrac{27}{8}x^4 - \dfrac{81}{80}x^6 + \ldots + \dfrac{(-1)^n 3^{2n}}{(2n)!}x^{2n} + \ldots$

  d i $-x - \dfrac{x^2}{2} - \dfrac{x^3}{3} - \dfrac{x^4}{4} + \ldots + -\dfrac{x^n}{n} + \ldots$

    ii $2x - 2x^2 + \dfrac{8}{3}x^3 - 4x^4 + \ldots$
    $+ \dfrac{(-1)^{n+1} 2^n}{n}x^n + \ldots$

  e i $x + \dfrac{x^3}{3!} + \dfrac{x^5}{5!} + \dfrac{x^7}{7!} + \ldots + \dfrac{x^{2n+1}}{(2n+1)!} + \ldots$

    ii $2x + \dfrac{4x^3}{3} + \dfrac{4x^5}{15} + \dfrac{8x^7}{315} + \ldots$
    $+ \dfrac{2^{2n+1}}{(2n+1)!}x^{2n+1} + \ldots$

  f i $1 + \dfrac{x^2}{2!} + \dfrac{x^4}{4!} + \dfrac{x^6}{6!} + \ldots + \dfrac{x^{2n}}{(2n)!} + \ldots$

    ii $1 + \dfrac{x^2}{2!} + \dfrac{x^4}{4!} + \dfrac{x^6}{6!} + \ldots + \dfrac{x^{2n}}{(2n)!} + \ldots$

2 $2 + \dfrac{1}{4}x + \dfrac{7}{64}x^2$

3 a Proof.   b 0.324 (3 d.p.)

4 a i $f'(x) = -2xe^{-x^2}$; $f''(x) = -2e^{-x^2} + 4x^2 e^{-x^2}$;
      $f'''(x) = 12xe^{-x^2} - 8x^3 e^{-x^2}$;
      $f^{(4)}(x) = (16x^4 - 48x^2 + 12)e^{-x^2}$

    ii $1 - x^2 + \dfrac{1}{2}x^4$

  b $\dfrac{23}{30}$

5 a $1 - x^2 + \dfrac{1}{3}x^4 - \dfrac{2}{45}x^6$

  b $x^2 - \dfrac{1}{3}x^4 + \dfrac{2}{45}x^6$

6 a i Proof.

    ii $f'''(x) = \dfrac{\cos x}{(1+\sin x)^2}$;
      $f^{(4)}(x) = -\dfrac{1 + \sin^2 x + \cos^2 x}{(1+\sin x)^3}$

  b $x - \dfrac{1}{2}x^2 + \dfrac{1}{6}x^3 - \dfrac{1}{12}x^4$

  c 0.116 (3 d.p.)

7 a i $f'(x) = \dfrac{1}{1-x}$; $f''(x) = \dfrac{1}{(1-x)^2}$;
      $f'''(x) = \dfrac{2}{(1-x)^3}$

    ii Proof.

  b $\dfrac{80}{81}$

8　a　Proof. 　　b　$\dfrac{x^n}{(n-1)!}$

9　a　Proof.

　　b　$5^n x^n$

10　a　$x + \dfrac{1}{6}x^3 + \dfrac{3}{40}x^5 + \ldots$

　　b　i　$f^{(n)}(x) = -g^{(n)}(x)$

　　　　ii　Proof; $k = \dfrac{\pi}{2}$.

11　a　$f(0) = \dfrac{1}{2}$, but in the diagram the y-intercept is not at $\left(0, \dfrac{1}{2}\right)$.

　　b　$f(x)$ is an increasing function at $x = 0$, but the first derivative of the series is negative at $x = 0$.

WORK IT OUT 10.1
Solution 2 is correct.

EXERCISE 10B

1　a　i　2　　　　　　ii　$\dfrac{1}{3}$

　　b　i　0　　　　　　ii　0

　　c　i, ii　Limit doesn't exist.

　　d　i　$\dfrac{3}{4}$　　　　ii　1

2　a　1　　　b　$-\dfrac{1}{2}$　　　c　$\dfrac{1}{2}$

　　d　$-\dfrac{1}{6}$　　e　$-\dfrac{1}{3}$　　f　$\dfrac{3}{2}$

3　a　2　　　b　1　　　c　1

　　d　4π　　e　6　　　f　$\dfrac{3}{4}$

4　a　$3x - \dfrac{9}{2}x^3 + \dfrac{81}{40}x^5$　　b　$-\dfrac{3}{14}$

5　a　-1

　　b　Limit doesn't exist.

　　c　Limit doesn't exist.

6　$-\dfrac{5}{8}$

7　$\dfrac{1}{4}$

8　Proof.

9　Proof.

10　a　$2x^3 + 2x^6 + \dfrac{8x^9}{3} + \ldots$　　b　2

11　$-\dfrac{1}{2}$

12　a　$f(t) = \dfrac{1}{1+t^2}$　　b　$x - \dfrac{x^3}{3} + \dfrac{x^5}{5} - \dfrac{x^7}{7}$

　　c　$\dfrac{1}{3}$　　　　　　　d　$\dfrac{304}{105}$

EXERCISE 10C

1　a　1　　　　　　　　　　b　4

　　c　Integral diverges.　　d　$\dfrac{1}{2}$

2　a　$p < 0$　　　　　　　b　$p > 1$

3　Proof; 4.　　　　　　　4　1

5　$\dfrac{\pi}{2}$　　　　　　　　　6　$\ln \dfrac{9}{16}$

MIXED PRACTICE 10

1　D

2　a, b　Proof.

3　$-\dfrac{1}{2}$

4　a　$f'(x) = (1+x)^{-1}$; $f''(x) = -(1+x)^{-2}$;
$f'''(x) = 2(1+x)^{-3}$; $f^{(4)}(x) = -6(1+x)^{-4}$

　　b　$x - \dfrac{x^2}{2} + \dfrac{x^3}{3} - \dfrac{x^4}{4} + \ldots$

　　c　$\ln 2$

5　a　Integrand isn't defined at $x = 0$.

　　b　Integral doesn't have a finite value.

6　a　$-\dfrac{1}{2}x^2 - \dfrac{1}{12}x^4$　　b　Proof.

7　$\dfrac{\ln 2}{\ln 3}$

8　a　$f'(x) = \dfrac{\cos x}{1 + \sin x}$; $f''(x) = -\dfrac{1}{1 + \sin x}$;
$f'''(x) = \dfrac{\cos x}{(1 + \sin x)^2}$

　　b　$x - \dfrac{1}{2}x^2 + \dfrac{1}{6}x^3$　　c　$-\dfrac{1}{2}$

9　a　$1 - 8x^2 + \dfrac{32}{3}x^4$

　　b　i　$\dfrac{dy}{dx} = \dfrac{-e^x}{2 - e^x}$; $\dfrac{d^2y}{dx^2} = \dfrac{-2e^x}{(2 - e^x)^2}$;
$\dfrac{d^3y}{dx^3} = \dfrac{-4e^x - 2e^{2x}}{(2 - e^x)^3}$

　　　　ii　Proof.

　　c　$-\dfrac{1}{8}$

10　0

11　Proof.

12　a　$x + \dfrac{x^2}{1!} + \dfrac{x^3}{2!} + \dfrac{x^4}{3!} + \ldots + \dfrac{x^n}{(n-1)!} + \ldots$

　　b　$\dfrac{x^2}{2} + \dfrac{x^3}{3(1!)} + \dfrac{x^4}{4(2!)} + \ldots + \dfrac{x^n}{n(n-2)!} + \ldots$

　　c　Proof.

13　a　i　Proof.

　　　　ii　$-4\sec^2 x \tan^2 x - 2\sec^4 x$

　　b　Proof.

377

c $px - \frac{1}{2}p^2x^2$

   d i $p = 3$

      ii 4

14 a i Proof.

   ii $4(1 + \sin 2x)^{-2} \cos 2x$

  b i Proof.

   ii $-x - x^2 - \frac{2}{3}x^3 + \ldots$

  c $1 - 3x - 2x^2 + \ldots$

11 Differential equations

BEFORE YOU START

1 $y = Ae^{\frac{1}{2}x^2}$

2 $e^{3x} + 3xe^{3x}$

3 $e^x(x - 1) + c$

EXERCISE 11A

1 a i For example: $\frac{d^2y}{dx^2} + 2\frac{dy}{dx} + y = 0$

   ii For example: $\frac{d^2y}{dx^2} + 2\frac{dy}{dx} + \cos y = 0$

  b i For example: $\frac{d^2y}{dx^2} + 2\frac{dy}{dx} + y = 0$

   ii For example: $\frac{d^3y}{dx^3} + 2\frac{dy}{dx} + y = 0$

  c i For example: $\frac{d^2y}{dx^2} + 2\frac{dy}{dx} + y = 0$

   ii For example: $\frac{d^2y}{dx^2} + 2\frac{dy}{dx} + y = x$

2 a i Second order linear non-homogeneous.

   ii Second order linear non-homogeneous.

  b i Second order non-linear homogeneous.

   ii First order non-linear non-homogeneous.

  c i Second order non-linear non-homogeneous.

   ii Third order linear homogeneous.

  d i Second order linear homogeneous.

   ii First order non-linear non-homogeneous.

3 a i $y = 2x^2 + 4$ **ii** $y = 8\cos x - 2$

  b i $y = e^{-x} + 3x$ **ii** $y = 6\ln x - 2x^2$

  c i $y = 3x^2 - 2x$

   ii $y = 10\sin x + 5\cos x$

  d i $y = 3e^{2x} - e^x$

   ii $y = 10\sin x - 2\cos x$

4 a $y = \frac{A}{\sqrt{x}}$ **b** $a = 1, b = -2$

  c $y = \frac{5}{\sqrt{x}} + \ln x - 2$

5 a $y = \frac{A}{\cos x}$ **b** $a = 0, b = 2$

  c $y = \frac{A}{\cos x} + 2\cos x$

6 a $a = 5, b = -2, c = -4$

  b $y = 3e^{-4x} + 5 - 2\sin 2x - 4\cos 2x$

7 a $y = Ae^{e^{-x}}$ **b** 2

  c $y = Ae^{e^{-x}} + 2$

EXERCISE 11B

1 a i $y = \frac{1}{3}e^x + ce^{-2x}$

   ii $y = -\frac{1}{3}e^x + ce^{4x}$

  b i $y = -\cot x + c\,\text{cosec}\,x$

   ii $y = \frac{x + c}{\cos x}$

  c i $y = \frac{\ln|x|}{x} + \frac{c}{x}$

   ii $-\frac{1}{x^2} + \frac{c}{x}$

2 $y = \frac{1}{2}e^x + \frac{1}{2}e^{2-x}$

3 $y = x^2 \ln|x - 3| + cx^2$

4 $y = e^{\cos x}(x + c)$

5 $y = -\frac{2}{x^2} + \frac{3}{x}$

6 $y = (x + 2)\cos x$

7 Proof.

8 $y = \frac{x^2 + c}{2(x^2 - 1)}$

9 a $\frac{dz}{dx} - xz = -x$

  b $z = 1 + ce^{\frac{x^2}{2}}$

  c 1

Answers to exercises

10 a $y = -\sqrt{\dfrac{x^3}{4} + \dfrac{36}{x}}$

    b $\sin y = \cos x (\ln(\sec x) + c)$

11 a Proof.

    b $y = A\left(\dfrac{x^4}{4} + x\right) + x^2 + B$

EXERCISE 11C

1 a $\lambda^2 + 5\lambda + 6 = 0$
    b $y = Ae^{-3x} + Be^{-2x}$

2 a $\lambda^2 + 4 = 0$
    b $y = A\cos 2x + B\sin 2x$

3 a $\lambda^2 + 2\lambda + 1 = 0$ b $y = (Ax + B)e^{-x}$

4 a $y = Ae^{4x} + Be^{2x}$ b $y = e^{4x} + 4e^{2x}$

5 a $y = (A + Bx)e^{-2x}$ b $y = (1 + 2x)e^{-2x}$

6 a $x = e^t(A\cos t + B\sin t)$
    b $y = e^t(\cos t - \sin t)$

7 a $x = Ae^t + Be^{3t}$ b e^2

8 a $y = (A + Bt)e^{3t}$ b $y = pte^{3(t-1)}$

9   $y = Ae^x + e^{2x}(B\sin x + C\cos x)$

10   $y = (A + Bx + Cx^2)e^{-x}$

11   $y = Ax^3 + \dfrac{B}{x^3}$

12 a $\dfrac{d^2y}{dt^2} + \dfrac{dy}{dt} = 0$
    b $y = A + Be^{-t}$
    c $x = \sqrt{3 + e^{-t}}$

EXERCISE 11D

1 a $Ae^{5x} + Be^{-x}$ b $-\dfrac{1}{9}e^{2x}$
    c $y = Ae^{5x} + Be^{-x} - \dfrac{1}{9}e^{2x}$

2 a $Ae^{-5x} + Be^{-4x}$ b $3x - \dfrac{27}{20}$
    c $y = Ae^{-5x} + Be^{-4x} + 3x - \dfrac{27}{20}$

3 a $Ae^{-x} + B$
    b $\dfrac{1}{2}\sin x + \dfrac{1}{2}\cos x$
    c $y = Ae^{-x} + B + \dfrac{1}{2}\sin x + \dfrac{1}{2}\cos x$

4 a $A\sin 3x + B\cos 3x$
    b $y = A\sin 3x + B\cos 3x + 2e^{-x}$
    c $y = 4\sin 3x + 5\cos 3x + 2e^{-x}$

5 a $y = (A + Bx)e^{-2x} + 3x - 3 + 3\sin x - 4\cos x$
    b $y = (7 + 18x)e^{-2x} + 3x - 3 + 3\sin x - 4\cos x$

6 a $y = e^{2t}(A\sin 2t + B\cos 2t) + 4t^2 + 4t + 1$
    b $y = e^{2t}(-\sin 2t - \cos 2t) + 4t^2 + 4t + 1$

7 a $(A + Bx)e^{5x}$
    b Proof.
    c $y = (A + Bx)e^{5x} + \dfrac{1}{2}x^2 e^{5x}$
    d $y = (4 - 18x)e^{5x} + \dfrac{1}{2}x^2 e^{5x}$

8   $y = 2(1 - x)\cos 2x + x\sin 2x - \dfrac{e^\pi}{2}\sin 2x + \dfrac{e^{4x}}{2}$

9 a Proof.
    b $y = A\sin^2 x + B\sin x\cos x - \dfrac{1}{3}\sin 2x \sin x$

MIXED PRACTICE 11

1   A

2   B

3 a $\lambda = -5, -1$
    b $y = Ae^{-5x} + Be^{-x}$

4 a Proof.
    b $y = e^{-x}\left(\dfrac{x^2}{2} + c\right)$

5 a $Ae^{-2x} + Be^{-5x}$
    b Proof; $q = \dfrac{1}{18}$.
    c $y = Ae^{-2x} + Be^{-5x} + \dfrac{e^x}{18}$
    d $y = \dfrac{34}{18}e^{-2x} - \dfrac{35}{18}e^{-5x} + \dfrac{e^x}{18}$

6 a $q = \dfrac{1}{3}$
    b $y = A\cos 2x + B\sin 2x + \dfrac{\cos x}{3}$

7 a $e^{-3x}(A\cos 4x + B\sin 4x)$
    b Proof; $p = 2$, $q = -\dfrac{12}{25}$.
    c $y = e^{-3x}(A\cos 4x + B\sin 4x) + 2x - \dfrac{12}{25}$
    d $y = e^{-3x}\sin 4x + 2x - \dfrac{12}{25}$

8   $y = \dfrac{5}{2}e^{-x} - \dfrac{1}{2}xe^{-x}$

9   $y = A\cos 2x + B\sin 2x + 2x^2 - 1 + 3\sin x$

10 a $\dfrac{A}{x^3}+\dfrac{x}{4}$

  b Proof.

  c $y=\dfrac{B}{x^2}+C+\dfrac{x^2}{8}$

11 a $y=A\cos x-2\cos x\ln|\cos x|$

  b $y=5\cos x-2\cos x\ln|\cos x|$

12 a Proof.

  b $y=\dfrac{1}{x}\left(e^{-3x}(Ax+B)+2x-\dfrac{4}{3}\right)$

13 a $u=(3x+c)(x^2+4)$

  b Proof.

  c $y=12\ln x-\dfrac{4c}{x}+\dfrac{3x^2}{2}+cx+d$

14 a $A=1,\ B=-1$

  b $y=\dfrac{1}{2}x^2+3x+\ln|1+x|+1$

12 Applications of differential equations

BEFORE YOU START

1 $y=Ae^{-4x}+Be^{-x}+\dfrac{x}{4}-\dfrac{5}{16}$

2 $4.8\,\text{m s}^{-2}$

EXERCISE 12A

1 a Proof.

  b $v=\dfrac{1}{\lambda}(g-(g-\lambda u)e^{-\lambda t})$

2 a, b Proof.

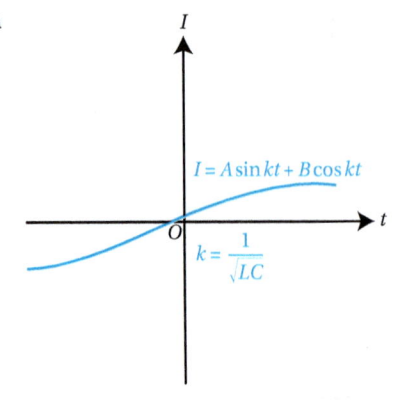

3 a $I=A\sin kt+B\cos kt$, $k=\dfrac{1}{\sqrt{LC}}$

  b $I=e^{-kt}(A\sin bt+B\cos bt)$, $k=-\dfrac{R}{L}$, $b=\dfrac{\sqrt{CL-R^2C^2}}{CL}$

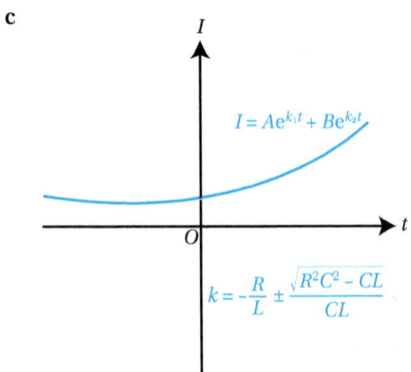

  c $I=Ae^{k_1 t}+Be^{k_2 t}$, $k=-\dfrac{R}{L}\pm\dfrac{\sqrt{R^2C^2-CL}}{CL}$

4 a $\dfrac{dY}{dt}=200\,000\times e^{-t\ln 4}$

  b $12\,144\,270$

  c A natural net birth rate of the population.

5 a $\dfrac{dT}{dt}=k(25+20t-T)$

  b $T=20e^{-0.5t}+20t-15$

  c $185\,°\text{C}$ (3 s.f.)

  d Different parts of the chicken are likely to have different temperatures.

6 a $\dfrac{dR}{dt}=kR(N-R)$

  b $\dfrac{N}{2}$

  c For example: interest in the rumour remains constant, the number of students who know the rumour is modelled as a continuous variable, there are no external people spreading the rumour, students mix freely and do not get grouped.

7 a This is proportional to the surface area of the bacterium. Larger surface areas make the bacterium more efficient in taking up nutrients so it will grow faster.

  b $V=\left(2-e^{-\frac{t}{3}}\right)^3$

c

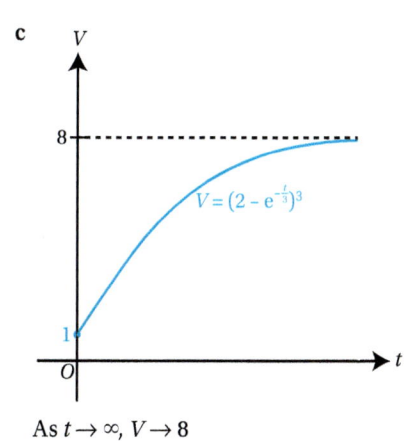

[Graph: V vs t, curve $V = (2 - e^{-\frac{t}{3}})^3$ approaching 8; starts at 1]

As $t \to \infty$, $V \to 8$

EXERCISE 12B

1 a i $A = 4.5$, $T = \frac{2\pi}{3}$; at rest.
      ii $A = 3$, $T = \frac{\pi}{2}$; equilibrium.
   b i $A = 2.6$, $T = 6\pi$; equilibrium.
      ii $A = 5$, $T = 8\pi$; at rest.
   c i $A = 3.2$, $T = 3$; equilibrium.
      ii $A = 10.4$, $T = \frac{10}{3}$; at rest.

2 a i $x = 0.6 \cos 10t$
      ii $x = 3.4 \cos 14t$
   b i $x = 0.7 \sin \frac{t}{3}$ ii $x = 1.3 \sin \frac{t}{5}$
   c i $x = 12.1 \sin \frac{4\pi t}{5}$
      ii $x = 0.3 \cos \frac{10\pi t}{3}$

3 a i $\frac{2\pi}{5}$ ii $\frac{2\pi}{3}$
   b i $\pi\sqrt{2}$ ii $\frac{\pi}{\sqrt{2}}$
   c i $\frac{2\pi}{\sqrt{3}}$ ii $\frac{2\pi}{3}$
   d i 2π ii $\frac{2\pi}{\sqrt{5}}$

4 a 0.183 m   b $1 \, \text{m s}^{-1}$
5 a −0.0768 m   b 0.131 s; $7.2 \, \text{m s}^{-1}$
6 a $1.2 \, \text{m s}^{-1}$ b $0.465 \, \text{m s}^{-1}$; $16.6 \, \text{m s}^{-2}$
7 a 3π s   b $0.0596 \, \text{m s}^{-1}$
8 a −0.595 m   b 0.0524 s
   c $5.20 \, \text{m s}^{-1}$; away.
9 a 7.20 s   b 0.497 m
10 a 0.3 m; 15.7 s   b $x = 0.3 \cos 0.4t$
   c 4.78 s   d 0.0032 N
11 a Proof; $\frac{2\pi}{q}$. b $0.6q$; $0.6q^2$
   c 0.520 m
12 a Proof.   b 15 m; 2880 N
   c 1.96 s

13 a $2.4x$ b Proof.
   c $x = 0.04 \cos 2.19 t$
14 a 0.1 m   b $0.1 + x$; proof.
   c Proof; $\frac{2\pi}{\sqrt{10g}}$ s.
15 a $19.6 \, \text{N m}^{-1}$
   b i   Proof; $h = -49$.
      ii, iii Proof.   iv $0.7 \, \text{m s}^{-1}$
16 a Proof.
   b i   Proof.   ii 2.8 s (2 s.f.)
      iii $2.17 \, \text{m s}^{-1}$
17 a, b Proof.   c $\frac{2\pi}{5}$ s
   d $0.433 \, \text{m s}^{-1}$ e $x = 0.1 \cos 5t$
18 a Proof.
   b $x = -\frac{14}{165} \sin 7t + 0.4 + \frac{49}{330} \sin 4t$

EXERCISE 12C

1 a i   Light.   ii Heavy.
   b i   Critical.   ii Light.
   c i   Heavy.   ii Critical.
   d i   Critical.   ii Light.
2 $n = \frac{8}{3}$
3 a Proof.   b $k = \frac{6\sqrt{2}}{5}$ c Heavy.
4 a $m\frac{d^2x}{dt^2} + 5c\frac{dx}{dt} + 4nx = 0$
   b $n = \frac{25c^2}{16m}$
5 a $x = 0.9 e^{-2t} \sin 3t$
   b Light.

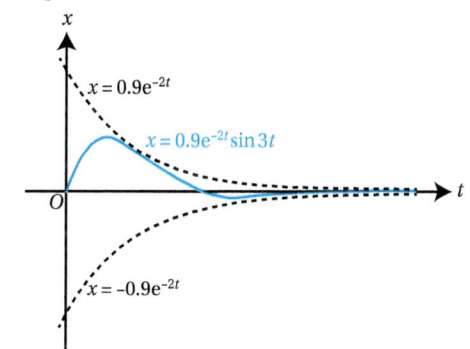

[Graph of x vs t with envelopes $x = 0.9e^{-2t}$ and $x = -0.9e^{-2t}$, and curve $x = 0.9e^{-2t}\sin 3t$]

6 a Proof.   b $x = 1.2 e^{-t} - 0.2 e^{-6t}$
   c Proof.   d Heavy damping.
7 a Proof.   b $k = 0.45$
   c $x = (0.8 + 0.72t)e^{-0.9t}$
8 a 0.4 m
   b Proof.

c Light; $x = -0.4e^{-4t}\left(\frac{4}{3}\sin 3t + \cos 3t\right)$

d 0.4 m

e 0.07 m s^{-1} (1 s.f.)

9 a Light.

b $x = \frac{5u}{3c}e^{-\frac{4ct}{5}}\sin\frac{3ct}{5}$

c Proof.

10 a Proof.

b $x = e^{-0.1t}(15\sin 0.7t - 20\cos 0.7t) + 20$

c $\frac{15\pi}{14}$ s

11 a–c Proof.

d $x = 2fe^{-t} - \frac{f}{4}e^{-2t} + \frac{f}{4}(6t - 7)$

EXERCISE 12D

1 a i $\frac{d^2x}{dt^2} - 7\frac{dx}{dt} + 12x = 0;$
$x = Ae^{3t} + Be^{4t}, y = Ae^{3t} + \frac{B}{2}e^{4t}$

ii $\frac{d^2x}{dt^2} - 2\frac{dx}{dt} - 3x = 0;$
$x = Ae^{3t} + Be^{-t}, y = Ae^{3t} - Be^{-t}$

b i $\ddot{x} + 2\dot{x} + 5x = 0;$
$x = e^{-t}(A\cos 2t + B\sin 2t),$
$y = \frac{1}{2}e^{-t}((A + B)\cos 2t + (B - A)\sin 2t)$

ii $\ddot{x} - 2\dot{x} + 5x = 0;$
$x = e^t(A\cos 2t + B\sin 2t),$
$y = 2e^t((A - B)\cos 2t + (A + B)\sin 2t)$

c i $\ddot{x} + 3\dot{x} + 2x = 3e^{-3t};$
$x = Ae^{-t} + Be^{-2t} + \frac{3}{2}e^{-3t},$
$y = Ae^{-t} + \frac{3B}{4}e^{-2t} + \frac{1}{2}e^{-3t}$

ii $\ddot{x} + \dot{x} - 2x = -26;$
$x = Ae^t + Be^{-2t} + 13,$
$y = 2Ae^t + \frac{B}{2}e^{-2t} + 17$

2 $x = Ae^t + Be^{-t} - \cos t,$
$y = Ae^t - Be^{-t}$

3 $x = Ae^{4t} + Be^{-4t}, y = -2Ae^{4t} + 2Be^{-4t}$

4 $x = 12 + 5\cos 4t, y = 7 + 4\sin 4t$

5 a $\frac{d^2x}{dt^2} - \frac{dx}{dt} - 12x = 0$

b $x = 3e^{4t} - 2e^{-3t},$
$y = 3e^{4t} + 12e^{-3t}$

6 a Proof; $\frac{dy}{dt} + 2y = 0.6e^{-2t}.$

b $y = 0.6te^{-2t};$ proof.

c 11.0 cm

7 a $\frac{dS}{dt} = 0.1F - 0.2S + 1; \frac{dF}{dt} = 0.2F - 0.5S + 4$

b $\ddot{S} + 0.01S = 0.2$

c $S = 20 - 3\cos 0.1t + 4\sin 0.1t,$
$F = 30 - 2\cos 0.1t + 11\sin 0.1t$

d $S = 20 + 5\cos(0.1t - 2.21);$ first shark peak at $t = 22.1,$ first fish peak at $t = 17.5.$

e The populations oscillate with the same period ($20\pi = 62.8$ time units), and with a phase delay of 4.6 units of time between fish population peaking and shark population peaking.

8 Proof.

MIXED PRACTICE 12

1 C

2 D

3 a $\ddot{x} = 2\sin t$ **b** 5.72 m

4 a 1.8 m s^{-1} **b** 1.34 m s^{-1}

c 3.24 N

5 a Proof.   **b** Proof; $\omega = 3.$

c $A = 0.3, B = 0$ **d** 0.9 m s^{-1}

6 a Proof.   **b** $\frac{5\sqrt{5}}{2}$ m s^{-1}

7 a Proof.   **b** Proof; $A = 0, B = 3.$

c $\frac{\pi}{5}$ seconds

8 2.3 months (2 s.f.)

9 $x = \cos 4t - \frac{1}{2}\sin 4t, y = \cos 4t + \frac{1}{2}\sin 4t$

10 Particle Q ($x_P = 33.3$ m, $x_Q = 73.2$ m).

11 a Proof.   **b** 0.785 rad s^{-1}

c 0.148 N

12 a Proof.   **b** Proof; 3.2 m s^{-1}.

13 a, b Proof.   **c** 0.75 m s^{-1}

14 a $x = 5\cos t$

b 1.57 seconds

c $x = e^{-\frac{5}{13}t}\left(5\cos\left(\frac{12}{13}t\right) + \frac{25}{12}\sin\left(\frac{12}{13}t\right)\right)$

d The second model (after 2.13 seconds).

15 $x = e^t(A\cos(t\sqrt{2}) + B\sin(t\sqrt{2})),$
$y = e^t\sqrt{2}(A\sin(t\sqrt{2}) - B\cos(t\sqrt{2}))$

16 4000

17 a Proof.   **b** Proof; $\frac{\pi}{2}.$

c 0.566 m s^{-1}

18 a i Proof.   **ii** $\dfrac{2\pi}{n}$

   b i Proof.

     ii $x = \dfrac{2U}{3n}\left(e^{\frac{-nt}{2}} - e^{-2nt}\right)$

     iii

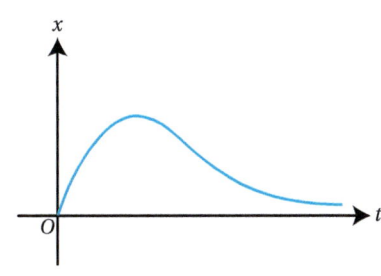

Heavy damping.

19 a Proof.   **b** $x = \dfrac{g}{4} - \dfrac{ge^{-2t}}{4}(1 + 2t)$

   c $x \to \dfrac{g}{4}$ **d** $\dfrac{g}{2e}$

20 a The force decreases at a constant rate. In reality the force will vary over each stride; he might be more motivated towards the end.

   b $2000\ddot{x} = 1000 - 100t$

   c $x = \dfrac{1}{4}t^2 - \dfrac{1}{120}t^3$; 33.3 m

   d Bill (Mike's distance is 14.7 m but you don't need to find this. A sketch of both forces makes it clear that Mike is never pulling harder.)

13 Numerical methods

BEFORE YOU START

1 3.31 (3 s.f.)

2 1.4720 (4 d.p.)

3 $y = 3e^{x^2-1}$

4 $y = \dfrac{3}{2}(3e^{-2x} + 2x - 1)$

5 $\dfrac{d^2y}{dx^2} = 3y - 2x + 9x^2y - 3x^3$

EXERCISE 13A

1 Answers are given to three decimal places.

   a i 1.425   **ii** 1.429

   b i 13.167   **ii** 13.472

   c i 7.053   **ii** 7.061

   d i 2.874   **ii** 2.858

2 Answers are given to three significant figures.

   a i 2.01   **ii** 2.00

   b i 0.883   **ii** 0.883

   c i 1.26   **ii** 1.26

   d i 1.41   **ii** 1.41

3 i, ii

	Exact	2 Approx.	% error	4 Approx.	% error
a	2	2.013082	0.654%	2.005461	0.273%
b	0.88208139	0.8842	0.240%	0.882789	0.0802%
c	1.26262726	1.211272	−4.07%	1.262919	0.0231%
d	1.40633517	1.41764	0.804%	1.409269	0.209%

	8 Approx.	% error	16 Approx.	%error
a	2.002147	0.107%	2.000814	0.0407%
b	0.882269	0.0212%	0.882129	0.00540%
c	1.262967	0.0269%	1.262713	0.00679%
d	1.407076	0.0527%	1.406521	0.0132%

   iii In most cases, doubling the number of intervals reduces the error by between a half and three quarters.

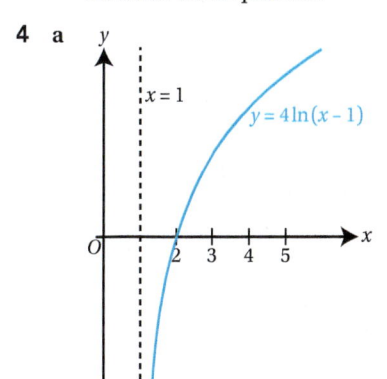

4 a

   b 5.20 (2 d.p.)

   c Overestimate because the curve is concave.

5 a 2.005 (3 d.p.)

   b Use more intervals.

6 a $\left(\dfrac{\pi}{2}\right)^{\frac{1}{3}}$

   b 0.9937 (4 d.p.)

   c Overestimate because the curve is concave.

7 a $a = \pi^2$, $b = 4\pi^2$ b 2.51 m (2 d.p.)

EXERCISE 13B

1 Answers are given to three decimal places.

   a   i   1.434   ii   1.433

   b   i   13.813   ii   13.744

   c   i   7.330   ii   7.061

   d   i   2.871   ii   2.847

2 Answers are given to four significant figures.

   a   i   2.000   ii   1.995

   b   i   0.8818   ii   0.8820

   c   i   1.244   ii   1.260

   d   i   1.406   ii   1.406

3 i, ii

	Exact	2 Approx.	% error	4 Approx.	% error
a	2	1.97179	−1.41%	1.989931	−0.503%
b	0.882081	0.829944	−5.91%	0.881812	−0.0305%
c	1.262627	1.175794	−6.88%	1.244406	−1.44%
d	1.406335	1.404456	−0.134%	1.406168	−0.0119%

	8 Approx.	% error	16 Approx.	% error
a	1.996425	−0.179%	1.998734	−0.0633%
b	0.882066	-1.8×10^{-3}%	0.88208	-1.1×10^{-4}%
c	1.26227	−0.0283%	1.262627	-4.0×10^{-5}%
d	1.406323	-8.6×10^{-4}%	1.406334	-5.6×10^{-5}%

   iii In most cases, doubling the number of intervals reduces the error by a factor of 5 to 10 (or more).

4 a

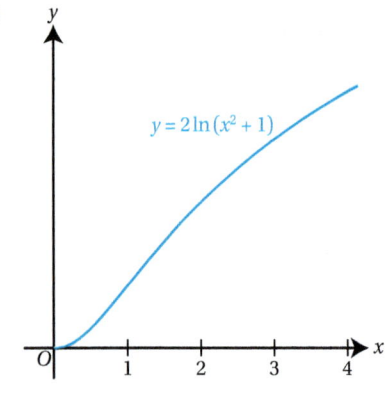

        $y = 2\ln(x^2 + 1)$

   b 11.442 (3 d.p.)

5 a 3.40 (2 d.p.)

   b Use more intervals.

6 a $p = 0.25\pi^2$, $q = 6.25\pi^2$

   b 59.933 (3 d.p.)

7 a $A = \dfrac{1}{2}\pi$

   b   i   Proof.   ii   1.555 (3 d.p.)

   c 3.110 (3 d.p.)

EXERCISE 13C

1 a   i   0.708   ii   2.32

   b   i   1.57   ii   1.07

   c   i   2.89   ii   1.45

2 1.629 (3 d.p.)

3 a 1.3007 (4 d.p.)

   b $y = 0.3 + e^x(x - 1)$

   c   i   7.15%   ii   Use smaller h.

4 a   i   0.615 (3 d.p.)   ii   Use smaller h.

   b $y = \dfrac{1}{2}e^{\frac{1}{3}x^3}$; $g(1) = 0.698$ (3 d.p.)

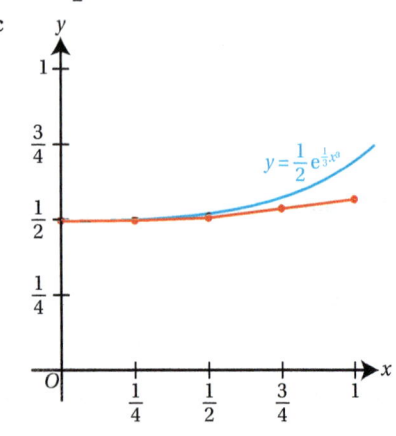

   c

The tangent is always below the curve (curve is convex).

5 **a** $\dfrac{dy}{dx} = 4 - 3e^{-x^2}$

b 2.58 (2 d.p.)

EXERCISE 13D

1 Answers are given to three significant figures.

a **i** $y(1.1) = 3.32$; $y(1.2) = 3.70$

ii $y(2) = 4.24$; $y(3) = 8.47$

b **i** $y(2.1) = 0.2$; $y(2.2) = 0.460$

ii $y(\pi + 0.2) = 0.8$; $y(\pi + 0.4) = 0.643$

c **i** $y(0.01) = 1.03$; $y(0.02) = 1.06$

ii $y(2.1) = 1.35$; $y(2.2) = 1.39$

d **i** $y(1.01) = 0.01$; $y(1.02) = 0.020$

ii $y(0.1) = 1.2$; $y(0.2) = 1.40$

2 **a** 1.15 (3 s.f.)

b 1.30 (3 s.f.)

3 **a** $y(1.1) = 1.3$ (2 s.f.)

b $y(1.1) = 1.315$ (3 d.p.)

c Part **b**: It is a convex curve, so the improved Euler formula is more accurate than the Euler method.

4 **a** $y(3.1) = 0.3 + 1.1c$

b $c = 0.8$

5 **a** $y(1.1) = 1.87$ (3 s.f.)

b $y(1.2) = 1.7916$ (4 d.p.)

c **i** $y = \dfrac{\sqrt{7 + 2x^2} - 1}{x}$

ii 0.312%

MIXED PRACTICE 13

1 D

2 3.990 (3 d.p.)

3 0.5948 (4 d.p.)

4 0.491 (3 d.p.)

5 9.786 (3 d.p.)

6 4.820 (3 d.p.)

7 **a** 2.1 **b** 2.34 (3 s.f.)

8 **a** 2.6238 (4 d.p.) **b** 2.6494 (4 d.p.)

9 **a** 1.4841 (4 d.p.) **b** 2.019 (3 d.p.)

10 B

11 **a** 15.358 (3 d.p.) **b** 15.372 (3 d.p.)

c 0.0902% **d** Use more strips.

12 **a** Proof.

b Curve is symmetrical about y-axis so estimate for $0 \leqslant x \leqslant 1$ and double. More accurate; effectively using 8 strips for the whole interval instead of 4.

13 **a** Proof.

b $\displaystyle\int_{k_1}^{k_2} ax^3 + q(x)\,dx$

$= \displaystyle\int_0^{k_2} ax^3\,dx - \int_0^{k_1} ax^3\,dx + \int_{k_1}^{k_2} q(x)\,dx$

for quadratic $q(x)$ and, by part **a**, the Simpson's rule estimate of the first two integral values will be exact and Simpson's rule will fit a curve exactly to any quadratic so the third term is also exact.

14 **a** **i** 1.2249 (4 d.p.) **ii** 1.2

b A smaller step will lead to a more accurate answer.

15 **a** 2.541 (3 d.p.) **b** $0.75 - \ln 4$

16 **a** 4.49 (3 s.f.) **b** 1.51

17 2.449 (4 s.f.)

18 19.9%

19 **a** $c = 1.5$ **b** $y = 0.75(2x - 1 + 3e^{-2x})$

c 6.45%

20 **a** 2.069 (3 d.p.)

b **i** $\dfrac{d^2y}{dx^2} = 2\ln(x+y)$

$+ (2x+1)\dfrac{1 + (2x+1)\ln(x+y)}{x+y}$

ii $y(x) \approx 2 + x\ln 2 + x^2\left(\dfrac{1 + 5\ln 2}{4}\right)$

iii 2.080 (3 d.p.)

FOCUS ON ... PROOF 2

1 Proof.

2 $\sqrt{\pi}$

3 $\sqrt{2\pi\sigma}$

FOCUS ON ... PROBLEM SOLVING 2

1. Proof.

2. The tangent to the chain at $x = 0$ is horizontal; proof.

3. $y = \dfrac{T_0 L}{gM} \cosh\left(\dfrac{gM}{T_0 L} x\right)$; moving the chain vertically does not change its shape.

4. Proof.

5. Proof.

6. Investigation (using graphing software). The distance between the end-points ($2D$) has to be smaller than the length of the chain (L).

FOCUS ON ... MODELLING 2

1. For example: all fish and sharks are treated as equivalent so that the effects of age or disease average out over the population; there is no randomness which might be OK if the populations are large enough; there are no external populations (i.e. no other predators or sources of food); there is no seasonality so the birth rate stays constant over time.

2. $F = 0$, $S = 0$ or $F = \dfrac{k}{c}$, $S = \dfrac{a}{b}$. The second solution is the biologically relevant one.

3. The equilibrium value of the fish goes down when k goes down. The equilibrium value of the sharks goes up when a increases.

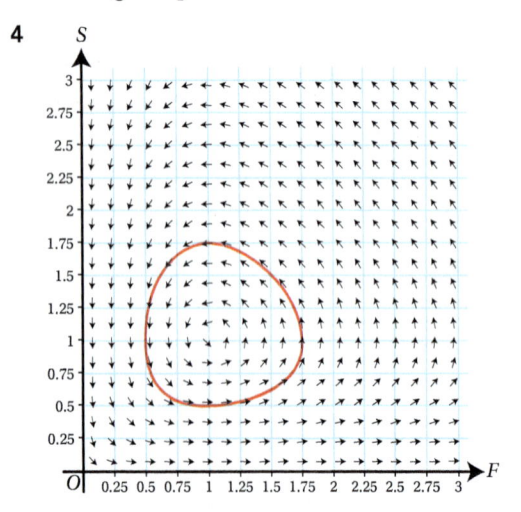

4. Maximum fish population is about 1.75 million.

5. [graphs of F and S against t]

6. When F is small the aF term will be relatively more important. When F is large the eF^2 term will dominate, meaning that when the population is too large there is a net death, as would be expected with internal competition.

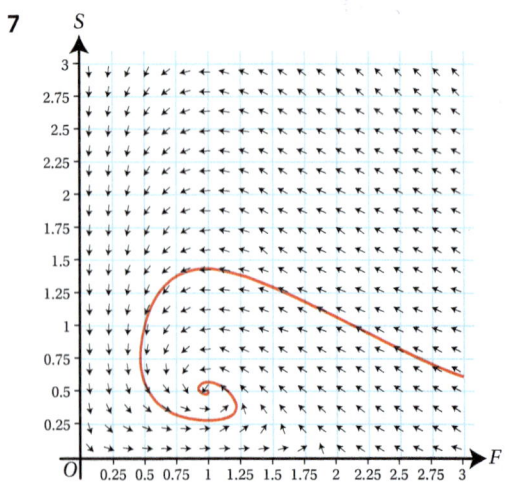

7. The systems tends to an equilibrium at $F = 1$, $S = 0.5$.

CROSS-TOPIC REVIEW EXERCISE 2

1 a $r^2 = a\sin 4\theta$ (rose curve with 8 petals along $\pi/4, 3\pi/4, 5\pi/4, 7\pi/4$ directions from origin O, with axes labelled $0, 2\pi$; $\pi/2$; π; $3\pi/2$).

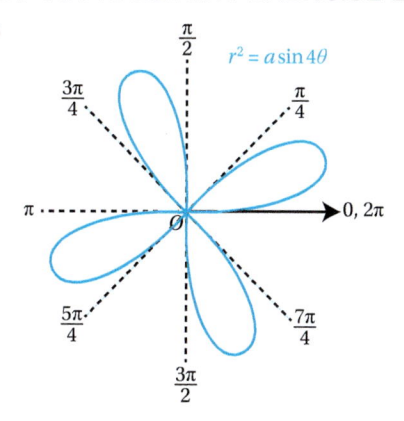

b a

2 a Asymptotes $y = 1$, $y = -1$; graph of $y = \tanh x$.

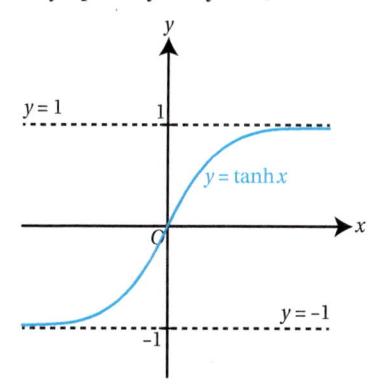

b Proof.

c $x = \tfrac{1}{2}\ln 3$, $\tfrac{1}{2}\ln\tfrac{1}{5}$

3 a 3 **b** 4

4 a $p^{-2} - q^{-2}$

b i Not finite. **ii** Finite; $\tfrac{1}{4}$.

5 $\ln(3 + \sqrt{10})$

6 a Proof. **b** 18 seconds

7 a $3x - \tfrac{9}{2}x^3$ **b** $-\tfrac{3}{10}$

8 a 25.6 (3 s.f.) **b** Smaller.

9 a 1.173 (3 d.p.) **b** 1.335 (3 d.p.)

10 a i $x^2 + y^2 = 2(x - y)$

 ii Centre $(1, -1)$, radius $\sqrt{2}$.

b i $\tfrac{33}{2}\pi$ **ii** Proof. **iii** $\tfrac{29}{2}\pi$

11 a Proof. **b** $k = \ln\sqrt{3}$

12 a Proof. **b** $\dfrac{9\text{e}}{2} - \dfrac{65}{2\text{e}}$

13 a Proof. **b** $s = \dfrac{\text{e}^2 + 4 - \text{e}^{-2}}{2}$

14 a Interval of integration is infinite.

b $\tfrac{1}{4}\text{e}^{-4}$

15 a, b Proof.

16 a $9 - 2(x - 1)^2$ **b** $\dfrac{\pi\sqrt{2}}{8}$

17 a Proof; $k = 2$. **b** Proof; $p = \tfrac{9}{8}$, $q = \tfrac{3}{4}$.

18 a $\dfrac{\mathrm{d}y}{\mathrm{d}x} = \dfrac{2\sec^2 x}{1 + 2\tan x}$;

$\dfrac{\mathrm{d}^2 y}{\mathrm{d}x^2} = \dfrac{(1 + 2\tan x)(4\sec^2 x \tan x) - 2\sec^2 x(2\sec^2 x)}{(1 + 2\tan x)^2}$

b $2x - 2x^2 + \ldots$

c -2

19 $y = \text{e}^{-x}(3\cos 3x + 4\sin 3x) + 2\text{e}^x$

20 a i, ii Proof.

b Proof.

c $y = A\text{e}^{x^2} + B\text{e}^{3x^2} + x^2 + \tfrac{4}{3}$

21 a $\tfrac{\pi}{2}$ s **b** $0.693\,\text{m s}^{-1}$ (3 s.f.)

c $s = 0.2 - 0.2\cos 4t$ **d** $0.262\,\text{s}$ (3 s.f.)

22 a $P\left(2, \tfrac{7\pi}{6}\right)$; $Q\left(2, \tfrac{11\pi}{6}\right)$

b i $\left(4, \tfrac{\pi}{6}\right)$ **ii** $2\sqrt{3}$

 iii Angle $OQA = 90°$ (since Pythagoras theorem holds) so AQ is a tangent.

c $\tfrac{1}{6}(33\sqrt{3} - 14\pi)$

23 a, b Proof.

24 Proof.

25 a Proof.

b $\operatorname{arsinh} x - \dfrac{\sqrt{1 + x^2}}{x} + c$

26 a $x\arcsin x + \sqrt{1 - x^2} + c$

b Proof.

c i $p\arcsin\sqrt{p} - \tfrac{1}{2}\arcsin\sqrt{p} + \tfrac{1}{2}\sqrt{p - p^2}$

 ii $x\arcsin\sqrt{x} - \tfrac{1}{2}\arcsin\sqrt{x} + \tfrac{1}{2}\sqrt{x - x^2} + c$

27 $\ln \frac{3}{2}$

28 a $\sqrt{1+(f'(a))^2}$ b Proof.

29 a Proof.
   b $y = \sqrt{x}(A\cos(\ln\sqrt{x}) + B\sin(\ln\sqrt{x}))$
   $+ 2 + 2\ln x + \frac{1}{2}(\ln x)^2 + \frac{1}{\sqrt{x}}$

30 a Proof.   b i, ii Proof.
   c i $x = e^{-2nt}(A + Bt)$ ii Critical.

31 a $4\cosh^4 t$
   b i Proof.   ii $S = \frac{8\pi}{3}(\cosh^3 1 - 1)$

32 a i Proof; $k = 4$.   ii Proof; $p = \frac{1}{2}$, $q = \frac{1}{4}$.
   b i Proof.   ii $S = \frac{\pi\sqrt{5}}{8} + \frac{\pi}{16}\sinh^{-1} 2$

PRACTICE PAPER

1 D
2 C
3 $k = -3$
4 Proof.
5 $y = \dfrac{2\arcsin x + 1}{\sqrt{1 - x^2}}$
6 Proof; $a = \frac{1}{4}$, $b = \frac{7}{5}$.
7 a Proof; $p = a$, $q = 1$.
   b Translation by $\begin{pmatrix} a \\ a \end{pmatrix}$.
   c i

   ii $\dfrac{a^2 - 1}{a} < k < a$

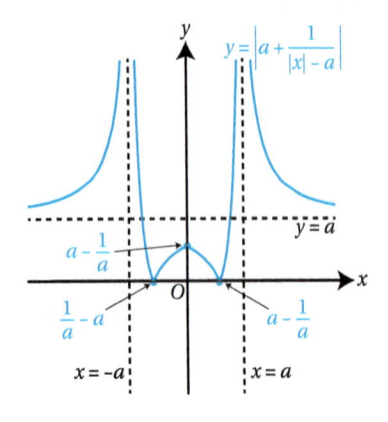

8 a Proof.   b Proof.   c $1, \frac{1}{2} \pm i\frac{\sqrt{3}}{2}$

9 a Proof.   b $\dfrac{752}{1215}$

10 a Proof.
   b $k = 2$; $\mathbf{r} = \begin{pmatrix} 1 \\ 0 \\ -1 \end{pmatrix} + \lambda \begin{pmatrix} 1 \\ 2 \\ 3 \end{pmatrix}$

11 a i Proof; 2, 5.
   ii $\begin{pmatrix} -3 \\ 1 \\ 4 \end{pmatrix}, \begin{pmatrix} -2 \\ 1 \\ 0 \end{pmatrix}, \begin{pmatrix} 1 \\ 1 \\ 0 \end{pmatrix}$
   b $\mathbf{r} = \lambda \begin{pmatrix} -3 \\ 1 \\ 4 \end{pmatrix}$ is a line of invariant points.
   $\mathbf{r} = \lambda \begin{pmatrix} -2 \\ 1 \\ 0 \end{pmatrix}$ and $\mathbf{r} = \lambda \begin{pmatrix} 1 \\ 1 \\ 0 \end{pmatrix}$ are invariant lines.

12 a i $f'(x) = \text{sech}^2 x$;
   $f''(x) = -2\,\text{sech}^2 x \tanh x$;
   $f'''(x) = 4\,\text{sech}^2 x \tanh^2 x - 2\,\text{sech}^4 x$;
   $f^{(4)}(x) = -8\,\text{sech}^2 x \tanh^3 x + 16\,\text{sech}^4 x \tanh x$
   ii $x - \frac{1}{3}x^3$
   b $1 + x + \frac{1}{2}x^2 - \frac{1}{6}x^3 - \frac{7}{24}x^4$
   c $\frac{1}{2}$

13 a Proof.   b 0

14 a Proof.
   b i $x = 5e^{-kt} - e^{-2kt}$
   ii Heavy.

Glossary

amplitude (of an object moving with SHM): The maximum distance from the central line.

angular frequency: The constant ω in the simple harmonic motion equation $\frac{d^2x}{dt^2} = -\omega^2 x$.

auxiliary equation: The quadratic equation $a\lambda^2 + b\lambda + c = 0$ associated with the second order differential equation $a\frac{d^2y}{dx^2} + b\frac{dy}{dx} + c = 0$.

central line (in SHM): The average position around which the object oscillates.

characteristic equation: The polynomial equation $\det(\mathbf{M} - \lambda \mathbf{I}) = 0$ satisfied by the eigenvalues of a matrix $\mathbf{M}$.

cofactor: The minor of an element multiplied by $(-1)^{i+j}$, where the element is in the ith row and jth column of the matrix.

cofactor matrix: The matrix of cofactors.

complementary function: The solution to the associated homogeneous differential equation.

conic sections: The collective name for a group of curves that can be obtained as cross-sections of a cone.

consistent (system of equations): A set of simultaneous equations that have a solution(s).

cross product: See vector product.

damped simple harmonic motion: Simple harmonic motion in which a resistive force proportional to the object's velocity is added, causing the amplitude to decay with time.

De Moivre's theorem: A theorem for finding powers of complex numbers: $z^n = r^n(\cos n\theta + i \sin n\theta)$ for any integer n.

dependent variable (in a differential equation): The variable on the top of the derivatives.

diagonal matrix: A matrix which has zero elements everywhere except from the lead diagonal.

diagonalise: The process of expressing a matrix in the form $\mathbf{UDU}^{-1}$, for some matrix $\mathbf{U}$, where $\mathbf{D}$ is a diagonal matrix.

eigenvalue: A scalar λ such that $\mathbf{Mv} = \lambda \mathbf{v}$ for some matrix $\mathbf{M}$ and vector $\mathbf{v}$ (the associated eigenvector).

eigenvector: A vector $\mathbf{v}$ such that $\mathbf{Mv} = \lambda \mathbf{v}$ for some matrix $\mathbf{M}$ and scalar λ (the associated eigenvalue).

Euler's method: An iterative method that approximates the solution of a differential equation.

exponential form (of a complex number): A way of expressing a complex number, z, in terms of its modulus, r, and argument, θ: $z = re^{i\theta}$.

general solution (of a differential equation): The solution involving all the necessary arbitrary constants.

homogeneous differential equation: A differential equation in which every term involves the dependent variable.

Hooke's law: A law which states that the extension in a string/spring is directly proportional to the force applied.

improper integral: An integral where either the range of integration is infinite or the integrand is undefined at a point within the range of integration.

improved Euler method: A refinement of Euler's method to give a better approximation to the solution of a differential equation.

inconsistent (system of equations): A set of simultaneous equations that do not have a solution.

independent variable (in a differential equation): The variable on the bottom of the derivatives.

integrating factor: A function that is multiplied through a first order liner differential equation so that the side containing the dependent variable can be expressed as the derivative of a product.

irreducible quadratic: A quadratic that does not factorise.

lead diagonal: The elements on the diagonal of a matrix from top left to bottom right.

linear differential equation: A differential equation in which the dependent variable only appears to the power 1 in any expression.

l'Hôpital's rule: A rule for finding the limit of a function which is of the form $\frac{0}{0}$ or $\frac{\infty}{\infty}$.

mid-ordinate rule: A method that approximates a definite integral by fitting a series of rectangles to the mid-points of each interval that the function passes through.

minor: The determinant of the submatrix of an element.

non-homogeneous differential equation: A differential equation in which at least one term doesn't involve the dependent variable.

normal vector (to a plane): A vector that is perpendicular to the plane.

order (of a differential equation): The largest number of times the dependent variable is differentiated.

oscillating behaviour: Behaviour in which the particle moves from side to side of a fixed point.

particular integral: Any solution of the differential equation.

particular solution: The general solution but with the values of all constants now having been found to fit a set of specific conditions.

period (of an object moving with SHM): The time after which the motion repeats itself.

plane: A flat, two-dimensional surface.

reciprocal hyperbolic functions: The functions $\text{sech}\, x = \dfrac{1}{\cosh x}$, $\text{cosech}\, x = \dfrac{1}{\sinh x}$ and $\coth x = \dfrac{1}{\tanh x}$.

reciprocal transformation: A transformation that turns the graph of $y = f(x)$ into the graph of $y = \dfrac{1}{f(x)}$.

reduction formula: An iterative formula that reduces the complexity of an integral.

roots of unity: The n solutions of the equation $z^n = 1$, where z is a complex number.

row operation: One of three possible manipulations that can be performed on the rows of a matrix.

simple harmonic motion: Oscillating motion where the force applied is proportional to the displacement from a central position and is in the direction opposite to that of the displacement.

Simpson's rule: A method that approximates a definite integral by fitting a quadratic through the two distinct and one shared end-point of any two successive intervals determined by the given function.

spring constant: The constant of proportionality in Hooke's law (also called the stiffness of the spring).

stiffness: See spring constant.

submatrix: The matrix formed by deleting the row and column of the original matrix containing the specified element.

surface of revolution: The surface formed by rotating a given curve around an axis.

transpose: A matrix formed by swapping the first row of a matrix with its first column, the second row with the second column and so on.

vector (or cross) product: A way of multiplying two vectors **a** and **b**. The direction is perpendicular to both **a** and **b** and the magnitude is given by $|\mathbf{a} \times \mathbf{b}| = |\mathbf{a}||\mathbf{b}|\sin\theta$, where θ is the angle between **a** and **b**.

Index

amplitude 274
analysis 229
angles
　between lines and planes 101
　between two planes 102
　between two vectors 101
　formulae for small 333
angular frequency 273
arbitrary constants 249
arc length 220–2, 332
area scale factor 116
areas
　between two curves 171–2
　elements of 312–13
　enclosed by polar curves 167–9
　sector 331
　surfaces of revolution 223–5, 332
　triangles 79, 83
Argand diagram, roots of complex numbers on 12–13, 16
arithmetic series, formulae 333
arsech x 184–5
auxiliary equations 257–60, 273, 281–2

binomial expansion 42–3
　formulae 332
boundary conditions 249

calculus 201–26
　area of surface of revolution 223–5, 332
　differentiation of inverse hyperbolic functions 204–5
　differentiation of inverse trigonometric functions 202–3
　length of arc of curve 220–2, 332
　reduction formulae 214–17
　using inverse trigonometric and hyperbolic functions in integration 206–9
　using partial fractions in integration 211–13
Cartesian equations
　conic sections 48
　plane 89–91
central line 274
chain, finding shape of 314–16
characteristic equations 138
　for 3×3 matrices 139–41
circle
　combined transformations 55
　length of arc of 222
cofactor 115
cofactor matrices 117
complementary function 249–51, 261–4
complex conjugates 9
complex exponents 7–10
complex numbers 1–27, 31–44
　complex exponents 7–10
　De Moivre's theorem 2–6
　　extending proof of 154–5
　exponential form 8
　formulae 330

geometry of 22–4
in multiple-angle formulae derivation 32–3
powers of 2–6
powers of trigonometric functions 37–9
roots of 11–13
roots of unity 15–18
in solving polynomial equations 34–6
trigonometric series 40–3
using to describe rotations 156–9
conic sections 47–55, 58
　combined transformations 53–5, 58
　enlargements 52
　formulae 331
　parametric form 48–50
　polar form 48–50
　rotations 51–2
　see also ellipse; hyperbola; parabola
cosech x 183, 184
coth x 183, 184
coupled first order differential equations 285–7
critical damping 282
cross product *see* vector product

damped oscillations 281–2
damped simple harmonic motion 281–2
damping 281–2
　critical 282
　heavy 282
　light 282
De Moivre's theorem 2–6
　extending proof of 154–5
definite integrals 240
　using Maclaurin series in approximating 232
determinants 79
　of 3×3 matrices 114–17
　factorising 122–4
　using to calculate vector product 124–5
diagonal matrices 143–6
differential equations 248–66
　applications 270–88
　arbitrary constants 249
　auxiliary equations 257–60, 273, 281–2
　boundary conditions 249
　complementary function 249–51, 261–4
　coupled first order 285–7
　dependent variable 248
　forming 270–1
　general solution 249
　homogeneous 249
　independent variable 248
　initial conditions 249
　integrating factor 253–5, 304
　linear *see* linear differential equations
　non-homogeneous 249
　numerical solution 302–6, 332
　order 249
　ordinary (ODEs) 248
　partial (PDEs) 248
　particular integral 249–51, 261–4

particular solution 249
　for simple harmonic motion 273
　terminology 248–51
differentiation
　formulae 329, 333–4
　from first principles 234, 334
　hyperbolic functions 188–90
　implicit 202
　inverse hyperbolic functions 204–5
　inverse trigonometric functions 202–3
domain
　hyperbolic functions 180–1
　inverse hyperbolic functions 181–2
　reciprocal hyperbolic functions 183–5
drag force 281–2

eigenvalues 137–41
eigenvectors 137–41
ellipse
　Cartesian equations 48
　combined transformations 53–5, 58
　enlargements 52
　formulae 331
　parametric equations 48–9
　polar equations 48–50
　rotations 51–2
enlargements 22–3
　conic sections 52
equations
　auxiliary 257–60, 273, 281–2
　Cartesian *see* Cartesian equations
　consistent systems 130–5
　　finding solution sets to 134–5
　differential *see* differential equations
　inconsistent systems 130–4
　of line 82
　modulus 70–3
　numerical solution 334
　parametric *see* parametric equations of plane
　　Cartesian 89–91
　　vector 85–91
　polar *see* polar equations
　polynomial 34–6
　simultaneous *see* simultaneous equations
　using hyperbolic identities to solve 186–7
Euler's formula 7–9
Euler's identity 7
Euler's method 302–4, 332
　improved 305–6, 332
exponential form 8
exponents
　complex 7–10
　see also powers

factorisation, polynomials 20–1
foot of perpendicular 104
forces
　drag 281–2
　on hanging chain 314–16
　resistance 271

391

formulae 329–34
Fourier series 40
functions
   complementary 249–51, 261–4
   modulus 66
   trial 261, 263
   trigonometric see trigonometric functions

Gaussian integrals 312–13
geometric series 41–2
   formulae 333
graphs
   modulus 66–7
   reciprocal 62–3

Hooke's law 275–6
hyperbola
   Cartesian equations 48
   combined transformations 53–5, 58
   enlargements 52
   formulae 331
   parametric equations 48–9
   polar equations 48–9
   rotations 51–2
hyperbolic functions 178–97
   differentiation 188–90
   domain 180–1
   formulae 331
   integration 191–3
   inverse
      differentiation 204–5
      domain 181–2
      range 181–2
      using in integration 206–9
   range 180–1
   reciprocal 183–5
      inverse 184–5
   using hyperbolic identities to solve equations 186–7

identity matrix 138
improper integrals 240–4
   diverging 241
   where integrand is undefined at point within range of integration 242–4
   where range of integration extends to infinity 240–2
indices, rules of 7–9
induction, proof by 3
inequalities, modulus 70–3
infinite series 230
initial conditions 249
integrating factor 253–5, 304
integration
   by parts more than once 214–16
   formulae 329, 334
   hyperbolic functions 191–3
   numerical 334
   in polar coordinates 167–72
   powers of trigonometric functions 39
   using inverse trigonometric and hyperbolic functions in 206–9
   using partial fractions in 211–13
interference 40

interval of convergence 230
inverse hyperbolic functions
   differentiation 204–5
   domain 181–2
   range 181–2
   using in integration 206–9
inverse matrices, of 3×3 matrix 117–18
inverse reciprocal hyperbolic functions 184–5
inverse trigonometric functions
   differentiation 202–3
   using in integration 206–9
irreducible factors 212

Leslie matrices 160
L'Hôpital's rule 236–9
limits 234–9
   important ones often occurring 236
   using l'Hôpital's rule to find 236–9
   using Maclaurin series to find 235–6
linear differential equations
   definition 249
   general solution 250
   homogeneous second order with constant coefficients 257–60
   inhomogeneous second order with constant coefficients 261–4
linear systems with three unknowns 127–8
lines
   angles between planes and 101
   intersection between planes and 94–5
   perpendicular 78–81
   vector equations of 82
logarithmic spiral 158–9
Lotka-Volterra model 317–18

Maclaurin series 230–2
   in approximating definite integrals 232
   in finding limits 235–6
   formulae 330
   general term 230
   generalisation 302–3
matrices 113–49
   characteristic equations 138
      for 3×3 matrices 139–41
   cofactor 117
   determinants of see determinants
   diagonal 143–6
   diagonalisation 143–6
   eigenvalues 137–41
   eigenvectors 137–41
   formulae for transformations 330
   geometrical interpretation of 3-variable simultaneous equations 129–35
   identity 138
   inverse, of 3×3 matrix 117–18
   lead diagonal 139
   Leslie 160
   powers of 145–6
   rotation 156
   row and column operations 120–5
      using determinant to calculate vector product 124–5

      using to factorise determinants 122–4
   solving linear systems with three unknowns 127–8
   submatrices 115
   symmetry in 123
   transposes 114
mid-ordinate rule 295–6, 298, 301
minor 115
modelling
   Leslie matrices 160
   Lotka-Volterra model and phase planes 317–18
modulus equations 70–3
modulus function 66
modulus graphs 66–7
modulus inequalities 70–3
moment of force 79
multiple-angle formulae derivation 32–3

Newton-Raphson iteration 334
Newton's second law 276
numerical methods 294–307
   Euler's method 302–4, 332
      improved 305–6, 332
   formulae 332, 334
   mid-ordinate rule 295–6, 298, 301
   Simpson's rule 298–301

orientations 116–17
oscillating behaviour 273
   damped oscillations 281–2

parabola
   Cartesian equations 48
   combined transformations 53–5, 58
   enlargements 52
   formulae 331
   parametric equations 48–9
   polar equations 48–9
   rotations 51–2
parametric equations, conic sections 48–50
partial fractions, using in integration 211–13
particular integral 249–51, 261–4
period 274
phase planes 318
planes
   angle between two 102
   angles between lines and 101
   Cartesian equations of 89–91
   coincident 129
   distance between point and plane 104–5
   intersection of three 96–8, 129–35
   intersection of two 95, 129
   intersections between lines and 94–5
   parallel 129
   vector equations of 85–91
   ways to describe 88
polar coordinates 167–74
   area between two curves 171–2
   area enclosed by curve 167–9
   integration in 167–72

Index

polar equations, conic sections 48–50
polynomial equations, solving 34–6
polynomials, factorising 20–1
powers
  of complex numbers 2–6
  of matrices 145–6
  of trigonometric functions 37–9
  see also exponents
problem solving
  finding shape of hanging chain 314–16
  using complex numbers to describe rotations 156–9
proof
  elements of area and Gaussian integrals 312–13
  extending proof of De Moivre's theorem 154–5

range
  hyperbolic functions 180–1
  inverse hyperbolic functions 181–2
  reciprocal hyperbolic functions 183–5
rates of change 248
reciprocal graphs 62–3
reciprocal hyperbolic functions 183–5
  inverse 184–5
reciprocal transformation 62
reduction formulae 214–17
reflections 58
  of point in plane 104–5
resistance force 271
reverse chain rule 192
right-hand rule 79
roots
  of complex numbers 11–13
  of unity 15–18
rotation matrix 156
rotations 22–4
  conic sections 51–2
  using complex numbers to describe 156–9
rules of indices 7–9

sech x 183
sheaf 96
shear 140
simple harmonic motion 273–6
  damped 281–2
  differential equation for 273
  Hooke's law 275–6
  period 274
  relationship between velocity and displacement 274–5
Simpson's rule 298–301
simultaneous equations in three variables 127–8
  geometrical interpretation 129–35
slope field diagram 303
spiral, logarithmic 158–9
spring constant 275
stiffness 275
stretches 58
submatrices 115
summations, formulae 330
surface of revolution, area 223–5, 332

TABLE function 296
tangents, plots of 303
Taylor series 303
transformations 22–4
  combined 53–5, 58
  curves 51–2
  reciprocal 62
  shear 140
  in three dimensions 116–17
  see also enlargements; reflections; rotations; stretches; translations
translations 58
transposes 114
trapezium rule 295, 296, 298, 301, 334
trial function 261, 263
triangle
  area 79, 83
  equilateral 23–4

triangular prism 96
trigonometric functions
  inverse
    differentiation 202–3
    using in integration 206–9
  powers of 37–9
  special values 17–18
trigonometric identities
  formulae 333
  in reduction formulae derivation 216–17
trigonometric series 40–3
trigonometry 31–44
  multiple-angle formulae derivation 32–3
  in solving polynomial equations 34–6

unity, roots of 15–18

vector product 78–83
  magnitude 83
  of parallel vectors 81
  properties 81
  uses 79
  using determinants to calculate 124–5
vector triple product 127
vectors 77–107
  angle between two 101
  angle between two planes 102
  angles between lines and planes 101
  base 79
  distance between point and plane 104–5
  equation of plane 85–91
  formulae 331
  intersections between lines and planes 93–8
  perpendicular 78–81
  position 85
velocity, in simple harmonic motion 274–5
volume scale factor 116

Acknowledgements

The authors and publishers acknowledge the following sources of copyright material and are grateful for the permissions granted. While every effort has been made, it has not always been possible to identify the sources of all the material used, or to trace all copyright holders. If any omissions are brought to our notice, we will be happy to include the appropriate acknowledgements on reprinting.

Thanks to the following for permission to reproduce images:

Laguna Design/Getty Images; Chris Clor/Getty Images; Lisa Romerein/Getty Images; rzarek/Getty Images; Philippe Bourseiller/Getty Images Scott R Barbour/Getty Images; Anna Bliokh/Getty Images Hani Alahmadi/EyeEm/Getty Images; Massimiliano Ricciardolo/EyeEm/Getty Images; AlterYourReality/Getty Images; Nobi_Prizue/Getty Images; Image by cuppyuppycake/Getty Images; Andrey_A/Getty Images

AQA material is reproduced by permission of AQA.